OUR BROTHERS IN CHRIST

Henri Daniel-Rops: *History of the Church of Christ:*

OUR BROTHERS IN CHRIST
1870–1959

by

H. DANIEL-ROPS

TRANSLATED FROM THE FRENCH BY
J. M. ORPEN
AND
JOHN WARRINGTON

EDITED BY A. COX AND
J. HETHERINGTON

LONDON: J. M. DENT & SONS LTD
NEW YORK: E. P. DUTTON & CO. INC.

H. Daniel-Rops: *L'Église des Révolutions:
Ces Chrétiens nos Frères*, first published in
France by Librairie Arthème Fayard, 1965.

Nihil obstat: Michael Richards, S.T.L., B.Lit., *Censor.*

Imprimatur: Patrick J. Casey, *Vic. Gen.*

Westminster, 10th May 1967.

The *Nihil obstat* and *Imprimatur* are a declaration that a book or
pamphlet is considered to be free from doctrinal or moral error. It is not
implied that those who have granted the *Nihil obstat* and *Imprimatur*
agree with the contents, opinions or statements expressed.

TRANSLATORS' NOTE

This volume is translated from *Ces Chrétiens nos Frères*, which
forms the third book of the sixth volume of M. Daniel-Rops's
Histoire de l'Église du Christ.

CONTENTS

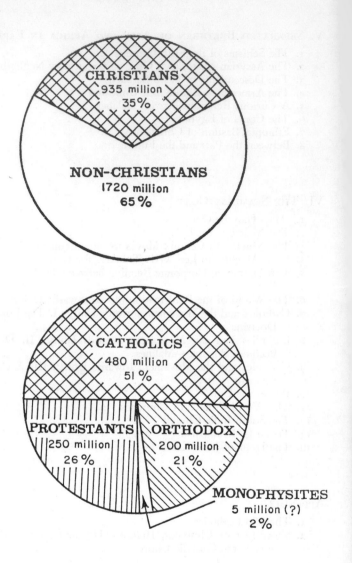

CHRISTIANITY'S PLACE IN THE WORLD

CHAPTER I

DAUGHTERS OF THE REFORMATION

1. FOUR FACETS

HARD blue sky, the rocky landscape of the Cévennes. In the distance, ridge upon ridge, piled like the sea, frozen into immobility. The church is the poorest building in the village: an old stable, it seems, long, low, bent-backed; crib and rack remain. The walls, stark, unadorned, are whitewashed. The end wall has a cross on it; on the side walls biblical verses, stained to the white, proclaim: 'For my thoughts are not your thoughts, neither are your ways my ways, saith the Lord' (Isa. lv. 8), and: 'He hath done all things well' (Mark vii. 37).

The congregation—men on the right, women on the left—number about one hundred; all are dressed in heavy, sombre clothes. The tone is stiff, even a little stilted. Standing in front of the white wooden table which takes up the end of the room, a Bible beside him on a small pulpit, flanked by two sprays of flowers, a man is speaking—the minister. He wears a black gown, which reminds one of a barrister's robe rather than a cassock. Collarless, the clerical band sits uneasily on his neck. 'Grace and peace are the gifts of God, Our Father and of Jesus Christ Our Lord. Let us invoke His help. . . .' Great simplicity marks the tone. The sonorifics which stress the local accent do not detract from the fervent conviction of the prayer. For an hour the service continues in the same key. Worship, reading from the Bible, confession of sins, profession of faith, Bible readings again. . . . From time to time an Amen resounds as if with one voice, and sometimes, though not often, a chant.

But there are two moments which are significant in this otherwise staid service: the sermon and Holy Communion. In neither case do they break with the tradition of restraint and simplicity. The minister speaks without emphasis, quoting from the Old and New Testaments with an ease that has something slightly mechanical about it. But there can be no doubt that his listeners pay attention nor that the simplest allusions to the Gospel awaken responses in them. Then the communion: a slowly moving file approaches the table, where each person sits for a moment on the bench before it, receiving the bread in half-closed hand and the wine in a small pewter goblet. One is reminded of a rustic meal, not at all of a sacrifice, still less of a mystery. A final prayer to which everyone listens standing, and, to end the service, the benediction of St Paul in his epistle to the Colossians: 'And let the peace of God rule in your hearts, to the which also ye are called in one body. Amen.'

The service is over. With the same simplicity as before the minister removes his robe and the clerical neck-band. In a grey jacket, he is no different from the men around him, a son, as they are, of the hard soil which saw the *Dragonnades* and the ambushes of the *Camisards*. The congregation pours out into the narrow lane, which echoes with their sing-song voices.

A Sunday in Norway. It is summer, but the sky is so pale that its blue has become pearly. The sea glistens in the distance over the roofs of the low houses, like a jewel held between the cliffs. A flight of gulls indulge in a noisy ballet overhead. The service has already begun, in the street, when the 'bishop of the region' (such is his title) comes out from the parish house to walk to the church at the head of a solemn gathering of men, all dressed in grey. He has a fine figure, white-haired, clean-cut of features—with his heavy gold-rimmed spectacles one is reminded more of a university professor than a priest. He wears a wide cape of purple velvet, adorned at the bottom and in front with Protestant motifs. Around him are four clerics. They have no capes, though they wear, as he does also, alb and chasuble. This is the form which Catholics call 'Gothic'. All have, embroidered at the back, a cross with oblique arms, in the centre of which can be seen a special motif, symbol of the Glorious Resurrection. But the most unexpected feature of this Nordic procession is the ruff which all five wear round their necks.

The bells have begun tolling. The church is full—always so when the bishop pays his annual visit; on an ordinary Sunday there is not such a crowd. It is an old building, squat, with strong foundations. The inside is vaulted Roman; on the walls are frescoes of biblical scenes; there are figures cut in the stained-glass bays; decorating the pillars, simple paintings or statues such as one sees in Sicily or Spain, evoking saints and martyrs. The altar is in the centre of the choir, agleam with candles; it is covered with an embroidered altar cloth. There is no tabernacle, the baptismal fonts being close by. At the entrance to the choir, as in Catholic churches, the communion table is but a long wide wooden barrier, fronted by a long cushion of imitation leather.

The Mass begins, the *högmässa*, entirely in Norwegian. But its arrangement is almost Roman; the sequence is traditional—introit from below the altar, prayer, reading from Epistles and Gospels, finally a very long sermon. A simplified Gregorian chant follows, popularized in form; Norwegian has no trouble in adapting it. Today it is to be a special Mass, with consecration and communion; this takes place only every fortnight or three weeks, depending on the parish. The communicants file to the communion table, where they kneel; the celebrant touches each forehead in turn, murmuring the words of the absolution, then holding out the Eucharist which some of them touch.

The file of communicants then proceeds to a kind of gilded buffet from which the minister takes a very small ciborium, which is brought close to each communicant's lips. The chant, which now resembles a psalm, is resumed. The *mässa* is almost ended. A few prayers, a benediction. The end seems abrupt, telescoped; to any Catholic present there is the impression that there is a curious resemblance to the service with which he is familiar. Yet, all the same, is it the tone of the service? The appearance of the congregation? Something incomplete in the order of liturgy, in its presentation? He senses a fundamental difference. One is certainly in another world.

Paris: a populous district, a soulless street. It is Saturday evening. In small groups men and women direct their steps down a cul-de-sac towards a doorway, indistinguishable from the entrances of the neighbouring workshops. They pass through two courtyards piled with assorted junk and scrap metal, finally reaching a brick-built edifice from whose high windows a flood of harsh neon light glares. Above the entrance is a banner, slackly held, proclaiming: 'Assembly of Christ the Liberator.'

The place is crowded: lower middle class, artisans; one might be at a trade union meeting, except that all ages are represented, even small children. One gets the impression that everyone knows everyone else, just as though they belonged to the same family group. At the end of the hall, on a raised platform, is a table flanked by five or six chairs painted in red and white, like those one sees in cafés. The table is strewn with Bibles, Gospels, tracts and propaganda leaflets. Behind it a man is speaking, with a profound sense of conviction. His theme is simple enough: Christ came to offer men His love but they would not accept it. 'Do you realize what men have done with the love of Christ the Saviour?' Then follow questions about the atomic bomb, world hunger, the atrocities in the Belgian Congo. Love one another! We must love one another! The touch of the Holy Ghost is nothing other than this power of love universal. 'If you do not want Paris one day to become another Hiroshima, the spirit of the Holy Ghost must enter into you and fill you with love!' The tone has risen now; through the congregation passes a tense collective shiver. Now there is a drumming of feet, and the whole congregation joins in a refrain: 'The Holy Ghost has spoken! Christ has saved me!' A man, then another, then a woman, come up to the table; they are introduced to the congregation by the speaker. They are going to 'bear witness' and to tell their brethren what the Holy Ghost has meant to them. It is a simple story, somewhat stereotyped: 'Evil held me in its sway, I was a sinner. I didn't observe the laws of God. I did not know of the existence of the Assemblies of God. I had no love for my fellows. But, one day, I felt the Spirit pass into me. . . .' Bravos and hurrahs from the throng and more drumming of feet, accompanied by cries of 'The Holy Ghost has spoken! Christ has saved me!'

A large basin is now brought to the front of the dais; just the kind of thing one sees in gardening advertisements for folding plastic swimming-pools. 'Who wishes to receive the baptism of repentance?' cries the leader. 'Who will bathe in the waters of the Jordan?' No— today no one wants to. But at this moment there is a cry from the back of the hall. The congregation parts to let a young woman through to the dais. Everyone at the back is standing on tiptoe to get a better look. She throws her arms out to the heavens, head thrust back, while a stream of unintelligible sounds comes from her, which the leader seems to understand, which he 'translates'. Sister Helen has been granted the supreme gift: a spark of fire from the Pentecost has fallen on her and has set her aflame; like the early Christians, she speaks with tongues and what she says is a vehement appeal to repentance, to universal love, to the Christ who alone can save. The woman falls silent, acclaimed, surrounded, embraced; then, anew, the drumming of feet, and the congregation repeats its *leit-motif.*

An English shire. The bells call from the church tower. The faithful, many of them with heavy leather-bound books in their hands, stream into the church. The church is a very ordinary Gothic style, fairly similar to those which served as models, under the Second Empire in France, to the builders of a whole series of Catholic churches; here perhaps a little more decorated and ornamented. Near the door is a red marble basin filled with holy water—here the visitor may dip his fingers. The nave is painted in red and gold, with many of the Christian symbols on it—fish, lamb, wheatsheaf, vine, and often the Alpha and Omega enclosing the *chrisma.* The general impression is one of studied comfort—pews in polished black oak, cushions along the front rows, heavy jute carpet covering the flagstones—which reminds one of the Catholic churches of Holland. The altar stands in the centre of the choir, with a tabernacle covered green—in the liturgical colour of the day. There are stained-glass windows; along the walls the fourteen stations of the Cross; at the end of the choir a great mahogany cross stands, on which is a Christ, peaceful in expression. To left and right, chapels on Cistercian lines parallel to the choir; the one on the right is blazing with light—a Virgin in painted wood is holding the Child, and there are at least a hundred candles lit for her. Candles are everywhere: on candelabra at the entrance to the choir, on the altar where the gilt gleams, and the purple chrysanthemums stand out in splendour. As they pass in front of the altar the members of the congregation genuflect.

The service begins. There are a celebrant and two clerics, all three in green chasubles decorated with embroidered motifs, lined with salmon-coloured silk. Four choirboys serve, wearing white albs heavily starched. The liturgy is no different from that of the Roman Catholic: ante-communion, readings, canon, consecration. Only the *Gloria* has been repositioned; now it is after the communion. The organ plays Bach or Handel or else accompanies the choir's talented singing. The only striking difference to a Catholic is that, until very recently, the entire service is conducted in English (according to the ancient 'Sarum rite').[1] But what one hears is strikingly in accordance with Catholic piety, such as the prayers which the minister intones before the canon.

Where are we? The foreign visitor would be at a loss to say. What is there to differentiate this service, correctly carried out as it is, from a solemn Mass in France, Italy or Spain? Perhaps there is something a little too studied in giving the liturgy its full import, as though celebrant and communicants, priest and faithful, had not become familiar with religious usage such as can only be acquired over a thousand years. But this is a small point, and it is not the essential one. Who, in all honesty, after the service is over, with the priest's final benediction having been given, would feel that he had been to a Protestant service? And yet . . .

Protestant. The four facets that we have just seen are all taken from Churches which sprang from the Reformation; all of them demonstrate one aspect of the Protestant phenomenon. The first one, Huguenot, was from French Calvinists, authentically traditional. The second in a part of Scandinavia which remains the bastion of Lutheranism. The third took the reader to a service of the Assemblies of God, normally called the Pentecostal Movement, which certain Protestants refuse to recognize as one of their Churches, but which are so none the less, in spirit as well as actions, and are one of the most lively elements of Protestantism. And as for the fourth, those who make it up would not consider it Protestant, yet their Anglican 'High Church' retains Protestant dogmatic formulae, takes part in the Protestant Missions Council, and its American counterpart is called Protestant Episcopalian. Four different aspects, all astonishingly different; one could depict thirty or forty without once departing from the framework of what is less an obedience than an attitude of mind, the Reformation.

[1] Modifications introduced by Vatican II will bring the Anglican and Roman Catholic liturgies closer.

2. PROTESTANTISM, THE SECOND OF THE WORLD'S CHRISTIAN BLOCS

Under the denomination 'Protestant' one will find many different aspects of Christendom. Statistically the Protestant bloc is the second largest in the world, far smaller than the Catholic, but considerably greater than that of the Eastern Orthodox Church.

It is not an easy matter to establish its numerical importance. The *World Christian Handbook*, which one can take as an official source, gave a total in 1954 of 260 million 'followers', among whom it stated were 70 million 'communicants'; the American magazine *Life* quoted 254 million, and the most recent figure from the Protestant historian Émile G. Léonard was one of about 206 million. The Catholic writer Jean Guitton, a specialist in ecumenical questions, did, however, put forward the figure of 280 million. The median gives us therefore some 250 million Christians who, practising and believing in greater or lesser degree, consider themselves Protestants.[1] Even this uncertainty with regard to numbers at once brings out one of the characteristics of Protestantism: a certain lack of precision in the outlines, a kind of porousness of all its outer walls, radically differentiating it from Catholicism, with its rigid framework, its well-defined limits, all springing from its very nature.

The term Protestant itself is curiously limiting and equivocal. In 1529 the Emperor Charles V, somewhat disquieted by the ideas of a certain Martin Luther which militated against the Church, summoned the Imperial Diet to Speier to consider the situation and to re-establish unity. The delegates soon realized that this was out of the question, and by a large majority decided to maintain things as they were. This *status quo* meant that the enthusiasts of new ideas and the traditional Catholics were certain of not being bothered further, even if they lived in an area dominated by their adversaries. But the innovators were not satisfied with this, for they were convinced that their movement was irresistible. The decision taken at Speier halted their progress; they were forbidden to continue with certain lines of propaganda, such as, for example, the criticism of the Eucharistic dogma. Five powerful nobles and fourteen cities refused the compromise. What? Tolerate the celebration of Mass, this Popish idolatry? Limit the right of their preachers to proclaim the truth? A *protestation* was published, whose vigorous tone seemed to echo the strong feelings which were present in the religious revolution then taking place: the term *protestant* took on a symbolic value.

[1] See table on p. 59.

Historically speaking [1] a Protestant is a Christian who protested against the decision of the Diet of Speier in 1529!—and by extension, against the errors of the Catholic Church. But it would be wrong to say that the great religious movement that is Protestantism is thus defined by its name in a purely negative sense. Even if it is true, as we shall see, that anti-Catholicism is one of its constants, it does not define itself by this alone. It is a protestation against Rome and Catholicism because it takes itself to be a protestation of faithfulness to the true Christianity, a testifying of conscience. Let us quote the etymological definition: *pro-testari*, to witness, or testify.

The historical links which bind the many denominations of today to the protesters of Speier are, however, strong. We are reminded that all that we call Protestantism is an issue of, and springs directly from, that event which took place in Germany from 1517 onwards, and in which all Western Europe was involved and which no historian doubts was the most important religious event for nine hundred years; more important even than the Greek Schism of 1054—the Reformation. In the deepest sense of the word, every Protestant is a son of the Reformation. He would not have been had there been no Reformation, or he would, in any case, have been different. Amidst all the different variations on the theme of Protestantism, now at least we have the link which leads us to speak of Protestant unity.

3. THE REFORMATION: MARTIN LUTHER

What then was the Reformation? 'A religious movement which took place in the sixteenth century, separating a great part of Europe from obedience to the popes, and gave rise to the Protestant Churches.' This is what the Larousse dictionary tells us. The definition is brief, makes no allusions to the causes, deals only with consequences and does not tell us why the word has a capital letter, nor why the usual sense of the word is not joined to its new meaning, a 're-forming' or 'a change for the better'.

In point of fact definition of the Reformation depends on one's point of view. For Protestant authors the Reformation is akin to a normal and legitimate reaction of the Christian conscience, not only because of the scandalous aspects which the Church was then presenting, but equally because of the deviations which had been introduced into practice and even dogma. Catholics have laid emphasis on political and moral causes: the cupidity of certain lay powers, pride, or an excessive taste for freedom attributed to the rebellious clergy. Marxists, for their part, applied to the phenomenon the principles of historical

[1] See *The Protestant Reformation.*

materialism, and saw in the Reformation the consequences of change entailed in the deep economic and social transformations of the age which resulted, according to the normal rules of dialectic, in the ruin of the old civilization of Christianity. Following Lucien Febvre,[1] more recent historians have remarked that in order to account for a religious phenomenon one must seek religious causes. In their view the starting point of the crisis that shook the very foundations of the West will be found in the personal struggles of certain believers. So far we have four explanations, but they appear to be less contradictory than complementary, all of them being true both partly and simultaneously.

We are at the beginning of the sixteenth century. A young German religious is going through a crisis of soul-searching. He is a tall thin lad, square-faced, with thick eyebrows and eyes that are by turns brilliant with passion and then obscurely sombre. He is a little over thirty, and yet in his Order (the Augustinians) he already shows promise. Neither success nor the real influence which he exercises can calm his anguish; only his closest friends know that it is unceasing and terrible. Sinner! He feels a sinner, racked less by carnal temptations than by those of spiritual revolt, that great denial whose other name is despair. As the result of an incident in which his life seemed endangered, he sought to escape it by entering a monastery and so into the protection of a Rule. But his anguish did not leave him; if anything, it became more acute during communion, for the very thought of Christ, as represented there, pronouncing judgment on the Last Day, was enough to make him blench. All whom he met, as well as himself, he asked: 'What must one do to be saved?'

His name was Martin Luther; but there were many other Martin Luthers in Christendom. In Bohemia, in Alsace, in Flanders, in Switzerland, in France, there were many who asked themselves the same agonizing question. It was in tune with the age. An age weary with wars and violence, with frightful crimes and with sins of every description. An age when the Dance of Death was a familiar theme to artists, when the unbalanced turned to necromancy and magic. An age when impious minds had begun to deny God, to pit against Him the man of 'Humanism', master of his own fate. But that man was here on earth, heavy with the poignancy of his misery, conscious of the gulf which separated him from sovereign justice. To the question which the Martin Luthers were all asking, who would reply?

It should have been the Church—Mother Church—who understands and comforts; but in the disorder in which the world was foundering her institutions were unstable. The Papacy had emerged weakened from exile at Avignon and the Great Schism; on return to Rome it was to be too intimately concerned with the intrigues and

[1] See article in the *Revue Historique*, vol. xli, 1929.

bloody conflicts of Italy; meanwhile it was manifestly attracted by that proud intellectual movement known as the 'Renaissance'. It was a situation which a twentieth-century Catholic historian has no hesitation in describing as grave. For having denounced it, perhaps too roundly but not without truth, Savonarola, twenty years before these events, was burned at the stake. . . . Throughout the ecclesiastical hierarchy similar causes had similar effects: too many bishops had lost the sense of spiritual responsibility; too many priests and religious, though not corrupted, were ignorant and listless, uncritical of superstitions which verged on sharp practice. The presence within the Church of the great figures of saints and of masses still humbly faithful did not lessen the distressing aspects of the scene.

What reply could the Church, so lacking in example, give to Martin Luther and his companions in anguish? Of course had they possessed in a measure equal to their faith that humility of the spirit which makes real saints, they would have recognized under the uninspiring crust of appearances the pure face of the Bride of Christ, and in spite of everything they would have remembered that the gates of hell cannot prevail against the holder of the Promise. But it must be admitted that, while they were misguided, they had some excuse. To calm their anguish they were offered a collection of largely paltry practices, of meaningless routine, of devotions which amounted to little more than magic formulae. Everything in that decadent system appeared to have been emptied of its religious content. Prayers to the saints were multiplied, too often regardless of the fact that there is only one mediator between God and man—Jesus Christ. Men bought indulgences to procure salvation, forgetting that without the spirit of repentance indulgences have no more value than words carried away by the wind. What relation was there between the gesture of putting a florin in the collector's box and the soul's aspiration to rise to God? And now we know why on 31st October 1517 Martin Luther was to nail a long *factum* against indulgences on the door of the chapel of the castle of Wittenberg, and in so doing he unleashed the most serious religious revolution of all time.

Did he not act too hastily? Could not the reply which he sought have been found among the learned men who asserted that they could explain the mysteries of God? Alas, was not theology that part of the Church's fabric that showed the most piteous state? Medieval scholasticism was in full decline: it seemed like a machine operating in a vacuum, incapable of recognizing the reality of the Word of God. The doctrine in vogue was, and had been for a century, that of the Franciscan Ockham, a system stressing an excessive naturalization of man and an infinite supernaturalization of God. In the universities it had so far replaced Thomism that Luther and his emulators could believe that it was the official doctrine of the Church. The most recent of Ockham's followers, Gabriel Biel, taught that one might defeat sin by one's own volition, but that this in no way constituted anything meritorious in the eyes of God. God must accept the work of man and accept it as worthy of merit. In this system grace is no longer conceived as a universal principle which raises spiritual forces to the plane of divine justice and good works as elements in salvation. Destiny seems as if it is ruled by the icy mechanism of a despot; the soul is disarmed.

Since Mother Church was in no state to reply, her practices acting as a screen to the truth rather than leading to it, her doctrines driving him to despair, Martin Luther—and others too—was to establish his own system. The elements he takes from St Paul—Paul the great sinner whom Christ touched in his heart. The verses of the Epistle to the Romans, a hundred times re-read, at last give the answer in a flash of inspiration: 'The just shall live by faith' (i. 17), and 'Therefore we conclude that a man is justified by faith without the deeds of the law' (iii. 28). Beside this, what matter the heartrending sense of misery which the sinner feels? It is true that he is 'incapable of overcoming his sin alone' and it is true also that compared to the righteousness of Christ, 'virtues themselves are sins before God'. But Christ is there, who answers those who call upon Him. The sinner is as if covered by a shaft of light; basically he remains unchanged, but he is carried towards God by a power greater than all those of Hell. Believe! Have faith! That is all that is needed. To him who truly believes, be he the greatest of sinners, God will impute the righteousness of Christ.

Such was the discovery of Martin Luther, through which he found deliverance from his anguish and a peaceful heart. To make up for the shortcomings of theology, he made this the starting point of a complete new system. In salvation, in religion itself, God alone must be considered; one should not count on the support or even the co-operation of man. Nothing is of value except grace. All 'good works', whether of charity or of penance, may be valuable in themselves, but they are of no account in salvation. All intercession, such as that of the Virgin Mary or the saints, is inconceivable. Only the Word of God, as it is found in the Scriptures, is of value. 'No other interpreter of the Divine Word but the author of the Word,' insists the reformer; in any case, has not St Paul said, 'The Spirit itself beareth witness with our spirit' (Rom. viii. 16). From this follows the exclusion of authority and mediation of the Church, either through faith by teaching, or through grace by the sacraments. Of these Luther retained only three which he considered originated in the Scriptures—Baptism, Penance and the Eucharist—divesting them of their operative virtue: the rite would act no longer in itself. Thus the entire doctrinal edifice of the Church was turned upside-down in this vehement dialectic where 'free inquiry' was to be opposed to 'tradition', direct recourse to God set against ecclesiastic discipline, the Spirit against the letter. . . .

How could the Church accept such subversion? The quarrel over indulgences pales beside this, for it is the whole content of religion which is in question now. To the innovator the Church replies: 'It is true that, in the work of salvation, everything emanates from God and His grace is indispensable; but Christ, our Mediator, has said, "Except ye be converted . . .", or, in other words, that He seeks our collaboration. And St Paul, so dear to Luther, said, "Work out your own salvation with fear and trembling" (Phil. ii. 12). And had he not proclaimed that by his trials he was completing that which was lacking in the passion of Christ? (". . . and fill up that which is behind of the afflictions of Christ . . .") (Col. i. 24).

'Faith is indispensable, but justification is achieved only by charitable acts or penance and by the receipt of sacraments instituted by Christ to bring us to salvation. Turning now to the Word of God, if it be true that it is Alpha and Omega, it has been given into the sacred keeping of the Church. It is that which, in its entirety, has received the blessings of the Holy Ghost; it is that which traditionally explains and legitimately extends the teaching of the Scriptures; it is also that which, in associating the humblest sinner with the righteousness of the saints, draws its members towards salvation.' Term for term, between the Catholic and the Lutheran doctrine, one can distinguish a fundamental opposition.

In systematizing the revelation which came to him—'the just shall live by faith'—Luther preached 'a separate opinion', to use an early Christian phrase, a doctrine which was no longer that of the Community. In Greek terminology such an opinion was 'heresy', a noble heresy—an error of *more* just as there are errors of *less*: God alone! Faith alone! The Scriptures alone!—but none the less dangerous, if not more dangerous, since there will be a measure of temptation for more demanding souls. When it became clear, three years after the incident at Wittenberg, that this was no quarrel between monks nor a scholarly discussion, but struck at the roots, and that Christians in ever-increasing numbers were identifying themselves with the new doctrine, the Pope condemned Luther and excommunicated him. He answered this publicly by burning the Bull directed against him. It was the final break, a result that the young Augustinian religious could not have foreseen when he nailed his ninety-five theses on indulgences to the door at Wittenberg. Did not one of them, the thirty-eighth, affirm, 'The remission, however, imparted by the Pope is by no means to be despised, since it is, as I have said, a declaration of divine remission'? But it is in the nature of 'separated opinions' that those who hold them should recede ever further from the shores which they have left. . . .

Meanwhile other factors had arisen, and Luther was drawn into powerful currents. Within ten years of the famous incident Germany was thrown into confusion, and neighbouring countries also felt the shock. The astounding success of the Lutheran theses was not to be explained merely by religious reasons; here we must consider the other explanations which Catholics and Marxists put forward.

In many parts of Germany, especially in Prussia, and elsewhere also —e.g. in Sweden and later in England—it was the rulers that decided when a change of faith should take place among their people. In order to enrich themselves at the Church's expense and establish their autonomy, powerful nobles and sovereigns, driven along by the upsurge of national feeling, adopted new ideas. All this was made easier by the disorganization of the world, which was going through a social crisis due to the emergence of capitalist economies and to an intellectual crisis due to the rapid expansion of knowledge. Sexual freedom also granted to the clergy by the Reformer—do we not read of married Apostles in the Scriptures?—had some influence on the speed with which certain clergy adopted the new theology. Pure or impure, all these forces were going the same way. In face of this formidable assault the Church appeared to confine herself to mere condemnations of principle, as though inertia and routine impeded her from effecting of her own accord those reforms which so many of her best sons proclaimed were necessary, from carrying out in fact what she had so often carried out in the course of her long history, by taking the lead in the movement for reform and thus directing it. Later she was to do this, but too late, at the Council of Trent; meanwhile over-zealous spirits would despair of her and Western Christianity would cut itself in two.

Luther's movement, of which he was the protagonist, now manifested signs of disunity and a certain insufficiency. The radical individualism, which is the basis of the Reformation, favours far too much those tendencies which lead to divergencies; other reformers had arisen meanwhile, some of them carrying to extremes theses similar to his. Thus, in popular circles, the Anabaptists rejected all practice excepting the sacrament of baptism, which they administered to adults, in order to stress it in all its aspects as a profession of faith. These were the same Anabaptists whose many-branched movement was to blossom into strange subversive forms. Zwingli in Zürich appeared to be close to a similar radicalism, although later on he was to rebut this. In Strasbourg Martin Bucer, in Basel Oeclampadius, were attempting to stabilize the doctrine midway between Luther and the extremists. The sacramentarians set aside the dogma of the Real Presence in the Eucharist, which they regarded as only a symbol, a memorial; and this angered Luther, for though he refused to admit 'transubstantiation', he believed in 'consubstantiation', in other words, that Christ, in the

Eucharistic host, is present *with* the bread. What confusion! Even on a practical plane disorder is manifest. The peasants, who were being ruined by the economic crisis, and who had heard much about Christian brotherhood and a redistribution of wealth, rose in revolt and risked setting all Germany aflame; to re-establish order it was necessary to invoke the secular power. Luther not only approved this step, but indeed advised it, thus confirming the princes in the authority of which he had deprived the Catholic hierarchy. It was necessary for the Reformation to organize itself if it were not to founder, a task which one man was about to accomplish. On the dogmatic plane he would go much further than the German Augustinian: it was now the hour of John Calvin, a Frenchman.

4. THE WORK OF JOHN CALVIN

'The second patriarch of the Reformation', as Bossuet calls him, was eight years old at the time of Luther's emergence. He thus belonged to that second generation which, in most religious or political movements, arranges the elements supplied by the first generation and provides them with their full impact. Cold, organizing, logical were the attributes that Calvin evinced; but despite an apparent shyness he was also of a speculative turn of mind, capable of tackling the most abstruse problems. He had the soul of an apostle, the character of a leader and a clarity of expression to which modern French literature owes much. He may have been converted suddenly to the new ideas which were abroad, or it may have been a gradual process—Calvin himself is not explicit on this point—but in his twenty-seventh year he changed his opinions. He assimilated, developed and enlarged the reformers' system of thought, especially that of Luther, transforming it into an entirely new system, stricter and more coherent. He set it out in 1536, in his *L'Institution de la religion chrétienne*, a key work which was an immediate and enormous success. Subsequently, through a combination of circumstances in which he discerned the hand of Providence, he became the spiritual leader of Geneva and then proceeded to give effect to his ideas—in an earthly city he experimented with the Church of Heaven as he conceived it. It was not without certain stresses and strains, but it was to serve as a useful example. For long Geneva was to remain in Protestant eyes a prototype of the perfect Christian community. A second wave of the Reformation was under way with Calvinists taking over from Lutherans.

What was Calvin's contribution to his forerunner's work? Not a great deal. As Luther had done, he insisted that man's salvation rests entirely on faith. Like Luther, he conceded that the Scriptures had value only when interpreted freely by each man, not according to his intelligence but through the presence within of the Holy Ghost which each man possesses. Similarly he rejected what Catholics call Tradition, or the totality of dogma and practices which the Church has garnered from the Scriptures and which she holds as guarantor. Similarly too he would have no intermediary between the soul and God. But the basic tenets of the Reformation are pushed by Calvin to their extremes with a deductive discipline which reminds one of Descartes. He gave Protestantism method and organization, in which Luther had taken little interest. For this reason Calvin must rank among the great figures of religious history.

As for dogma, the terrible logic of his system was to lead even Calvin to say that it was an 'appalling doctrine'. The desire—practically an obsession—to affirm the sovereignty of God in every respect, and in consequence to reject every aspect of human endeavour, was to lead to a radical thesis, so radical that its present-day inheritors have abandoned it—predestination. 'In the eternal Council of God, every man at birth is destined either for eternal life or eternal damnation'—a logical thesis, since God is all-powerful and omniscient. From this statement of principle the rest follows. For example, there is the definition of the Church, which cannot be other than a gathering of saints, of the predestined, leaving without all the sinners whom the 'Council of God' condemns. But what can earthly man do if he is to admit such a dreadful idea, condemned to damnation perhaps without knowing it, without being able to find any defence? Might he not be literally in despair? Not at all, for while it is horrible enough to believe oneself damned, it is singularly exalting to persuade oneself that one is predestined to meet God face to face; and it was this feeling that was to endow the Calvinists with the driving force of their apostolate and with courage in the trials they would have to face. What signs determine one's predestination? Calvin's reply was: The saintliness of one's life. In his view the operation of the Holy Ghost is not by way of illumination, as it was with Luther, but by way of an appeal to lead a saintly life. To practise virtue is not, as the Catholics aver, to acquire righteousness in the eyes of Heaven, but is rather to undergo the vital experience of the Kingdom of Heaven; it is to carry the sign of Christ upon one. Such was the idea that the 'Procurator of God' applied in Geneva with unfailing severity; this too was the mark of Calvinism and later of all Protestantism, giving it a moralizing role, not excluding a certain degree of Pharisaism.

Calvin applied the same strict, deductive principles to all his tenets. A man of the Bible, he accepted only what was found in the Scriptures. Of the three sacraments retained by Luther, he abandoned one, that of Penance, which he could not find in the Gospels; he considered it to be included in baptism, and refused to interpret in the Catholic sense the famous saying of Christ to his Apostles: 'Whose soever sins ye remit, they are remitted' (John xx. 23). He removed from the sacraments of baptism and communion all their sacramental value: the first is no longer anything but the 'sign of our Christianity'; the second, if it is not a symbolic memorial as for Zwingli, at least evokes a presence which faith alone may possess. The 'consubstantiation' which Luther admitted, and everything which recalls Christ's sacrifice, all are finally suppressed, together with everything that had been slowly added by tradition to the original fundamentals of Jewish prayer. No more incense, no more candles, no more liturgical formulae, no more stately ceremonies. In austere buildings the service was reduced virtually to a ministry of the Word; the ministry of the altar, retained by the Lutherans, was abandoned and communion in both kinds with the communicants seated around a table was to resemble a meal as closely as possible.

It was thus a new style which Calvin gave to Protestantism, as well as a new order. Luther had retained several elements of Catholic organization. Among these was the episcopal hierarchy, the bishops remaining as regional heads of the Church, though shorn of the power to ordain the priests whom they appointed. In Calvin's system the 'pastors' were men who had felt the call to spread the Gospel, and whom the community of adherents charged with that duty. Every Church, every parish was free; the councils or consistories were far from holding the same dogmatic or disciplinary powers possessed by the Catholic hierarchy. A democratic system was set up, founded on the same lines as the early Church. But Calvin, who had an authoritative nature, and who knew well the aberrations of sinners, would not allow the Church of the saints, as seen on earth, to abandon itself to any emotional excess. 'Free inquiry' for him had certain limits, and the Christian community, the 'Church', must help all of its members, if necessary by force, into the right channels of faith and to conduct themselves according to the sacred principles. The citizens of Geneva, and some wrongheads like Michael Servetus, were to experience this. And so it was that, in this striking synthesis of the spirit of authority and democratic freedom, the reformer set out to 'educate' the Church.

It is scarcely necessary to emphasize that Calvin's deductions and innovations were, even more than Luther's theses, 'separated opinions', unacceptable to the Catholic Church. On every essential and principal point Catholicism has opposite views. It does not admit that God is a kind of despot who damns or saves as the whim takes Him; that the blood of Jesus Christ was shed only for certain men; that good conduct, heroic efforts to practise virtue, all count for nothing in salvation; that the lost sheep so dear to the Good Shepherd are not expressly a part of the Church; that Christ is not really present in the bread and wine of the Eucharist; that 'vocation' suffices to entrust a priest with a sacred mission without this being received from on high and transmitted by the Church through a direct filial link with the God-Man. When Calvin died in 1564 the break between the new Christianity and the older forms of the Christian religion was complete and appeared to be irreparable.[1] The Church of Christ was now split. Subsequent events which, from the outset of the Reformation, the humanist Erasmus had prophesied would entail 'a frightful carnage', would only enlarge the gulf and deepen the abyss. And four centuries would not be too long for Christians to feel deeply about the scandal which this split represents.

In 1564, then, we can say that the Reformation had acquired its fundamental characteristics. It is impossible nowadays to consider one or other of the aspects which it adopted without discovering, in substance, at least some of the tenets of Luther or Calvin. The conviction that man is wise enough to embark unaided on spiritual exploration; the recourse to faith as the sole—or at least the primary—means to salvation; the veneration for the Scriptures and complete confidence in the Word of God which they transmit; the practice, somewhat too open, of virtues, or, in any event, loudly proclaimed moral principles —these will constitute the basis of Protestantism. To them must be added a common hostility towards Catholicism which ranges, according to circumstances, from mistrust to hate, a feeling which can be explained by reasons which are both spiritual and temporal, Protestantism being born, as to its thought and as to its institutions, in opposition to the Catholic Church. Only very recently has this feeling diminished.

5. 'VARIATIONS' AND SPLITS IN THE FABRIC OF PROTESTANTISM

Sons of the Reformation, linked together by the same great set of principles; why have the Protestants tended during the last few centuries to break up into different Churches? Why do they present a spectacle of disparity, whose four aspects, which we saw earlier, have already set the scene, and which, in any case, do not merely present cultural differences? Bossuet supplied the answer to this question in his famous work, *Histoire des variations des Églises protestantes*, an answer to which no Protestant will take exception: 'The variations in the

---

[1] Orthodox Christianity is opposed, as regards both doctrine and organization, to Protestantism no less than to Catholicism. See Chapter VI, section 11 for a statement made by the Orthodox Church at the Evanston World Council of Churches meeting in 1954.

Reformation spring from its very constitution.' Is it the genius of Protestantism that it can go on subdividing to infinity?

At the moment of the outbreak of the religious revolution it was possible to see that it had several starting points, and that it did not everywhere have the same characteristics. Luther may have been the most important of the heralds of the Reformation, but we must not forget Zwingli, Bucer and Oeclampadius. Before the end of the sixteenth century it was felt that the two great rivers of Lutheranism and Calvinism would absorb all the little streams of the Reformation, as it had in most cases even the older ones, older than Luther himself, such as the Hussites of Bohemia and the Waldenses of the Alps and Provence. There remained, in any size, only the Anabaptists, or at any rate those who had survived catastrophe, and these, made wiser and organized by Menno Simons as a coherent system, both simple and mystic, were shrewdly adapted to popular outlook; persecutions did not seem to trouble them and they did not disappear. In England, where the Reformation had established itself in a rather special context, it was too early to decide if Anglicanism would join with one of the great rivers or would constitute a variation of its own.

But there was in the very substance of Protestantism a ferment that would not allow it to develop along lines laid down by a straightforward plan: this was the principle of 'free inquiry'.

Both Luther and Calvin had admitted that the human conscience, in order to come to God, had no need to be guided along its route by a *magisterium* capable of preventing it from falling into error. This was to open the door to individualism. From the moment that no infallible authority exists who can say that this or that is true or false, all doctrinal deviations end up necessarily as a split, with very often the founding of a new group. Even the best-intentioned initiatives, if presented in an original way, upsetting normal customs, have the same result. Had Wesley been born into the Catholic Church he would have made his 'Methodists' a third order within the Church. The forces which urge the Reformation to infinite division seem to be irresistible.

That unchecked individualism risked incurring spiritual anarchy, and subsequently political and social anarchy, was well understood by the great reformers. Though their conceptions were different, Luther and Calvin had sought to establish Churches with leaders and discipline, and even to impose a minimum level of beliefs common to all in Confessions—Augsburg and Calvinist. By these means they had, wrote a liberal Protestant in 1871, 'restrained the liberty of their adherents by indicating more or less formally how they should understand the Scriptures'.[1] But this re-establishment of a creed was evidently contrary to the spirit which gave birth to the Reformation. The

[1] Maurice Vernes, *Quelques Réflexions sur la crise de l'Église réformée*, Paris, 1871.

same arguments which were used against Catholic orthodoxy were used against the new orthodoxy. New 'protestations' were heard, a second wave of protestations as it were, just as legitimate as the first ones. And against the former revolutionaries, by now conformists, now arose new nonconformists.

Even those reformers who appeared more noble, willing to enter fully into the Christian adventure in order to help man to rise above himself, contributed also to a multiplication of dissensions and splits. The theme *Ecclesia reformata semper reformanda* is one of the most cherished in Protestant conscience, and one of the most eloquent. And it is profoundly true that, in institutions as in souls, reform is always necessary to fight against the dark forces that draw man towards ease, routine, evil. The Reformation, born of the spiritual awakening of Martin Luther, has always accorded great importance to these movements, these revivals which, from time to time, have taken hold of its adherents. Certain souls, in the grip of a driving desire for the absolute, feel ill at ease in their own Church; they yearn for a return to the original principles, to discover anew the force of the Reformers; they also believe that the Holy Ghost has called them. Not all feel in this way, for it is not easy to admit that one needs a revival, and innovators are frowned upon. So it comes about that new movements are born either within one and the same Church, as 'Free Churches' hostile to the Established Church, or as new Churches, as, for instance, Methodism, or yet again as sects such as the Quakers or, nearer our own times, the Pentecostal Church.[1]

So it was that, following a dialectical process so flawless that one might have supposed it to be invented to prove Hegel right, the centuries that followed the Reformation gave rise to many and varied forms of religious expression, all claiming kinship. Yet within these various religious elements themselves, other divisive factors intervened. The geographical and political factors were not the least of them. Luther had expressly associated the lay authorities with religious administration in Germany. Feudal fragmentation brought in its train the setting up of some thirty-five Lutheran Churches, and even Prussian centralization failed to unite them. Elsewhere social factors played their part: there were some churches which catered for and were an expression of the lower middle and middle classes; others were of a working class, popular nature. In the U.S.A. racial questions entailed similar divisions: there were black Baptists quite separate from white Baptists, black Methodists quite separate from white Methodists. The debates which centred on ideas born in the nineteenth

---

[1] The case of the Methodists is especially significant, for Wesley obstinately refused to separate from his original Church, but his successors found themselves forced to it by the logic of their action.

century [1] had similar results also, the heritage of the Reformers being exploited in two different ways, by those who insisted on free inquiry and those who concentrated upon the great dogmatic themes of the sovereignty of God. A liberal Protestantism defended its Churches against rigid orthodoxies. Theoretically there is no limit to this process of fragmentation, since the Church as a whole is present, thanks to the Holy Ghost, in the smallest of parishes and, as is proclaimed in the Constitution of the Church of Geneva in 1910, 'each pastor teaches and preaches the Gospels freely, on his own responsibility, this freedom being unrestricted by any profession of faith or by any liturgical formulary'.

Does this constant division present advantages which may compensate for its obvious inconveniences? Many Protestant thinkers are convinced that it does. According to them this division allows the totality of the movement that sprang from the Reformation to grasp the whole of the Christian experience in all its diversity much better than Catholicism, whose framework seems to them to lack suppleness.[2]

Nevertheless the most striking character of Protestantism, as this has emerged from the end of the sixteenth century, does appear to be its multiplicity, its division. Is it possible to express this in figures? Only with difficulty. In 1954, in the U.S.A., official statistics revealed *263 religious denominations*.[3] But this was not the whole story, for among the American Negroes the number of sects and minor Churches was virtually impossible to determine. Let us say nothing of Africa: some authorities assess the number at 1,600 sects, all Christian to a greater or lesser degree. Protestants themselves disagree on the treatment to be accorded to this or that group: the Mormons, for example, are considered by most as heretics, since they added another book to the Bible; the Pentecostal Church, not admitted by some sections and graced by such men as Marc Boegner, is considered the leading wing of Protestantism in South America; and when the Methodists began spreading over France certain pastors, such as Réville, declared that this was the negation of true Protestantism! The lack of precision is made more obvious still by the use of identical terms to indicate very different realities. Thus the qualification 'evangelical', which may be claimed by all the Churches of the Reformation, is often applied to Calvinistic Churches hostile to liberal Protestantism; yet there exist numerous groups of Baptists and even Pentecostalists who claim it. In Anglicanism, moreover, the term has an altogether different meaning.

---

[1] See Chapter III, section 7.
[2] To which the Catholics reply that they too know as many different attitudes, and are as open to all forms of spiritual experience, but that they are directed towards a visible unity. . . .
[3] The Roman Catholic Church was the biggest with (in May 1964) some 45 million adherents.

The complexity is therefore already considerable, even if we are to consider only those groups which are well delineated. Further, within the same Church there may be Churches independent one from another, with still more differences between them; there may have been little difference among the thirty-five Lutheran Churches which still existed in the Germany of 1914, but the differences are more marked in the case of the sixteen Baptist Churches of the U.S.A.

We must not, however, rely on statistical evidence merely in order to be clear about the divisions of Protestantism. A great many of these 'denominations' have only minimal importance. Some groups are strictly local, others have only a very few adherents—they are only scraps of Churches compared to the big battalions. Between such and such a 'Church' the differences are so slight that they can exchange their adherents without any doctrinal difficulties: it will be seen that in the U.S.A. it is quite common for a man or a woman to change his or her 'denomination' for matrimonial or residential reasons. A closing of the gap between groups, and even a merger sometimes, takes place, as in south India.[1] Against the trend to still more division, a trend which prevailed until the middle of the nineteenth century, there is now a trend to what Jacques Courvoisier calls 'the Protestant concentration'. Nowadays this is the prevailing trend. Results have been achieved on two planes, and first within the larger Churches. Within the bosom of Anglicanism, for example, the Lambeth Conferences since 1867 have guaranteed unity. Again the World Presbyterian Alliance includes the traditional Calvinist Churches; it dates in Scotland from about 1875 and underwent considerable expansion between 1890 and the establishment at Geneva in 1948. There is also the World Lutheran Alliance, set up in 1900. The tendency towards concentration was no less clearly marked on another plane—that of a drawing together of common principles of faith, particularly for joint defence of common interests, among various Protestant groups in a particular country. Organizations were set up which included representatives of very different groups; the *Fédération protestante de France*, founded in 1907, supplies us with a typical example, and this was imitated elsewhere. In short one can recognize a hierarchy among the Protestant denominations, some half-dozen of them being the most important, two or three being in the second rank, and the rest representing trends or currents which are more or less divergent or excessive; but it is not an easy matter to establish the precise meaning of such terms as church, community, confession, denomination, sect. All are disputable and equivocal, covering (according to circumstances) very different realities: the first is employed with reserve by a Catholic speaking in an everyday and non-theological sense; the last has acquired a disparaging meaning.

[1] See Chapter VI, section 11.

The most highly qualified among authors confess themselves powerless to establish an entirely adequate vocabulary. Classification of Protestant terms must therefore be of necessity arbitrary.

6. The Most Important of the Protestant Churches: the Lutherans

The first-born of Protestantism, Lutheranism is also the most important numerically. It is difficult to establish precise numbers—different authorities give different figures, varying between 63½ million and 80 million in 1958. In 1963 Émile G. Léonard spoke of 90 million. The median is probably around 75 million, which means to say that about one Protestant in three is a follower of the Augsburg Confession.

This seems surprising at first glance. When one thinks of Protestantism, and tries to imagine the religious life of one of its adherents, it is not Lutheranism or a Lutheran that a Frenchman, an Englishman or an American takes as a characteristic example. It might be thought that the heirs of the first of the reformers have remained inside certain limits exercising an influence on the destinies of Protestantism. Such a view would be quite false for several reasons. Lutheranism indeed has made less stir than other Protestant groups; it has not gone through the same violent crises or suffered the same divisions as others. Again Lutheranism is commonly considered as inextricably bound up with Germany. The expression *Luthertum ist Deutschtum* is often on German lips. It is at once both true and false. True in that modern Germany has largely sprung from Luther; that, as Nietzsche said, 'Luther is now and always the major event in German history'; and that Fichte and Bismarck, as well as Kant, Hegel and Nietzsche himself, are all disciples of Luther. It is not coincidence that, on the eve of the vital decisions which were to result in a united Germany, there were national demonstrations in favour of a monument to Luther in 1868. But it is none the less true that the Lutheran field of conquest extends far beyond the German world, so far indeed that one Lutheran in two is a non-German.[1]

Lutheranism took root first of all in the German world, and it is there that it has entrenched itself. The *Landeskirchen*, first established in the sixteenth century by the princes, have survived the disappearance of feudal Germany and the coming of Bismarck's empire. However, other 'confessional' Churches, sprung from purely religious needs, have joined with them without upsetting the Lutheran framework.

[1] Firstly, because Catholicism in Germany is a very important element; after its victory in the *Kulturkampf* it took an active part in the destiny of Germany—see previous volumes.

The attempt by the Prussian monarch in 1817 to unify all the reformed Churches in his States [1] did not profoundly modify the general
character of German Protestantism, which remained Lutheran in
substance. From Germany, Lutheranism spread quickly to countries
farther north—to Denmark, Norway and Sweden. Its success was
virtually complete; for today it represents some 90 per cent to 98 per
cent of the population of those three countries. Thence it spread to the
Baltic States and to Finland, where it has an almost equally impressive
record. There were less important outcrops in Bohemia, Austria and
Hungary. In France the drive towards Calvinism left little territory to
Lutheranism, save in Alsace and the Montbéliard region, which until
1801 was a part of Württemberg.

Today the most important group of Lutherans outside Germany is
found in the U.S.A. Eighteenth-century immigration brought small
groups of German and Scandinavian Lutherans to America, and they
have remained uniformly loyal to their faith. At first they were
separated by the vast distances of the American continent, but during
the nineteenth century they reformed into tighter groups and became
strongly organized. Lutheranism is one of the most important
denominations in the U.S.A., numbering some 10 million, and on the
world scale of Lutheranism it carries considerable weight.

All Lutherans adhere to the Lutheran catechism and the Augsburg
Confession, which Melanchthon drew up for presentation to the Diet
in 1530 with the obvious intention of avoiding a complete split by
stressing the points of agreement with Catholic doctrine rather than the
stumbling-blocks. A Catholic theologian has said that 'the Lutheran
Churches are the most level-headed members of modern Protestantism'.[2] This does not prevent differences of opinion between areas, even
between Churches. As we saw in the second of the Four Aspects, it is
in Scandinavia that Lutheranism comes closest to pre-Reformation
Christianity. The liturgy is largely unchanged: decorated and even
sumptuous churches, liturgical vestments, the retention of the altar, the
use of candles and incense—all are astonishing to rigid Calvinists. In
Sweden the service is called '*Mässa*' and whoever presides at the
liturgy is indifferently referred to as 'priest' or 'pastor'. The bishops,
though they do not claim Apostolic Succession in the sacramental sense
of the term, have very wide powers. Traditionalism goes further than
one might assume at first sight. The Scandinavian Lutherans, while
they are hostile to Rome, have no feeling that continuity has been
broken. Their bishops consider themselves as the successors of those
in pre-Reformation times. Their Gregorian chant is scarcely modified.
Though their priests marry, they have nevertheless been slow to admit

[1] See Chapter II, section 3.
[2] Georges Tavard, *A la rencontre du Protestantisme*, p. 24.

women as priests. This has caused no great difficulties in other forms of Protestantism.

German Lutheranism has a much more pronounced Protestant character. The altar remains, but Mass has vanished, liturgy has been simplified, the teaching of the Scriptures and the chants have been made more important. The *Landesbischof* is more of an ecclesiastical functionary than a successor of the Apostles. He encourages both adherents and pastors, he urges them towards charitable works, he watches over the training of priests, he has a representative role. At his side a lay committee has important duties. However, belief in the presence of Christ in the Eucharist—which is not, let us remember, the Real Presence—is very widespread. And since the 'ritualist' renewal of the last century the liturgy and the decoration of churches have once again become the custom in many parishes. In other European countries Lutheranism has adapted itself to prevailing circumstances, though not without undergoing some Calvinist influence. In France, for example, it is run by synods who elect for life their 'ecclesiastical inspectors', not 'bishops'.

One of the traits which for long were characteristic of the Lutheran Churches in Europe, doubtless due to their origins, was that of being State Churches, 'Established Churches', whose faith, in principle, was that of all the inhabitants of the same country. *Cujus regio, ejus religio,* according to the Reformer's doctrine, taking into account national temperament and the circumstances in which the Church developed, the Church has been absorbed by the State. During the nineteenth century, when the concept of the State developed along democratic lines, control of religion by the State somewhat declined. Nonconformists and Catholics were able to obtain guarantees. The history of the Churches was largely one of 'disestablishment' as the doctrine of separation of Church and State gained ground. There is today no country where the idea of a State Church is in vogue.

Turning now to American Lutheranism, we see that it has adopted a fairly distinctive form. Being out on their own, having to bow neither to prince nor king, having brought with them no bishops, the early immigrants organized themselves spontaneously on democratic lines. Government is taken care of by synods, which enjoy considerable authority. In the main, American Lutheranism stresses strict morality and the integrity of doctrine, while at the same time attaching much importance to liturgy; all these being characteristics which outwardly bring it close to Catholicism, whereas in fact it constitutes one of the anti-Roman Catholic bastions of the U.S.A.

Differences such as these between the various branches of Lutheranism are not vital. The two main issues of free inquiry and dogmatic affirmation are both to be found in it, as in all other forms of

Protestantism. Among German Churches and American synods we shall find some of liberal tendencies, some confessionist; between theologians of both persuasions there are lively discussions but no splits.

The most original facet of Lutheranism is the persistence of a pietist movement. This sprang from the pastor Johannes Arndt at the end of the sixteenth century and was developed sixty years later by Jakob Spener, author of *Pia Desideria* and organizer of the 'Collegia Pietatis', as a reaction against the frozen orthodoxy of the Churches and the vanity of controversy. In the eighteenth century pietism was to be personified by the great Count Nicolaus Ludwig von Zinzendorf, a mystic and leader, at Herrnhut, the village of 'The Guard of God' where sincere souls might seek to live wholly in God. The movement was recognized by the Lutheran Church; Zinzendorf was granted the title of bishop, and Herrnhut exercised a deep influence on foreign reformers such as Wesley as well as on German thinkers, notably Schleiermacher, early in the nineteenth century.

Pietism was the medium with which Lutheranism in greater or lesser degree absorbed certain groups which had existed prior to the Reformation, such as the Moravians who are linked with the Hussites. One of Huss's disciples, Chelczich, assisted by Rokycana, parish priest of Kumwald in Bohemia, had founded there in 1450 a Community of Brethren separated from the Catholic Church. In 1467 they had their new priests ordained by a Waldensian bishop; then towards 1500 they reorganized under the leadership of Bishop Lucas of Prague. They now numbered several hundred thousand, mostly in Moravia. They were dispersed after the defeat at White Mountain near Prague in 1620. Many emigrated. Those who remained under Germanic influence vegetated until Count von Zinzendorf became interested in their fate. Nearly all of them then accepted the Augsburg Confession while retaining their autonomy in relation to official Lutheranism. Today the Moravian Brethren are divided into five branches: Bohemian, German, English (the largest in Europe, with some forty-three communities), North American (where it is called the Moravian Church and has more than a hundred communities) and South American. These groups were reorganized in 1918 as the 'Czech Protestant Church of the Moravian Brethren' and has worked unceasingly to retain all the links with the Czech past, particularly as regards the famous Bible of Kralice, originally translated by the Brethren, one of the outstandingly great works of Czech literature. Numbering only some $1\frac{1}{2}$ million, the Moravians have exercised an influence out of all proportion to their size. They are in the forefront of Protestant missions.

Lutheranism thus shows no splits in its structure. A tendency towards concentration is rather more noticeable, especially since the middle of the nineteenth century. In Germany the number of Churches was reduced to sixteen through amalgamation. In the U.S.A. two large groups have emerged, the National Lutheran Council and the Synodical Conference. The idea of a world union was first mooted by a German pastor who had emigrated to the U.S.A., one Wyneken, founder of the Missouri Synod. Taken up in Hanover, the idea gave birth in 1868 to the General Lutheran Evangelical Conference, in 1900 to the Lutheran Alliance or Lutheran Unity Action, and in 1923, thanks to the efforts of Pastor Morehead and Pastor Ralph Long, to the World Lutheran Convention, which subsequently became through the efforts of Bishop Nygren the World Lutheran Federation. This has a permanent directorate and has defined a common doctrine. The federation has not succeeded in gathering together all the Lutheran Churches; thus in the U.S.A. the Synodical Conference and certain South American Churches in alliance with it are standing aloof, but a serious effort at unity was begun in earnest in 1952.

Lutheranism is far from occupying the back seat often assigned to it by common opinion. The 'confessionalism' of some of its Churches exercises a certain influence on other Protestant groups, while several of the greatest thinkers and theologians of modern Protestantism were Lutherans: Kierkegaard, Schleiermacher, Bultmann. The 'Inner Mission',[1] which played a considerable part in the renovation of Protestantism in the nineteenth century and at the beginning of the twentieth, sprang from German Lutheranism; yet social Protestantism, which seems contrary to Lutheran doctrine, is largely Lutheran in origin. The Protestant missions are largely the work of Lutherans; Brazilian Protestants are mostly Lutheran; and the most powerful contemporary organ of propaganda wielded by Protestantism is the 'Lutheran Hour', an American programme broadcast in thirty-six languages over 1,500 stations. It is moreover a fact that the driving force of the last fifty years among the Reformed Churches towards the formation of the World Council of Churches [2] is due in large measure to the efforts of Lutheranism, especially in Scandinavia under Archbishop Nathan Söderblom.

It would be an exaggeration to say of Lutheranism, because it has retained a number of elements from the liturgy and tradition of the Catholic Church, that it constitutes a 'bridging-Church', as Anglicanism aspires to be. Certain Lutheran countries, e.g. in Scandinavia, were the last to suppress laws against Catholicism. But the most recent work of theologians has demonstrated that in the theses of Luther there are more elements which are acceptable than was at first thought, and that in certain matters the divergences were of vocabulary rather than of doctrine.

[1] See Chapter III, section 8.   [2] See Chapter VI, section.

7. In Calvin's Wake

As a religious element Calvinism has not spread to anything like the same extent as Lutheranism; from the start it never had the same well-defined geographical area. Even numerically it is very much less imposing. But this first impression is not the correct one, for the heritage of the 'second patriarch of the Reformation' is richer than that of the first. His message is transmitted to us today through many Churches which have no original link with the Reformation in Geneva: some because they have become absorbed, e.g. that of Zürich (the creation of Zwingli) or that of Scotland (transformed by Calvinism), while others, e.g. the Anglican Church and above all the 'Dissenters', have been no less strongly influenced by the thinking of Calvin.

Calvinism first spread from Geneva to France, where it was adopted by small groups of Lutheran evangelists. Its dream was to conquer all parts of the kingdom, but was prevented by the Capetian dynasty at the price of bloody religious wars. Despite persecution, however, it remained vigorous in some sectors. At the same time it penetrated to Flanders and the Low Countries, where it became associated with anti-Spanish patriotism and took root among the masses. In England, while it did not manage to absorb the national Church created by Henry VIII, it did succeed in giving it a distinct hue, especially after Elizabeth I came to the throne, and in Scotland, where it was introduced by John Knox, it found favourable soil. Its tendrils spread to Bohemia, Austria, Hungary and the Rhineland Palatinate, though not to Italy or Spain. Checked at the end of the sixteenth century, the advance began again in the seventeenth, carried by the Dutch and the English in the course of their maritime explorations, and the movement continued to spread in the eighteenth and nineteenth centuries in North America, South Africa and (to some extent) throughout the British Empire. Its geographical field was now established.

It should be noted that, unlike Lutheranism, Calvinism was almost never implanted in a territory at the invitation of a ruler; more often social or economic factors helped it to become established. Thus in Holland it served to link the small traders and seafarers against Spanish Catholic business interests. Less specifically, one might say that Calvinism was the religion of the small trader class as it groped towards a capitalist economy. Calvin considered material success as proof of divine election, and this view (it agrees with the teaching of the Bible—see the Book of Job!) helped to accelerate the process. 'Gold and silver are useful things which can be applied to good ends.' This of course was far from the Franciscan ideal of holy poverty. Its democratic nature and ecclesiastical organization established links between Calvinism and democratic regimes as they emerged from the revolutions that were to follow. The democratic and liberal-capitalist republic of the U.S.A. was congenitally Calvinist.

There is no Church as such that one can call Calvinist, this being quite contrary to what we have seen of Lutheranism. In most of Western Europe—France, Switzerland, Germany, Central Europe and Holland—the usual term is the Reformed Churches, and this denotes a curious misuse of the term, for it would seem that the Calvinists went further along the road of Reformation than their forbears, the Lutherans, and that they are more deeply Protestant.

The other term employed does not concern dogma, but rather ecclesiastical organization. Firstly in Scotland, then in all British territories, and thence to the U.S.A., authentic Calvinists meet as Presbyterians. This word is from Calvin's system of Church government: the *presbyterium*, a council of elders charged with the task of assisting the pastor. This system, often backed up by the 'synodal' organization, broken down into councils, parishes, consistories, provincial and national synods, is different from the two other systems of Church government, the Episcopalian of the Anglican (and to a certain extent of the Lutheran), and the Congregationalist of the independent Churches, which limit authority to the local Church level, to the parish community.

The Reformed Presbyterian Churches number some 35–40 million adherents of whom some 12 million are in Europe. On these figures, Calvinism will be seen to be far behind the Lutherans and other Protestant Churches such as the Baptists and the Methodists—about the same as the Anglican Communion.

In principle there is a considerable degree of uniformity of doctrine among the followers of Calvin. Yet there is no common Confession, as that of Augsburg for the Lutherans. It was Calvin's wish that each group of Churches should have their own Confession; there are thus some half-dozen of these, in Geneva, Scotland, Hungary, France (La Rochelle) and Holland (Utrecht), all of which are formally allied to the doctrine set out in *L'Institution Chrétienne*, excepting the famous thesis on predestination, which has lapsed today. For the rest, the main items have remained intact. The two sacraments which Calvin retained, baptism and communion, are administered as the Reformer laid down. Even followers of Zwingli have abandoned their founder's radicalism to return to the fold of Geneva, to the middle way. This conception of the sacraments sees more or less only the outward sign of lively discussion in the Protestant world, especially with Lutherans, all in the best scholastic style but without stirring the least interest among the mass of adherents.

The Calvinist service is characterized by its austerity and simplicity. In bare churches, without altar, candles, images or incense, the service is very restrained, just as we saw it portrayed in the first of our Four Aspects. The celebrant is scarcely distinguishable from his congregation, save for his clerical collar and the black gown; in some churches even these distinctive signs are abandoned. Liturgy, prayers and readings are all of the simplest; the chants are either of rhyming psalms, or paraphrased biblical canticles. The observance of Sunday is, as we all know, strict, giving it an air of gloomy boredom.

With these features Calvinism stands out as fundamentally anti-Catholic. A good Reformed Churchman, a convinced Presbyterian, has nothing but contempt for the pomp of Catholic liturgy—'sensuality' as one of them called it—and hence for all those Protestant denominations which have retained such elements. He considers as essential only the Word of God, as this is found in the Bible. He has nothing but hostility for all hierarchic systems, especially for that of the Roman Catholic Church and for its leader, the Pope. In this respect then we can say that Calvinism has long been the shield of Protestantism against any attempt to 'Romanize' it.

But this is not its most striking trait, which is rather to be found in its moralizing character. The latter springs from Calvin's original idea of moral precepts, the practice of virtues being a sign of the better of the two predetermined destinies. Calvinism, with its systematic strictness, demands submission, at least outwardly, to moral rules and religious discipline; everything is implied by the term 'puritan', which appeared first in sixteenth-century England. This is an attitude of mind rather than a doctrine, and is not an exclusive feature of Calvinism, or even of Protestantism: the Jansenists were, in essence, puritans. But it has become incarnated, historically speaking, in certain Presbyterian elements: first in England in the seventeenth century with the Roundheads of Cromwell, equally hostile to both the Pope and the king; later in North America with the Pilgrim Fathers. There may be no puritan Churches, but there is a considerable puritan influence throughout the greater part of the Protestant world. Most of the movements which oppose the Established Churches, principally the Quakers and the Methodists, have puritan tendencies. Puritanism has imparted a certain tenor, a certain way of life, with a touch of primness which is astounding to Catholics. This moral attitude, of which puritanism is the extreme example, has aroused and still arouses intense faith and exemplary conduct, as witness the descendants of the *Camisards* or of the Dutch rebels against Philip II. But it can also go along with quite different conditions of life (still in accordance with Calvin's justification of material success), even reaching conditions of some luxury. The '*Haute Société Protestante*' in France and the big business circles of the U.S.A. offer perfect examples of this curious alliance between Mammon and the God of Righteousness.

Calvinism exercises an influence upon the Protestant world out of proportion to the number of its adherents through the way of life it lays down, rather than the dogmas it reaches. One can even say that, until recently, it had penetrated circles which, doctrinally, were foreign to it. This is true of Methodism, whose doctrine of achieving saintliness on earth is far removed from Calvinism, but whose extensions, in the U.S.A., for example, are separated with difficulty from those of the Presbyterians. A similar 'Calvinization' of Anglicanism was seen at the beginning of the nineteenth century, and today the Anglican 'Low Church' bears a close resemblance to the Presbyterian 'dissenters'.

Because of the autonomy which Calvin gave to each of his churches (an autonomy, let us remember, which in principle is found at parish community level), Calvinism has had to suffer few divisions in the course of centuries. It has not given rise to any movements comparable to Methodism, which is an offshoot of Anglicanism and which has become more important than the latter. Only one split occurred, towards the end of the sixteenth century, during the course of the epic struggle which took place in Holland between Arminius and Gomar over the question of predestination. The latter triumphed at the Synod of Dordrecht in 1619, but this did not stop the Arminians from continuing to live, although severely persecuted. Today there are still some small Arminian Churches, comprising about twenty-five thousand adherents, in Holland. The descendants of Gomar are no longer addicted to predestination. . . .

Certain stresses have been noted within the Calvinist movement, but nothing approaching a split in recent times. Some of those stresses were brought about by external influences—Darbyism, for instance.[1] This sprang from Anglicanism, and later exerted some influence on certain Calvinist sectors, especially in France, where its missionary zeal resulted in a type of reinforced Calvinism. The Salvation Army,[2] a missionary and social movement, has influenced certain aspects of Calvinism, especially in Holland. Other divergencies were due to purely internal reasons. There was the revivalist movement [3] at the beginning of the nineteenth century, a reaction to which was the setting up of 'Free Churches', separated from State Churches but none the less Calvinist. Later, liberal Protestantism [4] was to set one faction against another without bringing into question the theoretical unity of Calvinism. Within the 22 million strong fold of Calvinists one finds factions with strong differences of opinion on dogma, at least in its essentials. The Dutch Reformed Church has a million adherents as

---

[1] See section 13 below. [2] See p. 203.
[3] See Chapter III, section 3. [4] See Chapter III, section 7.

against the official Netherlands Church with 3 million. In France today there are 'liberal' parishes and 'orthodox' parishes. These tendencies were just about balancing out until the arrival on the scene of Karl Barth.

At the extreme of Calvinist heterodoxy is the curious little movement called the Hinschites. One wonders whether Calvin would have recognized them, so strange are their characteristics. Founded in the mid nineteenth century by Coraly Hinsch, a Provençal middle-class Calvinist, with the assistance of her nephews, Pastor Kruger and his disciple Armengaud, who married her, the 'Hinschite Evangelical Church' stressed the blessings which flowed from the Holy Ghost and the role of the prophetic ministry of the Church. She taught a sort of dualism, mainly Manichaean or Albigensian, which represented life as a struggle between God and Satan. The founding prophetess busied herself with social works, and in particular she created the first workers' sea-bathing association. Groups of Hinschites are still to be found around Montpellier in France.

Though there may be forces tending to divide Calvinism, there are equally forces which seek to consolidate it. Since 1875, under impulsion from the Scots, the World Alliance of Reformed Churches, following the Presbyterian system, has been in operation, firstly from Edinburgh, then from Geneva; the title subsequently became the Reformed Churches World Alliance. This includes more than half of all the Calvinist Churches and has even absorbed non-Presbyterian elements, such as American Congregationalists. Opposing this alliance is the Ecumenical Reformed Synod, stricter in outlook, which emerged from 'separated brethren' in Holland. This numbers only about one-fifth of the Presbyterian Churches. The two organizations, until quite recently, treated each other coldly, the synod reproaching the alliance for not following Calvin's dogma closely enough, and worse, for allowing some of their members to give ground before a certain touch of 'episcopalianism'. In the climate of ecumenicalism which reigns today, the two organizations have drawn a little closer together. Despite internal differences, and 'variations' or 'deviations', or perhaps even because of them and the 'pluralism' that is the hallmark of the movement, Calvinism has exhibited a great deal of vitality. For a long time and all over the world the heirs of Calvin's message have been in the van of Protestantism, and exercise an influence which is far more apparent than that of the Lutherans, notwithstanding the fact that the latter are three times as numerous. In theological and spiritual matters there is a degree of animation in the Calvinist world, a sort of ferment, which emerges in various ways, such as a dogmatic revival (the work of Barth) and a renaissance of monasticism, the finest example of which is the monastery at Taizé, founded by a young Genevese Reformed pastor. The importance of the role held by Reformed pastors in Protestant ecumenicalism is no less revealing, pastors such as the Frenchman Marc Boegner and the Dutchman Visser't Hooft. Calvinism continues to act as a ferment within the world which developed from the Reformation.

8. The Most Independent of Protestants: the Congregationalists

Although many of them are Calvinists, one must consider the Congregationalists quite separately. Under this denomination, in reality, one could classify the Lutherans, as well as the Calvinists, the Baptists and a large part of the Methodists, not to mention the adherents of the majority of movements and sects that our age has produced. For the term defines a system of ecclesiastical government which presupposes a certain theology. This concept can be traced back to Luther, to certain points from the Calvinist doctrine, even to certain little-known reformers like François Lambert, a Franciscan at Avignon who, in 1522, being won over to the ideas newly come from Germany, threw his habit into the Rhône and went off to Wittenberg to marry. According to this doctrine the abundance of the spiritual power of the Church rests upon the local churches. Each community is responsible to itself, not only in matters of discipline but also in doctrine. It is therefore the will to enjoy full freedom which here finds its fullest expression. The absolute autonomy of the local church is the only authentic form of the invisible Church. Congregationalists are against all hierarchical regimes, either Presbyterian or Episcopalian, allowing only a Federation of Local Churches.

It was in England that Congregationalism first took root, in defiance of the Anglican Church. In 1570 Robert Browne first voiced the idea and was followed by a certain number of adherents, thus incurring the wrath of the official Church. He was exiled to Scotland; thence the Presbyterians drove him to Holland, where most of his adherents remained, and finally to submission to the English authorities. But his ideas had aroused the interest of an Anglican parson, John Robinson, who systematized them; in his turn he also was obliged to flee to Holland, where the movement prospered. Puritan elements then rallied to the cause and gave it the puritanical colouring that it has retained. It was largely in Holland that the preparations for the celebrated expedition of the Pilgrim Fathers were to be carried out.

Congregationalism proper has developed mainly in two countries, in England and in the U.S.A. In England a friend of John Robinson, Henry Jacob, newly returned from Holland, had founded Congregationalist Churches in secret. The king's police treated these as badly as they treated the Catholics and other dissidents. The title of 'Independent', which began with Robert Browne, and of which they felt so proud, was not to the liking of monarchs, who wanted to feel that they were the masters of their own Church. St Paul's words [1] sustained the small communities of the movement: 'Wherefore come out from among them, and be ye separate, saith the Lord, and touch not the unclean thing.' To whom did this apply? To nothing less than the Established Church. But under Cromwell the Congregationalists were left in peace. They prepared a profession of faith, the Declaration of Savoy, so called from the palace where it was worked out, which they presented to the government a short while after the dictator's death. On one point at least they were right: this was their refusal to allow King or Parliament to intervene in religious affairs. A further wave of persecution began, and it was not until 1689 that the 'independents', like other 'dissenters', obtained full religious liberty. And so the Churches of this particular movement were able to develop along their own lines, yet such was the extreme spirit of individualism that chaos would have ensued had not some moves towards unity been undertaken in 1833. The Congregational Union of England and Wales was founded, whose Council favoured mutual information and co-operation. There are today some 800,000 adherents.

In America, Congregationalism was mainly the work of the Pilgrim Fathers. Most of them were ex-Anglicans, others ex-Presbyterians, all of them fundamentally puritan. The success of this little group in the coastal areas of the east, where they were to settle, made of them a sort of aristocracy whose influence was to be considerable. Little by little other Protestant elements were to adopt Congregationalism. The need was felt mainly, as in England, from an organizational standpoint. The Cambridge Synods of 1648, Boston in 1680 and 1865, and especially the National Council of Oberlin in 1871, resulted in the setting up of a Central Council; but this had no special influence. It was too much for some, however, and these, led by W. E. Channing, left the movement, adhering to the ultra-liberal theology of the dissident Unitarians. But the Congregationalists continued to expand and to hold a preponderant place in American Protestant society. Today they number some 1½ million, but with more influence than this number might suggest. They were the first to organize missions to heathen regions, the American Board of Commissioners for Foreign Missions being set up in 1810. In politics and the press they are both numerous and active.

Outside England and the U.S.A. one can include with the Congregationalists those 'Free' or 'Independent' Churches which exist, e.g. in Holland, Scandinavia, Italy and France (Calvinist in these two last

[1] 2 Cor. vi. 17.

countries), the whole numbering a little more than 5 million throughout the world.

9. THE ANGLICAN COMMUNION

The reforms which gave rise on the continent of Europe to the great Churches separated from Rome all had roots in the dogmatic systems of one or more reformers. But it was quite different in England. Set in motion by the will of one royal personage, the country was soon to be strongly Protestant and almost completely cut off from Catholicism. It would be too simple a matter to repeat Voltaire's phrase: 'England separated from Rome because Henry VIII was in love.' The causes of the split were deeper than that. The fact that Wycliffe in the fourteenth century was not condemned as a heretic proves that his hostility towards Rome corresponded to a general and nationalistic tendency which the king was to use to serve his ends. The love affair with Anne Boleyn and his divorce from Catherine of Aragon supplied Henry with an excuse for breaking with the Pope, but the true reason is clearly set out in the declaration of 1532: 'Nowhere in the Scriptures is it said that the Roman Pontiff has been granted by God any more authority or jurisdiction than is granted to any other foreign bishop *in this realm.*' *In this realm.* It was in order to be master in his own realm that Henry VIII was proclaimed *Supremum caput ecclesiae.*

In this first stage of the split nothing indicated that England would turn to Protestantism. Henry VIII, who had lately so well refuted Luther that the Pope had invested him with the Golden Rose, considered himself as the most orthodox of Catholics. But there were Protestant influences at work around him, especially that of the Archbishop of Canterbury, Cranmer, son-in-law of the German reformer Osiander. These influences were to increase.

Amid a series of oscillations, now towards Protestant innovation, now towards Catholic tradition, a new form of Christian Church, the Anglican, was launched.[1] Under Edward VI, Henry's successor, who gave asylum to Bucer, the Strasbourg reformer in exile, the pendulum swung heavily towards Protestantism. The Prayer Book, official basis of the religious service, was published in 1549, and removed the character of sacrifice from the Mass, leaving it only with that of memorial and communion; later revisions only accentuated Calvinist traits. Then the pendulum swung back again violently towards Catholicism with Mary Tudor, whose reign, brief but severe, brought

---

[1] 'The history of the words Anglican and Anglicanism has yet to be written. I do not know when the expression Anglican Communion was first employed. The first mention of Anglicanism, cited in the *O.E.D.*, was from Charles Kingsley in 1846' (G. Neill, *Anglicanism*).

the kingdom back into the Roman fold. With the accession of Elizabeth I Protestantism returned, moderate in intention if not in execution; a new prayer-book was edited, and in 1563 the Church Assembly voted the Bill of the Thirty-nine Articles, a *résumé* of the religious principles which Her Majesty's subjects were to observe, or rather a list of doctrinal points which must not be overstepped. In sum, the 'Elizabethan compromise' allowed an approximate balance to be maintained between Catholics and Protestants. A new Church was 'established', with the queen as its head, doubtless to signify by this new title that she intended to rule both the men and the institutions of the Church, rather than to concern herself with sacramental and dogmatic matters. Would a Catholicizing reaction follow? Not entirely. James I was well aware that it was better to adopt a middle way, not to return to Rome, nor to give way to the pressures of integrationist Calvinists, which had triumphed, for example, in Scotland. So the Anglican Church was born, a national and an official institution, as hostile in principle to 'dissenters' who refused to submit to the Acts of Uniformity as to Catholics who denounced the break with Rome.

In effect this solution, which had much to commend it from the point of view of the individualism and insular nationalism of the English, was not an immediate success. The Protestant pressure was so strong that the pendulum swung again towards reform, bringing the puritan Oliver Cromwell to power, and chopping off the head of King Charles I. But the future belonged to Anglicanism, re-established in 1660 by Charles II; nor did he dare to suppress it when he entered personally into communion with Rome. Later James II was no more successful in establishing Catholicism (an attempt which cost him his throne) than William of Orange, a convinced Calvinist, who neither could nor would impose the full Genevan doctrine upon London. In 1688 Anglicanism had won: the pendulum was stayed at its centre; faced with a very small remainder of Catholics, but with a strong minority of Protestants of differing denominations, the Anglican Church now appeared to become an integral part of England, of her dynasty, her traditions and her interests.

One cannot include Anglicanism among the many forms of Protestantism without some reservations, without stating that it occupies an entirely separate place in the list. Many of its external aspects signify its closeness to Catholicism. No longer is the service in Latin, but the liturgy has remained so Catholic that anyone taking part in it could easily make a mistake. The last of our Four Aspects will demonstrate this fact clearly. The clergy have renounced celibacy, but the episcopal organization remains, including the character of the consecration governing the appointment of bishops.[1] The nomination of priests is

[1] See Chapter VI, section 5.

similar to that of the Catholics. There are Anglican religious orders. Going a little deeper, it can be said that Anglicanism approaches Catholicism in its fidelity to tradition, a fidelity which is pushed sometimes also to literalism, even medievalism, which leads one to say jokingly that some Anglicans regard their Church as the only one that has not been reformed, the Catholic Church having been reformed at the Council of Trent. The Anglican view of the sacraments is not invariably a Catholic one, but most Anglicans are attracted to the concept of the Incarnation, to the presence of Jesus Christ, to a theology of the Church as a body—all Catholic traits. The Anglican Church, however, is distinctly Protestant in its radical separation from Rome, by the hostility which it has, almost unanimously until very recently, shown towards 'Popery', by its refusal of *magisterium*, by its desire for freedom of thought and belief, more tolerant even than the majority of the Reformed Churches.

Finally, it must be said that one of the principal traits of Anglicanism is its love of the Bible. This is derived from Protestant influences, but has taken on a much more important aspect. The fervent wish to dwell in a biblical climate is so strong that Old Testament names are sometimes given to children at baptism; ironic spirits have made play with the extravagant use of this 'Canaanite patois'. But it must also not be overlooked that among Anglicans the biblical text is intimately connected with its liturgical usage, much more so than among the Protestants, which gives *pietas anglicana* its peculiar characteristics.

The alternating swing of the pendulum, during the course of which Anglicanism emerged, tends to prove the English genius, to which Cartesian logic is alien. It entailed a curious consequence, one which still determines the principal characteristics of Anglicanism: the coexistence within the Church of tendencies which appear to be contradictory, but which have never sought to eliminate each other over the last three hundred years. The first of these is Catholicizing and traditional; the second Protestant and puritan; the third, which emerged in the late eighteenth and during the nineteenth century, is liberal, critical, even rationalist. The English are proud of what they call the 'comprehensiveness' of their Church, or the peaceful acceptance of the coexistence of these three tendencies, where no higher authority seeks to synthesize them. An Anglican may be of one or other of these tendencies; for all that, he still belongs to the Church of England and accepts the validity of the Prayer Book. Since the publication of Paul Thureau-Dangin's classic, *The Catholic Renaissance in England* (1899), it has become common to define these tendencies as High, Low and Broad Church, the partisans of the first having friends in the House of Lords, those of the second being most numerous in the House of Commons. The formula is disputable, since it seems to indicate that there are three Churches, which is not the case since the same organization and the same hierarchy cover Anglicans of all three tendencies.[1] Nowadays, ever since the 'ritualist' trend (which followed the Oxford Movement) prevailed upon the High Church to adopt most of the externals of Catholicism, the tendencies are styled Anglo-Catholic, Evangelical and Liberal or Broad.

From its beginnings the Church of England has remained a State Church. Its supreme head is the monarch, who enjoys religious privileges and honours, as the impressive coronation ceremony reminds one when each new reign commences. The monarch appoints the bishops, the chapters having merely to endorse his or her choice. Convocations, local parliaments of clergy with upper and lower chambers, deliberate upon all matters of interest to the Church, but their decisions are applicable only if Parliament and the monarch approve. The same procedure applies to the Church Assembly, founded in 1919, except that this has a third chamber composed of lay members.

This officially admitted type of latitudinarianism has not been without its dangers. To see a succession of articles of faith imposed by authority, to find that apparently irreconcilable positions of principle coexist within the same Church, entails different reactions, now sceptical, now pietist and mystic. This accounts for the fact that England and later the U.S.A. both proved to be fruitful ground for numerous religious movements of a separatist nature, of which some were to blossom into Churches or sects. At the end of the eighteenth century, for example, when the official Church was sunk in routine and conformism, there arose violent separatist tendencies. Some of these thrust 'liberal' criticism to the point of negation of essential dogmas and joined the Unitarian camp.[2] Others, with Wesley, sought to awaken spiritually the old Church of England; not succeeding, they ended by constituting their own independent communities, the Methodists, who were disavowed by the Established Church. Later the Oxford Movement, after having begun well as a revival within Anglicanism, saw some of its leading figures, among them Newman, enter the Catholic fold.[3] Others, with Pusey, remained within the Anglican fold, but introduced innovations.[4] The power of the Anglican Church to absorb heterogeneous elements is therefore not limitless.

Taking only the British Isles into account, Anglicans today number about two-fifths of the population, some 20 million; but that figure must be understood to include members of three Churches distinct

[1] The degree of separateness is much more marked among the Episcopalians of the U.S.A., see Chapter III, section 6.
[2] See p. 38.
[3] *The Church in an Age of Revolution*, Index.
[4] See Chapter III, section 6.

from the Church of England—the Church of Wales, the Church of Ireland and the Episcopal Church of Scotland.

But Anglicanism has not confined itself to the British Isles. It extended its field as and when the sovereign extended the frontiers of empire. It is implanted in all the Commonwealth territories. It has even succeeded, at the price of minimal adaptations, in surviving the departure of the British from the U.S.A. and India. There are therefore Anglican Churches in Canada, in South Africa, Australia and India, as there are in the U.S.A. For long the situation of Anglicans overseas was precarious. They had no bishops and depended on those in the homeland. From the eighteenth century onwards, first in Nova Scotia then in India, sees were created. After the War of Independence in the U.S.A. the Anglicans of the new republic constituted themselves as a Church, independent of the Church of England, under the title of Episcopalians. These, with some 2½ million adherents, were to be the second largest group of Anglicans in the world. Their official title, let us remember, is and has been ever since 1873 the Protestant Episcopal Church, the first word distinctly indicating their separation from the Catholics.[1] The second word indicates their differentiation from the Congregationalists and the Presbyterians, to whom, geographically, they are linked. The same tendencies can be discerned as in Britain, although slightly less accentuated; the High Church tendency being for long represented by Bishop Seabury, Low Church by Bishop White of Pennsylvania, the liberal, latitudinarian tendency by Bishop Pruvost of New York. The American Episcopalian Church, drawing its strength from among the wealthier elements of the eastern states, is a force to be reckoned with.

All these scattered Anglican Churches have none the less managed to keep fairly strong links with one another. Today they all have the same creed—despite an attempt at Protestantization by the Episcopalians at the beginning of the nineteenth century—which has no links with any particular Reformation doctrine, allowing only as official doctrine all that is enshrined in the Prayer Book and the Thirty-nine Articles. In practice they have even tightened the links during the last 150 years. At regular intervals, ever since 1867, and in principle every ten years, representatives of all these Churches meet at Lambeth Palace, the residence of the Archbishop of Canterbury, to discuss everything of interest to their adherents. The number of representatives has never ceased to increase: in 1867 it was 76; in 1908, 194; in 1930, 252; and today it is 475.

The Anglican Communion thus consists of some 30 million baptized spread over 430 dioceses, and it shows considerable vitality. Anglicans have been in the forefront of battle in every field. The

[1] There was periodically talk of dropping this, but now it seems to be official.

exceptional quality of their translation of the Holy Bible, the famous 'Authorized Version', has contributed not a little to the success of their efforts. They have also been the spearhead of missionary activities. In the painful debate on *apartheid* in South Africa they have taken a courageous stand as leaders of the liberal attitude. The crises concerning the Prayer Book, the ritualist counter-move to the Oxford Movement and discussion with the Catholics on the subject of unity, as well as the noisy battles in which traditionalists and fundamentalists were opposed to the more daring spirits, have all helped to vitalize these Churches.

Anglicanism was long considered with suspicion in the Protestant world because of the Catholic traits which it retained, but this has now vanished. Anglicanism indeed, by virtue of its very constitution, holds an important place in the Protestant world. The moving appeal for Christian unity made at the Lambeth Conference in 1920 had notable repercussions. *Faith and Order*, one of the two movements which inaugurated Protestant ecumenicalism, originated largely among the American Episcopalians. It was the Anglicans, too, who made the greatest efforts towards unity with the Lutherans and with the Old Catholics, going so far as to envisage reciprocal recognition of titles and orders. Many Anglicans, however, are saddened by this collaboration with Protestantism; in the U.S.A. they dislike the word 'Protestant' in the title Protestant Episcopal Church. They have a feeling of continuity between the Church of the Middle Ages and their own, that they represent a sort of 'third force' between Catholicism and Protestantism—possibly even a 'fourth force', for they have made real efforts to re-establish links with the Orthodox Church. It was in this sector of Anglicanism that the tendencies towards total ecumenicalism, including Catholicism, have been seen; they were also the first to respond to Pope John XXIII's appeal and to visit him. The famous expression 'bridging-Church', which many Anglicans apply to their communion, is somewhat ambiguous, since links which bind it to Catholicism vary in strength. But it all adds up to a state of mind which we would do well to consider as sincere, and which could be of great importance for the future of Christianity as a whole.

10. THE UNITARIANS, MODERN ARIANS

In the distinguished circles of New England, where Anglicans and Congregationalists were numerous, Anglican latitudinarianism, no less than Congregationalist anarchy, resulted in the spread of a doctrine which the Protestant faithful viewed with some misgiving. That doctrine is known as Unitarianism, a name it has borne since the nineteenth century, but which appears in fact to be the extension or resurgence of a whole current of heterodoxy going back almost to the origins of Christianity.

The Church was not two centuries old when the relations of the Three Divine Persons of the Trinity became a matter of dispute. The Monarchianists and the Patripassians had affirmed that the Father and the Son were one Person; then the Sabellians had introduced the dualism of Good and Evil into the concept of the Trinity. Later, Paul of Samosata and then Arius had denied the consubstantiality of the Son. They were followed by Macedonius, a violent enemy of the Holy Ghost. The Council of Nicaea and the first Council of Constantinople had condemned those opinions, which, however, had never wholly disappeared. In the Middle Ages Abélard and Joachim of Flora were accused of teaching anti-Trinitarian errors; they were condemned, but their opinions survived. The danger of heresy was such that, in the Confession of Augsburg, Luther anathematized those whom he called 'old or new Samosatians', and Calvin had Michael Servetus burnt at the stake. But amid the turmoil of new ideas it was inevitable that those ancient errors should emerge with renewed vigour, and here Socinus, uncle and nephew, enter upon the scene.

Rejecting the dogma of the Trinity, the divinity of Christ, original sin and the Redemption, they reduced Christianity to a kind of humanitarian moralism. The Rakow Catechism, so named after the Transylvanian town where the younger Socinus had settled, spread these theories throughout the Christian West.

In England the doctrine had a certain success, despite the opposition of nascent Anglicanism which sent several anti-Trinitarians to the stake and imprisoned the Socinian leader John Biddle, who owed his life to Cromwell. Punishable by death, the movement, which was now being called 'unitarian' since it recognized only one unity in God, got under way in earnest in the eighteenth century with Lindsey (1725–1808) in London and Priestley in Birmingham, strongly tinged with the rationalism of the 'Age of Enlightenment'. At the beginning of the nineteenth century it reached the U.S.A., where it found a favourable climate.

Boston and Harvard formed as it were a kernel of Unitarianism, a chapel dominated by intellectuals and university men. W. E. Channing and Theodore Parker embraced and in turn spread Unitarian ideas. They were joined by others from several denominations: Anglicans, Baptists, Episcopalians, and Emerson's conversion set a seal upon what the poet had called 'the religion of the intellectuals'. The expansion of liberal Protestantism was favourable to the growth of Unitarianism (henceforth its official name) which was regarded by many as the extreme of liberalism, the expression of a Christianity freed from dogma, myths and mysteries unacceptable to reason. This then was the doctrine of Harvard's Faculty of Theology, which inspired a great part of the 'Social Protestantism' of which W. E. Channing was an eloquent spokesman. Among an impressive array of eminent persons sympathetic to or convinced by it were Presidents Adams, Fillmore and Jefferson, Benjamin Franklin and writers such as Hawthorne. Today there are some 300,000 adherents of this broad creed, this spirit of universal tolerance and mutual help which is Unitarianism. Debates on the Oneness of God, the non-existence of original sin and the non-inspiration of the Bible have all slipped back into second place. Paradoxically the Unitarians have retained their churches, their architecture being among the most interesting in the U.S.A. Unitarianism exercises a sure attraction for all those who see in Christ the exemplary man, the prophet of humanity on the march towards spiritual progress.

In Europe and elsewhere there are fervent adherents who have grouped together as Freethinkers in Associations of Freethinkers. There are some 40,000 in England; members have included such distinguished men as James Martineau, Stopford Brooke, J. Estlin Carpenter and L. P. Jacks. Transylvania, once the home of Socinus, has also produced Unitarians of note, men who in our own day have sought to find agreement, under the Soviet regime, between their creed and Marxism. There are some small groups in Brazil, India and Japan; in Italy there was Gaetano Conte, one of the most interesting representatives of Unitarianism, which he named, significantly enough, 'Christian Progress'.

11. METHODISM: PROTESTANTISM WITHOUT DOGMA

Indifferent to intellectual speculations and the strictness of dogmatic definitions, drawn rather to a simple and sincere piety, Methodism occupies a special place among the several forms of Protestantism. John Wesley (1703–91) was undoubtedly divinely inspired when, from 1739 onwards, he drew vast crowds to his meetings, holding them spellbound by the hour. Thin, pale, the son of an Anglican minister, he longed to regenerate the Established Church with new spiritual life; but that Church was crippled with routine and indifference. As a student and young deacon he set out to convince a small circle of friends that he had *method* to offer as a means of attaining the love of God. The nickname 'Methodist' was applied to him by his comrades at Oxford, and it stuck. But his quest soon led him from the fold of Anglicanism, even from that of all other Protestant denominations, to seek salvation in the simple practice of the Gospels, without any reference to dogma and with a great outflowing of charity. Two phrases summed up his thoughts: 'Be Papist or Protestant, so long as you follow true religion, that of Thomas à Kempis, Bossuet and Fénelon'; and 'I look upon all the world as my parish.' This breadth of vision, of fraternal fervour, found an echo in thousands of souls. He never hesitated to speak of subjects which interested him passionately, such as alcoholism, prostitution, the welfare of prisoners and social injustice; and together with his brothers in arms, among them George Whitefield, he saw the crowds grow at each of their field preachings. Bitterly criticized by the Anglicans of the Established Church and by puritan Presbyterians, even persecuted for a time by the authorities, the Methodists had nevertheless won their battle by the time of Wesley's death. Not only in England, but also in the U.S.A., they were to be one of the most active of Protestant groups, with the most brilliant future, a view that half a century of history has amply confirmed.

Throughout his life, however, Wesley retained an unreserved affection for the Anglican Church. A clergyman of the High Church, son of a clergyman of the High Church, brought up from the earliest years in strict obedience, he never believed for a moment that his audacious views would put him beyond the pale of the Anglican Communion. But his denunciation of social injustice, his marked indifference to dogma, his way of seeing in the Christian message only a generous moralism, and the unrestrained manifestations that took place during the Methodist Assemblies, all were to cause disquiet to the Church. The tension mounted; the Methodists themselves, due to the ever-growing extent of their following, were obliged to organize into circuits, districts and a General Conference, as though they were constituting themselves into a Church. Then, when American groups demanded priests, and when the Episcopalian hierarchy refused to provide them, Wesley, overstepping his power as a mere priest, himself proceeded to confer ordination. On his death in 1791 the break between the Anglican Church and Methodism was virtually complete. It was definitive by 1828.

Even as Wesley was moving away from Anglicanism, the Methodist system was undergoing the process so typical of Protestantism, that of variations, of splits and divisions. During Wesley's own lifetime internal dissensions could be seen: Whitefield had come closer to Calvinism; in America some circuits had demanded their own bishops; everywhere the relationship between local churches and the Conference had aroused dissensions. After Wesley's death the process of dislocation became more rapid. Won over to the idea of a strongly democratic organization, the Methodist New Connection (1797) followed Alex Kilham; opposed to remuneration for the clergy, the Independent Methodists (1805) formed their own Church; then followed the revivals of Bourne and Clowes on the one hand, William Bryant (O'Bryan) on the other, who set up respectively the Primitive Methodists (1811) and the Bible Christians (1815). There was an attempt to give a doctrinal basis to the movement, but this merely entailed the breaking away of the Wesleyan Methodist Association (1835). There is something a little distressing in seeing the heirs of one who desired that the world might be his parish losing themselves in petty rivalries. The question of organization served only to increase the divisions; partisans of the old democratic system would not accept the episcopate, and the Methodist Episcopal Church chose freedom (1816). When the tragic problem of the freeing of the slaves came up the Methodist Church, which had made substantial progress among coloured people, found itself divided anew and there emerged African Methodist Churches, Coloured Methodist Churches, Southern Methodist Churches and yet others too. One is lost amid this confusion, especially when it is noted that on various occasions these separated Churches regrouped themselves into the Methodist Connection, the Methodist Protestant Church and the Congregational Methodist Church (1872), from which last was to issue in 1881 the New Congregational Methodist Church.

It must, however, be stated that since the end of the nineteenth century the tendency has been in the opposite direction. This fact would not prevent further divisions, especially in Negro Methodist Churches, nor would it prevent rivalry such as that between the Southern and the Northern Churches in the U.S.A.; but groups have emerged which for twenty-five years have resisted the forces of division. The New Methodist Church, founded in 1939 in Kansas City, includes around three-quarters of all Methodists in the U.S.A. in six great sections, five on a territorial basis, including 119 Conferences, the sixth covering all coloured adherents. In Canada the same effort has been made since 1925. In 1951 the World Methodist Council was set up, to which the majority of Methodists belong. There are some 30 million adherents at least, of whom some 12 million to 14 million participate actively in the life of the forty Churches (twenty-two of them in the U.S.A.) which profess to follow Wesley.

All have a very broad and adaptable creed; the founder accepted a shortened version of the Prayer Book and twenty-five of the thirty-nine Anglican Articles, and it is certain that all today's Methodists observe these minima. In any case one can hardly speak of official doctrine with reference to a creed which states clearly that it rejects no one upon doctrinal grounds. If there is mistrust of, even hostility towards, Catholicism, long manifest among Methodist circles, this is explained by the fact that Roman discipline has been held up as slavery, radically opposed to the wide ideals of freedom proclaimed by the

Methodists. In the main, the Methodist Churches teach and believe that in order to be accounted a good Christian it suffices to live by the 'Book' (the Bible), to conduct oneself honourably, in a spirit of fraternity towards all men, and to bear witness faithfully to the Holy Ghost. Confession is sometimes practised; but the weekly communion recommended by Wesley has become obsolete in almost all churches. With such a wide creed it is not easy to single out the average Methodist. In some countries such as France there are for all practical purposes no Methodist communities left, most of them having become Calvinist. But this form of simplifying pragmatism is undoubtedly agreeable to the Anglo-Saxon mind.

As for Church organization, this has remained substantially as laid down by Wesley. Divided into two main trends, episcopal (in the U.S.A.) and nonconformist, the Churches have nevertheless the same administrative framework. They are grouped into 'circuits', each of these joining together regionally to form Conferences, the Supreme Conference directing the whole. Some of them have, alongside the clergy proper, a number of 'stewards' comparable with deacons. In all of them the role of lay preachers is prominent. These bear public witness to the Spirit; for, as in the Baptist and Pentecostal Churches, the Spirit may act directly on each person. Both ministers and preachers constantly change pulpit and audience, in accordance with the itinerant feature of Methodism so dear to Wesley.

By its indifference to doctrine, as well as by its insistence on personal experience, Methodism remains fruitful ground for religious revivals, and in this respect it constitutes a redoubtable force in the Protestant world. It can canalize the good intentions of those people who, in a stricter Church, might find them discouraged, and of all those who, though caring little for dogma and metaphysical precision, will not accept a materialist creed. The zeal with which, ever since its foundation, Methodism has tackled social problems has linked it to the more general wave of social advance that has stirred the world for more than a century. Some indeed have suggested that Marxist Socialism has failed to penetrate the Anglo-Saxon proletariat precisely because Methodism has offered it a gospel of freedom. For the same reason the Methodists are, along with the Baptists, in the forefront of the battle against segregation in the U.S.A.

While Methodism played the part of a leaven in the Protestant lump, the Evangelical movement, a by-product as it were of Wesley's activity, though on a more intellectual plane, exercised a profound influence in many circles. It originated in the late eighteenth and early nineteenth century with Isaac Milner, Charles Simeon, Venn and Wilberforce. Again it was from the Methodism of the 'New Connection' that there emerged in 1865 the Salvation Army, the most famous charitable institution of the Protestant world. This was less a separated Church than an organization for social work, a sort of Protestant religious order. The Methodists too played a specially active part in missionary work by using the printed word. In Wesley's own time the Christian Library was founded, spreading works by a number of religious writers, even Catholics such as Tauler or Fénelon. This was followed in America by the Methodist Book Council (1789), which in 1939 became the Methodist Publishing House, the largest religious publishing house in the U.S.A. and one of the most flourishing in the world.

It goes without saying that Methodism was predestined to occupy an important place in the ecumenical movement. Was not its most characteristically Wesleyan principle that of universal acceptance? From 1881 the Methodist Ecumenical Conference declared that it accepted the idea of Protestant ecumenicalism (as it was to be achieved later in the World Council of Churches). In 1951 this same conference, meeting at Oxford, launched an appeal for the unification of all spiritual forces to defend the Christian religion 'challenged by a rival ideology', and declared that 'Methodists everywhere are committed to the world movement' towards Christian unity. From 1958 the great voice of Pope John XXIII found warm echoes among the Methodists.

12. DISSIDENTS OF DISSIDENTS: THE BAPTISTS

Apart from the two great groups which are usually considered as the main products of the Reformation, there are others which have existed from the beginning, in Germany and elsewhere. Some were the issue of very old tendencies which the Catholic Church had unsuccessfully tried to eliminate. Several of them sprang from the Middle Ages, through Joachim of Flora and Jacopone da Todi; they were of the same spirit as the fifteenth-century groups in Holland, the *alumbrados*, who in the sixteenth century so exercised the Spanish Inquisition. All these reformers, though outside the main stream of the Reformation, had several basic ideas in common: belief in divine inspiration from within by direct operation of the Holy Ghost, in a Church which was to be purely spiritual and composed solely of saints. These ideas were to be found more or less in Calvin and Luther, but all were carried to an extreme of violence and exaltation. To these were added other facets, temporal in nature, which challenged the established order as had the medieval *spiritualism*, those vehement partisans of radical changes in the Church. These anarchic reformers were not clerics like Luther or Calvin, but men of the people, artisans such as Loiet of

Antwerp and John of Leyden, or peasants such as Thomas Münzer, leader of the celebrated Peasants' Revolt which so shocked Luther.

These currents, opposed unceasingly by all the Established Churches, have nevertheless managed to survive into our own day under different names and in various guises, inspiring millions of Christians who, for the most part, have forgotten that they descend from virulent spiritual revolutionaries. In the sixteenth century these people were commonly known as Anabaptists, a name derived from their practice of baptizing only adults, and even of 're-baptizing' children, upon the grounds that since faith alone (as Luther said) makes a Christian, it should precede baptism. Such an idea was not unreasonable if all operative virtue were denied to the sacrament and the Church no longer recognized as an institution. In quite recent years such outstanding personalities as Kierkegaard and Karl Barth have advocated adult baptism.

In the sixteenth century Anabaptism suffered a terrible ordeal, hunted down in Alsace, associated with the Peasants' Revolt, swept along with the rebels in their rout, and thence to the dreadful massacre at Münster (1538) following John of Leyden's attempt to establish the City of God. Even in Switzerland, where Zwingli had at first appeared to be reasonably favourable, the Anabaptists were destined to be drowned or hanged. So strong, however, was the current of faith that upheld them that they were not all annihilated, and reappeared a little later.

The saviour of Anabaptism was Menno Simons (1492–1559), a one-time Catholic priest from Holland. He understood that it was useless and dangerous to mix social demands with the great plans for reorganizing the world upon purely spiritual lines, and also that it was absurd to wield the sword while preaching the Gospel. A cultured and well-read man, he had no truck with the more popular and dangerous leaders of Anabaptism, but joined rather with small 'spiritual' circles which existed in Germany, and likewise with certain theoreticians at Zürich, especially Conrad Grebel. Under his influence Anabaptist-type groups came into being, yet different enough for them to be called Mennonites, a name which has stuck. Mennonism demanded no more from its adherents than that they should live according to the precepts of the Sermon on the Mount. The Schleitheim Confession (1527) and that of Dordrecht (1532) were very simple, retaining only baptism from the old sacraments, this being reduced to a ceremony as of entry to the Church, and Holy Communion. At the same time they insisted on the simple life, moral rectitude, work, the avoidance of oaths and the condemnation of any form of violence. On these bases, organized by 'shepherds' rather than by priests, the Mennonites expanded.

In Holland they numbered 160,000 in 1700, spreading to Germany, Switzerland, Poland and France, where there are still some four thousand. In the eighteenth century they spread to Dniepropetrovsk in Russia, and thence to the Caucasus, Siberia and Central Asia. As conscientious objectors they were exempted from military service, being placed in civilian organizations. Very roughly handled by the Soviet authorities, forced to bear arms, many of them fled to the Altai regions and to Kazakhstan, where they are to be found today. But the heaviest emigration of Mennonites was to the U.S.A. Large groups settled first in Pennsylvania, then spread to the interior, while others reached Canada. Almost everywhere, because of their doctrine, they took to agriculture. Their movement was fortunate in finding strong personalities to lead them and strengthen the Mennonite doctrine (the Mennonite Biblical School at Saint-Christchona has a special reputation), and this gave them a much-needed impetus. Like all forms of Protestantism, Mennonism in the Americas has succumbed to the same law of division: some 250,000 adherents in the U.S.A. and Canada are split into seventeen different varieties, classed in two large Conferences, which the Mennonite Central Committee has been trying to harmonize ever since 1940.

Some Mennonites settled in South America, mostly in Brazil. The strangest venture here was that of the Hutterites who, as we saw earlier, were founded in the early seventeenth century by the Lutheran mystic Hutter, and who, because the Churches were disloyal to the teachings of the reformer of Wittenberg, fled from Germany after the defeat in 1945 and settled in Paraguay, where they had immense success. They number some 450 communities and are very close to the Mennonites.

Though small in numbers, the Mennonites still maintain missions, and are very active in the U.S.A. both through the press and through other media. Their refusal of violence and their conscientious objection in time of war have brought them much into the public eye, and their services in devastated Germany after the Second World War were notable. One of their thinkers, Guy F. Herschberger, is among the most original of pacifist thinkers; it has even been suggested that 'social law', as defined by G. Gurvitch,[1] may have its roots in the Mennonite communities, which attempt to live according to the Beatitudes. . . .

Anabaptism, however, gave rise not only to Mennonism. Based on the same fundamental issue, adult baptism, there arose at the end of the sixteenth century certain communities which, despite the weak links which bound them, were categorized as Baptists. In view of their imprecise doctrine, of the absolute liberty upon which these resolute Congregationalists insisted for their local churches, and, it must be said, because of the strength of their missionary endeavours and

[1] *L'Idée du droit social*, Paris, 1931.

undoubted moral qualities, Baptists today, after three centuries, form the second largest Protestant movement in the world; in 1958 they numbered some 18 million baptized, a figure which corresponds to some 40 million adherents. This is a very large group, but confused and without structure, difficult to perceive in the round. The Baptist religion appears strangely enough to be both a meeting place of converging faiths (as soon as a certain degree of unity has resulted), then a splitting up into Churches and sects, each anxious to retain its individual liberty. The sole doctrinal link of any substance remains the baptism of adults, conferred only on those who make an open confession of faith. The one source of faith common to all is the Bible, but since each may interpret this as he wills, as the Holy Ghost so dictates, every concept is admissible, some finding in it the most rigid Calvinist predestination, others the free access of all to salvation. Others are convinced upon scriptural grounds that observance of Sunday as the Lord's Day is heresy, and that one must observe the Jewish custom of the Sabbath. One can imagine to what anarchy such a multitude of denominations, Churches, movements and sects will lead. It is even impossible to discover today just how many there are—ten or fifty!

The Baptists can be identified rather by their internal organization, this being of a strictly Congregationalist type. Each community is independent. The admission of new members to baptism is done by election, and in some communities the vote must be unanimous. Each community elects its leader, now called pastor, now elder, now bishop. The service itself is everywhere very simple, a considerable time being devoted to collective singing, with periods of silence for private meditation.

Although their origins are hotly disputed, it was undoubtedly in England that the Baptists first appeared, after the arrival of Anabaptist elements and also of Arminian Calvinists subsequent to the victory of the Gomarists.[1] Among the principal founders were J. Smyth and T. Helwys. Suspected by the Established Church, accepted by Cromwell, persecuted by the monarchy on the Restoration (when John Bunyan spoke out for them) and finally authorized to live in peace by the Act of Toleration (1689), they could scarcely be said to form a Church, but at once adopted the form which we have seen, a loosely linked collection of small communities. The two principal groups were the General Baptists, so called because of their broad, Arminian views on the question of Predestination, and the Regular Baptists, more Calvinist in outlook. The union of the two branches in 1813 to form the Baptist Union did not stop the process of division, for very soon various groups seceded and set up on their own, e.g. the Seventh Day

[1] See p. 29.

Baptists, the 'Free' Baptists, the 'Free Will' Baptists, etc. But this was nothing compared to the divisions which emerged in the U.S.A.

The appearance of the Baptists in North America was the work of William Rogers (1599–1683), a former Anglican minister who was obliged to seek exile for his nonconformist puritan views. Hostile to every ecclesiastical system which he found in the colony, he criticized them all so ruthlessly that he was forced to decamp to Rhode Island, where he founded the town of Providence. With his friend Ezekiel Hollyman he organized the first Baptist communities, along the lines laid down in the 'six principles' of the Epistle to the Hebrews (vi. 1–2): repentance, faith, baptism, the laying on of hands, the resurrection of the dead and eternal judgment. From this tiny seed there grew the mighty tree which occupies a pre-eminent position in American Protestantism; 80 per cent of the world's Baptists are Americans, and they represent the second largest group in the U.S.A. after the Catholic Church. They show great initiative. For long the bulk of them were recruited, according to Siegfried, from the 'little people from rural communities and towns of third-rate importance'. They have now penetrated both to the black proletariat of the South and to the higher managerial classes, for which latter they have built many universities. The crowning achievement of their efforts could be said to be the fact that John Rockefeller joined their ranks.

But here again this wave of success was accompanied by an increasing fragmentation, in accordance with the twofold process which we have already seen. Many new groups joined the Baptist fold, in the same way as those who founded the Disciples of Christ. Simultaneously divisions appeared, produced by three great questions. The first was dogmatic: that of the interpretation of the Bible, which some wanted in literal fashion, setting aside all criticism, while others were broader in their approach. Between 'fundamentalists' and 'liberals' no agreement was possible. A second question of a more practical nature, namely slavery, brought about other splits at the time of the Civil War; the Northern Baptist Convention and the Southern Baptist Convention arose, with a certain number of Negro communities joining the National Baptist Convention of the U.S.A. Then there was the question of missions, some adherents wishing to heed Christ's apostolic appeal by founding the General Mission Convention and the Home Mission Society; others were content to let God choose whom He should elect. In addition to this, outside the ranks of the Regular Baptists, who represent some four-fifths of the total, we find not less than twenty American Baptist organizations with different names, all rather hard to distinguish from one another.

Two of the most interesting are the Primitive Baptists of the Southern States and the Disciples of Christ. The first number some

7 million Negroes, all desirous of preserving the true faith and all having a certain mistrust of all other forms of Protestantism. They contend that it is not essential to train their ministers, to pay them salaries or to bother with any missionary activity. Their teaching is exclusively biblical, but their understanding of the Bible is simplistic and resolutely 'fundamentalist'. One must preach the Word of God as it is written, verse by verse (from translations that vary in quality), emphasizing the more striking features such as the blood shed by Jesus, the agonies of Hell, the joys of Paradise. And the gatherings are provided with hymns which have equally striking imagery and an insistent rhythm. This is the religion of the Negro spirituals, and that which, since the end of the Second World War, renewed and shorn of such imagery, has led the fight against segregation with Martin Luther King at its head.

The Disciples of Christ, numbering some 11 million adherents, represent diametrically opposite views. Their founder was Thomas Campbell (1763–1853), a puritan pastor from Northern Ireland who desired to live wholly according to the concepts of early Christianity, and who emigrated to the U.S.A. in 1810 with his son Alexander. They set up the 'Primitive Church of Christian Society', based on the Baptist faith. At the same time a Presbyterian minister, Barton W. Stone, after breaking with the Established Church, founded another whose members modestly referred to themselves merely as 'Christians'. The two movements joined forces in 1838 and were subsequently known as the 'Disciples of Christ', also called the Reform Baptists. The Disciples immediately set out to spread the Gospel along the New Frontier of the American West.

Despite a split in 1906, which separated the more orthodox elements who founded the Church of Christ, the movement prospered. But then a singular evolution took place, leading these 'Early Christians' towards rationalist criticism. Their progress was made easy in intellectual circles where religion, which was regarded as essential, was reduced to a liberal Protestantism, without dogma but with a strong moral structure and a high social sense of responsibility. Twenty-five universities are run by the Disciples, and the Seminaries of Colgate and Rochester and the Divinity School at Chicago are allied to their liberal views, as are also several American Christian social leaders, such as Walter Rauschenbusch.

Turning now to the rest of the world, outside the missionary territories properly speaking, there are not many Baptists. There are some in Germany, Denmark, Sweden, Norway, Brazil, China and Japan. In France there are only a few thousand, in four groups and with one independent Church whose tabernacle was for long at Montmartre. One group is to be found in Russia, where the Baptists, few in number before the Second World War, have expanded rapidly since 1944, when they merged with the former 'Christian Evangelists' or *Pachkovsti* (founded in 1895 by Colonel Pachkov, a Guards officer), and with the small evangelical communities which flourished among the Ukrainian peasantry. In 1960 they were estimated at some 560,000 baptized, which means some 3 million adherents in all. The anti-religious Communist press often reiterates the danger that they represent for militant atheism.

The Baptists are perfectly well aware that their fragmentation impedes them from playing the full role to which their large numbers entitle them. But they have made efforts to unite. In 1812 they set up the Baptist Educational Society to train the right type of pastor for each of the different denominations; but at least one-third of the total of the communities have never been near the seminaries run by this society. Certain alliances were made, resulting in the Baptist Federation, the Evangelical Association of Baptist Churches and (in 1905) the Universal Baptist Alliance; but even this last has so far failed to assemble all the Baptists of the world. It need hardly be said that Baptists are very mistrustful of all forms of ecumenicalism. The majority of their communities are members either of the World Council of Churches or of the International Council. But in their eyes, according to William Carey Taylor, a Baptist missionary, 'the two Councils are both unionist; both defend erroneous doctrines; both would destroy Baptist life if once they penetrate deeply into it'. Are the Baptists then *a fortiori* hostile to any form of unity with non-Protestants? In some of their circles, often marked by narrow nationalism or systematic anti-Communism, the most virulent anti-Catholicism has been maintained until quite recently in the U.S.A.

13. Sects or New Churches?

With some Baptist groups one is not far from what is called a 'sect'. The latter is a very ambiguous term. The dictionary definition is cautious: 'Those who have separated from or seceded from one of the great Churches'; but it has a different meaning when used by different people, 'laudatory to those who belong to the sect, pejorative to those who do not'.

It is difficult to establish what constitutes a sect, in what way a sect is differentiated from the great Churches. By its character as a minority? Then the Baptists would be considered a sect in France, whereas in the U.S.A. they are unquestionably recognized as a Church, and the Pentecostal sects are on the way to becoming Churches in the full sense of the word, admitted to membership by the World Council of

Churches. By its claim to represent the only true form of Christianity? But this conviction is formally part of the expression of many great religious groups, such as Methodism, and perhaps of all movements that sprang from the Reformation. It has been suggested that the word 'sect' should be dropped in favour of 'New Church', but this has the disadvantage of making all other existing Churches 'Old Churches'.

In any event the multiplicity of sects was one of the main features of religious history during the nineteenth and twentieth centuries. There has been an 'offensive by sects' in our day. They have emerged from nearly every Church, even the Catholic Church. The majority of them are linked to Protestantism, but not all Protestants are willing to admit them to their ranks. Christian Science, which formally declared itself to be a Protestant Church, is regarded as heretic by the majority of Protestant authors, and the adherents of the Pentecostal Churches are considered as *illuminati* by many Reformation groups. But, as we have said, the Methodists were for long treated as dangerous agitators by the pastors of the old Churches. . . .

The 'Sectarians' in fact spring almost always from Established Churches for reasons which are basic to Protestantism itself. All of them were the issue of 'revivals', a typical phenomenon of the Reformation. All of them laid emphasis on the inspiring presence of the Holy Ghost, and this bears, according to Calvin, not only upon the doctrine of justification as taught by Luther but also upon the entire divine oracle which is the Bible. This may explain why Lutheranism has been so little penetrated by sects. Illuminism finds fruitful ground in a doctrine which allows that each person may receive irresistible individual illumination.

The most important sect nowadays is fully representative of these three views: to await the guidance of the Holy Ghost, to awaken the soul and to withdraw from the rest of the herd in order to form a community of saints. That is what the shoemaker, George Fox (1624–1691), had in mind when in the middle of the seventeenth century he founded the Society of Friends, which was soon to be known more widely as the 'Quaker' movement.[1] According to Carl Heath, one of the movement's thinkers: 'The Society bases itself neither upon theological dogma nor upon any literal interpretation of the Bible, but upon an inner experience of the soul, which it invites men to share.' It has no Established Churches, no sacraments, no clergy—only universal priesthood, open to women also. The religious service is replaced by 'silence meetings', where each meditates in an inner light. Austere morals, forswearing of allegiance of whatever sort, refusal to take part in war or violence, even in legitimate self-defence, are enjoined.

[1] Fox once called upon a judge to 'quake before God'.

All this is a far cry from traditional Protestantism, the Quakers rejecting the Lutheran doctrine of grace as they do Calvinist predestination. Persecuted at first, the Friends ,nevertheless made great strides in England; William Penn launched them later in Pennsylvania, where their reliability, their culture and their industry worked wonders. The eighteenth century, however, marked a decline: turned in upon themselves in order to preserve their original purity, the Quakers were soon no more than a small group, virtually asleep in a form of quietism. Then, at the beginning of the nineteenth century, they were revived by a whole series of personalities: two Frenchmen, Antoine Bénézet and Étienne de Grellet; John Woolman and John Whittles, both Americans and fervent advocates of the liberation of the slaves; and a remarkable woman, Elizabeth Fry, who reformed the prisons of England. This renaissance brought the Society of Friends up to some 200,000 members, split into four groups—mostly in England and the U.S.A. They abandoned Fox's well-known costume of buttonless leather coats and large hats. They also eliminated the sometimes curious manifestations which took place at their meetings. But they retain the doctrine, the simple 'service' and the teaching of their founder. They have founded missions in astonishing numbers. Since the First World War the Quaker Relief missions have become famous and were so valuable during the Second World War that in 1947 two of their committees were granted the Nobel Peace Prize.

The 'revivalist' movement which shook the Protestant world at the beginning of the nineteenth century, the same movement that was to awaken the Quakers from their torpor, had, among other consequences, that of producing its crop of dissidents. The British Isles, that blessed plot of nonconformity, were to be their chosen territory.

The first dissident group was that of Edward Irving (1792–1834), a Scots Presbyterian minister who had studied the Bible profoundly and come to the conclusion that all ecclesiastical organizations, without exception, had cast aside the primitive Gospel spirit, and that it was now time to revive the 'Catholic Apostolic Church' and return to the old customs, not forgetting charismatic phenomena, 'the gift of tongues' and miraculous cures. Basing his ideas on St Paul's Epistle to the Ephesians (iv. 11) he set up twelve apostles, followed by prophets, evangelists, pastors (also called angels) and teachers; and in each small Catholic Apostolic community there very soon flourished the gift of tongues, with prophets announcing the imminent return of Christ to earth. Illumination from within, the inner light of the Quakers, was to replace dogma. But, oddly enough, to this subjective concept of religion, Irving was to add a theology of seven sacraments (very close to that of the Catholics) together with the Mass. This went hand in hand with a sumptuous liturgy, more Byzantine than Roman, with chasubles and copes, incense-swinging and a precisely regulated 'choreography'. All this was calculated to heighten the senses of the congregation, rendering them more receptive to divine revelation. Since the death of the last 'apostle' in 1901 the Apostolics have declined continually; lacking their own churches, and therefore sometimes obliged to take part in Protestant services, they now number no more than fifty thousand (less than a hundred in France).

But an offshoot appeared in the shape of the New Apostolic communities, which emerged from dissident Irvingites and gave them a new lease of life. In 1860 half the 'apostles' lived in Germany. Certain difficulties arose, and the Berlin 'prophet' Geyer, together with the 'angel' Schwarz, set up another college of twelve apostles, thus founding the 'Christian Apostolic Mission'. On Geyer's death Schwarz joined with the 'apostle' Krebs and they launched a large propaganda campaign. But the real breakthrough was due to Hermann Niehaus, Krebs's successor, a man of iron, spellbinder of crowds, and also to J. G. Bischoff, a one-time Catholic from Frankfurt, who was no less enterprising and energetic. From 1906 onwards the official name became the New Apostolic Community. Its principal doctrines were similar to those of Irving: the conviction that this was the one true Church and the certitude of inner illumination; but the sacraments were reduced to three—baptism, communion and a type of confirmation. More emphasis was laid on the role of the 'apostle' now become an 'apostle-patriarch', a kind of pope, much more powerful than the Roman pontiff in that he was able to guarantee the soul's salvation! Bischoff, the 'apostle-patriarch', announced several times that he would witness Christ's return before he died. His death in 1960 obliged his disciples to modify their doctrine on this point. Nevertheless there are some 540,000 of them, spread over fifteen countries, including France, where some 14,000 adherents are to be found in Alsace and Lorraine and around Paris.

The Darbyites are closer to traditional Protestantism. Their founder, John Nelson Darby (1800–82), was just as hostile towards the Established Church as Irving. A one-time member of the Church of England, he left it because he could no longer accept the idea that a society founded by Christ should submit to the authority of an earthly sovereign. He encountered small groups of evangelists, led by John Walker, who called themselves Plymouth Brethren. Darby subsequently took them over, and with his talents as an orator and writer he soon launched this movement upon a new and upward course. He preached in Geneva and Lausanne and among the Waldenses, and from 1844 in the south of France, everywhere spreading copies of his literal translation of the Bible, and extending his field of activity to Germany, Italy, Greece, U.S.A., Australia and New Zealand. Darby appeared as messenger for a new form of Protestantism, simplified, based on personal fervour and fraternal love. His doctrine was clear: all Churches were abodes of Satan, where souls died; the true Christian community had no organization, no hierarchy, no pastors, no written confession of faith; every adherent, having received inspiration from the Holy Ghost, could baptize and give communion. The service was extremely simple, merely a meal of bread and wine, readings from the Scriptures and witness by whomsoever was moved to it after meditation. Baptism is conferred at thirteen years only. Mistrustful of all forms of established order, the Darbyites take no part in public service. Today there are some 300,000 of them, about 10,000 of whom live in France.

Both Irving and Darby incorporated the doctrine of Christ's return to earth. This, however, was not their central theme; other reformers laid greater stress on it, giving rise to various sects which revived the Millenarianism of earlier centuries.

In 1840 an impoverished farm worker of Pittsfield, William Miller, who had read the theories of the theologian Bengal on the Millennium, left the Baptist Church to meditate alone upon this problem. In the Book of Daniel (viii. 14) he read that 'unto two thousand and three hundred days; then shall the sanctuary be cleansed', and, taking as reference date the return of Esdras to Jerusalem (457 B.C.), he concluded that the event would take place in 1843. He announced this in a pamphlet, as well as in a periodical entitled *Signs of the Times*, and many people believed him. Proved wrong thrice, the prophet saw most of his 50,000 adherents drift away from the hill in Massachusetts where they had gathered to await the event. But now a prophetess came upon the scene—Ellen Gould White (1827–1915), a former Methodist who had joined a Seventh Day Baptist Church, where the Lord's Day was observed on Saturday instead of Sunday. This extraordinary woman was an excellent missionary, and a visionary also. She announced that a vision had given her the reason for Miller's error: the year 1843 was indeed the 2,300th day of the prophecy, but it was not the end of the world; it marked the entry of Christ into the Holy of Holies, that period preceding the *Parousia*. It was therefore necessary to prepare the faithful for the approach of the Day of Judgment. Thus was born the sect—or Church—of Seventh Day Adventists, claimed to be the only guardian of truth and alone capable of leading the faithful to salvation. She travelled widely, preaching in America and Europe, even as far afield as Australia, organizing hospices and publishing houses. She gave the movement an impetus that it has retained, though she was unable to prevent divisions which resulted in five separate groups. But the overall results are impressive: 1 million adherents spread over 230 countries—even in Soviet Russia, where there are 30,000 of them—led by 40,000 pastors or evangelists, running 170 hospices or sanatoria, 3,500 schools and more than 500 papers and reviews in every language. All is done on businesslike lines, headed by a General Council in Washington with funds provided by each member's tithe. Adventism was for long a combative organization, violently attacking Catholicism and the Pope through its press. Its best known feature is the celebration of the Lord's Day on Saturday instead of Sunday, which has led to difficulties with the authorities in the U.S.A. Its disciples have become the advocates of special nutrition and diets of a natural character, and its propaganda is very well organized. Its doctrine is distinctly biblical, 'the Bible only', but the Bible as annotated by Ellen White. As with Catholics and Protestants, she accepted the Holy Trinity, the divinity of Christ, the Incarnation, the Resurrection and (up to a point) original sin. As with the Baptists, she insisted upon baptism by immersion, and communion as a symbol. The latter takes place every three months, preceded by washing of feet. But Adventists also entertain a peculiar notion of the hereafter: the dead sleep until the Last Judgment, which will be the triumph of the elect (the Adventists themselves) and the downfall of the wicked. Despite these rather odd views, the Adventists are claimed by Protestants as of their camp, and they participate in the work of the World Council of Churches. One cannot honestly inveigh against the Adventists on the grounds that they have given rise to other millenary sects, with doctrines vastly inferior to theirs and which, in fact, the Protestants categorically disown. Catholicism itself is not free from such spontaneous outgrowths where truth becomes singularly distorted. In the last analysis it might be said that the multiplicity of divisions within Protestantism springs from its very basis, whereas if analogous divisions were to take place within the Catholic Church they would be contrary to the nature of Catholicism. In any event the Adventists are followers of those who believe in freedom to interpret the Bible in their own way, and in total reliance upon the Holy Ghost, convinced that every man receives illumination directly; and these ideas have given rise, since the beginning of the twentieth century, to a group whose activities have urged Protestantism forward in many sectors, and which are known generally as Pentecostal Movements.

According to their adherents these have no founder; or rather, no human founder, for the only one they recognize is Christ, who promised his faithful followers that the Holy Ghost would come among them. The most fateful day for all humanity was therefore the day of Pentecost, on which the first Christians, gathered in the cenacle, saw tongues of fire descend upon them and knew that they were granted the gift of tongues, were able to perform miracles and to proclaim their faith. The main feature of Christian experience devolves from this

'Baptism of the Holy Ghost', which renews the inner spirit and assists those baptized towards the acquisition of spiritual blessing. This doctrine can be traced to the theology of St Paul, who emphasizes the vital part played by the Holy Ghost. But in Chapter VIII of his first Epistle he warns the Corinthians against assuming that the gift of tongues and the working of miracles is the essence of Christianity. To this temptation, however, some—e.g. Montanus, Priscillian and Donatus—succumbed, as also, among Protestant sects, have to some extent the Quakers, Methodists, Irvingites and Adventists. But no group has made it the king-pin of their religious system as the Pentecostal Churches have done.

Recourse to the Holy Ghost as the single enlightener of souls was basic to the 'revival' which took place at the beginning of the twentieth century in America and Wales. Here in 1904 a humble miner named Evan Roberts, a loyal Methodist, was the recipient of visions which filled him with longing to preach the message of the Saviour throughout Wales. In this he was assisted by the minister of his church, one Seth Joshuah, and a young girl of outstanding beauty. Crowds were soon spellbound by his missionary fire. At about the same time, first in Kansas then in California, revivalist meetings were being held, 'so charged with charism that the participating Christians had the impression that they were taking part in a new Pentecost'. The Negro Baptist pastor W. J. Seymour now entered the movement and provided it with a new impetus. Los Angeles was its capital. In Scandinavia, Lunde and Barrett founded a similar movement. The 'Assemblies of God' multiplied in number. The fanaticism of some of their members, allied to the caution of older Churches, was to have a result contrary to that sought by the Pentecostal Movement: instead of 'reviving' their sleeping brethren and so launching a 'Reform of the Reformation', according to the well-known formula, they led to division and to the setting up of a new Protestant denomination, and the Pentecostal Movement proper was born.

Merely embryonic in 1906, they are now the most original and active sectarian group. They are also the largest in numerical terms, varying, depending on the source of figures, between 4 million and 10 million, of which there are 2 million in the U.S.A. Introduced by a Baptist minister, the movement spread first to Scandinavia, where it was joined by a number of Lutherans and where it absorbed the Baptist Church. Through Hungary and Poland it reached Germany, where it absorbed numerous New Apostolic communities and reached the figure of some 50,000 adherents. Entering France through Le Havre, with the English pastor Douglas Scott in 1929, it spread quickly, reaching all the main French cities, thence spreading to Belgium and Switzerland and then to Italy, where in 1954 it numbered five hundred centres. The same year, at the Vélodrome d'Hiver in Paris, the movement managed to assemble some ten thousand adherents or sympathizers in one gathering. From America it spread with astonishing rapidity to Chile, Brazil, Mexico; and its progress continues.

What is this movement? Or rather, what are the Pentecostal Movements? For the particularity of this sect—or new Church—is that it affirms its plurality, each group leading its own life under the inspiration of the Holy Ghost, some of them being wide open to strangers, others shut in on themselves. A 'World Centre' exists at Springfield in Missouri, but it has little authority. Alongside the principal movement, the 'Assemblies of God', which accounts for nine-tenths of the membership, there are various subdivisions—Jaffrey, Apostolic, Final Deluge, First Pentecost and also Bethesda, which all the others view with suspicion.

Yet all of them have twelve 'basic truths':

(1) Complete confidence in the Scriptures;
(2) Faith in God One and Triune;
(3) Original sin;
(4) Redemption flowing from the blood of Christ;
(5) Necessity of baptism, which is granted to penitents and administered by immersion;
(6) Necessity of 'second baptism', the Baptism of the Holy Ghost;
(7) A strict moral code, in order that each may be as saintly as Christ;
(8) Faith in 'divine healing';
(9) Practice of the breaking of bread in memory of the Last Supper;
(10) Belief that the return of Christ is imminent;
(11) That eternal judgment will cast into hell those whose names are not writ in the book of life; and
(12) Practical experience of *charismata*, the gift of the Holy Ghost.

Many aspects of this creed are orthodox, others come from Calvinism, Baptistry, Adventism. Some are proper to the movement, especially those relating to the gift of tongues and miraculous cures, both of which are present when the assembly has been aroused to the required pitch of religious fervour. As for the service itself, it is very simple, as we saw from one of the 'Four Aspects' at the beginning of this chapter: readings, hymns, 'witness', sometimes baptism and even spectacular healings. . . .

How do the Pentecostal Movements fit into the Protestant framework? The French weekly *Réforme* has denounced their *spiritocentrisme*, which shifts the centre of gravity of Christianity: it is no longer Christ who saves, but the Holy Ghost. Many Protestants too are suspicious of these meetings where people shout, sing far too loudly and where very strange things happen. But Protestantism cannot cast aside such a large mass of sincere believers who show such astonishing missionary zeal, who multiply the number of home and foreign missions at such a rate, whose moral qualities, especially charity, are so exemplary and who, according to one of their current leaders, Arthur G. Osterberg, 'want to be Protestants and to work with the Protants'. In 1954 they sent observers to the World Council of Churches at Evanston. This was symptomatic, though it is too early to say whether a more settled Pentecostal Movement, better organized, will become a great new Protestant group, or whether the movement will give new life from within to other groups, as is the case with the Southern Baptist Church in the U.S.A.

The history of the Pentecostal Movements is significant. It reveals men's unconscious desire for spiritual nourishment in this twentieth century as a counter to the anguish which they feel at the *Âge de la mort de Dieu*. It is not only the Assemblies of God, but all sects, all Churches of recent origin that are asking the Established Churches a searching question. If men and women of goodwill, who cannot all be crazy or weak in the head, turn to religious groups with such diverse doctrines, it is obviously because in the Established Churches they do not find what they are seeking. Sects seem to be a form of historical judgment pronounced on the older Churches, not only the Protestant Churches but the Catholic Church too, which also loses members to these new movements as well as to Jehovah's Witnesses.

This *exposé* of the sects will have shown what is unacceptable in them. But it must be admitted that alongside suspect tendencies there are certain factors which spring from a true spirituality. The religion which is preached is founded on piety, personal experience of God, search for direct contact with Him and the necessity of bearing witness in public to the supernatural realities which each adherent has experienced. Much of the success depends on the degree of enthusiasm, fervour and joy engendered; their aim, according to Jonathan Edwards, 'is to touch your heart, not fill your head'. This means an excessive appeal to sentiment, and it may be that these sects lead their devotees along strange paths; but they have merit in that they oppose routine, conformism and pharisaism, and that they sometimes arouse that 'inner warmth' which the disciples at Emmaus felt when the resurrected Jesus spoke to them. Furthermore it is remarkable that, breaking with Protestant tradition, most of the sects have restored to a place of honour the mystics' devotion to the Precious Blood and Holy Wounds; so much so that certain Pentecostal and Catholic hymns are almost identical. This appeal to sentiment stands out in fact as a warm humanity which, it must be said, is not the main characteristic of the *Haute Société protestante* in their Reformed Churches, nor of the vast Catholic parishes of our great cities. All Catholic observers who have studied the sects have agreed that in the twentieth century they show a true spirit of fraternity among members. The new Churches recruit their members from among the lower classes, the humble and the disinherited, at least to begin with; for this aspect becomes less noticeable as they become more firmly established, as happened with the Quakers and the Methodists. Here again the sectarian phenomenon poses an important question to the Churches, rather like the question posed to the Catholic Church by the Protestant Reformation. As 'witnesses' of a faith and as opponents of the older Churches in the dialectic of history, in the full sense of the word the sectarians are 'pro*test*ants'.

MAIN PROTESTANT GROUPS

Lutheran	about 75 million
Calvinists	about 37–40 million
(including Reformed and Presbyterian—but excluding Congregationalists—1–3 million)	
Anglican Communion	about 30 million
(Anglicans and Episcopalians)	
Methodists (numerous varieties)	at least 30 million
Baptist Groups (Anabaptists, Mennonites, Baptists, numerous varieties, e.g. the Disciples of Christ)	about 30–40 million
New Churches and Sects (Quakers, Irvingites and New Apostolics, Plymouth Brethren and Darbyites, Seventh Day Adventists, Pentecostal Movements)	between 4 and 10 million
Grand Total	about 250 million

14. THE ESSENCE OF PROTESTANTISM

Now that we have seen something of the main Protestant groups it is time to ask what common bond unites them. There must be some constant, some common heritage claimed by all of them; for religious men of such different views as the Methodists, the Episcopalians and the Pentecostal Churches define themselves as Protestant. But what is this common heritage?

It is a difficult question to answer. The easiest and simplest reply is that all—Churches, denominations, sects—are daughters of the Reformation. Even those who find some difficulty in affirming their allegiance to Protestantism, e.g. the Anglican Communion, cannot deny this link. What in fact does this signify historically? What remains, among the sects, of the great Reformers' teachings? The 'pious country priest' Réville, whom we mentioned earlier, wrote in 1842 that ever since the death of Calvin 'all or nearly all have abandoned the Augustinian doctrine of grace', and this is still truer of our own age. The tragedy of human nature constantly battling with sin, which evokes the greatness of the drama at work within such men as Luther and Calvin, has been very much dulled in the various forms of Protestantism where religion is now reduced to moralism vaguely tinged with Evangelism. The rejection of righteousness, of the idea that good works are of no account in salvation when compared with faith, is much less current since liberal Protestantism on the one hand and the dissident movements on the other (Quakers, Methodists and Baptists) have laid great emphasis on social welfare work. All these Churches, denominations and sects were generated by the Reformers; they have preserved their heritage very unevenly.

Not one of the basic tenets of Christianity, as the Reformers conceived it, has been left undenied in one or other of the Protestant groups; if indeed there be such a one, it has been so enfeebled as to be unrecognizable. Apart from the existence of God, of the one God, creator and judge, there is not one principal dogma which this or that Protestant has not contradicted. Even the divinity of Christ and the immortality of the soul have been disputed. Of the sacraments, some have retained all those present in Catholicism; others three, two or none. It may be said that extremist positions are those of isolated cases, of individuals or groups, and that the greatest groups have all preserved intact the basic elements of the Christian faith. But it is none the less curious and significant that extremist positions have been taken up by men who remained steadfastly within the framework of Protestantism, men whom the great Churches criticized, even penalized, but whom they rarely if ever excluded altogether. Certain liberal Protestants have turned to agnosticism and the Unitarians to Arianism without ceasing to be members of the great Protestant family.

There is, however, one irreducible kernel of convictions which all Protestants have in common, a minimum of articles of faith which unite them in a common destiny. All things considered, they can be reduced to four:

(1) A true Protestant is a man who believes in God, who sees God's presence in all things, 'in, for and through the actions of men', a man for whom nothing counts save contact with God, either through faith alone or through human virtues, moral perfection and charity.

(2) The Protestant wants this contact direct. One Catholic historian has said that a Protestant is a man who 'believes that each man's conscience is strong enough to seek religious experience unaided'. There must be no intermediary between him and God, no mediator save one, the only rightful one, Christ—who is not, for all Protestants,

necessarily God, nor even the Son of God—sent upon earth precisely for this purpose by His teaching and sacrifice, one or the other being in the forefront, depending on the doctrine and the obedience.

(3) The way of salvation, that which leads to contact with God, has been revealed by God in the Bible. To read the Word of God, and to learn all of the moral and spiritual lessons which it contains, is thus a basic duty for every believer. This fidelity to the Bible is one of the characteristic traits of Protestantism which we find deeply ingrained in all its 'variations'. A Protestant is above all a man of the Bible, be he a Lutheran, a Methodist, a Quaker or a member of the Pentecostal Church; and in this respect the Anglicans are thoroughgoing Protestants. Irony might say that the Protestants believe in the Bible before they believe in God.

(4) Last but not least, the Word of God must come direct to the Protestant. It is in fact the corollary of the axiom that contact with God must be direct, without intermediary. 'Every Protestant must heed and read the Bible for himself,' said Pastor Édouard Fontainès in a sermon in 1875; 'he has no need of the intervention of priest or scholar, nor of the Church's explanations. He hears in his own heart a voice more persuasive than theirs, with more authority, that of God.' This was expressed by Voltaire as: 'Each Protestant is Pope, Bible in hand.' A Protestant is therefore more than merely a man of the Bible, for he reads the Bible *alone*, in the conviction that he is illuminated by the Holy Ghost—that, as St Paul says, 'The Spirit itself beareth witness with our spirit' (Rom. viii. 16).

Here is the point at which the Protestant and other Christians part company. Oscar Cullmann speaks of a 'gulf' lying between them. For Catholics and Orthodox, whatever may be their reliance on the Bible as the Word of God, however great may be their desire to establish contact between man and God, the absolute autonomy of man in this matter is wholly unacceptable. The message of salvation, that which indicates the means of man's attaining God, has been granted by Christ to an institution in which the Holy Ghost 'beareth witness' more powerfully than in each individual spirit. The Church possesses guarantees against error which no mere man could claim to possess. Moreover she has received power to explain the message to her members and to comment upon it so as to help them to live it. This is the stumbling-block, so much so that, at the World Council of Churches' meeting at Evanston in 1954, the representatives of the Orthodox Churches issued a declaration in firm tones concerning the role of the Holy Ghost 'who bears witness through the life and experience of the Church'. Refusal to recognize the Church as a divine institution invested by God with powers of spiritual *magisterium*, of judgment upon men, is basic to all forms of Protestantism; it is when certain Churches return, by various means, to traditional ecclesiastical concepts that they become suspect to the mass of Protestants.

This, in addition to historical reasons, will explain one final trait which a Catholic is forced regretfully to acknowledge as common to every branch of Protestantism (even though less marked among some). The fact that it finds expression only too often in such absurd phrases as 'Peter's chair, which superstition has made a throne' and 'a herd of slaves prostrate at a man's feet' are of little importance in themselves; ignorance and stupidity are not the prerogative of Protestant polemists. But they all point to a reality: the substantial volume of anti-Catholic feeling apparent in Protestantism. In its search for God and for the understanding of His message Protestantism has taken its stand, both doctrinally and institutionally, upon hostility to the Catholic Church, and has been diametrically opposed to everything that the Catholic Church believes and teaches. Protestant polemics have recently lost much of their virulence; both sides have made a real effort to understand each other, to regard each other as brothers, and they have emphasized those things which unite rather than those which separate them. But the opposition has not diminished, for reasons which are basic to both sides. Perhaps a new Pentecost will be necessary in order that what seem insurmountable difficulties may be overcome in the light of that Truth which is love.

CHAPTER II

THE PROTESTANT WORLD

1. The Geographic Expansion and Division of Protestantism

ALTHOUGH Protestantism has split up into too many Churches, sects and denominations, there still exists a Protestant world with a certain amount of common dogma, a number of common principles and above all a reasonably constant spiritual attitude. Where is this world? What sort of area does it cover?

If one looks back to the end of the eighteenth century—that is, to the threshold of the modern era, in which Protestantism and all other forms of religion are finding themselves challenged by a new destiny— one can see that this Protestant world was not very big. It may be divided up into three parts. In the first the Reformation had so entrenched itself that it included a majority of the baptized; for the most part this comprised the northern half of Western Europe from Geneva to Scandinavia, including most of Germany and also Britain—a special case. Of the remainder of Western Europe, Spain and Italy had insignificant minority groups, France and the Danube basin fairly important ones. The third Protestant bastion lay beyond the Atlantic along the coast of what had only recently become the U.S.A.; in actual fact Protestants played such a large part in the development of this young country that their religion would almost appear to be a birth-mark. Elsewhere the religion of reform appeared only as pin-pricks on the surface of the globe.

The nineteenth and twentieth centuries were to prove the great period of expansion for Protestantism; while the eighteenth gave little in terms of territorial gains, it was the time of a double planting of seed in new ground—both in North America and in other continents.

The area covered by Protestantism grew quickly; at the same time the reformed faith maintained and even strengthened its grip on ground already conquered, and in some areas where it was already a minority it added to its converts. By 1958 Protestantism occupied an impressive position on a world map of religions.

It goes without saying that when one talks about the 'Protestant world' one does not mean an organic unit complete with an organized hierarchy such as Catholicism. The law of constant division, which— it is only too well known—springs from the very genius of Protestantism, played as great a role in new lands as in those from which the faith had come; in this regard the case of the U.S.A. is very revealing. But that is not all: the conditions under which the ideas and actions of the Reformers had become realities of life had themselves led to a further division. This confusing schism within Churches already doctrinally divided came from the birth of national Churches.

Let us refer back to the origins of the Reformation. The new religion had survived only when taken over by a State, which defended it against adversaries, or when taken up by a group powerful enough to defend itself. In Germany, for example, Protestantism triumphed only in the towns and States whose leaders were converts. In France only the organization of the Reformers into a militant political party brought eventual success against their opponents. But of course the State, or party, adopting the Reformation put its own stamp on it. In Germany each prince wanted his own Church; the result was that in 1789 there was not one Lutheran Church but twenty-six! [1] In France, Protestantism was to retain—perhaps, it could be argued, to the present day—something of the character it had at the time of the *Dragonnades* and *Camisards*. Religious forms resulting from the Reformation developed, therefore, diverse characteristics that depended on the country in which they grew up. Sometimes a reformed faith and a nation reached a veritable state of symbiosis—as is the case with Sweden, where it has long seemed that the national consciousness cannot be separated from Lutheranism; or in Holland, where Calvinism has strongly conditioned a large part of the country. One can, however, talk of 'French Protestantism' or 'German Protestantism', for each one has its own marked characteristics as well as its marked divisions. There is even an American Protestantism with pronounced national features in spite of its numerous 'denominations'.

An obvious consequence of these geographical divisions is that one cannot write a history of Protestant Churches in the way one can of Catholicism. In the latter the differences and diversities (which exist, that no one can deny) are reduced by a tightly structured unity, and in order to categorize a succession of events, one is always able to turn to a number of axes around which all facts can arrange themselves. (Is this not the history of the Papacy?) To follow, however, the historical development of the world born of the Reformation, one has to study each of its parts in succession.

2. SCANDINAVIA, BASTION OF LUTHERANISM

The Scandinavian countries in northern Europe form the most compact, monolithic Protestant bloc in the world. The sister countries

[1] See Chapter I, section 6.

of Denmark, Norway and Sweden, whose destinies have so long been intertwined, together with Finland across the Baltic, offer a special example of a geographic and cultural whole which is almost completely faithful to the Reformed faith.

The percentage of Protestants is everywhere over 90 per cent; in Finland it is almost 99 per cent. The Scandinavian world, with its 16 million Lutherans, is as Protestant as Spain is Catholic. It has been said that here one finds Protestantism 'in its pure state'. It is certainly here that one becomes aware of the union of the Reformed faith with ethnic and psychological realities which have been determined by biology and by history.

The way in which the Reformation triumphed in these countries explains the characteristics which Protestantism has retained there. It was the first, the Lutheran, wave which covered all four Scandinavian countries. It encountered virtually no obstacles; sovereigns and princes launched it for strictly temporal reasons, but the ordinary people almost everywhere embraced it freely. In Norway and Denmark the priests remained at their posts, bishops were given the title of 'superintendents'; but the ordinary people took little notice of these changes of title. Many worthy Christians were not even aware at the time that the rumoured dispute between monarch and Pope had ended in schism. In Sweden, where things did not go quite so smoothly, where some eighty Protestants were the victims of Catholic reaction, events moved quickly and brutally. Bearing in mind that the Augsburg Confession, the basic rule of faith in Scandinavia, is the least anti-Catholic of them all, one can understand the external likenesses which Protestantism retains there.

The national Church, that of Denmark, Norway and Sweden, is in the common view the Church of the Middle Ages, in communion with Rome, with all its old saints—Olaf, Brigid and the rest. The Lutheran Archbishop of Uppsala, Primate of Sweden, claims apostolic filiation. To this he is entitled, unlike his Danish and Norwegian colleagues who are descended from 'superintendents' consecrated by a friend of Luther—Bugentragen—who was not even a bishop. Whereas in Germany the suppression of Mass might appear to be an indisputable sign of victory for the Reformation, in Sweden one continued to talk of 'Mässa', and the celebrant was always called 'priest' or 'pastor'. Traditional liturgy remained, with incense and candles. In churches with painted walls, before richly decorated altars, one continued singing Gregorian chants, to which the Swedish language was well adapted. The use of the national language in liturgy, communion in both kinds, and especially a married clergy—these constituted the only really distinctive differences. And so things remained until our own day, although in the nineteenth century, under the influence of 'revivalist' movements and sects, a slow process of Protestantization began. But from 1900 onwards this was opposed by a traditionalist and ritualist reaction, which was felt especially in what one might call the 'High Church' in Sweden.

The manner in which the Reformation established itself in Scandinavia determined also the character of the Established Churches, which assumed certain national features. These Churches are true State Churches, officially recognized as such, the monarch disposing of theologically assured powers. At the end of the eighteenth century such a situation was accepted without discussion. The links between the Lutheran faith and the State, the regime, the crown, were so well established that when the French general Bernadotte succeeded as Charles XIV (1818–44) he hastened to proclaim himself a Lutheran and conducted himself in every way as a true Protestant. But during the nineteenth century the establishment was undermined and dislocated. Secular ideas, issue of the Revolution, ill accorded with that Erastian and Constantinian regime. The various forms of mysticism which agitated the Scandinavian soul, ranging from Illuminism to Pietism; the appearance of 'revivals' such as that of which Grundtvig was the herald; and the prophetic activity of the Danish genius Sören Kierkegaard—all these brought in their train a questioning as to the basis of the official Churches which were accused of being mere administrations. Throughout the nineteenth and twentieth centuries, in all three kingdoms, there was a whole series of measures designed to diminish, even to break entirely, the submission of the Church to the State. Today the King of Norway is still considered as '*summus episcopus*', but a draft law places an ecclesiastical council at his elbow. In Sweden Lutheranism is still officially proclaimed as the State religion, even though the government has been for long both Socialist and anticlerical, even though one frequently hears some religious personality saying that Church is closely linked with the State but wishes to be free, and even though a draft law was laid before Parliament in 1956 with the aim of studying the possibility of separating Church from State.

Among the signs which prove the weakening of links between the State and the official Church is the fact that throughout the nineteenth century there was first a slackening then an abolition of the laws against Catholics and 'nonconformist' Protestants. The Catholics were subject to severe rules forbidding them all missionary work, and imposing stern penalties, even exile, upon converts and those who aided and abetted them. Protestant nonconformists and revivalist preachers fared no better: early in the nineteenth century Hans Nielsen Hauge, a Norwegian peasant, was imprisoned for a long time for having transgressed a law of 1741 which forbade the laity to preach. In

Sweden the bishops demanded the application of a law of 1826 which forbade the activities of sects. In Denmark Grundtvig, a patriotic pastor, was forced to conduct secret meetings so as not to anger the official Church. And, to escape the rigour of the laws, the 'dissenters' emigrated to America. But such rigours were scarcely compatible with the democratic ideas which were steadily gaining ground in Scandinavia, to such an extent indeed that the regimes there later became models of social equality. First Norway in 1845, then Denmark in 1849, granted equal status to all religions, this being enshrined in the Danish Constitution of 1886. Sweden took longer to reach that stage (in 1858 six women were exiled for conversion!), but by slow degrees —in 1860, 1870 and 1873—full equality was achieved. This altered climate meant that Catholicism could make a small but significant advance; only the Jesuits were forbidden. All the 'recognized nonconformist Churches' obtained administrative powers over their members, especially in matters affecting their civil status. The Baptists, the Methodists and later all the smaller sects and Churches expanded throughout the four Scandinavian countries. But the totality of Catholics and nonconformists represent a mere fraction alongside the official Churches.

Various differing trends, however, made themselves apparent in the official Churches. Wisely the latter made no attempt to crush them, even accepting certain curiously liberal measures, such as that voted by the Danish Parliament in 1868, which authorized certain dissatisfied members to form 'autonomous parishes', provided they numbered at least twenty and assumed responsibility for paying their pastors. Such parishes nevertheless remained within the national ecclesiastical framework. Pietist circles and the 'High Church' movements, especially active in Sweden and Denmark, are no longer looked on with suspicion by the episcopal authorities. But this has not prevented some from envisaging the development of a 'Broad Church' separated from the State Church.

The religious climate varies from one country to another. In Denmark today three distinct aspects can be discerned:

(1) The 'Inner Mission', to which most of the practising laity belong and which reminds one of traditional revivalism, of Norwegian pietism or of the movement which for half a century has provided the motive power for French Catholicism.

(2) A theological trend inspired by Karl Barth and more recently by Bultmann, strongly Protestant and anti-Catholic.

(3) A ritualist movement in which the Anglican High Church and Anglo-Catholicism are highly regarded.

The Church of Norway appears simpler, steadier its Lutheranism; the leaders and many intellectuals are of 'liberal Protestant' and even rationalist tendencies. The mass of the faithful have not forgotten the pietist campaign of Hans Nielsen Hauge and his successors; they care little for theology, but spiritual life is very active. As for the Bible, 'fundamentalist' theories are taught (Catholics would call them 'integritist') under the direction of a special theological faculty at Oslo. Norwegian pietists show great mistrust towards ecumenicalism even in a Protestant setting; so much so that they have refused the inclusion of the International Council of Missions in the World Council of Churches.

In the Swedish national Church the situation is much more complicated. At the apex is a 'High Church' liturgical and theological movement which stresses apostolic filiation and has strong ties of friendship with Anglo-Catholicism. Uppsala University plays a leading role here, and one of the two streams which gave rise to Protestant ecumenicalism started from here under Nathan Söderblom. At Lund the university has been engaged since the beginning of the century on a veritable renaissance of Lutheranism, with Anders Nygren as one of its protagonists. But there is also a strong pietist trend, springing from the disciples of the peasant mystic Erick Jansen (c. 1840), and from the still more numerous disciples of Professor Waldenstroem (1877), whose heterodoxy on the question of the Fall was such that he was prosecuted. On a more popular level, piety was linked to a rigid formalism, such as that which required the pastor to preach with a large handkerchief in his hand.

Lastly, in Finland, where the State is 'non-denomination', Lutheranism embraces all opinions, but seems in fact to be sliding towards a moralism tinged with religiosity. The Church has no seminaries; theology is not greatly respected, and serious dissensions have arisen to such a point that Osmo Tülilä, professor of dogma at Helsinki University, has left the Church and had his name inscribed on the 'lay' register, hoping thus to revive his Church and bring it to a clearer understanding of its needs. The people, however, retain their Lutheran traditions, and there is no lack of interest in the Bible, which is read in the sixteenth-century translation by Michael Agricola.

Lutheranism thus remains deeply rooted in all the Scandinavian countries. It is a part of daily life, of its customs and of its culture. Literature and life are closely linked to it. Ethnic and national peculiarities became marked towards the sixteenth century and were essentially Protestant in character. The democratic traditions which led these peoples towards freedom and the participation of all citizens in government became identified with Protestantism, a conviction which was driven deeper by the idea that Catholicism was necessarily anti-democratic! The close links between the nation and Lutheranism were made even more obvious during the Second World War in the upsurge of patriotism against the occupying power by the Churches of Norway and Denmark. In Norway Bishop Bergrav was imprisoned by the Gestapo; in Denmark the writer and pastor Kaj Munk was murdered by that organization. A whole book has been written about the northern Churches during the world crisis. Fidelity to traditional religion for long entailed a virulent anti-Catholicism. This took the form of press campaigns, in which the worst bits of gossip were too often repeated, and in which Catholicism was compared to Communism, both being denounced as being totalitarian. Only the shining figure of Pope John XXIII managed to modify certain points of view.

. . . Danes and Scandinavians, as Christians, wish to retain their specific characteristics and not to lose them in the Protestant mass; the recent dispute concerning women priests has its deeper side, revealing the strength of traditions which, through so many links, join the Lutherans to the pre-Reformation Churches.

What is the level of faith in this Lutheran bastion? It is difficult to say. Dechristianization appears to be widespread. Church services everywhere are poorly attended. At the election of priests in Finland only about 1–5 per cent of the congregation trouble to vote! The secularization of society is glaring—in Sweden, of every hundred marriages fifty end in divorce. There is talk also of a progressive demoralization consequent upon the loss of faith, and proof is found in the fact that few girls are virgins at the time of marriage. To deduce from this, as it is often done, that Scandinavia is heathen would be going too far. Many travellers have noted the religious fervour of packed churches, where sonorous chorales from the '*Psalbok*' are rendered. Ninety-eight per cent of Swedes are inscribed on the church registers, and would not think of being christened, married or buried outside their religion. The proportion is virtually the same in the other three countries. There is an *élite* of the highest religious quality; it includes Bishop Nygren of Lund in Sweden, one of the leaders of the ecumenical movement, who has successfully embarked upon an important theological renewal.

The real strength of the Churches in Sweden cannot be measured by the attendance figures at church services. In many Pietistic circles the 'meeting' replaces the church service, but has doubtless a higher religious value. And the Scandinavians on average give more than the faithful of the U.S.A. to maintain Protestant missions. Important also in the field of charitable works and popular education, the northern Lutheran Churches are by no means likely to abandon the ground that they have occupied so firmly for three hundred years.

3. Shocks and Tragedies in German Protestantism

No other national Protestant community has suffered so many shocks and witnessed so many tragedies as that of Germany. Shaken by the Napoleonic tempest, then by the forces of liberation and unification released by the Revolution, the ancient land of Germany gave its sons the dream of European domination. This led them to two world wars and two defeats, the second of which came about after that dream served as the motive for one of the worst totalitarian dictatorships in all history, and left them faced with a future filled with uncertainty and danger. All these events have had their repercussions on the faith in which most Germans believed during the sixteenth century and to which indeed Germany believed her fate was linked.

On the threshold of the contemporary period, Germany was a Protestant country both outwardly and at heart, though according to statistics she was not entirely so. One-quarter of her inhabitants remained faithful to Rome, but the majority of German Protestants did not think that Catholicism had much future in their country, nor that it fitted into the national '*Weltanschauung*'. Nothing surprised them more than to find that the Catholic Church showed astonishing vitality during the nineteenth century and increased its membership. The proportion between Protestants and Catholics was not the same everywhere. In 1800 the religious map showed areas almost entirely Protestant in the north and centre of the country, including Berlin and Hamburg. Others were the reverse, almost entirely Catholic, such as Bavaria and the Rhineland with Munich and Cologne, not forgetting Poland, which was still annexed. In other areas, such as Hesse, the Duchy of Baden, Württemberg and the Palatinate, the balance was equal. To a lesser degree, taking into account the free movement of people ordered by the Imperial Government after 1871, this proportion is still to be observed, though it is no longer a matter of tightly compressed blocs but rather of powerful majorities. Its effects are still to be felt in the religious situation prevailing today in Germany.

The Protestantism which dominates Germany is that of Luther. But it is not the only one; for after the Reformation a part of the German world abandoned Lutheranism in favour of Calvinism. When speaking therefore of German Protestantism one must distinguish between strict Lutheran Churches, others of the Reformed type and even (since 1871, in circumstances which we shall examine later) intermediary or mixed Churches, where the two confessions associated uneasily. But it cannot be denied that Lutheranism has provided German Protestantism with its guide lines and continues largely to direct it. Has not Lutheranism driven its roots deep into German soil? Has it not answered two calls of the German soul—a mystical piety often charged with anguish, and a need for discipline and organization? Furthermore was it not around Prussia, that ancient citadel of Lutheranism, that German unity and the German Empire of the nineteenth century were built? Of all the twenty-six Lutheran Churches, the Church of Prussia was already the most powerful and had the most adherents, but it also gained in authority when it became the Church of the emperor.

German Lutheranism, in sum, has remained faithful to Luther's teachings. The Augsburg Confession and the Large and Small Catechisms are the articles of faith. Practice, especially that of the sacraments, is what the former Augustinian would have desired. Ecclesiastical administration has remained unchanged, with its bishops and its territorial distribution, though synodal tendencies, derived both from the Baptists and from the Calvinists, have become progressively more marked. Yet this type of Lutheranism is, in externals, less like Catholicism than that of Sweden or Norway. It did not impose itself on the German people without some trouble—it triumphed only in suffering and often in blood. It was therefore opposed to Catholicism, which explains why it rejected Catholic forms and underwent a sort of Calvinization. Its Churches are still more stark than those of Scandinavia, its liturgy less complex; and its bishops are of the 'Herr Doktor' type.

Being part and parcel of the German people, or at least the majority of them, Lutheranism was obliged to minister to the innate need which they have of a rigid social and political structure. This need Luther himself had observed. Having invested the lay sovereigns with responsibility for maintaining order, which was threatened by rebel peasants, the reformer accepted the necessary relationship between the freedom of Christian life within and the protection of a strong and disciplined State without. It followed that since the State avowed itself Christian, the Church was integrated into the State, practically given divinity. The idea of a universal Church gave way to national and territorial Churches. The State exercised control over its Church. The scene was the same as in Sweden or Denmark, but caesaropapism had taken on more weighty forms. In Coburg Castle there is a seventeenth-century fresco depicting the marriage procession of Duke John Casimir; among the falconers, huntsmen and musicians are the two delegations of 'temporal' and 'spiritual' counsellors—perfect symbol of the fact that the two are merely servants of the prince!

Such was the regime which ruled the religious life of German Protestantism until 1918. In Prussia, for example, the monarch was *summus episcopus*. By virtue of his *jus episcopale* it was he that made decisions on matters affecting the Church. He appointed the members of the Supreme Evangelical Council which, from Berlin, directed the nine ancient provinces, and even the members of the consistories responsible for the three new provinces (Schleswig-Holstein, Hanover and Hesse-Nassau). His orders to the Church were channelled through 'general superintendents'. He it was who summoned the synods. At the General Synod one member in five was appointed by him, and the measures voted were never carried into effect unless he approved them. The pastors were paid civil servants, preaching unconditional obedience. Every German who belonged to a church must have himself officially inscribed on the register, this obliging him to pay the religious tax which the State collected for the church's benefit. The subservience was such that Catholics, a disdained minority, carried less weighty chains . . . And in numerous small States, which still managed to exist within the empire, the situation was similar.

The history of German Protestantism in the nineteenth century is thus dominated by submission to a lay sovereign, more complete than that under any Catholic monarch, even Louis XIV or Philip II. The circumstances in which Germany emerged from the revolution of 1789–1815 contributed still more to strengthen this situation. The evils entailed by that crisis, the unpleasantness arising from the French occupation, gave Prussia the will to resist and considerable prestige in her unhappy but heroic situation. Subsequent victory further enhanced her primacy. The defeat of the French ogre was the work of two Protestant peoples, the English and the Germans; why, then, not extract all the glory possible? Why not present Protestantism as the Christianity of the future? Lutheranism was thus reinforced by the Restoration in Germany and the authority of the victorious monarch over the Church. More, it was neither ancient German traditions nor political events alone that brought this state of affairs about; Hegelian philosophy also played its part. Hegel's dialectic was designed to show the all-powerful role of the State, and his disciple Marheineke declared that Church and State were but two facets of the same institution.

The ruler who embodied Lutheranism and Erastianism together was William III of Prussia, the vanquished man of Jena and Auerstadt, who had become, through his own energy and that of his wife Queen Louise, the victor of Waterloo. Forty-two years on the throne, from 1797 to 1840, gave him time to consolidate his authority at every level, including that of religion. Convinced that 'the name of the king must be sanctified' he took measures which increased his power as Pope-King. One of these suppressed, for a time, the Consistories; another brought the affairs of the Church into the orbit of the police. He went further still in ecclesiastical affairs. At the tercentenary celebrations of the Reformation in 1817 he decided to merge all the Churches of all the States, whether they were Lutheran or Calvinist, in order to form one 'National Evangelical Church', in which minor faiths would be set aside, embracing only reformed Christian principles. Proclaimed at the General Synod at Nassau, the 'union' was supported by the Princes and rallied a certain number of States. But the theologians of the two confessions were hostile. Their opposition crystallized around the new cultural formulary, the *Agenda*, which William wished to impose. It was accepted by only one-sixteenth of Prussian pastors. A serious crisis followed, which was to last until the end of the reign, especially serious in Silesia. It was all very well to adorn docile pastors with the splendid ribbon of the Order of the Red Eagle (*non propter acta, sed propter agenda*, said the wits), to imprison the recalcitrant ones and forcibly to restrain those disgusted members of their flocks who wished to emigrate to America; but all such measures were of little avail. The only tangible result was to create a Third Church—'united', half Lutheran, half Calvinist, undistinguished, which survives to this day.

The check to royal designs was significant, demonstrating the vigour of those forces which opposed the German soul's love of discipline and its natural submission to power. Revolutionary and liberal forces, stirred up by French ideology, acted on a political plane but did not intervene in the religious sphere, for democratic ideas had only a loose hold on the Germans of yesterday. But religious forces properly speaking now came into action. Germany, as we saw, was the scene of a vigorous pietist movement, of which Zinzendorf was the protagonist. After 1789 another movement started under the inspiration of Johann Gottfried Herder in the form of a 'revival' addressed to all denominations. At the same time Schleiermacher, who put forward a system founded on inward experience rather than on dogma, set to work to revive the old Lutheran theology. Then came Wichern's 'Inner Mission'. In Germany, as elsewhere, these currents resulted in a challenge to the Established Churches themselves as well as to caesaro-papism.

Curiously enough, it was a monarch who became the champion of ecclesiastical freedom—Frederick William IV (1840–59), successor to the authoritarian monarch of 'Union', a worthy and likable personality and a true believer. His life was to be darkened by mental disease, but that did not prevent him from setting a fine example of resignation and faith. On taking the throne he at once set about ending the conflict, freed the pastors still in prison, satisfied the adherents of the Church in Silesia who wanted an autonomous Church, and extended to those Protestants who rejected the National Protestant Church the same rights and titles as were enjoyed by members of the latter. He would have liked to go further. 'The territorial establishment and the episcopate of the sovereign', he said, 'are of such a nature that one alone of these institutions would suffice to kill the Church, if it could.'

And he added: 'If your mother were your slave, what would you do?' In fact this man of goodwill was up against forces greater than his own. In politics, having shown himself favourable to the liberal and national cause, and having granted a constitution to his people after the revolution of 1848, he was converted to the use of force as a means of re-establishing order, while on the religious plane he saw that to give total freedom to the Church would be to deliver it to heterodox theologians and rationalists. He therefore carried out a duty which he found loathsome. He appointed an *Oberkirchenrat* with the task of directing religious affairs, summoned a General Synod with the object of re-establishing order in Lutheranism and vigorously opposed the 'liberals'. It was his dream to succeed where his father had failed, but his Union of Protestant Churches, run by an elected assembly, was moribund. He who was known as the Prussian Hezekiah died in the knowledge that he had been found wanting in his task, that he, the Pope-King, had failed to lead his people to God.

Events were now under way which were to lead to the unification of Germany in Bismarck's Prussian grip. He was a sincere Protestant, married to a fervent Lutheran, hostile by conviction as well as by political considerations to everything that was Catholic. Germany's Protestant character was strongly influenced by Bismarck, as is clear from the importance attached to the unveiling of a colossal statue of Luther on 18th June 1868, when the King of Prussia was acclaimed as head of Protestant Germany. At the same time as her Protestant character was being affirmed, so also was caesaropapism. The 1848 Constitution had somewhat reduced the religious powers of the monarch, to the advantage of both Government and Parliament; but in point of fact nothing had been altered. In 1876 the Minister for Religious Affairs said: 'In the Evangelical Church the State is empowered to determine all religious laws, for all laws are born with its help.' The Constitution of 1873–6 further confirmed this ministerial and parliamentary caesaropapism. Taking his role as *summus episcopus* with great seriousness, Bismarck opposed the 'Protestant Association', which was founded by liberal and rationalist professors, but encouraged the setting up of the 'Evangelical Alliance', in which all Protestant Churches united to present a common front to Catholicism. The *Kulturkampf*, that great offensive against Rome, set the seal on Bismarck's endeavours; but though it pleased the Protestant masses it disquieted the more clear-sighted of Lutheran pastors, the secularization established by the May Laws being as damaging to Protestant Churches as to the Catholic.

In the last years of Bismarck's domination unequivocal signs of new trends were seen: a demand by both theologians and parliamentarians for greater independence of the Lutheran Church; newspaper articles criticizing the official doctrine of devotion to King and State as the first duty of a Christian. Was a change heralded?

Not under William II (1888–1918). That emperor, with his unlimited ambitions, would not yield any means to power. He proclaimed himself a true Protestant, though it was impossible to know what he really thought. Lutheranism was too much a part of the great German tradition for William II to ignore it. Was not Pan-Germanism, one of his most cherished dreams, the goal which, after having steered Christians away from the universal Church towards a merely national Church, would also bring them to the idea of German universalism? Later, under Hitler, this was to eliminate every Christian element. William II therefore behaved as Pope-King, as his predecessors had done. He stated that, profoundly disturbed by the increasing disbelief of his people, he would fight irreligion with 'blows of stone', in other words by building churches. In 1903 he intervened in the matter concerning the setting up of the 'Central Commission for the Evangelical Churches in Germany'; he also took sides against the liberals Naymann and Troeltsch, who wished to see a more democratic and less clerical constitution in the Church. His relations with the famous court preacher Stöcker demonstrated his authoritarianism in religious affairs. After having roundly approved the young Social Protestantism movement at a time when he thought of himself as more Socialist than the Socialists, the emperor suddenly changed his attitude when he thought that order might be threatened, and the unfortunate Stöcker was held up to obloquy. Until the First World War nothing really changed in the German Lutheran Church, the Church of the State.

This submission of Church to State was clearly unfavourable to any profound or even active religious life. The official Churches, with their civil-servant clergy, were all too often bodies without souls, and their façades of pomp and ceremony ill concealed their internal dilapidation. The faithful were well aware of it. It was common to read attacks on the Churches, which were 'more concerned to work for the safety of the throne and the safety of money-bags' than for the cure of souls. The result was progressive dechristianization, helped on by the wave of new ideas. Germany in the nineteenth century was the workshop, after all, where doctrines most hostile to religion were hammered out. Germans like Hegel, Marx, Feuerbach and Nietzsche were the mouthpieces of atheist humanism. Was the straightforward subjectivism of Schleiermacher's theses, which exercised a great influence on religious thought in Germany, to be no more than a *Schwebetheologia*, a nebulous theology incapable of keeping the soul true to the faith? To this religion of the heart the critical school held up the example of the Jesus of history; David Strauss, Harnack and Christian Baur pushed their arguments very far, even to negation of the main dogmatic truths.

Liberal Protestantism, which found fruitful ground in Germany, undermined the supernatural, and turned more and more towards a simple moralism. Wherever one looked it seemed as if the forces of dechristianization would win the day.

There were many pointers to this process of dechristianization. Frederick-William IV tearfully lamented the lack of piety of his people. William II grew indignant at the progress of irreligion. Already in 1818 the pious Baron von Kottwitz had spoken of the 'powerful forces of heathenism' at work among his compatriots; in 1827 Hengotenberg declared that the masses were 'listless'; in 1830 a Hamburg pastor denounced 'the misery of heathen souls'. The great cities were certainly heathen. At Berlin in 1880 59 per cent of marriages and 80 per cent of burials were secular. Elections to the Consistories interested only one adherent in every ten. Protestantism flourished only among the nobility of the rural areas and the peasantry, especially where Catholics were numerous, for they had to be shown a united front. It would be wrong to suppose that sincere Lutherans made no efforts to react against this situation. To the partisans of radical scriptural criticism were opposed the orthodox, of whom Claude Harms was the most able spokesman. 'Professing' Churches sought to establish themselves outside the framework of official and territorial Churches. The pietist current surged forward again, and Wichern's missionary activities increased. From about 1880 the sects and other dissident religious groups also began to manifest this reaction of other souls, sects and groups abroad—e.g. Methodists, Darbyites— and those sprung from the ancient depths of Germanism, such as the Baptists. Shortly before the First World War the desire for a theological revival made itself felt.

The empire's collapse brought about a decline of Lutheranism. The Evangelical Protestant Church had been too closely linked with the fallen dynasty not to be injured by its fall. Competition from Calvinism, to which belonged the greatest theologian of the era, Karl Barth, a Swiss who had settled in Bonn; from Catholicism, whose progress had been continuous for a century; from the sects, especially the newer and more active ones. All were working against it; so also was the swing of its own adherents towards indifference and free thinking. An effort was made, however, to remedy the situation. There were twenty-eight Lutheran Churches, of which nine were in Prussia, as well as a dozen other denominations; in 1922 a German Churches Federation was set up in which German Protestantism was fully represented and in which every Church retained its autonomy. The Weimar Republic now ensured a uniform set of regulations which governed the life of the Church as well as its relations with the State. There was now separation of Church and State, but the Churches became 'official bodies', recognized and protected by the authorities, the pastors continuing to be treated as civil servants and the faithful to pay the ecclesiastical tax levied by the State. Were the Churches freer or more united than under Bismarck? Perhaps they were a little stronger in defending their rights, especially in matters affecting teaching and when they were faced by a government which had no desire to bully or interfere unduly. But pluralism and dependence on the State remained serious causes of weakness, which did not help them to mount a common front when they were confronted by a more redoubtable adversary.

Hitler's rise to power in 1933 brought the German Protestant Churches face to face with their most serious crisis. Unlike Catholicism, which was to be protected in some measure by the Concordat signed in the first few months of the new regime in Germany, and also by the worldwide authority enjoyed by Pope Pius XI, the Protestant Churches were disunited and isolated. In the early days there were many good German Protestants who found in National Socialism some aspects which were not displeasing: the 'positive Christianity' that it wished to set up, based on German blood and German soil (*Blut und Boden!*), on a common destiny and social brotherhood—all seemed in no way unacceptable. The patriotism of the Brownshirt leader who prided himself on his declared ambition to put Germany 'over all' could only please a people who had never accepted their defeat in 1918. As for Hitlerite anti-Semitism, this did not fall on altogether stony ground. The love of discipline and of *zusammenmarchieren* all served to bring the masses together under the Nazi swastika.

The National Socialists at once took advantage of this favourable situation and used it to codify the status of Protestantism in the new State. In July 1933 a synod meeting at Wittenberg laid down the bases for a merger of all the Churches in the *Deutsche Evangelische Kirche*. Ludwig Müller was elected 'Bishop of the Reich'; and the Führer appointed him as his representative with the Church, with the task of 'breathing new life into the corpse of ancient Christianity'. The watchword was: 'One State, one People, one Church.' Very soon the Protestant Churches were made to fall into step; everything that was in any way Jewish was rooted out—e.g. the 'Society for Biblical Research' was suppressed; the Nazi theoretician Alfred Rosenberg, himself a Lutheran, criticized the Lutherans for lack of faith in Luther; in the churches the *Horst Wessel* song alternated with the chorale *Ein fest' Burg ist unser Gott*.

The work of domesticating the Churches showed no outward signs of persecution, as was the case with the Catholic Church; and this explains why the majority of German Protestants did not see any danger to their faith. But some pastors and some intellectuals did soon realize that there was an absolute incompatibility between the National Socialist doctrine and Christianity. Foremost among them was Karl Barth, whose glorious place in history is assured as much because he was the renovator of Protestant theology as because he was the first in the Reformed Churches to react against the National Socialist heresy. Against the 'German Christians' now rose the group known as *Pfarrernotbund*; seven thousand pastors out of a total of eighteen thousand joined it, and in a meeting at Barmen on 31st May 1934 they set up the *Bekennende Kirche* (the German Confessional Church). The 'Confession', which was prepared by Karl Barth and voted unanimously, can be bracketed with the Encyclical *Mit brennender Sorge* in which Pius XI condemned National Socialism. In particular it rejected 'the false doctrine according to which the Church must accept as a source of revelation, alongside and in addition to the Word of God, other so-called truths'. The movement won such a following that the *Reichsbischof* Müller resigned. Arrests then began and internments and executions increased. Martin Niemöller, a one-time submarine commander and now pastor of the Berlin suburb of Dalhem, who had been one of the leaders of the Confessional Church, was arrested in 1937 and thrown into a concentration camp, from which he was not to emerge until after the Second World War. For seven years the leading elements of German Protestantism existed in semi-clandestine shadows, resisting the Nazi grip, their services ill-attended by the masses. Other pastors were to become famous in this conflict, e.g. Vogel and Niesel, and the clandestine Church was to have its martyrs. The finest of these was Dietrich Bonhoeffer (1900–45), who returned voluntarily from America to Germany to lead the struggle. As a pastor in the poorer quarters, as director of a seminary and as spiritual author of the highest calibre, he did so with such a radiant personality that after his imprisonment in 1943 his jailers themselves used to take him to those of his companions who were the most distressed. He was hanged on 9th April 1945, probably because members of his family were implicated in the generals' plot against Hitler, as were others such as Bishop Hans Lilje and Dr Gerstenmaier.

On the collapse of the National Socialist regime the Confessional Church, fresh with the glory of its heroes and its martyrs, made attempts to reorganize the whole of German Protestantism along new lines, to harmonize the Lutheran Churches, the Reformed Churches, the United Church of the 1817 Reformation and the sects. An Evangelical Church in Germany was set up—but on paper only, for pluralist trends were stronger. The 'free' Lutheran Churches held themselves aloof from an organization which seemed to them to be too administratively inclined. The majority of the territorial Lutheran Churches formed their own association; the sects refused all associations. But the Evangelical Church in Germany (E.K.D.) remained and has tended lately to assume a more important role.

German Protestantism, however, has had to cope with other and more serious problems since 1945. The division of Germany affects it directly, for the lands on the other side of the Iron Curtain are Lutheran, especially Prussia. Of the situation of German Protestants in Eastern Germany only the most contradictory news emerges. Now the talk is all of persecution, now of rumours that a concordat is being studied. In Western Germany another problem arises: Catholics and Protestants are now roughly equal in numbers, so that Protestantism has lost the preponderant position it occupied in the former German State. After having fought Hitler in alliance, and having also joined forces in Christian democratic action, the two denominations witnessed the growth of tension between them in 1958, a tension which could not be explained away by the presence in the government of a Catholic Chancellor and many Catholic ministers.

On the religious plane, properly speaking, it would appear that since the end of the war German Protestantism has undergone a renewal, the style of which is not unlike that which took place in French Catholicism. There are worker-priests, there is a movement for liturgical renaissance, and a considerable pastoral effort is being undertaken. Was the *World Christian Handbook*, which in 1962 gave 10,576,885 practising members and 45,968,401 'sympathizers' as being the figures for German Protestants, out of touch with the true situation? It is difficult to say; but there is certainly a noticeable spiritual activity which is manifesting itself by the reappearance of neo-Lutheranism, in passionate discussions between theologians of different tendencies, the adherents of Barth against the adherents of Bultmann. The part played by Germany in the ecumenical movement for the last twenty years is also indicative of its vitality.

4. TWO MICROCOSMS OF PROTESTANTISM: THE SWISS CANTONS AND HOLLAND

Together with Germany, the two countries where the Reformation had established itself most securely from the outset were Switzerland and Holland. In both these small countries today Protestantism remains a force which has stamped them with its seal, but it also encounters problems—the relations of Church and State, the ecclesiastical 'establishment' and doctrinal differences—which are everywhere being met by the Churches deriving from the Reformation in such a way that both appear as microcosms of a sort where one can observe the Protestant phenomenon in all clarity.

Switzerland passed through the revolutionary crisis without too many upheavals. At one time a sister republic of France, under the supervision of Napoleon for the duration of the Empire, she was not the victim of unhappy consequences. In Geneva, for example, Protestantism was not shaken: the revolution of 1792, imitating that of Paris, attempted to establish equality between all believers and unbelievers, but a vote went against it and it was recorded in the text of the 1796 Constitution that 'no religion other than that of the Reformed or Protestant was allowed in the republic'. A part of France in 1798, within the *département* of Mont Blanc, Geneva was proud to be proclaimed the first Protestant city of the *Grande Nation*, which entitled its ecclesiastical delegate, Martin-Gourgas, to harangue the emperor in the name of French Protestants. This was to be the role of the Genevese Calvinists in their new country, and it led very quickly to a feeling of mutual distrust between them and the French.

After the revolutionary and imperial period Switzerland returned to its own destiny. The Protestantism of Zwingli as well as of Calvin was the religion of three-fifths of the population, with Zürich and Geneva as its two main centres. But the division between denominations emerged on to the political level in the cantons, where some were officially Protestant and others officially Catholic. This gave rise to tension, slight at first but more serious after 1830, mostly for political reasons. A dispute arose concerning the setting up of a nunnery at Lucerne; another regarding the appointment to a chair of theology of David Strauss, who was notorious for his theories about Christ; another concerning the revolutionary incidents which took place at Geneva in 1842; another concerning the foundation of the Protestant Union, this being openly directed against the Catholics; yet another concerning the expulsion of the *curé* Marilley from Geneva and the recall to Geneva of the Jesuits. Finally, in 1845, the seven Catholic cantons joined together in a defensive association, the *Sonderbund* (an imitation of the radical *Siebenbund*), which the Federal Diet declared illegal in 1847, at the same time decreeing the expulsion of all Jesuits from the cantons. Civil war broke out, the last religious war in history, but was quickly ended by the defeat of the Catholic troops of Salis-Solio at Lucerne by Colonel Dufour. The 1848 Constitution proclaimed the equality of religions, though in fact the governments of Protestant cantons were to make Catholics feel their authority. Despite the efforts of certain high-minded spirits such as Alexandre Vinet, the mistrust between Catholic and Protestant did not diminish; it exists even today.

Swiss Protestantism as a whole has always preserved a more radical appearance than that of Lutheranism. Its characteristics are severity, starkness of liturgy, austere attitudes and moral rigidity, together with a reserve, a hauteur and a coldness that were long considered the distinctive marks of the Huguenots. But the usual dissensions were to be found underneath those common traits.

Switzerland was one of the countries where the revivalist movement, which led to Protestantism at the time of the Restoration, exploded with the greatest force. Touching only briefly on the memory of Madame de Krüdener, who nevertheless exercised considerable pietist influence, the cantons, especially Geneva and Vaud, witnessed the rise of numerous spiritual organizers who set their seal on the epoch, e.g. Cellerier, Malan, Gaussen and, above all, Alexandre Vinet. The Established Churches, for the most part, were none too pleased at the criticisms levelled at them by these new apostles, who reproached them for their routine, their barrenness and their lack of true faith. The tension between the 'revivalists' and the authorities became such that a break was inevitable. Free Churches were then set up, first at Geneva then at Lausanne. German Switzerland followed in strength and set up a 'Union for Free Christianity'. Soon all the cantonal Churches found themselves facing 'Free Churches', which were quickly followed by others established by foreign missions (German Pietists, Baptists, Methodists), then by the propagandists of the sects. 'Pluralism' was in full swing, and the founding of a Federation of Official Churches did nothing to halt it. The Free and nonconformist Churches were accepted in the Protestant community, but they were poor relations, disbarred from the multitudinous liberality which the State bestowed on the official Churches.

The problem of the link between Church and State was thus raised in Switzerland as it had been in Scandinavia and Germany. Such links appear as indispensable to conservatives. But democratic ideas were strong in the cantons, and the Church/State system was more and more severely criticized. In 1848 Turrettini in Geneva declared it to be 'diametrically opposed to the spirit of modern Protestantism', and shortly afterwards the *Compagnie des Pasteurs*, often called the Protestant Pope, lost its authority to a consistory made up of only twenty-six lay members and six pastors. A new step was taken in 1873: total freedom of belief was decreed in all Protestant Churches, the Consistory intervening only in matters of faith, and the professors of the faculty of theology were appointed by the State Council. In 1905 a party demanded the separation of Church and State; this was obtained in 1907 and became effective two years later. The State would continue to recognize the Churches, and to help them, but would no longer intervene in their lives, the pastors being elected by those members inscribed on the registers of each parish. But what had happened in Geneva had no influence on other cantons. Basel, for instance, retained the reformed religion in its official state, though it accepted full responsibility for paying the salaries of Catholic priests as well. Others, e.g. Bern, reinforced the authority of the State to such a point that lay authorities took part in theological quarrels, which led to the birth of Barthism. Others again adhered to the Zürich Constitution of 1869, which made provision for freedom of worship and the non-interference of the State in religious matters, though it did permit its intervention so far as payment of the clergy was concerned. It can thus be said that the Swiss cantons demonstrated all the various forms of disestablishment of the Church; there is even an *Église libre de la côte aux fées*, of pietist tendency, which was founded in 1848 and which is completely independent, composed entirely of laity.

Pluralism also appeared in a striking manner among religious groups themselves. For a hundred and fifty years Swiss Protestantism has harboured every shade of theological opinion and every type of spiritual attitude; the field is vast, ranging from the Genevan pastor Élisée Gasc, who in 1800 scandalized the Faculty at Montpellier by denying the divinity of Christ, to Alexandre Vinet with his fervent meditations on the Passion, to the cold severity of the Huguenots in the churches of Bern, to the services of the young pastors of the French-speaking cantons of *Église et Liturgie*. Liberal Protestantism has many adherents in the cantons; it has even brought about the division of certain Free Churches into two parts—into two separate Churches—one liberal, the other orthodox. The influence of Barth has been considerable in this his native land, but Emil Brunner and Oscar Cullmann have their place.

Social Protestantism has also had a strong philanthropic influence on the people, one of whose sons was Henri Dunant, founder of the Red Cross. Powerful movements aided the official Church: in 1830 the *Société évangélique*, in 1871 the *Union nationale évangélique*, in 1898 the *Association chrétienne évangélique*. The sects continue to progress; the part played by Switzerland in Moral Rearmament is well known, one of its centres being at Caux. Faith and practice have undoubtedly declined in the big cities, but remain traditional in the rural areas. And there has been a *rapprochement* between the official Church and the Free Churches in cantons such as that of Vaud, which can only assist the process. On the whole—and taking into account the fact that each pastor is his own master in deciding what he teaches—Swiss Protestantism, which closely resembles French Protestantism, seems to be veering towards a more reasonable form of Calvinism, dropping the Reformer's more extravagant theories, retaining the dogmatic bases, evangelical and at the same time with a wide sense of humanity.

The situation appears to be no less complex in Holland, which is another small bastion of Western Protestantism, though it has not the same geographical and administrative divisions as the Swiss cantons.

Catholics are numerous—38 per cent in 1958 as in 1789, after a drop to 36 per cent in 1870; they are not confined to certain well-defined areas as in Switzerland, but are widely scattered, in greater numbers inland than on the coast, and in the south and south-east than in the north and north-west, increased by mostly Catholic Belgians between 1815 and 1830. But divisions appeared within Protestantism itself. Holland was, from the beginning of the Reformation, one of the areas of conflict between Lutheranism and Calvinism; where different currents were to expand rapidly, such as Anabaptism, then Mennonism; where violent theological controversies were to rage between Gomarists and Arminians; where the ferment of liberal ideas, soon followed by rationalist ideas also, were all to be very active. The ground had been well prepared, and during the nineteenth century there followed a great deal of confusion, entailing many splits and so offering the new Churches and the sects a ready terrain for their ideas.

At the outbreak of the French Revolution, which had violent effects in Holland also, there was in theory one Church in Holland— the Dutch Reformed Church, governed by a constitution handed down from the Synod of Dordrecht (1618–19), in theory synodal and Presbyterian but in fact closely linked to the secular power. Outside this, however, there existed a large number of communities varying in size and refusing to recognize its authority. Among them were the Walloon Churches of the south, where French was spoken and a brand of French Calvinism practised, this latter being considered purer than that of The Hague.

French intervention in the Netherlands in 1795, followed by the installation of a French administration, first republican then monarchical, with Napoleon's brother Louis, entailed various consequences for Protestantism. The official Church found itself freed from control of the State until 1815, when William I took it in hand again, though respecting all its ancient privileges. Unofficial communities took advantage of the situation to enlarge their scope. The Walloon Churches, after hoping that the presence of a Frenchman on the throne would grant them more favourable treatment, soon saw that this was not to be the case, for King Louis wished to be a good Dutchman, even to the point of himself adopting those mistrustful feelings which the autochthonous Churches harboured towards them. Their autonomous synod was suppressed in 1810 and they found themselves incorporated in the official Reformed Church. During the 1795–1815 crisis there was continual agitation; the most audacious ideas were spread about, consistories assumed the appearance of clubs and societies supposedly secret, e.g. that of *Christo Sacrum*, all gave the theologians free rein.

After the Restoration, under the amiable tutelage of the House of

Orange, the official Reformed Church returned to its proper paths. It was a traditional Church, on whose registers more than half the believers were inscribed and to which the sovereigns proved themselves entirely faithful. Its organization had become synodal in reality, though in fact the authorities continued to exercise a certain supervisory role through the pastors, who were paid by the State. And so the situation remained until 1848, when the separation of Church and State was made law. In practice this separation bore little relationship to the situation in 1900 in France, the clergy continuing to draw their salaries from the State and creeds coming under ministerial administration. Separation did at least ensure freedom of opinions and beliefs. It is true also that the official Church had not waited for this law to declare that confession of faith was not compulsory for anyone, that each pastor was free to preach as he wished, and to accept into the Church all 'tolerants' of whatever conviction.

Such a state of affairs was hardly conducive to true faith. But it was favourable to supranaturalism, rationalism and moralism, which little by little were supplanting authentic reformed Christianity. More demanding believers rose in opposition. A first counter-offensive was launched by Zeeland pastors who founded the Restored Church of Christ in 1820. Then the great movement of revival, which was sweeping the whole of European Protestantism, reached Holland and made great inroads. It took on two forms: one was orthodox 'revival' under the converted Jew da Costa (author of the famous poem 'Watchman, what of the night?') and Pastor Molenaar. The other form, of liberal tendencies, was led by a number of professors, among them Hofstede de Groot, who set up the strongly nationalistic 'Groningen school', affirming their attachment to Erasmus and to the first Dutch reformation. Relations were soon strained between both forms and the official Church. Persecuted, some of the orthodox 'revivalists' broke away. . . . Those of Groningen were the object of an indictment by the 'seven gentlemen of The Hague', all ultra-conservatives of note, for whom religious liberalism was the forerunner of revolution. But this indictment, rejected by the court, only resulted in an increase of authority for the theologians of Groningen and helped to spread their simple, active, social and missionary evangelism, which was to have a profound effect on official Dutch Protestantism.

A fourth wave of revivalism was at hand, having a neo-Calvinist, more dogmatic character. In 1852 the liberals, rationalists and secularists had procalimed that the State would henceforth be impartial in matters concerning the Church. But they later banned religious teaching in the schools, and, not daring to close the faculties of theology, forbade the teaching of dogma. Against them convinced Calvinists now rose. In 1830 there had been an attempt to set up a 'Christian

Reformed Church', but this had not attracted more than some four thousand adherents. The real Calvinist restoration came with Abraham Kuyper (1837–1920), a great mind and a man of culture, a writer as well as a theologian, a politician as well as a journalist. For his theological movement he was able to enlist the support of the lower middle class and the artisans, all of sound Calvinist traditions, led by several aristocrats and intellectuals hostile both to religious and to political liberalism. Under its fiery chief, the counter-revolutionary party increased in importance. Its most resounding success was the foundation of the free university of Amsterdam, of which Kuyper was the first vice-chancellor, and where all teaching was neo-Calvinist. Despite the opposition of the official Church, the university was able to force the State to recognize its degrees. The break came soon afterwards, and the *Gereformeerde Kerk* ('Re-reformed Church'), founded in 1885, became totally independent. Numerous communities soon joined it, to found in 1892 the 'Reformed Churches of the Netherlands'. Even outside these Churches Kuyper's influence was to be profound upon all aspects of Dutch Protestantism, at least until the Second World War, after which new trends appeared along with efforts at regrouping.

This may seem to be all very complicated, symptomatic of the law of division which one finds everywhere and always at work within Protestantism. But it is necessary now to refer to the existence in Holland of many communities whose numerical importance is very varied, and whose convictions range from the strongest Pietism to extremes of philosophic liberalism (rationalism and Unitarianism) together with Anabaptists, Mennonites, Baptists, propagandists of Methodism and Quakerism, and the Salvation Army. There are also those which spring from former French Jansenists and Old Catholics, hostile to Papal Infallibility, as well as more recent sects, all of which have Dutch branches. Religious pluralism has had one excellent result. Along with political liberalism, which the rulers of Holland have shown for many years, the State has practised a policy of pluralism which is an outstanding example of wisdom and justice. Catholics no less than other religions have benefited from this policy. In 1920 an educational law was passed which distributed State subsidies according to the wishes of the families involved. No other country in the world has so wise a law. More recently another law has given all the major denominations a say in the running of the State Radio Organization.

It should not be concluded, however, that Protestantism has become weaker in its ancient Dutch bastion. If the habit of religious practice is lessening, as it is elsewhere, it can still be affirmed that all social groups are in greater or lesser degree imbued with Calvinism. The grave mien, the unmistakable show of austerity (oh! the dismal silence of the Dutch Sunday!), the reserve—these characteristics belong not only to the

Protestants of the official Church, nor those of the Reformed Church; the Catholics themselves, especially in the north of the country, have adopted a similar style, while the Socialists at their political meetings sound as though they were chanting psalms when in fact they are singing militant songs. Nevertheless Dutch Protestantism is the most open, generous and understanding in the world, for all its superciliousness and defensiveness. Within it was born one of the men whom Protestant ecumenicalism was to recognize as one of its leaders Dr Visser't Hooft, who has shown the greatest understanding of Catholic efforts towards a real and full ecumenicalism.

5. ENGLAND OF THE ANGLICANS AND 'DISSENTERS'

Across the North Sea, the British Isles offer another good example of a country upon which the Reformation left its stamp. But here the inherent complications of all that sprang from the sixteenth-century revolution have been made worse by specific differences.

On the threshold of the contemporary era His Majesty's kingdom showed three distinct religious characteristics, and a question hung over each. The Church was an established Church, officially the Church of the State, whose head was the king, with even wider religious powers than those once enjoyed by the German princes or the Scandinavian monarchs. Was this caesaropapism to last for ever? The official Church did not contain all the religious sheep in its fold: at least a third of the baptized belonged to other denominations whom the powers of the Establishment treated with disdain, even hostility, and whom the Test Act kept out of public employment; would the dissenters continue to accept this state of affairs for long? Anglicanism, the doctrine of the official Church, had been established as a compromise during the sixteenth and seventeenth centuries, between Protestant innovations and Catholic traditions. Might it not now once more be called in question? The history of England from 1789 until today shows that these three problems were raised in turn unendingly.

At the end of the nineteenth century it would not have been out of place to draw a comparison between the pitiable state of the Anglican Church on the one hand and the only slightly better state of the French Catholic Church on the other. The former, while retaining the fidelity of rural areas, save in Scotland and Wales where dissenters held sway, exercised only nominal authority over its adherents, and this did not make for a living faith. It was still the era of stout and jovial clergymen, foxhunting in the shires, with laden tables and heady beer —butts of the satirical novelist. The upper ranks of the clergy were well provided for; it was not unusual for a bishop to receive £40,000 per annum, whereas the majority of the four thousand parish priests received less than £50. This secure Church was firmly attached to the established order from which it derived so much benefit: it was the sworn enemy of the electoral reform demanded by the proletariat of the cities and towns, totally uncaring of social problems, weak in its theology, non-existent in its missionary endeavours, and with no more effect on the masses than to create indifference tinged with rationalism. But all was not lost in Christian England. Both within the Established Church and in the nonconformist groups one common religious basis remained: veneration for the Bible, preoccupation with Eternal Life and the rewards of Heaven, moral austerity, scrupulous respect for the Day of Rest. Those were the main themes. Signs of renewal could even be observed.

One of these, the most astonishing, was Evangelicalism, a movement born within the Established Church and modelled upon Methodism. It began at Cambridge University with Isaac Milner and Charles Simeon, who were joined later by John Venn, vicar of Clapham, and William Wilberforce; its organizer was Zachary Macaulay, father of the great historian, whose strict moralism and philanthropy exercised a considerable influence on the governing classes, and whose efforts to spread the Bible and to establish missionary societies earned him a considerable reputation.

The French Revolution drove the English into a form of piety which the Protestant historian Émile G. Léonard has described as 'practically obsessive'. In the fight against the impious French, the help of supernatural forces was not to be considered useless! Apologies for Christianity increased in number; Bibles and psalters were distributed by the million; in the great universities a question often set in examination papers was: 'Prove that a State cannot live without religion.' The Holy Scriptures of course provided unquestionable proof that revolutionary France was the incarnation of Satan. Certain *émigrés* were converted to Protestantism, among them Étienne de Grellet (1773–1855), who became a Quaker, and Pierre de Pontavice (1770–1810), who was inspired while attending a Methodist meeting and who returned to France as soon as possible, was received as a Calvinist pastor, but continued to propagate Wesley's Methodism. Once the crisis was over the British were exhausted, yet filled with satisfaction at having fulfilled their duty and, on the spiritual plane, ready to embark on that era of ferment that the nineteenth century was to be.

The Evangelicals, who had laboured so hard during the dark years, now profited from the situation; their works were to enjoy great notoriety. There were the Church Missionary Society, societies for the conversion of the Jews and for the betterment of the poorer folk, the Bible Society, founded in 1804, reorganized in 1816, and many others.

Until about 1870, when the movement became embroiled with conservatism and integritism, the Evangelicals guided the Church of England. They exercised a similar influence in Scotland, where the official Presbyterian Church was no less dormant. There the brothers Haldane and Thomas Chalmers played the same role as Macaulay and Wilberforce had done in England. But at the same time, outside the official Churches, there was a revivalist movement similar to those in Switzerland, Germany, France and the U.S.A., but having a more emotional and popular appeal. Its main field of activity was Wales, where there had been several such movements in the eighteenth century. Its theoretician was Charles G. Finney (1792–1875). There were also the extremists, whose operations resulted not only in divisions but also in the founding of 'new Churches' or of more or less heterodox sects, such as the Irvingites and the Darbyites. All of this indicated a spirit different from that of the eighteenth century—a true revival not unlike that of French Catholicism with Maistre and Lamennais.

The basic problems remained in England, and the spiritual vitality of the dissidents contributed to a heightening of their desire to enter into a new relationship with the Established Church. Various incidents showed on which side opinion lay. Since the dissenters were mostly poor, the parliamentary votes in 1816 and 1824 of large sums for the building of unnecessary Anglican Churches aroused indignation. To indemnify the nonconformists, whom the Test Act had barred from public employment, subsidies were voted; but Catholics were excluded from these benefits. The Anglican hierarchy opposed every liberal measure. The founding by dissenters of independent schools, then of a secular university, aroused the anger of the bishops. In 1828 the Methodists were expelled from the Anglican Communion. But the movement of liberation was now well on its way, and the dissident Protestants were to receive help from unexpected allies—the Catholics, particularly those of Ireland. Led by Daniel O'Connell, the Irish were striving by every legal means to put an end to the laws which reduced them to mere pariahs on their own soil. In 1829 Wellington, the victor of Waterloo, and Peel, his Home Secretary, prepared for the abolition of the Test Act in three stages. In accordance with Lord John Russell's suggestion, a simple declaration was to be substituted for the oath sworn on an Anglican Bible by anyone canvassing for a public post. From 1833 nonconformists, Jews and Catholics were no longer barred from becoming Members of Parliament.

But despite all this the situation was still not clear. The nonconformists had seen what strength they possessed, and they looked upon the Established Church with ever-increasing severity—upon its wealth, its sterile conservatism. Nonconformity drew its strength from among the richest and most active elements in the nation, traders and industrialists, and its influence could not but increase. A campaign was launched against the Establishment, so violent that the Anglican historian Kilson Clark likened it to a jet of steam shot from a boiler. Articles, tracts and cheap books now appeared, denouncing this extraordinary state of affairs in which money was graced with the name of Christianity. Disquiet reigned in the Anglican Church. Thomas Arnold, the famous educationalist and father of Matthew Arnold, expressed it in these terms: 'In her present situation the Church cannot be saved by any human power.' Shortly afterwards he published his *Principles for a Reform of the Church*, wherein, starting from the assumption that the existence of a national Church is a blessing for the righteous, he proposed to set up 'a truly national Church, truly united, truly Christian, admitting all those who held a common faith, believing in the same Saviour and the same God'. But this idea, generous as it was Utopian, was rejected by both the Anglicans and the nonconformists.

The question of the Establishment was not to be resolved in this manner, and it might even be said that the abolition of the Test Act had merely complicated matters, because nonconformist, Jewish and Catholic members of Parliament could intervene in the affairs of the Anglican Church when these were debated in the House of Commons. Crises arose. The first warning came from Scotland, where Thomas Chalmers (1780–1847), one of the leaders of the revival in his country, an intelligent and respected man with generous moral and social ideas, and a minister of the established Presbyterian Church, had for long been a resolute supporter of that Establishment. But when he suspected that it was being rotted by rationalism, when he judged that the suggestions it put forward for dealing with social problems were irreconcilable with Christian principles, he broke away from it, instigating the Disruption in the name of 'the rights of the crown of Our Lord Jesus Christ'. Four hundred and forty-seven ministers followed him, and in 1843 the Free Church of Scotland was founded, with Chalmers as the central figure in an 'Evangelical Alliance' which attempted to embrace all the 'Free' Protestant Churches. The shock produced by this secession was severe. In 1838 the Prime Minister, Gladstone, in his book *The State in its Relations with the Church*, had vigorously defended the Anglican Church's absolutism; but a few years later he became a partisan of disestablishment, which he was to bring about in Wales and Scotland.

The most thorny problem, however, was Ireland. Here the regime was both odious and absurd: the Anglican Church included no more than 12 per cent of the island's population as adherents, yet its twenty-two archbishops and bishops drew more than £150,000 in revenues from the Catholics! In 1861 disestablishment ended this absurd situation.

Only the old Church of England remained faithful to the regime of the Establishment. But even she had still to face the problem, and efforts were made to reduce State pressure. From 1852 onwards Convocation met regularly. The bishops protested against the appointments of parish priests who were doctrinally suspect. They also protested against the replacement of the Court of Delegation by the Judicial Committee of the Privy Council. There were several instances, however, which demonstrated what strength the State possessed in maintaining its religious authority. There was the Gorham affair, where a candidate for a parish was refused it because he denied regeneration through baptism, but won his case on appeal to the Privy Council; then the Colenso affair, where this same council upheld a South African bishop who had been excommunicated by his archbishop. But this same council felt perfectly competent to condemn an Anglican minister who had knelt at the consecration and had lit two candles on the altar! It was not until the end of the nineteenth century that the Church was allowed to decide upon questions of faith, and at least, in the first instance, to adjudicate in matters of worship. At the same time the principle of the confessional State now yielded ground; e.g. payment towards the Anglican Church for those who were not its members was suppressed; the ancient rules requiring university posts to be filled by Anglicans were abrogated. There was thus an evolution taking place; but between the two wars there were violent debates concerning the revision of the Prayer Book, and these served to demonstrate the serious inconveniences which resulted from an Established Church, as well as the deep attachment which the majority of the English people had for it.

To these debates on disestablishment there were also those on purely religious grounds. A new spiritual ferment which emerged in the middle of the nineteenth and continued into the early twentieth century affected Anglicanism as well as the nonconformist Churches; and even Catholicism was to profit by it. The many attempts made to stem the tide of scientific rationalism and to halt the dechristianization of the proletariat led to increased vitality within the Churches. On behalf of Anglicanism much work was done by Bishop Samuel Wilberforce (1805–73) with a view to endowing both the episcopate and the lower clergy with greater piety and greater pastoral zeal. Missioners travelled from parish to parish; theological studies were revived; the field of biblical and early Christian history was opened, with Lightfoot as one of its most distinguished workers; and in 1884, after fifteen years' labour, the Revised Version of the Bible was published. Religious music and architecture took a new lease of life. Foreign missions flourished, and a monastic revival looked back to the oldest traditions for its rules and customs. A social trend followed, similar to that which we have observed in other sectors of Protestantism, a trend supported by men of very different views and beliefs; and the Young Men's Christian Association, founded by George Williams, expanded rapidly.

Amid all this ferment of new ideas, two events deserve special mention. First, the advent of Frederick Dennison Maurice (1805–72), a curious person who appeared to some of his contemporaries as 'a hazy and confused mind who writes nothing worth reading'. But there were others who admired 'his vast intellect, which ranges over so many fields'. He considered that between the 'High Church', the traditional, episcopalian and established side of Anglicanism, and the 'Low Church', Protestant and more popular, there was room for another, more intellectual, which would help the Church of England to adapt itself to the modern world. In this respect Maurice reminded one of Lamennais, the author of *Paroles d'un croyant*. His theories were so liberal that they approached latitudinarianism, and for that reason he was dismissed by the University of London where he taught. But the idea of a 'Broad Church' still found support; Maurice's views, tinged slightly with the Christian Socialist beliefs of his friend Charles Kingsley, continued to exert some influence—as they do today, e.g. in the Industrial Christian Fellowship.

The second notable event was the Oxford Movement, which, as we have seen, is as much a part of Catholic as of Anglican history. The ideas underlying John Keble's sermon (1833) on 'national apostasy' reached the general public through the famous *Tracts for the Times*, and the Tractarian movement soon began to exercise an immense influence on the young English clergy. It received a fresh orientation and a fresh spirit from John Henry Newman (1801–90), and shook the whole Establishment. With a view to reforming the Church of England, the Tractarians looked back to pre-Reformation and Patristic tradition, and so to Catholic custom and even to Catholic dogma. While Newman and others went to the logical conclusion of their thinking and entered the Roman Catholic Church, others were of the opinion that it was better to steer a middle course, continuing their activity within Anglicanism. Such was the attitude adopted by Edward Bouverie Pusey (1800–82), canon of Christ Church and professor of Hebrew, who gathered round him groups of those who were known as 'ritualists'. They taught a return to original traditions, and exercised such a profound influence upon the High Church, upon its liturgy and even upon some of its doctrinal elements, that the habit of referring to 'Anglo-Catholicism' soon arose. This development was not without some lively reactions from the Low Church: denunciations from the pulpit, demonstrations accompanied by cries of 'No Popery!', letters to the newspapers and so on. Actions were brought against certain clergy adjudged too 'ritualist' by the authorities, and certain condemnations pronounced even in secret council. At the end of the century the wave of emotion roused throughout Anglicanism by Lord Halifax's efforts to reunite the Church of England with Rome was proof enough of the strength of Anglican feeling.

Religious stirrings were not absent among the nonconformists. Ever since freedom had been granted them in 1829 they had continued to make steady progress. More and more schools were opened, Presbyterian as well as Methodist, and they were even granted State subsidies. They took over university chairs in force. Westminster College, seminary of future Presbyterian pastors, was to give an example of moral dignity and sound theological training. All the nonconformist Churches vied with each other and the Church of England in setting up mission stations in Asia and Africa. In the second half of the century nonconformity had preachers of great talent: the Congregationalist R. W. Dale of Birmingham, apostle of secular priesthood, who bracketed St Gregory the Great and St Thomas Aquinas with Luther, Calvin and Wycliffe; Charles Haddon Spurgeon (1834–92), son and grandson of Baptist pastors, whose magnetism, straightforward eloquence and flashes of wit drew crowds of ten thousand at a time; James Martineau, descendant of a French Huguenot, a Unitarian mystic and professor whose effulgence rivalled that of Newman. The foundation of the Salvation Army by William Booth, a Methodist, was another sign of this spiritual animation, which contrasted so vividly with the steady wave of indifference. Early in the twentieth century there were other proofs of this new revival in Wales, where William Ward, influenced by the Congregationalist pastor Blackham, set up the Brotherhoods; these were both study circles and mutual help societies. There was also Frank Buchman, an American Lutheran who had settled at Oxford and whose famous Oxford Group led to the Moral Rearmament movement.

At the outbreak of the First World War the religious situation in England was in general much better than it had been a hundred years earlier. Statistically there were probably fewer churchgoers in the Anglican Church, and the moralists were probably right in their contention that, since the accession of Edward VII, there had been a decline in moral standards, even in those of the Court. But, in general, the religious spirit remained and pervaded all customs; fierce disbelief was the exception. The Anglican Church still had the largest membership, though this was declining in favour of the nonconformists, the 'new' Churches and the sects. Dissidents represented some 45 per cent of the baptized, but by now the terms 'dissident' and 'nonconformist' were used much less frequently than 'Evangelical Free Churches'. It was under this title that the Presbyterians, Methodists, Baptists and Congregationalists had set up a National Council in 1892. In 1940 they formed instead the Free Church Federal Council. Outside those organizations were the younger groups whose keenness was having its effect on the older Churches, especially the Pentecostal and Adventist. There were also the Catholics, who had been strengthened since 1847 by the influx of Irish immigrants fleeing from the potato famine, and by the conversion of several leading figures in the Oxford Movement which had considerably enhanced the Catholic Church's prestige. Their London cathedral, hard by Westminster Abbey, seemed like a challenge to the National Church.

It was precisely what one might call 'the Catholic question' which was not to require an answer; it was a question of balance within the Anglican Church—between two trends, one Catholic, the other Protestant. After the First World War the Anglo-Catholic trend gained still more ground. The Protestant spirit was still there, but aspects of worship had become less and less Protestant. The contacts which many British had made on the Continent during the war helped to accelerate this trend. Certain theologians went further, reopening such questions as that of transubstantiation, and celebrants in some cases adopted the Catholic habit of 'the Reservation of the Sacrament'. But the Prayer Book of 1662, basis of Anglican worship, expressly condemns transubstantiation and forbids the reservation and transport of the Eucharistic host. Were the new customs illegal?

In 1927 a project for the reform of the Prayer Book was mooted, to incorporate certain Anglo-Catholic innovations. Convocations approved the new text with a large majority, and the House of Lords likewise. But Bishop Barnes of Manchester launched a critical campaign, and the new text was thrown out by the House of Commons by 217 votes to 205. This demonstrated how ill adapted the established system was since the admission of non-Anglicans to Parliament. Out of the 217 votes against, there were 65 nonconformists, Jews, and some agnostics—the Catholic members had discreetly abstained from the vote. The Archbishop of Canterbury, Randall Davidson, amended the text, watered down the 'Anglo-Catholicisms', and the project was taken up again in 1928. The Church Assembly accepted it by 396 votes against 152; but again the House of Commons threw it out, this time by 226 votes. So the 1662 Prayer Book remained as it was, disallowing many Anglo-Catholic opinions and practices. But this did not stop the Anglo-Catholics from persevering in their task, nor the bishops from recommending their dioceses to use the revised, and rejected, Prayer Book! The Episcopal Church of Scotland, sister of the Church of England, went one better—it disregarded the decision of Parliament and adopted the Revised Version. Confusion reigned and since that time nothing has been attempted to settle the matter officially, though a *modus vivendi* has been tacitly accepted so as to permit all tendencies to express themselves in speech and worship.

Despite the Catholicizing aspects which the form of worship has taken on, it would be wrong to suppose that the Anglican Church has lost the essence of its pro*test*ant character; its opposition to Rome is no less categorical, and until quite recently nothing happened to affect it. The failure of the Malines Conversations between 1921 and 1926, when Lord Halifax and Cardinal Mercier attempted to re-establish contact with Rome, provides proof of this. At the time all the groups and leagues and associations for defence of the 'Protestant heritage' took action to frustrate any attempt at Catholicization; they were led by the Protestant Alliance (founded in 1845 by the Earl of Shaftesbury)—a rich source of dark stories concerning the Jesuits and the untold wealth of the Vatican.

Despite the projects for disestablishment which have cropped up from time to time, and which have been successful only in Wales, where since 1920 the Church has been completely separated from the State, the Anglican Church remains an established one in England itself. All one can say is that since the creation of the Church Assembly in 1919 the official Church takes far more notice of the views of its lay adherents, and this, up to a point, provides a counterweight to State action. Moreover, since the setting up of the Anglican Communion, which includes every Church in the world having the Thirty-nine Articles and the Prayer Book as basis of its faith, and since the inauguration of the Lambeth Conference in 1867, Anglicanism has assumed a character much greater than that of a merely national confession. But it must not be forgotten that behind this splendid façade of unity there lie barely concealed discords, nourished by the independent spirit of the British temperament, by the wish for 'free inquiry' inherited from the Reformation, and perhaps by a certain taste for theological controversy. In 1937 the publication, after fifteen years' work, of the *Corpus*, in which the high clergy set out its doctrine, showed that in the final analysis each is free to believe whatever he pleases. . . .

Since the end of the Second World War England has not shown any significant change in its characteristics of earlier years. The Established Church continues to have the greatest number of adherents, although some observers affirm that the 'Free Churches' and the sects have now overtaken it in this respect. It has the best possible relations with the Free Churches; in concert with them it has even undertaken joint missionary works. In 1950 a congress was held, attended by representatives of all the great Churches in England; in 1952 it was decided, in principle, to open discussions with the Presbyterian Church of Scotland, with the Episcopalian (Anglican) Church of Scotland taking part. There was also the most interesting experiment with the Church of South India in which the Anglican Church and the Free Churches collaborated, an indication of one of the ways open to the future for Christian England.

On other counts we can see the same symptoms appearing as in other contemporary Christian groups, including the Catholic Church: greater attention to apostolic problems; efforts to find pastoral formulae suitable to modern needs; a tendency towards liturgical revival even among the old dissidents least attracted by ritualism; and expansion of sacramental practices. In 1957 the *News Chronicle* concluded a series of articles giving the results of a long and detailed study of faith among the British with these words: 'Heathen Britain? Absurd!' Even taking into account the well-known British respect for others, this peremptory assertion does not seem unjustified.

6. French Protestantism

Of all Protestant communities in predominantly Catholic countries, that of France is the most vigorous and the most interesting, despite the fact that it amounts to no more than 2 per cent of the population. It is little known by the rest of the French and is considered by some as a more or less foreign element. Even its own adherents look upon themselves as detached from the rest of the community. Their thinking differs from the rest of their compatriots, and they are more at home spiritually with foreigners—with the Swiss, the Germans and the Americans. This element of distinction emerges in their customs as well as in social and political life. André Siegfried (a past master of this form of analysis) called it, *cum grano salis*, a physiological type. It is precisely because of its awareness of this that the French Protestant minority has survived and asserted itself with such vigour.

The history of the Protestant community in France has been, as everyone knows, one of persecution, and this has had a profound psychological effect upon it. In fact for a century after the revocation of the Edict of Nantes (1685) every Frenchman who believed in the Reformation was obliged to consider himself as an outlaw, now tolerated, now hunted down, always kept out of the main stream of the country's affairs. Twice violence, with official blessing, broke out: once in the period between 1685–1715, under the Sun King Louis XIV, and again between 1745–60, unleashed by the Catholic authorities in face of the rapid expansion of Protestantism. From 1752, with the edict against the *Assemblées du Désert*, there was more agitation, and the difficulties of the Seven Years War made things still more dangerous for the government. The common sense of several leading pastors, Paul Rabaut (1718–94), for example, and of certain royal administrators such as Marshal Mirepoix, served to avert a general revolution. The distribution of Protestantism immediately prior to the Revolution was the result of persecution. This distribution was to last until 1900—five-sixths of Protestants were to be found in only a quarter of France, in a wide band running from the Pyrenees to the Alps, south of the Massif Central, with two branches reaching out to Alsace and the Charentes. It was persecution also that largely determined the political attitude of the Protestants, their mistrust of authoritarian regimes and their loyalty to ideas referred to as liberal (for which the French Revolution took credit), as well as their taste for all forms of resistance to the power of the authorities. This differentiated them from their co-religionists in Germany, Scandinavia or England, all so closely linked to the State. In the fullest and noblest sense French Protestantism is a religion of the persecuted, of martyrs for their faith.

When the Revolution broke out there had been no persecution for thirty years; the Protestants had no reason any more to feel outlaws. Tolerance was the order of the day; the Huguenot women imprisoned in the famous 'tour de Constance' had been freed by the Prince of Beauvau in 1763, Protestant prisoners and galley slaves in 1775. Worship had resumed in general without constraint: from the desert of the seventeenth century a second desert was now attracting adherents. First Turgot then Malesherbes drew attention to the urgent necessity of settling the Protestant question once for all. Finally, in November 1787, an edict of Louis XVI was signed (promulgated in 1788), which gave all non-Catholics legal civil status, independent of the clergy's registers.

The Protestants welcomed the Revolution with the same fervour as the rest of France. They looked to it for a definite status and for social advancement. Many of them served in the revolutionary units; one of them, Rabaut St-Étienne, wrote to his father, Paul Rabaut: 'The President of the Constituent Assembly is at your feet.' The Declaration of Rights enshrined the principle of the liberty of opinion, and the Constitution of 1791 acknowledged the right of all men to worship as they pleased. But things soon began to go wrong. Bloody affrays took place in various provinces, either because the Protestants were seeking vengeance for their former persecutions, or because the Catholics were reacting against the freedom of worship for other denominations. In the spring of 1790 a small religious war had broken out in the regions of Montalban, Bordeaux and Nîmes. Now came other points of discord—the Civil Constitution of the clergy and ecclesiastical property. At Nîmes riots resulted in 134 deaths. As the Revolution moved towards irreligion and greater severity the Protestants began to feel uneasy. Provincials, most of them were Girondins and Federalists rather than Montagnards. The steps taken towards secularization, such as the introduction of the revolutionary calendar and the confiscation of Church property, shocked them as much as they did the Catholics. But in general they put up little resistance. The churches closed; pastors were dismissed; in the Gard, fifty-one out of seventy-five voted to suspend services of worship; church plate and vessels were handed over to the authorities. Pastors like Rame and de Vauvert bowed to the goddess Reason, others like Marron composed odes to the worst tyrants. At the other end of the scale was Marat, whom Charlotte Corday, once a Protestant herself, was to assassinate. But there were exceptions. Pastors emigrated; others, e.g. the aged Rabaut and the famous Oberlin, were imprisoned for protesting against the anti-religious steps taken, and some of these died from the conditions in prison. Some had courage enough to harbour resistant Catholic priests or to lead worship in secret; a dozen were beheaded. But in general it was a weakened Protestantism which faced Napoleon later on.

He was to declare several times during his conflicts with the Papacy that it was to his regret that France, and indeed the entire world, was not Protestant. He declined to follow the advice of Huguenot counsellors of state who urged him, at the time of the Consulate, to fly the flag of Protestantism. But he did not wish to revive the fury of religious wars. When he undertook to bring the Churches into his system of autocratic government he took care not to forget the Protestants. The Organic Articles, published on 8th April 1802, applied to both denominations, Reformed and Lutheran. They were officially recognized but brought under tutelage. The pastors, paid by the State, became civil servants; several of them received the cross of the Legion of Honour immediately this Order was created. The Geneva Academy and the Strasbourg Faculty of Theology were reconstituted, and came under the State; the Montauban Faculty of Theology was opened in 1809. Outwardly, in general, such steps seemed favourable to Protestantism. Under the Concordat the Churches found peace and the guarantee of a secure future; churches and seminaries reopened. The only black spot was that the type of organization imposed by the State required that before a circumscription could be set up and elect a Consistory it must have six thousand members, and this was contrary to the fundamental conception of Protestantism, where the local church was the basis of the religious system. In four big towns, Nîmes, Bordeaux, La Rochelle and Paris, this did not apply. Furthermore the Synod was not re-established. But there was worse to come; as the French theologian Louis Dallière saw, the Church which had accepted the Concordat was diametrically opposed to the perse-cuted Church, to which true Protestants were faithful. Was there to be a serious break away from the traditions of the French Reformation? Was there to be State Protestantism, a middle-class Protestantism, embracing liberal and rational ideas? In the higher administrative cadres of the Empire there were indeed Protestants of note—Boissy d'Anglas, Rabaut-Dupuis, Arnal de Jaucourt. In every province zealous pastors resisted this dangerous trend as best they could.

Protestantism emerged without undue trouble from the revolu-tionary and imperial epochs. The Restoration could well have been fatal to it, strongly marked as it was by intransigent Catholic reaction; but it proved instead to be a favourable period. Louis XVIII was no fanatic and he did not forget that he owed his throne to England and Prussia. Protestants like Jaucourt, Boissy d'Anglas and Chabaud-Latour were associated from the beginning with the regime, as was the young Guizot (1787–1874), son of a Huguenot victim of the Terror, who began his brilliant career as Secretary-General at the Ministry of the Interior. The Charter guaranteed freedom of conscience and worship; the Organic Articles were maintained. Here and there, in various *départements* of the Midi, the *Terreur Blanche* brought about Catholic reaction which caused some hundred deaths and the burning of a dozen churches, but the trouble soon died down. Guizot and Pastor Marron, departing from their previous position, set to work to pacify those concerned. Even under Charles X the situation grew no worse; neither official propaganda nor the intrigues of the *Congrégation* brought the position of the Protestants into danger. They were obliged to put up with certain affronts when there was a procession or some important event, but this did not stop seven Huguenots from taking their seats among the peers, nor did it prevent Guizot or the illustrious naturalist Cuvier from performing duties in the highest ranks of the administration. The aged Oberlin was to receive the cross of the *Ordre du Lys* from the king, as well as that of the Legion of Honour; the pastor Samuel Vincent was to render homage publicly to the good faith of the sovereign.

This, however, did not prevent the majority of Protestants from following the general movement of French opinion when the 1830 Revolution overthrew the monarchy. It is true that Louis-Philippe had the advantage where the Reformed Churches were concerned: during his exile he had often met Lutherans, and he was on familiar terms with the Calvinist Chabot-Jarnac. Guizot, Cuvier and Benjamin Constant rallied to the Orléanist regime. There was still greater satisfaction when the three Protestant marriages of the royal family were taken into account: that of Princess Louise with the Lutheran Leopold I of Saxe-Coburg-Saalfeld, that of the Duke of Orléans with Helen of

Mecklenburg-Schwerin and that of Princess Marie with the Duke of Württemberg. This bourgeois monarchy was a period of prosperity for the Protestants, and the upper classes were to come into their own during this time, to be known later as the *Haute Société Protestante*, made up of higher government officers, university people, intellectuals, lawyers, bankers and business men. At the head of the government was Guizot, a Protestant—or, to put it more trenchantly, the living incarnation of Protestantism. Everything would have been satisfactory if only the traditional synodal system of government had been reinstated also.

Taking advantage of such a favourable situation, French Protestants between the years 1815 and 1848 sought to expand their movement. Many churches were opened, especially prior to 1830, since dissensions within the Protestant Churches were later on to slow down the movement. Faculties of theology went ahead: that of Montauban was to become well known. Protestant organizations emerged, most of which continue to survive. Thousands of Bibles were distributed, some even being destined for converts among the Catholics. Evangelists and distributors went assiduously around all the provinces carrying either the Scriptures or anti-Catholic tracts; if the police sometimes arrested them it was not for this particular activity, but rather for political reasons. In 1841 the pastor Vermeil created deaconesses in imitation of Catholic nuns. Perhaps Lamennais was exaggerating when he wrote in *l'Univers* (4th December 1847): 'Protestantism has got its grip on Catholicism the better to devour it.' But his words contained a grain of truth. . . .

Protestantism, however, although in full swing, was roughly shaken by discord within its fabric. The progressive rise to affluence of the Protestant society could not but disquiet convinced Huguenots, especially as for many of these affluent gentlemen faith was reduced to what Rabaut Saint-Étienne called 'humanitarian deism', in which there were 'no limits to the perfectibility of Reason'. Reaction then set in, similar in principle to those revivals which were taking place almost everywhere,[1] assisted by two foreign influences: that of the revival in Geneva, which sent several of its leaders, including Felix Neff, French in origin, to work in France; and that of Methodism, implanted by Pierre de Pontavice in 1809 and expanded after 1815 by the English pastor Charles Cook in the Midi, the Hautes Alpes and the Charente. This French revival provoked, as everywhere else, the resistance of too comfortable Churches sunk in comfortable routines. Splits appeared: Free Churches were set up in opposition. French Protestantism, more so even than that of other countries, because of the love which the French have of logical ideas and clarity, developed

[1] See Chapter III, section 1.

several tendencies which, however, the Concordat regime was to keep in check until 1905.

When the 1848 Revolution brought the spirit of liberty and fraternity to France, the Protestants thought that their hour had struck. Pastors and priests alike rejoiced. Organizations invited Protestant speakers to address them, and the younger Athanase Coquerel was elected to the Chamber of Deputies. It was perhaps a propitious moment to reinstate the traditional synodal and Presbyterian organization. An assembly was held in Paris in May 1848 to discuss the matter; a still larger gathering met in September of that year. But the conception of the Church itself proved a stumbling-block, for this had always been a vexed question among Protestants. What constituted the Church? The professing members who adhered formally to a confession of faith, or the mass of those who declared themselves to be Protestants? The greater part of the official Church opted for the second conception, but were opposed by the professing members under the leadership of Frédéric Monod and Agenor de Gasparin. A split ensued, giving rise to the 'Evangelical Reformed Churches', which joined forces with others already in existence. In 1873 there were forty-six of them. Confusion abounded and was made worse by doctrinal divergencies. We shall see [1] how the spread of so-called liberal Protestantism would arouse lively controversy among all the Reformed Churches in the world, and especially those of France; for such liberalism brought into question the fundamentals of Revelation and of faith.

Discussions between 'liberals' and 'orthodox' became super-imposed on those between the partisans and the adversaries of Established Churches. Complications abounded, for the Free Churches were not necessarily liberal; that of Adolphe Monod described itself as orthodox, whereas that founded by Athanase Coquerel was liberal. As for whatever hopes there were of returning to the former state of affairs, these vanished with the 1851 *coup d'état*.

Whilst the dictatorship was being prepared for, the Protestants were among those who opposed the prince-president. The young journalist Auguste Nefftzer of *La Presse* had been imprisoned; distributors and evangelists had been arrested by the police. On 2nd December there were riots in several Protestant regions—that of Vernoux in the Ardèche was the only one to vote No in the plebiscite. Such an attitude was not calculated to endear Napoleon III to the Protestants. A decree dated 26th March 1852 determined the organization of Protestant Churches: it was the work of Charles Read, vice-chairman of the Paris Bible Society, one of the founders of the *Société d'Histoire du Protestantisme Français*. The parish was restored after its suppression since the Organic Articles had been introduced, and a

[1] See Chapter III, section 7.

central council created, made up of Protestant notables chosen by the government: there was no more talk of elected synods.

The Empire retained until the last an ambiguous attitude towards Protestants. While missionary activities were blocked, while Methodist or Baptist evangelists were frequently arrested, there were wealthy Protestants in high places, such as the Minister of Finance, Achille Fould, a converted Jew so zealous that he even attempted to convert the emperor; and churches were built with the help of the State, e.g. that in the Rue Roquépine in Paris. Auguste Nefftzer was free to found the newspaper Le Temps in 1861. Protestant chaplains accompanied the troops into battle; conservative Protestantism was looked upon favourably, the other kind not. As the Empire developed it became less strict. In 1859 'creeds not recognized by the State' (Methodists, Baptists and others) were authorized; from 1860 onwards, while the pinpricks of over-zealous administrators did not stop altogether, the atmosphere became more favourable. In intellectual circles sympathy towards Protestantism was shown by those who, though anti-Catholic, had no wish to reject all Christian faith: Taine was one example. The black spot was within the Protestant Churches themselves, where opposition between liberal and orthodox tendencies was intense. It was at this time that Strauss's controversial book appeared in France and Renan published his Life of Jesus. Protestant intellectuals, such as Jean Bon and Félix Pécaut, were turning towards a religion without dogma and towards freethinking. The orthodox reacted. In 1864 Athanase Coquerel was struck off the list of Suffragans of the Oratory—but several hundred fervent souls supported him. Altogether 121 pastors of the Nîmes conference broke away.

Antagonism remained unabated throughout the Third Republic. It was even strengthened by the altered conditions in which the Protestants were placed by the new regime. The collapse of the Empire distressed them little, and in 1871, with the prestige that came from resistance to tyranny and from the reflected glory of heroic soldiers such as Denfert-Rochereau, the defender of Belfort, they hastened to take advantage of the situation. Thiers authorized the setting up of an assembly to study a return to traditional organization. Evangelical Christians of every denomination, every creed, liberal as well as orthodox, were invited. This synod met in Paris in June 1872—the first of its kind since 1659. There was immediate opposition. The orthodox, under Guizot, wanted the Assembly to set out a basic doctrine for Protestants, and this was formulated in the Declaration of 1872. The liberals retorted that this was contrary to the spirit of free inquiry and that it was impossible for them to sign something contrary to their beliefs. During the second session in November 1873 the Free Churches broke away. They did not expect the authorities to recognize their autonomy, and set up only a provisional organization, but the break was no less complete.

While these dissensions were painful to believers, they did not stop Protestantism from developing. Circumstances, however, were not very favourable. The loss of Alsace-Lorraine had brought their numbers down from 846,000 to 580,000, the only compensation being the arrival in Paris of vigorous Protestant elements such as the Fallots, the Siegfrieds and the Boegners. Then, when 'The Moral Order' was in power under MacMahon, aided by the 'Protestant banking world, drunk with joy', as Pressensé expressed it, there were anti-Huguenot scenes in various provinces, particularly violent in the Gard. As it turned out it was this reaction which brought the Reformed Churches into favour with the Left. André Siegfried spoke of this as showing the true character of French Protestantism. From left of centre to radicalism, and later on to Socialism, the Protestants were to constitute a whole range of left-wing political opinions.

The Third Republic was a period very favourable to Protestantism. From the first it took a leading part in political life. In the Assembly of 1871 there were seventy Protestant deputies, or 10 per cent of the total (instead of the normal six or seven). The first cabinet formed by Jules Grévy in 1879 had five Protestant ministers out of nine! A line of Protestant politicians and higher civil servants appeared, which has continued up to our time. The Ministry of Education was one of their special fields: it was the Protestants Ferdinand Buisson, Jules Steeg, Félix Pécaut, Charles Wagner and Mme de Kergomard who set up the non-denominational school system, as laid down by the Third Republic, sacrificing all the 1,535 schools which their fathers had opened during the nineteenth century. The republican State showed goodwill towards the Reformation in many ways such as the installation of the Strasbourg Faculty of Theology in Paris when Strasbourg became part of Germany. The prestige of Protestantism grew from year to year in intellectual circles: Renan came round to it following his marriage to the daughter of the Reformed Church painter Ary Scheffer; Taine entrusted the religious education of his children to Pastor Hollard, who was also to officiate at Taine's funeral. The Goncourts declared that Protestantism was 'the socially desirable religion'. Quinet, Renouvin, Jules Fabre, Prévost-Paradol made no secret of their sympathy with it, and, later on, Alphonse Daudet, whose l'Évangéliste was not particularly acceptable to the Huguenots. Subsequently Guizot and Droz after him were elected to the French Academy. The deputy Mahy and the pamphleteer Eugène Reynaud, author of 'Protestant Peril', both protested against the prominent part played by Protestants. Furthermore it was doubted whether these political and official features of Protestantism, with its accent on the importance of middle-class acceptance, should be part of the Reformed Churches' activity at all.

Apart from Protestantism in government, banking and academic circles, there was another branch of Protestantism which followed lines previously laid down. It was now that Charles Babut set up the 'Inner Mission' at Nîmes modelled upon the Catholic missions; that Eugène Réveillaud launched the 'Itinerant Mission'; that the English pastor MacAll, profoundly disturbed by what he had witnessed in Paris in the wake of the Commune, set up Mission Halls and the Popular Evangelical Mission, opening workrooms, dispensaries and centres of education; and that the Salvation Army,[1] led by Catherine Booth, daughter of the founder, established bridge-heads in France. It was also at this time that the Alsatian Tommy Fallot (1844–1904), whose generosity knew no limits, launched the *Société d'Aide fraternelle et d'Études sociales*, an organization in the front rank of the fight against social evils such as prostitution; then Charles Gide (1847–1932), uncle of the celebrated writer André Gide, published *le Christianisme Social*.[2] The Protestant press took on an unwonted importance: seventy-five publications, of which some were notable, such as *le Christianisme au XIXᵉ siècle*, which is still flourishing. French Protestant missions outside Europe multiplied.[3] New Churches and sects began to assume a more important role in French religious life: the Baptists with Ruben Saillens; the Mennonites, who had reorganized themselves in the Montbéliard region; the Darbyites, who were proselytizing in the Midi, with their austere form of piety; the Seventh Day Adventists in Paris in 1900. The massive upheaval which took place in the Catholic Church during the last quarter of the nineteenth century, under Pope Leo XIII, was to have its counterpart among Protestants also.

A new religious life was to open in France in the twentieth century. The separation of Church and State, voted by Parliament on 9th December 1905,[4] applied to Protestants as well as Catholics; on the whole, they all accepted it without difficulty. Some of them had joined the League for Independent Schools, alongside Catholics, to fight against the secularization of education, but these were rare exceptions. Separation itself was in the line of thought of Calvinism. Since the synods of 1872 several speakers had spoken for it. The Association for Worship which provided that the administration of Church property should come under secular commissions, was accepted without trouble, and congregations paid their own pastors. A Protestant,

---

[1] See Chapter III, section 9.
[2] On Social Protestantism see Chapter III, section 8.
[3] See section 11 below.
[4] *A Fight for God*, Chapter V, section 2.

Louis Méjan, the secretary to Aristide Briand, was reputed to be the instigator of the measures taken to bring about a peaceful solution.

Protestants in France continued to be regarded favourably by the Republic. In the *Chambre des Députés* as well as in the government itself, always on the left politically, they still enjoyed more power than their numbers warranted. They continued to play a most important part in the higher echelons of the ministries of Education, Finance and Foreign Affairs. The Protestant Bank expanded considerably. The newspaper *Le Temps*, which, without being formally linked to Protestantism, retained strong bonds with the *Haute Société Protestante*, became the most important French newspaper, at least in authority. It was now far from the time when Protestants looked upon themselves as outcasts. Twice they had been called upon to bear national burdens: in the First World War twenty-five pastors were killed. Among the Huguenot dead were the sons of emigrants exiled by Louis XIV, who had remained faithful to their country. During the Second World War many Protestants joined the Resistance. Among those killed was Yann Roullet, a young pastor who was arrested with his grandfather, Léonce Vieljeux, Mayor of La Rochelle, executed at the time of the German rout in the infamous Struthof camp.

The Protestant presence in France was not confined to government or administration. A considerable amount of intellectual activity was also in evidence. Publishing and the press were very active between the wars, although publishing lost ground after 1945. Newspapers were launched, such as *Réforme*, which is still pursuing its independent policy. The use of radio since 1939 and television since 1945 has ensured that Protestantism makes its presence felt—the title of one of its broadcasts is called *La Présence Protestante*. The older Churches are running into competition from younger and newer Churches and sects in these fields.

The spiritual leap forward which Protestantism took in the last quarter of the nineteenth century gathered momentum in the twentieth century. Doubtless Protestantism, like Catholicism, has suffered from the pressures which seem to be turning man ever further from revealed truths, and practice has declined greatly. But, as with Catholicism, there are hopeful signs. One of the most significant was the founding in 1910 by François Puaux and Edmond Hugues of the *Musée du Désert*, a few kilometres from Anduze. Here are the relics of the *Camisards*, and here, every year, some fifteen thousand pilgrims gather on the first Sunday in September. Protestant apostolic organizations re-formed, especially after the First World War; one of these, *La Cause*, founded in 1920, soon came to the forefront, but the older *Société centrale d'Évangélisation*, founded in 1833, is still as active as ever. In 1946 the French Bible Society was set up, which took over all the activities concerned in Bible distribution in concert with the British Bible Society. The Inner Mission has continued, assisted by other groups, especially that of worker missions, which, from 1945 onwards, at the time of the worker-priest experiment, adopted the worker-pastor formula still in existence. Protestant spiritual ferment goes side by side with that shown by the Catholic Church for more than thirty years. One of the most remarkable points is the appearance of religious vocations within the Reformed Churches. The Taizé community, founded from modest beginnings in 1940 by the young Genevan pastor Roger Schutz, has attained great spiritual value and worldwide renown during the past twenty-five years. To it come young men from all types of Protestantism to practise monasticism, together with believers of every faith.[1] Among all these signs of religious ferment, mention should be made also of the extraordinary progress made by the 'young' Churches, the sects, Adventist and Pentecostal Churches, all of whose methods may seem out of the ordinary but all of whom nevertheless are imbued with zeal and sincerity.

The most remarkable fact which emerges from the history of French Protestantism in the twentieth century is the emphasis which has been placed on consolidation as against schism, however great the difficulties appear to be. The separation of Church and State after the Concordat also had the effect of breaking the links between orthodox and liberals. The Reformed Church was split into the Evangelical Reformed Churches union (orthodox), and the Reformed Churches (liberal). The Free Churches union and the Methodist Churches union remained apart, as did the Lutherans. But soon there was a movement to end this obviously dangerous fragmentation. The number of Free Churches declined, from forty-nine in 1873 to thirty-five in 1935. The strong worldwide Protestant urge towards ecumenicalism from 1927 onwards,[2] had its effect on the French Reformed Churches. In 1933 the first steps were taken towards the formation of a common front, and these resulted in 1938 in the birth of the French Reformed Church, in which Churches and parishes of different tendencies, including Methodists, were grouped. It was pointed out that no one was obliged to toe the line, and a small minority declined to conform to this and became independent evangelical Churches. Nineteen former Free Churches took back their old names, and five Methodist Churches remained outside, together with the Reformed Church of Alsace-Lorraine, one of the Concordat Churches. Nevertheless some 90 per cent of Calvinist or Methodist Protestants belonged

---

[1] On Taizé see Chapter III, section 14, and Chapter VI, section 13.
[2] See Chapter VI, section 11.

to the French Reformed Church, with the exception of those in the two eastern provinces.

At the same time other efforts were being made with the object of uniting all Protestants in a common defence of their rights. It began in 1903, prior to the separation, and was launched by Pastor Wilfred Monod. In 1905 the bases were laid for this group. The first plenary Assembly of the French Protestant Federation was held at Nîmes; this was presided over successively by Edmond Gruner, a layman, and by pastors Élie Morel and Marc Boegner (from 1929 to 1961). It included all those who were of practical importance in French Protestantism. One or two small groups or sects remained outside, totalling some fifty thousand adherents. The two principal elements remained the Reformed Churches and the Lutherans.

These have retained their place in the history of French Protestantism. In 1789 they were for the most part found in Alsace and Lorraine, some small communities being scattered in Paris and in some provincial towns. In 1802 their number was increased by the return to France of the Montbéliard territory, where Mennonites were also established. Under the Empire they were granted by Napoleon the right to found a Consistorial Church. From that time until today they have shown great vitality, influenced by pietist currents which, since Soener in the seventeenth century, have always had their place in Alsace. This development ceased under the German occupation and the number of French adherents fell to some seventy-five thousand, but this Lutheran Church showed a remarkable will to survive, setting up, through strong private backing, many missionary and charitable organizations. After the First World War it was cut in two, as Alsace and Lorraine had retained the Concordat regime whereas the rest of French Lutherans since 1905 had adopted the separate regime. There are thus today two Lutheran Churches: that of the Augsburg Confession, and the Evangelical Lutheran Church which was founded by the union of the Montbéliard and Paris regions in 1872.

Both Churches have conserved many ties, especially as regards the recruitment of pastors. Several attempts have been made to unite the two, but the Lutherans, however much they were in the minority, always declined. They feel that their own services and chants, their reading from Epistles and Gospels and a broader conception of religion than that of the Calvinists bring something of unique value to Protestantism in France, apart from the fact that they are affiliated to the French Protestant Federation. Protestants, though still evidently a minority, are of great importance in present-day France. How many are there? It is difficult to answer this question, since the number of practising adherents does not necessarily determine actual numbers. It is probable that there is a maximum of some 850,000 in all, of whom

some 300,000 are Lutherans, and some 50,000 Baptists and members of
'young' Churches. Geographically,[1] the Protestants have altered the
appearance of the map of France considerably in the last one hundred
and fifty years.

Socially speaking, the distribution is of great interest. Firstly, there

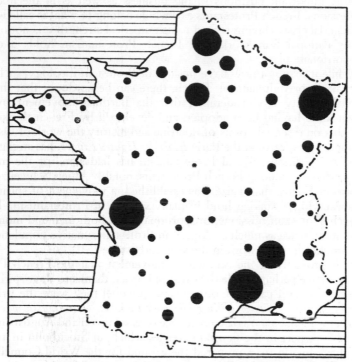

MAP SHOWING DISTRIBUTION OF PROTESTANTS IN FRANCE

The black circles indicate Protestant concentrations and their
relative importance.
(Taken from *Les Actualitiés Religieuses*.)

is a marked contrast between the rural communities of the Cévennes,
the Gard, the Charentes and the Alpes regions, where all classes are
represented, and the urban parishes which are almost exclusively
middle class. It is incidentally of interest to note that there are practically no working-class Protestants, except in Alsace and the Montbéliard region, where the expansion of the Peugeot and Sochaux
automobile works and the influx of foreign workers is modifying the

[1] See map.

traditional Lutheran and Mennonite character of the area. Everywhere, even in the villages, Protestants occupy important positions. André Siegfried attributed this to a knowledge of the Bible, which 'provides the equivalent of culture'. In point of fact pastors receive more comprehensive training than Catholic priests. Middle-class Protestants occupy important positions in big business as well as in the liberal professions. French Protestants as a whole belong to what is called the managerial class. Having regard to its numerical strength it is not only in its national framework that French Protestantism holds a disproportionate place.

While it may not now have masters of Protestant theology, such as Karl Barth or Bultmann or Tillich, there can be no doubt that theological activity is considerable, that the Barthian movement owes much to its having been adopted and developed by French thinkers, and that on essential points of doctrine and history the work of Oscar Cullmann, professor at the Paris *École des Hautes Études*, has strengthened the position. Liberal Protestantism has had some of the most active elements among French Protestants, notably Albert Schweitzer.[1] It was in France that Taizé was established, a movement of spiritual renewal which is taking hold in many spheres of Protestantism. The French Protestant missions, proportionately in both men and money, contribute twice as much as American Protestants; native populations are brought into the work in the very early stages.

It is probably in the ecumenical movement that the French Protestants have perhaps made the greatest impact, thanks to their spirit of enterprise. With pastors Gounelle and Jezequel they were the prime movers of the *Alliance Universelle pour l'amitié internationale par les Églises*, which, by a tragic coincidence, was set up on 2nd August 1914. They took part in the first conferences which, at Stockholm in 1925 and Lausanne in 1927, prepared the ground for the World Council of Churches.[2] Pastor Marc Boegner was to be one of its six presidents, and in citing his name we should not forget that amid all the efforts that have been made towards ecumenicalism, which His Holiness John XXIII has designated to all Christians as their common goal, an *élite* of French Protestants have held and still hold a pre-eminent place.

To sum up, it is a vigorous Protestantism, rich in future possibilities, that France presents in the world of that Christianity which sprang from the Reformation.

[1] See Chapter III, section 7 *ad fin.*
[2] See Chapter VI, section 6.

7. Minorities Expanding or on the Defensive

In the rest of Europe Protestantism appears in minority forms, among Catholic or Orthodox populations, its importance depending on the historical conditions in which it was implanted or the vitality of its adherents. Were these minorities exposed to hostility during the nineteenth century? Are they still so exposed? Now and again works appear which inveigh against Roman Catholic 'totalitarianism' without being very convincing. What is more serious is the persecution to which the sons of the Reformation have been subjected in truly totalitarian countries, not as Protestants but as Christians. In every case it is heartening to note that not only have they survived, but they have expanded.

Spain is certainly the only country where anti-Protestantism has survived into our age, not only in a vigorously polemical way but also as an official line of policy. Almost unknown in the Hispanic realm at the end of the eighteenth century, Protestantism felt that it stood a reasonable chance under Charles III (1759–88), the monarch who expelled the Jesuits and called upon German and Swiss colonizers to open up the Sierra Morena; then under Joseph Bonaparte (1808), who, while maintaining Catholicism as the State religion, put into practice the ideas of the French Revolution. As it happened, this alliance with the French was unfavourable to the Protestants; the return of Ferdinand VII opened up an era of troubles for them. These ceased with the anticlerical reaction of Espartero (1840–3) and the somewhat hesitant period of Isabella's reign. Towards 1850 Protestantism made a little progress, due to the efforts of evangelists from Gibraltar. In 1860 the arrest of a converted officer, Maramoros, and his sentence to the galleys, brought on a certain reaction. The brief Republican period of 1868–71, during which Emilio Castelar demanded rights for the Reformed Churches, resulted in new persecutions, less severe but none the less vexatious. Without the support of foreign Protestants, and in particular that of the German pastor Fliedner and of an American mission, the situation would have been grave. It grew less sombre with the 1876 Constitution which allowed churches to be founded and Bibles to be distributed; the Methodists and the Darbyites entered the scene. Official tolerance continued under Alfonso XIII (1886–1931); Protestantism boomed in Spain, mostly in the large cities; intellectuals such as Miguel de Unamuno made no secret of their sympathies. Protestantism was then in four categories comprising some dozen denominations. There were the Evangelicals, the Reformed (Anglican type) inspired by Cabrera, Baptists and other Churches and sects; in all some thirty thousand adherents and less than fifty thousand sympathizers—a very small flock. The 1936 Revolution once again confused the situation, and the historian Léonard states unequivocally: 'The Spanish Protestants were Republican.' Franco's regime, which was aimed at tightening the unity of Spain, could not be other than mistrustful of the Protestants. Though officially tolerated, their services were allowed only in private or in duly authorized chapels; they were forbidden to proselytize in public; they were obliged, until quite recently, to seek the assistance of the Catholic clergy for all civil status formalities; their publications were censored by Catholics; their seminaries and schools were closed—those of Madrid in 1956—and they were the object of attacks by a certain section of the Catholic press and by certain members of the hierarchy. Foreign observers considered these attacks ill-adapted. There have been various incidents also, the most violent at Seville in 1952, when 'Molotov cocktails' were thrown during a service. It is only during the last few years that the situation has changed towards a slackening of tension.

In Portugal the Protestants are more numerous in proportion to population (20,000 adherents, 25,000 sympathizers). They too have had their difficult times, but these were not so serious as those of their neighbours in Spain. Insignificant in numbers in 1789, Protestantism only began to develop under the influence of Anglican and Presbyterian chaplains attached to the British forces sent to fight Napoleon. In 1809 a Bible Society appeared; the distinctly anti-Catholic trend of Portuguese politics and the influence of freemasonry were all favourable. The first three-quarters of the nineteenth century were to see it expand. The most celebrated propagandist was Dr Kalley of Scotland, who worked in Madeira, Brazil and in Portugal itself; his emulator was Manoël Veira, a native Portuguese, a great apostle of the Bible. At the same time a split inside Catholicism, fomented on two occasions (1840 and 1867) by banned Spanish priests, resulted in the setting up of the Lusitanian Church, which became the most important of all denominations: an Anglican-style Church, which linked itself to Anglicanism through the English Church of Ireland. Reaction began in 1886, and in 1901, during the Regency of Amelia of Orléans-Braganza, real persecution broke out. From 1906 the situation improved and the republican Constitution of 1910, followed by the separation of Church and State in the following year, gave Protestantism its chance; it was to exploit this to the full during the anarchic republican period. Salazar's regime has not affected the legal situation; nor has it interfered with the distribution of Bibles (financed by the Americans) and the establishment of the most recent sects, both Adventist and Pentecostal.

Italy is no less Catholic than Spain, but her attitude towards Protestantism is altogether different. It is a little-known but well-established fact that Italy is one of the countries in Europe where

Protestantism has progressed most rapidly during the last century, and its progress increased. Catholic reaction to the reformed faith's propaganda during the sixteenth century was no less violent than in Spain. For all that it did not succeed in eliminating the heterodoxies which existed before the Reformation, or the survivors of medieval heresies, still called Waldenses. Hidden in the high valleys, close to the frontier, they lived in small patriarchal communities and looked upon themselves as Protestants. It was from here that the new Protestant offensive began after the French Revolution. In 1848 they were granted civil equality and, reorganized, founded a Faculty of Theology, colleges and schools throughout the peninsula, providing a solid intellectual and moral basis for Italian Protestantism. There was a second wave generated by small societies of thinkers, among whom, during the eighteenth century, Jansenists, Gallicans and liberals rubbed shoulders with Protestants of various origin; then a third wave of foreigners, Anglo-Saxons and Germans, who came to live in Italy during the romantic period. From the middle of the nineteenth century there was an invasion (though limited in the numerical sense) of various types of Protestantism. The anti-Roman trend which the unification movement took in Italy helped Garibaldi, whose chaplain was a pastor. The Italian monarchy, in dispute with the Pope, left the field open to the English and American Protestants who were anxious to help their Italian brethren. From the 32,000 of 1861, they rose to 59,000 in 1871 and 56,000 in 1901, their extreme fragmentation remaining always one of their most striking points. After the First World War, on the advent of Fascism, they numbered some eighty thousand adherents spread over a thousand communities, split into at least twenty-five denominations. Mussolini's regime hesitated between mistrust and favour, the latter being more in evidence when things went badly with the Vatican. Most Protestants were none too pleased with the regime. At the end of the Second World War a new wave of Protestants arrived, led for the most part by the sects—Adventists, Jehovah's Witnesses, Pentecostal Churches and, to a lesser degree, by Methodists and Baptists, assisted by the Americans. The number of pastors rose from 549 in 1945 to 1,071 in 1955, the number of churches from 677 to 1,272, and adherents inscribed on church registers rose from 90,000 to 265,000. The conversions of Catholics to Protestantism reached 8,896 in 1955. United since 1946 in a National Council, the main Churches are working, along with the sects and young Churches, to exploit their success, increasing the number of missions and publications (these are often very anti-Catholic), setting up correspondence courses in religious matters, even going so far as to 'assist' conversion financially. One of the most recent innovations has been the setting up of a seminary to 'gather in' those Catholic priests who have left the Church. One understands why it has been called the 'Protestant peril'. It is still too early to foresee the consequences that may follow from the ecumenical climate which has prevailed since 1959.

In Belgium there are some thirty thousand adherents, and here too the rise of Protestantism has been remarkable. When the kingdom was created in 1830 there was only one tiny Reformed Church in Brussels, run by the Swiss, and several communities of Dutch origin. As the first King of the Belgians, Leopold I, was a Lutheran and a practising Lutheran at that, the first impetus was automatic, and in 1839 there were sufficient Protestants (some two thousand) to set up 'The Union of Evangelical Protestant Churches' which the government recognized and established. But one small group, hostile to the tutelage of the State, set up a Free Church, named the 'Belgian Christian Missionary Church' (1848), which devoted its ministry to the miners of Borinage; within fifty years it had some eight thousand adherents. The traditional characteristic of Belgium as a meeting point also manifested itself on the religious plane; foreign influences—French, English, Dutch— were felt; a liberal Church was established; Anglican communities under the Bishop of Fulham in England appeared; *Gereformeerde* groups, in Dutch style, also appeared.[1] After the First World War the Americans set up a Presbyterian Evangelical Mission, very fundamentalist in nature, and a Methodist Church. In 1924, the necessity for consolidation becoming apparent, the main Churches came together in the 'Federation of Protestant Churches', along the same lines as that in France. But in the meantime all the younger Churches and the sects had entered the scene. One of them, the Pentecostal Movement, showed such vigour and such missionary fire (well adapted to the humbler classes) that in 1914 it was the third Belgian denomination in order of importance. In 1955 it became the second, on an equal footing with the Evangelical Mission, the Christian Missionary Church remaining the first in importance. Progress continued and fragmentation did not prevent the Belgian Protestants from getting together to finance a Faculty of Theology and schools, nor from obtaining their rights from the authorities as further proof of their vitality.

Protestant vitality, paradoxically enough, shows its most surprising aspect in Russia. Introduced into the czarist empire at the beginning of the sixteenth century, it had only a minor place until the end of the eighteenth century, except in certain peripheral areas among non-Russian peoples. Under Alexander I (1801–25), whose friend Mme de Krüdener was in contact with the Moravian Brethren and the Swiss Revivalists, not to mention Theosophists and many other zealous purveyors of surprising theories which added to the general confusion, a

[1] See Chapter II, section 2.

group of Protestants established a duly authorized Bible Society (1812). Rivalry between two of the Czar's ministers led to its closure, but the Russian translation of the Holy Scriptures continued intermittently, finally appearing in 1876 under the auspices of the Orthodox Holy Synod. In the meantime the Protestant Churches were basking in a reasonably favourable climate throughout the empire. German influences were also at work on their behalf through the *Stundists* (Students of the Bible). The law of 1832 recognized the Reformed and Lutheran Churches. The Baltic provinces, especially Lithuania and Finland, were to see Lutheranism expand there. In most urban centres the two great Protestant bodies were represented by fairly active communities, even in such a far-away place as Tomsk in Siberia. In 1914 of 90 million inhabitants there were some 4 million Lutherans and Calvinists.

Their numbers increased in a somewhat haphazard manner. Russia was prepared to welcome those sects which had sprouted from Protestantism and to make room for those who were at the crossroads of Orthodoxy and Protestantism, and sometimes even for those of other indeterminate schisms. The government also was prepared to admit Protestant communities in difficulties in their own countries. Thus the Mennonites founded colonies from the Volga to central Asia, on the understanding that they would be exempt from military service, but available for forestry service.

Baptists and Methodists settled in the Ukraine and in Byelorussia, in the Caucasus, even in St Petersburg. During this time, within the aristocracy, a new evangelical movement was created by a Colonel Pachkov of the Imperial Guard; the movement was looked upon suspiciously by the Czar's police. Other evangelists, sprung from the Doukhobors, themselves a breakaway, dissident group from the Orthodox Church,[1] penetrated the Don Cossacks. Even the revolution of 1917 did not stop this sectarian upsurge. In 1920 the Pentecostal movement with American preachers entered the scene under the aegis of famine relief campaigns and soon split up into rival groups. The Seventh Day Adventists, who had been there ever since the end of the nineteenth century, although small in numbers, now expanded rapidly, and during the Second World War Jehovah's Witnesses arrived in their turn. What estimates can be made of the numerical strength of all these movements? In 1928 official statistics quoted 4½ million, but this figure seems a little excessive.

The Communist regime treated the Protestant minority no better than the adherents of the national religion; it was subjected to the same cycle of persecution and tolerance as the Orthodox Church.[2] The

[1] See Chapter IV, section 14.
[2] See Chapter IV, section 15.

bigger Churches were the ones first to be attacked, both Luther and Calvin being denounced as upholders of the bourgeoisie. In 1928 pastors were deported, worship was reduced to furtive gatherings and the movement lost much of its vigour. In 1938 the Russian Lutheran Church was declared dissolved. Lutheranism retained its power only in Latvia, Lithuania and Estonia and among the Baltic and German people who have been deported to Siberia. The Reformed Church retained only the Hungarians of the sub-Carpathian Ukraine. But the Marxists did not find things so easy with the sects, as these had no churches and no structure, but it was not for want of trying on the part of the authorities! Persecuted since 1925, the Mennonites emigrated in large numbers to the U.S.A., but a sufficient number remained in Russia to cause disquiet to the authorities—there were two waves of persecution. Yet some forty-five thousand remained in the Altai and Kazakhstan regions. The Pentecostal movements were twice persecuted; some adherents fled, but those who remained moved from one region to another, exercising a certain fascination upon youth and even penetrating the ranks of the Red Army. The Adventists, after developing and expanding rapidly from 1919 to 1928, and despite declarations of unconditional loyalty to the regime, were to find difficulties increasing between them and the authorities—especially concerning the observation of the Sabbath. But police interference did not stop their missionary activities or their ecstatic wait for the end of the world.[1]

The most extraordinary venture was that of the Baptists. In the early days of the Soviet regime they were treated with a certain amount of goodwill because they had been persecuted by the Czar's police, and their simplicity, their stark way of life, all seemed to fit in with Communist ideology. They were authorized to set up Christian kolkhozes, and even a Khristomol (Christian Youth) similar to the Komsomol. They published a Bible and newspapers and undertook a huge programme of missionary work. In 1929 this happy period came to an end. As with other Protestants, they saw their communities decapitated, but they had so well dispersed themselves throughout the Soviet Union that they were able to continue to lead a clandestine existence, made still easier because their religion dispensed with outward signs. When, for reasons of national unity, calmer times prevailed in religious life during the Second World War, the Baptists found themselves well placed to take the lead in a great movement. On 29th October 1944 a Baptist Union was formed, including various kinds of evangelists, liberal Protestants, Methodists and even some members of the Pentecostal movement. The Union was administered by a Pan-Unionist Council and launched a systematic propaganda campaign, kept within

---

[1] In 1949 all the Adventist members of a kolkhoz sold all their goods, dressed in white, left the town and awaited their ascension into heaven from 25th May to 15th June.

bounds to some extent by the Soviet authorities. They were authorized to resume the publication of their Bible and to publish various religious works; the Baptists increased their meeting places, organized each local community in strong units under the presbytery system and succeeded until the most recent wave of persecution in publicly celebrating Christian feasts five times a year. Observers, whether Protestant, Orthodox or Communist, all agree in stating that their prayer meetings draw crowds among whom are many young people. Estimates give some 4 to 5 million adherents. Periodically the atheist press complains of the vitality manifested by this obscurantist offshoot.

8. The Leading Protestant Country: the U.S.A.

The two greatest events in the history of contemporary Protestantism did not take place in Europe. Both sprang from a process which had practically ceased since the end of the sixteenth century—the development of those Churches which emerged from the Reformation. This recommenced outside the framework of the Old World. Firstly, as will be seen, by setting up, in the non-Christian world, missions analogous to those which the Catholics had had for a long time already; secondly, and this is the most important point, by taking part from its inception in the upsurge of a new country and making it the world's leading Protestant country.

The origins of the U.S.A. are, as we know, Protestant.[1] Today's Americans like to recall that the discovery of their continent by Columbus in 1492 was followed only twenty-five years later by Luther's discovery of religious 'truth'. In fact it was rather from Calvin that the immigrants took their faith, immigrants who at the beginning of the seventeenth century were to found the Thirteen Colonies. These were to be the kernel of the future U.S.A., Calvinist in nature or taking after those reformers of the second or third wave, who in opposition to the Established Churches, especially Anglicanism, were to give an impetus to religious movements of quite another type. Anglicans under Captain John Smith took over Virginia; the Presbyterians and Congregationalists from among the Pilgrim Fathers of the *Mayflower* installed themselves in New England and Massachusetts; the Quakers founded Pennsylvania, open, in theory, to all forms of Christianity; the Baptists evangelized the Southern States, both the Carolinas and Georgia; here they were to be joined a little later by the Methodists, who thence spread all over the colonies. Meanwhile the Dutch, Calvinists and Mennonites, were building the city that was to become New York. There was one exception to this process of

[1] *The Church in the Eighteenth Century*, Chapter III, section 10.

Protestantization: Maryland, where Catholicism was implanted by one of King Charles's Catholic gentlemen. All these immigrants had the feeling that their Protestantism conferred blessings and imposed duties upon them. 'God', said one of them, 'has sifted the nations and allowed only the best to come to the virgin lands here.' And throughout the colonial period, in several of the old colonies, civic rights were strictly reserved for those who were, at any rate outwardly, exemplary Reformed Christians.

The stamp of Protestantism remains strong today in the U.S.A. In an impressive analysis of the U.S.A. which André Siegfried made in 1926 he described Protestantism as the 'sole national religion' and claimed that 'to ignore this fact is to get a false impression of the country'. In 1953 the Catholic historian Th. Maynard admitted that Protestantism 'has to be accepted as the national religion'. Today this assertion might have to be qualified but, by and large, it remains true. It was so in any event throughout the nineteenth century and the first third of the twentieth. 'Our country is a Christian republic,' said S. M. Campbell in 1867, 'and our Christianity is of the Protestant type.' He added, with a gracious air, that 'the non-Christians and those people who call themselves Christians but are not Protestants, who find this arrangement displeasing, have only to try their luck elsewhere'.

Statistics prove that the U.S.A. is a Protestant country; if further proof were needed it would arise from a study of the moral and spiritual climate, as well as the customs and traditions. In 1953 out of 94·8 million Americans with religious affiliations 55·8 million declared themselves to be Protestants—some 60 per cent. But this figure does not give a true picture of the place taken by Protestants in American life, for among those who were not affiliated to any religion the majority were Protestants; on the other hand the majority of Catholics were all duly inscribed on their Church registers. Furthermore the way of life indicates this, for Protestantism has stamped itself on American life and thought. Society has a religious background, this springing from the tents of Calvin at Geneva. On a 10-cent piece is the inscription: 'In God We Trust'. The most important of all national holidays is Thanksgiving Day. Congress has a special room where Senators and Representatives may meditate, in the manner of the Quaker meetings. At Conventions, where each party nominates its candidate for the Presidency, a pastor pronounces a religious discourse with the object of calling down divine blessing on the elected member of the party. The Bible is present everywhere: in hotel bedrooms, where it is deposited by members of the pious society known as the Gideons; in the civil registers, where there are many Rubens, Benjamins, Ruths and Deborahs; in the names of localities, Bethlehem being found in six states, along with Jerusalem, Canaan, Nazareth, Jericho; in the speeches of politicians; and in newspaper articles, where quotations from the Bible abound. Everything conspires to create a distinctly Protestant atmosphere; at any rate, certainly a non-secular atmosphere.

The State itself is religious, its background Protestant. In nearly all the states of the Union the Constitution opens with an invocation to God. The President-Elect has to swear oath on the Bible. Theoretically there is no constitutional clause against anyone becoming president whatever his religious convictions, but in point of fact thirty-three presidents have been Protestants. It was necessary to await our own age before the Catholic President Kennedy came to power; his successor, President Johnson, is a Protestant, a member of the Church of the Disciples of Christ. Every president and a great number of public men have invoked divine authority to justify their actions, internally as well as internationally. 'Without Protestantism', said Siegfried, 'President Wilson is incomprehensible.' The Bible has been cited many times to justify the prohibition of alcohol.

This State, where God is invoked unceasingly and whose rulers flatter themselves that they are devout members of a Church, is none the less a secular State. Politics and religion are kept strictly apart in principle, at least, for it would not be difficult to cite instances where this 'neutral' State was partial to Protestants, and we are well aware of the effect which the Protestant sectarianism of President Wilson had on the destinies of Europe at Versailles. But it is no less true that the principle of the separation of Church and State, as well as complete religious liberty, is basic to the U.S.A. and has been ever since its beginnings. The Constitution had hardly been adopted when the legislators, considering that not enough protection had been accorded to individual liberties, incorporated amendments in the Bill of Rights. The first amendment stated that: 'Congress shall make no law respecting the establishing of religion or prohibit the free exercise thereof.' The Protestant Churches, totally separated from the State, were thus never to bring into question their relations with the authorities, as was the case with all European countries dominated by Protestants. Always they have felt free, but equally they have never counted for help on other than themselves. All the Churches which emerged from the Reformation, even including the most outlandish sects, have been able to expand and develop in the Union in absolute freedom. Only competition has provided a motivation to advance, just as it has entailed risks.

9. Four Questions Confronting American Protestantism

The events which have shaped American Protestantism during the last two centuries, giving it the aspect which we can now see, were religious events. At the threshold of the modern world the most significant event was the Revival,[1] a descendant of that other revival of the eighteenth century, which stirred so many consciences throughout the first third of the nineteenth century. Among other consequences, new tendencies appeared amidst the older Churches, leading to dissident groups such as the Disciples of Christ, founded in 1830 by Presbyterians hostile to the rigidity of the institutional and administrative framework of their Church, and by Baptists with Methodist principles at heart. But also, as occurred in nearly all the older Protestant groups, without taking into account the barriers which were erected between them by the organization of the Churches, the revival contributed to the faithful of each Church the idea that these barriers were not insurmountable, and that personal salvation was not dependent upon this or that creed. Under slightly different forms, the revivalist movement got under way in two stages with the inevitable reactions. Today many observers are asking themselves whether the most important issue for the future of American Protestantism is not the appearance and success, when bolstered up by new revivals, of those movements which some disdainfully qualify as 'sects', whose faith, charismatic and resolutely 'spiritual', is modifying the physiognomy of American religious life.

This spiritual ferment has not been the sole determinant in the history of the American Protestant Churches. They have been faced with problems which, in themselves, have nothing religious about them, but which, on the religious plane as well, have required solutions. And from the solutions decided on, other consequences followed, all very important for American Protestantism. The first problem was that of what was called the 'Frontier'. As everyone knows, soon after they had achieved their independence the young United States, formerly grouped along the Atlantic coast, were to push inland, towards the Mississippi and its immense basin, to the far west, and thence to the Rockies and the Pacific: the drive west, a legendary epoch so dear to movie audiences of 'Western' films. The conquest of the continent was not carried out in any systematic manner, still less administratively, the government confining itself to granting land to those who were willing to work it as pioneers. Adventurers of every nationality set off to conquer the unknown, either singly or in groups,

[1] See Chapter III, section 1.

driven by the desire to take over lands which hitherto had belonged to no one; or, still more urgently, in pursuit of gold. Against them were the Indians, the celebrated Redskins of Fenimore Cooper, now hostile, now peaceful and finally intermixing with the colonists. All this was to make up a race apart, whose conditions of life and climate marked it with strongly individual features. Moving from east to west, the Frontier, like a wave, swept across the continent between the civilized east and the ocean of the unknown Pacific coast, leaving in its wake a new people, the American people.

The Protestants, then installed along the east coast, soon realized that if left to its own devices the Frontier would soon degenerate into something barbaric. It was therefore indispensable to send evangelists. But in contrast to the Catholics who, though spread all over the Union in small groups, were working actively to convert the natives and the pioneers, the official Protestant Churches, well established as they were, had not attempted anything like this; the question of the Frontier did not interest them greatly.

To plunge into the Wild West among the badmen and the savage Red Indians, carrying the Word of God which He reserved exclusively for the elect, appeared laughable to the distinguished Presbyterians and Congregationalists of the *Mayflower*, and just as much so to Anglicans, now become Episcopalians. It was the Baptists and the Methodists who took on the job, both more or less representing the religion of the poor and disinherited. In any event it was not stone temples nor ecclesiastical institutions which commanded their attention. Their faith, renewed by the revival, was a personal, internal and demanding faith. To face up to the conditions reigning on the Frontier they remodelled their organization, adapting it to changing situations. The Disciples of Christ, as soon as they were organized, set off likewise to carry the Word to the men of the Frontier. It was now the heroic age of the itinerant preachers who went from camp to camp on their horses, carrying to the adventurers and to the Redskins the Good Word, an often rudimentary Gospel, scarcely theological, but which touched the hearts of those tough populations. This intimate association of the new America with certain forms of Protestantism was to have very important results, and these can be seen still in the religious structure of the U.S.A. There was a change in the balance of power of the various Churches. At the end of the colonial era the Congregationalists and the Presbyterians were first and second respectively in the list of Protestant Churches in both number and influence. In 1850 the Methodists were in the lead, followed by the Baptists and the Disciples of Christ, not twenty years old. Religion itself took on a different guise. The puritans saw it as a communal activity where everything was under God's hand and allowed individual theological views where each could come to God in his own way. Free inquiry thus returned to its former rights, and all official formularies, institutions and liturgy lost their value. Along the Frontier more importance was attached to acts, to a virtuous attitude, than to dogma and ecclesiastical discipline. Here was one of the great features of American Protestantism.

Another trait was etched in by the solution which was found for the second great question which history set the Protestant Churches: that of the immigrants. Between 1790 and 1840 18 million Europeans arrived in the U.S.A., and from 1840 to 1890 some 9 million. Thereafter the tide of immigrants declined, but still remained considerable until the outbreak of the First World War. Legislation during the years 1920 to 1930 stopped it. For a long time immigrants had been mostly Protestants. They ceased to be in the majority around 1840, when the potato famine of 1845 in Ireland drove hundreds of thousands of Irish from their homeland. Italy and Germany also sent Catholics. This rapid change in the balance of forces, brought about by the changes of origin of the immigrants themselves, made the Catholic percentage rise and brought about little by little a change in the balance between Churches, a decline in Protestant numbers compared with those of the Catholics, a feature which is so obvious today.

At the same time, within Protestantism itself, there was a new difficulty. The immigrants belonged to none of the Churches installed in America. Even if they had been adherents of one or other of the European mother Churches they had their own peculiar national characteristics.

They sought to preserve these national characteristics in their adopted country by remaining in their own national groups. Thus communities of Germans, Dutch and Scandinavians were built up, and so consequently their Churches were set up there too. Even when they belonged to the same confession of faith the immigrants from different countries did not mix, and still less did they join up with the Protestant masses. The most striking case was that of the Germans, who brought with them their own national Churches. The feelings of common origins were so strong that some German-speaking Reformed Churches and Lutheran Churches envisaged the possibility of union and the setting up of a university together, while at the same time they remained apart from the other Reformed Churches or other Lutheran Churches. If this splitting process had continued one wonders what would have become of the American national image.

In fact this delicate question was solved by the way of life itself rather than by any human decisions. Among the Catholics, however, it was much more serious, for it threatened the unity of their Church itself. It was solved by the categorical refusal to split up along ethnic lines. The German Cahensly was condemned, there were the patient efforts of Cardinal Gibbons, and these measures led the way to a complete merger.[1] Among the Protestants this was not possible. But it was soon noted that among the second generation of immigrants there was one overriding desire—to Americanize themselves as soon as possible, giving up their national language and many national practices. Some of them abandoned their national Churches to join others more American and with greater prestige. But the third generation, Americanized in their way of life and in their language, saw in reverting to their origins, to their national Church, a way of preserving their individuality and not resembling all the others. So there survived German, Dutch and Scandinavian Churches, all seemingly cast in the same mould, but which nevertheless accentuated the slightest differences in dogma or liturgy as a form of defence and opposition. The result was quite the reverse from that of the old Frontier days: the older Churches from Europe tended to split up into watertight units, whereas movements previously regarded with suspicion by the Established Churches, and considered as sects of a sort, now became true Churches.

In 1860 American Protestantism seemed to be more or less set in its main lines, but it was then to meet two new problems which were to change it fundamentally. Neither of these has been resolved, and both weigh on the future of all Churches. The tragedy of the Civil War (1861–5), in which the U.S.A. achieved unity only at the price of much blood and many tears, suddenly revealed to American opinion that there was a Negro question, and that this was linked to yet another, less explicitly formulated but more serious still, the hidden opposition between North and South. The Negro question had been there of course ever since the first slaves arrived to cut sugar-cane. They had proliferated considerably, and now constituted a large slice of the population, living cheek by jowl with the whites. The Churches were very little preoccupied with the Negro slaves; not even, one must admit sadly, the Catholic Church, so active in other missionary fields. The Baptists, alone or almost alone at first, and then the Methodists, seriously concerned themselves with those abandoned folks. So deeply did they penetrate among the Negroes that today 65 per cent of the latter are Baptists, 22 per cent Methodists; all other denominations, including the Catholics, share the remaining 13 per cent.

During the colonial era, and at the commencement of independence, there were very few Churches which were exclusively Negro. In the South several big landowners encouraged their workers to found their own Churches, hoping thereby to inculcate a peaceful attitude among them with the promise of a better hereafter. Mostly the Negro workers attended services at the same time as their white masters, peacefully

[1] *A Fight for God*, Chapter X, section 4.

herded at the back of the church. The wish to keep the white race pure and to maintain the correct social hierarchies worked together to establish segregation as a general principle. In 1787, in Philadelphia, one incident demonstrated the depth of these feelings. A freed slave, Richard Allen, famous for his extraordinary gifts as a preacher, had been invited by the elders of the Methodist Church to speak from the pulpit. His sermon was a brilliant success. But some time later, when he came to worship in the same church in which he had preached, he sat in the pews near the front and the whites attacked him and drove him from the church. This was enough for Allen to decide to quit the white Methodist Church, and in 1816 he founded the African Episcopal Methodist Church, today a powerful organization.

The problem became still more serious after the Civil War. Slavery was indeed abolished on 20th January 1865, but at the same time there were many whites who felt that one of their vital safeguards had been lost. The constitutional articles were often violated, especially in the South. White defence organizations sprang up, like the Ku-Klux-Klan in 1866. The segregationist current became a torrent. The consequences for the Protestant Churches were serious. The emancipated slaves set up their own Churches, whose success was considerable. In 1958 more than 75 per cent of the 15 million Negroes enumerated declared their adherence to one or other of them. But in the white Churches, where Negroes were admitted, these numbered only 1 per cent. So there was a total racial cleavage between white and black Churches despite the protests of many ecclesiastical leaders, despite the generous efforts made by many organizations led by the whites: the Federation of the Churches of Christ, the Y.M.C.A. and the Christian Students' Federation.

The zeal which the Negroes show for their Churches has something disquieting about it. In itself such fidelity is admirable: a recent poll revealed that 96 per cent of Negroes who belonged to a Church stated that they were regular attendants, that 49 per cent of them went once a week. It means that the Church, their Church, represents for these descendants of the slaves, these people who still feel despised, something irreplaceable, something unique; the link through which they feel attached to the world of men, in which they have the right of expression and freedom to face their Creator. In the Bible they found much that reminded them of their plight, many verses which gave them courage. The refrains of the famous Negro spirituals [1] told them that an oppressed people had once conquered the Promised Land, that Daniel had been saved from the lions, that David had slain Goliath. All this was calculated to imbue them with supernatural hopes: the Promised Land was the paradise where, as in the famous film, the Good Lord

[1] See Chapter III, section 18.

would lead the humble Negroes towards his Green Pastures. When the moment came and the millions of blacks acquired confidence in their strength and demanded not only freedom, often theoretical and illusory, but true equality, it would need only a minimal modification for this spiritual hope to become part and parcel of political aspirations. The black Churches supplied the desegregationist movement with one of its most active leaders, the famous Baptist pastor Martin Luther King, Nobel Prize winner, a man of faith, uplifter of masses, for whom religion is one and the same thing as the justice which he demands for his people.

The Negro question has been a very serious one for the American Churches. Not only has it speeded up the process of fragmentation which, in itself, in the Protestant world, has no great importance, but it has brought about a kind of distortion within the white Churches themselves. Some, such as the Episcopalians and the Methodists, have taken a courageous stand against segregation, but the instructions of the leaders of these Churches are now always obeyed. In the South the majority of white Protestants remain hostile to racial integration, the pastors themselves resisting it. In the North opinion is against segregation and is determined to have done with it. The great Protestant theologian Reinhold Niebuhr has not hesitated to face the fact that in the 'Black Revolution' lies the reason for the astonishing upsurge in Black Catholicism, rising in ten years from 350,000 to 700,000 adherents. Nor must we forget that the increases in coloured adherents to the Pentecostal-type sects, such as the Sanctified, the Lord's Faithful, the Friends of Christ and some fifty more—all have the same reason. Finally, and still more serious (André Siegfried's opinion still holds good, perhaps even more so after forty years), in affirming their superiority over the blacks, in proclaiming their disdain of the blacks, far too many Christians have lost not only the sense of human values which the U.S.A. hold high in their national life, but also the consciousness of precepts without which there is no Christianity. Those precepts were jeopardized at the same time by another fact—the social transformation of the U.S.A. Prior to 1865, 85 per cent of the population was rural, in 1900 it was still 60 per cent, in 1920 it was no more than half, and today it is scarcely a third. This rapid urbanization is of course the result of the industrial age and of the prodigious expansion which the U.S.A. has undergone during the last hundred years, accelerated even more by two world wars. The fabric of society was profoundly modified: the towns saw a massive growth of working classes quite different from the old order. Social pressures no longer weighed heavy upon agricultural labourers in the east, white and black, nor upon the colonists of the Frontier areas, but upon the mass of workers in the towns, subjected to Lassalle's brazen law of wages paid by the 'robber barons'. The U.S.A. had ignored political revolution, but it was faced with technical revolution. At first social problems had to be dealt with, and, when these had been largely solved by the general rise in wealth of the population, there arose a moral problem, for this prosperity entailed profound changes in outlook.

The Churches found conditions vastly different from those in which they had first been established. Formerly they were occupied with small towns and villages of a few thousand people; now they faced industrial populations in which all trace of social structure had vanished, where every race and every nationality were intermixed.

The challenge of this new urban frontier found the Churches in no condition to meet it. The older Churches, used to their settled social structure, had not the slightest idea how to reach the masses of immigrants and rootless ex-rural populations now swarming in the ever-growing cities. Like Methodism, which had so brilliantly succeeded in the Frontier days, they were now comfortably settled in middle-class routine. The itinerant preacher of the Wild West camps had no counterpart in the little mining suburbs. The more prosperity increased, the more the old movements transformed themselves into bourgeois Churches, where the accent was on individual piety without much thought of communal responsibility. American Protestantism thus ignored the social problem just as European Catholicism did, and one could say of it, as Pius XI was to say of the Catholic Church, that it had 'lost the working classes'. In 1898 a pastor, the Reverend Francis Perry, questioning workers as to the reasons for their turning away from the Churches, was told: 'Because my comrades and I have come to think of the Church and the clergy as apologists and as defenders of the harm which is being done to the interests of the people'; and: 'The eloquence of theologians militates against the practical efforts of the workers themselves to get out of the mess they are in.' A Socialist in Europe would not have put it in any other way.

In face of this obvious danger the Protestant Churches attempted to set up a form of 'social Protestantism',[1] similar to that which was developing in Germany and Britain. It is a curious fact, but the oldest and most firmly established Churches were the first to undertake this —Presbyterians, Congregationalists and Episcopalians. Very soon, however, all denominations were involved; when the Federal Council of Churches was founded in 1908, representing twenty-five denominations, one of its main tasks was to tackle the social question. Theoreticians such as George D. Herron and Walter Rauschenbusch worked to adapt Protestant individualism so that a message of social redemption would emerge. A type of social evangelism—the social gospel— penetrated more or less all the religious groups, giving American Protestantism one of its most striking traits.

[1] See Chapter III, section 8.

Has the result been satisfactory? Has the dechristianization of the urban masses been halted? It does not seem so. Statistics show that two-fifths of Americans dispense with Churches, and that belonging to one particular Church is often merely nominal. Religious affiliation is on the upswing today, but this is probably due to reasons of conformity, the social advancement of the worker, who has now become a middle-class citizen, being signalized by his inscription on the registers of this or that Church. For the rest, it seems that all Protestant Churches are in a state of virtual powerlessness before the problem of the 'urban-industrial frontier'. The great movements which animate the consciences of the urban masses are not those of the organized Churches. The revivals that have influenced them are the work of individuals, usually outside any Church—the day before yesterday it was Dwight L. Moody, yesterday it was Billy Sunday, today it is Billy Graham. And here again we find Baptists at work in many different forms, their simple theology being easily assimilated by ordinary people; and also the sectarian movements, which were started in America at the moment when industrial civilization was being created—Seventh Day Adventists, Jehovah's Witnesses, Pentecostals. All of these have great success in the poorer quarters of the big cities, whereas they have little appeal to the middle classes, well established in their organized Churches. To the fourth question, set to the Protestants by the Sphinx of History, there is as yet no answer.

10. THE RELIGION OF THE AMERICANS

In recalling the historical evolution of American Protestantism, one can see to what extent there were forces at work contributing to splitting and fragmentation. In effect there were its origins, the climate with its insistence on liberty in which the Union was formed and grew, the revivals, the changes imposed by the Frontier, industrial development, the Negro question, the social question, all of which tended to exacerbate the tendency to division. Thus it is that the U.S.A. is the country where 'denominations' are the most numerous, and, despite repeated efforts at concentration and consolidation, new divisions appear unceasingly—it is hard to see what other country could beat their record.

In 1930 the highest record was reached: there were 263 religious denominations listed in the U.S.A. Of these 250 were Protestant. But official statisticians did not presume even then to have included all the sects, as indefinite in outline as they were ephemeral in life, which flourished unendingly among the Negroes. Here we have a religious pluralism pushed to extremes, astonishing enough for Europeans, even Protestants. This shows no sign of abating: when the Oak Ridge atomic plant city was being built the inhabitants were promised that every creed would have its place of worship; it was found that the minimum number of churches which would satisfy this promise was thirty-seven (for thirty thousand adherents).

However, this fragmentation should not lead us into any false views; let us once again remind the reader that, as has been said already concerning Protestant divisions, statistics and official enumerations do not make much sense in themselves. It seems a little odd to include in the same list of religious denominations the Roman Catholic Church, with its 40 million adherents in 1958, and a tiny Pentecostal Negro sect with scarcely five thousand! Among the Protestant groups the seven largest alone represent more than nine-tenths of American Protestantism, the Baptists leading with 23 million, the Methodists next with 16 million, then the Lutherans with $8\frac{1}{2}$ million, the Presbyterians with $6\frac{1}{2}$ million, with the Episcopalians and the Disciples of Christ, plus the Pentecostal movements, making up the rest. To the previous observation we must hasten to add another, in the opposite sense— that a designation such as 'Lutheran' covers in fact eleven Churches, 'Methodist' at least twelve, and that how many varieties of Pentecostal movements there are is virtually unknown.

In spite of this diversity—or perhaps because of it—the Americans evince the need to belong officially to a Church. In the beginning it was not so; in 1800 only 10 per cent of the Union's Protestant citizens appeared on the census forms as belonging to this or that Church; in 1900, it was 32 per cent, while today it is 64 per cent, and the percentage is always increasing. In reality it is more and more essential to belong to a religious denomination in American society if only to establish oneself socially. In 1953, when General Eisenhower entered the White House, he carried out a duty which, although while commanding the armies in Europe had not seemed to him to be essential, became vital before he could govern the U.S.A.—he had himself baptized and inscribed on the registers of the Presbyterian Church. This changing way of life corresponded to a tendency of Churches to become more organized, and figures prove that a solid framework increases the number of adherents. This has the effect of inducing even those least favourable to ecclesiastical organization to adopt one, even the Baptists!

This has given rise to a compartmentalization of social life, which has been superimposed on religious compartmentalization, just as though each of the different categories of Protestantism corresponded, on the spiritual plane, with a particular social or ethnic group. André Siegfried has already mentioned this; and things have not changed greatly since 1926. The Baptists continue to recruit their adherents among the lower classes, both whites and blacks, from the countryside and from the smaller towns; the Methodists, who are no longer the humble ones of their modest beginnings, among the 'well-to-do shop-keepers whose business has been blessed by God'; the Episcopalians, among the well-heeled older wealthy families, proud of having had George Washington and Franklin Roosevelt as their equals; the Congregationalists and the Presbyterians, among the cultivated and puritan aristocracy of the *Mayflower* era; and the Quakers always have many wealthy business men in their ranks. There is then not simply a juxtaposition of denominations, but a superimposition, depending on the social scale.

Yet in face of these divisive forces, others have arisen, especially since the beginning of the twentieth century, all driving towards concentration. On a practical plane, the American reconciles his individualism with his taste for mass action through political federalism and the organization of cartels. So too on the religious plane. It is quite often said that if the Churches wish to become efficient they have only to organize themselves along the lines of big business, vertically and horizontally. This spirit was demonstrated by the Americans at the World Council meetings at Lund and Evanston, much to the surprise of European Protestants, more concerned with theology. . . . The tendency towards union has always started within the larger denominations. The Lutherans, the Baptists and the Methodists have all set up federations, which, whether loosely knit or not, have all gathered in a certain number of Churches; in some cases even mergers were carried out, as in 1939 between three Methodist Churches. There has also been *rapprochement* between Churches of different creeds; in 1908 the Federal Council of Churches was founded, in which twenty-five great denominations were represented, accounting for two-thirds of all American Protestants. More and more it appears that the search is on for 'the reality which unites, not the shibboleth which separates'. Thus older organizations such as the Foreign Missions Conference (1893), the Home Missions Council (1908), the Missionary Education Movement and others have joined together in the National Council of the Churches of Christ, to which the Federal Council belongs, and which in effect it controls. This federalist tendency is all part of the American make-up, though it seems still to be insufficient to many, and there is a move towards a still more radical inter-Church union as was proposed in 1960 by the theologian Eugene Carson Blake to the Presbyterian, Episcopalian and Methodist Churches, and to the United Churches of Christ. This move may considerably modify American Protestantism, and even world Protestantism also. There are those who say that it would succeed more quickly if all the denominations had not top-heavy administrations providing a living for innumerable clergy, to say nothing of hierarchies jealous of their rights.

Not everything has been said concerning American Protestantism and its complexity unless mention is made of another matter, more spritual in content than the dialectics of divisiveness. For the U.S.A., engaged as it is in the race towards modernity, with all its attractions and its dangers, has been a special terrain for the great battle between the two tendencies which, in the twentieth century, have commanded Christian consciences; one accepting modern thought, the other rejecting it. What is elsewhere called modernism or Protestant liberalism has split the Americans fundamentally, and the split can still be seen today. On the one hand, what is called orthodoxy in European Protestantism has come to be known in the U.S.A. as Fundamentalism, 'a mixture of strict orthodoxy and pietism', says Fr Tavard, where formulations of faith are brief, where all the dogmas of the Reformation, or those which are imagined as being such, are jealously retained. Fundamentalism stands for 'the religion of the fathers', rejects all scientific hypotheses when these are not reconcilable with the letter of the Scriptures and proclaims that the Bible's lightest word is truth. It was the Fundamentalists who, in 1925, opposed the teaching of the theory of evolution in the schools of Tennessee and four other states. During the court case which followed, the former Secretary of State Bryan, a convinced Fundamentalist, proclaimed that he firmly believed in the story of Jonah and the whale. Faced with this integritism, liberalism took on all sorts of shades, from the wish to widen the religious framework the better to adapt it to modern conditions, through a type of Protestant 'modernism', to a spiritual humanism in which every positive creed founders. The gulf between the two tendencies is present both outside and inside the Churches—the Baptists, for instance, are in the main Fundamentalists—running more or less along the dividing line between the North and the South, the South being inclined towards Fundamentalism, the North towards liberalism.

Taking into account all these different divisions, one question springs to mind: 'Is there, nevertheless, an American Protestantism?' Yes, there is. There may be a wide gap between a Southern Baptist and a New England Presbyterian, but there are none the less many common points, transcending all their differences. The most obvious one is fidelity to the Bible, which we have seen is an essential element in Protestantism, and the importance of which in American life we have also seen. Even in those circles where religious practice is almost nil, there is an almost fetish devotion, evidenced in a thousand little ways, towards the Holy Book. Another trait common to all forms of American Protestantism is its puritan aspect; this spring from its origins, the greater part of the pioneers who founded the Churches having been strongly marked with puritanism. This has declined during the twentieth century, but it is far from having disappeared altogether. It is puritanism that imposes a moralistic principle, to which there are many exceptions in practice but which is still seen in such customs as the 'Sunday dinner',[1] and in administrative measures which astound a European.[2] This type of Yankee Protestantism carries the conviction that it has the benefit of divine approval and that it is, in all its various aspects, the highest form of Christianity. On this plane the predestination of Calvin has not been forgotten. Its most obvious application lies in the political field: Protestantism and freedom—they mean the same thing. Ralph Barton Perry, professor at Harvard University, has devoted himself for many years in lectures, and recently (1952) in a substantial book, to showing that 'puritanism and democracy' are substantially associated. All Protestants in the U.S.A. are convinced that it is because of their faith that they have the most perfect system of government in the world, according to Senator La Follette. They also believe that this same faith demands that they 'give an example of devotion to the great principles of justice which spring from the revelations of the Holy Scriptures', as President Wilson was so fond of saying; to fail in this would be to commit a mortal sin. In a word, the Protestant faith goes hand in hand with national pride, which it sustains, and justifies the assumption, at the cost of many great sacrifices, of the leadership of the world.

One of the less happy consequences of this conviction has been the hostility shown to all heterodoxy, especially Catholic. Anti-Catholicism has been, until quite recently, one of the most marked traits of all forms of American Protestantism. It comes out in different degrees, less virulent in some cases than in others, sometimes reaching brutality, but inspiring all who come in contact with it with a profound detestation of Catholicism. All average Protestants are agreed that they are against the Pope, whom John Adams, Washington's successor in the White House, referred to as an 'ecclesiastical tyrant'; against the Vatican, considered as the most redoubtable of the enemies of liberty and against Roman Catholic 'idolatry'. It was not so long ago that the American Legion opposed the hanging of the Stars and Stripes in a Catholic Church. And when, in 1928, the Catholic Alfred Smith was running for the presidency, the cry went up: 'Keep the Pope out of the White House!' which was pleasing to Protestant ears. It is true that this cry came from the Imperial Grand Wizard of the Ku-Klux-Klan, a

---

[1] According to the strict rule of Sunday rest the catering trade should suspend its activity on that day, but the religious law is accommodated by serving single meals at double price in restaurants.

[2] The puritan U.S.A. invented strip-tease, yet their hotels will not receive unmarried couples.

clandestine association founded in 1866 for the purpose of 'defending the white race against the black', which at the time of its resurrection in 1915 added to its other aims that of fighting against the progress of Catholicism.

American Protestantism presents a united front even more as regards its external aspects than in more fundamental points. These are so constant that for a non-American it is almost impossible to distinguish denominations from their external appearance. All employ the same methods to attract adherents, using publicity media such as the radio and television wherein this or that famous preacher is to conduct the service. A type of commercial competition is carried on between Churches. They are in favour of tangible achievements, comfortable places of worship and well-equipped meeting rooms. Powerful denominations pay for a well-heeled clergy, who drive about in large cars; it is moreover an obligation that they should if they are not to be discredited. Only the more recent sects present a more modest appearance: elsewhere one is inclined to the view that the Churches are too easily persuaded that they have domesticated Mammon. . . .

All this does not mean that there are not some good sides to the picture. There is generosity. One hundred million Americans each contribute 50 dollars annually to the needs of their religious community. Enormous funds are set aside for the building of churches; in 1958 this reached a total of 500 million dollars. On average there is one church for every four hundred white adherents and one for every two hundred black adherents, and another twelve are built every week. The millionaires, when their fortunes were finally made, all made haste to help their Churches: Jay Gould, Rockefeller, Armour, Vanderbilt. In 1956 John D. Rockefeller junior gave away 10 million dollars for the development of Protestant seminaries all over the Union. The total separation of Church and State has meant that the Churches can count only on their adherents, not only for the clergy's stipends, but also for the upkeep of their seminaries, schools, hospitals and universities. It is one of the glories of all believers in the U.S.A.—whether they are Catholic or Jewish or Protestant—that they are for the most part responsible for the finance needed for all these institutions. Protestant missions in heathen regions also benefit from this generosity. At least half of these throughout the world are kept going with American money; at the present time there is an enormous effort being undertaken in South America. To this must be added the funds for missionary work provided through the generosity of adherents to their Churches; there is not one Church, however small, which does not possess its own publications; the bigger denominations control some of those which are most read; in 1958 there were more than forty thousand religious broadcasts on radio and television; the American

Bible Society distributes 15 million Bibles in 228 languages or dialects throughout the world.

These achievements can be accounted for by one quality which the Americans, a race of pioneers and dynamists, have always placed high on their list: efficiency. And no one would deny that the American Churches are efficient. But is this not in itself a danger? It became ever more evident as America grew industrially and technically. A change took place in the older Protestantism. Emphasis was no longer laid on piety, on the search for a relationship with God, but upon the values inherent in action. Calvin appeared to justify this evolution, for his doctrine pointed to material success as a sign of divine election. Christ, in this perspective, is no longer the victim offered as redemption, but becomes the man of greatest virtue, the conqueror of souls, a super-man who is held up as a model. 'If you would have power, ask it from Christ!' cried a Boston preacher. And Siegfried assures us that 'American literature has often delineated a businessman Christ, a journalist or trade unionist Christ'. One is left wondering what remains of the God incarnated for the salvation of the world, of the Man suffering, of the victim and redeemer, in all these absurd images. The agony of the sinner, the feeling of tragedy in life, which are elements of the grandeur of the Reformed faith, give place to sickly optimism. In 1847 Bushell and Ward Beecher based the whole of religious life upon the certitude of the greatness of divine love; later the 'universalist' sect was to teach that every soul would be saved. The pietist revivalists reacted against such deformations of the faith. But in our own day the famous Billy Graham also exudes optimism: one of his sermons is entitled 'The Winning Life'.

Even the pietists, the revivalists, the fundamentalists all agreed with the other denominations in accepting another step along the road which still further distanced American Protestantism from its dog-matic bases. The logical consequence of this Rousseau-type of thought was that the real justification for religion is to christianize society so that the natural goodness of man may be brought forth. Its teaching then was to emphasize the improvement in the life of society, the practice of civic virtues and the sense of responsibility towards the human community. Christianity was no longer a doctrinal organism, still less a code of rules as the puritans still believed, but a mere attitude of conscience faced with all the problems of social life. Under these circumstances there was no mystery as to what happened to faith. In 1897 the Protestant paper *Arena* wrote: 'The creeds collapse, actions take their place. The religion of the future lays more emphasis on life than on dogma.' In the battle for success, in sum, it will be relegated to the role of umpire or of Good Samaritan. One might as well say that all creeds are the same. 'Our government has no sense unless it is founded on a deeply felt religious faith, though it matters little what faith this be,' declared General Eisenhower.[1]

Who benefits from this break-up of Protestantism, this Protestantism which has been called 'as soft as butter'? Not the Established Churches, seemingly interchangeable; one could leave one to enter another for any haphazard reason, because this one is considered better than that one, or because the place of worship is a little closer to one's home. Protestantism itself loses because of this, and all observers are agreed that from the twenties onwards there was a general decline, both in Church affiliations and in practice as well as in church-building. Concrete materialism, that which appears not as a denial of God but as unconscious elimination of Him from all aspects of life, has continued to make progress, even though it has been a thousand times denounced from the pulpit. 'Our faith today is more that of scientism, rationalism, materialism than of Christianity,' writes the Methodist Hervey Seifert. 'We owe our real allegiance to new cars and fashionable dress, more than to the Sermon on the Mount.' According to Will Herberg, this process has already had one further result, which marks the fall of Protestantism from its exclusive place as a national religion; for the American of today Protestantism, Catholicism and Judaism are 'three aspects of the same spiritual values, which American democracy is supposed to represent'.[2]

To counter this disintegration of true Protestantism into activism and middle-class civism, there has been a reaction, similar to that which we can see in European Protestantism; it came late—Karl Barth has been studied seriously only for a short time now—but it is progressing at a regular pace. Liberal Protestantism and the social gospel have retained their importance, though they are declining, and there are indisputable signs of a religious renaissance. Let us note three of these. Since the end of the Second World War there has been a theological revival. Teaching in seminaries has veered away from exegesis and history and is now increasingly devoted to courses and lectures for the laity, covering a theology which is influenced by Karl Barth and Kierkegaard, the chief exponents being Reinhold Niebuhr and Paul Tillich. There has also been an evolution in both the conception and practice of worship, especially marked in the traditional Churches, Lutheran and Episcopalian, with the liturgical revival. This has brought about, fairly generally, the restoration of Holy Communion as a central feature of worship, whereas in many Churches it had been relegated to an unimportant place in favour of the ministry of the Word —the sacrament being celebrated only once or twice a year. Finally, there has been an increasing emphasis on missionary activity during

---

[1] The New York Times, 23rd December 1952.
[2] Protestants, Catholics, Israelites, 1955.

the past twenty years. This is shown in several ways: a renaissance of evangelism, which can be likened to a Revival, where emphasis is laid on an inner change rather than on right conduct, a form of evangelism in which Billy Graham, despite his evident activism, is the most note-worthy representative; a search for new methods of converting souls, methods often inspired by those which are used by Protestants and Catholics in Europe; community and proletarian parishes; itinerant and worker missions. Finally, there has been an impressive upsurge of new Churches and sects, charismatic in character, where the prime objective is spiritual conquest hand in hand with true fraternal feeling. This upsurge has helped the Pentecostal movement to reach the highest ranks in the Protestant world among the seven chief denominations.

After the decline between 1920 and 1940, American Protestantism has now recovered. During and after the Second World War there was an astonishing religious revival; Catholicism and to some extent Judaism also benefited. The causes were complex: they range perhaps from man's existentialist anguish faced with the dangers of atomic destruction to the desire already mentioned of scaling the social ladder by becoming an adherent of a Church, and perhaps also to the increase of leisure. In 1940 50·7 per cent of the population aged over fourteen years were members of a Church; in 1958 the figure was more than 65 per cent. In 1958 251 religious denominations had 109,557,741 adherents. A Gallup poll indicated that on a given Sunday 47 per cent of adults had taken part in a religious service and 95 per cent of these declared their belief in God. The degree of interest in religious matters is considerable; there is proof of this in the ever-increasing flow of books, reviews and religious journals. It is natural that Protestantism should take advantage of this movement, which, however, has a keen rival in the Catholic Church. The latter has the advantage of her serenity in faith, her long traditions, her transcendance as opposed to the narrowness of particularisms, her generous firmness in the matter of racial problems, her unswerving intransigence with regard to Communism and the prestige she derives from her intellectual and political leaders. In 1958 61,504,669 Americans declared themselves Protestants. The future will show if this strong and vigorous Pro-testantism will continue to increase and grow, spurred on by Catholic rivalry. It will also become evident in what measure it has been able to take the right road, which all its sons in each of the 241 denominations can follow together, or whether it will not split in two, with the driving Protestantism of the fundamentalists, the pietists and the members of the younger sects on one side and, on the other, that type of moralizing civism characterized by the vague wish to enter into communication with higher things, which so many take to be the 'religion of the Americans'.

11. The Great Era of the Protestant Missions

While it was expanding on American territory, Protestantism was associated with British expansion in what was to be the Empire and later the Commonwealth. There it took on a variety of forms, not unlike those observed in the U.S.A. It is not there, however, that we must look for the second great feature of Protestant expansion, but rather in the astonishing spread of missionary activity in non-Christian countries during a period of 150 years. This brings us to a subject deserving of our highest admiration. Catholics, who are so badly versed in even their own missionary history, are entirely ignorant of the work accomplished by their separated brethren in this field. They have heard only of certain unpleasant incidents, in which the weaknesses or mediocrities which are part of human nature become a ready excuse for crying scandal upon the divisions among Christians. But how many of them have any idea of the greatness of soul, the true spirit of faith which drove these pastors, often accompanied by young wives, into the adventure of missionary work, beset with dangers and suffering? To look upon them as irksome competitors, without recognizing the love of Christ in them, would be to traduce that very love.

The Protestants were slow to awake to missionary duties. The leaders of the Reformation, from Luther onwards, had, in general, imperfectly understood the obligation to go forth and preach to all nations. There were even theological arguments put forward against missionary work: the era of apostolic expansion being over, none could presume to reopen it; God, who had pre-destined all men, had willed that the heathen should be rebels. Theodore Beza said that 'the evangelization of those people must be left to those grasshoppers thrown up from Hell who hypocritically flaunt the name of Jesus'. Only Bucer, among the first generation of reformers, was of a contrary opinion. But at the beginning of the seventeenth century several thinkers, mostly Dutch, had formulated the outlines of missionary theology. Various attempts were made by the Frenchmen Villegagnon and Jean de Ribault, by the Dutchmen Eduardus and Dorenslaer, by the Englishman John Eliot, imitator of Jesuit methods among the Indians, and by the Dane Hans Egede, lone hero among the Eskimos. The trend was thus reversed, and in the eighteenth century Protestants began seriously to embark on missionary work. Among the Methodist ranks was Dr Coke, a follower of St Francis Xavier. Five years after founding his pietist centre at Herrnhut, Count von Zinzendorf sent the Moravian Brethren to the harshest lands. There were Protestant missions among the Redskins, in Ceylon, Oceania, China, Mongolia, Greenland, Labrador and South Africa. But still the movement was sporadic and the effort minimal. There were scarcely fifty mission stations and maybe a total of some two hundred missionaries; at the same time, Catholic missions were far from successful. ...

But the real effort was about to begin. The spiritual renewal which accompanied the revolutionary crisis in many Christian countries was expressed in the Protestant world by the creation of missionary societies. The first was in India in 1792: the Baptist pastor William Carey, whom we shall meet again later, joined with twelve colleagues, all as poor as himself, to found the Baptist Missionary Society, their initial capital being about £10. Three years later, in 1795, several hundred nonconformist English pastors founded the London Missionary Society, of whom Livingstone was one of the leading personalities, and who, in the following year, sent the *Duff* to India with thirty missionaries aboard. The Anglicans followed these examples and in 1799 founded the Church Missionary Society. The movement was now launched: it was joined by the Dutch in 1797, by the Americans in 1810, by the Swiss from Basel in 1815, by the Danes in 1821; also by the Methodists in 1813 and 1819 and by the Episcopalians in 1820. In 1821 a report stated with pride that there were now 12 missionary societies, 252 mission stations and 520 missionaries in the heathen regions of the world.

The number of missionary societies multiplied year by year. Every Protestant country spawned them; every Protestant Church, every community, every sect wanted its own. There were soon too many of them, badly organized, financially unsound; but zeal could not be said to be lacking. Some of these societies had a great future before them, e.g. those of Paris and Berlin. In 1913 there were 365 societies; in 1925, 380. This last figure subsequently dropped to 360,[1] which is nevertheless considerable, especially if, in order to obtain an overall picture, one adds the auxiliary and independent societies, numbering 398 and 48 respectively.

This missionary movement, however, great though it was, had encountered stiff resistance within the Protestant world. It was quite the contrary in the Catholic world, where critics never assailed principles but only methods. The theological arguments against missions continued to be urged by the more narrow-minded orthodox or fundamentalists; regular campaigns of surprising virulence were launched against the missions and the missionaries. In 1831 Canon Sydney Smith, a far-sighted and liberal Anglican (he was one of the most active partisans of Catholic emancipation) said, with that irony for which he was famous: 'The veriest tinker, if he be devout, is infallibly sent to the East, and his absence is of greater value to us than his sermons are to his Hindu listeners.' Even today the dispatch of Negro

[1] No complete list is possible here. For the most important see the accompanying table.

missionaries to Africa raises vehement protests in America, while the Pentecostal missions, whose success in South America we shall notice later,[1] are from time to time the objects of sarcasm and bitter criticism.

Protestant Missionary Societies

1792. Baptist Missionary Society (W. Carey).

1795. London Missionary Society (Livingstone).

1797. Dutch Missionary Society for the Propagation of Christianity among the Heathen.

1799. Church Missionary Society for Africa and the East.

1810. American Board of Commissioners for Foreign Missions.

1813. Wesleyan Methodist Missionary Society. (The Methodists had set up missions in 1786 in the Antilles.)

1814. American Baptist Foreign Mission Society.

1815. Basel Mission Society.

1819. Board of Foreign Missions of the Methodist Episcopal Church.

1820. Domestic and Foreign Missionary Society of the Protestant Episcopal Church in the U.S.A.

1821. Danish Mission Society.

1824. Paris Evangelical Missionary Society. Berlin Missionary Society.

1826. Lausanne Evangelical Missionary Society. (In 1917 this became the French Switzerland Missionary Society.)

1835. Swedish Missionary Society.

1836. Leipzig Lutheran Evangelical Missionary Society.

1837. Board of Foreign Missions of the Presbyterian Church in the U.S.A.

1841. Board of Foreign Missions of the General Synod of the Evangelical Lutheran Church in the U.S.A.

1842. Norwegian Missionary Society.

1847. Presbyterian Mission Committee of the Presbyterian Church of England.

1848. Association for the Propagation of the Gospel in the Dutch Possessions Overseas.

1856. Free Church of Scotland's Foreign Missions Committee; Swedish National Evangelical Mission.

1858. Finnish Missionary Societies. Dutch Missionary Association.

1863. Syrian Protestant College. (American University of Beirut.)

1865. China Inland Mission.

1878. Swedish Missionary Union.

1881. North Africa Mission.

1894. American Friends' Board of Foreign Missions.

1897. Christian and Missionary Alliance (U.S.A.).

1903. Belgian Protestants Missionary Society for the Congo.

---

[1] See section 14 below.

Such resistance, significant but minimal, has not prevented the Protestant missionary effort from achieving impressive results. The number of mission stations has steadily mounted, and although the creation of organized dioceses since the beginning of the twentieth century has slowed down that rate of increase, the missionaries themselves have continued to multiply—there were 18,000 in 1900; today there are more than 30,000. Some of the Protestant Churches have given splendid examples of devotion to the apostolate: the first prize in this context would surely go the Moravian Brethren, one of the smallest of Protestant groups, who during the nineteenth century maintained an average of 2,000 missionaries, a ratio of one missionary in every 92 adherents. The Lutherans, on the other hand, had only 2,770 missionaries for 75 million baptized, while the other Protestant Churches had a ratio of one missionary in every 5,000–7,000 adherents. These tremendous undertakings were based on a firmly organized foundation, with special seminaries (some of them interdenominational), a system of rotating the pastors between parishes in Europe or America, financial aid and a missionary press. From small beginnings in 1789, missionary work has become one of the essential elements in Protestantism, just as it is in the Catholic Church.

As with Catholic missions, Protestant missions benefited throughout the nineteenth century from the process of European colonial expansion. Upon the heels of Her Majesty's soldiers came Anglican, Presbyterian or Methodist missionaries, increasing their field of activity as the empire itself grew. The conception which the Protestants held of their relations with the State helped to associate the missionary cause with that of the State. Nationalism was infinitely more dominant among Protestants than among Catholics, especially as certain governments (e.g. the British) found it useful to confer on the missionaries official titles such as that of consul. In the Dutch colonies of the Sunda Isles, in the German colonies in Africa before 1914, the association of the missions with the official administration was marked. There were incidents, such as the famous Pritchard affair,[1] which demonstrated the danger of this kind of association. In cases where Protestant missionaries were working in areas which were not politically dependent on their country of origin, the fact that they were officially attached to a certain nationality was bound to create awkward situations. A Catholic missionary, whether Italian, Belgian or French, was at the service of the Catholic Church, the Universal Church; but a Protestant missionary was a German, a Swede or an American. The confusion is evident in the words addressed by a native to a French colonial official in French territory: 'I shall not obey you—I am an American!' He had been baptized by an American missionary. During the last few

[1] See section 13 below.

years in South America, hostility towards the U.S.A. has slowed down the progress of Protestant missions, which are accused of allying themselves with neo-colonialism and Yankee capitalism.

On the whole, however, there can be no doubt that the Protestant missions have long benefited and still do benefit from financial means far greater than those available to the Catholics. The fact that the world's richest country is also the world's leading Protestant country is a stroke of luck for the Protestant missions, particularly as the majority of its millionaires are Protestants also. Auxiliary societies have bloomed almost as quickly as the missions themselves, even more quickly in some cases, and the current figure of 398 is not the upper limit. The Friends of this or that Church are innumerable; many of these societies assist every mission and do not confine themselves to those of one particular Church; the General Eldership of the Church of God and some other similar organizations are cases in point. The figures are impressive: in 1955 the totality of Protestant missions disposed of some 3,500 million gold francs, of which half was contributed by the U.S.A.

Operating methods are not always the same as those employed by the Catholics. The Protestant missionary pastor holds a position different from that of his Catholic counterpart; at least in general, for there are substantial variations between missionaries of different denominations, an Anglican or a Presbyterian on the one hand and a Baptist on the other. The Catholic missionary is regarded by the natives as a consecrated man; the very isolation imposed by his celibacy sets him apart. Again, he teaches a dogmatic religion, with an imperative creed, whose rites command the natives' attention, whose solemnity attracts them. The Protestant missionary cannot, without betraying his faith, represent himself as sacred. On the other hand he receives inestimable help from his wife, who can more easily make friends with the native women, and his home serves as an example of the Christian ideal of hearth and home. Thus he appears more as an elder, a guide in the tasks which are both everyday and supernatural, rather than as a priest, a fact which has both advantages and disadvantages. Some of the Catholic missionaries' sacrificial actions have astonished their Protestant colleagues. The case of Fr Damien, for example, much criticized, despised even by the pastors of the isles around the Sandwich Group, is typical: one must truly believe in the Communion of Saints to become 'a leper among lepers'. The liberty of action given to Protestant missionaries, besides the distribution of Bibles, which are unceasingly supplied to them by numerous Bible societies in every language, is most useful, for they can be distributed far from the pastor's place of work; but this system has its problems. If it is difficult enough for the average Briton or American to understand the Bible, one is inclined to ask what the bush native in Africa is going to make of it. Free inquiry seems scarcely to be adequate in this instance, and, as we shall see, it can have curious consequences.[1] Many Protestants today admit that there has been too great a hurry to declare Christian those who, without any special preparation, have been baptized and presented with a Bible.

For the rest the operating methods employed by the Protestant missions have been the same as those employed by the Catholics, especially as regards schools and hospitals. Protestant activities in the work of preparation for grace—which is, in the final analysis, the only effective method—has followed the trail laid by the Jesuits, the Sisters of Charity and other Catholic congregations. But it must be admitted that as regards medical and hospital services the Protestants have gone further and faster than the Catholics. Perhaps because they had greater resources; perhaps also because other missionary means were not open to them. From the middle of the nineteenth century those of England, Germany and America have worked to set up medical assistance for missions, whereas the Catholics, despite some sporadic attempts at the end of the nineteenth century, did not adopt those methods until after 1920. In 1925 there were 1,200 doctors, both men and women, and nearly 3,000 nurses, male and female, at work in the missions. Many of the pastors' wives were qualified nurses. Inter-denominational Protestant institutes were founded to train the staff of mission hospitals, such as that which opened in Mexico in 1925, financed by twenty-seven American denominations whose graduates are destined for South America. And everyone has heard of one of the greatest figures of modern Protestantism: Albert Schweitzer, doctor and apostle.

The school also has been considered as a missionary tool by the Catholic missions since their inception; Protestant missions make use of them systematically. No sooner has the jungle been cleared in any missionary area than a school house is built. In many cases, in India, Madagascar and the Loyalty Islands, the school has served as the weft in the cloth of Protestant Christianity. In 1925 statistics showed that there were nearly 2½ million children in Protestant primary schools in Asia. Then there were secondary and higher schools, some of them very ambitious, such as the inter-racial 'college' (i.e. university) founded by Alexander Duff in India, or the Anglo-Chinese college at Malacca, subsequently transferred to Shanghai. In China alone, in 1900, the Protestants had 1,819 schools, 138 secondary teaching establishments and 22 higher education, among these last Hong Kong Medical College, where Sun Yat-sen studied and where he was baptized. There are, however, a few innovations which deserve attention. For example, the Zenanas in India, founded by the daughter of the

1 See section 13 below.

Swiss pastor Lacroix for the purpose of making contact with the native women and bringing the younger girls into domestic science schools; in Uganda the reading rooms, connected with the public libraries and the people's university, which give evening classes. At the same time an enormous effort has been made, especially since 1900, to set up 'biblical and theological schools', veritable seminaries for the training of the native clergy. There were 461 in 1925 with 9,000 students of whom one-third were girls; but the love of system had been perhaps pushed too far, for many of these schools had enrolled teaching staffs long before they had any students.

If one is to get an idea of the power, the wealth, the strength of Protestant missionary methods, one could not do better than visit Mangalore in India. Here the Basel Mission has built a complete missionary village, with its own shops, where Christians from the surrounding countryside can buy all they need at reasonable prices; houses for catechumens and recent converts; a native seminary; schools of all grades, including technical and domestic science schools and a special school for the daughters of Brahmins; workshops making everything necessary for the local people there—textiles, bricks, furniture; a publishing house and a polyglot printing shop; all surrounded by farms belonging to the mission and leased only to Protestant converts. The Protestant missions, then, have enjoyed great success. Perhaps too great a success. Some observers wonder if all this brilliant organization does not hide a spiritual void. Half a century ago a reaction set in, under the name of the New Crusade, emphasizing the true religious training of the native—this comes closer to Catholic ideas on the subject. It was the brain-child of Charles Studd, a collaborator in China of the great missionary Hudson Taylor.[1] Today the Pentecostal or Adventist missions which are at work in South America attach much less importance to organization, schools, hospitals, than to the inner revelation of the Holy Ghost.

This very strong organization in the Protestant missions should not blind us to the men whose spirit of faith, courage and strength creates the grandeur of the whole edifice and ensures its successful operation. There have been many of them, and no Christian would seek to deny them the admiration which they deserve. If it is true that on average, in proportion to the personnel involved, the Protestant missions have had far fewer martyrs than the Catholics, there have been many none the less, spread over all the missionary fields: the Anglican Bishop Hannington in Uganda, the French pastors Escande and Winault, massacred in Madagascar, the Englishmen John Williams and John Paton in the Pacific.

The great Protestant missionary pioneers form an even longer list.

[1] See p. 141.

Many of them are almost legendary in the Churches to which they belonged. For instance, there was William Carey (1761–1834), a poor Nottingham cobbler, rachitic and unlettered. After reading accounts of Captain Cook's voyages he resolved to go and convert the heathen. He became a Baptist pastor and, despite numerous difficulties, established his humble Baptist Missionary Society, helped by Mrs Wallis, and left for India. Here he was authorized to stay only as an indigo planter, but proceeded to accomplish a colossal task, controlling all his mission's enterprises, translating the Bible into Bengali, founding schools in Calcutta and Serampore, reaching such a degree of influence that the British Government agreed to introduce a ban on infanticide and suttee. Then there was Charles Gützlaff (1805–51), the German missionary who, after an abortive attempt in Siam, went off to China, took advantage of the Opium War (1839–42) to establish himself in Hong Kong, and conceived an immense project for the Lutheranization of the whole empire, inspired by earlier Jesuit methods and helped by teams of native preachers. The scheme eventually failed, despite the help of the English Society for the Evangelization of China which he founded. He was traduced and duped by his Chinese collaborators, but always remained devotedly attached to the idea of a Christian China. Then there was Hudson Taylor (1832–1905) and his wife; he has been compared to St John Bosco in the fervour of his missionary zeal, the apostle of inland China, founder of the China Inland Missionary Society. It was while practising as a doctor in Shanghai that he first became aware of the appalling material and spiritual misery of the Chinese masses. He had no other thought but to bring them to God and to the charity of Christ, and to this end he recruited the services of as many men and women of like mind as possible; 600 missionaries responded to his appeal, plus 700 unmarried women missionaries, rather similar to the Sisters of St Vincent de Paul (who were entering China at the same moment), and also 190 doctors. Nothing was to stop him in his drive, neither criticism nor misunderstandings, nor even the Boxer Rebellion. On his death Protestantism had been implanted in half the Chinese Empire.

From Asia let us turn to Africa, where two figures stand out from among all those who have set out to implant Protestantism in the black continent. At the beginning of the nineteenth century Theodore van der Kemp (1747–1811), a cavalry officer, doctor and specialist in ancient and foreign tongues (he knew seventeen), came to missionary work through a tragic stroke of fate. Sailing on the Meuse one day his boat was overturned and his wife and daughter drowned, and Kemp offered his services to the London Missionary Society. He was sent to South Africa, where a very small community of Moravian Brethren had been founded. Kemp went straightway into the bush, first among the Kaffirs, then among the Hottentots. He may or may not have read the story of the Jesuit conquest of Paraguay; but his achievement at Bethelsdorp was a triumph. There he founded a community where a thousand natives worked, lived and prayed under the direction of the head of the mission and his assistants, who controlled them in all respects. The head lived just as simply as they did, sharing their meals with them. He went further, even to marrying one of the native women, and this set off a fine scandal among the whites who had strict views on *apartheid*. But Kemp cared little for insults: at sixty-four he was about to set up a mission in Madagascar when he died, leaving an unforgettable memory to the Christians of South Africa.

But of all the great Protestant missionaries, one is particularly famous: David Livingstone (1813–73), hero and discoverer and explorer of Africa, who throughout his life felt the urge to fight for true Christian charity where there was most need for it and who, in pursuit of this essentially missionary goal, accomplished an immense task which brought him fame and a final resting-place in Westminster Abbey. He was the son of a poor tailor of Blantyre in Scotland, the eldest of seven children, and he started work at the age of ten in a spinning mill. He was self-educated, learning Latin and history and imbibing the spirituality of the Bible in the evenings. Gützlaff's example inspired him towards a missionary life, and as soon as he was old enough he entered the service of the London Missionary Society. He was sent to Kuruman in South Africa to assist Pastor Robert Moffat, whose daughter he married. Africa was a revelation to him— the revelation of a frightful evil, of a running sore: the slave trade. It was at its height, Zanzibar being one of the chief transit centres. For thirty years the great powers had been talking about its suppression, but what in fact had been accomplished? David Livingstone vowed to devote his life to its abolition. He found that it was the Negroes themselves who supplied the slave traders. Obviously the natives must have some honest trade which would allow them to live decently, and also it would be necessary to implant white missionaries among them to guide them. Livingstone set out for the heart of Africa, discovered the Zambezi Falls and crossed the continent on two occasions. His journeys were voyages of discovery, besides civilizing and evangelizing; the three tasks were all one to him. Cutting short his exploration he came to London, gave talks on what he had seen, of the drama that was being played out in the dark continent, entreating governments to act once and for all against the slave trade. On his return to Africa he was to find a tragic situation: his wife dead, his companions decimated by fever. Should he abandon the enterprise now and accept defeat? By no means. He returned to England to seek reinforcements. Now his fame as an explorer was so great that he was asked to set out to discover the source of the Nile; to leave it undiscovered was to ignore something of the greatest importance to Egypt. Livingstone was tired. He was over fifty, but he set out again and for seven years he carried on his task in west and central Africa, the same task as in the south; he discovered not the source of the Nile but, without knowing it, that of the Congo; wherever he could he paved the way for the missionaries who were to follow. Africa finally defeated him; the man of iron was eaten up with fever, at the end of his strength, able to continue only if he was carried on a stretcher. He was given up as lost, to be discovered by Stanley. On the morning of 1st July 1873 his porters found him at his bedside, head in hands: feeling the approach of death, he had knelt down to pray.

12. An Example: the Paris Evangelical Missionary Society

Among the innumerable missionary societies which sprang up during one hundred and fifty years within the Protestant world, that in France, the pride of French Protestants, is of special interest. Founded by a very small community, it never received State aid, but it was very active and in many ways it was very successful.

Preoccupation with missionary matters, which the pious pastor of Charenton, Charles Drelincourt, had sought to encourage among French Protestants, was in evidence after the revolutionary crisis was over and new conditions were set up under the Organic Articles. In 1820 some citizens of Toulouse united to set up the small association known as the *Amis des Missions*. This became known in Paris and was taken up and developed. On 4th November 1822 the '*Société des Missions évangéliques parmi les peuples non-Chrétiens*' was founded by a combination of different social, ecclesiastical and even geographical groups. Their idea was to place the whole enterprise outside the framework of any particular Church, an idea which was much advanced for those days. It encountered strong criticism, from Lutherans as from Calvinists, from the orthodox as from the liberals. But the society flourished, and in 1824 it opened a seminary. In 1832 a mason came to offer his help to the missionaries; he was enrolled on probation alongside the young pastors. It was a happy chance, for it underlined from the outset the principle of lay collaboration. A publication was started with the object of arousing interest in the whole missionary adventure. The same movement then which was urging the Catholics to missionary work in non-Christian areas was also at work among the Protestants. There was a moment when the movement almost failed, and during the troubled year 1848 the seminary was closed. But the society had already sent its first missionaries to Africa. On learning that all was not well at headquarters, one of the pioneers of Basutoland, Pastor Casalis, returned at once to France. He took over and injected such vigour into the enterprise that the seminary was reopened in 1856, and soon afterwards there came a flow of pastors to China, Tahiti, Senegal, Mauritius. The impetus had been given; from now onwards it would not falter. The seminary was installed in the Boulevard Arago with Alfred Boegner at its head. Recruiting continued, always half clerical, half secular. Despite the disruptions caused by the two world wars—during the first of which it received help from two generous English people, Captain and Mrs G. A. K. Wisely, and immediately after the second from the Americans—the society has never looked back.

One of the most important of its missions was that of Lessouto. In 1829 the French society decided to send a mission to South Africa, to that part settled by the Huguenots, descendants of those who had been exiled by the revocation of the Edict of Nantes. In agreement with the London Missionary Society three pastors—Bisseux, Rolland and Lemue—arrived at the Cape. One enterprise among the Kaffirs was not a success, another in Bechuanaland failed through lack of support. But in 1832 three young missionaries, Casalis, Arbousset and Gosselin, sent as reinforcements, heard a strange tale. Beyond the Drakensbergs, among the Basutos, lived a chief named Mosheh. He had told a white hunter that he was prepared to pay several hundred head of cattle—the currency of those days—for a Christian missionary to come to his territory. By this means, he said, he would be safe from raids from the more obstreperous neighbouring tribes. The three pastors set off for Lessouto and began their work among the forty thousand subjects of the chief. Their first mission station they called Moraji, or Epiphany. But difficulties soon beset them. These sprang from the monogamy which the pastors urged upon their charges and partly from the pressure of the advancing Boers, who were being pushed ever farther into the interior by the British. The chief was wise, and aided by the three pastors the Lessouto people were protected from dangers, both external and internal. Agriculture expanded, the country grew rich, modern medical practice stopped the spread of endemic diseases. Inside four generations the Lessoutos grew to 500,000 people. There were difficulties—Mosheh's son was not so friendly as his father had been, and the Boer War shook the missionaries' little world. But now the roots were strongly implanted. Schools, hospitals and orphanages had been founded; all the baptized members contributed to the common effort by paying a voluntary tax, the *kavelo*. A theological school was opened at Morija for the training of native clergy. Under the British protectorate from 1884 the French missionaries continued their work. In 1890 the first African pastor graduated; in 1898 the

Seboka, a part European, part African assembly, was set up to run the Church. Some years later a group of American Negroes, the emissaries of a political group, came to this area with the slogan 'Africa for the Africans' and were greeted with laughter when they told the African pastors that they too would have their freedom, their own cheque books. Since each parish disposed freely of its own funds, this would be nothing new. The development of the mission continued, and in 1932, at its centenary, there were some 30,000 adherents, 28,000 children in its schools, 12,000 catechumens, spread over 37 parishes (26 of these being under the control of African pastors), 341 annexes, in which there were nearly 1,000 schoolmasters and catechizers. One of the converts, a pupil of one of the schools there, Th. Mofolo, was to show just how important a place Lessouto had taken in Africa by writing, firstly in his native tongue, then in French, *Chaka,* an historical novel on the Zulu warrior, published later by the *Nouvelle Revue Française* in 1939. 'It was among the Lessouto that French missionary work was formed,' the great missionary Maurice Leenhardt has declared.

It was the Lessouto missionaries who first conceived the idea of setting up the Cross in those countries across the Upper Zambezi to which Livingstone had drawn attention. An earlier attempt by the London Missionary Society had not succeeded. An English missionary and a Christian chief did, however, aver that evangelization was possible. One of the Lessouto pastors decided to attempt this. He was François Coillard, obviously a man in the great African tradition. In 1878 he set out to reconnoitre the terrain, an exploit which earned him the gold medal of the Geographical Society, and he was delighted to find that the local chief, Lewanika, was willing to receive missionaries. After many difficulties had been overcome the mission was established in 1885 by Coillard, his wife, his niece and Pastor Jeanneret, a workman and several Basuto evangelists.

In 1925 the mission station, under eight pastors, numbered some 500 Christians, as many catechumens and 1,700 children in the schools. In 1955 all these figures had been increased by 50 per cent, and four native pastors worked alongside their white colleagues.

In Madagascar, the third of the main fields of activity of the Paris Missionary Society, there were many difficulties, but they were not of the same order as those encountered in the upper Zambezi area. Protestantism first came to the island in 1813, when two Welshmen, David Jones and Thomas Bevan, arrived at Antananarivo with their families. The climate, unhealthy though it was for women and children, did not stop Jones, who stayed on alone, from continuing his task; ten years later the seeds had been well sown. But then persecution broke out, fanned by Queen Ranavalona I, who called herself Protestant but was no more than a cynical tyrant. All missionaries, whatever their denomination, had to leave, and some native converts perished. This state of affairs continued for twenty-five years. When the Christian king Radama II, her son, came to the throne missionaries, Catholic and Protestant, returned; Norwegian Lutherans, Anglicans and Quakers also arrived. Protestantism was very successful—Queen Ranavalona II (1868–83) was converted, a church was built in the precincts of the palace itself and the dynasty's ancient idol solemnly burnt; the number of adherents increased; the future queen became a pupil of one of the mission schools.

The French protectorate changed the scene. Following the first war in 1883, when the question of French occupation arose, the Missionary Society had considered the advisability of sending missionaries. In 1895 Pastors Krüger and Lauga were dispatched to reconnoitre, and to see what steps should be taken to relieve the British, Norwegian and other missionaries there. But in fact the established missions never agreed to leave the entire field to the French, and they remain to this day at work, complicating matters in the eyes of the natives, despite agreements for splitting up the territory which came into force in 1900. The Evangelical Mission came up against yet another problem: the rapid advance of Catholicism, directed by the Jesuits, which had immense success. The untutored native masses turned against the Protestants, reasoning that 'a Catholic is French, a Protestant is English'. A small-scale religious war broke out in which there were Protestant casualties. It was under these difficult conditions that the Paris society sent out missionaries in 1897. The intervention of General Galliéni, the island's governor, eased the situation—both Protestant and Catholic missionaries then went about their work, concentrating on evangelization only, and better progress was made on both sides. The French mission wasted no time: native pastors were ordained and the Church was allowed considerable freedom, until it became virtually independent. This was also the tactic of the Norwegian Lutheran mission in the island. A classic type of revival now took place, observable even among the Malagasy; but a new halt was called to this admirable progress. Unintelligent anticlerical measures were taken by the governor, Augagneur, in 1905. Mission schools were closed and conversions slowed down. Progress was resumed after the First World War, and Protestantism reached distant regions like Diego-Suarez. Great efforts were made to organize the training of native pastors; many hospitals were opened; the Manakavaly leper centre was placed in charge of the Evangelical Mission. The Second World War and the temporary occupation of the island by the British did not stop progress, though there was a period of difficulty stemming from inter-racial relations within the Churches. After some seventy-five years' work, the French mission today has some 1,545 churches and 350,000 baptized; this compares with some 600,000 from the other six Protestant missions and some 750,000 Catholics. There are 13 white pastors, 130 Malagasy pastors and 250 native evangelists at work.

Lessouto, the upper Zambezi and Madagascar are considered to be the three feathers in the Paris society's missionary cap. But it had other fields of action in Africa: Senegal, where it had been established since 1861; the Gabon, where it took over from American missionaries; Dahomey, Togo and the Cameroons, where it took over from German missionaries. It likewise established itself in New Caledonia in the Loyalty Islands and in Tahiti.

It was in 1865 that they arrived in Tahiti, on the heels of the London mission which had succeeded in converting King Pomare II and which considered (the Pritchard affair was proof enough) that missionary endeavours were closely linked to the interests of His Britannic Majesty. Consequently the French missionaries had a difficult task in avoiding a strongly anti-British reaction and in setting up the native Church. This was done in 1880, and five years later the establishment of the French protectorate enabled them to increase their activities and to reach out even out to the Marquesas. In competition with Catholic missionaries, the society's three white and sixty native pastors have been so successful that nine out of ten Tahitians are Christian—three of them Protestant, six of them Catholic.

The Paris society has fully justified the hopes of the 800,000 Protestants in France, who have contributed to its work by their generosity, in both money and men. Missionary work has a high place in French Protestantism. Catholics view with admiration the rotation system whereby pastors exchange posts in metropolitan France with those in distant places. The system was introduced more than fifty years ago, and there is no lack of applicants for the work.

13. FIELDS OF ACTIVITY AND SOME PROBLEMS OF MISSIONARY DEVELOPMENT

To apostles of the calibre of a Livingstone, a Taylor or a Coillard, the world is neither so large nor so harsh as to prevent the faith from taking root. Protestant missionary effort is no more than a hundred and fifty years old, and yet Protestantism has become firmly established in a large number of non-Christian countries, achieving, all things considered, an expansion rate scarcely less than that of the Catholics, who have had twice as much time at their disposal. In 1957 it was estimated that there were 37 million Protestants in missionary countries. It is an undoubted success, and the sons of the Reformation can justly feel proud of their efforts.

The Protestants have shunned no area of the world—the whole world is, in Wesley's words, their parish. But this very fact has raised a grave and even distressing problem, that of relations with the Catholics, a problem that has existed ever since the Reformation. While divisions within the Church of Christ may be shameful in themselves, they are even more so in missionary countries, flaunted before intended converts and confusing them with discord and divergent opinions. Newly arrived on the missionary scene, many of the Protestant missions settled in territories where Catholics were already installed. In many cases they brought with them the worst methods of anti-Papist polemics. In some cases rivalry led to conflicts, as that in Tahiti in 1842 with the Pritchard affair, when an English missionary intrigued against the Picpus Fathers, provoking a diplomatic crisis between London and Paris.[1] Throughout Polynesia there was bitter antagonism between Protestants and Catholics, with conflicting national and colonial interests. There were also similar incidents in Madagascar, and in Uganda where the White Fathers came up against the Anglican missionaries who wanted this territory for themselves and who appealed to Cardinal Lavigerie for support. Today it is in South America that the Protestant missions, often led by keen proselytizers, are openly hostile to Catholicism.

Protestant missions had developed in all parts of the globe, either under the guidance of missionaries from Europe or from groups of Reformed Churches installed in the U.S.A. and the Commonwealth. There is one important fact that needs mentioning also: the role of the native converts themselves in this development. At a very early stage Protestant missionaries taught these new Christians to assume responsibility for their own Churches and established a coloured clergy. It is of course true that they were not restricted by the vow of celibacy, nor even a rigid dogmatic formula, which, in the Catholic Church, gave rise to the famous dispute concerning rites.[2] For the Protestants all methods were valid, or nearly all. There were native auxiliaries in all the first Dutch missions of the seventeenth century and native pastors in the first years of the great period of expansion at the beginning of the nineteenth century. For the next hundred years the number rose enormously. In Africa alone, including Madagascar, the total of African pastors and evangelists was 22,000 in 1903, and 43,000 in 1925. Communities were asked to contribute towards the cost of evangelization, and their financial assistance soon reached a significant figure. Also, Protestants with their ecclesiology, which saw in each

[1] *The Church in an Age of Revolution*, Index.
[2] *The Church in the Eighteenth Century*, Chapter II, section 5.

national or local Church the embodiment of the Church as a whole, were far more inclined than were the Catholics to set up native Churches which would soon become autonomous. In 1864 the Anglicans consecrated the first bishop of Nigeria, the freed slave Samuel Crowther. In 1899 the Anglican bishop Hinne wrote: 'The aim is the creation of an indigenous Church in the best sense of the word, independent of all European influence and adapted to all the particular conditions of the race and the country—a Church which is their Church.' In Madagascar the French Lutherans created an indigenous Church. They were followed by the Presbyterians, with whom several other groups had joined forces. The same movement could be seen in India, in the Pacific and in China. Having first of all exported the confessional and traditional aspects of their European Churches, the Protestants aimed to plant the seeds which would flower into independent Churches on native soil. 'Christianity in seed form, not in pots,' according to one Protestant in India. Perhaps because it was undertaken too rapidly this policy suffered some reverses, as will be noted; nevertheless it led to rapid expansion in every continent.

For it is indeed in every continent that Protestantism has established itself, even in those areas which were thought at first to be unfavourable, such as Latin America. It would be almost impossible to draw up a complete geographical plan showing all the Protestant missions, because of the perpetual divisions which exist between the different missionary societies, each an exponent of a different confession. Let us merely note the main ones with their general characteristics.

According to the *World Christian Handbook*, an authoritative American publication, the largest group of non-European Protestants is to be found in India; there are some 8,875,000 adherents plus some 100,000 whites. To this large figure must be added the million or so practising Protestants of Ceylon, the same number or more in Burma, though there are few of them in Pakistan. Then there is India, the territory of Carey, Judson and Duff, where immense enterprises have been carried out by the missions of a dozen Churches—educational as well as social. These efforts were not always understood by the British authorities, and the missions were themselves threatened with expulsion in 1947 when India became independent. But they held on despite difficulties, launching out on a great campaign of evangelization under the National Missionary Society, and, as has been seen in south India, aiding the unification of all Protestant branches in India with a view to establishing an Indian Church.

Indonesia, during the Dutch colonial era, had provided Protestantism—especially Dutch Calvinism—with immense opportunities. Even the granting of independence seems not to have diminished these, for in 1957, at a meeting at Siantar in Sumatra, some 120,000

Christians, with President Soekarno himself, came together to affirm their faith.

For a long time Japan held out the best hopes of being the most promising territory. The ground, opened up in 1859 by American missionaries posing as school teachers, was busily cultivated after 1872 (the date when official tolerance was proclaimed), especially by the great Japanese evangelist Nisima, founder of the Doshisha College (later a university) and of the association of 'those who have but one goal'. Immense assistance was forthcoming from American millionaires, Rockefeller among them, and Japanese Protestantism grew considerably during the first half of the twentieth century, from 80,000 adherents in 1901 to 155,000 in 1925 and 500,000 in 1939. Religious culture was at a high level; there were radiant personages at work such as Kagawa,[1] the apostle of social evangelism. The Second World War brought all this to a halt. The atomic bomb on Hiroshima and the American occupation produced a climate conducive to counter-apologetics; the Kyodan, or United Japanese Church, is at work amid the working masses, but in a population of some 86 million there are only some 400,000 Protestants (540,000 according to the *Handbook*).

In China of course the situation has become much more difficult since Communism appeared and took over the old Celestial Empire. But what splendid work the missions carried out. China was the field of Morrom, Taylor and Gützlaff, of the China Inland Mission and of the English society. Aided by large amounts of sterling and dollars, Protestantism in China rose from 112,000 to 800,000 adherents between 1900 and 1927; the number of missionaries rose to 6,400, that of evangelists and catechists to 28,000. Everywhere there were schools, colleges and universities with thousands of students. Newspapers and publishing houses all helped with a flood of propaganda. The decline after the Second World War was rapid. In 1945 the country was still non-Communist, but there were only some 850 white Protestant missionaries. However, the million Protestants in China when Mao Tse-tung came to power had become used to living a self-sufficient life, with their own pastors and their own evangelists. The Communist regime persecuted them but did not succeed in removing all trace of them. A national Church was created, or rather two of them, one more strictly controlled by the regime, and in which Christianity is associated with Marxism in some curious ways. In Korea, at least in that half protected by the Americans, and in Formosa, where many of the ex-China missionaries have settled, the situation is favourable, as it is also in the former French colony of Indo-China, still spared from Communism.

The Pacific has been one of the areas most favoured by Protestant

[1] See Chapter III, section 16.

missionaries. Australia and New Zealand must be treated separately as being areas peopled for the most part by whites, where missionaries have had little enough work in view of the very small number of natives. But the islands are another story. Systematic programmes of evangelization have been undertaken; the work has been intense and martyrs not a few. The results have been impressive. In Tahiti, the Loyalty Islands and New Caledonia, the Paris society has established missions as well as in the archipelagos, strongholds of English and American missionaries. Evangelization has managed to secure great zones for Protestantism, despite severe competition from Catholic missions. It is estimated that there are now some 9 million adherents throughout the Pacific islands, of whom some 2·8 million are practising Protestants.

In Africa, where we have already seen the efforts of the Paris society, the work undertaken by other societies has also been immense. There is not one African territory where Protestantism has not been implanted. Virtually insignificant in the Somalis and Libya, minimal in Algeria, Tunisia and Morocco, it is far stronger elsewhere; e.g. in the Congo and in Ruanda-Urundi, where there are some 765,000 adherents apart from the Republic of South Africa and Rhodesia and Malawi, where Protestantism owes as much to white settlement as to missionary activity. In West Africa, where in 1785 there was already a colony of freed Negroes run by evangelists who had founded Freetown, Protestantism made impressive advances. When the French arrived in the Gabon they found American Presbyterians who had been there since 1841. The London Missionary Society sent its men everywhere in Africa, helped by—in some cases in competition with— the Germans, the Dutch, the Norwegians and the Finns. Every type of Protestant denomination was to be found in Africa, and it was split up into territories among them. Today the best settled areas of Protestantism are to be found in the Congo; in Tanzania, where the Lutherans are dominant; in Kenya, where the Mau-Mau crisis slowed down the work; in Uganda, where the Anglican episcopate has adroitly associated itself with the autochthonous auxiliaries; in the Cameroons; in Liberia and in Nigeria, which has an African archbishop. From 1925 to 1950 the Protestants in Africa have risen from 2½ million to 11 million. The various Churches and communities have a sufficiently well-developed awareness of their own interests to have held a Pan-African conference at Ibadan in 1958 to discuss common problems.

This touched upon one of the most interesting aspects of recent missionary history among the Protestants—the drive towards unity. Many missionaries were aware of the absurdity of attempting evangelization with a divided and competing number of denominations. It was seen that there was a real necessity to harmonize their efforts, and so the ecumenical spirit was present within the younger Church long before the European and American Churches created the World Council. In 1872 a large number of societies decided to inaugurate a decennial conference. The International Council of Missions was set up in 1910, and three-quarters of the missionary societies joined it. It has met regularly since then, a co-ordinating organism for all evangelization work. In 1947 the movement towards unity became much stronger. In that year, in south India, four indigenous Churches—Anglican, Methodist, Presbyterian and Congregationalist—decided to unite, despite the theological and ecclesiastical differences which separated them. Bitterly criticized by some, warmly applauded by others, this initiative was followed over the next ten years by seven other countries. These types of union are not without risks, but they are indubitably in the line of Protestant thinking in the mid twentieth century. The missions, it has been said, have set an example to the Churches.[1]

Nevertheless there are many thorny problems left for the Protestant missions to solve. Many of these are common to the Catholics also. Others are specifically their own, stemming from Protestant theology or ecclesiology. Free inquiry and the personal interpretation of dogmas may have the advantage of making propaganda easier and allowing many adjustments to be made, but they also run the risk of causing confusion, ending in unacceptable syncretisms. In India, between 1870 and 1884, a Brahmin convert, the Protestant Ram Mohan Moy, incorporated in Protestantism certain elements from the Koran and the Vedas, so that all believers in India might find something to their taste. What was still more surprising was that this syncretism was approved by white theologians, by pastor Leblois of Strasbourg, and later by Professor R. E. Hume of New York. A too literal attachment to the Bible is not without its dangers; in 1917 in the Cameroons native pastors rose, in the name of the Holy Scripture, against the European dogma of monogamy, and taught their people, as did the Mormons of old, that the teaching of the Bible authorized polygamy, and that henceforth they would authorize it. Christianity almost collapsed after this curious schism, which continued until Catholic missionaries arrived.

But these are not the most difficult problems: others, which are well known to the Catholics also, are the constant preoccupation of missionary societies. Despite the advantages over the European clergy which the pastors have in matters of marriage and the rotation of posts, missionaries are lacking everywhere. The lack is made good by employing more evangelists and catechists, whose main role is the

[1] See Chapter VI, section 12.

distribution of Bibles. New methods, some of which are copied from the Catholics, seek to make better use of pastors by grouping them in a central residence from which they can cover a particular region and direct a team of evangelists. The Anglicans are in the lead in this respect with the so-called Bush fraternities. The spectacular success which Protestant missions have had has not always led to conversion in depth, and Protestant Christianity, even more than Catholicism, very often finds itself faced with persistent heathen customs, with a refusal to admit the Christian values in marriage—the dowry custom in equatorial Africa is very hard to eradicate—and with the periodical reappearance of witchcraft.

For thirty or forty years Protestant missions, as with Catholic missions, have been faced with the upsurge of native nationalism, which, since the end of the Second World War, has given rise to violence. Decolonization has presented the Churches with very serious problems. Non-whites are less and less inclined to accept a white clergy. For Protestantism the problem has been solved through the appointment of autochthonous clergy in those areas where the supply was sufficient and where the degree of development was appropriate. But elsewhere, what place does the white missionary have now? In the Congo, at the time of the crisis of 1960, the Protestant missionaries were in greater danger than the Catholics, for, because of their nationality, they were thought to be in collusion with the capitalist Anglo-Saxon powers. The emancipation of the various Christian communities founded by missions is inevitable, and it is interesting to note that the main theme discussed at the Pan-African conference at Ibadan was: 'What is the Church?' This gave the delegates the opportunity of demonstrating that, theologically, emancipation was in the main stream proper of the Reformation. In the same way the Catholic Church, yesterday white, is called upon today to hand over more and more of its responsibility to the non-white Churches, hierarchically constituted, which it has built up within itself, just as the Protestant Churches have to envisage the handing over of the missions to black-skinned or yellow-skinned Christians.

Serious problems are being encountered today, but Protestant missionary work is an immense undertaking—with its 25–30 million adherents it has become a considerable force, an essential part of Protestantism and regarded as such. 'Missionary work', wrote Pastor Marc Boegner, 'is not something apart from the Church, an enthusiastic side issue—it is the Church itself, obedient to the laws which created it . . . carrying out its fundamental task. . . .' Perhaps the original reformers would be surprised to read such words. Nevertheless they express that unquestionable truth on which Luther and Calvin established the future of *their* world.

14. AN ASTONISHING STORY: PROTESTANTISM IN LATIN AMERICA

In this geographical outline of the Protestant world, a special section must be devoted to Latin America, where Protestantism has developed on a most impressive scale. That development has taken place not in pagan territory or in countries dominated by non-Christian creeds, but at the expense of the Roman Catholic Church, amid Catholic (or at least nominally Catholic) populations. In 1927 the Abbé Dedieu wrote: 'Protestant expansion seems to have failed entirely in Latin America.' This was wrong in so far as Brazil was concerned, but true in other former Spanish colonies. The same opinion was expressed at the end of the nineteenth century by the Protestant *Lichtenberger Encyclopedia*, which, in a survey of Protestantism in Spanish America, gave 'nil' as the number of Protestants in many countries. Today even the least pessimistic Catholic statistics indicate that there are thousands of Protestants of every denomination in all the states. In Chile there are some 800,000, out of a total population of 6 million inhabitants, and 4 million in Brazil. The increase has been rapid: in 1900 there were only some 8,000 Protestants in the small countries of central America; today there are some 150,000.

The root cause of this phenomenon is well known: many far-sighted Catholics have voiced it. In far too many places in Latin America Catholicism has been implanted by summary, even questionable, methods. These have only succeeded in thinly covering the upper crust of pagan beliefs, and this veneer has gradually worn away. All that remains in many cases now is a faith with no real roots, often superstitious, generally in conflict with current ethics, and useless against the vices of poverty-ridden populations. A continuous apostolate would be needed to correct this situation; but no such work is possible, because there are too few clergy. Some figures will illustrate this statement: one-third of the world's Catholics live in Latin America, which has only 8 per cent of the world's priests, some of whom have parishes as extensive as a French *département*. There are some Christian communities which have not set eyes on a priest for thirty or forty years. It is a miracle that one can still find, alongside superstitious practices, a lively desire for baptism and faith in the Cross. But were the delegates at the Inter-American Catholic Conference in Lima wrong when they assessed at 10–25 per cent the total of true Christians among the millions of baptized?

In these conditions the *evangelicos* have a smooth path. A Protestant missionary team has only to arrive in one of these disinherited areas, or to penetrate those other sectors where material and spiritual misery reign among the proletariat of large cities, speaking of Christ and His message in terms readily understood by all, and it will straightway acquire converts, who in all probability will not make any distinction between the new teaching and that vaguely recalled from olden times. Propaganda began with isolated evangelical missions with no fixed terms of reference, and then, when the great Protestant Churches saw possibilities of success, they went into action on a grand scale, opening information offices, building seminaries and giving the operation sound financial backing. The International Missionary Conference in Edinburgh in 1910 and then the Latin-American Committee, founded at New York in 1913, were the prime movers. In 1938, at Madras, representatives of four-fifths of the Protestant Churches stated that America was now the most important of all missionary areas. After the Second World War the U.S.A. took great interest in Latin-American problems, and this helped to strengthen the movement.

Expansion could not be achieved in the same way in the Spanish-speaking countries and in Brazil. In the former it met with constitutional difficulties or administrative measures (in Argentina, until 1958, the Protestants were denied access to State broadcasting services and parish meetings were subject to authorization before they could take place), and sometimes there was open violence, such as that which broke out in Bolivia in 1951 or that which occurred on several occasions in Colombia between 1948 and 1956. Because of this, Protestant propaganda has assumed markedly popular characteristics throughout Spanish America. It is directly associated with social demands and is often openly anti-Catholic, denouncing the Church of Rome as a conservative and reactionary force, incapable of helping the people in their longing for justice. Moreover in the majority of left-wing political movements there is a Protestant element. This does not mean that Protestantism predominates among the industrial proletariat, for its strength lies mostly in the country and especially among the lower middle classes, all very poor, who are held down by the wealthy classes above them.

Protestant proselytism in Spanish America has been extremely well organized during the past thirty years. The number of missionaries increased and each is assigned a particular area; cultural centres have been set up, which are in fact Protestant parishes in disguise. Material assistance, often considerable, is given to the converts. For example, the missions guarantee the solvency of those who wish to buy machinery, equipment or tools on credit. Seminaries have been opened, the Protestant Institute in Costa Rica supplying excellent teachers. One important fact about all this is that the sects have taken a leading part. In Chile, where, as we saw, the most impressive advances have been made, one-third of the Protestants belong to sects, especially to the Pentecostal movement with its 180,000 adherents. The success of the sects has many causes: simplicity of doctrine, appeal to mass audiences and mass emotions, undoubted charity towards all men and a system of strictly autochthonous pastoral recruitment. For while the Presbyterians, the Episcopalians, the Methodists and others all undertake a vigorous missionary programme, it often happens that the powerful American missionaries fail where the poor half-breed *evangelicos* succeed. Catholic observers have stated that the Pentecostal movements in Chile formed the most national and the most devoted of all groups; and the historian Léonard has noted that a certain type of propaganda, employed by American missionaries who treated their catechumens as 'natives', has had only poor results. One might question whether the destiny of Protestantism in Spanish America will not depend on the future of the sects, and what future these sectarian communities will have when after one or two generations their members demand a less simplified religion.

The situation in Brazil is quite different. It is in this part of the continent that Protestantism has experienced the fastest growth and now has the greatest number of adherents. At the beginning of the nineteenth century there were none. There had been sporadic attempts during the sixteenth and seventeenth centuries by the French and the Dutch, but nothing remained of these. The first large-scale Protestant colonization was carried out by German Lutherans in 1824 in the south, but it did not spread. In addition the local Churches were troubled by disputes between the indigenous preachers and the pastors sent later from Europe. Today they are known as the Lutheran Church of Brazil, and are aloof from the main stream of Protestant life. However, Protestantism germinated here and there, almost spontaneously, in the distant *fazendas* which were not often visited by a Catholic priest and where nevertheless true piety managed to survive. Around the head of the family—even a Negro slave—a circle grew, but this form of purely lay piety soon lost contact with the Church. Another favourable circumstance was the action of Father Feijo, to whom the Emperor Pedro II entrusted the regency when he was obliged in 1841 to go to Lisbon as king. Feijo was a liberal-Jansenist, a 'crypto-Protestant' shall we say, who talked of reforming the Brazilian Catholic Church and of inviting the Moravians to evangelize the Indians, and who actually allowed an American Methodist Mission to establish itself in the country. The hidden conflict which the Emperor Pedro II carried on with the Catholic hierarchy, and which continued under the republic, was very favourable to Protestantism. Sporadic attempts to hold up its expansion came to nothing. Other American missionaries arrived, mostly Presbyterian, carrying out a strategic campaign of evangelization, based on the dollar. It was in some respects successful.

The efforts of Joseph-Manuel de la Concepcion, an ex-Catholic priest turned Protestant, but retaining his former religious name, directed the programme of evangelization towards the humbler strata of society. Alone, he led an immense missionary enterprise in the wildest areas, teaching a purely evangelical form of Christianity, quite simple, eminently suited to the poorer classes. When he died, worn out with his labours, Joseph-Manuel left not only a memory of unstinted generosity, but also a whole chain of Protestant communities.

From 1870 onwards Brazilian Protestantism increased quickly and consistently in spite of a number of complications. Taking advantage of the new freedom which was offered them, many societies sent their missionaries to Brazil; Methodists, Presbyterians, Moravians, Baptists, Episcopalians—almost all were to be found there. But fragmentation and division now appeared, aggravated by the theological conflicts that emerged. Miguel Vieira Ferreira, at loggerheads with the Catholic Church, founded the Brazilian Evangelical Church, which showed certain illuminist tendencies. The tutelary role adopted by many American missionaries brought about reactions—some severe, especially that which led the pastor Eduardo Carlos Pereira to found the Independent Presbyterian Church. Among Baptists and Methodists, Americans from the Southern States of the U.S.A., exiled after the Civil War, provoked similar reactions. The sects now quickly began to make their influence felt. All of them were represented: groups from the older Protestant Churches, such as the Plymouth Brethren and the Darbyites, as well as the younger illuminist movements, Pentecostal and Adventist. Brazilian Protestantism became almost as complicated as that of the U.S.A.

This, however, did not stop its progress. In 1922 the total of all denominations was 300,000 practising adherents. In 1940 it was more than 1 million and in 1958 $1\frac{1}{2}$ million, which indicates more than 4 million followers. Today there are two quite separate forms of Protestantism in Brazil. On the one hand, that of the middle class and intellectuals separated from the Catholic Church, who are on the registers of the Episcopalian, Congregationalist, Presbyterian and Methodist Churches; on the other hand, that of the Baptists, the Pentecostal and the Adventists, who are making progress among the distressed populations of the Amazon, of Minas Gerais and along the Matto Grosso, and who are attempting to penetrate the shanty towns in the great cities. Two thousand pastors, trained in twelve Faculties of Theology, are not too many for this work.

Protestantism gives the impression of having embarked on the conquest of all Latin America. There are more than enough would-be pastors, and the number of Protestant cultural centres will soon be more than the number of parish churches. Will this progress be maintained? During the last few years there have been signs of a slowing down. The ever-increasing antipathy towards the North Americans, noticeable throughout Latin America, is beginning to affect the Protestant missions, which are held to be associated with the North Americans. But it must not be assumed that Catholicism will gain from this reaction; the real benefit may accrue before long to Fidel Castro and a more or less nationalistic form of Marxism tomorrow. On the other hand, the undoubted efforts made during the last twenty years by the Catholic Church, efforts which continue to grow in scope, the heroic devotion of priests and bishops in the shanty towns of Rio, in the Amazon jungles and in the poorest areas of the north-east, are bearing fruit. It has often been observed that small Baptist or Pentecostal communities will return to the Catholic fold if a priest will only visit them and talk to them. A regenerated Catholic Church, made manifest as that of the poor, would raise a barrier to the expansion of Protestantism far stronger than the faintly slanderous charges of yesterday.

15. PROTESTANTISM ON A WORLD SCALE

Due to its enormous growth in the U.S.A., and through its missionary expansion, Protestantism has undergone a complete transformation since the end of the eighteenth century. Firstly in geographical terms: in addition to the compact area in Western Europe, there is now another of virtually equal size in America. On the other continents there are a whole series of small areas of different sizes, which together equal the first two. From the material point of view, twentieth-century Protestantism, like Catholicism, is now of world stature, much more so than is the Orthodox Church, whose area is more circumscribed and virtually limited to territory in the East and in Russia.

In sheer weight of numbers, Protestantism has a considerable say in the destiny of the world. It acts, directly or indirectly, at political and social levels, as well as in moral and intellectual fields; it determines a way of life, imbues literature with its spirit and inspires music. This influence is seen not only in countries where it preponderates, as in the U.S.A. and South Africa, but also in countries where it is only now gaining a foothold, such as Latin America.

Protestant expansion has resulted in the emergence of a truth hitherto little understood—that Protestantism was not an exclusively European plant, sprouting in Germany and transplanted to France, but that the spirit of the Reformation would spread to all races, all countries and all civilizations.

For a long time it was said that the Protestant message was more suited to the north-western area of Europe; but then why has it been taken up with such fervour by the Negroes of the U.S.A. and the mestizos of Latin America? It is fully universal, and accessible to all for the very reason that in its many different ways of expressing itself it can adapt itself to practically all forms of civilization and to all levels of intellectual and moral development. It is not linked to any hierarchical organization with a clearly defined centre or one associated with a particular race of people. In this, much more than the Orthodox Church, it is a rival of Catholicism, its chief competitor, in the effort that both consider a necessity, to keep alive the message of Christ in a world that denies it.

To carry this out, and above all to check the process of division, Protestantism has been led to strive for certain forms of union.[1] Even in its own interests it would have embarked on this course, but there were other imperatives. In missionary territories, realizing the effect that their divergencies were having on evangelization, the various forms of Protestantism have been driven to collaborate and sometimes even to unite. The ecumenical movement, whose importance will be discussed later, springs from identical considerations, but on a world scale; but here too the risks are great and various. One Protestant—Émile G. Léonard—sees these in uniformity, and prefers 'the union of truth and love'; another, the Anglican Bishop Barnes, sees them in a confusion of values and a contempt for principles, to which tend such undertakings as the union of south India. It is between risks on one side and imponderables on the other that the future of Reformed Christianity lies.

The Main Protestant Groups in the World

(The figures given are those for 1958. Those countries where Protestants are in the majority are shown in italics. The letters following each number in Europe show the different denominations present: A—Anglican, B—Baptist, L—Lutheran, M—Methodist, O—Other, P—Presbyterian.)

EUROPE:

Czechoslovakia	1·8 m.	POL
Denmark	4·2 m.	L
Finland	4·3 m.	LB
France	·8 m.	PLOBM

---

[1] See Chapter **VI**, section 6.

Germany	45·0 m.	LPOBM
Great Britain	33·0 m.	APMOB
Holland	4·0 m.	PLO
Norway	3·2 m.	LO
Sweden	7·0 m.	LOBM
USSR	4·0 m.	OBLP

ASIA:

Burma	1·0 m.
India	8·0 m.
Indonesia	6·0 m.
Japan	·65 m.
Korea	2·5 m.
Philippines	3·2 m.

AFRICA:

Cameroons	·5 m.
Congo (Ex-Belgian), Ruanda-Urundi	·7 m.
Ghana	·8 m.
Kenya	·8 m.
Madagascar	1·4 m.
Nigeria	1·3 m.
Rhodesia-Malawi	1·6 m.
South Africa, Rep. of	7·2 m.
Tanganyika (Tanzania)	·8 m.
Uganda	·9 m.

AMERICA:

Brazil	4·0 m.
Canada	6·2 m.
Chile	·8 m.
Mexico	·88 m.
U.S.A.	66·0 m.
Western states	1·0 m.

OCEANIA:

Australia	5·7 m.
New Zealand	1·5 m.

CHAPTER III

THE SOUL AND SPIRIT OF PROTESTANTISM

I. A Spiritual Revolution in Geneva

THERE was much excitement and no little indignation in the city of Geneva when a mere student, a greenhorn who still suckled at the breast of his foster-mother, the Faculty of Theology, dared to criticize that most venerable of Genevan institutions, the Pastors' Commission. The pamphlet—prudently printed at Baden across the frontier—bore a lofty theological title: 'Considerations upon the Divinity of Jesus Christ'; and it was widely read, if only because it called in question the highest authority in the land, and contained all the elements of scandal and revolt. Some protested loudly at such insolence; others, less vociferous, believed that Henri-Louis Empaytaz was not far from the truth. The dignified calm of Calvin's city was shattered.

These events took place towards the end of 1816; but the religious and secular authorities of Geneva had been for six or seven years conscious of agitation in student circles. Instead of being content with learning to be pastors, the young men discussed the thorniest problems among themselves, problems which daunted even the most experienced theologians. Worse still, they were questioning the authority of the Pastors' Commission and even its teaching. The leaders of this movement were known to the police—Amy Bost, Empaytaz, Lhuillier, Gonthier, Pyt, Guers and Gaussen. The authorities had cautioned them on more than one occasion, but with little effect. The *Société des Amis* included the more uncompromising members of the movement; it also organized propaganda. Naturally enough, the more serious-minded treated them with nothing but disdain; and though they received encouragement from Professor Demellayer and from the pastors Cellerier and Moulinié, everyone knew that the last had bizarre ideas on the end of the world and that the theology of the other two was questionable. No one believed that a handful of young men could really shake the established order laid down by the reformer.

But that order was exactly what Empaytaz, Bost and the others were contesting: the fact that the city still conformed with Calvin's principles. Outwardly the institutions were what they had always been: the French occupation and the Napoleonic regime had scarcely disturbed them, and in 1815 everything had returned to normal. All that emerged was that the Commission had gained in authority over the lay Consistory. Appearances may have indicated that Geneva was still the headquarters of Calvinism, but in reality, spiritually speaking, it was far from so. It was like a hollow nut, the outside perfect, but the inside shrivelled and dry. Among the people practice was now no more than a routine; furthermore the strict moral code which Calvin had laid down was being broken. Among the ruling classes the rationalism of the Century of Enlightenment had made great inroads, oscillating between the scepticism of Voltaire and the emotional pantheism of Rousseau, both of whom, as we know, were quasi-Genevans. The situation was even more serious among those who should have been the guardians of faith, the pastors in their parishes and the professors of the ancient academy founded by Calvin. The best of them stood for a moralistic deism, which poured from the pulpits each Sunday. The Bible was now discredited, it was never read by the rank and file; at the faculty the Old Testament was never opened except with a view to acquiring a smattering of Hebrew. As for the New Testament, one student of theology, Frédéric Monod, stated that for him it was *terra incognita*. What remained of faith? *The Liturgy or Manner of Celebrating Divine Service*, published in 1807, took care to avoid calling Jesus God. Rousseau's stricture on the pastors still seemed to hold good: 'One does not know in what they believe nor in what they do not, nor even in what they pretend to believe.' So too that of d'Alembert, in the article on Geneva in the *Encyclopédie*: 'Some ministers have ceased to believe in the divinity of Christ.' The official Catechism of 1814, to the question, 'What do we owe the person of Jesus Christ?' gave the astonishing answer: 'Respect!'

It was against this weakening of faith that the young men of the *Société des Amis* were reacting. There had been various influences at work on one or other of them, all of a pietist nature. One of these influences was the Moravian Brethren,[1] who meditated upon Christ's Passion with such emotion that tears ran down their cheeks. Another was that of Mme de Krüdener, who during her brief stay in Switzerland had led the young Empaytaz towards mysticism. There was also that of Robert Haldane, a Scot who had pitted himself against the Established Church in his own country. Lastly, that of the Methodists, who were then infiltrating all levels of Protestantism on the Continent. The young men of Geneva sought inspiration from all those sources; they even went to breathe the incense-laden air of the Catholic parish of St Germain, and occasionally attended masonic lodge meetings.

It was in this curious atmosphere that there took place in 1816–17 what Protestant historians have called the Swiss Revival. Empaytaz's pamphlet signalled its beginning. Thenceforward the Genevans were aware that those whom they had taken for trouble-makers were in fact

[1] See Chapter I, section 6.

the apostles of spiritual renewal, that they wished to lead their compatriots away from the torpor in which souls wilted, that they intended to return to the precepts of Calvin, that they believed in a theology which was both more soundly based and more orthodox than that of the majority of preachers. It soon became evident that these young men were not content with simple effusions dear to the pietists; they created a Sunday school to popularize their faith and undertook schemes to 'succour the poor and the afflicted with every means that the Lord might grant them'. A new spirit had entered the Genevan Church; furthermore the city's political and social edifice had been rudely shaken.

Everything might have returned to normal had not another personage now appeared on the scene, a young pastor, César Malan (1787–1864), a descendant of the Waldenses who had taken refuge in Provence, and an advocate of revival. He was of the stuff of which leaders are made, the great-grandson of Reformation martyrs, a democratic leader, sure of himself, authoritarian. An inner experience had converted him from conformist religion to a more living expression of faith, and he felt that he was the herald of a new revival. He preached a sermon at the Madeleine on Easter Sunday, 1817, during which he unfolded the pure doctrine of Calvin's justification through faith. He had to admit that he was heard in silence and with displeasure. Obviously this was a far cry from the usual moral exhortations to which the Genevan middle classes had been accustomed. His family and his wife felt that he had gone too far; but some of his hearers had been reached, and a small group was formed fervently resolved to revive the spirit of the Reformation. Alongside the pietistic revival of Amy Bost, Empaytaz and the *Amis* there was now another more dogmatic, strictly Calvinist. This division was not in the best interests of either movement.

The authorities were violently opposed to both. The Commission was not going to admit that it was in need of a revival; as for the theological theses, these appeared to be in accordance with free inquiry, and were left to the judgment of each individual.

Calvin had indeed taught predestination, justification through faith, the vanity of works in the light of grace; but certain of a master's postulates have always been watered down by his disciples so as to render them more easily acceptable. No one now offered the left cheek after the right had been struck. The Commission felt itself justified in issuing an edict which forbade the preaching of Calvin's doctrine and the declaration that Arius was a heretic.

The young leaders of the revival did not feel bound by this ukase. Those who had not yet been accepted into the pastorate refused to swear the oath required by the edict; some ministers adopted the same attitude. César Malan, who stated that he wished to remain faithful to the national Church, was barred from the pulpit. There were various court actions in which the Commission had the disagreeable surprise of not being upheld by the judicial authorities. The most it could obtain was an order requiring all foreigners who took too strong an interest in the Revival to leave the country. But the heart of the problem had still not been reached. The leaders of the national Church had acted in this way to avert a split, but in fact how could they impose their will? They were not infallible! Repressive actions had the opposite effect to that desired: the split occurred, or rather two splits. The old *Amis* formed a pietist group with a Congregationalist organization, based on the authority of the community as a whole; this was known as the Church of Bourg de Four. César Malan and his disciples, on the other hand, founded another, very dogmatic and Calvinist, on Presbyterian lines, which they called the 'Church of Witness'. The two revivalist movements accused each other of being insufficiently Christian and relations were generally bad.

This revolt in Calvin's city, in opposition to established authority and in defence of what was considered as true spiritual values, took place at the beginning of the nineteenth century, so often quoted as being indifferent to religious matters. For many years the dispute continued between the Established Church and the small groups which disagreed with its theology. Hundreds of pamphlets, tracts and brochures were printed by both sides; there were a few lighter incidents which pleased the gallery.

For example, some candidates for the pastorate when asked for a confession of faith handed in the text of the *Confessio Gallicana*, virtually the fundamental basis of Calvinism, and this was rejected by the official theologians as heresy.

There were scenes of violence, and several times the little church at Bourg de Four had to be protected by troops. But in spite of all its troubles, the revival slowly forged ahead. Some of its converts were well known and their conversion had its effect on public opinion. There was the case of Felix Neff, a young soldier and a pillar of the Established Church, who had been sent to protect a 'heretical' church service. He announced his intention of running his sword through the first 'heretic' he met, but far from doing this he was converted and became one of their best propagandists. The ideas of the revival seeped into the very heart of the Established Church. In the old days scoffers had found a word to indicate these agitators: *Mômiers*, or mummers, as actors were then called. But history will not forget Bost, Empaytaz, Malan and other 'mummers' who gave Protestantism a new lease of life by rescuing it from the position in which routine, indifference and rationalism had placed it.

2. 'ECCLESIA REFORMATA SEMPER REFORMANDA'

The revival is one of the most significant spiritual aspects of contemporary Protestantism. The phenomenon springs from a well-known psychological fact. The father of Methodism has explained its mechanism so clearly that this has come to be known as Wesley's Law.

In itself, the phenomenon of revival is not confined solely to the Protestant world. The Reformed Churches have often quoted the dictum 'Ecclesia reformata semper reformanda', and this is applicable to all religions. The Catholic Church is equally certain that it is unceasingly being renewed, reawakened and reformed, and has been so throughout its history. During the Middle Ages these movements can be traced to those who had responsibility for the Church and the clergy. One revival followed another—the Gregorian, the Cluniac, that of St Bernard and that of the Mendicant Orders. In the fifteenth century, having delayed too long before reacting against what had become mere routine, Rome watched a reformation taking place before undertaking the same thing at the Council of Trent. Other revivals of less importance were effected during the nineteenth century, heralding those which are now in progress.

The essential difference between such movements in the Catholic and in the Protestant fold is that both proceed in different ways, according to the spirit and fundamentals of each faith. When there is revival or reform within the Catholic Church one of two things happens: either process is rejected by authority, in which case its promoters either submit to or leave the Church, or it is accepted and applied. In the Protestant world an attempt to reform the reformers merely conflicts with customs and principles, none of which is indisputable, none of which has been laid down by any infallible authority. As we have seen,[1] this is one of the basic reasons for Protestant fragmentation. It also explains why all such movements arouse bitter criticism, as was the case in Geneva, and why their effect is, in the final analysis, so limited.

Of what are the revivalists accused? Not of breaking away from habit and upsetting routine, but of taking their stand on personal experience rather than on principle, and especially the Bible. All the revivalist movements in Protestant history, even that of the seventeenth-century Quakers and of eighteenth-century Methodism, sprang from the religion of the Spirit, a situation which has both advantages and disadvantages. On the one hand, only recourse to the Spirit offers any bar to the forces of inertia which thrust man downwards to all that is evil; on the other hand, a spiritual self-interrogation, which is

[1] Chapter I.

uncontrolled and without a definite framework, always runs the risk of leading the soul to unhappy and unreasonable experiences.

The revivals that swept through Protestantism during the nineteenth century all arose from a vehement and sincere desire to bring believers back to more urgent spiritual demands. They emerged in conditions vastly different one from another, and all had vastly different results. Some, that of Switzerland and later that of Oxford, were the reactions of small groups of university scholars who were attempting to reason out their position within their own Church. Others, for instance in Denmark and Sweden, were the result of action by leading figures of the national Church, anxious as to its future. Elsewhere revival took the form of theological renewal, as was the case in Germany. It also sometimes happened that instead of rousing the *élite* it affected the masses, arousing fervour over vast areas, ending in our own day with the mass meetings of Billy Graham. Three great waves followed one another: the first one at the beginning of the nineteenth century, up to about 1830, the second during the last years of the nineteenth century and the beginning of the twentieth, and the third in our own age.

What results can be expected of these great spiritual movements? They will vary. Some, operating within the framework of the Churches proper, will revive those Churches; others, thrusting further ahead in the search for freedom of the Spirit, will become free Churches or even sects. In both cases they will play an important role, either by reminding those in authority in the older Churches that it is of no use preaching the Law without love, or in demonstrating that lapses in spiritual authority drive men to substitute beliefs. Revivals are never very long lived (and here we should remember Wesley's Law), just in the same way that, in the Catholic Church, gains made by successive reforms have never been final. At the same time the majority of spiritual upheavals in Protestantism have brought in their train a number of good works, and these have lasted. For example, in the early part of the nineteenth century there was one which contributed largely to the foundation and expansion of Bible societies and missions, either at home or in pagan countries. In the structure of the Reformation these stand out as the manifestation of a spirit of permanent reform, which largely explains its vitality and its success.

3. THE GREAT REVIVAL AT THE TURN OF THE CENTURY

Observers and historians are agreed that at the beginning of the nineteenth century Protestantism in all its forms was in a seriously weakened state. Jacques Courvoisier spoke of the 'distressing spectacle' which the Churches presented. 'They are,' he said, 'on the whole, organizations without much spiritual life. Orthodoxy, in the long run, has not been able to stand up to Enlightenment. Within its limits, it is soon stereotyped; the framework remains, but scarcely anything else. Rationalism has won, and if the confessions of faith of the sixteenth century are still to be seen, it is rather as museum pieces. . . .' Samuel Vincent, one of the most vigorous heralds of the revival in France, had already spoken of 'a deep sleep which resembled indifference' and had written a celebrated passage depicting life in France under the Huguenots at the end of the empire: 'The preachers preached, the people listened; the consistories met; worship retained its outward forms. Apart from that, no one bothered, no one cared; religion was something apart from the average man's life.'

This scene was further darkened by the obvious decline in ecclesiastical standards, varying in character from one country to another. Church of England parsons were considered frivolous, too much concerned with worldly things; Lutheranism and Calvinism seemed to be dominated by the spirit of the eighteenth century and by Rabaut Saint-Étienne's belief in the unlimited perfectibility of human reason. The weakness, not to call it more than that, of French pastors faced with the French revolutionary Terror, and later with the Napoleonic dictatorship, appeared likewise in the docility of German and Scandinavian Lutheran ministers towards the civil authorities. It was high time the clarion call of revival sounded.

Signs of a forthcoming revival had been observed during the eighteenth century. In Germany a spiritual renascence was effected by Pietism, initiated by Spener, developed by Francke and the Moravian Brethren at Halle and fully organized by Count von Zinzendorf at Herrnhut in 1750. In England there was Wesley and Methodism; at first this was attempted within the framework of the Anglican Church, but soon overstepped it. The essence of religious life, Wesley insisted, was a seeking after direct experience of God. Pietism and Methodism had few adherents at the beginning of the century. But in the U.S.A. the revival had assumed more important aspects and covered a wider field. The Great Awakening had begun in 1735 in western Massachusetts with the Congregational minister Jonathan Edwards, and had then swept through all the villages of the Connecticut valley. Five years later the arrival of the Methodist George Whitefield, Wesley's companion, was to light the fuse. America was a perfect place for those great open-air meetings which the Methodists liked so much; Whitefield's success was rapid, and the revivalist movement spread all along the Atlantic coast. At the end of the eighteenth century a third wave was unleashed, starting from the frontier states of Tennessee and

Kentucky, under the influence of Presbyterians such as McGready, the originator of camp meetings, and of Baptist farmer-preachers.[1]

It was all very sporadic. But, during the first thirty years of the nineteenth century, all or nearly all branches of Protestantism were to experience impressive revivals. This phenomenon was substantially similar to that which was seen in the Catholic Church, perhaps more striking since the situation in the Protestant Churches was much worse. There was talk of a veritable spiritual resurgence, all the more welcome since Protestantism's success on the temporal plane, accompanied by territorial expansion, might well have put it in great danger of becoming middle class. The revival, contrary to what French historians of Protestantism have said, was not confined to France and Switzerland. It sprang up everywhere, in different forms in different countries. In Germany there was more emphasis on doctrinal problems, in France and Switzerland more on questions of faith, in England more on worship and the Church, but in every case showing the same impetus.

In Switzerland the impetus of the first two movements was felt in a concrete manner. The two Free Churches there had declined. But in the meantime a new wave had arisen. Adherents of the national Church, deeming it to be too slow in reacting, were joined by sympathizers of the revival, none of whom had been drawn to one or other of the two original movements. They now attempted to avoid the anarchic individualism of the first movement as well as the blunt dogmatism of the second. And so it came about that in 1831 the *Société Évangélique* was created, whose organizers were pastor Louis Gaussen and the historian Merle d'Aubigné. The society founded the short-lived paper, *Le Protestant de Genève*, various missions both at home and abroad and a school of theology. The national Church reacted against this new organization as it had done against those of Empaytaz and Malan. The society set itself up as an autonomous Church to which the best elements in Genevese society were drawn. In 1849 the majority of the remnants of the other movements joined it and it was then renamed the Free Evangelical Church, and exercised a deep influence on religious life in Geneva up to modern times. The national Church also became aware of the necessity of reawakening spiritual life, and under the guidance of James Fazy it underwent a revival in its turn.

The Swiss revival was not confined to Geneva, for the most powerful figure in that movement was Alexandre Vinet (1797–1847). He was nothing if not modest, a distinguished university man who, if he did not particularly impress his students, was highly respected in the city. Apart from a dispute with the authorities of the canton, which resulted in his exclusion from the Chairs of Theology and of Letters, he led an

[1] See Chapter II, section 9.

uneventful life. But beneath a calm exterior there lay a fiery soul. He followed in the steps of Pascal, with a stern conscience, a love for saintliness and a wide-ranging mind capable of seizing on essentials. He was prepared to sacrifice everything for his convictions. Sainte-Beuve, his contemporary at the University of Lausanne, held him to be a man of promise. Even if today his teaching is disputed, there can be no doubt that for many years his work had a profound effect on Swiss Protestantism, even influencing that of France and other countries. A man of the Reformation, Vinet wished to adhere neither to the sentimentalism of the Bourg de Four type nor to the dogmatism of Malan. He went beyond them in affirming that the Christian life fulfilled the most exacting demands of the era, and that in the Gospel alone would his contemporaries find the solution to their problems. In this respect his views were far in advance of his time, especially on such problems as the relations of Church and State. It was said of him that he was less of a reformer than an initiator in religious affairs. It was in his religious experience that this sincere and tormented man made the most impact. After the manner of Pascal, he demonstrated the painful void of the heart, which only the revelation of God incarnate and sacrifice can fill. Deeply Protestant, because of the individualism to which he subscribed, he yet transcended Protestantism on several counts, taking up a position which every Christian could accept, e.g. in the role which he assigned to personal sanctity as an appeal to grace. Alexandre Vinet was one of the finest examples that Protestantism has to offer.

One of the pastors of the Bourg de Four—Guers—once told of a dream in which he saw a star of great brilliance which broke into shafts of light, each one illuminating a part of the Earth. This to him signified the Revival, and the imagery is well conceived. Far from being confined to Calvin's city, the movement of renewal was to be felt in many other countries, forming a sort of revivalist 'Internationale'.

France was one of the countries affected by it. As we have seen, Protestantism was in a sorry state there at that time. It is probable that, at the end of the revolutionary crisis, there were several centres of true believers in existence, especially in the rural areas. But the renewal did not begin until the effects of foreign intervention were felt, particularly that of the English Methodists who from 1820 onwards took a real interest in France. The pastors were not mistrustful of them, and within ten years they were able to hold meetings and to preach freely; one of them, Charles Cook (1787–1858), left an abiding memory.

At the same time, Swiss teams went into action. A national society was formed in Geneva to carry the torch abroad. Pastor Guers, whose dream was now coming true, took charge of the French sector. At least a dozen apostles were soon at work, travelling from parish to parish with missions similar to those of the Catholics. Some of them were to undergo singular experiences: Amy Bost, one of the initiators of the Genevese revival, driven from Strasbourg by the Lutheran clergy, devoted himself to missionary work among convicts. Felix Neff,[1] the one-time soldier, converted at Geneva, wore himself out travelling on foot throughout the Alpine regions, especially in the Queyras area. These itinerant missionaries brought back the watch-night prayer meetings which the peasants attended in private houses when their day's work was done, a habit which still exists to this day in the Cévennes area and in the Alps.

The first revival was accompanied by a second, the origins of which were to be found in intellectual and middle-class circles. It began in the Midi and in Alsace and soon reached Paris. The leaders in the first sector were from the university communities at Montauban and Montpellier, the guiding spirit being Daniel Encontre (1762–1818), a one-time resistant during the revolutionary era; it was also sustained by industrialists and wealthy wine merchants. In Alsace, where at the outbreak of the Revolution an admirable man, Pastor Oberlin,[2] had already combined social with missionary work, it was also in wealthy business circles that a pietist revival took place. The movement reached Paris in 1825 with help from different sources: there was that of a wealthy English cleric, the Reverend Mark Wilks, whose pious assemblies at the Château de Bellevue drew great crowds; that of a Swiss from Neuchâtel, Pastor Grandpierre, whose oratory was such that he was nicknamed the Revival's Bourdaloue. A free chapel was founded in 1830 in the rue Taitbout, where all the leaders of the revival came to speak, attended by many of the great names of Protestant high society.

This aristocratic and middle-class revival undoubtedly set off a renewal in those circles which now took on the work of holding it up to example, spending generously on works and missions, creating social Protestantism;[3] but this was not the case everywhere. In Lyons the movement produced the strange and fiery Adolphe Monod (1802–1856). The son of a pastor, 'awakened' by a sudden conversion, he was elected to the leadership of the Church at Lyons when he was thirty years old. He set to work to revive his flock with a zeal that was altogether praiseworthy, but not always with prudence or moderation. He was a considerable orator whose hearers compared him to Bossuet, and at first his success was great; but his star waned when he reproached the industrialists of his parish with 'taking advantage of the needs of the poor', and it faded completely when he refused communion to

---

[1] See sections 5 and 8 below.   [2] See section 8 below.
[3] Ibid.

those who seemed to him to be unworthy of it. Dismissed by the Consistory, he returned to his fervent adherents in an Evangelical Free Church before going on to teach at the Montauban Faculty.

All these different manifestations of revival bore fruit, even when they seemed to fail, as in the case of Adolphe Monod. Many of the centres of French Protestantism were affected—not only those which adhered to strict orthodoxy, but those of liberal tendencies. Pastor Samuel Vincent, the leading thinker of liberal Protestantism in France, played a major part as a revivalist. All this did not proceed smoothly, for the Established Churches, strongly entrenched in the Concordat regime, reacted in the same way as those of Geneva had done towards the Pastors' Commission. Pamphlets such as the Methodist Letters flooded France, aimed at all those who were concerned in the awakening, and protests thundered from the pulpits against these new-style apostles who were sowing seeds of doubt in men's souls. In 1848 the Assemblies attempted to put an end to this state of affairs as well as to the tensions between orthodox and liberal groups, and to regularize the position of Protestantism as regards the State. This only resulted in the creation of Free Churches. But the impetus given by the Revival was to make itself felt right up to our own day throughout French Protestantism.

The upsurge was even more strongly marked in the British Isles; for a long time there had been considerable signs of upheaval. At the commencement of the nineteenth century there were two groups of apostles preaching revival: the Methodists, whose great leader, Wesley, died in 1791, and whose followers were continuing his work with vigour; and the Evangelists, with Sydney Smith, Charles Simeon, and later with William Wilberforce (1759–1833) and Henry Thornton, who were at work on a higher social plane. Their work was carried out by numerous apostles who travelled throughout the country. The most vigorous campaign was carried on in Scotland, in Presbyterian and puritanical Scotland, where David Hume had affirmed that his Church had become deist and unchristian. Strong personalities arose: the Haldane brothers, Robert (1764–1842) and James Alexander (1773–1851), who launched the Scottish Inner Mission, founded the Continental Society, which the Genevans adopted and developed, founded schools, preached at great meetings called Tabernacles a faith that was drearily Calvinist. There was also Thomas Chalmers (1780–1847), who burst the official Presbyterian Church asunder by his introduction of social questions, who became the apostle of the Glasgow poor, the protagonist of an educational programme for youth, and who finally broke with his Church to found the Free Presbyterian Church. The Revival spread to all Britain. It was not only a religious renewal, but conversion *en masse*, arousing emotional excitement rather than appealing to reason with a technique similar to that employed by Methodism.

The leading spirit was the Reverend Charles G. Finney (1792–1875), whose long life was devoted to indefatigably preaching a permanent revival; the main effort was concentrated in Wales, where, in the stamping grounds of the eighteenth-century Methodist revivalists, now started with an enthusiasm that was almost boundless the campaigns of the Anglican minister Daniel Rowlands, nicknamed the 'mad gentleman', and the lay preachers Pantycelyn and David Jones, whose psalms in Gaelic are the joy of the Welsh. This multifarious spate of activities gave rise to splits, to the creation of curious sects like that of the Catholic Apostolic Church, based on the Second Coming, founded by Edward Irving,[1] and later on of the Plymouth Brethren and the Darbyites, austere protesters against the general climate of apostasy. The Anglican High Church was shaken by all these different forces, and there came about from the thirties onwards in the University of Oxford, under the influence of the Reverend John Keble (1752–1866), and then of the young Newman, the famous 'Movement', which, after an attempt to renew the High Church, split in its turn into two groups, one becoming Catholic, the other remaining in the Anglican Church under Pusey.

These shocks were felt in all religious groups in the kingdom, and spread to practically every land where English was spoken, even to the remotest colonies. The nascent U.S.A. was not slow to feel it. The new wave of revivalism, starting from the frontier, swept across the states from 1800 onwards and ebbed and flowed for nearly forty years with the assistance of men such as James B. Finlay, Peter Cartwright and the blind William H. Milburn. Camp meetings of twenty-five thousand at a time became frequent. Methodist and Baptist preachers, odd in both their attire and their utterances, travelled the country with unstinted zeal. We have already seen what the soul of American Protestantism owes to this immense activity.

The Revival did not take on the same form, being less spectacular, as in the Anglo-Saxon countries; nor did it take on revolutionary forms as in Geneva or Lyons. In Germany it appeared in more intellectual guise, even, one might say, professorial in tenor, which fitted in with the characteristics of that country expressing itself in a return to theological and biblical studies. At the same time a new literary movement, Christian in inspiration, was also at work; it was similar to that experienced by Catholicism, from Maistre to Chateaubriand and Lamennais, along the lines traced by Klopstock, Novalis and Stilling, none of whom worried greatly about orthodoxy.

At the commencement of the nineteenth century the first of the great

[1] See Chapter I, section 13.

German revivalists died: Johann-Gottfried Herder (1744–1803). After an eventful life he became a Lutheran ecclesiastical superintendent. An able philosopher, he well understood the manner in which intellectual life was linked to religion and exercised his influence on many minds, less by his more ambitious work on anti-Kantian 'metacriticism' and the philosophy of history than by his pastoral letters, which are sensitive and straightforward theology. 'To acquire the sense of God and of divine matters', he said, 'is the only true aim of the study of theology.' His campaign to get the Bible read 'by men as a man's book' paved the way for a return to a less stereotyped knowledge of the Scriptures. While Fichte was losing himself in pantheistic mysticism, Hegel subordinating religion to philosophy and the young Schelling confusing faith and gnosticism, the wisdom of Pastor Herder appeared as the leaven which raised the lump of German Lutheranism.

He was followed by a number of professors and pastors who opposed the currents then in vogue, and at the same time a kind of apologetic based on aestheticism and utility so dear to Chateaubriand. One of them deserves particular notice—Daniel-Ernest Schleiermacher (1768–1834). Son and grandson of pastors, he saw his father turn now to Kantian rationalism, now to supernaturalism, before finally finding peace of mind among the Moravians, whom the official Church regarded with suspicion. As an adolescent he himself could well have succumbed to hypercriticism without the influence of his mother, who was a deeply pious Moravian follower. After a religious crisis the young Daniel acquired more assurance when, in his turn, he discovered Pascal's dictum: 'It is the heart which knows God, not reason.' In 1790 he became a pastor in Berlin, then a chaplain at the Charité and a preacher at Court; during all this time he acquired an immense quantity of learning, literary as well as philosophical and theological. His doctrine was enshrined in a series of striking works: *Discourses on Religion* in 1795, *The Christian Faith according to the principles of the Evangelical Church* in 1821. These two works enshrined the basic idea which he had developed since his youth: 'My religion is entirely a religion of the heart.' And to express this he made use of striking and persuasive forms, exalting religious experience as an essential function of man, taking many aspects from the great pre-Reformation mystics, justifying in a hundred different ways the contempt which he felt for dogmatics so as to bring back souls to the essential point: the vital impetus towards God. As we shall soon see, his 'pastoral' (as his enemies put it) theology had strange results.[1] But there can be no doubt that, following one of the most lively currents of Protestant thought, that of the personal experience of God, Schleiermacher was a staunch opponent of the rationalism then threatening. His ideas

[1] See section 7 below.

influenced many liberal Protestants, as well as such young neo-Lutherans as Claude Harms, who sought to rediscover the vital example of the Reformer. Outdated nowadays in the eyes of the disciples of Karl Barth, he remains none the less the man who gave twentieth-century Protestantism its most decisive thrust forward.

How far did this intellectual stirring penetrate the public at large and set off a true revival? There can be no denying that the sermons which he preached in Berlin for many years had a considerable influence upon his hearers; but it could not be compared to that of the great revivalists of the Anglo-Saxon world, nor even to that of the leaders of the Genevan and French revivals. But it undoubtedly helped to bring about the creation of Free Churches which at that time came into being for other reasons. Later, about 1840, when the measures taken by Frederick William IV gave semi-official character to the Revival, the spiritual heirs of Schleiermacher were not disposed to agree with this Hezekiah, who wished to lead his people to faith by following certain rules. But in the very conscience of that sincere monarch, was it not this appeal to the religion of the heart that had given rise to these good intentions? The revivals which took place in Protestantism covered a large area on the world map, generously studded and variegated. Even those countries whose language or geographical situation kept them at a distance from the world currents of religious renewal were affected in their turn. In Holland, for example, there were two revival movements: one orthodox, with Bilderdijk, Isaac da Costa (a Jew converted to strict Calvinism), Groen van Prinsterer and Henri de Coock; the other of a liberal type, close to Schleiermacher's ideas, sponsored by Hofstede de Groot and the Groningen school. Both of them helped to reanimate a faith that was well nigh foundering in torpor. In Scandinavia, where religious experience was often carried to an extreme mysticism—Swedenborg was an example—the Revival took on various forms: pietist in Norway with Nielsen Hauge, scholarly in Sweden with the 'Bible readers' and rigorous and orthodox with bishops Balle, Münter and Mynster. In Denmark, Nicolas Grundtvig (1783–1872) transformed his country from a feudal and militarist State into the exemplary nation that it is today. But towering above all of these was Sören Kierkegaard.

4. A Danish Pascal

The preacher mounted the pulpit; all eyes were fixed on him. An impressive congregation filled the church to overflowing. The king and queen were present, together with ministers, courtiers and the whole distinguished world of both palace and city. For the preacher was an illustrious theologian, an orator of great renown. But he seemed not to be quite himself. For a long time, in silence, he surveyed the assembly, then he began his sermon in a voice charged with resolution and with anguish. And his words aroused the astonishment and indignation of those well-dressed ladies and gentlemen to whom they were addressed. Were they Christians? Were they true Christians? No, answered the preacher's voice pitilessly, no, they were not. This gathering of worldly worshippers in this beflagged church, this self-satisfied society, upheld by well-paid clerics, was not Christianity. The Gospel was being betrayed! They were spitting on the face of Christ! These painful truths were answered with a shout: 'Down with him—out of here!' But the preacher thundered on: 'Before God, I hold you responsible—it is you whom I accuse—for it is the truth that I speak.' The wind of Revival passed over the hundreds of astounded listeners.

The author of this narrative—for it was an imaginary incident, published under the title *Situation*—was a little-known writer, except for his polemics with this or that journalist, whom Copenhagen took with little seriousness, partly because of the sartorial fantasies which he adopted. A thin, stooping figure, he gave the impression of being slightly hunch-backed; his 'front paws', as he himself described them, were ridiculously short. His voice was now harsh, now reedy, the voice of a eunuch. None of this was calculated to impress his hearers. But when one spoke to him in private, it was impossible not to be impressed by his presence.

His *Journal* and other of his writings provide clues to his way of life. From an early age he was submerged in a pietist atmosphere, which the Moravians had built up in several areas of Denmark. His father, Mikael Pedersen, had become one of them. The last-born of a numerous family, Sören was brought up in a dry and austere religion which had little time for consolations, and whose members had the deep-seated conviction that they lived more in God than the ordinary baptized. The criticism of everyday Christianity, which he placed in the mouth of the preacher in *Situation*, was one which he had often heard from the lips of his father. From him too he had received the conviction that Christianity without awe is valueless. Having reached manhood he suddenly understood this. The secret was to affect him 'like an earthquake'. One day while he was out walking across the Jutland countryside, pondering the eternal problems of life and death and the human condition, problems to which he could find no acceptable solution, Mikael Pedersen had solemnly cursed God. Here was something that provided an explanation for all the penitent austerity of the rest of his life, something that would forever sear the conscience of a son who held himself responsible for his father's blasphemy. There was too the staggering significance of the final piece of advice that the dying Mikael had given his son: 'Love Jesus!'

It was not through faith or spiritual impulse that the last-born of the Kierkegaards had responded to the objurgations of his father, nor through the pious remonstrances of his saintly mother. In adolescence he had estranged himself from faith and had gone through a phase of moral dissipation—a phase that he was later to call 'aesthetic'—where his models were Don Juan and Faust; during this period he had written on the weaknesses and cowardliness of Christianity in phrases that Nietzsche would not forget. Then, tiring of these deceptive experiences, he came to the 'moral' phase, during which time he attempted to lead a decent life; he became a pastor and got engaged to the innocent Regina Olsen, with whom, had he been more middle class, he could have been happy and raised a large family. But all this came to nothing. He soon realized that he was on the wrong track, that he was not cut out for parish work nor for a life of slippered routine. 'I had a splinter in my flesh,' he said in St Paul's words, and it was never to come out. Rather than attribute this to psychoanalytical causes one may see the recognition of the all-pervading depth of his anguish, of his uncontrollable inner awe, which is reminiscent of St Augustine or Pascal.

The course was now set. The curious ideas, the fits of melancholia which to outsiders appeared as vagaries, sombre daydreams, were for him 'pitiless creditors' whom he could never escape, but to whom he would be faithful to the end, for they would lead him to the eternal certitude of the infinite. His life now had found its basis: through anguish to God, and nothing was to deter him from this course. He led a cloistered life. Hardly ever leaving his town except for solitary rambles in the surrounding countryside or in the Gribskov forest, on which he wrote many admirable pages, he spent all the short years of his life in crying aloud the truths which he had discovered. Book succeeded book. Nothing counted for him but the problem of Christianity and Christian life. Was the world Christian? Was he himself Christian? How could one become a Christian?

This was his true vocation—to put these questions to humanity; to oblige it to make a choice. As he had once said, when speaking of Goethe, his own greatness also was: '. . . to have seen once, to have felt once, Something so incomparably great that everything else in comparison was as nothing'. That Something, so akin to that discovered by Pascal, Kierkegaard was to call 'the Christian future'. Away with philosophic idealism in the manner of Hegel! Away with the current spate of rationalism! Did not Luther's experience prove that the relationship of man to God is not to be found in the rational sphere? Away with the facile subjectivism of Schleiermacher, that 'faith choked with sentiment'. There was no more subjective person in the world than Kierkegaard: he analysed himself to the depths of his being, to the extremes of subjectivity, to find something other than sentimental consolations: the certitude of God's existence, of redemption, of the love of Jesus, of salvation.

Thus, taking existence as a starting point, which he called 'existential reality', he rediscovered Christianity. But it goes without saying that it was not Christianity pure and simple, of formularies and routines, as commonly practised. He felt that faith was born from the tragedy of life, bringing us not peace, but a sword—a constant reminder of the absolute, the eternal, and addressed to beings who lived in a transitory and temporal world. This explained why faith appeared to be discreditable as soon as one really tried to affirm it; yet to affirm it was so difficult that he asked, 'Has no one the right to write that he has faith?' Until his death this debate, the most dramatic in which man may be engaged, continued within him, while not preventing him from embellishing his works with beautiful and moving prayers that the most uncomplicated of pious believers could use as if they were his own.

Such an event in Christian experience obviously runs counter to what is ordinarily accepted. This was what Kierkegaard meant when he said: 'My task is to halt Christianity.' This, in his day, was called revival, renewal, awakening, but for him it took on the likeness of a campaign of the more prophetic kind—explosive, in which everything that the honest Lutherans of Copenhagen considered of firm foundation was brought into question. Their regular attendance at worship on Sundays—putting on their best clothes—their respect for the preacher's words, their generosity towards charities; none of these things had really any sense in light of that other agonizing Christianity which the new prophet was crying aloud. Giving up the unruffled tenor of their lives, they were to leave the steady everyday routine to reach the tragic, and live the madness of the Cross.

The logical consequence of this spiritual attitude may be imagined: it was the one adopted by the preacher in *Situation*. Official religion in Denmark, the Established Church—that is, the Lutheran State Church —appeared to the terrible polemist to be capable only of leading its adherents to paganism. Following Pascal, he saw in Christianity 'a society of people who, with the help of certain sacraments, are able to set aside the first requirement, that of loving God'. The struggle broke out over the death of Bishop Mynster, who had done all he could to awaken his flock, and who had published many pious works. Kierkegaard saw red when the bishop was lauded as a 'witness for truth'. For what truth? For this enfeebled Christianity as it was practised everywhere? What had this famous witness suffered for truth? Had he not maintained, unhappy man, that Christianity was not to efface nature but to ennoble? One might as well call upon heathen wisdom! And then the pamphlets appeared, blistering in content, reaching out to lash the whole Church, its pastors, its organization, its customs. Not only the Church, but Protestantism itself, for Sören, who was Protestant to his bones, steeped in Luther's doctrines, had no hesitation in writing that 'it is necessary to reveal what nonsense, what dishonesty, what corruption Protestantism is'. It would not be possible to go any further in destructive paradox and prophetic invective.

The battle which raged around the memory of Bishop Mynster was the last which Kierkegaard was to fight. His health had always been bad, and when he was thirty-five it became rapidly worse; a great peace descended on him. 'All my inner life is changed,' he wrote in 1848. 'I am no longer shut in on myself; the seal is broken. Almighty God, grant me grace.' He died on 11th November 1856 at the age of forty-three in Copenhagen Hospital.

At the time this inspired man was not heeded, but, little by little, the Danish Church absorbed his ideas and attempted to put them into practice. Protestantism was slow to understand the meaning of his message. He whom Rudolf Kassner has so justly called 'the last great Protester' was to wait until the early nineteenth century before being credited with injecting new force into the theology of the Reformation. The Protestant theological renewal of the last fifty years owes much to Kierkegaard, and in his early works Barth acknowledges the debt. In religious history he towers up as a man filled with certitude, strong in his whole-hearted drive towards God, the most important figure in modern Protestantism.

5. Lasting Fruits of the Revival

The Revival was not merely a flash in the pan, a spiritual tornado which for twenty or thirty years buffeted the Protestant soul. As is natural, the first flush of enthusiasm declined, but nevertheless it reappeared again and again in new revivals and new missionary endeavours. But lasting fruits remained in the form of institutions which today are still the most lively elements of the Reformation Churches.

In the front rank one must place the Bible societies. The Bible, as we have said, is the basis of every reformed faith. A Protestant is a man of the Bible. It is odd that in olden times there was not much desire to put this into the hands of the poor and humble. The movement can be discerned in embryo in German pietism which created the *Bibelanstalt* in 1710. At the end of the eighteenth century, firstly in Anglicanism, then among the dissenters in England, later among the German Lutherans, there was an awakening to missionary duties. This led to an increased interest in the Bible, since no Protestant apostolate is possible without the Holy Book. There was a dearth of Bibles. Mediocre organizations such as the Religious Tract Society and the Naval and Military Bible Society attempted to fill the gap as best they could. In 1804 representatives of the official Church and the dissident Churches met in London to found the British and Foreign Bible Society. Its aim was to distribute Bibles in all lands and in all languages, at the lowest cost. It was decided that, for those nations which already had their own Bible adequately translated, the existing edition would be reprinted; others would receive the Authorized Version of King James I.

The example was soon followed. Six months later a Bible society was founded in Basel, in 1805 one in Berlin, in 1812 in Stuttgart, in 1814 in Stockholm, then in Copenhagen, Oslo and in Holland; but none of them compared with the London society in size. In 1816 a second impetus was given by the foundation of the American Bible Society. It was vigorously led and soon covered all the Frontier area, where Methodist and Baptist pastors distributed copies in the pioneers' camps. When it was discovered that the only Bibles available in Latin America were Catholic translations, the American Bible Society set out to print these, duly stamped with the seal of approval. The society gave rise to the American Scripture Gift Mission, whose object was to give away Bibles free. France set up the Paris Bible Society in 1818, and in 1866 the French Bible Society was created, organized by pastors who were hostile to liberal tendencies. Finally, the World Bible Alliance was created in 1917, and, after a false start, emerged finally in 1946 with its head office in London.

The societies accomplished a gigantic task. The Holy Bible is now available in more than a thousand tongues; the London office alone has been responsible for its translation into seven hundred languages. In some cases it was necessary to create an alphabet and establish grammatical syntax before being able to embark on the translation. Sometimes new words had to be invented to render the meaning into dialects unprepared for theological precisions. The figures are staggering: more than 200 million Bibles and as many copies of the New Testament distributed in one hundred years. But it would be premature to suppose that the recipients of these texts are fully conversant with them, for, until very recently, Protestant Bibles, in accordance with the idea of free inquiry for every reader, carried no explanatory notes.

This effort, admirable in itself, was not only undertaken to propagate Bibles, but also had a missionary purpose that was equally admirable. Up to the end of the eighteenth century, the Protestant Churches had little understanding of the methods of religious propaganda used by the Catholics—the inner mission. They had no St Vincent de Paul, St Jean Eudes or St Grignion de Montfort in their ranks. But some groups, generally outside official circles, had demonstrated the necessity for undertaking some permanent form of penetration for the Christian message among the baptized populations; foremost among these groups were the English evangelists and the Methodists. The Revival aroused the idea of missions among Christians just as much as among heathens; it also demanded a particular brand of zeal.

The initial attempts were made during the revolutionary period and, oddly enough, first appeared in German Lutheranism, which had been interested only in individual salvation. Noble spirits like Spitler and Zeller launched the idea; it was taken up by Falk and Baron von Kottwitz, a model Christian. It was necessary, he said, to organize a mission to combat modern heathenism—a mission to the heathen of our country; 125 years later the Abbés Godin and Daniel were to make use of this same formula in their work, *France, pays de mission?* The idea was aired many times during the first third of the century in all countries affected by the Revival. The first efforts were those of the teams sent out from the Church at Bourg de Four to preach in the Genevan suburbs, those which Felix Neff set up in the Upper Alps *département*, the evangelical societies which from 1830 onwards emerged in Geneva, Paris, Lyons and Grundtvig's pedagogical foundations in Denmark.

One man now emerged who saw that all these different efforts needed co-ordinating. Missionary work needed an organization which was strongly based, not one made up of improvisations. This was Johan Heinrich Wichern (1880–81), a noble and enlightened soul of modern Protestantism. A poor student, a pupil of Schleiermacher at Berlin University, he became assistant of Pastor Rautenburg, the pastor of the poor in Hamburg; then he embarked on social and charitable work for delinquent and orphan youth, the importance of which will be seen later on.[1] His *Rauhen Haus* was a most impressive realization. But, influenced by Rautenburg, who had already spoken of the necessity of missionary work, Wichern realized that it was not enough to clothe and feed the poor; some deeper and longer-lasting action was needed: 'If the proletariat will not come to the Church, the Church must seek them out. Nor should it rest until it has brought the Word of salvation to them all.' The 1848 Revolution and its attendant riots convinced him of the necessity for speedy action. On 21st September 1848, in the Kirchentag at Wittenberg, five hundred delegates voted enthusiastically for the setting up of his Inner Mission.

Wichern's organization was to take up all his time and energy, and he was sustained in his work by the help of the King of Prussia,

---

[1] See Chapter III, section 8.

Frederick William IV. The movement, having spread throughout
Germany in a few years, is still alive today, strongly organized, with
specialist pastors at the head of each section, controlling lay evangelists
whom it has trained itself. From the start it distributed Bibles and
religious works, organized teams of preachers, and on Sundays held
special religious services in otherwise torpid parishes. It was very
similar to the Lazarist missions. Wichern's emphasis on charities,
orphanages and schools went hand in hand with his missionary work.
The charitable organizations that he created, such as the Deaconesses
and Brethren, supplied the Inner Mission with experienced collaborators. Some people were of the opinion that too much emphasis
was placed on charities to the detriment of the missionary side. Later
the mission was to react against this.

During the sixties the idea of an inner mission had spread everywhere. Not one of the great Protestant Churches was unaware of the
necessity of missionary work among the baptized. Some sects, such as
the Darbyites,[1] saw in this the main element of their work, and their
teams were to have considerable influence in areas such as the
Cévennes. Specialization now came into the work of the mission, which
adapted itself to particular circumstances, e.g. the urban mission of
Stöcker and the American worker missions of the type made famous by
Moody. But Wichern's basic idea was fundamental to them all—to
make Christ present to those who had forgotten Him.

There has been a third type of missionary activity lasting from the
time of the Revival into our own era, which has aimed at providing
Christian background to youth. Looking at the social works of Protestantism, it will be seen that works for children and adolescents are
very important. In England, as in Germany and France, welfare
projects such as schools and orphanages have been of prime
importance. But at this point came something different. Grundtvig's
high schools in Denmark were schools of life, aiming at instilling into
the young certain moral and spiritual attitudes. The same outlook is to
be found in the Young Men's Christian Association (Y.M.C.A.). At
its centenary in Paris in 1955, Marc Boegner defined it correctly as
follows:

'While the Churches confine their actions almost exclusively to
cultural and catechetical ministry and to charities, the Y.M.C.A. sets
out to interest all those young people whom the Church has passed by
in a search for true spirituality, allied to a real confrontation of all sorts
of problems which adolescents encounter at the age when they must
take on responsibility for their personal lives. The Y.M.C.A. has
developed with astonishing speed in Anglo-Saxon countries and in
Protestant Europe; it has flourished in Catholic countries; it is open to

[1] See Chapter I, section 14.

all young people regardless of denomination. In this respect it is the first youth movement to have an ecumenical character.'

There were various youth movements before 1855, such as that of Pastor Dürselen in Germany, and in Paris, with the union founded by Henri Dunant and eleven of his friends. But it was not until George Williams (1820–1905) took a hand that all these efforts were to rise above a limited range. His parents were Somerset farmers, members of the Anglican Church. When he was apprenticed to a cloth merchant he was told by this worthy that, since he was a strict Congregationalist, he required that his employees emulate his example. The perplexed apprentice sought counsel of his mother and was told: 'Follow both denominations!' The reply only served to emphasize that no Church was more important than another.

He was later employed in a large London firm, and this experience brought him into contact with the hardships and perils to which, in the Victorian age, thousands of young men were exposed. He was lonely and cut off and soon gathered a group of young friends round him to found the Y.M.C.A. At first there were only twelve members, but from year to year the movement grew, and its premises likewise in size and importance. Importers and banking houses became interested in it. In 1845 the association became a company, and was able to gather three thousand members at a meeting at Exeter Hall.

The movement never looked back. It was helped by Lord Shaftesbury, well known for his social work, and by members of the House of Commons. At the Great Exhibition of 1851 the Y.M.C.A. had its own stand. In 1855 it had covered the Continent and held its annual meeting in Paris. There was no lack of difficulties, however. These came from certain employers' organizations, disquieted by such a large body of young men, and from the Churches, who either looked upon it as competitive, or wished to absorb it—or at any rate exercise strict control over it. But George Williams wisely refused to be absorbed or taken over. He insisted that the Y.M.C.A. must be 'neutral ground where members of every denomination could meet in complete freedom and fraternity'. The Y.M.C.A. had three aims: to help the intellectual development of the young in what is known today as 'guided leisure', to watch over their moral training and to nourish them spiritually.

George Williams's movement exceeded all expectations. It became virtually an institution—it bought Exeter Hall—and had its own buildings, its own organization and its own publications. Williams was knighted and made a freeman of the city of London, and was buried in St Paul's Cathedral. There are at present some 4 million members in seventy countries. In 1955 the president of the association was a Negro from Liberia. Faithful to the principles of its founder, it is always ready to welcome any Christian young man of whatever denomination. It is open to non-Christians, such as Buddhists and Moslems. It played an important part in international welfare work after both world wars.

6. RETURN TO SACRAMENTS AND LITURGY

The renewed vigour of spiritual life which we have seen had another consequence, less to be expected than one might suppose: the return of certain of the principal elements of Protestantism to the two great Christian realities which Luther, and still more Calvin, had set aside—the liturgy and the sacraments.

In this it was the Anglican Church which provided the impulse. Within it the spread of what was called ritualism was, at the outset, expressly associated with a manifestation of Revival, in the same forceful way as it appeared in Scotland with Haldane and Chalmers, and in Wales. But, while the first currents of revivalism had shaken the Presbyterian Church and the most puritan elements of the United Kingdom, it was at the very heart of the Established Church, the Establishment, that the greatest upheaval took place at the beginning of the second third of the century through the Oxford Movement. Oxford, the city of learning, where half the nation's *élite* was educated, along with the higher echelons of the clergy, had been a century earlier the birthplace of Methodism. . . . The events which led up to the explosion—it is not too strong a word—of the Oxford Movement are well known.

The principal aim of the leaders of the Oxford Movement was undoubtedly to renew religious life in the Church of which they were members. Around them they could see spiritual collapse. Practice was no more than routine; living faith was rare. The bad example came from above, from the bishops, the professors and other churchmen who, as the challengers of Oxford put it, thought first of worldly things, and then of serving God.

The situation had come to such a point that in 1832 Parliament embarked on a fundamental reform of the Church; but this itself disquieted the young clergy, for it seemed to them that it was directed towards a secularization of the Church, whereas they were of the view that too close a link between Church and State was one of the causes of the spiritual crisis.

The followers of the Oxford Movement decided that in order to counter the forces of degradation (as other reformers before them had also decided), it was necessary to return to original sources. In studying the primitive Church, the Fathers of the Church and every aspect of holiness which was in existence before the break with Rome, they found the traditions which Anglicanism claimed to have kept intact and which it had allowed to tarnish. A certain puritan asceticism, a throwback to English Christian humanism and certain German pietist influences all became part of the movement, crystallizing into no less than an urgent demand to recover the true basis and direction of the Church. It was this complicated but attractive doctrine which the Oxford Movement's theologians preached through ninety tracts (from which the word Tractarian springs), through sermons and through books. This set off lively reactions in the established hierarchy, but the movement held its ground, and even gained some, eventually obliging its co-religionists to ask themselves if they themselves were still true to the traditions of their Church—whether they had not given in too much to what was being shown to them as 'Calvinist heresy'.

In reassessing the tradition of their Church, Newman, Pusey and their friends rediscovered the importance and the true significance of the sacraments and of liturgical rites. At the outset, Anglicanism had not, concerning the meaning and the range of the sacraments, taken up the radical positions adopted by Protestantism, and there was nothing, either in the Thirty-nine Articles or the Prayer Book, to oppose the liturgical usages of the ancient Church. The Oxford Movement was just such a return to these ancient customs. They were instrumental in creating sculptured stone altars, like the one which Newman had installed in the church at Littlemore, instead of the wooden tables normally allowed and which custom demanded. There was a return to embroidered altar cloths, to candles, to incense; and sacerdotal dress regained its original sparkling colours. To celebrate communion the minister stationed himself before the altar—as the Catholics do—instead of at the table, a change which signified that this was not a question of a meal but of a sacrifice. Newman and Pusey both taught that the eucharistic sacrifice is that of the Cross, that the Body and Blood of Christ are present in the bread and the wine. Still more surprising, and to the horror of all the Calvinist elements of the Church of England, the Oxford Movement's clergy confessed as the Popish priests did. The movement incorporated a whole collection of doctrines contrary to the Protestant main stream and had to be considered as pro-Catholic. In 1841 monastic orders reappeared; these had been absent since the Reformation. One can understand the displeasure of the official Church, whether High or Low. The Oxford Movement's ideas, however, were gathering adherents very quickly. The sermon which Pusey preached in 1843, and for which he was condemned with due ceremony, was taken up again word for word in 1853, and accepted without great reaction.

The Oxford Movement had gone through a severe crisis in the

meantime. Taking his return to origins to its logical conclusion, Newman became a Roman Catholic in 1845. More than two hundred clergymen followed him, some of them well known, such as Archdeacon Manning of Chichester. The Church of England was severely shaken by these events. Every method was used in an attempt to stop the flow of conversions, even an action against Newman, but this only served to make his name even better known. It looked for a time as if the cream of Anglicanism was returning to Rome.

In point of fact, apart from a brilliant start, the movement very soon slowed down. The responsibility for this can be ascribed to Pusey and to those who, like Keble, refused to doff their traditional clergyman's habit. It was not without distressing inner debate that a noble soul like Pusey made his choice (he spoke of the agony in which he lived). But once his choice was made, in spite of being a normally cautious man, he acted with speed and vigour. He told those who came for advice that Newman's experience was particular to him and that others should not try to imitate him, that it was not right to leave the Church of England, despite its defects; members should remain within it in order to remedy these defects and bring it back to its authentic Tradition. For his part, he abandoned none of the stands that he had taken up on questions of liturgy and the sacraments; he even founded the English Church Union, which he described as ritualist, to act as a vanguard within the national Church—a vanguard that would drive it into undertaking the necessary reforms. And people listened to him.

This new Anglican ritualism became allied with certain tendencies already present in the High Church, and the result was to emerge as Anglo-Catholicism. The established authorities were not too pleased with this development. The first clergymen to introduce vestments, candles and incense in the Catholic style were abused by their congregations or brought before the courts, as were Lowder and Machonochie. The Reverend Denison was dismissed and suspended for five years for having taught 'heretical' theses concerning the Eucharist. To combat the English Church Union Lord Shaftesbury created the Church Association, and in Parliament he denounced the ritualists. A commission was appointed to examine these delicate matters, and Parliament later adopted the Public Worship Regulation Act, which provided for the imprisonment of any minister who introduced irregularities into the religious service; a dozen delinquents were arrested. But the bishops had accused the ritualists of favouring 'those errors which the Anglican Church had already rejected', and Pusey, with his calmness and courage, then intervened. If it were his ideas that were being called into question he would accept the challenge, resign his post and then say out loud what he wanted to say. The hierarchy decided to push the matter no further, and the atmosphere became progressively less strained. A parliamentary debate found that Anglican priests might hear confession if they so chose.

Pusey died in 1882, and by then his influence had extended to every level of the High Church; liturgical rites and the practice of the sacraments—including confession—were now commonplace. From the Oxford Movement there remained the religious communities which had been reconstituted along the same lines as those of old. In 1839 Pusey had expressed the wish that a group of Anglican Sisters of Charity should be created. Newman, before his conversion, had even gone so far as to declare that the founding of Anglican religious orders was the only way to keep some of their adherents from becoming Catholics. In 1841 Mary Rebecca Hughes, aged twenty-four, took the three vows of poverty, obedience and chastity before Pusey, but remained with her family until 1849 when she gathered a small community together; this was the nucleus of the Sisters of the Holy Trinity, similar to the Poor Clares. Pusey's own daughter had thought of becoming a nun, but died before this could be achieved. On the day of her burial four pious women, after seeking counsel from their priest, formed the Sisters of the Holy Cross, a movement observing the strictest piety, which sent its members to work in hospitals for Crimean wounded. Despite the opposition of certain bishops the movement grew, and some twenty orders were founded over a twenty-year period.

Male Orders took longer—it was not until 1863 that the first of them, the Society of St John the Evangelist, was founded at Cowley by Richard Meux Benson. This was followed by others, and by the end of the century there was a considerable number.

During this time another great Reformation Church was going through the same ritualist and sacramental crisis as the Anglican: the German Lutheran Church. In 1848 a neo-Lutheran movement began in Germany, which opposed Kantian rationalism, sentimental pietism, the 'misty' theology of Schleiermacher, and became the enemy of all that made up liberal Protestantism. The movement's supporters proclaimed that the Church had a vital role to play in the life of the soul, that it was the guardian of dogma, and that in obedience to its authority inner experience must give way. This seemed to be contrary to what Luther had proclaimed ('Faith alone'). But the neo-Lutherans believed that Luther himself had erred in misunderstanding the role of the Church and that of the sacraments. For them baptism, in bringing man into the Church, would assure faith. From this sprang the sacred and consecrating character of the ministers who administered baptism as mediators between the soul and the supernatural. One point led to another, until they affirmed finally the importance of the altar sacrifice; this led in turn to a development of sacramental practice and liturgy, which, as we have seen, had been much less marked than in Scandinavian Lutheranism.

The movement got under way with Friedrich Julius Stahl, who brought to it certain contestable theses concerning Christianity as the State religion, and the ideas of the movement were much developed by Wilhelm Löhe (1808–72), a true believer and regular communicant, who avowed that he had never, since his first communion, taken the sacrament of communion without his 'soul being filled with adoration'. At twenty-nine he was appointed to the poor Bavarian village of Neuendettelsau, where he soon became famous and was invited to preach all over the region. Sought out by penitents, for he had restored auricular confession, he revealed himself as an incomparable spiritual adviser. This Lutheran Curé d'Ars, without leaving what he called 'his hole', exercised an enormous influence. With his *Ritual for Christian Communities of the Lutheran Confession* he restored liturgy taken from texts which antedated the Reformation. A liturgical and sacramental flood of ideas came from his pen.

His disciples went further still in what might be called the Catholic direction: Delitzch, Munchmeyer, who affirmed that the sacrament is efficacious in itself, and Detlev Kliefoth, a determined adversary of personal experience (who taught that the Church had the power and, through the sacraments, the means to ensure salvation). Standing a little to one side of this group was Christian Vilmar; his 'theology of facts' proclaimed that the sacraments were superior to the Word, that their objectivity was always self-sufficient and that their administration required sacred words and movements—in sum, a liturgy. The reaction which emerged with Vilmar—more or less anti-Calvinist—made itself felt throughout Lutheranism.

In 1870 the liturgical and sacramental current, if it had left purely Calvinist areas untouched, had nevertheless given a new look to some of the great Reformation groups. It reached the U.S.A., where the Episcopalians embraced it whole-heartedly and where part of the Lutheran Church submitted to the influence of Löhe. It had before it a future promise which would be fulfilled in our own age.

7. FROM LIBERAL PROTESTANTISM TO FREE CRITICISM

The Revival was, in all its various forms, substantially a reaction against the deadly routines which were sapping the spirit of the Reformation and against all the various forms of scholasticism which had ruled Protestant theology for two centuries. Pietism, which is found in greater or lesser degree in every revivalist movement, was mistrustful of speculation and also of institutions which were too firmly established. The danger was that mistrust was brought to bear not only on intellectual systems and ecclesiastical organization but also on dogmas. The reasoning was simple enough: if the official Churches were no more than the graveyard of souls, what was the purpose of the creeds which they taught? The renewal of fervour was the origin—or better, one of the origins—of the current which was finally to separate Protestantism from fervour and from faith.

This current merged with another, older one which sprang from the early days of Protestantism. The Reformers' heritage had been exploited by its successors in two different ways, one opposed to the other. The first, based on the principles of free inquiry and the direct influence of the Holy Ghost on each man taken individually, tended towards subjectivism and dogmatic anarchy, the Holy Ghost becoming identified with conscience. The second, faithful to the dogmatic affirmations of the Reformers, insisted on the other hand on the Sovereignty and the Transcendency of God, and thereby established orthodoxy. For three centuries Protestantism has been unable to escape the dilemma: either the freedom of the Spirit which leads to anarchy, or else the acceptance of an orthodoxy which in substance is contrary to the spirit of the Reformation.

The liberal current was strengthened during the eighteenth century by the climate of opinion then prevailing. The guiding lights which were followed owed everything to reason and little to faith. Dogmas were sapped. A rationalist deism ruled; it was accepted that a Supreme Being existed, but He was unknowable and inaccessible. Faith must be considered apart from intellect; it existed solely to inspire emotion and to satisfy feeling. If this philosophy was inadmissible to a Christian, there was perhaps nevertheless still a means of reconciling faith and rationalism in the interpretation of dogma. Here was a second source of what was called liberal Protestantism.

A third, less well known, was Unitarianism,[1] which was the doctrine of the Englishmen John Preston and William Ames and the German Johann Koch in the seventeenth century. In this everything was based on religious experience in an alliance—alliance between God and man, between God and the Church and between men in the bosom of the Church itself. It was operative within one's conscience and the Christian revelation was its manifestation. To be a complete Christian man had only to live according to his conscience; the light of God would illumine him. No formula of faith was therefore necessary—nor was any ecclesiastical discipline. The Unitarians, few in number, and whose ranks were filled almost entirely from the intellectual and upper classes, exercised a more or less secret, though considerable, influence in the U.S.A., where the theology of alliance became identified with the

[1] See Chapter I, section 10.

idea of the social compact and so brought faith down to a purely human scale.

All these theories and tendencies converged to make up a system of thought and a doctrine of religious life which came to be called (from 1875 onwards) liberal Protestantism. This seemed to be even more attractive when it appeared to find a solution to the problem faced by Protestant Christianity that had already confronted Catholicism: relations with the modern world. The Reformers were mistrustful of the modern world, even hostile to it; we know to what extent the humanism of Erasmus, the basic doctrine of the modern world, was regarded as suspect by Luther and Calvin. But, after the French Revolution, noting the advances made in knowledge and technology, attracted by the doctrine of progress, imbued with the idea of liberty, many Protestants looked upon the modern world more favourably. A French liberal thinker, Samuel Vincent, wrote in 1820 that man, brought face to face with himself through Revelation, had 'the presentiment of a religion which went hand in hand with civilization, without ever being jealous of it; with the sciences, without fearing their achievements; with industry, without being disturbed by the ease and the happiness of the peoples it enriched; with the advance of social institutions, without wishing to interfere constantly in their running, to hinder or abolish them'. Liberal Protestantism seemed to be the means to see this splendid programme through.

A large number of thinkers, philosophers and theologians helped this idea to spread and grow. Lessing (1729–81), more poetically than philosophically, enunciated a theory in which Christ's religion and the dogmas should be separated, the former being composed of true personal piety and aspiration towards holiness. Immanuel Kant (1724–1804) who, in his mistrust of reason, is akin to a lay Luther, had none the less reduced religion to the limits of pure reason by identifying it with the inner imperative of moral law. Hegel (1770–1831), a one-time theological student at the Tübingen seminary, wanted to save Christianity by emptying it of its supernatural content and by founding a religion based solely on the rationality of the Christian idea ('faith restored to the level of sentiment', as Kierkegaard said with contempt). Frederick Schelling (1775–1854), also a candidate for the priesthood, an anti-Hegel man, saw in religion a means of seizing hold of the world soul through Christ; this led Heinrich Heine to accuse him of having delivered philosophy into the arms of religion.

It was Schleiermacher (see above) who, more than anyone else, brought these elements together. In his view religion exists in every conscience—an accomplishment of the divine instinct. It is therefore essential to use this as a starting point if dogma is to have any firm bases. All metaphysical speculation is useless; what counts is the religion of the heart. Through the heart we can discover the truth, we can discover ourselves, we discover God; all are substantially the same thing. Conceived in this way, religion obviously cannot identify itself with a system, with a strict profession of faith; it follows the evolution of life, perpetually changes and progresses, and it is this experience, endlessly repeated, that gives it its meaning. What, in these circumstances, is Christian Revelation? None other than the revelation of our own conscience. But when we consider Jesus Christ, when we seek to imitate Him, do we not have a feeling of spiritual fulfilment, do we not ascend to the Divine? This is the real proof that Jesus was divine, and historical proofs are unnecessary. Since Christ was the most perfect of all religious Masters, then Christianity, of all religions, is the best. But its dogmas have no absolute value; they change, because they correspond to changes in conscience over a certain period and to the exigencies of the Church. It is scarcely worth observing that, of the older brand of Protestantism, founded exclusively on the Bible, outstanding in the tragic contrast between man the sinner and God the All-powerful, noble in its dogmatic and moral strictness, there remains but a nebulous theology in which everything dissolves.

Schleiermacher had many followers, though not all of them took his ideas so far. One was Neander (1789–1850), a former Jew who became a convert, an admirable man who resembled Vinet. He underlined the theory of Pascal, that to seek God is to find Him, and built up on a firm basis the history of early Christianity. Nietzsche tried to synthesize liberal theses and faithfulness to the Holy Scriptures in what he called 'practical theology'. Ullmann, taking a stand against excessive criticism, was one of many who inclined to the study of Jesus the man, of His psychology, of His holiness. Others, taking Schleiermacher's subjectivism and his theses on the real meaning of Revelation as a starting-point, set to work to criticize the Scriptures; among these were Davis Strauss, Christian Baur and Adolph Harnack, whom we shall come to later on.

A new impulse was given to the German liberal current in the 1870's by Albrecht Ritschl (1822–89) of the University of Bonn, author of a work entitled *The Christian Doctrine of Justification and Reconciliation*. He saw the danger that lay in a system of thought exposed to the arbitrary nature of unbridled subjectivism, and stressed that true knowledge of God rested upon a positive religion. He stressed, much more than his predecessor, the value of studying the Holy Scriptures, which he cleansed of all external influences by eliminating that which seemed to him to be valueless or open to doubt, especially the 'miraculous' aspects of Jesus's life, focusing everything on the person of Christ, 'revelation of God in his whole being'. He arrived at a 'theology of Christ', the sole explanation for everything, the only model, the sole basis of faith. Revelation became the supernatural response to man's deeper needs, to his most intimate aspirations, given as it was by such an exceptional Being that only the epithet 'divine' was adequate. Religion was, in sum, an instrument for conditioning and strengthening the consciousness of the self.

The German liberal current had its counterpart in France, and here it was perhaps still more active. From about 1830 there were many personalities who agreed with the ideas that it brought forth, personalities who were prominent in the Revival. Pastor Samuel Vincent at Nîmes was one of them. Certain of his observations remind one of Teilhard de Chardin. In 1850 the radical Scherer, in his book *Authority in Matters of Faith*, gave a condensed version of liberal theses. This had a considerable following—*avant-garde* pastors (the same pastors whom we saw combating the Established Church), together with Coquerel, Roberty, Astié and Raoul Allier. In 1882 Pastor Leopold Monod propounded theories fairly similar to those of Ritschl. Christianity was becoming more and more a plain fact in practical life; Albert Réville stressed this view in an incisive criticism of dogmas and the Scriptures, and Cougnard in a moral rationalism.

The leader of liberal Protestantism in France was Auguste Sabatier (1839–1901), whose *Esquisse d'une philosophie de la religion*, which appeared in 1897, was hailed by Pastor Ménégoz as 'the greatest work on dogma to emerge from Protestant theology since Calvin's *Institution*'. He was in fact more of a popularizer of German theories than an innovator, and while he moderated the excessive aspects of subjectivism he retained all the essential elements of Schleiermacher and Ritschl. Setting the religion of the Inner Spirit against the 'religions of authority', Sabatier found in the 'inner certitude which preceded and produces all Christian dogmas' a basis secure from the attacks of disbelieving science. No external authority could be acceptable. Even the Bible itself was open to question since one might, as with any secular work, dispute its origins. The Churches were not endowed with infallible authority, since history demonstrated that they were often proved fallible. Theology accorded with history: it was limited to the creation and the evolution of dogma. What then was left that was stable? Faith in Jesus Christ, the perfect manifestation of God in man, guarantee of salvation for those who possessed this faith—for those that is who gave themselves to God whatever their theological viewpoints.

These are the lines of the thinking which dominated liberal Protestantism. It is not a complete, logical system, still less a dogmatic one. 'Serene and wise,' as Pastor Chavel said, 'more philosophic than religious, more religious than Protestant, unless we define Protestantism as the spirit of research, of liberty in fervour.' At the highest point is that inner experience where each man is aware of the continuing message of the Gospel and sees the living image of Christ.

This type of religious experience should not lead to formulas unacceptable to one's intelligence. In the modern world liberal Protestantism has its part to play, without, for all that, letting slip its hold on the Gospels. Its aim—one might say it is a form of religious rationalism—is to express the Christian message in terms which are intelligible in this age of science and technology. The Christ of history is disputed; His existence is often denied altogether. In any case, so the more radical affirm, Jesus's existence has in itself no vital importance for faith, faith and reason not being in the same category. His divinity, or rather His 'divinization', are accepted, but not His 'Godhead'. The Gospel is regarded as purely human teaching: it is no longer Grace, the manifestation of the Almighty in man through the Incarnation, the Redemption through Blood, that it teaches but moral obligations, necessity for social work and the perfectibility of Nature. Between Jesus and an ordinary prophet, where now is the difference? Obviously we have come far from Luther and Calvin and have reached a slippery slope leading to moralism and pragmatism, towards belief in the myth of progress, towards a humanism akin to atheistic humanism. This is all very similar to what is known as Modernism in the Catholic Church. But this is a modernism which, restrained by no infallible authority, has developed unchecked and reached extreme positions.

Liberal Protestantism, although it may have drawn Protestant thought along very dangerous ways, has nevertheless certain positive aspects which it would be unjust not to place to its credit. It has played an essential role in apologetics, giving scientists a link with religion. By radically separating faith from reason it has justified this particular type of spiritual dichotomy, which can also be seen in other Christian groups, though they may not admit it. More especially, liberal Protestantism has focused much more attention on the Bible. Critical study of the Scriptures has provided a meeting-point for faith and science, making possible a scientific view of Revelation. It will be seen that this was not without its dangers, and of the numerous works on the Scriptures not all were favourable to faith. At least, however, there has been in all this an attitude of responsibility and a vigorousness which has given rise to an impressive revival. Among the constant objects of study have been Christ's human personality, psychology and virtues. That study has been carried out with a care and a zeal which have earned the praise of Catholic critics; the type of sentiments towards Jesus, by Renan, are a feature of liberal Protestantism. By insisting on the social aspects of the deeper of man's aspirations, by demonstrating the practical value of Christianity and by reducing evangelical teaching to a social message, liberal Protestantism has taken up a position at the source—or one of the sources—of the movement which led all the Reformation Churches to interest themselves in the creation of philanthropic works, as well as at the source of Christianity itself.

These incontestable and positive results are not sufficient to allow us to forget that liberal Protestantism, despite its intention of safeguarding Christianity by defending it against the hostile forces of the modern world, has been the ally and accomplice of men who, on the evidence, have contributed to the success of irreligion. In this connection the biographies of Jesus are a case in point; they flourished under liberal Protestantism. A large number of thinkers, philosophers, theologians and historians belonging to the liberal Protestant current of thought have devoted at least one book each to the life of Jesus. The presuppositions of their philosophic conceptions became apparent in these works just as much as their recital of historic truths. Schleiermacher, in line with his theology of the heart, postulated a mythical Christ, the expression if not the creation of human consciousness, a sublime manifestation of the most noble aspirations. David Strauss (1808–74) preferred the 'Jesus of History'—it is his own expression. Applying Hegel's theses wherein 'religion and philosophy have the same content, one in the form of images, the other in the form of ideas', he attempted to 'explain' Jesus's life and the miracles as mythical projections of the fervent wishes of the disciples. More rigid still was Christian Baur (1792–1860), an eminent exponent of the Tübingen school, whose exegetical works were for many years the basis of academic criticism; he disputed the texts themselves by stating that the Gospels originated in the second or third century and that Christianity was the result of the synthesis between the Jewish thesis postulated by Jesus and the universalist antithesis affirmed by St Paul. Ritschl retained from the Gospels only those parts which had any permanent degree of utility, and he transformed Christ into a social apostle. Adolphe von Harnack (1851–1930), after having undermined the New Testament as a source of divine revelation, concluded with the view that Christ was no more than an incomparable man of genius with great strength of soul and moral superiority—which is substantially the heresy of Arius, for whom Jesus the man was not God. After Harnack there was an entire school which taught the theses of 'free criticism'; among them were Bernard Weiss, Beyschlag and Wellhausen, and in France Renan, who reduced Christ to the level of a 'gentle Galilean prophet'.

Already in the year 1895 the *Gazette de la Croix* of Freiburg in Breisgau was asking the question: 'Are there two truths in the Evangelical Church? That taught by the pastors, and that—precisely the opposite—which is taught by the professors?' And this did not apply only to the studies of the life and message of Christ. At the end of this road, which liberal Protestantism was now taking, there lay far graver perils. Schleiermacher himself, although he was a deeply pious man, had written this astonishing sentence: 'A religion without God is perhaps preferable to one with God.' The way was open to a Christianity without Christ, redemption without Redeemer and, finally, a religion without faith. Itself a religious rationalism, liberal Protestantism was now logically forced to become more and more rational —and less and less religious. While it tended to become a moral school of thought it was losing all spiritual life. It would not be long before it was said that the real reason for believing in Christianity was that on a practical plane it was very useful. There was no intrinsic Christian truth any longer; in any case, had not the study of comparative religions shown that all of them possessed the same origins, that they were determined by the same psychological needs? It was pure rationalism which now ran through degenerated Protestant thought; atheistic humanism had begun to triumph over a great religion. Is it not significant that many of its leaders, from Heine to Nietzsche, were Protestant born? As time went on the 'twin verities' which had so worried the *Gazette de la Croix* became, to general surprise, one alone. Impious affirmations were even made from pulpits, and one can understand the distress of a Protestant believer such as Gabriel Monod who said: 'Protestantism is no more than a series and a collection of religious forms of free thought.'

This is not to say that there were none who offered resistance to this trend. The more curious theses on the person of Christ aroused (to the credit of Reformed thought) strong reactions from Adolphe Schlatter in Germany, Émile de Pressensé in France in his book *Jésus-Christ, son temps, sa vie, son œuvre* (Paris, 1866), and the famous statesman Guizot in his work *Méditations sur l'essence de la religion chrétienne* (Paris, 1864). One can even see that there is within liberal Protestantism more than mere nuances of thought; for instance, Ritschl opposed Baur, and was himself opposed by his former pupils, Karl Keim and Wilhelm Herrmann. The last named was Barth's master, and he followed Ritschl in dropping all the miraculous aspects of Jesus's life, though he affirmed, on the other hand, that historical and psychological knowledge are not in themselves enough and that revelation requires faith.

The opponents of liberalism constituted a veritable party, more strongly structured than their adversaries, sometimes using, especially in France, methods similar to those which, in Catholicism, were castigated as 'integritist'. In Europe they were normally designated by the term 'orthodox'. They were present in every country. In Germany, where they used political as well as religious action, they ranged from

Hengstenben to the doctrinaire Klaus Harms, who proclaimed: 'We regard the very words of our religion as holy. We do not look upon them as a cloak which can be removed from religion but as the body of religion itself.' In France, where the Montauban Faculty was its bastion, orthodoxy had some vigorous opponents. It was the same current, perhaps a little more tinged with pietism, which gave rise to what was called 'fundamentalism' in the U.S.A., the thunderous affirmations of which so astounded, and still astound, opinion in general.[1]

The clash was severe, and there was no authority to whom either side could turn to act as umpire. In France, where conflicts between ideas are necessarily violent, Protestantism was severely shaken from around 1860 until the outbreak of the First World War; the Church, it was said, had become a battlefield. Men like Pastor Ménégoz joyfully announced the 'death throes of orthodoxy'. Tragic episodes aroused passions, such as the 'treachery' of Edouard Scherer, a champion of orthodoxy, who crossed over to the liberal side. And the battle was no less hard in other Protestant countries such as Germany and Holland. In the Anglican Church it resulted in the formation of the Broad Church,[2] which attacked indiscriminately both the Calvinizers of the Low Church and the orthodox Anglicans of the High Church. It is a sad story which no Christian can regard with pride. Pastors brought up such audacious points in their sermons that they were howled down by their congregations; parish priests were dismissed by synods or consistories. Some of the scandals rang round the world: the case of Pastor Charles Byse in Belgium, that of J. W. Colenso in Natal who, condemned as a heretic by the majority of his colleagues (1863), dismissed from his episcopal see and banished from Cape Province, appealed to the Privy Council; he obtained satisfaction from this secular body. Later he set up a small independent Church. Incidents of this kind, distressing as they are, still continue.[3] One can understand why sober spirits have tried to establish a middle way between the audacious stands of liberalism and the severities of orthodoxy; these made up the Party of Conciliation, to which the Germans Richard Roth and Frederick Tholuck (the father of modern pietism), the Swiss Alexandre Schweizer, the Alsatians Reuss and Colani, all belonged. Auguste Sabatier later veered towards their ideas.

To what degree did liberal Protestantism penetrate the world of Protestantism in general? This is not an easy question to answer, since its influence is not seen in any overt way. Pastor Maurice Vernes in 1871 likened it to a baleful contagion which seeped through everywhere. Officially, the well-established Churches abandoned none of

[1] See Chapter II, section 10.   [2] See Chapter II, section 5.
[3] See Chapter III, section, 12.

the dogmas of the Reformation, with the exception of certain groups which attached themselves to the Unitarians. Many of the dogmas were passed over, however. Protestantism as a whole became an organism in which traditional beliefs and liberal theses coexisted without there being any effort to harmonize them. There was no apostasy, but faith became compromised with pragmatism, activism and rationalism. The same thing has been observed with a large part of American Protestantism. The confusion lasted until Karl Barth initiated a theological reaction at the end of the First World War. It was then understood that the right road lay beyond static orthodoxy as it lay beyond adventurous liberalism.

Though it has been buried many times, liberal Protestantism is far from dead. It even exists officially, in the form of an *Association Libérale*, whose president was Dr Albert Schweitzer and of which André Siegfried in France is a member, the organizer being Pastor Georges Marchal. One of the most comprehensive outlines of the liberal school was supplied by the historian Maurice Goguel in 1945, in the *Présence* series, under the title of *Protestantisme Français*. But there are still other proofs of the survival of liberal thought. One of the most famous of living Protestant theologians, Rudolf Bultmann (born in 1884), has resuscitated the old dream of all liberal Protestants by separating the essentials of faith from the myths and images which surround them. In America the social theology of the Niebuhrs and the theology of culture of Tillich are also close to this idea. It is curious also to hear some of the ideas of Ritschl or Sabatier taken up in the ecumenical statements made by those who seek to unite the Protestant Churches. Liberal Protestantism will last as long as the Reformed faith can accommodate contradictions.

Compare if you will the Protestant thinkers such as Leibniz, Kant and Hegel with Catholic thinkers such as Descartes, Pascal and Malebranche. . . . For so long as a Protestant Christian can declare his faith in the Resurrection of Christ while denying the historical authenticity of the fact of the Resurrection itself (as is the case with, for example, Maurice Goguel and Bultmann), then Protestantism will endure. It may not be liberal Protestantism, which today animates the thought and spiritual issues of the Reformation, but it will continue for a long time to occupy an important place in the Protestant world.

8. PROTESTANT WELFARE WORK

Welfare work was an outstanding feature of liberal Protestantism, although it was not the only source of the flood of charitable activities during the nineteenth century. The Revival, which regenerated the

Churches spiritually, also awakened the sense of fraternity. While the protagonists had as their principal aim the salvation of souls, they were not uninterested in the material misery which abounded. But it was chiefly because Protestantism tended towards a moral religion that it became a social religion. Prior to the Revolution there were many pastors who were more concerned to raise the material conditions of life of their parishioners than to lead them to the supernatural. Year after year the expansion of liberal Protestantism increased interest in social matters. It was a form of justification: to bring about social justice was to make God immanent and to make manifest the noblest aspirations of conscience in tangible fashion; it was also a method of applying the principles of the Gospel to society. It was one of Ritschl's dreams that the Reign of God should be apparent in social relationships.

Was this not something new within the Protestant world? In 1896 Hans Gallwitz wrote: 'Until now, it has not been possible to organize, within the framework of the Church, the various manifestations of Christian charity, because one could not establish any cause-and-effect relationship between the observance of Christian morality and the supreme salvation of a Christian.' The situation was quite different from that of the Catholics. For them the paramount factor of charity is the truth which rules conduct; one may forget it, one may traduce it, it remains nevertheless. The works which it imposes all have their part to play in salvation. Among Protestants, the Lutheran rejection of works and Calvinist predestination pulled in opposite directions. To direct Christian endeavours to ensure the reign of justice on earth was to distort the biblical idea of the Kingdom and to substitute God's works for those of man. Might it not also re-establish feelings of pride in righteousness among the faithful? This explains why social trends encountered resistance, firstly from the Churches, especially the Lutherans, where the pastor was bound to observe and not to over-step the rules: the teaching of the Word of God, and the administration of the sacraments. The sixth General Lutheran Conference at Hanover in 1890 made a special point of confirming these rules. Yet there were liberal Protestants who showed reserve: Adolphe Monod, normally uncritical, said of Oberlin, the leader of social Protestantism: 'He is a most respected pastor, but it is more a question of establishing whether the care which he has taken of temporal matters has not damaged, in certain respects, the development of spiritual interests.'

Despite these opposing views Protestantism embraced social improvements just as Catholicism did. As with the Catholics, the movement began with charitable and philanthropic works, with no clear distinction between social justice and welfare work. Critics soon arose against them, their paternalism, the bourgeois spirit which animated them and the righteous consciences which they bestowed on their movers and organizers. Alongside social Catholicism—and, let us not forget, of Marxism—a social Christianity developed, aiming at a social reorganization of society on a Christian basis.

Prior to the Revival, social Protestantism was foretold by Frederick Oberlin (1740–1826), one of the greatest Christian figures of the century, a Reformation saint. His apostolic and social vocation became clear to him when he was sent to the parish of Ban de la Roche in the Vosges, where the soil was poor and the climate difficult. Moral and physical misery abounded. He made it his business to improve the spiritual and material life of his flock. He remained there for fifty years, leading the fight for apostolic and social advance, terms which were synonymous to him. Agriculture was reorganized, craftwork was set up to make use of the slack period in winter, and schools, hospitals and rest homes were opened. Its fame grew, and innumerable visitors came to see for themselves. Even Czar Alexander spoke of his intention of visiting it. Throughout the century Oberlin's influence made itself felt deeply. The founder of social Christianity, Tommy Fallot, followed in his steps.

The lesson of Pastor Oberlin was heeded by many of those who took part in the Revival. One of these was Felix Neff, who was sent to the Queyras valley in the Upper Alps. He worked unceasingly among the ten villages in his care to promote better material standards as well as spiritual ones among his flock. Modern civilization had not made itself felt in these regions where the houses had no chimneys, where bread was baked but twice a year and where medicines were unknown. He took on the role of architect, gardener, engineer, doctor and school-master to the people of the Upper Alps. The task exhausted him, and in 1829, scarcely more than thirty years old, he died of tuberculosis.

Oberlin, Felix Neff and a few others were isolated cases. The profound indifference to social justice which existed among the majority of Catholics existed also among Protestants. Few people realized that there might be a link between the precepts of Christian morality and social organization. Only slowly was it realized that there was a duty to eradicate misery, and until 1848 only certain writers and intellectuals and statesmen were aware of it; and even they themselves spoke in the wilderness. In England, where the degree of misery brought on by the Industrial Revolution was immense, Charles Dickens's works had great influence, along with Hood's *Song of the Shirt* and Elizabeth Barrett Browning's poem *The Cry of the Children*. In Scandinavia, Andersen's voice helped to awaken the middle-class conscience. In Germany it was the pietist circles, particularly the Moravian Brethren, who were the first to act, along with the Quakers, Methodists and, as a general rule, other Christians not members of one of the Established Churches. In France it was mostly among the Protestant middle classes that a sense of social obligation arose, prompted by Methodist influences. There were some great figures among them, especially that of the young Catherine Cuvier, who founded the Protestant Welfare Association before her death at the age of twenty-two.

The awakening of conscience to social duties led immediately to active participation on the part of the Protestants. The first works were those of industrialists in Alsace and the Midi based especially on what was to be called 'paternalism'. The pioneer was Daniel Legrand, an owner of textile mills, who at Rothau and St Morand made his works into a sort of vast family where the boss ate with his workers. His example was followed by others. It was still a far cry from the idea of social justice in which the worker has rights, rather than being dependent for charity on his employer's goodwill. But none the less it was a step in the right direction—and it was in any event better than the icy indifference to human realities of economic liberalism.

From the second quarter of the nineteenth century onwards a movement began in almost all Protestant circles with the object of launching charitable undertakings. It is a story similar to that of social Catholicism—in the same year, for instance, as Ozanam founded the *Conférences de St Vincent-de-Paul*, the Lutheran pastor Louis Meyer created *Les Amis des Pauvres* with identical goals. It must be realized that, since they counted far less on the help of female orders than the Catholics did, the Protestants were obliged to set up many more organizations. In twenty-five years, from 1823 to 1848, French Protestantism founded no less than thirty-two organizations covering various aspects of welfare work. In England and Germany the movement was no less active. Though in the latter the Lutheran Church stood aside for a long time, the creation in 1840 of the General Association for Welfare gave promise of considerable future development. The work continued with unabated vigour until the outbreak of the First World War. It took root in America also towards the end of the nineteenth century and here it flourished exceedingly well, assisted by the State in the form of tax exemptions. It was only after 1918 that, with the progress of social laws and systems of social security in many countries, there was a slackening throughout the Protestant welfare movement; some of the schemes were even discontinued.

It would not be possible to draw up a list, even a brief one, of the many societies and works which for one hundred and fifty years bore witness to Protestant charity, nor even one showing those who founded and directed them. They are all extremely complex and their fields of activity are many and varied, covering every aspect of human distress. Some of the organizations are unusual, some of the methods also, as is the case with the Salvation Army. There were unusual characters such as Mme Armengaud-Hinsch,[1] who founded the Calvinist Hinschite sect and devoted a considerable amount of effort to helping the poorer classes to enjoy sea bathing; Gottlieb Hoffmann, a German pietist, who ruined himself by helping many of his poorer co-religionists to live in an agricultural colony which he founded; Baron von Kottwitz, who also ruined himself by pouring out his own funds for the upkeep of social workshops; Mme Andrée Walther of Paris, who turned her Versailles domain into an orphanage for boys where they were taught printing.

But if one had to choose one among all these noble figures, it would undoubtedly be Johann Wichern (1808–81). A Christian of the first rank, whose goodness knew no bounds. Clear-thinking and an excellent organizer, he was led to social work by the spectacle of abandoned and delinquent youth. At twenty-four he set up the *Rauhen Haus*, a hostel sheltering many who had been criminals. The organization grew, was recognized by the authorities and, one thing leading to another, soon covered delinquent youth, hostels, orphanages and nurseries, with other branches fighting drunkenness, prostitution and giving assistance to ex-prisoners. At the end of Wichern's life his organizations numbered several thousand 'brethren' and 'deaconesses'; his friend Professor V. M. Huber had systematized his social ideas and, moving from the purely charitable level to that of the apostolate, but bringing the two together, Wichern launched the Inner Mission.[2] Germany has never forgotten this exemplary man. Along with Monsignor von Ketteler he was one of the pioneers of social work, not only among his compatriots but also among all Western Christians.

In the field of social work there is not one sector that does not have a Protestant organization at work, or an outstanding figure worthy of admiration. Neglected children were one of Wichern's special fields, and in this he was followed by other leading figures. In France orphanages and special educational centres for difficult or maladjusted children proliferated. In England where, as stressed by Dickens, poor children were particularly badly treated, many generous spirits offered their help: Lord Shaftesbury (1801–85), an 'evangelist', was instrumental in amending the law to reduce the working day for children to ten hours and founded, along the same lines as Wichern's *Rauhen Haus*, the Ragged Schools; George Muller, a German pastor who had settled in Teignmouth, refusing all official help, managed a home for lost children and maintained himself on offerings from the congregation; Doctor Barnardo founded an institution for homeless children in the East End of London and assisted some sixty thousand during his lifetime; Florence Nightingale (1820–1910) devoted all her substantial

---

[1] See Chapter I, section 7.
[2] See Chapter III, section 5.

fortune to the assistance of the distressed, orphans as well as young soldiers, and reorganized the nursing corps.

Prisoners, whose fate was an unenviable one, as well as the inmates of the infamous workhouses, aroused the sympathy of many people. Wichern himself took an interest in their case, as did Theodore Fliedner, who founded the 'deaconesses'. But one name stands out from all others: that of Elizabeth Fry (1780–1845), a Quakeress, who discovered an ocean of distress in the prisons and set to work to reform them with unlimited zeal and enterprise. The resulting Society of Penal Reform was recognized by the British authorities and by the authorities of six or seven countries. Its first president was Samuel Hoare, grandfather of the statesman. Elizabeth Fry's example exercised an undoubted influence in this otherwise uncharted sector.

Hospitals were for many centuries another of the fields in which Christian charity was active, and they were not neglected in Protestant welfare work. Hostels, hospitals and institutions all had their part to play, each linked with this or that great Protestant name. Two principal figures are worthy of note: John Bost (1790–1864), who came to social work quite by accident when he was trying to find a roof for two homeless little girls. His organization grew from year to year from its first site near Bergerac and eventually became an immense undertaking, similar to that of the Little House of Divine Providence Turin where every form of human distress was alleviated. There was also Frederick von Bodelschwing (1831–1910), Wichern's spiritual heir, who, after working as an evangelist in the poorer areas of Paris and as a pastor in the Ruhr, was led to social activities through the grief occasioned by the death of his four children. In twenty years he had built up an enormous undertaking, the *Bethelanstalt*, which included even house-building associations and savings banks. He also found time to organize a society for mission work in Africa.

One fact must be underlined in Protestant welfare work. This is that the social leaders of Protestantism have been very conscious of the need to fight against social evils as well as against misery and suffering. Every sector of Protestantism has had its Temperance Society leading the fight against alcoholism. Prostitution also was attacked, and Josephine Butler (1828–1906) became famous through her campaigns against this evil with a multitude of articles, tracts, speeches and petitions; her campaign received the approval of Victor Hugo, Garibaldi, Mazzini and Garrison, leading to the setting up of an international federation for its abolition. At length the League of Nations took over the movement after the First World War. Josephine Butler's friend and follower in France was Pastor Louis Comte.

To assist all these various welfare and charitable works, the Protestants created a corps known as the Deaconesses. They are

particularly well known in Germany; today they number more than
thirty thousand. Their uniform resembles that of Catholic nuns, though
the habit is not so long nor the head-dress so distinctive. But they are
not nuns: they take no vows and can leave their work at any time to
marry; they must, however, remain celibate while in service. The
organization was the idea of Theodore Fliedner (1800–64), a German
pastor, and arose from a study which he made of the primitive Church.
In 1836 his school at the Presbytery of Kaiserswerth in Rhenish
Prussia was altered to this end; he also purchased a larger establishment and set about recruiting volunteers for this new vocation. One of
the most active of the 'young Lutherans' in the liturgical and sacramental renewal movement,[1] Johann Löhe, founded a movement with
aims similar to that of Fliedner. This included welfare and hospital
work organized by pious women, but it did not, at first, resemble an
order in its own right; the women did not live in communities. The
necessity of imposing discipline and maintaining stability, however,
soon led him to the same formula as Fliedner had adopted for his
deaconesses, and the success of the movement was thereafter assured.
In 1877 Löhe had 168 deaconesses, and his movement had spread to
the U.S.A. and Russia; later on, in 1894, it was further developed by
Frederick Zimmer of Elberfeld. A Frenchman from Nîmes, Antoine
Vermeil, pastor of the French Church at Hamburg, heard of Fliedner's ideas and brought them back to France, firstly to Bordeaux and
then to Paris. Here, with the help of Catherine Malvezin, he opened the
first centre for deaconesses in 1841, and both liberal and orthodox
pastors looked with astonishment and strong disapproval on this new
development. In 1877 there were thirty-two organizations in Germany,
and eighteen more elsewhere, of which seven were established in
France. The Protestant Sisters of Charity are still today a very large
organization, numbering sixty thousand, mostly in German-speaking
and Nordic countries. In France there are several hundred. In England,
real interest was not aroused until after the 1920 Lambeth Conference,
although there had been a modest beginning in 1860. It was decided
that the deaconesses would be formally dedicated; there was even
question of their receiving the canonical diaconates, with a view to their
becoming women priests at a later date. However, a petition, signed
by fifty thousand women, opposed such a move. Prior to the Second
World War there were one thousand from a training centre at
Hindhead who had been sent to every Anglican diocese.

One cannot but admire much of this powerful Protestant welfare
movement. It is of the same calibre of that of the Catholics during the
same period. There are, however, some special characteristics, one of
which is paternalism. This trait is much in evidence in American

[1] See Chapter III, section 3.

welfare work, often inclining towards a moralizing attitude. It should
be noted that apologetics are much more strongly stressed than among
Catholics. The great figures which we have seen—Oberlin, Felix
Neff, Wichern, John Bost and others—were zealous evangelists as
well as apostles of charity. Many instances could be quoted to show that
this or that social leader aimed at converting souls rather than merely
succouring the afflicted. Tommy Fallot, for example, headed the
movement which attempted to widen the bases of charitable activity to
establish as justice what was then seen as charity. For him, 'social
Christianity is a spiritual and ethical answer to universal anxiety and
restlessness, a manifestation of the Reformation'. The social apostle
and the preacher worked together. 'To rebuild human life was to
rebuild Christianity,' was the formula. Neither St Vincent de Paul nor
Ozanam, however, would have employed this without reservations.

9. WILLIAM BOOTH AND THE SALVATION ARMY

The interweaving of apologetic intention and social action is nowhere so clearly seen as in that institution which, in the eyes of the man
in the street, is the most striking manifestation of Protestant social
action: the Salvation Army.

One winter's night in 1888, in London, a man was returning home.
Through the mist from the river he noticed that the benches along the
Thames Embankment were all occupied by down-and-outs, wrapped
up as best they could in their ragged clothes. The scene deprived him
of sleep that night. The next day he called his son, who had already
helped him in his social work for many years, and said: 'Did you know
that there are hundreds of human beings sleeping out in icy weather
here?' His son replied that he was aware of it, but that he could make
no suggestions for giving them shelter. 'Do you mean that there are
too many?' said the father. 'We must do something; these men
are our brothers. Try to find some way of sheltering them all.'
From this conversation there sprang the world-famous Salvation
Army shelters.

The father's name was William Booth (1829–1912). Raised in
poverty in Nottingham, orphaned at an early age, he soon took an
interest in the Chartist movement, the forerunner of Socialism, which
aimed at a reorganization of social order. When he was twenty he went
through a religious crisis: the Anglican Church in which he had been
baptized seemed cold, empty of spiritual substance and of charity. He
turned to Methodism and threw himself into Wesleyan propaganda
with a zeal that his Methodist colleagues found excessive. The young
Booth joined the *avant-garde* Reformed Methodists. His reputation as

an orator was now well founded. He preached in London and later in the provinces, and discovered still more miseries in England's Black Country, which he called the 'slaughter-house of civilization'. His wife Catherine shared his hopes and his fears. She was an orator herself, who knew how to speak to crowds about Christ and His message of social justice. In 1863 William Booth was one of those itinerant prophets so well known to Protestantism during Revivals. His presence drew great crowds, and at Cardiff he and his wife were obliged to hire a circus 'big top' to accommodate the crowds eager to hear them speak.

The era, as we know, was one of great social misery. The economic crisis began in 1860, the same crisis which Marx studied for his work *Das Kapital.* Catherine and William Booth were now well launched in their vocation. Without attaching themselves to any particular faith or Church, they proclaimed the message of human love and social justice from the Gospels, preaching this in every slum quarter. At the same time they acted—food shops and soup kitchens were opened. But charitable organizations cannot function without money for long, and they soon realized that only dedicated men and women could render such an undertaking successfully. Where could they find these people, if not among the unfortunate, the fallen and the homeless touched by the Word of Christ? It was from this idea that William Booth, having separated from his Church, launched the Christian Mission.

He soon saw that, to make a success of this organization, strict discipline would be needed. He knew and admired the discipline of the British Army—why should he not adapt this to his organization? So the Christian Mission became the Hallelujah Army, and in 1877 the Salvation Army. The movement was now well launched. From every Protestant group men and women flocked to serve under the 'General'. Booth became famous. When he published his book *In Darkest England and the Way Out* (1890), on the situation of the proletariat and the reforms needed, more than 200,000 copies were sold in six months. Rich friends joined the Army, others left legacies to it, many of them donated large sums. And, in a never-ending stream, all sorts of institutions came from William Booth's untiring work—missionary stations, hostels, hospitals, rest homes, shelters and homes for delinquent youth. From everywhere in the world came requests for help and for the prophet William Booth. This immense enterprise was not to everyone's liking. Antagonists set up the 'Skeleton Army' for the express purpose of sabotaging the Salvation Army's meetings. In the U.S.A. the first women to join the Salvation Army were beaten up as heretics. But antagonism had no effect, for, when William Booth died at ninety-three, his Army was an obvious success and had spread to every corner of the world. A new colour had appeared on the Protestant palette.

The Salvation Army today is just as Booth conceived it originally. It is an army, run on military lines, with men and women soldiers and officers, with capes and caps for the men and long dresses and the familiar bonnets for the women. It has its Regulations and its Manuals. The magazine is called the *War Cry*. It has its own flag, blue for holiness, red for the Blood of Christ, the golden star for the Holy Ghost. But its most significant feature is its bands which are designed to draw crowds and provide an audience for the preacher.

Any converted man or woman can join the Army, but as soon as they have donned their uniform it is just as though they had joined a strict Catholic order, as strict, for instance, as that of the Franciscans or the Dominicans, even resembling the Jesuits in its asceticism. Alcohol is forbidden, only certain books may be read, no financial interest is allowed in any proscribed industry (such as the manufacture and sale of alcohol). Even in his ordinary life the Salvation Army member has to observe strict rules of humility and goodness. He must give the Army what money remains after his needs have been met. He cannot bring an action without the approval of his superiors. He cannot marry without permission. The rules are strict, but this is because in the early days the first members of the Army were ex-prisoners, drunkards and reformed prostitutes. Those who fall into none of these categories still accept the strict rules laid down, since the Army is still at work in the slums, and it would not be politic to have several levels of discipline. Strict though the rules are, they do not interfere with personal liberty in matters of the apostolate or in charity.

Can the Salvation Army be defined as a sect? Most Protestant authors present it as such, but this does not seem correct. The Army looks upon itself as a movement which transcends all other Protestant groups—it accepts members from any Christian group, even the Catholic—and imposes no particular creed and teaches no dogma. It recognizes the two sacraments which are common to all Protestantism, baptism and communion, but it has no doctrine concerning them and does not administer them. In spite of this, however, it would appear that there is a certain sectarian atmosphere in this warm and fervent world, where each member has the feeling—perhaps it is the uniform—that they stand apart from other Christians, as well as above them.

It is on the social level that the Army has had the greatest success. Here it bears unchallengeable witness to Christian charity in action. In 120 countries its 2 million soldiers and 30,000 officers are responsible for some enormous undertakings—hospitals, hostels, night shelters, soup kitchens and clothing shops. Everything that eases the lot and destroys the isolation of the poorest classes falls within the compass of the Salvation Army's operations. William Booth expressly placed these social activities before any attempts at evangelization, and requested—though this was not always observed by the leaders of Protestant institutions—that the two be kept separate. Adapting the words of St Thomas, he said: 'It is difficult to save a man if his feet are wet.' The Army's famous trilogy, soup, soap and salvation, has often had fun poked at it, but anyone who has visited one of the Army's hostels is well aware that, in curious ways, with no especial emphasis on doctrine, the Salvation Army carries out its work on a truly charitable basis.

10. SOCIAL CHRISTIANITY

All these institutions, including the Salvation Army, were obviously paternalist. Some of them were at the level of what were called 'soup kitchens' in Britain. But Protestantism did not stop there. The initiators based their works on the principles of 'social evangelism', whose connection with liberal Protestantism is obvious. All of them, as the Catholics Buchez, Armand de Melun and Albert de Mun had also done, carried out a critical examination of social injustices and of the established order which caused them. The idea of social duty was replaced by the idea of social rights. At the very moment when social Catholicism was emerging Protestantism saw the same current of thought arising within its framework.

This social Christian current took on different forms in each of the Reformation Churches, until they all merged into what was called social Christianity. It first appeared in Anglicanism, under J. M. Ludlow (a former pupil of a Paris lycée), an associate of Fourier, Cabet, Considérant and the Catholic Buchez, who had read Lamennais and Lacordaire. The idea spread rapidly in the light of the events of the 1848 Revolution in France, though it was not always smooth going—one pastor actually founded a 'Communist Church'. One association of vegetarian Christians turned to Socialism. There were even nudist social Christians. However, two men of great intelligence adopted the idea and attempted to systematize it, Frederick Dennison Maurice and Charles Kingsley.[1] Both were adherents of the Broad Church (i.e. between the High and the Low Church) and espoused liberal ideas. They took a firm stand against economic liberalism, as taught by Adam Smith—as they did also against the social indifference of those Christians who were satisfied with the *status quo*. Maurice propounded the thesis of which Marx was later to make such good use: 'We have used the Bible as though it were a police manual, a dose of opium to calm the beasts of burden bent under their heavy loads.' At first the social doctrines of Maurice and Kingsley had little effect, but they were soon

[1] See Chapter II, section 5.

to go deeper into circles far from the Broad Church. Bishop Westcott, founder of the Christian Social Union, drew heavily on Maurice's 'Christian Society'. The trade unions too became imbued with the idea, and the Labour Party owed many of its basic elements to it. In 1924 the Association of Christian Industrialists acknowledged its debt to the social Christians of the previous century, and in Sweden the International Conference on Life and Work in 1925 did likewise.

In the U.S.A. similar ideas were being expressed. W. E. Channing had announced, prophetically enough, the advent of economic liberalism and of its perils. George Ripley, who had read Owen and Fourier, set up as a social reformer and attempted to put his principles into practice by organizing a communal undertaking, the Brook Farmers. Sects set out to live according to social Christian principles (the Shakers with their communistic agricultural colonies are an example); the Mormons did likewise, though they stood a little apart from Christianity. There was even an 'Institutional Church', which received encouragement from Episcopalians and Congregationalists, proposing to teach social Christianity besides carrying out a whole range of social works. The Social Gospel sprang from all these diverse currents, in the period which Charles Hopkins determined as lying between 1865 and 1915.

Germany in its turn had given rise to a social Christian movement. After 1870 throughout the new empire there was a decline in religious life, as though the ancient gods of war had replaced Christ. The Bismarckian *Kulturkampf*, in theory directed only against the Catholic Church, tended in fact towards secularization of life, even among Protestants. Against this wave of irreligion several Lutheran pastors sought to establish a renewed form of Christianity, offering men a practical ideal of social justice. In Rudolf Todt's book, *German Radical Socialism and Christian Society*, the author attempted to establish, with some naïveté, that all concrete problems, even the smallest, could be solved with the aid of the Gospel. Adolf Wagner composed a plan of society based on Christian principles, justifying everything, including progressive scales of income tax, by quotations from the Parables. Adolf Stöcker (1835–1909) was soon to be accepted as the leader of this movement. A Court preacher, he preferred, when the choice had to be made, to throw up his easy life and join in the struggle for social justice. He was a man of iron, fire and unquenchable energy, a conservative in politics but a socialist in economic questions, theocrat yet anti-paternalist, anti-Semite, even though he acknowledged that Christianity had its origins in Israelite revelation. A convinced nationalist, he became the architect of the victory of a just, human and fully German Christianity.

The ideas of the Social Evangelical Movement were bound to meet opposition. The leaders of the established Lutheran Church stated continually that social questions were not their province and that the innovators were distorting the image of the Kingdom of God. In the early days the traditionalists, aided by Bismarck, held their ground and the new social movement could make no headway. But a new German emperor, William II, was convinced that if he were to adhere enthusiastically to the new social ideas he would gain popularity and at the same time be able to offer resistance to Socialism. He encouraged the Church to develop social Christian thought, hitherto neglected. The supreme Lutheran Council at once about-turned, submitting with docility to these royal wishes, and in 1891 recommended all pastors to take the Socialist movement into account and also to spread the evangelistic doctrine relating to property and work. In the universities the Church's social doctrine was now taught. Pastors worked as miners; publications on social evangelism proliferated; Stöcker was vindicated. His movement was the rival of the social Catholicism then in action in the Rhineland; he founded the Urban Mission, and as a Prussian *Reichstag* member it seemed as if he were about to embark on a huge programme of social Christianity.

But Baron von Stumm, styled the 'King of the Saar', who vaunted himself as an enlightened boss and indeed had many welfare works to his credit, became exasperated by the criticisms of these audacious young pastors. He was a friend of William II; he persuaded him that these Red Christians were playing the Socialists' game and he attacked social evangelism in the Reichstag. In 1895 the Kaiser banned the Social Evangelical Movement, stating cryptically that the term social Christian was meaningless. Stöcker and his friends attempted to ride the storm, but at once the official Church, always docile, attacked them. Under a variety of names the social movement stayed in being, only coming really alive in 1919 and in 1945. Along with social Catholicism, it has played a major part in the politics of the Bonn Republic.

French Protestantism was responsible for the clarification and systematization of the more or less confused ideas of other countries. The theories of the American Channing, of Dennison Maurice and Kingsley, Stöcker and Naumann were not unknown, but French thinkers were better at linking doctrines to principles and gave the movement a much more solid theological basis.

The starting point for this was what is known as the Nîmes School. There were, of course, other elements involved in the original doctrinal formulation, such as the campaigns of Charles Robert in favour of a scheme whereby workers participated in the profits made by their firms, the teaching of the Belgian Professor de Laveleye, the work undertaken by the Swiss Charles Secrétan and the concrete example of the de Guise colony, a true and happy Christian community.

Certain rapports with Le Play and social Catholics such as Armand de Melun also played a part. Nîmes was for many years one of the capitals of Social Protestantism, this being due to the efforts of three men: Édouard de Boyve, Auguste Fabre and especially Charles Gide (1847–1932). Co-operatives had been founded in the Gard *département* along the same lines as the British Rochdale Pioneers' movement. Gide became interested in this, and Fabre, who had visited the de Guise colony, exchanged views with him; from this conversation there sprang the *Société d'Économie Populaire* in 1885, along with a grocery co-operative, a printing co-operative, a training school—the first in France—and an employment exchange. Basing his conclusions on these undertakings, Gide decided that the moment had come when they must all be examined more deeply. To this end *La Revue d'Économie politique* and a journal, specially printed for the purpose, *L'Émancipation*, aimed at the public at large, were launched. A shoal of young pastors now gathered round the master, among them Louis Comte, Élie Gounelle, Wilfred Monod and Louis Gouth, who founded the Protestant Association for the study of social questions. Social Protestantism was born.

The example of Nîmes was followed throughout France. In the north, where Élie Gounelle settled, the *Solidarité* institution was opened, part charitable, part evangelical. In Paris Pastor Paul Doumergue, founder of *Vie et Foi*, opened a kind of independent social university and sent lecture invitations to Bergson, Henri Poincaré, Émile Boutroux, and of course Charles Gide; he also founded a school of social service which trained the young women who were later to be called *assistantes sociales* (welfare workers).

The most outstanding personality was Tommy Fallot (1844–1904), who succeeded Oberlin at Ban de la Roche, and who devoted the whole of his life to the cause of social justice. Since his early years he had been deeply conscious of the conditions under which the proletariat lived. His theology thesis was on poverty, and when he became pastor of the La Chapelle district of Paris he commenced his work by founding *La Ligue française pour le relèvement de la morale publique*; he then set about unifying all the various elements at work in French Protestantism in this field. At his request Gédéon Chastand launched *Le Revue de la théologie pratique*, which was later named the *Revue du christianisme social*. He was an enemy of all forms of theoretical theology—which he called a 'theology of tin soldiers'—and wanted Christianity to devote its strength to social reform. This would, he maintained, lead to 'converting Protestantism to the people, in order to convert the people to Christianity'. Employing formulas similar to those used by Social Catholicism, he proclaimed the social doctrine of the Gospel and demanded that all men be accorded the right to salvation, this being preceded by the right to enjoy social justice. He was a tireless worker, and the work which he undertook still lasts today.

Social Christianity, as defined by a Tommy Fallot or an Élie Gounelle, held to the idea, so dear to social Catholicism too, that neither the individual nor society could be saved alone, that there was an imperative in social salvation—cosmic salvation we should call it today perhaps—that each Christian must feel. Obviously we are a long way from the first Reformers and their stress on the confrontation between the sinful soul and the God who redeemed it. Sin is now collective, not individual, in this new dogmatic system. According to Gounelle, Christ was the archetype of human beings, the consummation of all humanity. Social Christianity demanded the necessary reforms in order to found a just social order. Based on the Sermon on the Mount, he viewed property as a service opposing the abuses of capitalism and demanded the christianization of relations between men, between classes and between peoples. He offered no practical solutions, looking upon himself as an inspirer rather than a combatant of the struggle.

Today social Christianity has not the same degree of importance that it had in the early years of the century. Perspectives have changed, and, as and when the original ideas became a part of the modern world, they were bound to lose a lot of their original force and appeal. It had both direct and indirect results. With a Shaftesbury in Britain or a Legrand in France it was direct, resulting in legislative action which led to an improvement in the lot of the worker. It was indirect also in its action upon a host of people, influencing them morally and intellectually.

In the last fifty years there has been a curious renewal of social Christianity. In Sweden Archbishop Nathan Söderblom founded the International Institute for Social Christianity in 1925. In the U.S.A. Walter Rauschenbusch in his books *Christianity and the Social Crisis* (1907) and the *Theology of Social Evangelism* (1917) tried to effect a synthesis of all social Christian ideas with contemporary economic and social doctrines, even going so far as to say that the principles of Communism seemed basically Christian. The brothers Niebuhr opposed the social indifference of Karl Barth and set to work to establish a theology of social action which would provide bases for the current of social evangelism then sweeping through American Protestantism.

11. The Protestant Crisis and the Expansion of the Sects

In the last twenty-five years of the nineteenth century Protestantism went through a crisis period, a period which all historians have examined and defined. It spread to the U.S.A. and to missions in non-Christian territories. The old formulas were overtaken by events, traditional Protestantism had to undertake a renewal, and the great institutions (charitable organizations, social welfare works and youth organizations) were all drifting away from the traditional, classic Reformation mould which placed religious experience on a purely personal plane. It seemed as if there was a lowering of spiritual tone and a great deal of activity at one and the same time.

The causes of the crisis were evident, and most of them have been examined in the previous pages. But there was one main one, serious too, in the Catholic Church; this was the decline in faith which had resulted from the progress made by atheistic humanism and scientism. The Protestant Churches had exactly the same problem here as the Roman Church; if the means used yesterday were no longer sufficient to retain a hold on the faithful then other means had to be found.

The Reformation Churches had other problems peculiar to them. The success of liberal Protestantism had, as we saw, been responsible for separating men from dogmas, lowering the value of the Scriptures, even threatening faith itself. By reducing religious life to the level of social and personal ethics, it emptied religion of all spiritual content. For this reason it aroused violent reactions, from both the Orthodox and the Fundamentalists, and no observer could fail to notice the underlying crisis. In France, for example, the arguments grew violent, involving—as was the case with Athanase Coquerel—personalities as well as ideas.

Another element in the crisis, observable especially in those countries where Protestantism was most securely established (besides being supported by the State), was the trend towards disestablishment, a trend noticeable almost everywhere. And everywhere also surged the opposition of the Spirit's aspirations to a religion that was too conformist. Free Churches arose in many places, and the old type of Protestantism lost many of its traditional characteristics.

One of the most striking aspects of the crisis was the proliferation and expansion of the sects. The nineteenth century was their hey-day, but the offensive was not yet spent. The conditions in which they arose and flourished are of little importance [1] compared to their proliferation. Prior to 1789 there were very few of them. There were the

[1] See Chapter I.

Baptists and two more, who were ascetic and spiritual at the same time, the Quakers and the Methodists. During the nineteenth century in the U.S.A. the Baptists and the Methodists expanded rapidly, acquiring stable bases as separate institutions. Between 1820 and 1830 the Darbyites or Plymouth Brethren arose as well as the Apostolics of Irving and the Mormons under Joseph Smith. Later, in 1840, William Miller set up, and in 1860 Ellen Gould White reorganized, the Seventh Day Adventists. Fifteen years later Jehovah's Witnesses arose. Then came the Salvation Army, an obvious indication that the old religious framework was outdated. Following these came the Christian Science of Mary Baker Eddy, which claimed to be able to heal sickness of both body and mind, and the sect founded by the healer, Father Antoine, who offered a *pot-pourri* of Christianity and metempsychosis and whose sect was tinged with Methodism. At the beginning of the twentieth century Wales was the scene of a Revival which led later to the creation of some of the most vigorous of the new sects, the Pentecostals.

The crisis within Protestantism was both obvious and indisputable, but not definitive. At the turn of the century there was a renewal which took on a variety of aspects—dogmatic, apostolic and liturgical —and resembled the renewal which took place within the Catholic Church; it is still in evidence today in a form of renovated Protestantism.

12. THEOLOGICAL RENEWAL: KARL BARTH

It was on the theological plane that the most impressive renewal took place, and this fact is of prime importance. It is a constant of religious history that any Church whose theology is in decline is a Church threatened, and spiritual renewal is only assured when the theological bases are secure. Protestant theology at the end of the nineteenth century was not in a very happy state. Not that there were any works lacking on the subject—they proliferated. Liberal Protestantism and its diverse forms had given rise to innumerable dogmatic systems. In a few well-chosen words Jacques Courvoisier defined the crisis precisely: 'Theology is less and less considered for itself and more and more in its relations with the disciplines of thought, mainly in philosophy, especially in psychology. Natural theology, as distinct from the theology founded on the Bible, has a vital place in Protestantism. The Reformers are either little known or altogether unknown. Protestantism now is something quite different from what it was at its birth.'

It was this disastrous situation at the beginning of the twentieth century which set off a reaction that could not be ignored. Thinkers of note now inclined towards the theology of the absolute sovereignty of God, the same as that of Luther and Calvin. In Scandinavia and Germany Lutheranism was regenerated. The same thing was observed in Calvinism, especially in Holland. Many pastors returned to the doctrinal commentaries of the Bible as the Word inspired: the courageous pastor Henri Monnier was one of them, remarking in 1906 that he preferred the Jesus of the Dominican Dido to all Loisy's science. Immediately after the end of the First World War this neo-Calvinist current became of some importance, influenced by a number of leaders who ever since 1895 had been preparing for a return to Reformation thinking. But all were overtaken by Karl Barth.

Born in 1886 in Basel, where his father taught theology, he was educated at Bern, a city whose heavy conformism he liked little. Barth's real training took place at the German universities of Berlin, Tübingen and Marburg during the period when Adolf von Harnack held sway. It was also the period when Wilhelm Herrmann was teaching his students the dogma according to which decisive religious experience owed everything to the personality of a Christ who was psychologically exemplary if historically untenable. As a young pastor Barth seemed likely to remain in the liberal realm, and at twenty-two he collaborated in the Protestant liberal review *Christliche Welt*. How did he change his views so quickly thereafter? He was appointed to the parish of Safenvill, and here he devoted himself to his parishioners, mostly workers, with such zeal that employers looked on him with disfavour, as a Socialist. Preaching and the cure of souls made him see the sterility of certain aspects of liberal theses. His friend Thurneysen, pastor of a neighbouring parish, exercised a neo-Calvinist influence on him, as did Christophe Blumhard, the great preacher. The world war also had its influence, and he asked himself what he should preach to his parishioners and in the name of what. Thus he began to understand the uselessness of preaching human or even religious values, and he saw that his sole duty was to transmit the Word of God. From this starting point he began to question the Protestant message. In 1919 the publication of a long commentary on the Epistle to the Romans demonstrated that the former liberal had returned to the fold. In 1922 the first issue of the review which he founded, the *Zwischen den Zeiten*, exploded like a second bombshell, and the liberal Protestant and free criticism camp trembled to its foundations. Henceforth Karl Barth's career assumed two distinct aspects: that of the theologian and of the man of action. In his view theology could not be separated from life; its subject was God and it had to carry its message to men, therefore it needed temporal implications. In his youth he had belonged to the Social Democrat Party and had helped the cause of trade unionism, besides becoming interested in the theology of politics. A professor at Münster and later at Bonn, he planned a new *Summa* of Protestant dogmatic thought in its principles and its applications in the twentieth century. In 1927 he published the *Doctrine of the Word of God*, the first step in a vast work, yet he quickly ceased to follow this line. Why? Because, influenced by Kierkegaard, and having read Dostoyevsky and Nietzsche, the one a friend, the other an adversary, he had started from the experience of a man aiming at God, whereas—as he soon discovered—man could only approach God through Christ; similarly a soundly based theology could succeed only when aimed at Jesus Christ. On this principle he began work on his immense *Ecclesial Dogmatics* in 1932, which, even thirty years and fifteen volumes later, is still unfinished.

Astonishingly enough Barth worked in no cloistered retreat, well protected from the noise of the outside world. In 1933 the National Socialist storm fell upon Germany. Barth saw at once that the Hitlerian doctrines, if taken to their conclusions, led to the heathen heresies in which man becomes the God whom he was trying to destroy. The founding of the German Christian Church [1] was a warning to him: one cannot praise God by singing the Horst Wessel song. He took over the leadership of the men who had undertaken to fight against National Socialism through the Confessional Church. A new review was launched, the *Theologische Existenz Heute*, a fine challenge to the ideology of 'earth and blood'. It was Barth also who issued the resounding declaration at Barmen in 1934. The reaction was not long in coming—arrest by the Gestapo, and expulsion to Basel, where he was born. From here the courageous prophet of the rights of God carried on his struggle, assisting with his writings the stand taken by his friends Niemöller and Vogel in their continuing fight within Germany itself. The German rout in 1945 allowed him once again to settle in Bonn, where he continued work again on the *Dogmatics*. Now world famous, he continued to serve the cause of God's justice on earth, imploring the Allies not to drive the Germans once more into despair, taking a firm stand against nuclear weapons, protesting against the persecution of Christians in Eastern Germany while declining to adhere to the anti-Communist front—slowly but surely Barth became one of the great men of his time.

Barth's thought consists of a system, just as the thought of St Thomas Aquinas consists of Thomism, and this system has been expressed in his *Dogmatics* and his other twenty-odd works. But Barth himself is cautious; at the beginning he presents his work as a kind of introduction to theology in general, a commentary which aims at re-establishing at all levels the truth of the radical and decisive statement: only God exists, only God acts, only God saves.

[1] See Chapter II, section 3.

Barth has taken the sovereignty of God to its extreme, and in this he is typically Protestant, radically opposed to Catholicism; a scholastic, he affirms that God is essentially different from man and that any analogy of man's identification with God, so dear to scholastic thinkers, is an invention of the anti-Christ. Only the Incarnation and faith in God incarnate have enabled man the sinner to resemble God; these alone re-establish unity, lost since the appearance of sin, with Him in the act of creation.

Barthian theology develops in a dialectic between human and divine standpoints; the relation of one to the other oscillates between present opposition and past and future unity. Grace is a power which will help man to recover this unity. This explains why discussion has centred on 'dialectical theology' or 'crisis theology' for it supposes that a constant tension exists between the two opposites.

Dialectic implies a synthesis of thesis and antithesis: the thesis is God, creator and organizer of the order created; the antithesis is man the sinner; the synthesis is Christ. Between God who speaks and man who is called upon to listen, there can be no other mediator than Christ. Theological dialectics are essentially Christological, and faith is seen as having no meaning other than in Christ. Barth's conception of Christ is an admirable one: key to the Cosmos, for whom worlds were created; so perfect a man that in imitation of Him we might accomplish all the intentions of our being; a unique product of the Predestination so dear to Calvin, for He is the sole predestined Being, through whom all becomes reality. He is also the only one to be condemned, for He has assumed all the guilt and despair of man, and is the only Being who could in all truth cry out: 'Why hast thou forsaken me?' For Barth, the Christian message is summed up in these words: 'Christians, rejoice, for Christ has come down to earth.'

The message of the great Reformers is thus taken up and renewed: faith is salvation. The analogy between creature and God can be found only through faith. Philosophical intuition and intellectual insight are useless; that which opens the field of knowledge is not science, nor progress, nor even conscience, but faith. St Anselm of Canterbury had already stated this fact, and Barth devotes many remarkable pages to him. Contrary to liberal theology, he acknowledges the value of faith as a means to knowledge. The famous battles between science and faith and history and faith seem to him to be outdated. History is dominated by faith in Christ, and to try to find the Jesus of history is never to find Him.

Barth's work led to a re-evaluation of all the basic Protestant standpoints: the transcendence of God, the open justification of the sinner, worship of the Word of God, the sense of sin. On certain vital points he disagrees with the Reformers; e.g. he approves the present-day dropping of the Calvinist doctrine of Predestination by considering only one predestined Being, Christ. But at the same time he discredits dogmatic liberalism, so taken up with psychological experiences, which finished too often as rationalism pure and simple. He guides the Reformers' heirs towards a type of theology quite distinct from the 'misty' or 'pectoral' ones of other theologians.

His influence has been immense. He induced Protestant theologians to return to Revelation and abandon Kantian or Hegelian postulates. He re-directed Protestantism towards a study of the Reformers; more attention has been given to them over the last thirty years than over the previous two hundred. He turned Protestant preaching away from rationalist arguments, bringing it back to the arguments of the Bible. He re-taught Protestants that, between natural religion, even where this produced noble and charitable works, and Christianity, there is one main difference—transcendency.

It is not only within Protestantism that Barth has exercised a deep influence. We have already seen the action he took against National Socialism—action which was neither empiric nor improvised but was the consequence of his theological conception of liberty. His theory of the 'occurrence', a manifestation of the Word of God intervening in the world, has entered into certain aspects of Existentialism. Catholics themselves have been very interested in Barthian thought. One thing is clear—Christian theology can no longer be the same as it was prior to Barth.

Despite Barth's influence, however, there is much to be done before Protestant theology as a whole becomes Barthian. He has adversaries of note, such as Emile Brünner, who has remained liberal, declining to admit Barth's opposition between nature and grace. Another, Friedrich Gogarten, sought to preserve immanence but inclined towards the National Socialist heresy. Others, such as Niebuhr, reproached Barth for ignoring the social aspect of man. Yet others, such as Jean Rilliet, asked if Heidegger-style Existentialism had not obliterated his thought altogether, or whether his 'occurrence' theory might not be a theological transposition of Hermann Cohen's philosophy. As well as having his 'crisis theology' formula misunderstood, Barth has been reproached also for his pessimism and for seeming more Lutheran than Calvinist. All these criticisms demonstrate nevertheless the importance of Barthism: no Protestant theologian of our age is not, in one way or another, 'post-Barthian'.

Paul Tillich (born in 1886) a German who fled from Hitler to the U.S.A. in 1933, has criticized Barth for having emphasized divine transcendence overmuch and driving man back to a type of fideism. His *Systematic Theology*, which appeared in 1941, made him one of the most influential theologians of the age. In his view religious experience no longer takes place within the framework of the Churches, but rather in the movement of secular thought, especially scientific thought; it therefore becomes necessary to define a Theology of Culture, as he has done in his compact work of the same title. Humanity requires a religion which can satisfy its deeper aspirations and answer the questions it asks itself. Away with abstract theologies! It is necessary to provide, in Existentialist words, a 'situational' theology. Tillich attaches no great importance to the message of the Bible or to religious and moral teaching. In his view God is no longer even that which Luther or Calvin or even Barth taught—a living Person whom man meets face to face—but a transpersonal Being, the basis of all that is, present throughout everything. Christ is not so much the Christ of the Synoptic Gospels but rather the *Logos* of St John, the cosmic Christ of St Paul. This doctrine—which accords in certain aspects with that of Teilhard de Chardin—is enjoying an ever-increasing success in the U.S.A., where Tillich has been compared to St Thomas Aquinas. Obviously it satisfies the deeper aspirations mentioned.

Tillich's views are shared by two other American-German theologians, the Niebuhr brothers, Reinhold (born in 1892) and Richard (born in 1894). Richard is the author of *The Kingdom of God in America* and of *Social Sources of Denominations*. But the youngest representative of post-Barthian theology, Nels Ferré (born in 1908), a professor at Andover Newton Seminary in Massachusetts, has boldly coupled an existentialist philosophy and a certain pietism to the theses of Barthian Dogmatics. And the Dutch Professor Dooyewerd is engaged in establishing a neo-Calvinist system upon solid bases.

Oscar Cullmann (born in 1902), a leading figure in French Protestant thought, theologian, exegetist and historian, stresses the fundamental basis of the revelation in the Church's keeping. In his work *Christ and Time*, a study of the relation of history to revelation, he stresses a little-known aspect of Protestantism—Tradition; and this leads him to adopt an attitude on the question of St Peter which arouses the astonishment of his co-religionists; he also highlights, in his immense work *Christology of the New Testament*, a Christ as far removed from that shown in strict orthodoxy as from that mystical and symbolical figure which neo-liberals such as Bultmann propound. His line of thought leads to an ecumenical goal, and it is not surprising that he was the first Protestant observer at the recent Vatican Council.

Of all theologians over the last thirty years who have worked to renew Protestant positions, the last and perhaps the most striking is Rudolf Bultmann (born in 1884) a professor at Marburg. Scarcely known twenty-five years ago, except by professional exegetists, he published an important article in 1941, *The New Testament and Mythology*. Since then such important works as his *Theology of the New Testament* and his study of primitive Christianity within the framework of ancient religions have developed theses which have shocked or been received with enthusiasm in the Protestant world. Numerous Catholic authors, such as the Jesuits Malevez and Marlé, have studied them carefully. Twenty years after the Barthian wave, the wave of Bultmannism in its turn broke over Reformation thought.

Rudolf Bultmann is distinctly outside that orthodoxy which 'makes dogma out of a confession of faith', in which he sees the greatest temptation for the Church. Yet he denies that he is solely a liberal Protestant of the kind who seeks to establish a scientific basis for the biblical revelation. In his view there lies between science and revelation an absolute gulf of opposition, with natural order on the one hand and supernatural, eschatological order on the other. In any conflict between the two science is always right, though only on its own plane, not on that of faith. Revelation has no need to concern itself with historical truth; it is a message. It has made use of mythical forms to express itself and only from itself does true religious experience emanate. Sacred texts must therefore be 'de-mythed' so that the true Word of God may be heard.

Such a doctrine resolves the conflict between science and faith while separating them at the same time one from another. In a world of science and technology Christianity may by this means return to its sovereign state. But it is contrary to the Catholic conception of a world created, informed and ordered by God, and in this respect Bultmann is the precise antithesis of Teilhard de Chardin. To be fair to him one should highlight his 'theory of occurrence' (this being both real and divine), the encounter with Christ, and man's response to God's appeal coinciding with man's discovery of his true nature. But one cannot be certain that the followers of Bultmann have not discarded this important aspect of his thought, retaining only the criticism of myths and, wanting to dispense with an out-of-date imagery, ending up by rejecting the Church's authority altogether.

With Barth, Bultmann, Tillich and Cullmann, Protestant theology appears to be in a state of crisis, seeking on the one hand to restore doctrine, but on the other hand afraid that too much importance may be paid to form and not enough to the content of its message. This is where its great interest lies.

13. EVANGELICAL RENEWAL: WALES AND CAUX

Dogmatic renewal is the most striking sign of increased vitality in Protestantism. There are others too which indicate efforts to rejuvenate

the Reformed faith. On the apostolic plane—pastoral to the Catholics'
evangelical to the Protestants—these signs are less obvious than those
on the theological plane, but are there nevertheless.

By the end of the nineteenth century revivalist activity was declining,
though there were a number of outstanding preachers such as Charles
Haddon Spurgeon, Adolphe Stöcker, Dwight L. Moody, Sam Jones
and Wilbur Chapman. In France the Baptist pastor Ruben Saillens also
exercised deep influence. But each of these men was an isolated individual, and their activity cannot be compared with the immense
Revival which swept across the Protestant world when well-equipped
teams were at work in each country.

There was, however, one exception, and that was Wales. In 1904 a
young miner, Evans Robert, threw himself into an immense apostolic
campaign. Soon he had a team of evangelists at work in the mines,
teaching a very simple and undogmatic faith with the accent on
fraternal charity, confession of sins, public affirmation of faith, and
especially opening the soul to the will of the Holy Ghost. Presbyterian pastors and Anglican priests looked on the movement sym-
pathetically, but took no part in it. It had a spectacular success with
conversions firstly in dozens, then in hundreds of thousands. Sales of
alcohol dropped in Wales. The national press sent reporters, and their
stories helped the movement still more. Election candidates told their
agents not to organize any meetings when Evans Robert or his
disciples were speaking, or they would have no listeners. Lloyd George
led the singing of Revival hymns at their meetings. Who gained from
all this activity? Principally it was the traditional Churches, one of
whose representatives estimated that 120,000 people returned to the
fold in five months because of the Welsh miner's preaching. But a
number of the converted joined the Pentecostal Churches, which were
then emerging also in Australia, Scandinavia and the U.S.A.[1]

With the exception of another smaller Revival, which took place
between 1922 and 1939 in France, this has been the only true-to-type
Revival in the twentieth century. The smaller of the two was the work
of a group of young French pastors led by Paul Eberhard, but the
impetus was insufficient for it to become of any significance.

The Inner Mission, however, was to last, one of the most useful
results of the Revival, and during the latter half of the nineteenth
century it showed remarkable development. In Germany the impetus
it received from Johann Wichern was such that it made itself felt until
Hitler came to power. Backed by a network of charitable institutions
and run by deaconesses and 'brethren', the mission was such a success
that many pastors belonging to the official Church, though at first
extremely suspicious of it, soon adopted its methods. One of the most

[1] See Chapter I, section 13.

interesting achievements was the holding of 'special religious services', sometimes at unusual hours, adapted to the different hours of work of each trade. In England both the High Church and the dissenters set up Home Missions, to be followed in their turn by Methodists, Baptists and later on by the Pentecostal Churches, who considered themselves as permanently in a State missionary activity. In the U.S.A. the Home Mission began along the lines of 'Institutional Churches' with a flourishing range of social works centred on the place of worship. In France, while the Central Evangelization Society maintained traditional missions, the American-German formula was taken up by the Popular Evangelical Mission, commonly referred to as the McCall Mission, from the Scottish Presbyterian minister of that name who founded it after the war of 1870. Its particular speciality was the 'Salles McCall', many of which were opened throughout France; these served as meeting-halls, hostels and even as relief centres, and were always to be found in the busiest areas. If one of them proved unsuccessful a move was made to a more promising site. There was no fixed programme governing the meetings, each being slanted to the disposition of the particular audience. Hymns were lively and had no special leaning towards religious music, being chosen rather to help memory to preserve the truth of the faith. Lectures and discussions rounded off the very simple type of service, well adapted to the needs of the humble gatherings for whom it was intended. The McCall Missions were very successful throughout Protestant France in the same way as the Catholic missions of the seventeenth century had been in rural areas.

Towards the end of the nineteenth century the Inner Missions were enjoying considerable success in all Protestant countries, and it followed that Bible Societies, also expanding rapidly, were of great help to them. One fact needs emphasis: the gradual development of the missions towards specialization. In Germany, for instance, Dr Stöcker generously lent his support to the Urban Mission, which was specially adapted to the apostolate in the suburbs of big cities. In England special missions were set up among seamen, miners and textile workers; during the First World War the Y.M.C.A. played the part of a permanent mission among the troops. New forms were tried out—e.g. the 'evangelical barge', which covered the canal ways of northern France and Holland and provided services of worship for the bargees and their families. An imitation of Catholic apostolic methods was ried out by the Anglicans in the Fiery Cross crusade of 1918, the cross being ceremoniously carried across England and solemnly acknowledged with due religious ceremony as it passed through each parish. These occasions were accompanied by a wave of fervour similar to that evoked by a Catholic procession of the statue of the Virgin Mary through a selected area. In recent years the Protestant apostolate has retained all its vigour. It has continued to seek ways to adapt itself to the different areas where evangelism needs to be revived. But in none of the great Reformation Churches has there been anything like Catholic Action, an organization which penetrates into every sociological sector for the purpose of reactivating and developing faith. This lack has been deplored by many pastors, and its absence is the more surprising since the Protestant conception of the role of the laity within the Church inclines very favourably towards the shared apostolate which Abbé Cardijn made a principle of the specialized branch of Catholic Action. Publishing and the propagation of the Bible benefit from a centrally directed organization; but pastors, clergymen and the directors of institutions are free to undertake independent apostolic work as they feel inclined. The growth of the sects, all of which are very active, has not led to any simplification of the problem, and between the missions set up by the Established Churches and those of the Adventists or the Pentecostal Churches relations are sometimes scarcely peaceful.

Missionary initiatives are very varied, and in many cases one has the impression that those who take them are not unaware of developments in the Catholic camp and are not slow to profit from them. In the liturgical renewal observed in several Protestant Churches—the German Lutheran, for example, or the French-speaking Swiss—this will give rise to what the Catholics call 'pastoral liturgy', or the systematic use of liturgy as a means of planting the verities of faith. The Central Evangelization Society has teams in about a hundred 'evangelization posts' in France; some twenty of these are to be found in working-class areas, and these have developed along the lines of the sacerdotal teams of the *Mission de France*. In the U.S.A. the larger industries have set up a series of chaplaincies rather similar to the Italian system for Catholic workers in heavy industries. In Sheffield the Anglican Canon Wilham, official chaplain to one of the biggest foundries, has set up an industrial mission along the lines of Father Loew's among the dockers. The 'community parish', so dear to Abbé Michoneau, has been introduced into American Protestantism, e.g. in Harlem, New Haven and in districts of Chicago and Cleveland; all this is bound to help the movement towards primitive evangelism, such a constant feature of Protestantism. A number of pastors and clergymen have even become 'worker-priests'. There are some in England, the U.S.A., Italy and Spain, but the most intensive effort was made in Germany where three young pastors took up work as coalface miners at Gladbach in the Ruhr. In France the brethren at Taizé are sent regularly to working-class areas where they take up employment alongside the other workers.

All these different types of missions are at work in Protestant Christianity in more or less small pockets, but Protestantism has not abandoned the idea of mass conversions. One can see proof of this in the vast effort of religious propaganda undertaken with modern techniques. In the U.S.A. there are thousands of Protestant religious broadcasts over the radio and on television. Even in France, where Protestantism is so obviously a minority interest, the Sunday morning service on the national radio network has become quite important; and, on transmitters just outside national territory, several sects have provided funds for additional broadcasts.

The last thirty years have seen the reappearance, in a modernized form, of the great evangelical orator of the past, always on his journeys to bring the Word of Christ to the world's millions and capable of exercising a magnetic influence on crowds, besides being fully conversant with the latest publicity methods. The new preachers have been at their most effective in the U.S.A., where they have many ancestors. Apart from the prophets who arose among the Negroes, some of whom aroused considerable mass fervour (sometimes leading Christianity along strange paths such as that of Father Divine), they have all made their mark, as Billy Sunday did some years ago and Billy Graham does today.

The man described by radio announcers as the 'greatest evangelist of the age' wanted to be a baseball player when he was young. But, as he has said so often, God called him, and he resolved to become a pastor in the Baptist Church. This was in 1939, and he was then aged twenty-one. The necessary aids to success were not lacking: natural manner, handsome appearance and a face that inspired confidence, together with an undoubted talent for oratory and an enthusiasm which was quickly communicated to his hearers. In 1949, at Los Angeles, Billy Graham realized, during the course of a mass revival meeting, that this was his destined career. His campaign took in town after town, and month after month he continued to refine his technique. At length he tackled New York, with immense success—there were two million listeners, the radio and television channels all carrying his speeches. The vast auditorium of Madison Square Garden was likened by a journalist to Sinai itself. Billy Graham was now fairly launched on his life's work.

Since then he has spared no effort in an apostolate where external publicity and business aspects should not give a false impression. The young apostle's crusade was organized precisely like a campaign for launching a new product, with press and radio advertisements and 'conditioning' of the public beforehand by teams of Billy Graham's advance guard. The annual budget soon reached one million dollars. The choir at his meetings had no fewer than 1,500 voices. Billy Graham himself received 15,000 dollars a month salary. And all this vast effort has succeeded, for audiences of 60,000–100,000 people are common at his meetings. In Berlin there were 65,000 fervent listeners; in Paris in 1954, at a meeting to which were invited pastors, the directors of institutions, welfare workers and propagandists, the 3,500 seats available in the Palais de Chaillot were far too few. The Billy Graham phenomenon is one which cannot be ignored.

What does this prophet have to say? In the final analysis, very true and simple things. That the world is dying under the attacks of rationalism and materialism and that it desires other sustenance; that the Gospel offers the only hope of salvation and that it must be brought to all, believer and unbeliever alike; that one must be a good wife, a good husband, a good father (Billy Graham often speaks of his wife and four children) and treat all men as brothers. However, he does not stop at this simple moralizing; he tries, often cleverly, to make his audiences understand the great Christian mysteries, and to this end he employs anecdotes or fables. For example . . . one day while out walking with his son in the country he accidentally trod on an ants' nest. He stooped to take a closer look; there were dead and injured ants everywhere and much damage had been done to their nest. He tried to help these unfortunate insects in their distress. Impossible; he was too big—only an ant can help another ant. And that is how he explains the mystery of the Incarnation. Another day he was stopped for speeding by the police. One of the police motor-cyclists recognized him and praised his work. The evangelist said to himself that maybe therefore the ten-dollar fine would be overlooked. Not a bit of it—the police-man, all too conscious of his duty, pulled out his book and noted the details of the fine; but, since he was a generous man as well, it was he who paid it. Which provides an excellent illustration of Redemption.

What success do these methods have? In the immediate aftermath results are spectacular. When Billy Graham invites all those who have heard the call to God to come up to the rostrum at the end of his speech, some 4–5 per cent of those present invariably do so. The secretariat of the Billy Graham enterprise keep a register of 'conversions': there are some 300,000 every year! The eight thousand letters sent to Billy Graham every day seem to testify to a real depth of influence, but he is concerned more with the problem of making the results of his action durable, and to this end he asks his listeners to set up Bible Clubs where they can meet to deepen the impact of his lessons. Some of the states in the U.S.A. have already a considerable number of these clubs. Indiana is one example. Here there are 1,700 of them, composed mostly of young people. Television is another of Billy Graham's means (his weekly appearance costs 60,000 dollars) of

maintaining contact with his adherents, besides gaining him new converts. Europeans are rather startled to see the Gospels boosted like
toothpaste or a make of car, but it would be pharisaical to take offence
at methods which after all are perfectly at home in a mass civilization.

Did the Revival movement, which was so characteristic of the
period immediately after the First World War, and which has grown
considerably since then, make any impact on the intellectual life of our
society? At first this new aspect was called the Oxford Groups movement (here a distinction must be drawn between this and the Oxford
Movement of Newman and Pusey), but in 1938 it adopted the name it
has today—Moral Rearmament. It sprang from the spiritual experience
and conversion of one man, Frank Buchman (born in 1878), an
American of Swiss origin who was a Lutheran pastor in Pennsylvania
—significantly the country of William Penn the Quaker. He was
thirty years old when, during a trip to England, he received the call to
God. He happened to be visiting in a Methodist Church listening to a
woman preach. She spoke of the Christ of the Cross who saved sinners
because He had taken the sins of the world upon Himself. Irresistible
hope surged anew in him, replacing the terrible feeling of anguish
which he felt as a sinner; even he, stiff as he was with pride, egotism
and malice, was being called by Christ to salvation. Kneeling at the foot
of the Cross, he asked the Lord to guide him. The response from
within was clear: to ask pardon from those whom he had wronged, to
humble himself. Immediately he wrote to six people with whom he had
quarrelled; after this had been done he felt considerably relieved. This
gesture of making amends was the essence of Buchman's movement.
He embarked on a new life.

He was for some time chaplain in the Y.M.C.A. of a large American
university, but he left this in 1919 to devote all his time to the movement. At Oxford, among the intellectual *élite*, he gathered several
Fellows round him, all of whom were convinced as he was of the
necessity of a direct contact of the soul with Christ. Little by little
groups of 'fraternities' sprang up in different parts of England, then in
Europe, America, Australia and New Zealand. These were constituted
along the lines of the primitive Church, so that everything was held in
common, material wealth as well as prayers and spiritual experience.
In the groups, as well as in public meetings, meditative prayer was of
great importance, and equal emphasis was placed on witness and
sincere affirmation of conversion. The doctrine was a very simple one:
there were four absolutes—absolute honesty, purity, unselfishness and
love—besides a reliance on guidance from the Holy Ghost.

In 1938 the movement was powerful enough for its founder to
consider launching out on a bigger scale. The stage was set for the
drama of the Second World War, and armament and rearmament were

being much discussed. One day while Buchman was out walking in the Black Forest he experienced a second revelation. The Holy Ghost spoke to him, saying that the only worth-while rearmament was a moral one and that the only way to save peace was to set up groups of men, spiritually and inwardly renewed, who would base their lives and actions on Christianity. M.R.A. was born.

The Second World War was a cruel blow to the movement's hopes of remaking the world on the basis of justice, honesty and love. But M.R.A. was very successful in the post-war years. Men of all classes and from every country joined it. The groups multiplied. European industrialists and bankers offered M.R.A. enormous sums of money for it to establish its centre in Europe instead of in Michigan; and so it was decided. Mountain House, once a neo-medieval hotel at Caux, above Montreux, was selected. Here each year since 1949 meetings or retreats have been held all through the summer; the most diverse types of men have come to stay for several days or several weeks in an atmosphere of brotherly friendship and love, taking their turns at cooking and cleaning, participating in guided meditations and listening to confessions from others at the centre.

M.R.A. has a type of clergy, if they can be so described: these are 1,500 permanent officials, specially chosen for their task, who have given up all their material possessions to work entirely for the movement to which they devote their lives. They organize the meetings and run the propaganda campaigns. Advertising and publicity are principal weapons in their armoury; there are numerous publications, radio and television programmes, films and stage shows. The intellectual content of their literature appears to be fairly undistinguished, but it cannot be denied that the fervour is readily communicated. It is an established fact that M.R.A.'s intervention has helped to avert a number of strikes in different industries, and that even on the international plane their intervention has proved useful. Lately the movement has declined somewhat, though in 1958 it was in full vigour.

What is the part played by M.R.A. against the backdrop of Protestantism? In his book, *Remaking the World* (1942 and 1947), Frank Buchman stressed that he aimed at launching a Christian revolution and setting up a living Christianity. Some observers see in this a call to spread a form of Christianity so wide, so all-embracing that it would flow far beyond the frontiers of today's Churches, Catholic as well as Protestant. Yet there are specifically Protestant elements in Buchmanism: the idea of direct contact between the soul and God without the intervention of any hierarchical authority, faithful adherence to the Bible (much read at M.R.A. meetings), the typical moralism of puritanism and a lack of interest in dogmatic formulas. All these aspects have contributed to the attitude of reserve formulated by the

Catholic hierarchy, and especially by Cardinal Suenens; other Catholics, however, have been impressed by the depth of the efforts made by M.R.A. to realize the ideals of fraternity and justice. As it stands, M.R.A. provides proof that the spiritual sap which moved William Fox, the Wesleys and William Booth and their like has not dried up in the old Reformation tree.

14. LITURGICAL AND MONASTIC RENEWAL: TAIZÉ

The third aspect of renewal in contemporary Protestantism is more striking. In certain ways it traces its being back to the ritualist and sacramental movement, which we saw grew from the Oxford Tractarian movement in England [1] and in Germany from the neo-Lutherans. But in other more basic ways it seems to be, within the framework of the Reformation, a very surprising innovation.

The love of liturgy, as defined by Puseyism, remained an essential part of the Anglican Church wherever the High Church, which today has become Anglo-Catholicism, returned to all the liturgical customs in force before the Reformation, even to certain dogmatic positions relating to the sacraments. To what degree did this return to sources go hand in hand with the impetus towards inner renewal, as Pusey and Newman would have wished? In 1933, at the time of the commemoration of the famous sermon by Keble on national apostasy, some fifty clergymen signed a statement in which they reproached the Anglo-Catholics with not having maintained the intense spirit of piety and fidelity to the Gospels exemplified in the first Oxford Movement. Yet the very existence of the apostolic and fervent sacerdotal community known as Pusey House seems to constitute sufficient answer to this grievance.

In Germany the liturgical and neo-sacramental current had lost some of its vigour during the glorious days of the *Reich* of William II. But after the First World War it was launched anew by Pastor Hausen when Germany, beaten and in ruins, sought spiritual realities to give inner meaning to its reconstitution. Pastor Hausen was one of the first to air the idea of pastoral liturgy; that is liturgy employed as a form of religious pedagogy along the lines of Russian Orthodoxy, which Hausen had studied. At his appeal Lutheran ministers sought retreat in Catholic abbeys in order to study the ancient liturgies. In Berlin High Mass was celebrated in German according to the liturgy in force in Luther's day. The High Church Association, presided over by Professor Heiler, and its sister organization *Die Hochkirche* evolved in

---

[1] See Chapter III, section 3.

a similar way. At Jena the Protestant Professor Hans Litzmann published a profound work entitled *Sacramentum Gregorianum*, the Roman Mass in one of its most venerable forms, declaring that: 'There are few things in the world which are so compelling in their fascination and so venerable as the Roman Mass.'

Brought up short by Hitlerism, the High Church movement only resumed its activities after the Second World War, and then it adopted new terms. Changes were made in services similar to those carried out in Catholicism, especially the greater participation of the congregation, and there was also a considerable development in sacramental practice. Here it joined with the monastic movement of which, as we shall see, Germany was a birthplace.[1] There was also a whole stream of theological thought stressing certain aspects of doctrine little featured in the past in Lutheranism, such as devotion to the Blessed Virgin and the veneration of saints, on which Pastor Lackmann has written a fervent work.

From Germany and England the liturgical movement spread to other sectors of Protestantism, especially the U.S.A. Löhe founded a Missions House to train pastors according to his theories, and the spirit of Neuendettelsau was transferred to the other side of the Atlantic, to the Lutheran Churches of the Ohio Synod, then to Missouri, finally totally reforming the Indiana Synod. The efforts undertaken to return to a purified form of primitive Christianity were accompanied by an insistence on dignity of conduct and an increased emphasis on sacramental practice and on the magnificence of the services. Episcopalian Anglicanism, under the influence of Puseyite ritualism, inclined more and more towards Anglo-Catholicism, with its magnificent cathedrals and stately ceremonies; it even led some to look down on other forms of Protestantism as lacking a sense of mystery and symbolism. The clergy of the High Church movement were drawn from among the most distinguished minds in the union, and this fact explains its actions. The increased worship of the Virgin and the use of an American Missal (becoming more and more evident) are two signs pointing to this conclusion. A parallel development can be observed even in those Churches where it might have been least expected—the Presbyterian, Methodist and Baptist. One can find in their places of worship ornate crosses, candelabra and stained-glass windows, all of which would be astonishing to the Huguenots of the Cévennes. In central New York the Reverend Fosdyck, a Baptist pastor, has built a church modelled on Chartres Cathedral; true, the chapels are not dedicated to saints, but to great humanitarian figures.

Today there can be no doubt that many sectors of Protestantism are tending towards liturgical and sacramental reform, and a return to a

---

[1] See below.

more mystical conception of religion. Frequent communion and prayers in piously maintained chapels are all part of the same trend. The Lenten sermons inaugurated by Pastor Marc Boegner in 1928, for example, have been taken up elsewhere. Liturgy and sacramental life have a pre-eminent place in the Taizé community as well as in all the women's religious communities. In Anglicanism a liturgical renewal may be observed today—indeed it is fast becoming a liturgical pastorality—under the guidance of such people as the erudite Dom Gregory Dix, Father Gabriel Hebert, W. K. L. Clarke and Canon Harris. In the German United Lutheran Evangelical Church a new ritual was laid down in 1956, covering not only the *Deutsche Messe* but Vespers and the Compline as well. In Sweden a movement is developing which has no hesitation in calling itself the High Church, after the Anglicans. Even in the most Calvinist of Reformed Churches there are undoubted signs of a similar trend. 'As a general rule', said Adolphe Monod, 'the use of liturgies is not advised,' the only valid one in his view being the Word of God. But this strict view is being forced out. At the end of the nineteenth century in Paris the Étoile's pastor, Bersier, caused a sensation by taking the lead in a liturgical movement, decorating his church and moving the pulpit to one side and the communion table to the centre instead. Today these cannot be classed as innovations any more than the siting of the cross behind the communion table. Whereas during the nineteenth century there was a powerful movement to abolish the pastor's robe, nowadays it is always worn. The author of a treatise on liturgy, Raymond Paquier, has voiced many people's views when he insists that more sumptuous sacerdotal vestments should be worn; white surplices, even the stole, are advocated. In 1955 there was a discussion within the French Reformed Church which was entirely in keeping with the new spirit of the times. A new ritual had been proposed, but there were many pastors who regarded it as too cold and too austere; they suggested instead the adoption of Max Thurian's, in use at Taizé, or that of Dr Bakhuysen van den Brink at Leyden. Where Holy Communion was once celebrated four times a year, it is now celebrated twenty-eight times. The liturgical and sacramental movement in many areas of Protestantism is thus indisputable. But it would be unwise to conclude that it constitutes a *rapprochement* pure and simple to Catholic positions. Pastor Hausen, the leader of liturgical renewal in Germany, stated categorically: 'It is not to the Catholic Church that Protestantism must return, but to Catholicity itself. It is not a matter of submitting to our brethren but to our Mother Church.' The Anglo-Catholics who are most close to Catholicism hold views no different from these.

The English ritualist renewal was, as we have seen, accompanied by a resurgence of Anglican monasticism copied from the Catholics. The movement was of particular interest to women, and many female communities arose during the period 1840–70; still others were founded later until there were 58 in all, spread among 238 convents throughout the world. Some adopted the Rule of St Augustine, others that of St Benedict; some are Franciscan or are called the Daughters of St Vincent de Paul. There is even a Cistercian monastery. All have adopted the custom of taking vows.

For men only one organization was set up before 1870—that of St John the Evangelist—but towards the end of the century a considerable increase was observed. In 1891 there was the Society of the Sacred Mission, founded by Herbert Kelly, with an essentially active character; in 1892 the Community of the Resurrection, led by Charles Gore at Oxford; in 1894 the (Franciscan) Society of the Divine Compassion; in 1898 the Benedictines of Caldey Isle, with a branch also for women. The spiritual drama which led to conversion *en masse* to Catholicism of these two latter organizations, under the leadership of the Abbot, Dom Carlyle, shocked England deeply; but in 1914 another community was installed at Nashdom and remained attached to Anglicanism under the Rule of St Benedict. Today there are about six hundred Anglican religious and monks, without taking into account the missionaries abroad who are under no particular rule. There is only one contemplative order—the Servants of the Will of God, in Sussex. This is similar in many respects to the Trappists. Indeed they are so little known that the Anglican Bishop Kirk of Oxford said in 1952 that he wished 'there was at least one contemplative order in the kingdom'.

Monastic renaissance in Anglicanism is not so surprising when one reflects that it has always claimed to follow Tradition, like the Catholic Church; but it is less to be expected in the Calvinist and Lutheran Churches. We remember with what violence Luther, in his *De Votis Monasticis*, took a stand against vows which he declared were contrary to the Word of God, to faith, to evangelical liberty, to the Commandments and to reason. As for Calvin, in his *Traité des Scandales*, his opinion of monks was that everyone knew their cloisters, cells and holes to be such loathsome places that he would not dare to go into the enormity of their deeper secrets. While not all the great Reformers are of this opinion, there is no doubt that Protestantism today is still influenced by these attacks. Pastor A. N. Bertrand in 1944 stated that the radical condemnation by the Reformers of monastic life is justified from the evangelical point of view.

Protestant opinion crystallized immediately after the end of the First World War. Seeing that social evangelism lacked spiritual force, several Reformed thinkers decided that if the Kingdom was to be realized it could not be on a material plane only, but that its spiritual foundations must be laid also. Social achievements were to go hand in hand with prayer. Wilfred Monod, a social leader and mystical thinker, was of this opinion. Having studied the Catholic Third Order formula he decided to introduce the principle into Protestantism under the name of *Veilleurs*. The organization was created in 1923, and Monod devoted all his energies to its success until his death in 1943. The idea consisted of gathering together groups of laity who continued to live and work in the outside world, but were firmly resolved to put Christian principles into practice and to devote a part of each day to prayer and meditation. Without taking vows they were to consider themselves bound by a solemn undertaking.

This was, in a way, the first step to be taken since the Reformation towards a resurrection of monasticism in the Protestant world. It met a need, for in the years following there were other positive signs in the same direction. In 1929 Mlle Antoinette Butte directed a *maison de retraites* firstly at St Germain-en-Laye, then in Paris, and became very interested in the monastic movement. She later gathered round her a group of people who were of like mind and founded a community. During the Second World War it was transferred to southern France and was soon famous under the name of *Retraites de Pomeyrol*. In 1931, at Grandchamp in Switzerland and under similar circumstances, another group was formed by three pious young women, helped by Mme Léopold Micheli. Thirteen years later this had developed into a true religious community. In Germany, at Darmstadt, while the Nazi tyranny was in full control in 1936, two young women who gave excellent Bible instruction courses, Klara Schlink and Erika Madauss, set up women's circles to combat by prayer and spiritual studies the increasing suppression of Christianity under Hitler's regime. The trend was so strong that among the deaconesses, who, as we have seen, were not strictly religious, some houses became communities and followed a particular Rule, such as that of Bethlehem at Hamburg. Yet all these achievements were surpassed by one which seems to incarnate all that is new in monastic renewal within the Reformation—the achievement of Roger Schutz at Taizé.

In August 1940 a young man arrived in a Burgundian village to settle in a large house that had stood empty for a long time. He was a French-speaking Swiss, a little reserved in manner as became a citizen of Geneva, but he soon became friends with the local farmers, although they too were unusually suspicious and withdrawn because of the German occupation. Taizé was located exactly on the demarcation line between occupied and unoccupied France. The empty house was a natural stopping place for illegal travellers between the two zones.

Naturally Roger Schutz did not come to Taizé specially for the purpose of helping escaping prisoners. He settled in France because he felt that his vocation would benefit from direct contact with human distress, and his vocation was to serve Christ in prayer and works. His sense of vocation was fairly recent. For some ten years he had lived without faith, but at the age of twenty he had begun to feel that the arguments of Lamarck and Darwin could not withstand the certitude that had grown in him. As a pastor's son he attributed the rediscovery of faith to his Calvinistic background.

It was while he was studying theology at the Lausanne Faculty, when he was twenty years old, that God spoke to him. He was preparing a thesis for his doctorate: the subject was St Benedict and the early years of monasticism in the West. While he meditated on that immense work of psychology and faith, a work governing the lives of monks, he wondered if the strictures of Luther and Calvin as applied to monasticism were well founded. It is quite certain that he was unaware of the monastic revival then taking place in Anglicanism, that he knew nothing of the *Veilleurs*, and that he had heard only vaguely of the experiments of Grandchamp. It was purely through his own inner conviction that he resolved to devote himself to a monastic life within Protestantism, and he set about this together with several friends.

He remained alone at Taizé for two years, and it was during this time that he conceived the idea of settling in this village when peace returned and setting up a community of young men resolved to devote their lives to the service of Christ in the Church and the world. He also intended to help the ecumenical movement, working towards the reunion of Christians of all denominations. In 1941 two of the apostles of Christian Unity, the Abbé Couturier and Father Villain, paid a visit to the young solitary at Taizé.

In 1942 he was forced to leave Burgundy, now occupied completely by the Germans. He returned to Geneva. Here he met three students who became enthusiastic about his ideas: Max Thurian, Pierre Souvairan and Daniel de Montmollin. In 1944 the Taizé Community was finally founded as both a school and centre for spiritual retreat.

Progress was slow. For five years the brethren were alone, living the type of life they had envisaged, meditating and planning future action. They discovered for themselves the two realities that really make a monk: submission to a Rule and the triple vows of celibacy, community and obedience. However, it was not until Easter 1949 that the real story of Taizé begins, for not before then had Roger Schutz considered that he and his friends were ready.

The name of Taizé has become famous during the last fifteen years. In 1958 there were forty members, in 1964 there were sixty-five. The brethren run workshops, and there is a co-operative farm run jointly by the brethren and Catholic laity from the canton. The village as a whole has been revitalized. An enormous number of visitors come to Taizé—cardinals and bishops, bearded archimandrites and popes, even soberly dressed Protestant pastors of every denomination. Its importance in Christianity grows daily; in the Protestantism of the twentieth century there is nothing quite so unusual or so promising.

The brethren of the Taizé Community are monks—or rather, less formally, they are akin to the Little Brothers of Jesus set up by Father Voillaume along the lines laid down by Charles de Foucauld, or to the members of certain other worker missions such as those set up by Father Loew among the dockers of Marseilles and Port-de-Bouc. Normally they wear ordinary dress, adapted to the tasks in hand— pottery work, printing and agriculture. Some carve icons or run the co-operative dairy. Thrice daily they gather for readings from the Scriptures, psalms, prayers and hymns. Their existence is regulated by a Rule. It is less rigid than any formal one, allowing some latitude and merely seeking to indicate the essentials of communal life, which are similar to those of the great Catholic orders from St Benedict to St Ignatius Loyola. Liturgy plays a large part in the life of the community, not so much in the length of time taken up by it as by the role which it assumes throughout the day, work being expressly conceived as an adjunct to prayer, being itself a manifestation of prayer. The services are personal and specifically directed, so that everyone feels individually involved.

But life at Taizé, as the prior himself insists, is based on a provisional conception. 'Here we make the conviction that everything that goes to make up the spirit of the community, everything that distinguishes us in our Rule and in our liturgy, will one day disappear. Our Rule and our liturgy are weak instruments in the struggle for unity. In certain respects these provisional aspects are called upon to disappear as soon as visible unity appears. When this happens the particularities of the community will cease to be, but not the bases which are common to all, for there is an immutability in this vocation, especially in our vows. These cannot be called into question, for they constitute not only the way of life we follow in the wake of Christ, but also the framework which holds us together in the same community.'

In many ways, therefore, the Taizé brethren are close to the Catholics. But let there be no mistake: they remain totally and wholly Protestant. The prior, Roger Schutz, asserts: 'The distinctive appeal of Taizé does not stop it from being whole-heartedly associated with the Reformation Churches. Within these, it seeks the path of visible unity among Christians.'

This sentence should be emphasized. It highlights the profound goal of the leaders of the community. Taizé is attached to no particular Protestant Church. Among the brethren are Calvinists, Lutherans, Congregationalists, Methodists, Anglicans and others, some eighteen Churches being represented; it maintains fraternal relations with the Catholics, and indeed counts many high-ranking Catholics among its friends. But it would be absurd to conclude from this that the brethren at Taizé are well on the way to conversion. What the community wants is to try, in a climate of friendship, to achieve some degree of *rapprochement* between all Christian brethren, at present so far apart.

This explains how Taizé has become an ecumenical centre, whose role became still more evident from 1959 onwards when Pope John XXIII showed especial interest in Roger Schutz's work. There have been official meetings at Taizé between Catholic bishops and Protestant pastors, and colloquies with dignitaries of the Orthodox Church—all emphasizing Taizé's role as a common meeting-ground between the separated brethren. Of course, it can play this role only because its brethren have provided the community with an authentic spiritual life of its own and a definite aim in view.

One of the principal spiritual works to appear this century is Roger Schutz's *Vivre l'aujourd'hui de Dieu*; it transcends all religious barriers, and every Catholic theologian is ready to acknowledge his debt to Taizé's principal leading theologian, Max Thurian, whose works on the Eucharist, Confession and the Visible Unity of Christians and Tradition, have given new life to Protestant positions on these subjects. Pope John XXIII was moved to observe one day in the presence of the author that this experiment, so full of hope, was 'a shining light'. No better summing-up could be made.

The experience provided by the Taizé experiment is great, but we should not because of this dismiss other monastic endeavours in the Protestant world. They are far from unimportant. Grandchamp, which is for women what Taizé is for men, has been a success under the wise guidance of Sister Geneviève, and vocations are not lacking. In 1958 there were thirty members.

The *Retraites de Pomeyrol* have retained a more independent character. After a difficult period during the war and liberation the community reorganized itself, and while it is numerically weak its influence as a retreat is considerable. Emphasis is laid on liturgy, inspired by that of the primitive Church, of Anglicanism, of Catholicism, of the *Veilleurs*, the Moravians and the Quakers. The Rule is the same as that of Taizé.

The *Marienschwestern* of Darmstadt have had a more difficult time. They were still organized only as members of a Bible circle when their city was razed by Allied bombs and their houses and books burnt. This they regarded as a sign from Heaven. A few weeks later fifteen of them met to consider embarking on a life of prayer and repentance. Little by little they became aware of the stern demands of monastic life. Seven of them, including the two founders, Klara Schlink and Erika Madauss, launched the movement on a new course—they took vows and modelled their order on that of St Benedict, with emphasis on prayer, meditation and liturgy. As well as this contemplative discipline they undertook missionary activities. There were seventy members in 1958 and further expansion has been limited only by lack of accommodation.

In 1950 their example was imitated by a group of young German women, formerly members of the Protestant guide movement until it was suppressed under Hitler. In 1942, on the eve of Easter, they determined to set up as soon as possible a community aimed at the training of youth and based on prayer. Without leaving their everyday employment they set up what Catholics would term a secular institution: the Castell Circle. They took the three vows, but wore religious habit only during services. Today there are twenty-five members, with their main centre at Schwanberg Castle. Other similar organizations have emerged in South America in Moravian circles.

While such beginnings are still small, the renewal of the monastic movement in the Protestant world seems to hold out excellent promise. Theologically Max Thurian's work had demonstrated its justification, affirming that, while it might appear contrary to the views of the Reformers, it was wholly in line with the basic spiritual tenets of Protestantism, and with the teachings of Jesus, the apostle and the Fathers. It is too early to say how it will fit in with Protestant thinking in our own age, but it is a fact that these experiments in faith and charity give cause for hope for the future.

15. The Life of the Soul in Protestantism

After this survey of the Reformation world and its development over the last 150 years, one question now arises: what is the place of spiritual life and faith in Protestantism? It must be answered, whatever religion is being examined, since to live according to the principles of a particular religion is not merely to affirm one's allegiance to a human society, as one might to a trade union or political party; the soul is guided according to the principles of that religion. And this is particularly true of Protestantism—a 'specific form of Christian life, viewed in its deepest aspect, in the attitude of the soul before God'. This means that the ecclesial and dogmatic conflict in which the Reformed Churches arose is an important consideration.

A study of religious practice supplies little information on this important aspect of the matter. As we saw earlier, from the statistical facts given, the various Protestant Churches define 'practice' according to different criteria. Some of them regard only those adults who attend Church regularly as practising adherents; others incline to the Catholic conception and accept only those who attend Mass a certain number of times in one year. In some of the newer Churches or the sects, attendance is obligatory at least several times a week. There seems to be a certain ambiguity in the word 'practising' as applied to a Protestant. One can feel that one is, and may truly be, a Christian member of one of the Reformation Churches without feeling obliged to attend church. Intense inner fervour may go hand in hand—at least in theory—with absence from Sunday service and from participation in the Mass. Some Protestants consider that it is the pastor's job to attend to the affairs of the parish and the church, these matters having little bearing on religious experience itself—on the issue of the soul face to face with God. An empty Protestant church does not necessarily mean—at least in theory—that the parish is apostate.

Scientifically based religious sociology is still in its infancy for nearly all the Protestant Churches; throughout the nineteenth century there were few reliable statistics to serve as evidence, though some are useful as indicators even if they are pessimistic. In Lutheran Prussia practice had fallen so low in 1848 that Frederick William IV bemoaned the fact openly. But worse was to follow, for in Berlin in 1880 80 per cent of burials, 52 per cent of marriages and 26 per cent of births dispensed with religious formalities. In 1851 a census revealed that in Anglicanism less than 22 per cent of registered adherents attended services. In 1955 a Gallup poll showed that the figure had fallen to 16 per cent, and this included not only Anglicans but members of other dissident Churches. In France, a country where Protestantism was in a minority, while in peasant areas practice was still almost universal in the large cities it had fallen to some 25 per cent in 1890. In many areas of the U.S.A. it did not even reach this figure for many denominations. And the slide continued. In Scandinavia, that Lutheran bastion, it touched 10 per cent. In Finland, in 1953, a poll indicated an 8 per cent attendance on Sundays and that only 15 per cent took communion once a year. In Sweden the situation was worse still, and a visitor, looking into one of that country's empty cathedrals on a Sunday, might conclude that it demonstrated clearly that the degree of secularization was total. In the Nîmes area of France, in 1958, one Protestant commune numbered some seven hundred members, all of whom contributed to their pastor's stipend; but only one hundred and fifty of them thought of themselves as parishioners. Only twenty of these attended church, and only two were men.

The drift away from faith in the modern world has affected all forms of Protestantism just as much as Catholicism. This fact is insufficiently known, hidden as it is by the 'inner' character of the Protestant religion. But those who are directly concerned with human realities are well aware of it; they say that, where religious practice dies out and where it ceases to be manifested publicly, the life of the soul fades quickly, defeated by routine and the prevailing public opinion.

One of the signs of the religious crisis among both Protestants and Catholics is the decline in recruitment to the ministry. It is more significant among Protestants than in the Roman Church where ecclesiastical celibacy is an obstacle to the vocation. Undoubtedly all the Reformation Churches can be thankful that the vocation of pastor is often handed down from father to son; this is especially true of the Baptists, among whom we can cite the examples of Martin Luther King or Billy Graham. The same thing occurs among the Calvinists in Switzerland and in France, where there are veritable dynasties of pastors, such as the Monods. But this does not necessarily help to fill the seminaries and the Faculties of Theology. In France, in 1958, there was one pastor for every 850 adherents, a proportion that satisfied the Protestant Church. But since then there has been a flight from the ministry, the young preferring to write, edit newspapers or run welfare organizations. Out of 167 trainee pastors during the period between 1946 and 1951, 29 of them declined ordination. In Germany the decline has continued for 150 years, with a catastrophic fall during the Hitler regime which still seems not to have flattened out. In the Scandinavian countries the admission of women priests has been but a palliative; and it set off violent controversy in Sweden. In the U.S.A., to help recruitment and provide better training for the young entrants, some Churches have pooled their efforts by setting up common seminaries or common Faculties of Theology. But as a whole, even among the most active sects, such as the Pentecostal Movements, there are complaints that religious leaders are lacking, especially in Latin America, where these movements are developing rapidly.

But there are positive aspects which testify to Protestantism's vitality. It is not possible to draw up plans demonstrating 'areas of fervour', as Canon Boulard has done for Catholic France, but there are out-of-the-way districts where attendance at Protestant services is high. Georges Goyau has shown that at the end of the last century in Protestant Germany every village church was full on Sundays and communion was common. It is still a true picture today. In Scandinavia a reliable witness has testified to the fact that the church at Leksand in Dalecarlia, for example, is always full on Sundays, tourists rubbing shoulders with woodcutters and farmers. And in France the author himself recalls that the small Protestant churches of the Queyras and Haut-Vivarais regions were full to bursting. Then there are the Negro Baptist Churches of the U.S.A., where attendance beats all records, figures of 93–95 per cent being common. The same applies to the newer Churches and sects.

There is yet another sign of Protestant spiritual vitality—the ever-increasing spread of the Bible. One must not forget that Protestant life has a biblical basis. It is the Bible which engenders, qualifies and determines its life. Spiritual life is born of the Bible and it rises or falls in proportion to the degree of attention paid to the Bible. At the end of the eighteenth century one of the most significant signs showing the decline of the Reformed faith was that Bible reading itself had declined. In the last 150 years the situation has altered completely, though not without certain difficulties. The attacks of 'free criticism' against its historicity increased the degree of disaffection for the Bible. In Lutheran Germany Luther's translation fell into such discredit that the theologian Paul de Lagarde was driven to admit that 'it was no longer read at all'. However, the emergence and the upsurge of the Bible societies brought about an entirely different situation. As we saw, these societies arose at the beginning of the nineteenth century, that of London being in the lead, closely followed by those of the U.S.A., all of them now linked in a common endeavour. The millions of copies distributed all over the world in almost a thousand languages exercise an immense influence. In mission territories, either in non-Christian lands or among nominally Catholic peoples in South America, the distribution of the Bible is normally the only way in which missionary work can be carried out. Lately help has come from radio broadcasts aimed at explaining the Bible to the least educated. In advanced countries translations of the Bible have been brought up to date, and in this respect there has been a large measure of collaboration between Catholics and Protestants over the last fifty years, especially in the case of the 'Jerusalem Bible', produced in France by the Dominican Fathers and due to be published in a Protestant edition. The Bible has once more taken its place in Protestant spiritual life; the theologians, whether Barth or Bultmann, stress the acknowledgment of its authority, even if they offer different interpretations of its texts. These details are small enough when compared to the Bible's present sovereign position, especially among the peoples of the U.S.A.

16. A PROTESTANT 'SAINT': KAGAWA

No Christian, whatever his obedience, can speak of Kagawa without emotion or affection. He has been called the St Francis of Japan and a Man of Christ. When he died in April 1960 even the Catholics celebrated Mass in his memory. He was undersized, weak-sighted and lacking in charm, yet this age would have been poorer had Kagawa not lived, for he had the same effect on it as a St Thérèse of Lisieux, a Charles de Foucauld or a Gandhi.

At eleven years of age he was sent to an Anglican Mission run by a family called Myers, and here he learned English and the ways of Western civilization. He related later on the substance of a conversation he once had with the pastor. 'Is it true that Jesus was persecuted by cruel men, that He was struck and spat on? Is it true that before He died on the cross He pardoned those who had harmed Him?' 'Yes,' the pastor answered, 'it is true.' Kagawa then kneeled, touched the ground with his forehead and prayed that he might be capable of imitating Christ.

When he was fifteen years old he became a Christian. At twenty he had determined his course and resolved to devote his life to God's service. But in the meantime he had made another discovery—the poor, and that the poor were, no less than Christ, ever present. A first attempt at sharing the lives of the people of the Kobe slums had ended in an attack of tuberculosis, but he recovered, finished his theological studies at a Presbyterian university and returned to the slums. At Shinkawa, with its ten thousand people living in shanty towns and tumbledown dwellings, he set up as 'pastor' to his parish, a parish which no Church would have attempted to create.

Shinkawa: a sublime experiment. Installed in a tiny hovel no more than six feet square, sharing his lodging in turn with lice and scab-ridden men, murderers and sufferers from trachoma, he became completely at one with them. Of his own money there remained nothing and all he got he gave away. When a drunk shouted at him that if he were a true Christian he would give away his shirt, Kagawa stripped it off and gave it to him, and tunic and trousers as well.

In the ordinary way this sort of conduct would have been looked upon as provocative enough, but it was more so in time of war when, a believer in non-violence, he stressed God's solemn commandment: Thou shalt not kill. Worse, he publicly denounced the prostitution racketeers and helped underpaid workers to organize themselves against exploiters. Legally, no one could take action against him, especially as he was well on the way to becoming famous, though there was always the possibility of a knife thrust in a dark alley way. Everything was tried against him, but he stood firm.

The very fierceness of the resistance to his ideas was enough to make him famous. His book, *Beyond the Frontiers of Death*, in which he wrote of the horrors of Japanese working-class life in the 1920's, led him to the leadership of the Workers' Trade Union, then of the Workers' Party. Under arrest for several days for leading a subversive movement, he was released by the pressure of public opinion. It was then he understood he would have to widen his field of action, and that political action was not to be ruled out in his campaign to help the poor. Before undertaking any new course of action it was his custom to go into retreat, and in long hours of prayer he would attempt to understand what Christ required of him.

The second act of his life now opened. Meanwhile he had married Haruko ('Miss Spring'), a workshop superintendent at the women's university. It was she who helped him to maintain his contacts with the workers' world, from which she herself came, and to remember his true vocation on behalf of the poor; for circumstances seemed to be driving him into ever-increasing and wider tasks of a political and social nature, even to status as an international figure. The Workers' Party, the Peasants' Union, the Co-operatives Federation, with all of which he was concerned, were designed to lift the poor from their misery. The Japanese social security system is a direct result of his efforts. At the same time efforts to stamp out prostitution, tuberculosis and syphilis all owe much to his drive in arousing public opinion against them. Naturally enough, all this was not plain sailing. Even in his own party extremists accused him of having sold out to the capitalists; the upper middle classes remained distrustful and envious of him. But there were compensations, such as when the emperor appointed him a member of the newly created Economic and Social Commission.

No one knew better than he that he would not end his life as a councillor in striped trousers. While he was directing the Tokyo welfare bureau (the city was still suffering from the effects of an earthquake and the unemployment figures were climbing steeply) he undertook a missionary campaign as well. Although he was only fifty years old his sight, which had never been good, had almost gone, and the after-effects of the tuberculosis, which had never had a chance to heal, had considerably weakened his body. But where the soul commands the body must follow. From youth onwards not a day had passed without his preaching the Gospel, without his speaking of Christ. One book followed another until at the end of his life he had written 180 in all—social novels, autobiographical sketches and works of the purest piety sometimes reaching into mysticism. Until the end of his life evangelism played the principal part.

His evangelical activities extended to the international level. Crowds came to hear him in Great Britain, the U.S.A., Scandinavia, Australia and even in Germany, despite the fact that he spoke only in broken English. In his voice, practical Socialism and Christianity went hand in hand: the world must be reformed, the established social order and the distribution of wealth likewise, but it was even more important to reform man himself, teaching him the lessons of the Gospels and to return good for evil. What he had to say to his listeners was scarcely theological. Many people claimed that it was wholly sentimental; but when he spoke of the necessity to live the total life of the Cross and of the complete acceptance that this demanded, he was convincing, for he himself had lived this kind of life. In a manner of speaking he still continues to do so, for the immense royalties that still pour in from the sales of his works go to the poor. One dream sustained him: the setting up of a corps of five thousand missionaries, covering Japan in the first place, then the entire world. But the undertaking was too vast in scope. After three years it failed, though it left some tens of thousands of conversions which remain permanent.

The succession of wars in which Japan was engaged saddened him. He kept silent, not wishing openly to condemn his country, which he loved and venerated. But when Gandhi reproached him for his silence he signed the manifesto condemning war, along with Gandhi, Tagore, Einstein and Romain Rolland. In Shanghai, where a pastor had been killed by a Japanese bullet, he publicly apologized to China in the name of the real Japan. This incident brought him a new spell in prison.

But he knew he was right. The Second World War was approaching, and his calls to peace, his appeals for universal love and brotherhood in Christ, became more and more insistent. His health was bad, but his soul was as strong as ever. Once more, in 1940, he was thrown into prison, once more he was freed—it would not have been politic to keep a Kagawa in prison while Japan was fighting for its life. 'Ah, my country—how heavy is your burden of sin!' he cried publicly. The tragedy of Hiroshima overwhelmed him, though he was scarcely surprised by it. After Japan's defeat, the emperor sent for him to help the country out of its distress. His party was electorally successful, though he himself had declined to participate in Parliament itself: instead he undertook a successful tour of the U.S.A. to plead in the name of Christ for American goodwill towards Japan. After this his activities slowed down and he resigned from all official posts, intervening in debates only to denounce atomic war. But he took up his pilgrim's staff once more to return to the poorer quarters of the big cities, there to speak of Christ and the rule of love. 'Stripped to the skin one marches best . . .' he said with his wonderful smile. In 1955, and again in 1959, it was rumoured that he was dying; on the latter occasion he had caught pneumonia while speaking to the poor of Shikoku, on the same island where sixty years earlier Pastor Myers had first introduced him to Christ. For a year he lingered on, dying on 23rd April 1960. To a pastor friend who was with him he murmured: 'For peace in Japan, for the salvation of the world.' A cloud blacker than night descended on the world at that moment.

17. PROTESTANTISM EXPRESSES ITSELF: I. IN ARCHITECTURE AND THE PLASTIC ARTS

It is a constant principle that the soul of a people who have recourse to prayer expresses itself in the arts, and that all the great artistic creations of humanity have been strongly influenced by the religious feelings then reigning in the society which produced them. Medieval Christianity and the Catholicism of the Council of Trent have, in cathedral architecture and baroque styles respectively, demonstrated typical expressions. In what way has Protestantism displayed in its artistic endeavours the depth and originality of its religious experience?

As regards architecture and the figurative representational arts, we must bear in mind that the Lutheran and the Reformed Churches, in many cases, have not had the freedom of expression necessary to create their own type of religious art. Where they gained ground they merely occupied what were once Catholic churches, and though these suited neither their taste nor their aspirations they had the merit of costing nothing. The Protestants merely accepted them, subordinating their own aesthetic tastes to what was available. St Peter's Cathedral in Geneva or the Gothic cathedral in Basel bear no relation to the Huguenot faith that is preached in them. Parisians attending services at the Oratoire Church find it difficult to imagine that the baroque nave is Calvinist and has been since Napoleon gave the church to the Protestant community at the request of Boisey d'Anglas.

It was only when the Protestants were obliged to build on their own account that they expressed their deepest convictions, and their sacred art became truly an expression of their faith. Luther and Calvin fought against ostentation in the churches, even against intrinsic beauty. For them paintings and sculpture were mere simulacra, and Calvin denounced them as likely to lead men into superstition. It was an unhealthy sign to decorate churches in any way. This rigorous attitude had a firm doctrinal basis, for there was of course no mediator between God and man, only the Word of God itself. To those Catholics who saw in the beauty expressed through art some spiritual portrayal, some reflection of the Divine, the Protestants replied: 'There can be no question of receiving through art any beneficial knowledge of the living God.'

Protestant architecture was designed to signify nothing else but the renunciation of sensuous religion. It was not a case of reflecting on the splendours of creation through appropriate forms, but rather of inspiring, through starkness, the austerity demanded by the Word of God. Among Calvinists, still more than Lutherans, the church was a meeting-place and should not be too large—was not the vastness of the Roman basilicas a sign of pride? It should have bare walls, adorned perhaps solely with biblical texts, and the cross as the sole ornament, though even this might be construed as excessive decoration. The pulpit occupied the principal position, and the communion table was relegated to one side, where it seemed to lack any majesty even when the opened Bible was laid on it. The Word was thus confirmed as superior to the sacrament. This aesthetic setting ruled Calvinist thought until the beginning of the twentieth century. The churches at Port-Royal and the Étoile can scarcely be called works of art, for they resemble comfortable conference rooms. Among the Lutherans the austerity principle was much less observed, and in Scandinavia naves are frequently ornamented with paintings, sculptures and stained glass. This applies also in Anglicanism, where fidelity to a tradition that pre-dates the schism has often led to restoration and pastiche.

Today there has been a marked reaction against too severe a stark-ness. For the past forty years, under the influence of various Protestant theologians and aestheticians, Protestant sacred art has been the subject of reconsideration. A similar movement to that which in the Catholic world led to a renewal of sacred art, as we have seen, has got under way. It has aroused discussions as lively as those which took place among Catholics. In 1950 an article called *The Decline of the Unadorned Church* aroused a public protest.

This particular aspect of renewal is linked to those we have outlined already concerning dogmatics and liturgy. The liturgical movement evidently cannot but go hand in hand with a developing religious art. Max Thurian has stated that 'it is pertinent to community renewal to make the faithful conscious of the nature of the Church. This very nature has a theological base which leads to true communal psychology and liturgical aestheticism.' Denis de Rougemont, a Protestant essayist of great authority, states that 'the form of Protestant art is linked to a dogmatic conception of faith' and that hence, 'the renais-sance and purging of that art will be conditioned by a corresponding doctrinal renewal'. Theologians such as Barth and Tillich, by widening the framework of Protestant dogmatics, touch upon art also. The decline of Protestant art has been attributed by Pastor Jean Bosc, a convinced Barthian, wholly to 'the emergence of a certain type of moralism which, forgetful of the doctrine of the creation and the cosmic significance of the Incarnation and Redemption, imputes unfaithfulness to the teachings of the Reformers, and especially of Holy Writ'. This is very strong language and it opens up a whole new perspective. Pastor R. Will has written that 'art must help the Christian community to be aware of the main theme of worship—union with the living God'. He also goes on to say—and this is so close to the Catholic thesis that it may well be confused with it—that 'a church is not simply a place where one speaks, but must be a place which speaks for itself'.

This then is the wider sense in which Protestant sacred art is now evolving. While the communion table takes up a central position, and sometimes becomes the altar, the pulpit moves more modestly to one side and the cross comes more into prominence, sometimes, though not often, bearing a crucified figure; the walls become covered with frescoes and the windows have their stained glass. Here and there one may see sculptures of prophets and apostles. And one wonders if all this has an ecumenical intention. In the church, where the Taizé community holds its services, two icons are much in evidence, and there is a beautiful statue of the Virgin flanked by fresh flowers. How are we to avoid stressing the ecumenical significance of this evolution of Protestant sacred art at the very moment when, as though by some spontaneous impulsion towards convergence of ideas, Catholic sacred art is tending towards increasing simplicity?

Here we have been looking at the internal decoration of churches. Where it has been found necessary to build new Protestant churches, architects have had to consider, as have Catholics, a new approach to form made necessary by the use of a new twentieth-century material—cement. In Germany, Switzerland, Holland, England and more especially the U.S.A., where churches of different denominations abound, there have been a great many different attempts to restate architectural forms. It is all a far cry from the rectangular meeting-room preferred by the Huguenots of past eras. Some of the designs have been so bold that in 1955 in the U.S.A. the pastors of ten leading denominations came together with the architects to try to lay down some basic rules. There are round, square, saw-toothed and triangular forms of churches, though each shape is linked to a particular symbol. One of them has been a success, based on the conception of the biblical tent, the dwelling of God's people in the wilderness. It adapted itself excellently to the new materials. This form has given rise to a slender and graceful shape, allowing a flood of light to enter through immense triangular windows at the end.

This type of church is illustrated by those built for the Congregationalists by Harold Spitz in Iowa and by Frank Lloyd Wright for the Unitarians at Madison, Wisconsin; there is another example at Hyvinkää in Lutheran Finland. All these examples indicate a new departure, resolutely turned towards the future, even in the case of the architect who, as in Coventry with the Anglican cathedral, built his new church on the ruins of the old and skilfully integrated both. These are the signs of a Protestantism which is looking forward, yet at the same time adapting itself to the preoccupations of the ordinary man.

Outside sacred art, properly speaking, and the little sculpture and painting accepted in Protestant architecture, can it be said that the spirit of the Reformation inheritance is being expressed in the work of great masters? Pastor Jean Bosc unhesitatingly answers no. If there are Protestant artists, one cannot say that as a general rule they seek inspiration for their work in their Church. There have been other views; Pierre Chazel, for example, maintains that great painters such as Bazille or Van Gogh 'painted in the Reformation spirit', but when we read, in reinforcement of his argument, that the characteristic traits of this art are 'accuracy of vision, firmness of touch, balanced construction, sense of the inner life', we feel compelled to ask if these traits are specifically Reformation ones. In any event, neither of these two great impressionists have taken their themes from the faith to which they belonged, unlike Dürer and Rembrandt before them. There are no figures in Protestantism like Maurice Denis, Desvallières or Rouault.

18. PROTESTANTISM EXPRESSES ITSELF: II. IN MUSIC

It is much more in music that one finds the force of Protestant faith, in that kind of imperious recourse to the Grace of God found among its adherents. Very soon after the split with the Catholic Church Protestants found expression in song. Doubtless this was because something had to take the place of the liturgical music of the chapters and the monasteries, which persisted only among the Anglicans and the Scandinavian Lutherans, and also because collective singing is an instrument of communal unity. It should not be forgotten also that the Reformation first arose among Germans, whose musical talents are famous. According to Pastor Appel: '. . . in the field of sacred songs, the heritage of the Lutherans constitutes an enrichment of Protestantism'.

At the end of the eighteenth century Protestant music was dominated by Johann Sebastian Bach (1685–1750). A deeply religious man, and an untiring worker, Bach provided the Lutheran Church with a great number of organ pieces, chorales and cantatas. In his austere *Clavierübung*, for example, he expressed all the aspects of the faith of the Lutherans in a series of twenty-one chorales. In his cantatas, conceived as a succession of choruses and recitatives, he evoked the great biblical truths and the meditations of man on his state and his supernatural visions. The great 'Passions' of Bach were so much in harmony with the spiritual climate at a time when the Gospel was widely read that their performance served to uplift the soul. Bach was a genius, and his genius flowed far beyond Protestantism (he also wrote Catholic Masses). He made such a deep impression on the Reformed

Churches' thought that even today there seems to be a connection between him and Protestant self-expression. Catholics themselves have been able to find a form of faith in his works which is not alien.

Yet Bach's music, and that of his imitators and successors, has always been for the specialist, who alone could properly interpret it. Of course it touched chords in every heart, but the ordinary church-goer could not participate directly. On an entirely different level, the idea of Luther was that everyone should participate in the solemn proclamation of faith through music, and this led to the birth of another form of expression—the hymn. It was not unknown to the Catholics, but they, as distinct from the Lutherans, did not make it a systematic part of the service. Revived during the seventeenth century by Paul Gerhardt, hymns became more and more important during the eighteenth century. Wesley made them into one of the principal apostolic instruments of his Methodists, and the Moravians and the followers of Zinzendorf also made use of them. Their simple phrasing and their occasional banality aroused the anger of the more intelligent, but an intellectual such as Taine enjoyed them, remarking that they combined all the factors necessary to bring men into direct contact with God.

The Calvinists produced very much less of this type of religious music. In France they preferred to adapt the translations of biblical psalms by Margot or Théodore de Bèze to a more serious and solemn musical cadence. But at the beginning of the nineteenth century every-thing changed with the coming of the Revival. The young Empaytaz in 1817 at Geneva first had the idea of translating and adapting Chris-tian hymns of various origins—Moravian for the most part—and this had considerable success, still larger editions of his work being pro-duced in 1824 and 1846. This principle was followed by César Malan in 1824 and resulted in a veritable anthology which in 1836 contained more than three hundred items under the name of *Chants de Sion*. While the words were emotionally satisfying the music was often of poor quality. In Paris in 1834 the Lutteroth family, members of the 'revivalist' circle of the Rue Taitbout, embarked on a new collection of Christian hymns, adapting the music of such masters as Haydn, Beethoven, Handel and Mozart. Henri Lutteroth selected poems from Racine and Corneille and from Revival figures such as Pictet, Felix Neff and Malan, and his wife arranged the music for them. The result was very successful; even today the Lutteroth collection remains in current use, in translation in Anglo-Saxon Protestant countries as well as in France.

The tradition of hymn singing is now so well rooted in Protes-tantism that there is not one Reformation group which does not have its own hymnal.

In one part of the world the Protestant hymn has undergone modification and renewal out of keeping with the traditions of the European Reformed Churches; this is in the Deep South of the U.S.A., where the Baptist and Methodist evangelists started the practice of singing verses from Psalms and prayers. From this came the habit of asking members of the congregation to sing rather than talk about religious subjects. Well-known themes were taken from the Bible, from personal confessions or direct appeals by the singer to God. The music was made up from old European hymns or ancient traditional themes from Africa, or even from the latest popular songs, which were thereby claimed to be specifically purified by the Holy Ghost. So the Negro spiritual was born. With its deep appeal to the slaves and the sons of slaves, it has covered every aspect of the Negroes' lives, their work, their troubles and hopes. Many of the songs have become famous— e.g. 'Deep River', 'Nobody but Jesus', 'All God's Chillun Got Wings' and 'Little David'. An authentic religious experience expresses itself in these naïve and tender songs with their insistent rhythm.

The hymn plays an enormous part in Protestant religious life, but it is not the only means of musical expression. It may be said that there is a correlation between the highest point of Reformation spirituality and great musical gifts or certain marked tastes for music. Dr Albert Schweitzer was a consummate organist and a composer of the first rank. There are innumerable pastors who are excellent organists. Karl Barth begins each day by listening to Mozart. The strong link between Protestantism and music can be observed in the music of those masters who, without necessarily wanting to rewrite church music in the sense in which the Catholics understand this term, have found in the faith and traditions of the Reformation the themes for their inspiration. For more than fifty years there has been a Protestant school of music developing in parallel to that of the Catholics. Some people have tried to include Wagner in this tradition, but Parsifal himself, the only hero of Wagnerian thought who can be accepted as formally Christian, is rather suspect. It was in France that the school had the greatest success, the most celebrated representative being Arthur Honegger (1892–1955). Honegger has even used Catholic themes successfully, e.g. in his 'Joan of Arc', yet has retained the Protestant mood in such works as the 'King David' oratorio.

19. PROTESTANTISM EXPRESSES ITSELF:
III. IN THE WORLD OF LETTERS

To what extent is there a Protestant literature today? It is not an easy question to answer, but one thing is certain: one cannot speak of a renewal in contemporary Protestant literature as there has been in the Catholic literature of France, for example. Among the Reformation Churches as a whole there are no specifically Protestant works.

Nevertheless a great number of writers who are members of Reformation Churches have made their mark on the literary scene of the nineteenth and twentieth centuries. It is not by sheer chance that the Reformers themselves were men who were masters of the art of writing. Luther was the father of modern German, Calvin was the author of *L'Institution Chrétienne*, a key work in the great classical manner. In England the Anglican translation of the Authorized Version of the Bible is a work of art which has moulded modern English. Nearer to our own age the most eloquent witness for Protestantism—a man who can be compared to the great Reformers themselves—is Sören Kierkegaard, a master of the written word whose influence now is stronger than ever. Protestantism has retained from its inception an intellectual character which leads it to find expression in literature. It is impossible to count the number of pastors of different nationalities who have been philosophers, poets, novelists or historians.

A very large part of Protestant literature takes its themes and its figures from among those of the Reformation world. It seeks to depict Protestant society or Protestant man, or evokes episodes in Protestant history. From Selma Lagerlöf of Sweden (1858–1940), the Norwegians Björnson (1833–1910) and Hamsun (1860–1952) to the Frenchmen Jean Schlumberger and André Chamson, there are innumerable novelists whose works have taken their themes from typically Protestant societies. In England, from Dickens (1812–70) to Galsworthy (1867–1933), there are many novelists whom one might call Anglican, because they depict a society permeated by Anglicanism. The Protestant pastor is a character who appears in novels to the same wide extent as the Catholic priest. He may not know of problems brought about by celibacy, but the novelists have given him and his family others to cope with. Some of these heroes of novels have been portrayed as types, such as the unforgettable Pastor Vickerath of Gerhart Hauptmann (1862–1946). One can hardly count the number of Scandinavian novels which have pastors as their central characters; in Finland Juhani Aho and Minna Canth have written a dozen works with titles such as *The Pastor's Wife*, *The Pastor's Daughter* and *A Family of Pastors*. In France there are the pastors created by André Gide, Roger Breuil, Raoul Stéphan and others. As for the great episodes in Protestant chronicles, it would be impossible to cite all the literary works which they have inspired.

One most striking characteristic of Protestant literature is its biblical basis. Sacred texts are almost always in evidence, at least in outline, in all Protestant writing. Protestant poetry is deeply influenced by the Bible, especially by the Psalms, whether it is the work of two such different men as Longfellow and William Blake. Quotations, references and allusions to the Bible are found everywhere, certainly in the works of every great English novelist.

Biblical training is so strongly entrenched that even those Protestants who were baptized into the faith and later elected to adhere to no particular dogma are unable to disguise it. André Gide is a case in point; his prose is filled with biblical phrases, he constantly refers to the teachings of the Gospels and the titles of his works often reflect his indebtedness to the Bible.

Yet it was not only by associating the Revelation of the Divine Word with the Book of Books that the Reformers exercised such an influence on literature. Once more it cannot be too strongly emphasized that the Reformation was a spiritual experience long before it became an historical event. Men questioned themselves in personal terms about the great problems confronting humanity and those concerning the soul's relation to God. This same experience was later taken up by others who laid stress on the tenets of Luther and Calvin—direct contact with God, the tragedy of a life destroyed by sin and the necessity of a return to grace. These are the great spiritual bases of all Protestant literature worthy of the name, and it is they which give it its distinctive atmosphere.

In many of the great works of the Protestants we find this expression of a direct recourse to God. It is the cry for help of a Kierkegaard wandering through the Jutland countryside, so intensely alone save for the presence of Christ. It applies to August Strindberg (1849–1912), driven to choose between the Inferno and prostration, to Matthew Arnold (1822–88), and to that seeker after adventure, R. L. Stevenson (1850–94), in his book *If This Were Faith*. Closer to us, curiously attuned to the discords of twentieth-century man, there is T. S. Eliot, who in *The Waste Land* best expressed the certitude that in a life without aim or sense man has as his last refuge the God of Salvation.

The conflict between sin and grace and its effect on human life has had still greater influence on literature. The Protestant writer is a master of the secret aspect of life; for him inner realities count more than events, and he unconsciously makes his characters enter into the fight between good and evil. Even when there is no formal reference to religion in them, we know some works to be typically Protestant because they could only have been written in the climate of the Reformation. One example is *Jude the Obscure*, by Thomas Hardy (1840–1928), and others are the New England novels of Nathaniel

Hawthorne, and the unforgettable *Wuthering Heights* of Emily Brontë (1818–48), in which the subject is carnal passion and the climate so evidently puritan. Nothing seems more secular than Ibsen's plays, based as they are on the conflict between passions and interests, or on philosophical speculations from which faith is absent; but it is none the less true that the works cannot be fully appreciated until one remembers that the action takes place in Lutheran Norway and that what we are witnessing is basically the 'theatre of the soul'. It is hardly necessary to stress that, after the crisis of *Inferno*, August Strindberg became converted.

Since the Protestant soul is one which subjects itself to self-scrutiny and feels a sense of sin, it has in expressing itself given a powerful impetus to psychological literature. This is not the only source, for the Jansenist tradition in the French classics of the age of Louis XIV also had their influence. However, it was Jean-Jacques Rousseau, a Protestant at heart, even though he quarrelled with the Pastors' Commission, who, with his *Journal Intime* (a model of complete sincerity but not without a certain cynicism), began the tradition in modern literature that makes a writer analyse a character's conscience to the extent of exposing his very soul. It is not by chance that one of the great figures of psychological literature, Benjamin Constant (1767–1830), was at his best in the atmosphere of Coppet at Madame de Staël's (1766–1817) on the shores of Lake Geneva; his *Adolphe*, even more so than his hostess's *Corinne*, has an almost Huguenot tenor, even though faith plays no part in it. It has been noted that the way in which Constant exposes the moral faults of his hero is altogether different from that employed by a Catholic like Chateaubriand, who is fairly indulgent to the sins of his *René*. From all this has come a flow of analytic literature, sharp and lucid, filled with a sense of the need for complete sincerity—the sincerity that man should feel face to face with God. It has led to works such as Gide's *L'Immoraliste*, where justification through intelligence takes the place of grace. This 'protestant' literature has its characteristic style, restrained, calculated, wary of brilliance, yet probing into the soul. In turning to Frédéric Amiel (1821–81), we see to what excesses this preoccupation with analysis of sin and distress can lead; here was a man who in analysing life used up his own and, as only a Calvinist tormented by conscience could, poured out the results of this analysis in eighteen thousand pages of his *Journal*.

One might also ask if it is not the fundamentally Protestant conviction that 'the Holy Ghost speaks through the spirit of man' which has produced that whole line of thought running through Protestant literature dealing with Christian mysticism, illuminism and gnosis. Often it occurs in the work of writers who are convinced that they are far removed from the Reformation Churches; yet they are none the less basically Protestant. Novalis (1773–1801), who rebelled against the Reformation, came close for a time to Catholicism, but his mystical lyricism was akin to the Protestant inspiration of the 'spiritual' sects and had a direct influence on Schleiermacher. William Blake (1757–1827) scorned the clergy and all the Churches, and his strange metaphysics dreamed of a marriage between Heaven and Hell, but he was Protestant not only in tenor, style and imagery, but also in his own abandonment to faith. Thus he is a blood brother to William Fox and Charles Wesley, two other inspired Protestants. The Protestant atmosphere is noticeable in Edgar Allan Poe, a man fascinated by the hereafter, in Henry James and in Rainer Maria Rilke (1875–1926), for whom the divine is to be seen in the mysteries of the created world as much as in the depths of the being destined to die.

The current of 'social evangelism', which as we saw arose and gathered strength during the nineteenth century, exercised a direct influence on a whole province of the world of letters: Dickens expressed it in his novels; it was conveyed in the warm pleading of Harriet Beecher Stowe for Uncle Tom, the oppressed black slave; it emerges today in the novels of Dreiser and Sinclair Lewis (though here there are other influences at work). Everything that may be considered as decisive in modern Protestantism—its basic issues, its striking aspects, its developments—has found adequate literary expression. This is one of the clearest signs by which the vigour of a faith can be recognized.

20. Here and Now

At the end of this examination of Protestantism as it is today we must conclude that it obviously has great vitality. Nietzsche's sinister prophecy 'God is dead!' uttered at the end of the last century was directed to it as much as if not more than to Catholicism. The Reformation Churches were thus condemned, it seemed, to disappear, just as the Roman Church. But Nietzsche's prophecy was not to be fulfilled. The followers of Luther and Calvin took up the challenge, as their Catholic and Orthodox brethren did also. For all of them, sixty years and more after the death of Zarathustra's messenger, God is not dead: He is very much alive.

The vitality of the Christianity of the Reformation Churches is not confined to statistics. If Protestantism shows every sign of vigour, this is due not only to its 268 million adherents (figures quoted by the *World Christian Handbook* in 1963), nor to its observable political and social influence, nor yet because its expansion over the past one hundred and fifty years shows no signs of abating—it is due also to the fact that the Reformation continues to be a vital and authentic spiritual experience for millions. We can disagree with some postulates and condemn certain of its conclusions, but cannot deny its reality.

Is it possible to determine the outcome of this undeniable force in the world, or to establish its contribution to the religious problems of humanity? A movement so vast and complex as Protestantism is not easily reduced to a few simple facts. The Reformation is not seen from the same angle by a liberal Protestant such as Albert Schweitzer, an American fundamentalist such as Senator Bryan, and a member of the Pentecostal sect of the Assemblies of God. Churches, denominations and sects are all different in their institutions, viewpoints and spirit, even if a closer examination reveals that they have a substantial affinity. A question such as 'Where is Protestantism heading?' needs quite a few cautions and distinctions before the answer can be attempted. All one can do is to indicate certain general lines along which Reformed Christianity seems to be proceeding, *hic et nunc*, as Karl Barth's disciples would say.

The Reformation, it must be stressed, was a religious revolution in the name of liberty. The basis of all the Reformers' thinking was that each man is able to undertake the spiritual adventure alone, and that he is free to do so since everything depends on the issue of the soul's confrontation with its Redeemer, on that inner dialectic of sin and grace. It follows that, in order to receive God's message, man has need of no other guide or mediator than Christ; he is also free to seek for himself in the Scriptures those rules of conduct which he needs. Such is the principle of 'free inquiry'.

We have seen that this call to liberty has had two important consequences, which despite certain astute attempts at justification have not proved very favourable to Protestantism. The first can be seen on the ecclesial level: the endless multiplication of Churches, denominations and sects—an unavoidable weakness of Protestantism. In Protestantism today, however, there is a reaction against this divisive factor. It is demonstrated by the institutional manner in which it is being carried out: through the numerous world federations—Lutheran, Baptist, Methodist and so on—and also in the concentrating factor which can be seen at work, e.g. in France, where all Protestants of whatever profession of faith are linking up for purposes of common defence and common action. It is also evident—and this is perhaps still more important—in the appearance of a new state of mind which transcends traditional divisions; the promoters of theological renewal, such as Barth, speak now not to any one Protestant Church, but to all, and therefore exercise influence over them all; the neo-liturgical and sacramental current has overrun the boundaries of each Church; in Taizé, the brethren come from twenty different Protestant groups; neither Billy Graham nor the leaders of M.R.A. are bound to any one Church. Everything is tending towards a state where Protestantism, without renouncing its characteristic diversity, is seeking to rediscover some sort of informal unity.

The second consequence is even more damaging. Free inquiry applied indiscriminately to all the basic elements of religion finally empties it of substance. During the first years of the twentieth century the sudden evolution of Protestantism towards liberalism resulted in a religion without dogma, which covered humanitarian ideologies of the time with a patina of evangelism. The mixture was so feeble that the true followers of the Reformers could not accept it. The result of their refusal was the renewal of all aspects of theological, scriptural, sacramental and monastic life, whose various facets we have already dealt with. Here is one of the decisive factors at work in Protestantism today: the reaction against the mortal peril of too great a degree of liberty of action.

It would be an exaggeration to say that all Protestants have seen the danger. The great majority of them will probably continue to move towards a sort of humanitarian and moralizing evangelism, as can be seen in the American way of faith. Others will rely on purely formal and mechanical biblicism, as can be seen among many of the Baptists. But it is of the greatest significance that the thinking *élite* of the Protestant world have accepted the need to be reminded of the exigencies of transcendency, whether it is that defined dogmatically by Karl Barth or that which Paul Tillich situates in the abysses of creation explored by science.

At the meeting-point between these two currents—the one seeking a certain degree of inter-clerical unity and the other the rediscovery of the very roots of the Reformed Faith—we find the most significant of Protestant movements, ecumenicalism. Its aspects will be developed later,[1] but let us note that it first saw the light of day in this century, inspired solely by the idea of bringing a degree of order into the prevailing chaos and being a means towards greater efficiency based on the principle that unity makes for strength. The ecumenical movement has evolved rapidly to a position that is much more interesting than the original one. One of the most active groups was *Faith and Order*, advocating order in the Christian world and at the same time a careful re-examination of faith. But it was impossible to embark on a *rapprochement* between the Churches without bringing up the question of the Church itself, and in association with ecumenicalism a concerted dogmatic reappraisal was carried out. The great champions

[1] See Chapter VI.

of the logical and spiritual renewal, from Barth to Cullmann, were all associated with the movement; Taizé itself, which sprang from a purely mystic call, became one of its strongholds.

Obviously the ecumenical current cannot gather together all the streams of Protestantism; there are anti-ecumenical groups, mature or in embryo. Those who hold to the old conception of the liberty of the Churches have far from disappeared and are not lacking in arguments to put forward against 'ecumenical confusionism'. Yet it does seem that contemporary Protestantism gains from the ecumenical attitude, for it is no longer possible to return to the old position now that so many steps forward have been taken, and now that—as in the case of the Churches in south India—new groups are the visible incarnation of ecumenical desires. This fact is of great importance not only for the future of Protestantism itself, but for all Christianity. There is always a necessary logical basis to every great human endeavour. In closing their ranks the Protestant Churches make possible other *rapprochements* which will be governed by principles higher still—faith in the sole Saviour, and closer ties with other Christian Churches which were not influenced by the Reformation. Even now, in the meetings of the World Council of Churches, we have seen representatives of the Eastern Orthodox Churches, and Catholic priests have been present as observers; and during the Week of Unity [1] Protestant and Catholic prayers have been united.

It is of course premature to try to make definite predictions from all this activity, but it is not impermissible to ask oneself in an ecumenical spirit not what the Reformation Churches have about them that is reprehensible or blameworthy, but what positive factors they might bring into the Universal Church. Again there is no point in stressing that, for a Catholic, Protestantism represents a divergent opinion, a heresy, and that the Universal Church becomes identified with that Church to which the power of the keys has been granted. But it is a part of faith also, since the Scriptures teach it, that the role of heretics is a useful one. Protestantism is not called upon to represent itself as the religion for modern man, as Taine accepted it, as the young Bergson tried to believe, as today Tillich tries to define it, but it can help Christians of the twentieth century to emphasize certain realities and truths of which not all of them are conscious. The infinite greatness of God, liberty in grace, the ever-active role of the Holy Ghost, the necessity for a certain degree of poverty to be apparent in the Church, the affirmation of a universal priesthood, which entails the definition of a laity participating much more in religious observances—all these points are highlighted by Protestantism. Naturally the Catholics find them in their own faith, but it is in no spirit of criticism that it may be

[1] See Chapter VI.

said that they have not always devoted an equal amount of attention to them.

Summing up briefly all that the Reformation stands for, Jacques Ellul wrote: 'It is a problem set for the Universal Church.' Did St Paul intend any other idea in his famous *Oportet haereses esse*? [1]

[1] The author would like to express his warm thanks to Professor R. P. Tavard of Mount Mercy College, Pittsburgh, and Monsieur le pasteur Marc Boegner of the Académie Française, honorary president of the French Protestant Federation, both of whom carefully examined the three chapters devoted to Protestantism.

CHAPTER IV

THE BYZANTINE HERITAGE—THE ORTHODOX CHURCH

1. Dom Pitra

In 1858 Dom Pitra, a learned Benedictine monk from Solesmes who three years later was to be appointed a cardinal and librarian of the Church, spent a long while at Bruges in Belgium with his friend Monsignor Malou. This bishop, one of the most cultivated men of his time (he had been one of the restorers of the University of Louvain), was an eminent authority on Byzantine history, one of those rare members of the Catholic hierarchy who had a profound knowledge of the Christian East. He had gathered together a unique collection of documents and works dealing with the Eastern Churches and the split with Rome. Dom Pitra, who found the question fascinating, spent many hours in his host's library. Profiting from his stay, he wrote later to a friend: 'Is it not rather surprising that we have all but forgotten the Greeks while there is such a plethora of works directed against the Reformation?'

It was an apt remark. However little the Catholics knew the Protestants, at least they had dealings with them, and relations, good or bad, did exist between the two faiths. The Christians of the East, also separated from Rome (those whom, as was the custom, Dom Pitra called the Greeks), were quite another matter. It was as if they lived in another world, shut in on itself, inaccessible, a world about which the average Catholic had only the haziest notions. If we are to judge by Joseph Le Maistre's work *Du Pape*, even educated Catholics knew very little about it. Was it the Russian Church, which was generally described in terms of contemptuous references to 'dirty and ignorant priests'? Was it Greek Christianity, renowned for its ridiculous fables of Stylites, hermits living in grottoes, and strange mystics whose prayers required them to concentrate on their navel? Despite Migne, the great tradition of the Greek Fathers had been forgotten, along with all the wealth of Byzantine liturgy. The lack of knowledge was of long duration and was only finally dispelled with the Russian Revolution in 1917 and the end of the Second World War, when the thousands of Russians and Eastern Christians who dispersed among the Catholics and Protestants of Western Europe and America brought back a better understanding. During the nineteenth century mutual ignorance was the rule.

This accounts for the astonishment felt by the Catholics when several popes, on various occasions, worried by the problem of the Christian East and West, made overtures with the aim of bringing about a *rapprochement* and were brusquely repulsed. On 6th January 1848, shortly after his accession, Pius IX dispatched his Encyclical *In Suprema Petri Sede* to the Greek religious authorities. This was intended as a call to unity. In 1868, when convening the Vatican Council, he addressed a letter to 'all bishops of the Oriental rite who are not in communion with the Apostolic See' inviting them to the Council. Twenty-five years later Pope Leo XIII made another attempt with his Encyclical *Praeclara Gratulationis* of 1894, followed up in the following year by the Encyclical *Orientalium*, in which he stressed that 'the Latins had not the least intention of undermining the rights, privileges and historical traditions of the Easterners'.

All attempts failed. The first attempt of Pope Pius IX was answered by Anthimus VI, Patriarch of Constantinople, in agreement with the three other Eastern Patriarchs, twenty-nine Metropolitans and also, it is thought, the Patriarch of Moscow. He delivered a veritable encyclical in his turn, in which he expressed the hope that the Pope himself might be converted to the true faith and so return 'to the true Church, Catholic, Apostolic and Orthodox'. He added, and here touched on the heart of the matter: 'Here, no patriarch, no council could ever introduce innovations, for the body of the Church itself—that is, the people—is the guardian of religion.' The majority of Eastern bishops answered the Council's invitation by keeping a contemptuous silence, others by a categorical refusal. The appeals made by Leo XIII, though they were infinitely more subtle, cautious and generous, were no more successful. In the meantime the dogma of the Immaculate Conception had been proclaimed and, still more serious, that of Papal Infallibility. Patriarch Anthimus VII stigmatized 'Roman innovations' in a decidedly acid tone.

These exchanges illustrated the depth of misunderstanding between the Christians of each camp. From the Latin point of view, the Easterners had broken the links which bound them to the Church because they had refused to accept the legitimate hierarchy as Christ had defined it; unity was only conceivable at the price of submission, poetically described as 'a return of the wandering sheep to the fold'. In their appeals for reconciliation the popes spoke of this, as was to be expected. But the Easterners, quite apart from feeling not at all like strayed sheep, considered that it was the Roman Church that had departed from tradition and even from the creed of the primitive Church, and that it was they who held these in sacred trust. Unity, in their view, could be achieved only on the bases of the indivisible faith of the early centuries, excluding everything which the Roman Church had added or redefined, particularly with regard to the authority of the Bishop of Rome. Obviously the two sides were irreconcilable, and so long as both maintained their positions there was no possibility of the slightest *rapprochement*.

2. ORTHODOXY OR CATHOLICITY

Against Catholicism, and against Protestantism also, there stood therefore another Christian community, though the antagonism was perhaps less violent and aggressive than that between Catholic and Protestant. It was a Church conscious of its greatness and of its strength, and which claimed for itself the sole honour of preserving the faith intact and of fidelity to the teachings of the past. This was borne out by the name it gave itself: the Orthodox Church, the Church of Orthodoxy.

This term must be understood in its historical context. Etymologically the word means to be of the true faith, not accepting any of the particular opinions or heresies that have arisen from time to time within Christianity. In practice, the adherents of one Church adopted this title during the violent disputes concerning the nature of Christ, which had shaken the Christian world during the fourth and fifth centuries and provoked the crises of Arianism, Nestorianism and Monophysitism.[1] In point of fact, to call oneself Orthodox was to imply solidarity with the decisions of the Council of Chalcedon in 451, which had decided that Christ was one Person, with two natures, united 'inconfusedly, immutably, indivisibly, inseparably'. It goes without saying that from this definition the Westerners were no less Orthodox than the Easterners. For both of them the canons of the first Ecumenical Councils, which from 325 to 784 established the rules of faith on the Holy Trinity and the nature of Christ, were indisputable. Eastern Christianity felt that it was no less 'catholic' than the Catholics of the West; that is, universal, according to St Ignatius of Antioch's qualification in the first century and the Nicene Symbol. At most there was a certain difference of emphasis. In the East stress was laid on orthodoxy, on fidelity to dogma, perhaps because it had so often been disputed; the West, for whom the conversion of the barbarians was of the greatest importance, stressed universality or catholicity. But while the two parts of Christianity remained on the whole on friendly terms no one thought to make an issue out of the two

[1] See Chapter V.

meanings or to make enemies between the Orthodox and Catholic factions.

The scene changed after the separation in the eleventh century. This clearly defined the two sides, and little by little the word orthodox took on the meaning which we know today. It arose from a whole era of historical evolution, for reasons in which the theology of the Trinity and ecclesiology were closely interwoven with politics and sociology. It is incorrect to say that the schism took place all at once through ill will, pride, ambition or the bad judgment of a few men; if there was in the first days any single group responsible, this group was driven by forces largely outside its control. It should be borne in mind that long before this, from the middle of the fourth century and into the eighth century, as a consequence of the crises that shook the Church in the East, Constantinople broke off relations with Rome five times and remained separated for 152 years! In point of fact it was the ebb and flow of life and history that brought relations to breaking-point. As long as the Church's leaders set unity as a prime factor, unity was safeguarded; but when ambitions or interests got the upper hand the break was bound to come.

In Diocletian's day the split in the Roman Empire that resulted, despite the juridical precautions taken to prevent it, in two great domains each presided over by an Augustus, showed that even in this immense area the forces of disruption were at work, and that the unity of the *Imperium* was a fiction. In taking over the leadership of the Roman world Christianity imposed its own unity, that of common baptism and adherence to the sole Church. But it was extremely difficult for it to reconcile unity with ethnic rivalries, the divergent ways of life and the interplay of political and economic interests, all of which tended to bring differences more and more to the fore. Barbarian invasions, which the East was spared for another ten centuries, modified the structure of Romano-Christian society. Proud of their ancient civilization, the Easterners tended to treat the Westerners as barbarians. The Westerners for their part, basing themselves on a simpler and less disputable faith, looked upon the East with disdain, always so ready as it was to challenge the truths of salvation. Differences of temperament also played their part. One was practical, active, juridical and logical; the other mystical, speculative, irrational and drawn towards a more synthetic conception of life. Low Latin, the language of the West, was an object of derision in the East; the Emperor Michael III in 864 described it as a Scythian dialect. As for the Latins, ruled more and more temporally as well as spiritually by descendants of the Germanic race, they had scarcely any notions of what the Eastern and Greek traditions had brought to the Church in the way of spirituality and theological speculations.

The conflict became inevitable with the founding, at the end of the eighth century, of the Carolingian Empire. Western historians tend to show Charlemagne as the restorer for his own ends of the Western Roman Empire, ruined by Teutonic invasions. The Easterners were not of the same opinion. For them the only legitimate Roman Empire was that of which Constantinople was the capital; Charles the German was a usurper. Tension arose within the Church owing to the growing importance of the Pope. He was upheld by the emperor, who had been crowned by him. For diplomatic reasons Byzantium recognized the new arrival, but with so much reserve and such obvious disdain that the Western emperor could not fail to notice it. If Charlemagne had failed to understand the situation fully, the Empress Irene's refusal of her hand enlightened him. He resolved therefore to destroy the Byzantine emperor's authority. To attain this object, and at the same time to stir up the Eastern Church, the emperor's ally and helper, Charles carried the attack on to the plane of faith. The Byzantine emperors were accused of being disloyal to the true doctrine, and this threw their rights to imperial succession into dispute.

The conflict thus broke out on the theological plane with the *Filioque* affair. The Nicene Council in 325 and the Council at Constantinople in 381 proclaimed, using the very words of the Gospel according to St John (xv. 26), that '. . . (even) the Spirit of truth (which) proceedeth from the Father . . .' But the Spanish Council at Toledo in 589, which had to fight Arianism, considered that this formula, in omitting the Son in this reference to the procession of the Holy Spirit, gave a weapon to those heretics who refused to consider Him as God, the equal of the Father. For this reason the word *Filioque* was inserted before the verb *procedit* in the Creed: 'the Spirit proceedeth from the Father and the Son'. Undoubtedly this was an innovation, even if the interpolation agreed precisely with theological truth. Those Christians who were attached to tradition, which all Easterners were, had a right to feel angry. It may be thought that the intelligence of the Emperor Charles was strained a little to follow such theological speculations. But none the less he saw that this was a weapon with which to attack the Byzantines, and, despite the reserve of the popes, *Filioque* became a part of the liturgy of the Frankish dominions and remains so to this day.

It needed only a spark to start the fire now. One such critical point might be the conflict between two men, one at Rome and the other at Constantinople, both of whom were firmly resolved to defend their rights. And another problem then arose; a matter of ecclesiology. Who should rule in the Church? Since the fifth century, tradition had had it that there were five regional leaders—the Patriarchs of Rome, Constantinople, Alexandria, Antioch and Jerusalem. The first of these was invested with primacy and the Easterners called on him for arbitration in disputes, but no one had ever clearly defined this state of affairs. In the middle of the ninth century the situation had changed. In Constantinople a new Patriarch by the name of Photius came to power. He was a man of considerable intellect, a former imperial functionary, and, as was to be expected, he sought to strengthen the authority of his see at least to equal that of Rome. Was not the Church of Byzantium the Glorious more venerable and powerful than that of the barbarian West? At that time the Pope in Rome was St Nicholas I (856–67), one of the strongest personalities of his age. (He had no hesitation in holding his own with the Carolingian emperor Lothair II in the dispute concerning the latter's divorce.) Photius was appointed in somewhat irregular circumstances, and the Pope, disregarding the recommendations of a Western Council, refused to recognize him. Aided by his emperor, Photius answered by accusing Nicholas of 'introducing dangerous innovations and having unjustified pretensions' and had him deposed by a vote in Council. The course was now set for a break, but the two protagonists disappeared from the scene— the Pope died and Photius was exiled to a monastery on the orders of the Macedonian Basil I, the new master of Byzantium.

The conflict was stayed for two centuries, but in the meantime the two halves of the Church continued their drift apart, and the rift became ever wider. The unity of the Church became less and less important to the majority of men, but on all possible occasions there were discussions and disputes on *Filioque* and on many other subjects, such as the marriage of priests, the relatively minor issue of whether priests should wear beards, or whether the Hallelujah should be sung at Easter. There were incidents concerning the Pope's intervention in the matrimonial affairs of the Basileis and concerning the Latin's activities among the Bulgarians, who hesitated to choose between two obediences. All official relations between Rome and Constantinople ceased: the Pope's name was no longer cited in official Eastern prayers; the Patriarch no longer even bothered to notify the Pope of his nomination. The rise of Byzantium under its Macedonian dynasty at that time served only to strengthen the pride of the Eastern Church. Had the Papacy not been going through a period of weakness at the time the break would certainly have come about, but the Byzantines could afford to ignore the Pope since he was in no state to assert his authority. It seemed quite normal for Benedict VIII to celebrate the coronation of Henry II, the Germanic emperor, according to the Frankish rite; that is, with the addition of the disputed *Filioque*. It was yet another proof of the low state into which the Roman Patriarchate had fallen.

The two halves of the Church might have continued to drift slowly apart for centuries, without any violent crises, had not the 'Gregorian Reform' once again restored the Papacy to its former glory during the eleventh century. In order to detach the Western Church from the clutches of the feudal lords, the Cluniac popes increased their authority over the bishops and declared their right to sit in judgment over the laity, emperors as well as common men. Their doctrinal infallibility was now openly spoken of. Obviously this strengthening of pontifical authority went against the Eastern conception of the Church's organization.

All the conditions necessary for the break were now at hand. It took place paradoxically enough in 1054, while an attempt at a *rapprochement* was being made by Rome in face of danger from the Normans. One man clearly bears a heavy degree of responsibility in this— Michael Cerularius, a patrician whose dream it had been to plot his way to power and who, once converted, became Patriarch in 1053. He maintained that his office was inferior to neither the purple nor the diadem, and in any event went so far as to propose to the Pope that they should divide the world between the two Churches, each being universal in its own sphere. The initiative shown by the Pope in fighting against the Normans he found disquieting. Leo XI had won over the Western emperor Henry IV; if he were now to ally himself with the Byzantine Constantine IX, what would his own position be then? He could see the Pope intervening in the affairs of the East. Stealthily he started a campaign to discredit Rome, once more reviving old quarrels, and he was behind riots in Constantinople itself in which Latin churches were desecrated.

It was unfortunate that, in order to hasten diplomatic negotiations and at the same time introduce some order into religious affairs, the Pope decided to send as legate to Constantinople the rough and obstinate Cardinal Humbert de Moyenmoutier from Lorraine. The legate was quick-tempered; the pinpricks of Byzantine polemics served only to reinforce his intention of bringing the Eastern Church to heel, using the same methods previously employed to 'reform' the Western Church. He threatened that the Eastern Church would become nothing more than 'an assembly of heretics, a conventicle of schismatics and a synagogue of Satan' unless it recognized the Pope's complete supremacy. The Patriarch refused all contact with him, so on 18th July 1054 the legate went to St Sophia's to pronounce a sentence of excommunication against Michael Cerularius. This gesture, as it happens, exceeded his brief. The break, carefully schemed by the Patriarch, was made certain by the legate's lack of diplomacy; everyone in Byzantium was now convinced that it was entirely Rome's fault. A synod anathematized the legates. The excommunication was publicly burned and Michael Cerularius was triumphant.

This painful episode, though accepted as the time from which the Greek schism dated, did not sever all relations between the Christians of East and West. Few were able to see the real significance of the disaster, except for the Holy Patriarch Peter of Antioch or the monk George the Hagiorite. 'Communio in sacris', however, remained in use by the faithful of both Churches and the Asiatic Patriarchates remained in touch with Rome, a necessary link in matters of pilgrimage. The Byzantine emperors even helped Western monasteries, that of Monte Cassino, for example. But anti-Roman polemics were not stayed because of such incidents; indeed they were accentuated. To the old accusations new ones, even more grotesque, were added. Without any great show of logic the Westerners were accused of eating unclean meat, which was contrary to biblical law, and even of fasting on Saturdays, which was nothing more than a continuation of the Hebrew Sabbath! The use of unleavened bread in communion also aroused indignation. A treatise on the Franks even went so far as to state that loose women disported with the priests during Mass!

The crusades served to make the break final, though not in the early days, for the first crusaders recognized the canonical rights of the Byzantine bishops, whom they delivered from the yoke of Islam. Little by little the Westerners replaced the Eastern clergy by Latin priests. Was it not a scandal that there was a Latin Patriarch at Jerusalem, and not a very estimable one at that? The scandal grew when the soldiery of the Fourth Crusade laid siege to and pillaged Holy Byzantium, removing to the West shiploads of precious booty and icons and installing a Venetian Patriarch on the throne of Photius and Michael Cerularius. From the year 1204 religious antagonism between Christians of East and West was strengthened by national hate which centuries were not to eradicate. Various attempts at unity, set in motion by Byzantine emperors in the face of growing Turkish danger, the Council of Lyons in 1274 and especially the Council of Florence in 1439, dictated by political necessities, all failed owing to obstinate Byzantine opinion, which preferred the yoke of the Turk to Roman apostasy. The two camps had now taken up their respective positions and these were to be maintained for centuries. It is a distressing story. Pope John XXIII stated that responsibilities for the break were equally divided between the two Churches.

These then are the origins of the quarrel between the Christians of East and West. Time served only to accentuate the differences and increase the antagonisms. In the eleventh century the Byzantines listed their grievances against the Latins: their pamphlet *On the Franks* detailed thirty-five of them. To those we have already noted were added others just as strange: the Latins, so it was said, refused to call the Holy Virgin 'the Mother of God' (an assertion that the text of the Ave Maria refuted); their bishops were dressed in silk and not in wool; they had no idea of the proper way to prostrate themselves; worse still, they ate impure animals such as tortoises, crows and mice! And from one century to another the list of complaints against them grew until there were 104 of them at the end of the fourteenth century and 150 in the nineteenth century, the newer ones being mostly concerned with minor points of liturgy.

The degree of misunderstanding grew greater, and the Easterners' conception of themselves as Orthodox took on a new sense. They were Orthodox in that they had resisted not only the ancient Christological heresies but also the Latins' dangerous innovations; they now represented the immutable faith of the past. For many years the term 'Orthodox' was unknown in the West and no one was sure how to describe this separate Christian entity. 'The Greeks', as Dom Pitra used it, was incorrect since the majority of adherents to the Eastern Church were Russians. A 'Graeco-Slav' Church was incorrect also, since it contained Arabs, Syrians, Rumanians and Georgians. Joseph de Maistre referred to it as the 'Photian Church', which was correct but somewhat erudite. Official documents used contorted formulas such as 'Churches of the Byzantine rite separated from the Apostolic See'. In his letter of invitation to the Vatican Council, Pius IX mentioned 'those Churches which call themselves Orthodox', which was a considerable concession, for in so doing he recognized them as Churches, a distinction he did not extend to the Protestants. It was not until the twentieth century that the custom became established of referring to them as Orthodox Churches, partly for the sake of simplicity and partly in recognition of an established fact, without giving the word any doctrinal significance. Pius XI used the term in this sense.

Let us leave the catalogue of Eastern grievances against the West. After eight or nine centuries of separation an attempt to set down the real points at issue shows that they are few. What separates Catholic and Orthodox is doubtless less important than what unites them. All the essential bases of faith are common to both, even if they are not seen in the same light. All the sacraments are common to both. For the Catholic Church Orthodox baptism is accepted without question as valid; whereas the Greek Church has for a long time rebaptized those Catholics who wish to enter it, on the reasoning that only baptism by immersion was valid. (The Russian Church also reconfirmed them.) Orthodox ordinations are valid, Apostolic Succession never having been brought into question. If a Catholic is unable to participate in Orthodox Mass, this is not because Eucharistic consecration is invalid —it is, without question—but because the word 'communion' itself implies a belonging to the same community, which is of course not the case.

This is the stumbling-block lying across the road to unity: the fact that the two Churches do not constitute a single and similar community. The question is here rather than in the dogmatic, liturgical or disciplinary discussions which arose during the past ages. The *Filioque* question has certainly lost its importance; at the Council of Florence the Greek formula, that the Holy Ghost 'proceedeth from the Father through the Son', was equivalent to the Latin formula. Orthodox theologians for many years now have not insisted on this point. There are, however, more or less deep differences on the doctrine of the Immaculate Conception; on the after life (since the Orthodox Churches differ from the Catholics in their conception of Purgatory); on the Bible (since the Orthodox Churches venerate the 'deuterocanonicals', using them in their liturgy, though they hold them to be inferior to others); on divorce, authorized in the East in several cases; and on the discipline of certain sacraments. But once more the real issue does not lie here or there. It has never ceased to be, since the time of Photius and Cerularius, the question of the Pope's authority—that is to say the question of the very conception of the Church itself.

For the Orthodox the Church is not a monarchical society directed by one man on whom the Spirit rests, the representative of Christ on earth. It is a juxtaposition of Churches each with its leader, but all obedient to the invisible leader, Jesus Christ. In their view the Apostles are all of the same rank, Peter's pre-eminence being merely honorific. His successor, the Bishop of Rome, could not therefore lay claim to the title of head of the Universal Church. *A fortiori* he was not to be vested with infallibility, which was enjoyed by all the Church collectively, reposing in the episcopal body as a whole. These positions were of course unacceptable to Catholics. But here it must be understood that the refusal of the Orthodox Churches to accept the Pope's authority is not due only to pride or their acute sense of the greatness of their Church and fidelity to what they consider the true tradition; it is strictly in accordance with their own conception of the Church, of religious life, of the reign of God and of faith.

3. THE HERITAGE OF BYZANTIUM

The Orthodox Church is proud of the fact that it springs directly from the early Church and that it occupies the same territory. Are not its ancient sees—great names such as Antioch and Alexandria—those which were glorious in the days of the Apostles and Martyrs? But its geographical area became smaller when considerable numbers of its adherents inclined towards the heresies of the fifth century and even more so when the Arab invasions overran Egypt and the Near East.

The torch was handed on to another Church whose see was the capital of the Eastern Empire, and here it found stability for many centuries. The heritage of early Christianity was taken over by Byzantium, which, through a sense of duty and because of its fitness for such a task, set to work to preserve it intact, though not without incorporating certain characteristics of its own. This ancient and traditional religion was taken over by Byzantium and spread by its missionaries in an attempt to convert Western Europe, from the Caucasus to the Carpathians, even as far as the Arctic Circle. Using a similar process the Church of Rome furnished Western Christianity with its methods, its style and its organization, widening its field of action in baptizing the Barbarians. If, in substance and not solely administratively, the Western Church is the Roman Church, then we may describe the Eastern Church as Byzantine.

Orthodoxy has preserved some of the more striking characteristics of early Christianity. The most important one is that the faithful play an active role in it, much more so than in Catholicism, in which clericalization has developed substantially in the course of the centuries, firstly in the Middle Ages at the time of the great struggles against interference by the feudal lords, and then after the Council of Trent, as the result of reaction against Protestantism. The Orthodox laity are much more conscious of belonging to a community. Not only do they play an active part in the running of their Church, but it is quite normal for them to intervene in theological matters which in the West are and have been reserved for the clergy. The use of the vernacular in liturgy has probably helped to maintain lay participation in religious life, particularly among those peoples whom the Byzantine missionaries converted and for whom they provided at the outset a liturgy in their own language. In various Orthodox Churches (though not in Greece) it is the laity who elect the priests. These, being married, are naturally close to their flocks, which has advantages and disadvantages. Above them, and considered as spiritually more advanced, are the monks; they are not married. They live outside the main stream of life in accordance with the customs of the primitive Church, where monasticism arose with the hermits of the desert and was later properly organized by St Basil and St Pachomius.

All these ancient elements were taken up by the Byzantines and were then incorporated into the Eastern Roman Empire, an empire in which Latin jurisprudence accomplished its finest work in the development of Codes of Laws, Digests and Pandects, and in which numerous Mesopotamian, Egyptian and Persian influences also played their part in investing the Byzantine emperors with the hierarchical pomp of Eastern autocrats. From Byzantium Orthodox Christianity received many characteristics, of which the most obvious was the dignity, solemnity, even majesty, of the Byzantine imperial regime and which, as we shall see later, corresponded to the conception of Christianity then held. From Byzantium it also received a rigorous traditionalism. Orthodoxy prided itself, then as now, on having never introduced any innovations. It is the Church of the Seven Ecumenical Councils, a Church which observes these canons defining precisely the Christo-logical message, the mystery of Christ, true God and true Man. The idea, so important to the Western Church, that there exists a history of dogmas (that is, a normal evolution of dogmatics dependent on human circumstances), and that it may be necessary to formulate a doctrinal point hitherto regarded as implicit, arouses the total disapproval of the Orthodox Church to such an extent that the beliefs which it held on such matters as the Immaculate Conception—a common subject in Byzantine poetry—have lost ground since Rome declared them to be dogmas. Orthodox religious art transmits this twin ideal of majesty and fixity through its icons, the techniques of which have not altered for centuries (in Greece the painters' guide is that of the monk Denys of 1450) and which so obviously impose a spirit of veneration.

It was also to Byzantium that Orthodoxy owed its especial attitude towards the State and secular society, an attitude determined by the profound respect for what is known as 'symphonia'. This entails the perfect balance of the two powers, so that there is no risk of caesaro-papism and theocratic ambition; so that there may be collaboration between civil and religious authorities on a footing of equality, inter-vention by rulers in Church affairs being balanced by the Church's moral and spiritual control over them. Such a system had been fore-seen by Justinian in his *Novellae*. In practice it leads to a kind of identification of temporal organizations and the Church, and a national Messianic spirit of which Russia offers the most striking example.

The faith which governs the Orthodox Church is basically the same as that of the Catholics and the Protestants. It has no other roots than those furnished by the Gospels and New Testament texts. But it does not have the same emphases. It stresses the hope of the supernatural, the vision of a future world, the action of the Word and the Glory of God. This is the faith of the Greek Fathers, whose thought has never ceased to nourish the Orthodox soul. The humanity of Christ, so essential to the medieval Western mystics such as St Bernard, is of course venerated, but it appears to have less prominence than His divinity or power. The Passion, an object of so many spiritual medita-tions in the West during the age of Louis XIV, inspires their icons with an inexpressible degree of love, but it is perhaps less contemplated than is the Resurrection: the faith of Easter, as Karl Adam has said, opposed to the faith of Good Friday. This is the faith proclaimed through the celebrated formula: 'Christ is risen!'

There is another basic characteristic of this faith: the Holy Ghost occupies a place unknown in Western Christianity. St Athanasius stated: 'The Word became Flesh that we might receive the Holy Ghost.' St Basil stressed on several occasions that 'the Spirit is present everywhere and in each man'. This explains why, immediately after baptism, the new Christian has the *myron* conferred on him, a sacrament similar to Western confirmation and known as the 'great unction of the Spirit'. It enables the Spirit to penetrate to the profoundest depths of the soul and to allow each man to acquire a resemblance to the image which baptism has restored in him. Every Christian is thus a bearer of the Spirit, a repository of a part of that divine power of which the Church is guardian. This explains why every Orthodox Christian, even the humblest of laymen, is empowered to manage the Church, to study and teach theology, even to preach from the pulpit. The gifts of prophecy and miracle-working (considered rare and strictly controlled by the Western Church) are considered as normal in Orthodoxy today as they were in the primitive Church, since they are manifestations of the Holy Spirit, always present. The sacraments are considered not so much as supernatural instruments for spiritual perfection leading to salvation—as they are in the Catholic Church—as the means by which man may become divine through the Word made Flesh, by the action of the Spirit which rules everything.

The idea that the Holy Spirit is unceasingly at work, that He speaks to man continuously, is a fundamental tenet in Orthodoxy. But this action does not take place under all conditions, and man has not the freedom to interpret its message in his own way. Here is the dividing line between Orthodoxy and Protestantism, especially as regards newer sects. During the Evanston meeting of the World Council of Churches in 1954 Orthodox delegates made this clear: 'The Orthodox Church cannot entertain the idea that the Holy Spirit speaks to us only through the Bible. The Holy Spirit is present in the whole of life and the experience of the Church. The Bible is given to us in the context of apostolic tradition, in which we also possess the interpretation and authentic explanation of the Word of God.' To these views a Catholic would fully subscribe.

It is this markedly spiritual view of religion that bears witness to the peculiarities of Orthodoxy: its ecclesiastical organization, the large part played by monasticism, the devotion to icons and especially the prime importance accorded to liturgy.

For an Eastern Christian the world is the image of the divine world; this is a wholly Greek view and is firmly in the Platonic tradition. The Church, which gathers together men living in the present world, is thus seen as a conception, a manifestation, a foretaste of the divine world. According to Father Sergei Bulgakov it is 'heaven on earth'. Through the sacraments man is enabled to enter into divine life; it has been said that this itself is 'an immense sacrament' or again 'the sacrament of sacraments'. From this conception spring two most important consequences. One is that ecclesiastical institutions are unimportant when weighed against the inner drive which carries man towards the divine, which raises the entire Church to the level of the Spirit. Whereas a Catholic tends to see his Church through its institutions, under a man on whom the Spirit rests and who is responsible for all the baptized, the Orthodox Christian will see its perfect expression rather in a monastic community, such as that of Mount Athos, entirely cut off from the world, living exclusively in God. The more the Catholic Church sought strength in rigid organization in order to resist Protestant assaults, the more the gulf widened between it and its sister Church of the East. And the matter was made still more difficult by the fact that the organization was centralized and hierarchic, both being far from Eastern conceptions. Orthodoxy, as a general rule, accepts the formula of St Paul to the letter: 'The Church of Christ which is in Corinth.' It considers that the Church as a whole is present in the smallest of local or national Churches, and that to give it visible unity serves no useful purpose since it has an invisible leader—Christ. There are thus two possible interpretations of the doctrine of the Mystical Body; the Orthodox Christian feels justified therefore in refusing to accept the Pope's authority over that system of Patriarchates and autocephalous Churches so different from the Roman system.

Monasticism, as we have seen, represents for the Orthodox the most perfect way of Christian life. A stranger to the everyday world, the monk lives in God, in a quasi-angelic existence. True holiness lies in this detachment from everything, in isolation and contemplation. The West admires and accepts holiness in action, labour in daily tasks, working for the coming of the reign of God through the exercise of charity; Orthodoxy does not ignore it altogether but accepts it rather as exceptional. The monk is the aristocrat of the Church, its most active and resolute member. Monasticism has always played the part of a spiritual citadel against seizures of power, doctrinal error—during the iconoclasts' quarrels, for example—and against secularizing tendencies. From it come the candidates to the episcopate, not from among the clergy. The monk is not a cleric; his function is on a higher plane than the administration of sacraments, although it often happens that he acts as a guide to innumerable souls. Within monasticism itself there are differences and degrees, although there is only one monastic society. One of the tendencies is towards a cenobitism (or group religious life similar to that of our Benedictines) vowed to liturgical prayer and submitting in the main to the rule of St Basil, codified in the ninth century by St Theodore the Studite. The other tendency is towards eremitism, life totally isolated, inspired from the solitary Hermits of the Desert of the first centuries.

Between the two extremes there are many variations, perhaps groups of four or five, within very large communities, guided by a spiritual Father. Eremitism is considered a degree above the other kinds of monasticism, for it allows one to ascend higher in the spiritual life. It may be based on a hut or a grotto or cave, or even the top of a column, the Stylites being still in existence in Syria only a hundred years ago.

To these higher forms is linked one religious practice which is characteristic of Orthodoxy: pure prayer or the prayer of the heart, also called the prayer of Jesus. It came into the Orthodox Church as a reaction against a too well-established monasticism. Violent elements having practically broken with this traditional type of monasticism, several zealous souls proposed to undertake reform to bring back the rebels. The 'prayer of Jesus' was the means employed. It developed in the Sinai monastery in ancient ages, and was systematized by Simeon the New Theologian in the year 1000, and later by St Gregory the Sinaite (1265–1346), and was then imposed on some of the monks of Mount Athos by Athanasius I. It was transmitted to Russia by St Nil Soraky (1433–1508). The spiritual school of thought which first advocated it is known as the Hesychast school (Greek: peace, calm). This practice has always had a profound influence on Orthodoxy. 'Pure prayer' is linked closely to the Eastern Byzantine conception of religion—to the rule, that is, played by the Holy Spirit. The goal of life, as St Gregory the Sinaite has put it, is to 'actualize the Holy Spirit'; each man is the Church of the Holy Spirit and its pontiff, and his heart must come to maturity in it. In order to achieve this state, he must give his whole soul over to the deep aspiration which drives him to enter into the Holy Spirit. It is not through mere understanding that this will be achieved, but by humble, permanent and constant recourse to that 'memory of God' which each carries within him. This necessitates prayer, a personal relationship between man and God, who alone can restore human nature to its true state. It is a simple type of prayer but, incessantly repeated, fills the soul. For example: 'Lord Jesus Christ, Son of the Living God, have mercy on me.' This prayer identifies itself with the aspiration of the soul towards God, 'coupling the name of Jesus with the breathing cycle', as St John Climacus puts it. It appears an easy matter, but in fact it is an art to be acquired only after years of spiritual discipline. It presupposes complete domination of the passions and thoughts, a true science of living; it even requires discipline in breathing accompanied by gestures which are reminiscent of yoga. The 'prayer of Jesus' has been practised by the highest

Orthodox spiritual leaders throughout the centuries, and contributes today to a renewal of Orthodoxy in its finest sense.

The Hesychasts are relatively unknown in Western circles. The cult of icons, however, is a distinctive feature of Eastern Christianity. There are enormous numbers of them in churches and monasteries, all seeming rather like one another. They play a special part in liturgy, to such an extent that the Catholics (and even more the Protestants) express astonishment. There has been talk of a 'worship of images', which is incorrect. The Seventh Ecumenical Council, in 787, put an end to the iconoclastic crisis by defeating those who wished to destroy the icons, and defined them as objects worthy of veneration, not of worship. This veneration is directed to representations of Christ (never to God the Father, and the Holy Spirit is represented only by the figure of a dove), of the Blessed Virgin and of the saints. It is justified by the fact that it is a theological factor linked to a spiritual conception of religion. St John of Damascus wrote: 'Since the Invisible appeared in the Flesh and became visible, it is necessary to portray the resemblance of Him who became visible.' The icon is a kind of affirmation of the Incarnation. To venerate an icon is to commune with the Invisible which it represents. Participation in the sanctification it communicates is, according to the constant ideal of Eastern spirituality, a step towards one's own divinization.

This is even more true of liturgy, which lies at the centre of Orthodox piety; it is religious reality in its most vital form, constantly present. It is through liturgy that the believer discovers 'heaven upon earth'. In those great liturgical services attended by immense crowds the Eastern Christian finds the nourishment for his spiritual life. Far more profoundly developed than Western liturgy, it constitutes true religious pedagogy—in Russia during the past five years this has been the means of teaching the faithful—and it requires that the entire Bible be read each year and the four Gospels during the first three days of Holy Week. Each liturgical cycle, like those of the West, is studded with hymns of exceptional beauty. With its stately entrances through the holy doors, its almost esoteric atmosphere, Eastern liturgy has a dramatic character which makes one think of it as an extension of the classical theatre. Byzantine in its vestments, its pomp, its processions and its censing, it gives the impression of being both more hieratic than the Catholic Church and also more popular, for the people all participate closely with their acclamations, the common chanting of numerous prayers (particularly the *Trisagion*) and the varying obeisances which are all carried out in unison and have an almost hypnotic effect. All present are familiar with the spoken liturgy. It is always in the vernacular, even in Russia, where the use of Old Russian or Church Slavonic (Palaeoslavonic) in no way hinders the congregation from following the service. Celebrated almost invariably according to the Byzantine rite, it is liturgy that constitutes the link between all the national Churches, each with its own language, and allows them to understand one another. The symbol of this unity is emphasized each year by the reading of the prologue to the Fourth Gospel on Easter night in as many different languages as possible. For, as is to be expected, it is at Easter that holy liturgy reaches its high point, with this feast to the glory of Christ, to the triumph of life over death, to man's salvation and divinization through Redemption.

To these positive elements in Orthodox religion, which have ensured its survival through the most difficult circumstances, we must add one negative aspect. Since it is a popular and scarcely intellectual religion, subjected to the yoke of Turk or Czar, more or less isolated from the rest of the world, the Orthodox Church has hardly been affected by the crises which so disturbed the Western Churches, both Catholic and Protestant. Not that the current of irreligion has passed it by, for there have been unbelievers among the Russian intelligentsia, and among the Greeks and Levantines. The influence of Western philosophers, from Comte to Taine, can be felt in some degree everywhere in the Orthodox world. Even Renan's *Vie de Jésus* was translated into Russian. In the Near East after the First World War, when France and Britain exercised their mandate over the Lebanon, Syria and Palestine, the most cultured centres were subjected to Western influences and thought. A certain degree of 'modernism' crept into theological studies. It would appear that today this is one of the major problems with which Orthodoxy has to deal. But the ordinary people were too unlettered to be bothered with arguments about the historicity of Christ! Thus, although these dangerous ideas were to have a definite effect, it was limited in scope.

4. PATRIARCHATES AND AUTOCEPHALOUS CHURCHES

As it is today, the Orthodox Church remains faithful to the conceptions which established its structure fifteen centuries ago. The system of Patriarchates has remained in force. The Pentarchy has gone since the Roman Patriarchate has been ostracized; but the other four remain —that of Constantinople in the first place, made up almost entirely of Greeks, and the three of the Christian East, in which the Greek element is dominated by the descendants of Syrians and Arabs who were converted during the early centuries and remained faithful to the Byzantine Church, so earning the name of Melchites or Royalists. In the Patriarchates, moreover, the Patriarch is far from being the master; his authority is in no way similar to that of the Pope in the Catholic

Church. If he has certain privileges and honours, the 'first of the bishops' is no more than *primus inter pares*. The real power has belonged since the 1639 reform to the Holy Synod, an assembly of bishops whose method of recruitment varies with each country. It is this body which elects him, counsels and advises and controls him, allowing him no power, in practice, to take any important decision without its approval.

The geographical division of the Church did not stop here. As soon as certain territories had their own leader others claimed the same privilege. Even before the system was canonically established one Church—the Church of Cyprus, in 431—made known the fact that it had appointed its own leader, had become in effect 'autocephalous'. When the Orthodox faith spread among the Slavs, the method most favoured for conversion necessarily brought demands for national autocephalous Churches. The Serbs and Bulgarians sought to have their religious independence recognized—the right, that is, to elect their own Primate. For example, the Bulgarians obtained a Church independent from Rome in 927, only to have this fall under Byzantine rule in 1020, though it was restored to them in 1204. The most notable example of independence cleverly won was that of Moscow. The Czar's empire, when Ivan the Terrible (1533–1584) had given it a solid and powerful basis, could not tolerate religious dependence on Byzantium, then under Turkish rule. Impecuniousness having driven the Patriarch to Russia in search of funds in 1589, Moscow took advantage of this to claim the patriarchal title. After this the spread of autocephalous Churches ceased; neither the Czar nor the Patriarch of Constantinople, who with the assistance of the Sultan was engaged in extending his authority to cover all Christians in the Balkans and the East, was favourable to them. Thus in 1767 the Bulgarian Church lost even its liturgical autonomy, and was to all intents and purposes attached to the Greek.

But the movement began afresh in the nineteenth century. One of the consequences of the great revolutionary drive, which was then enabling subject peoples to claim their national rights, was to multiply the number of autocephalous Churches. Those who cast off the Turkish yoke at once demanded their religious autonomy—the Greeks in 1833, the Rumanians in 1856, the Bulgarians in 1870 (not without a hard struggle against the Greeks of Constantinople) and the Serbs during the period from 1831 to 1879. After the First World War a new drive for independence began; while the older autocephalous Churches were reorganizing themselves—those, for instance, in Serbia and Rumania—other peoples who had recently acquired political independence, such as the Poles, Finns, Esthonians, Lithuanians, Letts and Czechs, were now demanding religious autonomy. Even Greece successfully acquired her independence from Constantinople. Albania achieved religious autonomy in 1937; Georgia, under the control of the Church of Moscow, took advantage of the collapse of the Czarist regime to declare herself religiously independent. Even the Orthodox community set up in the U.S.A. by Russian immigrants wanted its religious autonomy. There is therefore a total of twenty-six separate Churches.

This situation is fundamentally different from that of the Protestant Churches. A Baptist has not the feeling of belonging to the same one Church as Methodists or Quakers. On the other hand, all members of Orthodox Churches, because of their unity of faith, are convinced of the fact that they belong to one indivisible Church. Do they not glorify the same Father? Do they not recognize one and the same Christ? Are not the same graces conferred on them by the Holy Spirit? For them these considerations suffice, and they seek above all things a deepening of spiritual life, to the detriment of external unity. Officially the links between each of the Churches are very slack. When a new leader is elected he dispatches an 'Irenical letter' to the heads of all the other Churches, in which he makes known his election. The other Churches may or may not acknowledge it. Some Churches receive the Holy Chrism for the consecration of churches and altars from a sister Church. In olden times Constantinople had established a monopoly by sending chrism to every Church, but Moscow dispensed with this during the seventeenth century and Rumania in 1882. Today only the Churches of Alexandria, Jerusalem, Cyprus and Greece accept the chrism from Constantinople, all other Churches providing it for themselves. As for the authority of the Ecumenical Patriarch of Constantinople, it is now purely nominal. On several occasions during the nineteenth and twentieth centuries he has tried to give advice to this or that Church when problems have arisen, but on each occasion he has been rebuffed.

The lack of unity in this respect is not without certain disagreeable consequences. The excessive desire for independence may be roundly condemned as a heresy, but it remains strong nevertheless. There have been many examples of resistance to the Orthodox 'Vatican'—the Phanar—at Constantinople; the Serbs and Bulgarians even resorted to force of arms, as did the Georgians against the Patriarch of Moscow. The history of Orthodoxy since the early nineteenth century is marred by such disputes against authority. The Bulgarians were for a long time treated by Constantinople as schismatics simply because they demanded an autonomous Church, not only territorially but with authority over Bulgarians all over the world, though the other Churches maintained friendly relations with those who had been excluded. The Melchites of Antioch elected a Syrian Patriarch in 1899, but the Greek

Churches refused to recognize him. In Jerusalem the same thing occurred, even though the elected leader was a Greek, and it was twenty-three years before the Patriarch of Alexandria recognized him. In 1931–2 the two Patriarchates of Antioch and Jerusalem entered a new crisis. More recently the question of the attitude to be adopted towards the Catholic Church during the Vatican Council brought the discussion to public notice. The Ecumenical Patriarch, Athenagoras, was favourably disposed to fraternal contacts, but the bishops of several Churches, especially in Greece, protested.

Nevertheless a new trend has emerged, particularly noticeable after the Second World War, which seeks to renew communion and to organize a more visible unity. In various countries the Young Orthodox movements are working in this direction, and the Churches behind the Iron Curtain are becoming aware that they too must stand together in face of Marxist pressures. Ever since the end of the First World War there has been talk of an Orthodox Ecumenical Council. But the Pan-Orthodox Congress of 1923, which met at Constantinople to prepare the ground, could not command the attention of more than half the Churches involved. The Great Synod, scheduled for 1925, never took place. A study group met at Mount Athos in 1930, but advanced no further towards a general convocation. It was only in 1952 that the Patriarch Athenagoras took up the idea once more, and this resulted in the Pan-Orthodox Conference at Rhodes (September 1960–October 1961) where practically all the Churches except the Alexandrian were represented, including the Russian. Here the bases for a future Great Synod were laid.

5. The Ancient Patriarchates of Greece and the Near East

At the beginning of the contemporary era the Greek Orthodox Church was placed in a singular position. For over three hundred years the whole of its territory had been occupied by the Turks, but it was still very much alive. Its religion had in fact served as a defence against the inroads of Islam, and if it had declined somewhat the activity of the 'herd', as the Turks called those who practised it, was still considerable. There had even been an unexpected phenomenon: the revered Ecumenical Patriarch of Constantinople had become more powerful, with jurisdiction over an enormous territory stretching from the Carpathians and the Adriatic to the Persian border and from Russia to Crete. He had also compelled the other Patriarchates of the Near East to receive his accredited representatives. From the middle of the eighteenth century, whether at Antioch, Jerusalem or Alexandria, there had been only Greek Patriarchs and these, moreover, often preferred to reside in Constantinople rather than among their own flocks.

This state of affairs stemmed from the attitude adopted towards Christians by the Turks from the beginning of their rule. Islam did not take away from a conquered people the right to conduct their own affairs in matters of religion, but Koranic law regarded them as a nation in themselves with no differentiation with regard to origin, language or creed. It was the Sultan's wish that this Christian nation should have as a representative a responsible head, and since the time of Mahomet II this had been the Patriarch of Constantinople, whose title and rights had been confirmed by the conqueror. The Greek Orthodox head, as 'millet-bachi' or Ethnarch of the Christians, assumed the role of a Khalif, and the entire Christian hierarchy found itself with a power over its adherents that it had never possessed in the time of the Basileis. It was quite usual to confer imperial titles on the Patriarch and, with a mitre in the form of a crown, to enthrone him on a carpet bearing the Roman eagles. In his palace in the Phanar, on the Golden Horn, he could believe himself sovereign. At the same time, however, such prestige had its inconveniences. One was that the 'millet-bachi' and his subordinates took part in the corruption which was rife in the Turkish Empire. Patriarchal elections brought in money, and this encouraged the Sultan to see that they took place regularly. In the eighteenth century there were forty-eight in seventy-three years! Another disadvantage was that the Patriarch gave the impression of having too much in common with the Turks and of accepting the lot of the Christians too easily, confined as they were in a kind of ghetto under the perpetual domination of Islam.

The position was made worse when, following the crisis brought about by the French Revolution, the Balkan peoples began their liberation movement against the Turks. The resurgence of the Greek nation, spurred on both by the merchants in Greece and by emigrants who formed part of the *Hetaria* (a secret revolutionary party), brought irresistible patriotic fervour. The upheaval took place in 1821 with the first War of Independence, which was finally successful thanks to Western intervention, and the kingdom of Greece was finally constituted in 1830.

Faced with the uprising of its people against the Turk, the Orthodox Church could not remain indifferent. Its basic sentiments were well known, but at the same time it could not renounce the position that the Sultan had established for it, since the Christians would thereby be deprived of all legal rights. The horrors of the War of Independence, such as the massacres of Chios, rendered the situation intolerable. The Ecumenical Patriarch paid dearly for the authority vested in him by the sultans. On Easter Day 1821, as a reprisal for the insurrection,

Gregory V, who had just celebrated solemn Mass, was arrested by the janissaries and hanged on the carriage gate of the Phanar. In memory of his martyrdom (he was later canonized) the gate has remained closed ever since.

As a consequence of the wars of liberation the Sultan was led to amend the statutes affecting the Christian subjects who remained. Thus in 1889 the Galhani Charter introduced civil liberty, at least in principle. In 1856 political equality had been recognized by the 'Hatti-Houmayoun'. But these things in no way altered the paradoxical situation of the Patriarch, which persisted until the collapse of the imperial regime—that is, until the period immediately following the First World War. On the one hand, the Ecumenical Patriarch seemed to have interests in common with the Sultan; every territorial loss by the Turks meant a diminution of his territory, and in consequence of his authority, because of the appearance of autocephalous Churches. On the other hand, any steps by Greece towards full independence had their repercussions in the Phanar and brought problems. The Balkan wars caused tension between the Patriarchate and the Turkish authorities, and acts of violence against Christians. The Italo-Turkish conflict did not have the same effect, for here the enemy was a 'Latin' and the Orthodox Church was able to stand behind the national cause, whereas during the First World War it found itself in a distinctly embarrassing position fighting against 'Latins', Anglicans, Protestants and the elder brothers of its faith, the Russians. The Patriarch Germanus V stood unreservedly behind the Turks—at that time the 'Young Turks'—with the result that after their defeat he was treated as a common collaborator and deposed.

The last act of the Greco-Turkish struggle following the First World War was the campaign in Asia Minor, entered into so lightly by Athens; this resulted in the final breaking of the ties between the Patriarchate and the Turks. Monsignor Melethios made so little attempt to hide his sympathies that when the disaster of 1922 came about his own life and those of his faithful followers were endangered. He was only saved by the presence of allied troops in Constantinople, who allowed him to leave for Greece. Once there he was immediately dismissed from office. The Greek debacle and the population exodus imposed by the Turks brought about the decline of the Ecumenical Patriarchate. The whole of Asia Minor and eastern Thrace had gone and the Patriarchate now consisted of eight small dioceses, four in Turkey and four in the islands and western Thrace, a poor remnant of ancient splendours. A certain degree of authority with regard to Mount Athos remained, a nominal Patriarchate was allowed by Greece in the northern dioceses of her territory and a form of recognition came from the autonomous Church of Crete. This decline brought about a great deal of suffering. It is estimated that 4 million Christians under the Patriarchate of Constantinople were massacred or deported from Asia Minor between 1914 and 1924.

At the same time, however, the downfall of the Imperial Turkish regime and the setting up of the secular—and even secularizing—rule of Mustapha Kemal in 1923 brought about a radical change in the position of both Church and Patriarch. The new Turkey had no longer any reason to maintain the Christian Ethnarch, nor the privileges and duties which the sultans decreed. The new capital, Ankara, was purely administrative and secular; it replaced Constantinople, that venerable capital of Christian faith. In Kemal Atatürk's view, the Patriarch was merely the religious head of a foreign population and, as such, to be treated with caution. In the early days relations were mediocre. The government approved of the attempts made by a certain Father Efthym, an Orthodox Turkish priest, to found a national Orthodox Church with the liturgy in Turkish. In 1947 relations between Greek and Turk had improved and this Church disappeared, and the few churches which it had taken over were handed over to the Greek Church. But relations often degenerated into open conflict and a number of violent clashes between Greek and Turk occurred over questions of Ottoman nationalism, with consequent injury to Christians and clergy and damage to Church property.

A parallel can be found in the incidents in Cyprus after the Second World War, when numbers of priests and monks were among the victims. In September 1955, during anti-Greek riots in Istanbul, Turkish mobs set fire to thirty churches and monasteries and pillaged as many more.

Detached from the Patriarchate at Constantinople, recognized as autocephalous by the Phanar in 1850, the Greek Church has had a troubled history. From the start the problem revolved round its relations with the secular power. Under the monarchy it could hardly call itself free; the system originally adopted concerning its relations with the State was the same as that of Peter the Great with his Church —and that needs no further comment! The State's hand lay heavy on it. At the meetings of the Holy Synod, the members of which were named by the government, a procurator was always present by the side of the Metropolitan. Political influence was always present. In 1917 the Synod solemnly anathematized Venizelos for his opposition to the pro-German line taken by Constantine I. When the king was forced out by the Allies and Venizelos came to power, the Synod promptly associated itself with the change and dismissed the Metropolitan who had taken the lead against Venizelos. In 1923 an attempt was made to remedy this state of affairs by replacing the Holy Synod by an Assembly of Bishops, but two years later the government restored the old system. The 1938 Constitution placed the Church under tight control. Since the Second World War, however, there has been a distinct tendency to allow the Church its freedom, although the State does not hesitate to intervene in a crisis, as was the case in 1959 when there was a dispute among the bishops.

This was not the only question that brought trouble to the Church of Greece. From the beginning secular authority was hostile to the monks, possibly because of the power they represented. The smaller monasteries were closed and their inmates were housed in the larger monasteries; from a total of 593 in 1830, they were reduced to only 85, and the total number of monastics from 3,000 to 1,800. The same measures were applied in 1931 to those territories which were attached to the Athens Metropolitanate subsequent to the victory of 1912. In all there are 150 monasteries in Greece today containing 13,000 monks and 650 enclosed monks, a small number when one considers the great part played by monasticism in spiritual Orthodox life. In the meantime there was a considerable confiscation of the not inconsiderable areas of land owned by the monasteries. The last and most drastic seizure was for the benefit of a flood of refugees from Asia Minor after the defeat of 1922. Articles have appeared in the press concerning the 'uselessness' of monks, written in a style with which one is familiar in France; some monasteries have reacted against this criticism by taking up charitable work and by founding schools for the training of clergy, but they are very often hampered by lack of funds.

As we have already said, the Greek Church has not always had a peaceful existence. Towards the end of the period under review it underwent a very severe trial. The Second World War brought great suffering to Greece, not only under the German occupation but also later during the troubled times of the liberation. There was civil war during which gangs of Communist insurgents attacked the clergy and four hundred priests and deacons died; some of them were tortured and crucified. This baptism of blood, as is always the case, led to the spirit of renewal which this Church is at present manifesting.[1]

The importance of the Melkite Patriarchates of Syria, Palestine and Egypt is far from corresponding to the prestige which still clings to their titles. Symbolic of this is the Antioch of today, once the third city of the Roman Empire—'the City protected by God, the City of Cilicia, of Iberia, of Syria, of Arabia and the East'—now a large village on the Orontes in Turkish territory. The three Eastern Patriarchates never recovered from the loss of the mass of the inhabitants who in hatred against the Byzantines went over in the fifth century to the heresies of Nestorianism and Monophysitism. Then followed the Turkish occupation, much more severe in the outlying provinces than

[1] See Chapter IV, section 16.

in the capital. Time after time they were subjected to persecution and massacres such as that of 1860, when both Orthodox and Maronites fell to the Druses, or those which took place both during and after the First World War. Then, as we saw, other difficulties were caused by the Greeks who wished to keep the Eastern Patriarchates under the authority of Constantinople, helped in this by the Turkish Government. The struggle between Arab-speakers and Greek-speakers went on all through the nineteenth century, and in fact ceased only when Egypt, Palestine and Syria came under Western influence. Even then the rights of the indigenous Christians were not always respected.

The Patriarchate of Antioch, which covers Syria and Lebanon, has some 300,000 adherents, the largest mass of Christian Arabs. To this figure must be added some 200,000 emigrants, most of them now in the U.S.A., who remain attached to their land of origin by both emotional and charitable ties. Since 1899 their Patriarchs have no longer been Greeks, but autochthones (indigenous). There is no permanent synod to counsel them, but a two-week synodal meeting takes place every year and an Assembly of Bishops every four years. Divergent trends have been noticed in the Patriarchate; for instance, in 1937 the Archbishop of Homs attempted to set up an independent Church. The real problem for His Beatitude was that of recruitment and training of clergy, just as it is everywhere. An ecclesiastical school, opened in 1904, lasted only eight years. There are now only fourteen, and the total number of monks is less than a hundred. Czarist Russia had made its presence felt in the Syrian Patriarchate, notably in founding schools. The Soviet Government had carried on its policy and had even accepted a representative of the Patriarchate of Antioch with his own church in Moscow; it also pays an annual indemnity as compensation for lands confiscated in Russia. In 1950 relations were still further strengthened by exchanged of visits between prelates. But the renewal now taking place in Syria and Lebanese Orthodox Christianity is due to Western influences.

Jerusalem may have retained all its glory, but this is not due to the Orthodox Patriarchate. Over the years its flock has declined and is now no more than fifty thousand. It functions as the guardian of the Holy Places, to which duty it devotes itself with such rigour that during the nineteenth and twentieth centuries disturbances broke out between Catholics and Orthodox adherents. Real authority is in the hands of the Fraternity of the Holy Sepulchre, a very ancient body whose present organization dates from the sixteenth century. The Patriarch is chosen from among its members; it has seventeen monasteries in Jerusalem and eighteen others throughout Palestine. The only monastery outside this circle is that of St Saba, the oldest in Palestine, in an isolated corner of Judah, where the monks live a life of asceticism.

Domination by the sixteen-centuries-old Fraternity of the Holy Sepulchre has presented problems in that its recruitment is almost exclusively Greek; this has caused trouble with Arab adherents, discontented at being governed by a small minority. The British High Commissioner had to intervene on two occasions. The question had still not been settled when the Arab-Jewish war broke out. The war was followed by an exodus of part of the Christian Orthodox Arab population.

Without being identical the situation at Alexandria was in many respects analogous. Following the arrival of the British in 1882 there was an influx of Greek and Syrian elements, both wealthy and active, who overshadowed the autochthonous Melchite Copts. At the beginning of the nineteenth century the Patriarch could not reside in Egypt and was obliged to govern his small flock from Constantinople. This state of affairs improved under Mohammed Ali, and there was once again a Patriarch at Alexandria. On two occasions the Patriarchate was held by Greeks who were both intelligent and energetic, Monsignors Photius and Metaxatis. Between 1899 and 1935 they endeavoured to modernize and reorganize the Church and to provide it with its own schools. They also tried to improve relations with the autochthones by appointing some of their representatives to episcopal sees. The question is far from being definitely settled; the Greeks attempted to shed Patriarchal authority, but the government opposed this in 1954 by recognizing the Patriarch as sole leader of the Church. A remarkable effort towards renewal has taken place, due in large measure to sponsorship by the laity who have especial influences in the Egyptian Church. The three candidates for the Patriarchy are proposed by an assembly of seventy-two lay members and thirty-six ecclesiastics; an *élite* group of theologians has emerged and its role will no doubt become progressively more important.

The history of Greek Orthodoxy has been a troubled one. But, cut off from the main stream of the world, one small Church, whose independence was reaffirmed in 1782, has continued to dwell in the peace and solitude of prayer: the monastery of St Catherine in Sinai. The abbot has the title of archbishop and is responsible to no one. He resides for the most part at Alexandria. The twenty monks there carry on the old spiritual traditions of Orthodoxy, and the monastery's library contains a unique and priceless collection of manuscripts.

6. Two Strongholds of Faith—Mount Athos and the 'Philocalia'

Orthodoxy has not only survived in spite of conditions that could have eroded it, but has shown and is showing every sign of renewal.

There are two principal reasons for this: the instinctive fidelity of the Christians to their religion as a bulwark against Islam, and the essentially spiritual character of their religion, where liturgical and sacramental life holds a vital place, yet plays little part in external activities, pastoral work and even intellectual activity. It is this religion of the Spirit that has safeguarded the two strongholds that stand firm in Greek Orthodoxy, investing it with incomparable prestige—Mount Athos and the *Philocalia of the Saints.*

Mount Athos, the Holy Mount, has been sacred land for centuries. Here men have lived their whole lives striving to transform the 'mortal body' spoken of by St Paul into the 'spiritual body'. No Eastern Christian can hear the name of Mount Athos without emotion —what Rome is to the Catholics, Mount Athos is to the Orthodox, though in a slightly different sense: it is the visible image of the Church, the place where it is presented in its most perfect form, where one can hear its heart beat.

In the north-east of Greece the Chalcidic peninsula stretches its three rocky fingers into the Aegean Sea. The northern one is narrowed along its thirty miles' length to a width of two miles at one point. Six thousand feet up on the eastern side, where forest alternates with cultivated areas and olive groves, stands Mount Athos, which for a thousand years has existed as the most extraordinary republic Europe has ever known—all the inhabitants are monks and all the towns are monasteries.

In about 962 St Athanasius, the mystic of Trebizond and one-time chaplain to the imperial fleet, retired here, and with the help of several disciples built the first monastery, that of the Great Laura. He was soon joined by the hermits who for a long time had been seeking God in these solitudes. Other monasteries were built and more and more dedicated men flocked to this corner where, it was said, the Blessed Virgin rested before the Assumption. The beacon kindled by the monks on the Mount during the feast of the Transfiguration was a sign to all those who sought purification and ascension towards the light. The state of holiness which all men sought seemed possible on Mount Athos—the Holy Mountain was the visible antechamber of the invisible beyond.

For a thousand years Athos played a large part in the destiny of the Eastern Church. How many autocrats during the time of the Basileis came here to do penance between battles? How many empresses presented treasures, icons and manuscripts to its monasteries? Byzantine converts from many lands sent the best of their sons to pray here on its slopes. To the Greeks were added Bulgarian, Serbian, Rumanian and Georgian monks. The larger monastic foundations of the Orthodox world, especially those of Russia, took Athos as a model. Most of those who left their mark on the traditions of their Church had so-journed at Athos before going on to a life of action or asceticism.

It seems extraordinary that this society, whose very existence is a continual paradox, has been able to go on through the ages without some upheaval to change the course of its destiny. Even the Turks respected the Monks' Republic. It was not until the turmoil of 1821 in Greece that the Sultan, faced with the fact that the younger monks were siding with the insurgent patriots, was obliged to send troops to occupy the mountain; but this lasted for only nine years, from 1821 until 1830. When in 1913 the kingdom of Greece took possession of the territory, which included Athos, it instituted only a very light form of control over it. Since 1924 all the communities have been left with almost complete autonomy, the prefect delegated by Athens as governor being as discreet as possible, his men confining themselves to surveillance of visitors and traders who visit the small ports of the isthmus. The real power lies in the hands of the twenty large monasteries whose representatives meet regularly at Karyes and form the temporal and spiritual government. The Ecumenical Patriarch, under whose nominal authority Athos lies, hardly ever intervenes. No monastery or order in the West has ever known a similar independence.

At the end of the nineteenth century Athos was not what it was in the golden age of the fourteenth and fifteenth centuries, when there were 15,000—even, it was said, as many as 30,000—monks there. In the seventeenth and eighteenth centuries a decline set in and the numbers dropped to some 2,000. In the Great Laura, where once there had been 700, there were now only five. However, from the nineteenth century onwards a renewal took place side by side with the renaissance in Greece and the spiritual evolution in Russia. In 1913 a complete census gave the figures as a total of 6,345 monks, of whom 3,243 were Greek and 1,914 Russian. The revolution of 1917 put an end to the rivalry of Greek and Russian monks and slowed down the influx of the latter. After the Second World War the creation of popular democracies dammed the flow. The 'Russikon', which had 1,800 monks in 1917, had only 68 in 1958, and all of them were very old. Today the figure for the whole of Mount Athos is reckoned at 7,500, in itself an impressive figure. There are unmistakable signs of a renewal.

It is to Athos that one must turn in order to understand Orthodoxy fully, to acquaint oneself with the spiritual message that this Church brings to the world. Whoever sojourns on the Holy Mountain cannot fail to be sensitive to its divine atmosphere—the solitude of the woods, the murmur of water from ancient stone aqueducts. Man himself does little to break the supernatural silence. For hours on end, even in the larger monasteries, there seems to be no sign of life in the close-packed buildings; those monks who are not at prayer in shady corners keep their voices so low that they are lost in the lightest sea breeze. Occasionally a young monk appears in the courtyard carrying a form of gong made of cypress wood, which he beats loudly. A file of bearded monks makes its way then to the central church, and through an open door one hears a rhythmical chant which seems less to break the silence than to prolong it in the same consecrated design.

This then is Athos—a city of prayer where everything is ordered towards the consecration of life. It is quite different from the Trappist or Benedictine monasteries where one has the feeling of being in vast beehives. In the monasteries of Athos intellectual pursuits are relegated to a very modest place. They have never been, as in the West, considered beneficial or necessary; indeed they are almost suspect. The excellent libraries have for a long time now been frequented only by an occasional visitor—perhaps monks or laity engaged in classifying the rare manuscripts. Prayer, however, is constant and universal, taking on all the aspects culled from the traditions of the Christian East. All the forms of religious life practised under Orthodoxy are found at Athos: cenobitism, analogous to the way of life of Benedictines and Cistercians; 'idiorhythm', which groups its monks in a family circle around their leader with freedom of action in temporal or spiritual matters, though all forgather for common services of worship; eremitism of various degrees from groups of two or three to total individual isolation in the heart of the forest or in grottoes by the sea, accessible only by rope—places from which, only a little while ago, death was the only release.

In its role as a conservatory of prayer through the ages Athos has acted as a bastion of faith against which neither time nor events have prevailed. Just as the monastery buildings, whose architecture, external decoration in bright colours and solemn frescoes within have not changed over the years, so the prayer of Athos is today what it was three hundred, five hundred or a thousand years ago. Devotion to the Blessed Virgin, Panagia and Theotokos, is as live as ever. Is not Athos known as the 'Garden of the Mother of God'? And is not its seal on official documents her image? Since the reforms carried out in the middle of the eighteenth century by Eugene Bulgaris, abbot of Vatopedi, the life of prayer has progressed still further. In the last few years a good deal of interest has been centred on hesychastic prayer, directed both towards its historical development and to its spiritual significance. Despite losses, despite the attacks of the forces of irreligion, the Monks' Republic has retained its validity and remained faithful to its mission.

And it was in fact at Athos, within one of its communities, that the second bastion of faith was established from which, during the nineteenth century, the movement of renewal emerged in Orthodoxy, not only in Greece but all over the world. It was a bastion of a kind quite different from that of the monasteries and hermitages clinging to the side of the mountain. It was of ink and paper, like many others in Christian history: St Augustine's *City of God*, the *Summa* of Thomas Aquinas and the *Institution* of Calvin.

At the end of the eighteenth century there lived in the Dionysiou monastery in Athos a monk of singular qualities. He combined a high degree of asceticism with a rare and far-reaching intellect; he also had a passionate interest in all forms of literary work with a spiritual content, whether of the East or the West, particularly Loyola's *Spiritual Exercises* and the famous work of Scupoli, *Spiritual Combat*, both of which he translated into Greek. The monk's name was Nicodemus the Hagiorite (1748–1809). While deepening his knowledge of spiritual matters—and the libraries of Mount Athos offer immense possibilities for patristic research to the more erudite monks—especially with regard to the origins and content of pure prayer, he had the idea of gathering together all the texts of the great Fathers in one volume, so making them available to others in their search for the supernatural. He enlisted the help of his friend Macarius, Bishop of Corinth, and at Venice in 1782 there appeared in Greek the enormous anthology the two friends had compiled from those texts that seemed to them to represent the greatest beauty—the *Philocalia of the Saints* (*philo-kalos*: lover of beauty).

It is indeed an impressive work, a monument of faith which appeared at a time when the influence of the encyclopedists and Voltaire was being felt in the West. It covers the Fathers of the Desert, Evagrius of Pontus (fourth century) and the anonymous hesychastic monks of the fourteenth and fifteenth centuries. The aim of this work of contemplation was, according to Nicodemus, to indicate the shortest and simplest way to perfect prayer, the key as well as the way of return to the 'Inner Kingdom'. The texts were classified with this intention in mind. Some were adapted to the preparatory phase, the rule of life, which man must follow in order to live righteously in God's eyes; the second part was concerned with the 'psychotechnical' aspects of spiritual discipline, incorporating both the use of simplified prayer and sacramental practice. Nicodemus and Macarius were staunch believers in frequent communion. The final texts dealt with 'theurgical' experience, or the use of pure prayer, of short and fervent prayers combined with respiratory discipline and a concentration of all the forces of the soul in order to bring the worshipper wholly to God.

The work was a great success, firstly in the Greek Church. It ran into several editions, each one different because different editors added or subtracted certain texts to suit the spiritual needs of their readers. Velochkovsky (1722–94), a Russian monk on Athos, read the work and was so enthusiastic that he translated it into Russian in 1793. He added certain important texts that Nicodemus had left out, especially those of St Gregory Palamas. The work was read widely and other editions followed. In the famous *Tales of a Russian Pilgrim* [1] the anonymous narrator tells of buying the *Philocalia* for two roubles and greedily nourishing his soul on it. The *starets* Ambrose of the famous Optina monastery advised those under his direction to read it. Translations in Bulgarian, Rumanian and all the languages of Orthodoxy followed. In 1884 the Bishop of Tambov published an enlarged edition, which has remained the principal spiritual nourishment of the Russian monks, practically on the same level as the Gospels. Today there is increasing interest in the work, especially in Rumania, where a new edition is in preparation, and in Greece where the *I Zoï* [2] Fraternity constantly refer to it. The *Philocalia* provides a constant link with the past, a 'rediscovery of sources' of the kind so much talked about among the Catholics of today. Like Athos, the great anthology of the monk Nicodemus has in its turn contributed greatly to keeping the Orthodox faith on the correct lines.

7. SERIOUS PROBLEMS AND PROMISES OF RENEWAL

To what extent can these great spiritual realities—monasticism, the *Philocalia* and the prayer of Jesus—be said to ensure the future of Greek and Eastern Orthodoxy? There can be no question that as a general rule the clergy is not completely fulfilling its functions. One of the best authorities on Eastern Christianity, Père Rondot, has stated that: 'The Greek Orthodox clergy, especially in the higher echelons, do not escape criticism, largely because representatives of the faithful take part in the appointment of the Patriarch. The merits of the various Metropolitans are openly discussed by the public and the press. Many priests are reproached for their ignorance, some of them are scarcely lettered in Arabic, most of them are not conversant with Greek and the Eastern languages. There are more severe criticisms of their ways of life. Some are said to be freemasons. And, finally, the abuses of trust, the acts of violence and unscrupulousness attributed to the Orthodox hierarchy by the Bulever inquiry of 1860, are still in evidence today in too many cases.'

This opinion, even more justified a hundred years ago, should not be applied without qualification to all Christian communities of Greece and the East. One should not forget that there remained reserves of religious vitality in the ancient Church of Byzantium just as much in the healthier elements among the clergy as in the people, where faith

---

[1] See Chapter IV, section 10. [2] 'Life.'

was very much alive. One must above all not ignore the obvious signs of renewal which Orthodoxy is manifesting.

It is little realised in the West, but there have always been in Orthodoxy, even at the blackest hours of its history, those who were ready to fight against indifference or resignation on the part of their co-religionists. In 1820–30, for instance, at the time when the Christians of Greece were only interested in political freedom, an apostle arose among them, Apostolos Makrakis, who was a born preacher. He presented Christ in words of fire as the 'Universal Word', the link between God and the world, the centre of things, and he repeated unceasingly that independence was as nothing if the souls of his listeners remained sunk in inertia, doubt and impiety.

The impulse given by Makrakis has not been wasted. In any event during the past decades signs have multiplied and the renewal can be observed at almost all levels of the Greek and Melchite Churches. Even if it has not achieved so much as the Catholic Church over the last one hundred years, it has already had results in two important respects. The first is a desire for a return to original sources: it is the return to their most firmly established traditions—the *Philocalia*, pure prayer and the religion of the spirit—that the most distinguished of Orthodox Christians believe necessary in order to revitalize their Church. This return to source can be seen in the renewed interest in the *Philocalia*, in hesychastic prayer, in the movement towards a neo-Byzantine iconography, in the resurgence of monasticism and in the participation in all these things by intellectuals and the middle classes as well as by the common people.

In the second place, the Orthodox Church has undoubtedly turned its attention to the efforts undertaken in Catholicism and Protestantism and has profited by them, adapting them to its special circumstances with results that are already evident. The canonization of Gregory the Hagiorite in 1955 marked the degree of interest that the official Church had in this new departure.

In the Orthodox renewal there is one movement which has played the part of pioneers, the Fraternity *I Zoï*, in Greece. In 1906 five friends, worried by the situation in which their Church found itself and mindful of the lessons of Makrakis, formed a group. Three were priests and two were laymen, of whom one was a professor at Athens University. Their movement began as a community, but was soon to be known officially as a 'Fraternity'. For many years they studied the problems which the Greek Church faced, and in 1909 they published their views and their projects in a review of which they were the sole editors, *Anaplassis* ('Reform'). In 1911 they felt strong enough to appeal to a wider public and launched their weekly publication *I Zoï*. It was an immediate success. Its circulation reached 145,000 copies, an enormous figure for a small country such as Greece, where the peasantry read nothing. *Life* spread far beyond Greece. The movement was launched.

As the most outstanding of its founders, Father Eusebius Mathopoulos (1849–1929), had imagined it, the Fraternity was almost a type of monastic order. Its members took no vows, but promised chastity and obedience and were required to have had a sound education and a minimum of theological knowledge before being admitted to the Fraternity. Priests and clerics were not allowed to hold too great a proportion of places in the movement. In 1958, of 140 members there were only 35 clerics, all of whom undertook not to accept episcopal office. One month only in every year was spent in community as a kind of retreat; for the rest of the year they were engaged on the most diverse apostolic tasks. Later the founders conceived the idea of setting up a women's branch, and to this came many women students who undertook catechetic work. Another branch supplied nurses for hospitals.

After the First World War the Fraternity was in full operation. Its founder, who had died in 1929, was succeeded by one worthy of him, the Archimandrite Papacostas. The goal which the founders had set themselves was attained: to spread throughout Greece a ferment of authentically Christian life. Today it exercises considerable influence, through its friendships with various classes and professions and with the clergy, as well as through its ever-increasing number of good works. In every way open to them the Fraternity are working for a renewal of liturgy, for the generalization of sacramental practice, for the religious training of the faithful and deeper study of Holy Scripture. The ancient monastic ideal has been adapted by them to an apostolate which reminds one of Catholic Action and others of the same type in Italy.

Members of the Fraternity are in the main preachers, and many of them speak in churches according to the Orthodox tradition, which allows lay preachers access to the sacred pulpit; but preaching is only one aspect of an immense educational and cultural campaign. Catechistic schools have been opened all over Greece and Cyprus; today there are almost 7,500 of them.

The Fraternity organizes religious courses in settlements and holiday camps, and has created a higher institution for the training of preachers. It is engaged in spreading increased numbers of popular libraries, and provides scholarships for the poorer students of the Faculty of Theology. An enormous part of its activity is devoted to publishing with its own press: it publishes its own papers, weeklies and reviews for children as well as for intellectuals. It has made great efforts to distribute the Holy Scriptures: the pocket edition of the New Testament has run to 650,000 copies. It sponsors a large number of movements: the Students' Christian Union, the Young Workers' Christian Union and the Intellectuals' Christian Union. The last-named body has founded an engineering school, a department of which prints the great works of Christian literature of today and the review *Aktinès* ('Radius'). This is of high quality, and its articles have had a considerable effect in the Western world.

There is also a repercussion from the activity of the Fraternity. The hierarchy, usually suspicious of movements over which it has not direct control, has been seized with admiration and, emulating the movement's achievements, it has sponsored since 1946 an apostolic service founded by Basil Vellar, similar to Catholic Action. A university circle, a seminary and catechism schools in the main towns have also been set up. This service has its own publications and produces its own review, *Ekklesia*. The tension between the laity and the hierarchy has thus eased, to the benefit of the renewal movement in general.

It was in Athens that, after a long hiatus, the missionary idea again came to the fore. In 1936, at the first Congress of Orthodox Theology, one of the main subjects tackled was that of the missions. Reports from laymen were presented to the Congress, one of these being supplied by a member of the Fraternity. A committee was set up for promoting missions, and a Rumanian delegate suggested the founding of an Orthodox Missionary Institute. Twenty years later the idea was again taken up by the Greeks of the U.S.A. and a missionary society of the Greek Orthodox Holy Cross was founded in Brooklyn. It received the warm wishes of the Ecumenical Patriarch Athenagoras. Students from Africa, Ethiopia and Korea have been invited to universities and seminaries in Greece since 1948. An impetus has been given; the results are expected to be good.

The Greek Church, while it may be in a state of expansion compared to the rest of the Christian East, is not the only one to show signs of renewal. On Mount Athos, where the number of new recruits to monasticism is growing and where intellectual interest in the wealth of libraries is a new development, the *Athonias* school of theology was opened in 1953 in the Russian monastery of St Andrew and immediately enrolled some fifty students.

In the Patriarchate of Antioch, once so neglected, a new movement has been launched similar to the Fraternity in Greece, though neither has directly influenced the other. In the summer of 1941 a group of very young students from the Catholic colleges run by the Brothers of the Christian Schools decided after much discussion and meditation on a new move. True Orthodox believers, they were disturbed to note that their Church, once so famous, was reduced to the status of a merely social body, administratively alive but empty of religious spirit, desiccated by routine and ignorance, to all intents and purposes moribund. They felt that instead of indulging in recriminations against the hierarchy and the clergy, as was the common practice, they would do better to reform themselves and embark at once on the creation of a new form of Christian community by making themselves Christians. The two main leaders in this movement were George Khodr and Albert Laham, residents of Tripoli in Libya. But at almost the same time, at Latakiyeh in Syria, two other young men, Marcel Marcos and Gabriel Sahadé, were thinking and doing the same thing. Unaware of each other's existence, the two groups met, and from this meeting in Beirut, on 16th March 1942, the Orthodox Youth Movement was born. The Holy Synod of the Patriarchate recognized it in 1945.

The rate of growth of this young movement was comparable to that of the specialized branch of Catholic Action, the same degree of enthusiasm being expressed in a similar way. Soon there were new centres opened in various parts of the Lebanon and Syria, for the most part made up at first of young intellectuals, later by workers and artisans. Circles were set up in which studies were made of the Word of God, the Fathers of the Church and the wealth of liturgy. The young men undertook the development of sacramental practice, and, as with the Catholic Youth Movement of Monsignor Cardijn, they sought to prove themselves, in every aspect of life, worthy witnesses for God. An excellent review was launched: *An-Nour* ('The Light'). Other publications for the working classes were also printed. The movement, which had six main centres and fifty smaller ones, set up a biennial congress and a general secretariat. The basic unit was the team of a dozen members, and they all met regularly for prayers and at yearly retreats.

The movement now numbers some two thousand members. It has been the promoter of many new schemes, some educational, such as the founding of colleges and welfare schools, with dispensaries and welfare workers, and others with the object of training the young for church choirs. But above all it has concentrated on religious action. Its members undertake missionary work in the villages. The movement has been responsible for the resurgence of Syrian monasticism, which had completely vanished from the Levant. A convent was founded at Tripoli where the nuns devote themselves primarily to the religious education of villagers, and a monastery was founded at Beirut. Some of the prime movers of the movement have now become priests and exercise great influence in their Church. A central body, the *Syndosmos*, was created at Athens in 1952 to link up the Lebanese movement with the Fraternity and the Young Orthodox Students Movement set up by emigrants in the West. Undoubtedly the Orthodox Youth Movement will play its part in Greco-Oriental Orthodoxy.

Signs of renewal are not so clearly distinguishable elsewhere, but at Jerusalem and Alexandria some can be observed in the appearance of certain journals and reviews; the Monophysite Coptic Church [1] together with the Orthodox Melchite Church of Egypt have both shown signs of a new awakening. The latter has for several years shown an increased degree of activity in missionary work; it has also created sees in Accra and in Central and East Africa.

The idea that the Greek Orthodox Church is in decline must now be discounted. Its most ardent and forward-looking spirits intend it to become much more open and welcoming than it has been in the past. Efforts have been made to strengthen the bonds with the rest of the Orthodox world: the Rhodes Conference is proof enough. At the same time many links have been renewed with other Patriarchates, including that of Russia. The man responsible for this new approach is Ecumenical Patriarch Athenagoras I, since 1948 the organizer of the Great Seminary at Istanbul and leading spirit of the review *Orthodoxy*. His long stay in the U.S.A. at the head of the American Orthodox Church enabled him to take a wider view of the problems of religion, and his reflections on the matter, together with his relations with the Apostolic Delegate, Monsignor Roncalli, brought him to decide on the necessity for a *rapprochement* with the Catholic Church. His meeting with Pope Paul VI at Jerusalem in January 1964 bore witness to the real feelings of this man of God.

8. MOSCOW AT THE TIME OF THE HOLY SYNOD

The coronation of Czar Paul I in 1796 in Moscow was the occasion for a display of great pomp. The Metropolitan Plato had invited the Czar to lay his sword to one side before approaching the altar to be crowned. But the Czar anticipated his gesture and seized the imperial crown himself, placing it upon his head and crowning his spouse with a somewhat smaller crown to the accompaniment of ritual shouts of acclamation from the assembled crowds. A priest then read out the principal legislative Acts, laying each document on the altar for safe keeping by the clergy. Among the Acts was that which governed the succession to the throne. In the long list of titles accorded to the Czar was that of Head of the Church.

This close association between the two powers, so publicly manifested, indicates the fundamental character of the politico-religious system which had ruled Russia for a long time. It sprang directly from Byzantium, though official links had been broken since the year 1448 as an indirect consequence of the Council of Florence (1439–40); then

[1] See Chapter V, section 6.

the Metropolitan Isidore, a Greek, in agreement with the Eastern Patriarchs, had accepted union with Rome, a union which did not last very long. Since that time Moscow had not ceased to grow in ambition and prestige. Not content with being autocephalous, the Russian Church had aimed at the Patriarchal title. It had taken advantage of the impecuniousness of the Patriarchate of Constantinople, then under the Turks, to have itself recognized in 1589, though it was displeased at being classed fifth in the list of Patriarchates. It had aspired ever since to the role and the dignity of being the 'Third Rome', the rival of Byzantium and sole repository of the true faith and the greatness of the Church.

In point of fact the separation from Constantinople had in no way disturbed the interrelation of Church and State: the rights of the Church and those of the Czar were closely interwoven and balanced, though in fact it was the sovereign who ruled. In the seventeenth century an attempt had been made by the great reformer and Patriarch Nikon to put an end to this state of subjection. His failure with the masses, who had objected to liturgical reforms, his disgrace and his deposition signalled the end of ecclesiastical desires for independence. At the end of the century the young and very ambitious Czar Peter the Great had decided on a measure to stop such attempts in the future. For twenty-one years he forbade Patriarchal elections. To those who asked who would be the holder of the See of Moscow, he replied: 'I shall.' In 1721, at the instigation of the mysterious Theophanus Prokopovitch, an apostate Catholic with Protestant and freemason leanings, he published the *Spiritual Rules*, suppressing the Patriarch and establishing a college, the Holy Synod, with nominal authority vested in a group of bishops—later joined by one or two priests. They were assisted in their deliberations by one lay member, the Imperial Procurator, who was charged with the task of ensuring that the Church functioned properly, but who was in fact all powerful.

This regime was in operation on the eve of the French Revolution. It had even been strengthened by increased secular power over the Church. The Synod was under the control of the Procurator, who was commonly referred to as the Czar's eyes, and each member of it was obliged upon appointment to swear to defend the interests of the State in all circumstances. It was also obliged to accept the most damaging and disagreeable decisions for the Church: prohibition against building new centres of worship, the setting up of a special corps of police to watch over the bishops, the confiscation of a large part of ecclesiastical revenues and a limitation on the number of priests and deacons in order not to decrease military recruitment! The priests became merely government servants, and were compelled to spy on their parishioners, denouncing those who transgressed the law. Peter III had even considered confiscating all the Church's possessions. Catherine II actually carried out this operation in 1764, leaving the clergy with only its palaces and summer residences; she undertook to pay them salaries and reduced the number of members of the Great Synod to six, the better to control it. The Metropolitan of Rostov was deposed, imprisoned and exiled for having protested against confiscations. The word slavery hardly does justice to the humiliating situation of the Church in Russia at the time of the accession of Paul I.

The nineteenth century did not bring about any changes in the principles of Church-State relations. In vain the Metropolitan Plato had written a handbook of religion designed for the young Paul's use before he became Czar. Its object was to inculcate in him certain principles for his future role, and especially to remind him that 'the only true leader of the hierarchy is Christ'. No sooner had he become Czar Paul I than he in his turn claimed his rights as Head of the Church. A new law on the Church's possessions was promulgated in which it was laid down that the clergy owed to its sovereign, as its divinely elected head, faithful allegiance and obedience. It was obvious that the yoke was not yet to be lifted.

One question long at issue will show what rough treatment the Russian clergy received from the czars. Among the penalties inflicted was the ignominious one of the knout. In 1767 the Synod had forbidden the ecclesiastical tribunals to condemn priests. In 1771 this gracious measure was extended to deacons. Catherine II had agreed to it, influenced by her profit from the spoliation of the Church's possessions, but despite the intervention of Czar Paul I the practice had continued, the judges continuing to inflict penalties on priests and deacons. In 1801 a new decree was promulgated which officially put an end to this scandal. The families of priests were also exempted. But it was not until 1862, when serfdom was abolished, that the clergy felt sure that the practice was finally dead.

Each czar during the nineteenth century adopted the same tactics towards the Church, considering it as a department within the framework of the State. Only at the beginning of the twentieth century were any real changes to be noticed. Not that the same climate always prevailed, for the mystic Czar Alexander I (1801–25), after his defeat of Napoleon, dreamed of refashioning Christianity along ecumenical lines under the Holy Alliance and intervened in spiritual as well as practical affairs in the Church, compelling high functionaries to come to terms with the freemasons. When he tired of freemasons he turned to Protestant-type Bible societies and insisted that the Church's leaders took part in their meetings. There were rumours also that he wished to abjure Orthodoxy and lead his Church back to Rome.

His successors, less interested in dreams than he, continued to exercise strict control over the Church; and the Church not only did nothing to counteract this, but even actively agreed. Under Nicholas I (1825–55) the Holy Synod congratulated the Czar on having brought in—we know by what means—to Moscow's orbit millions of Uniate Ukrainians and Poles. Under Alexander II (1855–81), who initiated a series of political, economic and social reforms, the agreement between Church and State had its good points. The most important decision to abolish serfdom (1861), to which the nobility were hostile, and of which some clergy were afraid, was officially celebrated by the Metropolitan Philaret; it was he who drafted the statute of liberation of the peasantry in the name of Christian principles (the same principles which were invoked by Herzen the revolutionary), and who on publication of the ukase cried: 'Thou hast vanquished, O Galilean!' Yet the hand of the State remained heavy on the Church. While Alexander III (1881–94) was more diplomatic, he was no less a caesaropapist than his predecessors. The government's guiding rule was the same as that enunciated by Count Ouvarov: 'Orthodoxy, Autocracy, Nation!'

Nevertheless there were certain compensations under the Czar's autocratic system. The Russian clergy were in dire need of reform, and it is doubtful whether they would have carried it out alone. The State's control was unquestionably a help. The decree of 1869 was a case in point; in it the ancient custom of hereditary priesthood was abolished and the priesthood opened to all. The intervention of the State for the purpose of setting up 'academies' in which the upper echelons of the clergy would be trained was another happy case in point.

At the beginning of the twentieth century religious practice was compulsory: church parades were organized for the military, with officers taking evening prayers; no one could sit for an examination unless he produced a certificate stating that his religious obligations had been fulfilled; every unit in the army and navy had its chaplain, and these constituted a special hierarchy which reported directly to the Holy Synod. Every member of the clergy received a modest salary from the State. Despite successive waves of confiscations, churches, dioceses and monasteries still owned 2·8 million hectares of land, valued at 130 million gold francs. Religious teaching was compulsory in all schools and the Church had its own parochial schools. By right the bishops were entitled to sit on the provincial council, next to the governor, and were given all sorts of honours. But all this did not compensate for an almost total lack of freedom—practical, moral and even spiritual—for the Czar was the guardian of dogma.

At this time there was a trend towards greater freedom for the Church. The political crises which had shaken czarist Russia during the nineteenth century had not been quite strong enough to endanger the balance of powers within the autocratic framework of the State. It was another matter in 1905 when the nation was shaken by the crushing defeat administered by the Japanese, and twelve years later, partly as a result of this, the regime foundered. Nicholas II (1894–1917), under pressure from a great popular movement, was obliged to grant a semblance of a constitution and also to summon an assembly, the *Duma*. Religious measures were put into effect; freedom of worship was granted and an Orthodox Christian was at last able to change his faith if he wished. The great statesman Count Witte advocated changes in the Church-State relationship. The Procurator appointed to control the Holy Synod, the terrible Pobiedonostev, a stern believer in State control of the Church, was forced to resign. A religious and philosophical society was set up in St Petersburg where senior clergy and lay thinkers met to study reforms. The Church itself undertook a critical self-examination. Sixty-three bishops furnished official reports which were later combined into a five-volume work. In full Synod, the Metropolitan of Kiev spoke of the reforms necessary. A commission was set up to prepare them and came to the conclusion that it would be necessary to convene a council of the entire Russian Church. It also published five large volumes of critical studies and reports in 1912.

The movement towards greater freedom for the Church was not without its risks. The opponents of the idea indeed adopted it, but only to advocate the separation of Church and State. Discussions raged throughout the Church. Now that political parties had been authorized the bishops, prelates and members of the Synod increased their intrigues: the most reactionary among them obtained the government's permission to relegate five bishops to monasteries because they were of the 'conciliary' party. The disorder was immense; everything was in a state of flux and ecclesiastical structures themselves seemed as badly shaken as social and political life. In the middle of all this the Rasputin scandal broke. Rasputin (1864–1916), an almost illiterate *moujik*, a self-styled man of God, certainly had acquaintances in the upper spheres of ecclesiastical life and wielded a baleful influence over the imperial couple.

The collapse of the dynasty, and its replacement by a provisional government of moderate Socialists on 2nd March 1917, was received by the Church with equanimity. This may seem strange when one remembers the very close secular links between it and the czarist regime. The Synod's Procurator demanded allegiance to the new order from every parish. A dozen bishops known for their reactionary temperaments, and certain prelates who had been associated with Rasputin, were deposed. The Holy Synod's composition was altered. The Council, it was finally announced, would meet at last. The Metropolitans of Petrograd and Moscow were replaced by two excellent men both known to the working classes, Monsignor Kazansky (martyred in 1921) and de Vilno, a future Patriarch. On 15th August an all-Russian Council was held, for the first time since 1696. There were 564 delegates, more than half of them laity. Prudently the Council set aside all motions with a political flavour. On 28th October 1917 it voted unanimously to re-establish the Patriarchate. The new Procurator, Kartachev, assumed the title of Minister for Religious Affairs. For the Church a new climate now reigned in Russia, after two centuries of oppression under the czars.

But on 25th October the Bolsheviks struck against the Menshevik moderates of Kerensky, and when on 5th November Monsignor Tikhon was proclaimed Patriarch, Lenin was almost the undisputed master of Russia. On 7th November the Communist dictatorship began.

9. The True Strength of the Church

At the time when the czarist regime fell the Church in Russia was an imposing force—at least externally. There were 100 million adherents, 57,000 priests, 16,000 deacons, 21,000 monks and 73,000 nuns. There were perhaps too few dioceses—the administration was in the process of economizing on the salaries of bishops—with too great a mass of territory to cover, but the Metropolitans were helped in their tasks by 80 auxiliaries. There were nearly 55,000 churches and 26,000 chapels, where services were held regularly, and 1,500 monasteries.

It was all very impressive. It should be added also that the Russian Orthodox Church, like the Catholic Church of the Middle Ages, had strengthened its hold on its flock considerably by educating them. Since the eighteenth century in particular the number of parish schools had increased; these were the only establishments providing education for the people, and though it was doubtless only a rudimentary education, it was closely linked to religious instruction and helped to inculcate the faith in the masses. In 1914 there were 37,000 parish schools and another 3,000 establishments run by the Church where higher education was given.

All this is a far cry from the usual Western idea of a drunken and often debauched clergy incapable of leading their flocks because they were no better. It is certain that there were mediocre priests—Russian literature mentions them—but there were also others who were convinced of the dignity of their mission and whose closeness to their flocks made them more easily aware of their parishioners' troubles.

But not all the clergy were devoted to ordinary, everyday works.

During and from the seventeenth century the great seminaries were founded, then called Academies, beginning with that of Moscow in 1697. During the nineteenth century the term Academy was applied to higher schools of theology; ordinary seminaries increased in number. In 1914 there were four Academies: Moscow, St Petersburg, Kiev and Kazan, and fifty-eight great seminaries holding twenty thousand students, of whom about half were ordained. In the beginning the pattern of education was modelled on that in force in the West to such an extent that future clerics in the Russian Church studied in Latin. The system was modified in 1808, but had not totally disappeared until 1870. It had the good result of bringing to the attention of the more erudite Russian clergy the differences between their tradition and Western theology. In 1853, for instance, the Metropolitan Macarius published a five-volume work on Orthodox Dogmatic Theology based on Western textbooks. But a work entitled *Orthodox Theology* (1866) by the Metropolitan Philaret, Archbishop of Tchernikov, demonstrated a serious effort to reconsider dogmatic bases on traditional Russian lines and vigorously defended the certainties of the ancient faith against the critical hypotheses of German exegetes. Since then the Academies and ecclesiastical schools have turned out a steady stream of theologians, historians and liturgists, all of whose works were unfortunately to remain unknown in the West. In 1914 the greatest of patristic texts was in Russian. Who would have thought this possible?

But the Church's strength rested on the people rather than on the clergy. The very basis of Orthodoxy, as we have seen,[1] is to link the laity closely to the life of the Church, and this makes for a feeling of responsibility, though obviously one cannot put the *moujik*, the middle class and the nobility all on the same level. Since the eighteenth century the upper classes, all more or less imbued with Western ideals, had allowed themselves to be swayed by the philosophical ideas of Voltaire and the Encyclopedists, in whom Catherine II had shown great interest. In the nineteenth century Positivism and Socialism came to the fore among the cultured classes. Those who were concerned about injustices became irritated by the social order which the Church stood for and turned towards revolutionary action. Yet this current of irreligion—which was, as we shall see, far from being general [2]— affected only a small number compared with the great masses of the faithful.

It may sound like a cliché to say that the Russians are a religious people, but it is true none the less. We all know what Nietzsche had to say about this: 'In Russia, an atheist himself is a believer.' It is not without significance that the Russian word for a man of the soil is *krestianin*, a corruption of the word Christian, whereas in French

[1] See Chapter IV, section 3.   [2] See Chapter IV, section 12.

paysan comes from *paganus,* a pagan. The everyday expression 'Holy Russia' does not contain any idea of pride or indicate any standard of value—it simply expresses one of the deepest aspirations of the Russian race: the aspiration towards holiness. Many of Russia's writers have testified to this impulse: Dostoyevsky demonstrates it in the basest of his characters. The Christian faith is so deep rooted in the Russian national conscience that half a century of a godless regime has not killed it.

A popular religion such as this is not without certain characteristics which deserve criticism. It has, for example, superstitious elements which ethnologists maintain can be traced back to primitive taboo and magic. Traditionalism, exaggerated and grafted on to abysmal ignorance, assumes weird forms—this was seen at the time of the Raskol schism.[1] Such a faith has little influence on moral conduct: drunkenness and debauchery go hand in hand with outward observance and in no way invalidate devoted reverence to icons, prostrations or the strict observance of fasts. In popular folklore there is a well-known story of the drunkard arriving at the gates of Paradise. He is spurned by the Apostles, finally buttonholes St Peter and says to him that at least he never denied his Lord, even though he did drink too much; to St Thomas he says he never doubted and to St John that, according to his very own doctrine, every sinner had the right to mercy. Faith alone saves! Nothing better expresses the religious feeling of the Russians than this old French peasants' dictum.

This type of religion is obviously not one with strong theological bases. Catechistic instruction is reduced to a minimum. Illiteracy was widespread in Russia at the time of the czars, and the ordinary people were only just able to recite one or two prayers by heart. Theologians stress that according to strict Orthodox tradition dogmas are only the outward expression of an inner illumination from the Holy Ghost; this illumination is denied to no one who believes with all his soul, even to the lowest and the humblest. The danger is that this type of religion introduces an excessive stress on sentiment. 'The unfolding of liturgical action, the interplay of light and shadow, the aroma of incense, the drone of the chants all tend to induce in the practitioner the feeling that he is forgiven, is reconciled with God, and is regenerated through contact with celestial realities.' A certain feeling of self-pity is induced, and this, accompanied by a sense of sin and repentance, is nearer to quietism than to a demanding faith. In any case it does not stimulate the will.

Liturgy occupies the first place in this type of religion. As we saw, it is one of the main characteristics of Orthodoxy,[2] and is particularly marked in Russia. For the ordinary Christian it is the living faith, a

[1] See Chapter IV, section 14.　　　　[2] See Chapter IV, section 3.

synthesis of spiritual experience and religious pedagogy for those who cannot learn their religion. It has an honoured place in daily life; the poorest household has its icon, often only a cheap reproduction, before which the head of the family offers prayers twice a day. Yet it is at the service in church that the ordinary Russian's soul turns towards God, and through the sumptuous liturgy 'realizes' His mysterious presence. The long slow ceremonies, archaic and magnificent, are incomprehensible to the majority of believers. It is doubtful whether many of them are conversant with the canon or the rite governing the preparation of oblates. Nevertheless Russian liturgy today constitutes a whole of such great beauty and wealth that the humblest of the faithful derive immense benefit from it. It is impossible not to be affected by the fervour generated, for instance, in a cathedral filled to overflowing during a service; the light of candles, the smoke of incense, the volume of singing all contribute to an exalted feeling of belonging to a faithful community which is being called to salvation.

The Russian faith is, in all this, the heiress of Byzantium, a faith of absolute confidence in the power of the Holy Spirit and the infinite goodness of Christ the Saviour. The least ascetic of Russians is convinced that his true destiny is not to be found here on earth but rather in the hereafter. This explains the stress laid on the Resurrection in the Russian faith, a stress that is even stronger than that in other Orthodox Churches. The common salutation between two Russians: 'Kristos voskriegie!' (Christ is risen!) brings home the importance to them of the first of Christian dogmas of joy, fervour and hope.

Byzantine in so many ways, Russian Christianity nevertheless has its own characteristics. Orthodox tradition has become incarnate in the people, has taken root in them, but there are differences. Berdyaev has even maintained that the Orthodox Russian Christian is not only superior to his Byzantine co-religionist but owes nothing to him. In point of fact the Russian people are humbler, more gentle and of a more simple holiness than their Byzantine counterparts. Russian saints, for the most part of lowly origin, have a freshness of outlook very different from that of the great and awe-inspiring ascetics of Greece and the Christian East. Compassion plays a large part in the Russian religion, the compassion that man pleads for in the famous 'prayer of Jesus' and also the compassion that man gives to man, his brothers, the ever-present compassion of God. To Tolstoy, Christianity was essentially compassion; it contributed towards making religion a communal thing, on earth as in heaven, according to the dogma of the Communion of Saints. It is through this that one can find an explanation of one of the deepest traits of the Russian religious soul: the sense of universality, of the cosmic, of a mission upon earth. The true Russian believer knows that he belongs to a people who have been chosen by God, and that his role is to 'lead the salvation of the world', a grandiose idea which Communism took over, adapted and made to serve its own ends.

10. EARTHBOUND TRAVELLERS AND HEAVENLY PILGRIMS

The search for the divine absolute, which is such a marked feature of the Russian religious soul, tends to produce a great variety of different types of people. It may be pursued inwardly, in a monastery or hermitage buried deep in a forest. It may find an outlet in the kind of fever that drives a man restlessly out into the world: indeed the pilgrim, the eternal hunter of the absolute, is a typically Russian figure. The Church of Holy Russia offers innumerable examples. Early Christian ascetics undertook long and exhausting marches; they were wanderers, exiles from home, family and country, possessing nothing, not even a stone on which to lay their heads, as it was with Jesus Christ. Russian Christians have followed their example in every century. However far back we go in their history we find incalculable numbers of the pious wandering with their bundles on their backs— each bundle containing a loaf of bread, a lump of salt, a tea kettle and the Gospels. They prayed before venerated icons, in a monastery where some holy man lived, or even went as far afield as Mount Athos or the Holy Places of Palestine. In the nineteenth and early twentieth centuries this race of people was still flourishing, and we may conjecture that it is still alive today.

Some of the wanderers show strange characteristics, such that moderate people might consider due to mental derangement. The *strannik* we can accept—a wanderer who never stays in one place but is constantly on the march, who has no definite aim except perhaps to seek out the least trace of God. Stranger still is the *yurodivi*, the 'God-crazed', who purposely dresses and behaves so as to draw upon himself every insult and humiliation in imitation of Christ. This particular type of man is dear to the Russian soul. There is one in *Boris Godunov*, and Tolstoy's Gricha speaks of one he knew. The type is not unknown in Western Catholicism, but in Russian history it is quite natural and accepted. One of the finest basilicas in Moscow is dedicated to a *yurodivi*; and in Leningrad the eighteenth-century *yurodivia* Xenia is commemorated for her virtues.

Without going as far as the excesses of the 'God-crazed', there are many Russians who secretly desire to emulate these wanderers; the literature of the nineteenth century is full of such pilgrims, and they are always presented in sympathetic terms. Writers themselves have been fascinated by the nomadic life: think of Leontiev, Soloviev and

Tolstoy, who after abandoning his family set out, as Kologrivov puts it: 'like a wounded lion in search of a lair there to hide and die in peace'. Whether celebrated or unknown, all these pilgrims resemble each other in the strength of their faith and their hope. Anyone who has seen them at prayer in the Holy Places of Palestine, before the Holy Sepulchre or in Bethlehem, can judge the strength of the faith which drives them, and the depth of their piety.

One book in particular evokes this spiritual experience: *The Story of a Pilgrim*. Despite, or perhaps because of, the extreme frankness with which the author exposes his sins, it is admirable in its sincerity, and it is illumined by the faith that moves mountains, a faith knowing instinctively that, as Léon Bloy has put it, 'everything that happens is worthy of adoration'.

First published in 1865 at Kazan, it became famous only in the early twentieth century. The author is quite unknown. He was a simple peasant, aged thirty-three, who wandered across Russia and Siberia after the Crimean War, before the abolition of serfdom—at some period between 1856 and 1861—blessed with a lively intelligence, a certain degree of religious culture, but above all with a violent desire for salvation. It may have been a monk from Athos or Optina who wrote down the story from the facts supplied by the pilgrim. It is a literary masterpiece. It exposes all levels of society, from the prince who as a recluse expiates his life of debauchery and violence to the convicts, chained together, marching to distant Siberian prison camps. The Russian landscape is skilfully evoked. But the essence of the story is the spiritual witness of the pilgrim concerned. One cannot help a feeling of brotherly affection for this sinner and his people to whom the Kingdom is promised.

In contrast, the other important division of Russian religion is represented by the monk, garbed and hooded in black; and to a lesser extent the enclosed nun, less well known but none the less respected. Their roles are identical: prayer unceasing to God. The figures cited [1] demonstrate the importance of monasticism in Russian religious life, an importance greater than in the West for reasons connected with the very conception in Orthodoxy of religious experience. When one accepts, as Dostoyevsky puts it, that 'Christianity is not for this world, nor for the men therein', there is no alternative but to shut onself away from the world in some holy retreat, there to pray and await the end of time. The conception of monasticism as being in opposition to the actual world, which as we saw [2] is basic Orthodoxy, a logical result of its refusal to accept temporal ties, has nowhere else but in Russia known such a degree of conscious and radical expression. Leontiev, Rozanov and many other religious thinkers have said: 'Christianity

---

[1] See Chapter IV, section 9.   [2] Chapter IV, section 3.

finds its total integration only in the monastery. Christian society and the Christian family are problems. The monastery is a fact. Outside the walls of the monastery Christianity is in chaos. It is alive only in us!'

Monks are therefore essentially contemplative. The Western type of mendicant monk, whether Franciscan or Dominican, or a religious after the manner of the Oratorians or the Jesuits who take on certain specific apostolic tasks, is unknown in Russia. The monks there have— in theory—no other function but prayer, and it is in accordance with the degree and perfection of their prayer that we differentiate them, the eremites being credited with higher qualities than the cenobites, as is customary in Greek Orthodoxy. In decline in the eighteenth century, monasticism made considerable progress during the nine- teenth century. Better men were recruited; the abbots, chosen by the Holy Synod, were more devout; stricter attention was paid to obser- vances, especially in the larger monasteries, any erring monks being sent away to distant solitudes. It was above all with regard to the inner soul that the renewal was active, and here again we find evidence of the importance of the *Philocalia*, which was published in Moscow in 1794 and soon became the key work in monastic piety. It led to a resurgence of the custom of perpetual prayer, of the 'prayer of the heart' or 'prayer of Jesus', which during the great days of past ages had sus- tained the faith of the humble and exalted the mystics. The return to hesychastic practice [1] is one of the most striking characteristics of the renewal accomplished by monasticism.

This has led to certain consequences for the Russian Church as a whole. From the moment when the monastery was looked upon as a form of archetypal Kingdom of God, and was the home of men who could be venerated and imitated, the power of example played its part. The simple faithful could ask counsel and take lessons from the monasteries; monasticism could then become, as it did, the agent of religious ferment.

The man who began the movement for religious renewal through a revitalized monasticism died in 1794, but his work continues to have results today. He was Paissy Velochkovsky, a Ukrainian intellectual who, disgusted with worldly wisdom and discouraged by routine theology, went to live in the solitudes of Mount Athos, there to acquire considerable renown and influence, partly through his learning and partly through his charismatic gifts and his gift of prophecy. He re- formed the methods then employed in the life of prayer, drawing from the *Philocalia* and hesychastic discipline; on his return to Russia he founded monasteries based on his new ideas and thus began a long tradition of spiritual men and saints.

It is in relation to his work that we must consider the development

[1] See Chapter IV, section 3.

of a particular type of man, well known in Russia over the centuries, who came into prominence in nineteenth-century religious life: the *starets*. In theory he is an older monk, no different from others; he is not always a member of the monastic hierarchy, nor necessarily is he the abbot; but the saintliness of his life, his wisdom and sometimes his charismatic gifts are all so obvious that he stands out from the others. Young monks confide in him as in a spiritual father. Some of the *startzi* lecture on the writings of the great masters to the members of their communities; others prefer private discussions and counsel. The *starets* soon acquired a considerable reputation; from far and wide visitors come to him to listen, to confess their sins, to receive words of comfort in affliction. Before they leave he blesses them, gives them the kiss of peace. No penitents can resist tears on parting, the words of his farewell, 'Christ is risen!' ringing in their ears.

The development of the *startzi* in the nineteenth century is undoubtedly one of the dominant features of the Russian religious scene. The majority of officially recognized saints began as *startzi*; there is mention of them in Russian literature—in *The Brothers Karamazov*, for instance. As they became more famous so they became exposed to criticism. Some bishops, enthusiastic for real reforms, upheld the *startzi*; others viewed their influence with suspicion. 'It is their fault', they said, 'that the shepherd has no flock!' And they added that the crowds of visitors troubled the monastic calm. The greatest *startzi* were often at loggerheads with the bishops of their dioceses, particularly those of Optina.

To every Russian, Optina is a symbol of something great and holy. It lies in Kaluga, in a region so sparsely populated that it may be considered both temporally and spiritually a desert. At the end of the eighteenth century it had declined so much that there were only three monks left. Refurbished by the Metropolitan Plato of Moscow and taken in hand by one of Macarius's disciples, himself a disciple of Velochkovsky, it arose anew spiritually, and throughout the nineteenth century until the period of the Russian Revolution it was the most lively and celebrated centre of Russian religious renewal.

It was fortunate for Optina that it was led by men of high spiritual qualities—Theophanes, who reconstructed the monastery in 1800; Nagolkine (1763–1841), 'God-crazed', a man athirst for the absolute; Macarius Ivanov (1788–1860). Macarius Ivanov was a man of a quite different character. His cell was filled with books which he read and reread; he commented on the *Philocalia* and the works of the Fathers; he spoke slowly and meditatively, but his voice shook with emotion and his face streamed with tears when he celebrated the Divine Liturgy. His fame soon spread far from Optina, drawing penitents from every walk of life, including Gogol and the Grand Duke Constantine. From the year 1880 Optina was headed by 'the most important personage in Russian history at that time', Alexander Grenkov (1812–91), known as the *starets* Ambrose. He was another exceptional man; his wealth of spiritual experience was undoubtedly of great value to Orthodoxy and his influence was immense. (Dostoyevsky almost certainly had him in mind when creating the character of Father Zosima in *The Brothers Karamazov*, though the monks of Optina have never acknowledged the resemblance between their monastery and the monastery of the book.) Innumerable people came to Optina to see him: the imperial senator, the old peasant, the university professor, the socialite from Moscow—all were equal in his eyes, all were conscience-stricken souls whom he comforted as best he could. To this man of God there also came members of the intelligentsia such as Khomiakov, the greatest of lay theologians; Leontiev, who came to Optina to die; Dostoyevsky on two occasions; the young Soloviev in 1878. And it was in the desert of Optina that Tolstoy, on his way to the convent of Khamordina, where his sister was a nun, died in the little station of Astapovo. The saintly austerity and serenity of the *starets* Ambrose dominated Russian spiritual life in those years; he was the living expression of everything venerable in Orthodoxy.

11. THREE SAINTS OF HOLY RUSSIA

The Russian Church at the end of the eighteenth century, anaemic, fossilized and reduced to mere functionalism, was in full expansion during the nineteenth century, and under conditions that were by no means the most favourable. Several signs of renewal were noted, principally a greater depth of holiness. One of the basic tenets of Orthodoxy, as with Catholicism, is that holiness is the touchstone of the health of any religion, and that the history of any Church is above all the history of its holiness; and few would deny, whatever the canonical sense we give to the term, that the Russia of contemporary history has produced its saints.

The saints of Holy Russia are, in the main, monks—founders of monasteries, *startzi*—because the most exemplary religious life is that of the cloistered monk, alone in his quest for God. This is tantamount to saying that there is little variety in the gallery of Russian saints, at least as far as external appearances are concerned. Only rarely do we find any of them resembling the 'mystics in action' of the Catholic West: John of Kronstadt is perhaps the only one. But this does not mean to say that behind the austere similarities of external appearances there is no real diversity; every soul has a different path to salvation, and a different method of answering the call of the Saviour.

On the threshold of the age when Marx and Nietzsche proclaimed the death of God and the certain destruction of all religion, came St Seraphin of Sarov (1759–1833), the good saint beloved of the pious Russian masses, an amalgam of St Francis of Assisi, St Anthony and the great evangelists, a man exceptional in every way. After a long and mysterious illness he sought solitude as a hermit in the forests of Sarov. But this abnegation was still not enough. While the world trembled and the Napoleonic armies seemed about to reduce Holy Russia to servitude he undertook still more rigorous penitence in imitation of the old Stylites by kneeling for a thousand days and nights on a stone. Then this great ascetic, on the instructions of the Blessed Virgin, renounced his eremitic existence and became a spokesman for Christ. He welcomed the many people who came to his door; innumerable souls were touched by his infinite sweetness, his unbounded compassion and still more by the spiritual quickening which his very presence engendered in them.

Theophanes the Recluse (1815–94) was the spiritual brother and disciple of Seraphin, and professed the same doctrine of abandoning everything for God, of certainty in the Holy Spirit and of universal grace. But he applied his faith differently, just as his terrestrial life was different from that of the saint of Sarov. The brilliant student of the ecclesiastical Academy of Kiev appeared to have his route ready made before him. Later, as a monk, his studies terminated, he was obviously destined to become a bishop. He became a religious inspector, then Rector of the ecclesiastical school of Moscow where he demonstrated his talents as an eminent educator. A stay in Jerusalem then followed, and here he helped the Russian pilgrims in the Holy Places. Then he became Bishop of Vladimir and later of Tambov. He was an exemplary shepherd, devoted to his flock, helping the more unfortunate of them through times of stress, always ready to lend a hand in the carpenter's shop or the pottery. Suddenly, in 1866, he resigned all his offices and went into seclusion at the Vysun hermitage, remaining there for twenty-two years, to all intents and purposes cut off from the world, though in fact the volume of correspondence which came to him there showed that he continued to be conscious of the sorrows and miseries of many, and to be always ready with counsel and encouragement, even advising many *startzi* who sought his help. During this time he wrote his books, exegetics, commentaries on St Paul, the Psalms, and especially his *Way of Salvation* and his treatise entitled *What is Spiritual Life?* There was much of St Francis de Sales in him: he was simple, direct, deeply human, experienced in the preoccupations of ordinary man from his long period of pastoral activities. Orthodox theology and spirituality were through his efforts brought within the grasp of those faithful who were prepared to make the effort to understand; the ascetic way of life which he formulated pointed the way from the first stirrings of conscience up to the highest point of spiritual reality. The 'prayer of the heart' became through his efforts a means available to all. He was canonized on his death.

With John of Kronstadt (1829–1908) Orthodox saintliness took a new step forward, away from the walls of monasteries and hermitages —a step, one might say, towards the Western ideal. The roots of its spirituality were, however, the same as those of the other Russian saints, and with them he was concerned only to bring about the reign of the Holy Ghost upon earth, to equate human life to the grace which filled the three Apostles when on Mount Tabor they witnessed the Transfiguration.

In his view the search for God was not confined to a life spent in solitude and silence. These things he knew and practised, but they left room for love of the most active kind. The son of a poor priest, he had known misery and hunger. He was sent at the age of twenty-seven to take charge of the parish of Kronstadt on the Baltic. His parishioners were seamen and artisans, dockers and convicts from the penal settlement, all living in near-slums. His generosity became a byword, and although he was married he gave away stipend, clothing, food and crockery so selflessly that his colleagues intervened and had his monthly State stipend paid to his wife! In 1882 he opened his 'Work House', a town within the town, housing twenty-five thousand people and providing shelters, refectories, hospitals and schools, a settlement similar to that of Cottolengo at Turin and others. John of Kronstadt became famous; his miracles multiplied; letters flowed in from all over the world; the Archbishop of Canterbury came to see him. The priest was a wonderfully gentle man with a welcome for everyone, and he seemed to incarnate all that was brotherly and moving in Christianity. His popularity was so great that ten years after his death the Bolsheviks had his body removed from his tomb. But one wonders if this will erase his memory from the hearts of men or if people on that account forget the straightforward recital of his life's work in his book, *Life in Christ*.

12. THE 'INTELLIGENTSIA' AND GOD

Russian Christianity had witnesses other than the mystics, the *startzi* and the saints in the period we are examining. One of the most important features was the return of a considerable portion of Russia's 'intelligentsia', as it was called, to religion. This took place some time before the same current was observed in the West, where great literature turned towards Catholicism. An increasing number of writers found inspiration in the ancient Orthodox faith and in its spiritual traditions. The Russian religious soul was from then on reflected by the most reputable masters, and this meant that it became vastly better known outside Russia.

Like every other great creative current which has aroused the emotions and feelings of a people, this too had obscure sources. Why should the 'intelligentsia', who during the eighteenth century had almost completely embraced French ideas of Voltaire and the Encyclopedists, return in the nineteenth century to their Christian roots? Hegelians and Marxists would see dialectical principles at work here. Berdyaev, one of the last witnesses among us of the spiritual renewal of Russian letters, saw the cause in the intuition that catastrophe was not far off—the catastrophe in which traditional Holy Russia actually foundered. Since 1830, he said, Lermontov had been proclaiming the coming betrayal. The feeling of belonging to a condemned world, to a society out of step with the future, drove them to seek refuge in the forces which had in times past ensured the greatness of ancient Russia. Nearly all great Christian writers in our age are similarly affected, faced as they are with the end of time and the end of the world, and secretly torn between opposing principles; their concern for the future is that of a Dostoyevsky with his particular type of religious sensibility.

This current joined another, not at all religious, which sprang from certain historical conceptions. Emerging victorious from the Napoleonic onslaught, Russia sought to become the guide and leader of nations under the role assigned to it by the Czar, Alexander I, in the Holy Alliance. This conception fitted in well with her ideas of racial Messiahship. Russia had a special vocation: from its depths it drew its ethics, its way of life and its thought. The heiress of Byzantium, not only must it claim the role held by the Basileis, but it must gather together all brethren of the same blood and faith, except the renegade Poles.

Born of reaction against the revolutionary ideas of the French, the movement known as Slavophile was necessarily Christian and Christian Orthodox. The national Messianic dream now joined with that of the 'Third Rome', which had become current since the Patriarchate had been established in Moscow. Holy Russia would have to be rebuilt —on top of the secularizing reforms of Peter the Great, some said! The Russian people, the predestined guardians of the true faith, offered an example in their village community life of fraternal evangelistic existence. The monks, the pilgrims and the 'God-crazed', all were messengers of true Christianity. It was all very confused, but it was all very exhilarating and appealed to the common people. The movement gained ground among leading thinkers and writers.

In opposition to the Slavophile school of thought there was the pro-Western school, which was nothing more than an extension of Western rationalist movements. German idealism had great influence on this, as did Socialism and Marxism, the latter being well able to use for its own ends the deep Messianic aspirations of the Russian soul. Agnosticism and atheism soon took a firm hold on the pro-Western school; Ivan Karamazov's character was the perfect example.

The greatest of the Russian writers came to the fore in this struggle between religion and irreligion. Not that they were all Slavophile in the precise meaning of the term. Gogol (1809–52), the satirist and author of *Dead Souls*, was a mystic, frequently going on pilgrimages to Jerusalem. He was opposed both to the rationalists on the one hand and on the other to certain aspects of Slavophile thought in the matter of national religion, which he held was too often cut off from all Christian conceptions of social and personal life. Gogol's views aroused fury and he was accused of selling out to Rome. Lermontov (1814–41), another master of Russian prose, whose flamboyant life ended prematurely in a duel at the age of twenty-seven, declined to accept the Slavophile conception of Holy Russia led by its autocrats, and felt torn between mystical tendencies and intuitions of catastrophe; he was Nietzsche's predecessor.

From the middle of the nineteenth century the religious and national currents seemed to be carrying the day. Fedor Toutchev (1803–73) wrote the famous hymn to the soil of Russia that every Russian learnt by heart. It was also at this time that Alexis Khomiakov (1804–60), that pure and noble Christian figure, set out to establish the theology of the Slavophile movement and took up his stand as an adversary of Catholicism, yet at the same time proposed a mystic formula concerning the freedom of man within God, of love as a means to knowledge, which a Catholic could not but admire. He influenced several men of letters, among them Dostoyevsky and Soloviev—who owed his return to faith to him—and even Tolstoy, who after reading his work was almost brought back to the Church he had accused of lacking in love. Many writers thereafter were haunted by the problem of religion, and each of them according to their particular temperament set forth contradictory answers.

The two greatest of them were Dostoyevsky (1821–81) and Tolstoy (1828–1910). Are they truly representative of the Russian faith? There has been much discussion on this point. As for Tolstoy, the reply must be in the negative. In any case, both are unimpeachable witnesses of the imperious desire for the absolute, the passion for God which so many Russians have, the same passion which drives the 'God-crazed' along their wandering path or the penitent to sit at the feet of a *starets*.

Every Christian is aware of the debt owed to Dostoyevsky. This unhappy man, dogged by ill luck and misery, whose unprepossessing appearance disquieted the employees of the banks and money-lenders whom he approached for loans, was afflicted by the dreadful tragedy of man—choice between belief and unbelief. Like the characters of his novels, it was not so much his fits of epilepsy that disturbed him nor even the haunting fear of the morrow or the malice of others— but God. In the last analysis there is only one subject in his works: it is not the relations between men or their relations with society, but their relations with God. He does not find these relations a simple matter, as simple as they might be for ordinary men; for him, they are burning issues in a world where everything may be thrown into question at any moment. He himself said: 'My faith in Christ is not that of a child; it has been forged in the furnace of doubt.' He carried within him all the most contradictory desires. He descends to the uttermost depths of Russian mysticism; at the same time, he under-stands perfectly the aspirations of the nihilists and the atheists in the 'intelligentsia' of the Westernized movement. His type of Christianity is one of tragic and anguished conflicts, perhaps somewhat Manichaean. The conflicts between the characters in his works merely reflect his own inner conflicts. In the whole of literature there are no characters spiritually greater than the pilgrim Macarius in *The Adolescent,* Arch-bishop Tikhon in *The Possessed*, the *starets* of *The Brothers Karama?ov* and Prince Mishkin in *The Idiot*. At the same time, it would be difficult to find more resolute destroyers of God than Ivan Karamazov or Kirilov. No one understood better than Dostoyevsky the realities of radical atheism, not even Nietzsche, who greatly admired him. Yet out of all these conflicts, these contradictory postulates, this agon-ized realization of the distress of man without God, there emerges a strong and sublime song of faith which is most moving. In sum, he was a staunch believer, an Orthodox Christian, Slavophile by nature, convinced that all Russia was in Orthodoxy and that Orthodoxy was alone the source of all light. He was violently anti-Roman—the legend of the Grand Inquisitor in *The Brothers Karama?ov* proves this—and yet he was the spokesman for a new type of Christianity, a universal Christianity, in which brotherly love, issuing forth from Russia's monasteries where mystics prayed, would spread all over the world. Dostoyevsky was a Nietszche saved by the Blood of Christ.

For a long time the West saw in Tolstoy a typical representative of Russian Christianity. In actual fact he had certain communal ideas, a tendency towards sectarianism of a more or less rationalist kind, and reflected only the more popular side of religion. Of all the great Russian thinkers, he is certainly the most distant from Orthodox spirituality, the least touched by mysticism. Yet haunted by the problem of God he too, especially in his more mature years, came to discover the absurdity of life and the reality of death. In *Anna Karenina* his hero too is faced with the impossibility of living without knowing what he is nor why he is here. To this Tolstoy supplies an answer through the voice of a humble *moujik*, that one must not live for self, but for God. This God whom he finds so necessary he does not know how to seek with the humility and openness of heart that will enable him to find Him. While Tolstoy attempted to descend to the level of any common vagabond, to imitate the 'God-crazed' by setting out on the roads of Russia as they did, he was never able to experience misery, suffering and imprisonment as Dostoyevsky—though not from choice—had done before him. Tolstoy was driven to a total refusal of the Established Church, of middle-class society, of literature and of art; he substituted the rejected dogmas with a type of modernism which provided him with neither peace nor certitude. He was anguished by the fact that he could not surrender totally to the call. He was torn between the inner appeal which he could hear and which his rationalist inclinations could not altogether stifle. Tolstoy's conflict is that he could not follow Jesus for fear of abandoning himself; yet he admires the message of Christ and would have it become a universal rule of life. This leads him to evangelism without Christ, an untenable position admired by the rationalists whom he despises; he is the propagandist for Communism by what he denies, but its enemy by what he affirms. No true believer can contemplate his tragic end without infinite compassion; it seems to set the seal on his unsatisfied and desperate wandering. But above all the manifest insufficiencies there remains the great love for humanity which emerges from all his writing and which attains in some indefinable way the charity of Christ.

A finer image of Russian Christianity is shown in the works of lesser writers than Dostoyevsky and Tolstoy, who showed only rather deformed versions of it to the outside world. The most important of these lesser writers was Leontiev (1831–91), who was, according to the most traditional of the Orthodox, the truest representative of the faith. Of a fiery nature, avid for life, he was by turns officer, diplomat, traveller and civil servant. Turned away from agnosticism by a religious crisis, he was later as determinedly religious as he had once been irreligious, a pilgrim to Mount Athos (whose monks refused him admittance) and lastly a penitent at the feet of the *starets* Ambrose. He became a novice and later a monk at Optina, where he died. Leontiev embodied Russian Christianity in all its absolutism. He detested the modern world of progress with its social and egalitarian ideas; his system of thought was opposed to that of Tolstoy and Dostoyevsky. In his view truth sprang from the scrupulous observance of tradition, in the hieratism of a religion indomitably opposed to humanitarianism and liberalism, in which the ascetic struggle against sin went hand in hand with the fight against every innovation likely to damage religious observances. There is much of the stubborn monk in this great spirit, yet nevertheless he knew how to praise beauty and strength in Nietzschean terms. No other representative of the 'intelligentsia' gave, as he did, the impression of being a Byzantine transported to the modern age.

Soloviev (1853–1900) demonstrated the other aspect of Russian religious faith, a community and universal aspect found in the grandiose dreams of the Slavophiles and the Panslavists and in the mystical aspirations of the people towards universal brotherhood. He was an admirable and moving figure—his friends considered that he could have served as a model of Christ for an icon. He was a dialectician and a poet with a wide culture, able to understand both the genius of Russia and that of the West. He occupies a unique place in the world of Russian letters. Separated from his faith by the works of Renan and Strauss in his youth, he returned to it at twenty years of age after a spiritual journey which reminds one of Rimbaud's. He devoted himself throughout his short life to seeking out the spiritual bases of life, to rediscovering the means to attain perfect inner harmony. He was a Slavophile early on in life, but left this movement when he began to know the West better, aware of the fact that if Russia wanted to undertake a universal mission it could not be done merely through sterile opposition. The Orthodox Church appeared to him to be too narrow in its perspectives; perfect perhaps as the 'Church that prays', but of no use as the 'Church that acts'. He considered that Russian spirituality needed the addition of social action, of charity in action; moreover he himself put this into practice. Later he became convinced that to achieve unity in Christianity it would be necessary for all Christians to be reconciled in a united Church. This unifying element he saw in the Church of Rome, and he became converted to Catholicism without ceasing to be profoundly Orthodox in the original sense of the word, always regarding himself as the herald of reconciliation between the Eastern and Western Churches.[1]

The list of writers haunted by the problem of God does not end with Soloviev and the end of the nineteenth century; it continues today. But those who followed the great masters of the nineteenth century belonged to a society threatened by the approach of what many considered to be so near, the final catastrophe. Many expressed this in their writings, tinged as they were by apocalyptic mysticism, no stranger to the Russian religious mind. One was Vassili Rozanov (1856–1919), whom Berdyaev characterized as a garrulous genius, a kind of Léon Bloy of Orthodoxy, but a Léon Bloy showing himself at the same time as a vehement adversary of Christ and conducting himself as a believer; a curious personage, eternally at war with the world and himself, who

[1] See Chapter VI, section 4.

ended his life in misery. He died in the convent where his daughter was a nun. There was also Dmitri Merejowsky (1866–1941), another apocalyptic prophet. A sincere and true believer, he celebrated the coming of the Paraclete, but inclined to ignore the real hierarchies and sought to discover a more authentic Christ in the Apocrypha. Attracted by Julian the Apostate and the myth of the antichrist, he bears witness to a society eaten up by doubt and fascinated by suspect esoterics. Ivan Bunin (1870–1953) was yet another example: an ardent exponent in poetry and prose of Russia and its people, of ancient fealties, of all the sacred heritage of his country which he carried with him in his heart when the revolution drove him out. The sincerity and power of expression in his work, continued in exile, earned him the Nobel Prize for Literature in 1933.

The revolution did not put a stop to this flow of Christian literature. Just before it broke out there had been a religious revival among the younger writers, similar to that in France in the Bergson era. Staunch Marxists became converted first to Kantian idealism then to Christianity: Struve, Bulgakov, Berdyaev were among the best known. During exile they continued to bear witness to Russian Christianity, just as the 'intelligentsia' had done before them. P. B. Struve (1870–1944), an Encyclopedist, politician, historian, philosopher, philologist and critic, who has been compared to the famous nineteenth-century critic Bielinski, continued to exercise the same degree of influence in Paris, where he lived in exile from 1918, and where he died in 1944 after a sojourn in Nazi prisons. Bulgakov (1874–1944), a professor of political economy, who became a priest in 1918 in protest against the attacks of triumphant atheism, was known in Paris as Father Bulgakov and produced a considerable volume of controversial literary work— on Mariology, the role of St John the Baptist, the angels, uncreated Wisdom and the mystery of the Incarnation. Nicholas Berdyaev (1874–1948), the persuasive exponent of a New Middle Age—or of Christianity redefined in the light of our age—a profound analyst of Communism and of its role as 'arbiter' of a society insufficiently Christian, exercised an influence on many French thinkers from Jacques Maritain to Emmanuel Mounier. They were all witnesses for Christ and for Holy Russia. Even though Marxist materialism appears to have imposed its will on Russia, they may be thought of as witnesses who might still have brothers and emulators within the U.S.S.R., especially if we remember a recent Nobel Prize winner: Boris Pasternak was a Christian.

13. RUSSIAN ORTHODOX MISSIONS

'The only people who spread God's word are the Russian people,' said Dostoyevsky. The missionary activities of Holy Russia at that time did not seem to bear this out, though it could have been applied to earlier ages. As the Princes of Moscow extended their territorial grip, so the missionaries followed. In the fifteenth and sixteenth centuries they gathered in Kazan (1552), Astrakhan (1556) and the vastness of Siberia. Many of them were canonized by the Russian Church. In the seventeenth century the Metropolitan of Tobolsk had sent his emissaries as far as Kamchatka and Yakutsk; there was even a mission to Peking. But the expansion slowed down at the end of the eighteenth century and the missions lost ground in the same way as did the Catholic missions. The movement got under way again in the nineteenth century under the impulse of the empire's colonial ambitions and also inspired by grandiose ideas—interpreted by Dostoyevsky as the Russian vocation—of spreading the word of God throughout the world.

The man responsible for stirring up this sense of vocation was a layman, Nicholas Ilminsky, an outstanding polyglot who had a command of all the languages of central Asia. He was disquieted to see the progress made by Islam and set up at Kazan a study and training centre for would-be missionaries. An Orthodox library was set up for the Tartars and other tribes. He adapted the liturgy for some twenty autochthonous languages. He considered, just as the Catholics did, that in order to implant Christianity firmly, it was necessary to create autochthonous Churches with their own clergy, and he trained Asiatic priests, who received help from the St Gurij Fraternity. In 1899, for example, in the diocese of Samara, there were forty-seven priests, twelve deacons, and twenty readers. His efforts were seconded by those of Bishop Veliaminov, who set up missionary dioceses in Siberia, at Kamchatka and in the Aleutians, and who in 1870, when he was Metropolitan of Moscow, created the Orthodox Missionary Society.

Missionary expansion went ahead in all directions—first towards Siberia and central Asia, both of which were coming under Russian Government control to an increasing extent. In 1830 the Archimandrite Macarius founded the Altai Mission, which thirty years later had 25,000 Christians. In eastern Siberia, Father Veniaminov—whom we mentioned earlier—worked indefatigably, covering the most desolate regions with his emissaries; he could lay claim to having converted some 125,000 heathen. Alaska came next, by way of the Bering Strait, then part of western Canada, where Monsignor Coudert, the Catholic Bishop of the Yukon, referred to the presence of Russian missionaries with some annoyance. There were undeniably great difficulties, and one cannot doubt the high sense of missionary purpose shown by the missionaries in these territories. An interesting book, *Memories of Missions in Siberia*, written by a monk, Spiridon, gives lively details of his work among the natives and convicts.

In China, where for over two centuries the missions had been unable to convert more than a few hundreds, the movement expanded from the time when czars first began to display an interest in the country. The Patriarch of Moscow divided China into five regions, the whole presided over by an Exarch resident in Peking. The mission here was responsible for many important subordinate organizations, including some twenty schools for more than ten thousand Christians. After the 1917 Revolution many Russians emigrated to China and the influx strengthened Orthodox representation there. The Communist victory in China meant that both Orthodox and Catholic missions suffered the same fate. All the Russian members of Orthodox missions left. There remained an autonomous Chinese Church with its own Chinese clergy, notably the bishops of Peking and Shanghai. The three remaining dioceses had no one at their head. Today there are still two Orthodox monasteries and a catechetical school which the Communist authorities have allowed to remain open.

The Orthodox Mission was founded in Korea in 1897, but did not prosper. In 1912 there were 820 adherents spread over nine stations. After the Russian Revolution it ceased to function, but it was reopened after the Second World War by the Greek diocese in America, with two Korean priests.

It was in Japan that the best results were obtained. The mission founded in 1853 was given a considerable impetus in 1870 by Father (later Archbishop) Nicholas Kassatkin, who converted more than twenty thousand Japanese in twenty years. His first task was to translate the liturgy into Japanese and, as soon as circumstances permitted, to ordain autochthonous priests. At the end of the nineteenth century there were 219 Orthodox churches in Japan, the most majestic of them being the Tokyo cathedral, the most famous religious edifice in the capital—the Japanese still refer to it as *Nicolai Do* (the house of Nicholas). The first Japanese bishop was consecrated in 1940 and seventy Japanese priests care for forty-five thousand adherents.

Missions also went to the south—towards Iran, the Near East, even as far as Ethiopia. A mission founded at Urmia with the object of bringing the Iranian Nestorians back into the fold was destroyed in 1918 by the Turks; it was restored in 1922, but produced very few results. In Palestine, Russian Orthodoxy set up a mission, convents and rest-houses for pilgrims—there were 112 in 1912—which the Palestine Society has been responsible for ever since 1882; after the revolution the decline was rapid, and today there are only two monasteries and a few hospices, helped discreetly by the Soviet Government. But the most curious venture of Orthodox missions was that in Ethiopia. The Archimandrite Paissy, a former Cossack, after numerous campaigns in Central Asia, became a monk in 1862 and founded a hospice for pilgrims at Constantinople. Later he was charged by the Moscow Patriarchate with the task of accompanying the Ataman Achinov to Ethiopia, where the latter wished to found a Cossack colony near Addis Ababa. In this he had the support of the Negus. The mission was so well established that it still survives, and today there are several hundred Orthodox Christians in Ethiopia.

The story of the Orthodox missions denies the suggestion, too often heard, that the Orthodox Church was a servile instrument in the hands of the czars. The vitality it displayed on the spiritual plane—the same as was displayed by the leaders of the 'intelligentsia'—is evident. With the advent of the Soviet regime the missions suffered from political ups and downs; sometimes they were ignored, sometimes accepted, even assisted. In 1945 the Missionary Society was reconstituted. The missions seek to 'Orthodoxize', or rather to 'Russify', the Catholic populations which were annexed after the Second World War in the Baltic countries and the Ukraine, and it seems that the same sort of methods which were once used to bring the Uniates to heel have also been used here. The policy of setting up autochthonous Churches has continued; various Soviet republics have their own elected bishops and clergy. With regard to Korea and Palestine, Russian emigrants in the U.S.A. have shown a great deal of interest in missionary activities. Whatever the future may hold for it under the Soviet regime, Russian Christianity is still very much alive.

14. From the Raskol to the New Sects

No picture of contemporary religious life in Russia would be complete without some mention of the strange and often muddled story of the sects. A phenomenon analogous to that observed in Protestantism is also evident in Russian Orthodoxy, but for diametrically opposite reasons. Protestantism's Churches and sects stem from its basic principle, liberty—liberty of belief, liberty with regard to obedience. The Russian sects, on the other hand, were the result of reaction against authoritarianism and conformism in a Church under secular influence. The sects have always offered to those who felt themselves subjected to a too disciplined, too passive religious life, contacts that were more fraternal and of greater spiritual liberty. This explains why Orthodoxy, which had never been really badly disrupted by any of the grave crises of Western Catholicism—the Renaissance, the Reformation, the French Revolution, liberalism and lastly modernism—had, in the vacuum in which it found itself since the time of Peter the Great, undergone deviations natural to itself and bearing all the characteristics of the Russian tradition. These sects were not unimportant, for on the eve of the 1917 Revolution there were 20 million adherents.

The largest of the sects, more like a Church separated from the Church of Russia than a mere sect, had its own hierarchy and its own well-known edifices—this was that of the Old Believers. It emerged from the Raskol or schism of the seventeenth century led by the Archpriest Avvacum as a protest against the liturgical reforms of the Patriarch Nikon. Before this, Russia had known only minor heresies: the Strigolniki of the thirteenth century, or a type of Catharists with austere morals, hostile towards corrupt clergy; the Judaizers of the fifteenth century, who began in the Novgorod region, spreading all over Russia, even to the entourage of the Grand Duke Ivan III, and who based their faith upon a very narrow interpretation of the Bible. Raskol itself in the beginning was no more than a split with the Established Church, which it accused of being unfaithful to true traditions in liturgical matters—we know what great importance is attached to liturgy in the Orthodox world. The Old Believers observed old traditions, such as blessing with two fingers, singing the Hallelujah twice and not three times during Lent, prohibition of the use of mirrors by priests, even refusing the minimum modifications introduced by Nikon to the Apostles' Creed. They were looked upon as rebels by the imperial authorities, but they heroically withstood, under Avvacum, the trials of persecution, even going so far as to commit mass suicide rather than submit. All through the eighteenth century they were persecuted (only one czar, Peter III, left them in peace). The Raskolniki still lived and managed even to increase their numbers. Their undoubted virtues turned them into a rich middle class, as traders and ship owners on the great rivers. But the problem of recruitment of priests, always one which is presented to sects separated from their mother Church, brought about splits in their ranks.

It was only in 1905 that all the different varieties of Old Believers were officially accepted, immediately after the reforms introduced following the Russo-Japanese war. Reorganized in 1923, after the dark hours of the revolutionary period and having gathered together all the most vital elements of their faith, the Old Believers Orthodox Church appears to have recovered its place and now has some 20 million adherents. In February 1961 it elected, with much official pomp, its Patriarch.

Alongside this movement, which, despite certain excesses, deserves respect, past ages saw the birth of less responsible sects, which neither the passage of time nor persecution has managed to wipe out. The Russian review *Kommunist* remarked that even after forty years of re-education the Marxist regime had not succeeded in suppressing them. There are the Klysty, the Skakouny, the Subbotniki and the Skopsy. The last was fiercely persecuted under the czars and the Communists, but in 1930, according to the Great Soviet Encyclopedia, the sect still existed.

The Doukhobors are a type of sect quite different from the Old Believers. The first of them appeared in the Ukraine in 1750, and their doctrine spread rapidly under the influence of Kolesnikov. 'We do not worship the Christ of the icons but the Christ who lives in our hearts,' they stated. They destroyed their icons and refused to enter churches. Seeing in them a variety of revolutionary that he detested, Paul I led them a difficult life, but Czar Alexander I was more favourably inclined and allowed them to establish themselves in groups to live according to their faith. During the period from 1820 to 1826 they settled along the shores of the Black Sea, under the leadership of a former corporal, Kapustin, who had a gift for organization. The Czar himself visited their little agricultural republic, the forerunner of present-day kolkhozes; a delegation of Quakers also went to see for themselves the idealistic way of life they practised. The Doukhobors observed, among other things, the principle of non-violence. They declined to be enrolled as soldiers, and Nicholas I had them deported to the Transcaucasian regions. The Prince of Mingrelia, who was sympathetic to them, gave them lands in 1887. But 2,400 of them fled from Russia and settled in Canada, aided in this by Tolstoy and helped financially by the Quakers. The sect has survived, practising simplicity, equality and fraternity, according to principles which the Quakers themselves appreciated. There was even a type of puritanism among the sect's adherents, the 'milk drinkers', being so called because they said that they were nourished on the 'spiritual' milk of St Paul's First Epistle to the Corinthians (iii. 2). Roughly treated by the Communists during the great persecutions of 1930, the Doukhobors have survived nevertheless, treating all forms of government with equal indifference as a necessary evil, keeping away as best they could from collectivization, and increasing the number of illegal 'houses of prayer' in Azerbaijan and in the Caucasus. Some idea of their not insignificant spirituality may be gained from reading the works of an illustrious Doukhobor, Verigin, a doctrinaire exponent of non-violence whose *leit-motif* was: 'God is unlimited love. To love one's neighbour is to realize God in His love. Man is the Temple of God who is love.'

In the years preceding the revolution there emerged many other sects from the spiritual ferment which was then spreading over all Russia. Some ancient sects which were thought dead arose anew.

15. PERIOD OF TRIAL FOR THE RUSSIAN CHURCH

Late on 25th October 1917 the administrative capital of the czarist Empire, Petrograd, was in the hands of a group of resolute men, the Bolsheviks, led by Trotsky and Lenin. They were so called because the word means 'majority', and since 1903 they had enjoyed a majority within the revolutionary Socialist Party. The seizure of power, carefully prepared, had succeeded admirably. Trotsky's few men, a thousand at most, had occupied railway stations, telephone exchanges and power stations with scarcely a shot fired, while the liberal Menshevik government guarded the ministries. The next day, to cries of 'The war is over!', the sailors and most of the army rallied to the new regime. A new chapter opened in the history of Russia, and of the world.

Half a century has elapsed since that day. Although for many years its enemies—the liberal capitalists—were predicting its imminent downfall, the fragile Bolshevik regime has not only survived but has given Russia a degree of political strength which it had not known before. This changed situation was due to the characters of the outstanding and ruthless men who led the revolution, the men who set about applying the most stringent of Marxist principles with energy, subtlety, intelligence and Machiavellian plotting. First among them was Lenin (1870–1924), the little man who looked rather like a schoolmaster. It was his genius that brought Marx's theses up to date by applying them to the situation then ruling. Next was Stalin (1879–1953), the political fox whose arrogant cynicism went hand in hand with an acute sense of timing and opportunity and a profound awareness of Russian interests. After them came Khruschev (born 1894), who was dismissed in 1964, a man who combined the realism of the peasant with the subtlety of a diplomat and doctrinal inflexibility with a jovial appearance of good sense.

The history of this half-century has not been without its severe crises. In 1918 the Soviet regime was forced to accept the humiliating and disastrous Peace of Brest-Litovsk; its attempts to spread the revolution to Germany, Hungary and the Balkans were checked. Threatened from all sides, Bolshevism fell back on a dictatorship of terror. In 1919 the 'White' incursions were defeated and the Soviets reconquered Russia. In 1920–1, with the nation's economy in ruins and production at a standstill, famine stalked Russia and took 5 million lives. In the midst of immense disorder the regime had to reorganize the State and stabilize its position with the outside world. The rigorous attitude adopted towards the trading class and the peasants had to be modified and softened: the New Economic Policies were launched. In 1922 Lenin fell ill, and on his death in 1924 the regime was plunged into another crisis. With the last of the Mensheviks liquidated, Trotsky demanded an end to the N.E.P., which was driving the revolution into middle-class channels. After a desperate struggle Stalin emerged as the victor. He was then Secretary-General of the Communist Party. In 1924 a Constitution set up the federative system of states within the Union and the pyramidal organization of the workers' and peasants' 'soviets'; the Communist Party now controlled the country, and through it Stalin, with the help of the O.G.P.U. (later the N.K.V.D.), assumed full power.

The economic and diplomatic situation slowly improved. In 1927 Stalin the all-powerful sent Trotsky into exile in Mexico, where he was later assassinated. The Stalinist dictatorship superimposed the State's authority on collectivism, though this was mitigated somewhat by the co-operative system at work in the kolkhoses, the reinstatement of small landowners and the principle of private profit. Five-year plans (1927–33) were launched to get the economy into higher gear. In 1934 Stalin felt his position threatened and embarked on drastic 'purges' within the ranks of the Communist Party; even Lenin's closest collaborators were executed. In 1936 the Soviet Congress voted a new Constitution which ended the revolutionary era and proclaimed that the country was now a democracy. In 1937 the U.S.S.R. was once again a great power as much by its 170 million inhabitants as by its economy, and resolved to play a major role in the world's affairs. It had forged a new governing class of managers capable of assuming such a role. In 1938, to have his hands completely free, Stalin embarked on yet another purge in which even the chief of the O.G.P.U., Yagoda, was executed. In 1939 the outbreak of the Second World War offered Stalin the opportunity he had been waiting for—he encouraged Hitler in his ventures, partitioned Poland with him and annexed the Baltic States. He then judged it opportune to counter National Socialist expansion and was making plans to hold it when in June 1941 he was taken by surprise by the German invasion of Russia. In 1943, with the victory of Stalingrad to his credit, he made Russia into one of the Big Three. At Yalta in January 1945 Stalin obtained through Roosevelt's weakness a division of the world which eminently suited the Russian leader's ambitions. Eastern Germany, Poland, Hungary, Czechoslovakia, Rumania and Bulgaria all became Soviet satellites. Relations with the West became difficult and Stalin lowered the 'Iron Curtain'. In 1950 Russia was in a period of full expansion without having found it necessary to call upon help from the West; the regime, though it had dropped numerous Marxist principles, was none the less securely established. But Stalin's dictatorship inclined more and more towards despotism, and this nurtured the beginnings of an underground movement. In 1953, on 6th March,

Stalin died and was succeeded by Malenkov and four (later three) vice-chairmen, one of whom was Khruschev. The regime underwent severe shocks and there were new purges. The party of the 'Reformers' carried the day against the 'Stalinists', one of whom was Beria, the chief of police. All the Stalinists were executed. The Russian people looked forward to material improvements in their standard of living and the more intelligent among them advocated peaceful co-existence with the capitalist states. But the West had organized itself into the Atlantic Alliance under N.A.T.O. and the 'Reformers' in Russia were swept away in their turn and executed in December 1954. Under the theoretical presidency of Marshal Bulganin, Russia was in fact ruled by Khruschev.

It is in the light of this series of terrible events that Russian policy towards the Churches must be seen. Each of the crises has had repercussions on the relations of the Communist State with the Church, and these could not be other than hostile. Marxism is basically materialist and atheist, the enemy of religion. 'Marxism is a materialist creed, and as such is the sworn enemy of religion,' were Lenin's words, and for him as for Marx religion was 'the opium of the people', a type of spiritual narcotic through which the capitalist slaves forgot their human rights and their just demands for a life worthy of man. But from this principle two different attitudes emerge. The first, sustained by Marx, Feuerbach and Engels, even by Lenin himself on certain occasions, placed first and foremost the establishment of the perfect Communist society in which, the alienation of man being impossible, religion would disappear of its own accord. 'No Kulturkampf', said Engels, no persecutions. Lenin laid down that all religions were organs of capitalist reaction which helped to exploit the proletariat, and should be fought with all the weapons available. The ups and downs of the religious policies pursued by the Soviets and all their apparent contradictions can be explained by this dialectic.

From 1917 to 1958 there were periods of persecution alternating with periods of relative calm. The first crisis broke out soon after the Bolsheviks seized power, and it was spectacular in its effects owing to the terrible conditions then prevailing in the regime; calm was reached only in 1923. A few days after the revolution began, in Decem-1918, there were grave incidents. All religious schools and farms had been nationalized. Armed bands made attempts to pillage monasteries; at the Alexander-Nevsky Laura an elderly archpriest was killed and the police fired on those who had come to help the monks. In many instances summary executions took place. It was a period of violence and blasphemy. This was the period when Alexander Blok wrote his famous poem, *The Twelve*, in which were the lines: 'Have no fear, comrade, Seize your rifle, And put a bullet into Holy Russia, No more crosses, No more crosses!' Courageously, Patriarch Tikhon pronounced anathema against those responsible for such infamy.

The separation of Church and State on 20th January 1918 did not stop at breaking the traditional links of collaboration between the two estates and removing from the Church's province the registration of births, marriages and deaths; it also forbade any religious society from owning property, prohibited religious instruction in all schools, even private ones, and set to work to discourage the faithful from helping the Church financially. (The decree has never been abrogated.) It was followed by others forbidding religious instruction, even from pulpits, and limiting to three the number of children in one family authorized to receive courses of religious instruction. Acts of savage violence continued: in Kiev the ageing Metropolitan Wladimir was assassinated; but such acts were answered by the Church with equal vigour—the Patriarch Tikhon stigmatized 'the horrible, restrictive and evil nature' of Bolshevism. Certain intellectuals became priests, e.g. Sergey Bulgakov [1] and the poet Soloviev, nephew of the writer.

A degree of peace descended towards the end of 1918; attacked from all sides, the regime relaxed its severe grip a little. The People's Commissar of Justice donounced these acts of violence. But from the spring of 1919 the climate of violence returned again. The same commissar ordered that the tombs and shrines of saints should be searched and that any treasures found should be carried off to museums. Strict police security measures prevented any protests against such sacrileges. However, still hoping for the best, the Patriarch Tikhon declined to bless the 'White' armies which were then on Russian soil in the south of the country.

Such hopes were all in vain. As it felt itself becoming more secure, the Bolshevik Government increased the severity of its anti-religious measures. Administrative persecution was unleashed, increasing the number of vexatious and restrictive decrees. The Patriarch had launched an appeal for charity to ward off the effects of the famine then sweeping the country, but the Bolsheviks seized the funds so collected to ensure that the Church should not appear in such a worthy role. In February 1922 a decree was published which ordered the confiscation of all precious metals and stones in the churches for the benefit of the hungry. The Patriarch Tikhon authorized the handing over of all unconsecrated objects, with the exception of liturgical vessels. The Bolsheviks saw in this an excellent propaganda weapon—the Church was refusing to help in the struggle against famine! In many cities there were clashes between adherents and the police. In order to strike a final blow against the Church, the government brought a number of prominent Christians to trial. The trial of the '44' was held in Moscow;

[1] See Chapter IV, section 12.

nine priests and three lay members were found guilty and shot. The Patriarch Tikhon, who had come to court as a witness, was imprisoned in his residence and thereafter no longer exercised his functions.

At the same time, in order to attempt to divide the Church, the Bolsheviks set in motion a particular manœuvre which they were to use later in so many countries. It was designed to create a schism. The priest Vvedensky, accompanied by two ambitious bishops, set up the 'Renovated' Church, which asserted its loyalty to the regime. Those members of the hierarchy who protested were attacked: the ageing Metropolitan Agathange, the representative in Moscow of the imprisoned Patriarch, was exiled to the far north; in Petrograd an iniquitous trial was held in which eighty-seven Christians were charged, among them the Metropolitan Benjamin, a man who had always demonstrated charity towards the Church's enemies and who, shot at the same time as three other believers, set the seal on a saintly life with his martyrdom. At the end of 1923, sixty-six bishops were in prison or in exile. Trials similar to that at Petrograd took place almost everywhere; there were summary executions and other outrages and it was estimated that there were more than 8,000 religious victims, of whom 2,700 were priests, 2,000 monks and more than 3,000 nuns, to say nothing of the laity, the figures for whom are unknown.

The 'Renovated' Church nevertheless held a Council, in which the Patriarch was reduced to secular status. It permitted bishops to marry, and voted unconditional loyalty to the government. But this triumph was ephemeral. Split into three rival Churches soon, the members of the 'Renovated' Church saw that they were not attracting any great following, and several of their leaders returned to the true Church. This was in the period when Lenin was making ready to soften the regime with his New Economic Policies. The 'Renovated' members were abandoned by the government to their fate. It now looked as if a certain degree of peace would descend on the history of Church-State relations. As a result of unknown pressures on the old and still imprisoned Patriarch Tikhon—very probably a mixture of threats on the one hand and promises by the authorities on the other—he agreed to co-operate with the regime. It is not known whether the assassination of his own secretary had any influence on his decision, but not only did he agree to condemn the Extra-Territorial Synod of the Russian Church, which sponsored the anti-Bolshevik crusade, but in June 1923 he agreed to (or was forced to accept) the publication of a statement in which he said that he 'was no longer the enemy of the Soviet authorities'. A new chapter was opened in the relations between the Church and the Communist regime.

At the time this change of policy did not seem to be of much value. Without renewing the violent persecution of the period between 1918 and 1923, the regime nevertheless continued its policy of hostility towards the Church. Patriarch Tikhon was dead, but the government forbade the appointment of what is called, somewhat curiously, the 'locum tenens of the Patriarchal see'. The three successors designated by Tikhon had each been arrested, and it fell to the Metropolitan Sergius Stragorodsky of Nijni-Novgorod to occupy the Patriarchal throne, after an interregnum lasting two years. He was a remarkable man, an excellent diplomat and so much loved by the people that when he was arrested by the Bolsheviks the workers in his city went on strike until he was released. He directed the Church's affairs for many months from Novgorod. With the approval of the various members of the laity, such as Professor Popov and of several of the bishops deported to the far north, he made attempts to legalize the situation by negotiation with the Soviets on the basis of the statement made by the Patriarch Tikhon renouncing any intention of standing as an enemy of the Soviet authorities.

In 1927 therefore, while Monsignor Sergius was authorized to resume his functions in Moscow, a declaration appeared in which it was made clear that he accepted obedience to the State. He stressed the 'contradictions between the Orthodox Church and Communists' and condemned 'those who sowed a hatred of God.' But, realistically, 'without seeking reconciliation between the irreconcilable', he proposed to all Christians that they should not withdraw into a sterile climate of non-co-operation, but should bear themselves as 'exemplary citizens' so that 'the joys and successes of the Soviet Union, their country, became their joys and successes'. He went perhaps too far in suggesting that there were resemblances between Christianity and Communism: 'If the State demands the abandonment of property and the offer of self to the common good, is that not what faith demands of Christians?'

There is much to be said in defence of such an attitude. Confident of the faith of his adherents, tempered by trials undergone, the locum tenens was accepting a challenge that, within the Communist society in which it was accepted, the Church would be able to preserve the essential message of Christ. Such an attitude was not acceptable at all. There was a split towards the Right and the I.P.T. (True Orthodox Church) was set up. This was hostile to any *rapprochement* between the Orthodox Church and the Communists and was led by the Metropolitan of Petrograd, Monsignor Joseph Petrovsky, though it only assumed any degree of importance in some dozen dioceses. This Church also had its martyrs, among them the Metropolitan himself, who was shot in 1937, but it still exists today.

Events did not seem to bear out Monsignor Sergius's reasoning. Only a year after the 1927 declaration, in the Stalin era, a systematic campaign of persecution began, and lasted eight years. This time it was not a series of more or less legal outbreaks of violence, or trials or measures more or less strictly applied—it was nothing less than an attempt to stamp out the Church entirely by a series of laws and police measures. Stalin had just completed a reorganization of the secret police. All religious propaganda, considered now almost as a crime against the State, was forbidden. Priests and their families were compared with the kulaks, the detested private property owners, and were deprived of civil rights, which meant that they had no ration cards, nor were they allowed medical assistance or treatment. Crushing taxes were levied on them, and in the street hard by their own churches ill-clad priests were to be seen begging. One priest was observed ascending the pulpit in his underwear—everything else had been taken from him. Innumerable churches were closed and transformed into museums. A wave of destruction swept over Soviet Russia, similar to that in France during the Terror. Basilicas such as that of the Holy Saviour in Moscow and Our Lady in Kazan were burned down; so were five-hundred-year-old monasteries and innumerable churches. Icons and religious books were destroyed by the hundred. The Central Committee of the Communist Party, alarmed at this vandalism, appealed for calm, but the appeal went unheard.

During this time the government mounted a very strong ideological offensive against the Church. In 1922 the atheist movement had not had much success. The publication of *The Atheist* and *The Godless At Work* had not seriously disturbed public opinion. But in 1925 a Jew named Gubelmann, who used the pseudonym Yaroslavsky, had set up the League of the Godless, which received government backing. The organization's five-year plan was only partly successful; in 1932 the league numbered between 5 and 6 million adherents instead of the 17 million hoped for, but its *Manual of Atheism* sold some 800,000 copies. Every modern medium of propaganda was used to spread atheism: books, pamphlets, newspapers, films and exhibitions. Youth was duly indoctrinated in the schools. It must be said that the arguments used in the campaign were of very poor intellectual standard, scarcely worthy of M. Homais. The most outmoded scientism was advanced. But, nothing daunted, Gubelmann-Yaroslavsky announced that at the end of the second five-year plan all traces of the old superstition would have been eliminated from a new Russia.

In 1937 there was a census of the population. Among the questions was the following, which in any case was unconstitutional: 'Are you a believer?' The results were such that the government dared not publish the true figure—it was thought to be some 70 per cent; certainly it included more than half the population. The failure of the campaigns of persecution and of the godless was obvious. Marx had erred on this point: in Holy Russia the pillars which upheld the Church were neither the middle class nor capitalism, and Christianity, far from being the ally of the 'haves', had its strongest roots in the common people. And despite the massacres—thousands of peasants, all Christians, had perished because they refused to submit to the system of collectivization—because of these massacres even, the Russian people in the main refused to betray their faith.

From 1934 to 1937 there was a period of respite for the Church. Stalin needed stability in the regime internally before embarking on much wider plans externally. The 1936 Constitution gave priests civil rights. At the 1935 Congress of the League of the Godless Yaroslavsky was forced to admit that the number of clerics had risen, that militant atheists were declining in numbers and that the anti-religious campaigns no longer held any interest for anyone. Monsignor Sergius's gamble seemed, at long last, to be paying off.

Why then should the years 1937 and 1938 have been singled out as periods of the most terrible persecution? It was the time of the great purges of the Stalin era, a terrible period in which, as Khruschev has put it, 'no one was safe from arbitrary action or persecution'. It seems that the dictator was not driven by ideological reasons, but, sensing danger in increasing opposition to the cult of personality (his personality), simply struck out at everyone to produce a reign of terror. The Church was one of the victims. Thousands of churches were closed. Hundreds of bishops, priests and monks were once again sent to prison, from which they were not to return alive. Any excuse was good enough to set up trials in which, to say the least, the forms of Soviet law were scarcely respected. This man had attacked the 'Renovated' Church; another had invited young people to attend Mass; another had a confessional in his house. Many executions were carried out without any pretext: the Metropolitan Sergius's sister, a nun who was in his service, and his secretary were all killed. There were perhaps a hundred churches still open in all Russia. At Rostov the cathedral was transformed into a zoo.

On the eve of the Second World War, which he could see was threatening, Stalin was forced to realize that if the U.S.S.R. was involved at least half of the population would be hostile to him. He slackened his grip. From July 1938 to July 1939 he introduced various measures aimed at increasing the degree of tolerance; he was now all smiles. This policy continued throughout the war. But official figures showed just what the Church's losses had been throughout the last quarter-century. In 1917 there had been 54,000 parishes, 57,000 priests, 1,500 monasteries, 4 academies of theology, 57 large seminaries and 40,000 schools. In 1941 the respective figures were: 4,200, 5,600, 38 and all the rest were zero.

16. A Great but Threatened Renewal

Let us go forward seventeen years to 1958, the year in which this book closes, and allow the figures to speak for themselves. There were 30,000 churches, more than 35,000 priests, 80 monasteries, 2 academies of theology and 8 seminaries. Only in respect of schools has the Church not regained lost ground. Monsignor Sergius's desperate gamble in 1927 had been successful.

This vastly changed situation is due to only one thing: the war. It was because of the war that Stalin was forced to change his tactics, and it allowed the Church to achieve a spectacular renewal. In the first phases the occupation by the Red Army of the Baltic states, Poland and Bessarabia, where several million Orthodox Christians lived and whose Churches were intact, gave a much-needed boost to the Russian Church. Monsignor Sergius managed, more or less, to place them under his control. And the Soviet Government did not have the necessary time to bring them to heel before the turn of events made it too late to do so; it was forced to reconsider its whole policy regarding the Church.

When the German attack was unleashed Monsignor Sergius, then aged seventy-four, took yet another gamble. The head of a Church which had been persecuted almost out of existence, he could have seized the chance to turn against the regime and try to bring it down. But he did nothing of the sort. The day after the invasion he launched an appeal to his adherents, an appeal of the highest patriotic nature, calling on all believers to join in the sacred struggle against the aggressors, and he blessed the nation at war. On several occasions during the blackest periods he repeated his appeals. The faithful massed in Moscow's cathedral were more than a little surprised to hear him cry from his pulpit, like a captain from the bridge of a ship in danger: 'Every man to his post!'

The Metropolitan never swerved from his attitude of loyalty throughout the war. On every occasion he upheld government directives and sponsored collections for charities, even giving the State a column of tanks, financed by an immense collection. This was called the Dimitri Donskoi column and it flew the flag of Holy Russia. Taking refuge at Simbirsk from the German advance towards Moscow, he continued to preach resistance; his two closest collaborators, one in the capital and the other within encircled and famished Leningrad, did likewise.

The danger was too great for Stalin not to grasp this outstretched hand. In his turn, he launched an appeal to his fellow brethren in the flowing style that befitted the one-time seminarist he had been. There was a joke current in Russia at the time: 'How long would it be before *he* took part in a church procession!' New links were established between the religious and governmental authorities. One of the first results was the suppression of the League of the Godless, which in 1942 had planned to distribute more than 3 million books and pamphlets against religion. Its printing presses were turned over to none other than the Patriarchate of Moscow, so that its review could once again appear! The 'Renovated' Church was disbanded and all its buildings were handed over to the true Church. Everywhere services were again being celebrated and schools of theology were reopened. In this climate of sacred unity the miracle of reconciliation brought enthusiasm to all and washed away memories of the past.

On 4th September 1943 Stalin, accompanied by Molotov, received Monsignor Sergius and his two Metropolitans, who had come to request that relations between Church and State should return to normal. The dictator's reply was astonishing. After having praised the courage of the ecclesiastics at the front he said: 'I now call upon the Russian Orthodox Holy Synod to elect the Patriarch of all the Russias.'

The one-time seminarist still remembered the language of the Church. A council was convened; there were only eighteen bishops present since the remainder were still kept in their dioceses by the war, and many others could not be brought back from the prison camps in time. The traditional Church was reborn in the U.S.S.R. faithful in all respects to the canons and the rites of Orthodoxy. Monsignor Sergius had without any doubt won his gamble.

He died on 15th May 1944 after only three months as Patriarch. A council was summoned and appointed as his successor the Metropolitan of Leningrad, Monsignor Alexis Simansky. The descendant of a noble family with connections at court, he was a man of great culture, with a law degree taken before being ordained and undertaking studies in theology. His opposition to the 'Renovated' Church had meant his deportation to Kazakhstan, but his attitude during the war had been irreproachable.

The line adopted by the new Patriarch was exactly the same as that of his predecessor. Immediately on his election he sent Stalin a letter in which he pledged his complete allegiance, recalling the 'sincere love' of his predecessor for the dictator and assuring Stalin that his feelings were in no way different. From this position he never budged, demonstrating in all circumstances thereafter that he was the loyal citizen of the Soviet State; he published Stalin's photograph in *The Patriarchate Review*, accompanied by flattering remarks, and adhered in all respects to the attitude demanded of him by official propaganda, particularly with regard to the Korean war, the Anglo-French affair at Suez and the Hungarian uprising, where he accused 'dark forces of provoking the spilling of blood'. The Peace Movement could have wished for no more zealous propagandist. The Soviet Government showed its approval by investing him on three occasions with the Order of the Red Banner.

This attitude, which in the West was taken for servility, must be understood in the traditional framework of the Orthodox Church, so closely linked as it has always been to the secular power. It cannot be questioned that, in the view of the Patriarch Alexis and numerous other leaders in the hierarchy, the ideal goal was a sincere reconciliation between Church and State; this would allow the Church to collaborate fully with those who guide the destinies of Holy Russia today, just as the czars did in the past. For the moment, at least, there can be no doubt that submission to the State has paid off. It enabled Patriarch Alexis to ensure that freedom of worship was granted—a clause of the constitution lays down that anyone raising any obstacle to this would receive six months' forced labour!—and to carry out a discreet but thorough reorganization of his Church. It also provided the climate for the astonishing renewal, whose figures bear such eloquent testimony. The essential fact is that attitudes have changed, that the State no longer ignores the Church, and that an official council presided over by a minister looks after the affairs of the Church. In this new climate it has been possible to set up Patriarchal administration anew as well as the system of dioceses and seminaries, to undertake collections and the sale of candles, which provide enough money for the clergy to be financially independent, to open parish churches again and to authorize the opening of a certain number of monasteries. Renewal has been particularly marked in those provinces occupied by the Germans during the war.

But serious difficulties remained even in this new climate, areas of friction emerging immediately after the end of the war. As the Church reorganized it had cause to complain of mounting taxes. We already know the great importance that Orthodoxy attaches to monasticism; all the monasteries of former times were far from being re-established, those remaining open being for the most part in territories annexed by the U.S.S.R. in 1945. Authorizations for reopening were few and far between. It was learned from the Soviet press that certain peasants had signed a petition asking for the monks to be reinstated, and even that one monastery was disguised as a kolkhoz!

But, above all, the official reconciliation between Church and State did not stop the rebirth of the League of the Godless in 1947, nor prevent the government from giving it its support. It is now called the Society for the Development of Scientific Knowledge. Furthermore—and this while the country was locked in the war in 1943—Kalinin, then Head of State, made a speech to young people in which he explained that the abandonment of anti-religious policy was dictated by circumstances, and he entreated them not to betray their militant atheist convictions. The movement, although not very active in the beginning, continued to grow during the first eight years of peace. An intensive propaganda campaign was launched using all modern media. It was directed at all levels of culture, rehashing all those old arguments aimed at the masses, from Strauss on the non-historicity of Christ to the dragging out of old 'scandals' from Church history; and also directed to the intellectuals through the quality reviews such as *Science and Religion*. Even Communist intellectuals looked on this propaganda as 'flat and preposterous', but it stopped at nothing. Conjurors put on demonstrations in which 'the miracles of Christ' were re-enacted to show their falseness. One Communist, feigning conversion, had himself admitted to a seminary, and later published the story—which had some success—of his life there, exposing the depravities he was supposed to have seen; he later became a propagandist for the anti-religious movement. Even Stalin's death in 1953 and the reign of Malenkov, who was responsible for a 'de-Stalinization' campaign, did not halt the atheist campaign. It was not until 1954, under Khruschev, that the Central Committee of the Communist Party ordered a halt, condemned the excesses of the propaganda employed and praised the priests who took an active part in the life of the country and acquitted themselves honourably in their duties as citizens.

In point of fact the position of the Church in Russia is an extremely ambiguous one. Doctrinally the Soviet power has not abandoned any of the more rigid materialist and atheist attitudes of Marxism. There is not one Communist leader who has not repeated the weary aphorism of religion being 'the opium of the people', or has not proclaimed that Communism and religion are irreconcilable. A few weeks after the moderate statement of the Central Committee in 1954 the review *Kommunist*, very closely linked to the party, published an extremely violent article which, referring to the religious renewal then taking place, stated: 'The Church has always been the parasite of human misery.' The paradox is thus curious—a Church conducts itself with unconditional loyalty towards a regime that has sworn to destroy it.

What have been the concrete results of the policy of the outstretched hand? It is a very difficult question to answer. There is no doubt that the Church enjoys only relative liberty, that it has not the right to carry out its mission, nor to fight with equal weapons against the League of the Godless, nor to train or educate youth, nor even to run charitable or social works. It may be that the constraint on its activity and its rights may have beneficial consequences, for it is forced to channel its activities towards a deepening of its spiritual traditions, an authentic 'return to original sources' similar to that evident in

Catholicism today, towards a more profound study of its history, towards a renewal of the better liturgical customs. But to what degree is this activity efficacious, and who can answer such a question?

It is sufficient to read the testimony of travellers to the U.S.S.R. since the end of the war to see that there are serious contradictions in their stories. Nearly all of them will agree that churches are full on Sundays and that the piety of the congregations is striking and moving. But some reporters have observed in these masses at prayer only old women, 'babushkas and grandmas', as one has put it; others reckon the proportion of young people to be 12–15 per cent. The figures are unreliable. Are there in Moscow 33, 49 or 133 churches open for services of worship? The figures for believers are even more hypothetical: some estimate that there are 33 million practising adherents; but what of the number of the baptized, and what of those who worship in secret because their official status or their participation in the activities of some particular group or in the party precludes making known their convictions? If proof were needed that religion is very much alive in the U.S.S.R., it can be found in the writings of its enemies. Periodically there are articles in the official press bemoaning the existence of superstitions; we also learned from the press of the existence in Byelorussia of an increase in Christianization, and that Bibles and Gospels were being secretly imported. The review *Kommunist* found it necessary to undertake a survey of the remaining superstitions still extant; it found that devotion to icons was still widespread, that church weddings and burials were very numerous and that the most tenacious of those distressing superstitions, baptism, was so widespread that it was impossible to guess at the numbers involved. As for the degree of influence wielded by the godless, the leaders of the movement are the first to acknowledge that they still have much ground to cover. A turncoat priest, Ossipov, who has become one of the leading figures in the atheist crusade, let slip this significant remark: 'The clerics are not such fools as we thought!'

The failure of this movement, and perhaps also the preoccupations of the government with cold war politics, may help to explain why at the end of 1958 the first signs of a further change in attitude were observed. The growing power of one of the members of the Central Committee—Leonid Ilitchev, a clear-minded and resolute atheist with a sound grasp of the problems involved—brought about a stiffening in policy. Basing their attitude on a letter published on 11th November 1954, in which Khruschev advised the use of persuasion on all believers to make them abandon their superstitions, both party and government launched a campaign with the ultimate aim of gradually destroying the Church and stifling faith. Three out of eight seminaries and thirty-five out of sixty-seven monasteries were closed; bishops were forced to resign, baptism and the Eucharist were denounced as 'dangerous to public health' and administrators of the sacraments were arraigned. Such is the scene unfolded by the most recent events. The times of trial for the Russian Church are not yet over.

17. The Church Outside Moscow

Grouped round the Russian Orthodox Church—that is to say outside the Patriarchate of Moscow—is a series of Churches, each of which in theory is Patriarchal or autocephalous, but which for geographical or political reasons finds such independence difficult or impossible.

The saddest case is that of the Georgian Church, one of the oldest in the East. Early in the sixth century St Nino, a woman Apostle, converted King Miriam and he had his people baptized. At first the Church formed part of the See of Antioch, then it came under Constantinople, but declined to follow the neighbouring Churches of Persia and Armenia, who refused to accept the decisions of the Council of Chalcedon and turned to Nestorianism.[1] It remained firmly Orthodox, became autocephalous in the eighth century and elected its own 'Catholicos'. It played no part in the dispute between Rome and Byzantium; hidden away as it was behind the Caucasus and content with its own life, it made no move to formalize the schism. But unfortunately, at the end of the nineteenth century, this peaceful nation was attacked several times by the Persians. It called on the Russians for help in 1901. It was later annexed to the czarist Empire, its autocephalous standing was abolished and its 'Catholicos' exiled, an Exarch being sent from Moscow in his stead. During the Russian Revolution it took advantage of the confusion to strike a blow against the religious yoke imposed by Moscow, but it was not until thirty-seven years later that its autonomy was recognized. An integral part of the U.S.S.R., Georgia was subjected during the revolutionary era to the same tragic destiny as the Russian Church. The first reinstated 'Catholicos' was assassinated, the second was imprisoned. Most churches were closed; it was said that pagan cults had reappeared. The renewal that affected the Russian Church was less marked in Georgia: out of 2,500 parishes only 80 became active again. In Tiflis, the capital, the only truly Christian communities were those of the Russians, who had three out of the eleven churches. Native Georgians seemed to have little or no interest in their Church.

In the Balkans other Orthodox Churches underwent a similar fate. For many years the shadow of Turkey was cast upon them and also

---

[1] See Chapter V, section 1.

that of the Greek Patriarch of Constantinople, who as we saw [1] sought obstinately, with the help of the Turkish Government, to control all the Christians of the Balkans.

The most complicated situation was that of the Serbian Church. Baptized finally towards the end of the ninth century by the missionaries of Basil the Macedonian, the Serbs fell naturally into the orbit of Constantinople. When, however, during the twelfth century they became a kingdom under Stephen I Nemanya they very cleverly made use of their geographical position and their cordial relations with Rome to slacken their links with Byzantium. In 1220, taking advantage of the situation created by the capture of Constantinople by the crusaders in 1204, St Stephen II, 'the first crowned', had his brother St Sabas, a former monk from Mount Athos, enthroned as the Metropolitan of Serbia. While it came closer to the Greeks after the collapse of the crusades and even opted for the Orthodox schism and broke with Rome, the kingdom of Serbia, then at the summit of its power under Stephen Douchan, demanded its own Patriarch in 1346; his see was to be at Petch. In vain the Phanar pronounced sentence of excommunication. Until the Turkish conquest the Serbian Church flourished, but the disaster of Kossovo in 1389, in which Greater Serbia foundered, had very serious consequences for the country; for several centuries thousands of its adherents fled to the Austrian region of Karlovitz and the Greeks strengthened their hold. In 1766 they suppressed the office of Patriarch at Petch. The Phanar had no hesitation in exerting pressure on its new adherents.

In those areas not subject to Turkish domination the Church arose anew during the nineteenth century. The Serbs were, as we know, the first to rise against the Moslem yoke during a heroic struggle lasting from 1804 to 1929, and their religious independence was achieved in 1832. Their first Metropolitan was a one-time drum-major of the army of independence. The guerrillas of Montenegro, who had been harrying the Turks since Kossovo under the command of their Prince Bishop, also acquired their own Metropolitan, whose see was at Cetinje. In the kingdom of Hungary emigrant Serbs set up the Church of Karlovitz in 1741, which was very active and undertook missionary work, though this was sometimes in conflict with Budapest. In the provinces annexed in 1878 by Austria Hungary, Bosnia and Herzegovina, another Church was founded, but was never fully autocephalous and remained under Constantinople's control. This fragmentation ceased after the First World War when the new State of Yugoslavia was created in 1918. A Serbian national Church was thus brought into being. The Patriarchate of Belgrade was recognized by Constantinople in 1922, its authority extending over some 6 million adherents and 3,000 priests.

Chapter IV, section 5.

The Church was in close association with Moscow, whence it received the Holy Chrism. In the best Byzantine tradition the monarch took a direct interest in ecclesiastical life and too often the Church lent its aid to 'Serbianization' campaigns directed by Belgrade at the expense of Croatian and Dalmatian Catholics. In 1935 a concordat was arranged between Belgrade and Rome for the reorganization of Catholicism in Yugoslavia; the Orthodox Holy Synod excommunicated in advance any member of the Skupshtina who voted for it.

The Second World War was a period of severe trial for the Serbian Orthodox Church. Under German occupation the Serbs waged unrelenting guerrilla war. The Patriarch, bishops and other dignitaries were all deported. Taking this opportunity to get their revenge after years of humiliation, the Catholic Croats allowed the formation within their ranks of groups of terrorists, partisans of an independent Croatia who were helped by the occupying power. In circumstances in which it is difficult to disentangle political and religious considerations, there were widespread massacres; at Plaski the Orthodox bishop and 137 priests were shot. Some records have spoken of 700,000 victims. With the ending of the war the situation changed. In 1945 the new Communist regime proclaimed the separation of Church and State. There have been no overt persecutions similar to those in the U.S.S.R. and, especially since the break with Moscow in 1948, Marshal Tito has adopted a relatively moderate attitude. But the Orthodox Serbian Church declared itself violently hostile to Marxism, and in consequence was treated as an enemy, subjected to police surveillance and often persecuted. The Metropolitan of Montenegro and several priests were executed; public trials were held against members of the hierarchy, and in some cases sentences of forced labour were passed. A 'confraternity of priests' similar to the 'Renovated' Church in Russia attempted to bring about a schism and destroy the Church's unity. The situation improved only in 1954 when a more prudent Patriarch was elected.

The history of the Bulgarian Church has been dominated, much more so than the Serbian Church, by the question of its relations with the Ecumenical Patriarchate. From the time when Czar Boris (852–88) had himself and his people baptized, the Church had hesitated between the jurisdiction of Rome and that of Byzantium. We have seen how the persistent antagonism between Greeks and Bulgars often exploded into violent conflicts. In 1767 the suppression of the Metropolitan see at Ochrida appeared to confer victory on the Greeks, who set about destroying the Bulgarian Church, even to the extent of forbidding the use of Slavonic in the liturgy and ransoming the faithful to profit the Phanar. National awakening, which appeared early in the nineteenth century, was accompanied by a firm desire for religious independence. The Bulgarians obtained civil liberties from the Sultan in 1856, and in 1860 signalized this by omitting the name of the Ecumenical Patriarch during Mass. The question then arose of rejoining Rome. Russian diplomacy skilfully opposed this move, but the Greek bishops were forced to leave Bulgaria, and in 1870 a *firman* from the Sultan acknowledged the independence of the Bulgarian Church; it would have its own Exarch and would no longer be dependent on the Phanar. A long period of tension then began, almost of open war. A council at Constantinople excommunicated all Bulgarians, though only the Greeks took notice of this, obstinately making a point of treating the Bulgarian Church as schismatic. On the eve of the Balkan war of 1912 there were rumours of reconciliation; but the second Balkan war of 1913, during which the Bulgarians attacked their former allies, served to increase hate. Once more the Bulgarians turned their eyes towards Rome, and once again Russia intervened. It was not until 1933 that talks began in earnest, and not till 1945 that they were really fruitful. Constantinople agreed to recognize the Metropolitan of Sofia as Exarch.

The final episode in this story took place in 1953 when, under pressure from Moscow, the Bulgarian Holy Synod set up a Patriarchate without consulting the Phanar (who in any case did not recognize it).

But since the end of the Second World War another and graver problem has arisen. 'Satellized' by the U.S.S.R., Bulgaria has had to put up with Communist persecution, though it was less violent than in Russia. Church and State were separated; religious instruction in schools was forbidden; ecclesiastics were arrested, even Bishop Cyril of Plovsk; numerous monasteries were secularized, some of them being transformed into tourist hotels; and a National Priests' Association was set up within the framework of the Patriotic Front organization. The Patriarch of Moscow showed great solicitude for the Bulgarian Church: his dignitaries visited it frequently. During the 1950's the situation worsened, and the recruitment of seminarists became more difficult. But the Church shows an astonishing degree of resilience. The St Clement Academy at Ochrida is very active and its theologians are most distinguished. The Bible arouses a great deal of interest. Religious reviews have appeared, of which one is very highly rated— the *Academy Annual*. The Exarch Stephan, who was disgraced in 1948 for having dared to publish *The Social Problem Seen in the Light of the Gospels*, has left a profound impression. Officially, basing itself on the attitude adopted by Moscow, the Bulgarian Church is in full agreement with Soviet diplomatic policies and encourages the Partisans of Peace movement, under cover of which it strives to remain on as high a spiritual level as possible.

The position of the Rumanian Church is even stranger. The Rumanians are descendants of Roman colonists settled in the region by the Emperor Trajan; they have a strong admixture of Slavs, Bulgarians and Tartar races, as well as Greeks and Turks. They were baptized by Latin missionaries and were attached to Byzantine Orthodoxy, whose liturgy they adopted, by Czar Simeon the Great (893–927). They have been in fact a type of extension of the Bulgarian Church, for they came under the Greco-Bulgarian bishopric of Ochrida, and in common with their neighbours were obliged to suffer the domination of the Phanar.

At the beginning of the nineteenth century the Rumanians were split into three Churches, which corresponded roughly to the three political divisions of the country into Turks, Austro-Hungarians and Russians. Moves towards national independence were accompanied, as with all the other Balkan countries, by a desire for religious autonomy. This appeared firstly in the principality of Moldava, which was created in 1856 and which in 1862 declared itself independent of the Greek Patriarch. The movement spread to Bukovina, where Serbian religious authority was thrown off in 1873, and to Transylvania, where the Metropolitan Carlovitz's control was ended in 1869. Constantinople was forced to accept that Bucharest had acquired autocephalous status and recognized this officially in 1885.

The end of the First World War saw the emergence of Greater Rumania, and this allowed the three Churches to unite in one national Rumanian Church, to which the Orthodox Christians of Bessarabia also adhered. At one stroke, with 13 million adherents, the Rumanian Church became the second largest after the Russian. In 1925 it elected its own Patriarch. The Church was, in strict observance of Byzantine tradition, closely linked to the State; the Patriarch Myron himself presided for a time over the Council of Ministers. The collapse of the monarchy after the Second World War was a severe blow to the Church. In 1947 Rumania was taken over by the Communists. What would happen now to the Church?

Thanks to a remarkable man, the Patriarch Justinian, who was an able diplomatist and skilled organizer, Christianity was not swept away with the monarchy. The new regime did not proclaim the separation of Church and State; on the contrary it took over the role of the monarchy with regard to the Church. The law passed in 1948, which laid down general rules for the Church in Rumania, eliminated all religious intervention in the affairs of the State and in educational matters, but retained all the State's rights to intervene in ecclesiastical matters. The constitution recognized 'the Head of the Rumanian United Church'. A Minister for Religious Affairs was appointed; the bishops were required to take the oath of allegiance before him, to 'the People and the Popular Republic'. The dream of Monsignor Sergius in Russia had become a fact in Bucharest.

Relations, however, were not always very good between the two powers. In the beginning bishops were forced to resign, episcopal sees were abolished, priests were arrested and monasteries closed. Through the Russian press and radio it was learned that the Rumanian clergy were far from toeing the party line, and that very often priests omitted to read from the pulpit those passages in pastoral letters which contained government directives (for which crime 154 of them were arrested in 1952), and that the Peace Movement was being resisted.

But on the whole the official position of the Orthodox Church was not without advantages. Apart from the fact that it was able forcibly to absorb the Catholic minorities, it enjoyed a certain degree of freedom in some fields. Thus it has been able to keep a certain proportion of its property. It has two institutes of theology. It publishes a dozen periodicals, among them the excellent review *Studi Teologici*. The regime tolerates the fact that it maintains 'Schools of Cantors' which are nothing less than disguised seminaries. There is one priest for every 1,500 adherents—8,568 parishes and 9,400 priests. But, most importantly, there has been an extraordinary monastic renascence; monasteries have been reopened and now contain some ten thousand monks. The Patriarch Justinian has reorganized them on Benedictine lines, though with due regard to Socialist principles. The monks must undertake social service as well as intellectual and manual work; they must 'participate in that transformation of nature exalted by Communism, and yet give it the character of a mystical work of transfiguration of nature and of deification'. The Niamez monastery, made famous by the *starets* Velochkovsky,[1] has become a flourishing monastic seminary. Convents are equally flourishing; that of Agapia houses three hundred nuns. The publishing of the *Philocalia*[2] is yet another indication of the Church's vitality. The renewal is so much in evidence that in 1959, at the same time as the wave of persecution in Russia, the Communist government found it necessary to place the Patriarch under surveillance in his residence. One wonders for how long the Rumanian paradox will continue.

18. THE ORTHODOX DIASPORA

At the end of the eighteenth century there were no large groups of Orthodox Christians outside the Balkans, the Near East or Russia. The nineteenth and twentieth centuries have produced a diaspora of Eastern Christians. Greeks left their country, then under the Turkish yoke, to work in the ports of the West and of America, there to amass fortunes, some very substantial; Bulgarians, Serbs, Albanians, Greeks,

[1] See Chapter IV, section 10.   [2] See Chapter IV, section 6.

Syrians, Lebanese, Egyptians, Russians and Ukrainians emigrated to the U.S.A. in the early years of open immigration to that country; after the revolution of 1917 there was another exodus of the former Czar's subjects to countries that held out a welcome to them—in Europe, in America, even in China; and after 1945 and the setting up of Peoples' Democracies there was yet another exodus, though it was held in check by the governments concerned and was of less importance numerically. Today there are some 6 to 7 million Orthodox Christians dispersed around the world, belonging to different Churches.

In the last years of the nineteenth century there was a Russian Orthodox diocese in the U.S.A. which included Greek, Serbian, Albanian and Bulgarian parishes; between 1890 and 1901 Uniate Catholics, isolated in the midst of Orthodox Christians, joined the diocese. In 1908 the Greeks left it and placed themselves under the jurisdiction of the Athens Synod. In 1922 they placed themselves under the Ecumenical Patriarchate and constituted an ecclesiastical province of their own, with four dioceses; but this plan was over-ambitious and it had to be abandoned in 1931, the year in which the 'Archbishopric of North and South America' was set up, the head of which was styled 'Exarch of the Atlantic and Pacific Oceans'. He was assisted by nine auxiliary bishops. There was a split in 1924 which lasted six years, then another in 1933 which has yet to be settled. This vigorous Greek Church founded numerous seminaries and was headed by men of the first rank, such as the future Patriarch Athenagoras,[1] but its priests complain that their flocks are becoming more and more Americanized and secular in outlook. There is also a Melchite Church (Arab) and Serbian, Rumanian, Bulgarian and Albanian bishoprics. All tend to look for guidance to the Russian Church, which is the most important of them all.

It has been the Russians who, ever since 1917, have been the largest group in the Orthodox diaspora. Between 1918 and 1922 it is estimated that some 2 million people left Russia; at least 75 per cent of them were Orthodox Christians. To give this mass of faithful an organization adequate for their needs, some twenty prelates met at Constantinople in June 1920 and founded an independent Church which was set up at Carlovitz (Yugoslavia). The decision was not accepted either by the Phanar or by the majority of emigrant bishops. In opposition to this Synodal Church there arose a Patriarchal Church whose leaders, one at Paris, Monsignor Eulogius, and the other in the Americas, Monsignor Plato, were nominated by the Patriarch of Moscow. This first split was further complicated by repercussions due to internal politics in the U.S.S.R. While the Synodal Church became more rigid in its opposition to Soviet power, the Patriarchal Church adopted a more

[1] See Chapter IV, section 7.

flexible attitude, especially when Monsignor Sergius, the 'locum tenens' of the Patriarch of Moscow, adopted the stand towards the Soviets which we examined earlier.[1] Monsignor Eulogius thought it best to state that neither he nor his diocesans indulged in politics and that he remained loyal to the national Church. When he led prayers for the persecuted in Russia the break with Moscow was not long in coming, and he then rallied to the Patriarch of Constantinople, who appointed him Exarch of all the Russian Churches in the West. However, the intrusion of a Greek into Russian affairs brought about a wave of anger which led to a minor split.

After the Second World War, in the new climate of Sacred Unity which then prevailed, many Russian emigrants, especially those of the second generation, were filled with admiration for Russian victories and the economic development in Russia and decided that links should be renewed with the Patriarchate of Moscow—which was in any case now recognized by the Soviet Government. Patriarch Alexis sent emissaries to sound out opinion, and on the death of Monsignor Eulogius in 1946 made attempts to nominate his successor. It was in fact the Metropolitan Vladimir, designated by Monsignor Eulogius, who was appointed. From this incident there emerged a new, very small Patriarchal Church which was attached to Moscow. The Russian emigrants are thus split into three Churches—the Synod of Carlovitz, now installed at Manopac near New York; the Church of Monsignor Vladimir, recognized by the Ecumenical Patriarch of Constantinople; and the Church under the Patriarchate of Moscow. There is still another one in the U.S.A., made up of earlier Russian and Ukrainian emigrants from the period before 1917, and this Church recognizes none of the other three. Each of these Churches seeks to increase its activities. The most important of them is that of Monsignor Vladimir, which has adopted a middle way between vehement anti-Communism and obedience. The St Sergius Institute in Paris is one of its most lively centres; in the U.S.A. the St Vladimir seminary of New York, founded in 1938, became in 1948 a Faculty of Theology attached to Columbia University.

The situation is both absurd and distressing, and it is the young who suffer most from it, for they never knew the tragic years of the revolutionary era; they have grown up in the West or in America and see the problem from a different angle. Their fathers looked upon Orthodox religion as the vehicle of passionate worship, a relic of the Holy Fatherland now vanished. In emigrant circles Slavophile theses were often aired, according to which, in the Hegelian manner, Russia was the thesis and the West the antithesis, the synthesis being provided through an impregnation of the universal soul by the Russian soul.

[1] See Chapter IV, section 15.

The young have more clear-cut and less grandiose ideas. It is within the framework of the Western world that their plans lie for a faith which is now the subject of lively revival under the twin influence of a return to the sources of Orthodoxy and a confrontation with the pastoral achievements of Catholicism and Protestantism. The impetus came from the Russian Students' Christian Action Organization, which was founded in 1923 in Czechoslovakia. This was the first Russian Orthodox Church youth movement and it was supported by Bulgakov and Berdyaev; it took the form of an extension of the religious renaissance of the early twentieth century. Under the influence of a true apostle, Father Basil Zenkovsky (1881–1962), it became an authentic Inner Mission, with its own publications, working parties and annual congresses, polarizing the living forces of the Russian diaspora. Before 1939 it had taken a hold in all the countries of Europe, Canada and the U.S.A.; it was especially active in the Baltic States, Slovakia and France. It is only in France, however, that the movement has retained its pre-war vigour, even though several of its members had been in German or Soviet prison camps, notably those who had led the movement in the Baltic States where Christian Action had taken on the characteristics of a mass movement, particularly among the peasants. In France today (though there have been no students in it for many years) it represents the most active and clear-thinking element of the diaspora; one of its leading spirits, Nikita Struve, grandson of P. B. Struve, is the author of an excellent work on the Christians of Russia. It is no longer as a restoration of Holy Russia that its members see the future of Orthodoxy, but as a concrete contribution to the building of a Christian world in which each of the great obediences would have its part to play in combating atheism.

ORTHODOX CHURCHES

GREEKS

Patriarchate of Constantinople	225,000
Crete	350,000
Church of Greece	7,000,000
Church of Cyprus	400,000
Church of America	300,000
	8,275,000

MELCHITES

Patriarchate of Antioch	250,000
Patriarchate of Jerusalem	45,000
Patriarchate of Alexandria	150,000
Archbishopric of Sinai	100
	445,100

SLAVS

Patriarchate of Moscow	125,000,000 (?)
Emigrants	3,000,000
Raskolniks	20,000,000 (?)
Serbian Patriarchate	7,500,000
Bulgarian Patriarchate	6,000,000
Church of Poland	350,000
Church of Czechoslovakia	150,000
	162,000,000

OTHERS

Rumanians	12,000,000
Georgians	2,000,000
Albanians	160,000
Finns	70,000
	14,230,000

Grand total: 184,950,100

These figures are taken from the 1952 tables published in the *Catholicisme* encyclopaedia. Those for the U.S.S.R. and the Peoples' Republics might perhaps be a little optimistic. If they are reduced by 10 per cent the grand total is about 160 million.

19. ORTHODOXY THROUGHOUT THE WORLD

It was through the diaspora that Orthodox Christians and those of the Catholic and Protestant faiths made contact again. The veil of ignorance of which Dom Pitra spoke is now not nearly so much in evidence. Orthodox thinkers and theologians who had emigrated to the West have helped greatly to make their faith better known; some of them, such as Berdyaev, Bulgakov and Lossky, even exercised an influence on Western thought. The degree of interest in Orthodoxy can be seen by the number of publications which are concerned with its theology, its spirituality and its leading figures. The patristic movement so characteristic of Catholic renewal has also spread to Orthodoxy in so far as it is the direct descendant of the Greek Fathers. Organizations such as those of the Dominicans of Istina or the Benedictines of Chèvetogne [1] work not only for better understanding of the deep spiritual life of the Christian East, but promote the most valuable personal contacts. And, since the Orthodox Churches have participated in the ecumenical movement and are represented at the World Council's meetings,[2] both Protestant and Anglican circles have

[1] See Chapter VI, section 11.   [2] See Chapter VI, section 9.

in their turn shown greater interest in the Eastern Christianity inherited from Byzantium. There can be no question that in the middle of the twentieth century the situation is quite different from that prevailing in the middle of the nineteenth. The Christian world now takes account of the place occupied by Orthodoxy within it.

But the position nevertheless is a difficult one to establish numerically. Before the 1917 Revolution, by including four-fifths of the Czar's subjects, it could be estimated that the whole of the Orthodox Churches contained some 130 to 140 million adherents. Since the Communist regimes were set up in Russia and in the Peoples' Democracies it has proved extremely difficult to estimate the number of Christians in these countries. It varies with the criterion chosen—open practice, baptism and so on—and there are no ways of finding out how many there are who practise in secret, or within their family circle, and how many whose faith is an inner, personal matter. For Russia alone one observer gives a figure of 30 million faithful, another of 100 million. A comparison of five recent estimates gives a total figure of between 120 and 200 million Orthodox Christians throughout the world, and a true figure is more probably some 160 million. This establishes Orthodoxy as the third largest group in the Christian world, after the Catholics and the Protestants (who, it must be remembered, do not consider themselves as one single Church).

Though it is important in size, Orthodoxy is still more important in what it stands for in the way of tradition, theological thought and mystic piety; these three aspects, which for so long were presumed to be sunk in lethargy, are now, at least in certain sectors, undergoing an impressive revival. 'How could one fail to see an upsurge of new life', asks Olivier Clément, one of the best commentators on Orthodox spirituality, 'in the "mournful joy" of the Russian Church within the Communist world, in the renewal movements which prayer is bringing about in the Christian peoples of Greece and the Lebanon, in the higher thought of the Russian "dispersion" and the Rumanian Church, and in the birth of a vigorous American Orthodoxy?'

This renewal, as we saw earlier, has two aspects. On the one hand there is a return to sources, which is the best guarantee that in preparing for the future there will be no excursions into improvisation. The interest shown in the Fathers and the masters of the Christian East, of Greece and Holy Russia, and in methods of attaining spirituality such as hesychastic prayer, 'the prayer of the heart', only recently looked upon with disdain, show a new fidelity to authentic tradition. But on the other hand an obvious effort is being made—and many proofs of this have been noted—to widen and renew the methods used by the Christian West, or at any rate those methods which are acceptable. The severance of the ancient Byzantine link between Church and all-powerful State is almost universal. 'Religious power and civil power', as Soloviev put it, 'came together; they stretched out their hands towards each other. They found that they were linked to each other by an idea common to both: the negation of Christianity as a social force and as the driving power of historical progress.' This situation has now ended, together with the negation so well portrayed by the author of *Russia and the Universal Church*. Emerging from isolation, from a sort of mystical ghetto in which it had shut itself away, Orthodox spirituality in its purest form discovered, through action, the charity of Christ. We saw the same symptoms in Greece with the *I Zoï* movement, at Antioch with the Young Orthodox, and in Rumania with the monastic reforms of the Patriarch Justinian. Everywhere it is evident in increased missionary activity. Even in the U.S.S.R. the movement has had some success, despite the enormous difficulties which confront the slightest Christian advance into temporal affairs. In 1962, at the Komsomol Congress in Moscow, Sergei Pavlov, the First Secretary of the Communist Youth Organization, stated that he was disturbed to see the Church adapting itself too easily to present circumstances, seeking, as one of its preachers put it, 'to look upon the Communist society as a springboard to divine perfection'. Many articles in the Soviet press testify to the renewal in preaching, a trend that disquiets the Godless.

This widening of horizons is an excellent sign for the future. In rediscovering its role of Apostle, Orthodoxy may very well gain ground. It is certainly so in the U.S.A. Wherever they find ways to break out of their isolation the Orthodox Churches, because of their mystical spirituality and their austere and simple piety, exercise a salutary action on those souls wearied and disgusted by modern life. In the Syrian diocese of the U.S.A., for example, which comes under the Patriarchate of Antioch, one-third of the adherents were originally from other Christian faiths. The Russian St Vladimir seminary in New York, to give another example, now has students not only from all the Orthodox Churches but from many other denominations as well. Orthodox missions, after a severe testing time following 1917, have now begun, albeit hesitantly, to move forward again, especially in Japan. And still more astonishing: Orthodox Churches are springing up in places where one would not have thought it possible. In 1932, in the wilds of Africa, a group of Ugandian Christians left the Anglican Church and adopted Greek Orthodoxy. They were led by a remarkable man, Father Spartas, and soon the movement numbered some twenty thousand adherents. Father Spartas was appointed as their first bishop, and on his death another succeeded him. This small but very active Church sends the best of its young people to study theology at the Patriarchal College in Cairo or the Faculty in Athens. Since it is free from any colonial taint it attracts many African anti-colonialists. In the autumn of 1958 the international organization of Orthodox youth, *Syndesmos*, embarked on missionary activities based on a theology which was quite new.

Even in the West Orthodox Churches have sprung up. In London since the year 1920 there has been a Greek Exarchate to which have come various elements sprung from Anglicanism or from one or other of the different branches of Protestantism. In France certain thinkers and theologians have aimed at a 'Western Orthodoxy', which would adapt the spiritual traditions of the Christian East to the spiritual framework of the West. There is in Paris an Orthodox Church where the liturgy is entirely in French. Under the jurisdiction of Moscow, it is led by Père Lhuillier. Olivier Clément, a professor with an excellent knowledge of Orthodoxy, became a member of this Church. A few other Frenchmen, such as Père Léo Gillet, have also joined the ranks of Orthodoxy, first Russian then Greek.

There is in Britain an Orthodox spiritual group within the Anglican Church—the Fellowship of St Alban and St Sergius—which plays a part in the ecumenical dialogue.

Christians of every confession are aware of the eminent and unique position occupied by Orthodoxy in the Christian world. They are fully aware of the mysterious sacrificial role of the Russian Church, whose stubborn resistance to forces hostile to every faith sets a valued example of supernatural reversion. Both Catholics and Protestants will find positive elements in Orthodoxy. Close to the primitive Church, it brings all other Christians to a conception of faith and practice that is austere, concentrated on essentials, less juridical and more open to the breath of the Holy Spirit. Monsignor Dumont, the founder of Istina, bids us consider the profound and authentic sense that the East has kept of the 'mysteric' character of the Christian religion, the atmosphere of sacramentality which permeates not only its worship but the very expression of its faith, and even the exercise of its government. As regards practice, Catholics could profitably study the importance accorded by Orthodoxy to the liturgy, the use of vernacular languages, the role of the laity in government—married laity—and the urge towards the transfiguration and divinization of human nature which balances any tendency towards activism, from which neither Catholicism nor the Protestantisms are free.

But Orthodoxy is held back from playing its full part in the Christian world by a threefold burden: ultra-conservatism, voluntary isolation and disunity. In far too many strata of its society and its clergy tradition is too often confused with routine and a certain degree of necessary hieratism with mummification. Like the icons, which are still painted today as they were ten centuries ago and which almost entirely hide the precious blackened metal beneath, so Orthodoxy is very largely overlaid with customs considered sacred simply because 'they have been followed for so long'. Every attempt at reform is met with violent resistance. It is these same circles, stiff with sacrosanct routine, that see the Church as a ghetto or—if one prefers it—a fortress from which it is very dangerous to emerge. Protestant ecumenicalism has no more vigilant opponent than Orthodoxy; when Pope John in 1955 and later Pope Paul tried to narrow the gap between Orthodoxy and Catholicism, reactions were vigorous and caused an uproar. However, the press campaigns against Rome, the Vatican and Catholic schools in Orthodox countries have grown less frequent and less violent, though they have not died away altogether. In certain respects one can appreciate the deep disunity that divides the Orthodox Church, a disunity that, as we have seen, expresses itself in so many ways. Efforts are being made to remedy this state of affairs: the journals and reviews of many Orthodox circles express the ardent wishes of an ever-increasing number of faithful to see an end to the embarrassing disunity between Patriarchates and autocephalous Churches.

Without any doubt this is the heart of the problem of Orthodoxy and its role in the Christian world. Père Le Guillou, commenting on an observation by Père Schemann, wrote that the dissensions in the Orthodox Church during the last decades are all, in one way or another, linked to the problem of primacy—or perhaps this should be expressed as the absence of any conception that is both precise and common to all the Churches concerning the nature and functions of primacy. Furthermore this problem, still unsolved, is a major obstacle to a positive and fecund growth of ecclesiastical life in all cases where it is not darkened by open dissensions. Can the Orthodox Church resolve the problem of primacy? Precisely because it is essentially traditional it cannot forget that the glorious Patriarchates of olden times were five in number, that they were not limited to Constantinople, Alexandria, Antioch and Jerusalem, and that the first of them was Rome. It is in the universal Church, in which its mystic wealth will find a place within the juridical framework providentially established by Rome, and in which it can add its spiritual impetus for the promotion of Christianity throughout the world to that of the Catholics and the Protestants, that the Orthodox Church will find the solution to its triple problem of disunity, isolation and ultra-conservatism. The reorganization of the Catholic Church, which was proposed by John XXIII as one of the aims of the Council he convened, may perhaps help Orthodoxy to feel this necessity even more. It would not be purely by chance that Pope John, and His Holiness Pope Paul after him, turned their attention, full of respect and fraternal affection, to the Orthodox East.

CHAPTER V

SEPARATED BRETHREN OF ASIA AND AFRICA IN EARLIER AGES

1. THE SCHISMS OF THE FIFTH CENTURY

THE Orthodox Church is not the only separated Church in the East. Beyond it, in time as well as in space, lie other Churches, other Christian communities—some very small—which proudly claim complete independence from Byzantium and from Rome. For it was in the Byzantine East that they arose, at a time when the Church was still one and universal, more than six centuries before the schism of Michael Cerularius, for reasons which were not entirely connected with matters of discipline but which brought into question, to a most serious degree, the truths of revealed faith. Viewed as heretics as well as schismatics, the destiny of each of these Churches has led to the adoption of characteristics which have finally isolated them. Several among them decline to accept the interpretations which traditional theology gives of their creed, and even go so far as to dispute their classification as heretics. All this does not make things any easier in classifying these venerable but disputable survivals of a troubled past.

These Eastern Churches number some 5 million faithful in Asia and 9 million in Africa—with a small number in America and in the West, for the most part consisting of Egyptian, Syrian, Lebanese and Armenian emigrants—and may be classed in two branches, the Nestorians and the Monophysites. These two words evoke the violent clashes which disrupted the Church, especially the Eastern Church, during the fifth century, an extension and in one sense a conclusion to the terrible crisis of the fourth century with Arius. This Greek priest from Egypt, an austere and pious man, whose striking face and gifts of oratory had excited the crowds in Alexandria, had in the year 320 advanced a new interpretation of the mystery of the Incarnation which some greeted with enthusiasm and others with horror. It is of course impossible for the human mind to grasp how God took on human form and still more incomprehensible how the two natures, the divine and the human, were one in Jesus Christ. It is a definition of mystery that it should be irreducible by rational analysis and that it can only be understood by the soul illuminated by grace. Starting from a correct premise, that of the ineffable and sublime greatness of God, the absolute of Being, Power and Eternity, Arius had posed in principle that the essence of God was incommunicable and this led him to conclude that everything else was created. Everything—including Christ. Thus Christ was not in essence God, but a unique creature the living expression of increate Wisdom in whom the Word of God rested; a man who through his supernatural virtues had proven that he merited the title—to which each man could aspire—of the Son of God. Arianism was condemned by the Council of Nicaea and soon lost ground in the Byzantine East, already undermined by dissensions. Apart from the fact that the doctrine spread to certain barbarian Germanic tribes along the frontiers, who saw in this weakened form of Christianity an exalting of man which was flattering to their instincts, it continued to exercise men's minds, bringing theologians to question the relation of the two natures in Christ which the Council had proclaimed were both equally real but indissolubly united. Early in the fifth century the discussions were made even more lively, since they aroused a spirit of rivalry between the two great theological centres of that time, Alexandria and Antioch.

The problem of the unity in Christ of the two natures may be looked at in two ways. *Either*, as we are told in the famous prologue to the Fourth Gospel according to St John, in the beginning was the Word, and the Word was with God . . . and the Word was made flesh at a certain moment of time for the purpose of bringing salvation to the world: this was what was being taught at Alexandria, where metaphysics were held in high esteem. *Or*, we are to take the figure we see in the Gospel, with all the profoundly moving aspects which bring it so close to us, discovering in its bearing, and especially in the miracles, proofs of divinity: this was the theme preferred by the masters at Antioch, psychologists and mystics. The truth is that Christ is both the Word and perfect man, the 'Son of God' in the widest sense of the term, and God-created man. But depending on whether one gave importance to this or that detail of the argument, and thus neglected another, error was inevitable. This led in the fifth century to two main currents of ideas, two Christological heresies which troubled many consciences; these became known as Nestorianism and Monophysitism. To sum up, in the fourth century the dispute concerned Christ's divinity, which Arius denied, and in the fifth century it concerned His humanity.

In the years following 360 the virtuous and wise Bishop Apollinarius of Laodicea had striven vainly against Arianism by demonstrating that the Word was truly God increate; or in other words that the figure on the cross was really God, the Son of God; he had, however, deviated from the right doctrine in stating that the Word, in Christ, had taken the place of the soul, and that this explained why there was no trace of sin. How, he asked, could two such radically different natures as the divine and the human unite? Two halves of an apple may be rejoined and it may once again become a whole fruit, but this could not apply in the case of half an apple and half a melon. Therefore, he concluded, Christ was not a whole man: He was half man to which the divinity of the Word was joined. Several provincial synods denounced Apollinarianism, and it was finally condemned by the second Council of Constantinople in 381, the same which completed work on the Nicene Creed.

Since it happens frequently in history that an exaggerated thesis arouses an equally exaggerated antithesis, Apollinarianism aroused violent protests and definite statements for or against. Diodorus, the leading doctor of the Antioch school, who became Bishop of Tarsus in 378, stated that it was necessary to distinguish between Christ the Son of God, who was God, and Christ the son of David, born of Mary; between them, he averred, there was 'moral unity'. His best disciple, Theodore, Bishop of Mopsuestia, took a great deal of interest in what we should call nowadays the psychology of Jesus, and undertook an analysis of the virtues of this highest of models and stressed the temptations which were resisted, the feelings of tenderness or anger manifested, without mention of the divine aspects of His personality. It was all very cleverly formulated and no one had any idea that this attitude would lead to danger. But when the theses of Diodorus and Theodore were taken up, simplified and systematized by the most notable of their disciples, Nestorius, called in 428 to the See of Constantinople, they caused a sensation. In his view and in that of his friend and assistant Anastasius, a priest from Antioch, the two natures in Christ must be separated: it was necessary to distinguish clearly between the man and the God. No one had any right to attribute to God the properties, feelings and passions of Jesus the man. The logical consequence of this followed. No longer should one say: 'God died for us,' or: 'The Son of God was crucified.' The soothing formulas which the Nestorians used to envelop these more than disputable assertions did nothing to alter things. When Anastasius, proceeding with the development of his thesis, proclaimed from the pulpit that it was not the Son of God who was born of the Virgin Mary but a man to whose nature was added divine nature and that, in consequence, the Blessed Virgin had no right to the title *Theotokos*, Mother of God, but only that of *Christokos*, Mother of Christ, this caused a considerable stir. The faithful in their churches protested. Nestorius took his subordinate's side and attempted to settle the differences—though in a curiously muddled manner—but he himself was publicly taken to task. A layman, Eusebius, later Bishop of Dorylaeum, denounced him as a heretic. St Cyril of Alexandria, a respected if pugnacious theologian, attacked him violently, not displeased with the opportunity of striking at an upholder of the Antioch school. He brought the matter to the attention of the Pope and the two princesses who reigned in the name of the Basileus Theodore II, his wife Eudocia and his sister Pulcheria. The affair soon had political repercussions in Byzantium itself, where people believed devoutly in the *Theotokos*, and in Syria, where it was seen as a manœuvre by the Alexandrians and the Greeks to turn the tables on Antioch. A council then had to be convened at Ephesus in 431: St Cyril and the Pope's legate were carried in triumph by the crowd and Nestorius reviled. Condemned, he was later exiled to Petra and then to Egypt's great oasis, protesting to the last that his theses were correct.

However, during this time the pendulum began to swing back. The violent refutations of Nestorianism gave rise to yet another error, which could be traced back largely to Apollinarius. Very wisely St Cyril had decided not to push the Nestorians further into secession, but, in concert with the theologian John of Antioch, to find formulas acceptable to all. His successor, Dioscurus, an unintelligent man, stated that such moderation was criminal and proceeded to lead Nestorius's friends a very hard life, even though they had faithfully abided by the decisions of the Council. Dioscurus and his partisans formulated theses which took up an opposite stand from that of Nestorius, pushing these to the limits of reason. And so Monophysitism—the doctrine of the One Nature—was born; it might, however, be better expressed as Monophysitisms, for very soon this doctrine split into innumerable ramifications, the details of which need not concern us.

In the view of the Monophysites there was only one nature in Christ —and not two, associated (depending on the faith) by a hypostatic union. Humanity became absorbed by divinity, melted into it as a drop of water melts into the ocean. The formula of St John: 'The Word was made flesh' meant to the Monophysites 'The Word spread throughout the flesh.' Everything that was in any way human in the mystery of the Incarnation was annihilated, reduced to a vague symbolic state: could a God suffer and die as a man? In taking up their stand against the Nestorians, and demonstrating a Christ not merely apparelled in humanity but resplendent in divine glory, the Monophysites subtracted half the truth from Christian revelation.

The argument escaped from a purely theological plane to become a matter of public debate, when the Monophysites acquired a new leader in the monk Eutyches, whose intelligence and scientific knowledge were not on the same level as his ambitions, but whose nephew was all-powerful at court, especially as he had the ear of Eudocia, the wife of Theodore II. The affair became a battle between Eudocia and the sister of the emperor, who, furious at seeing her sister-in-law so successfully governing her weak brother, declared herself staunchly opposed to Eutyches's views. The struggle was carried on also by the same Eusebius of Dorylaeum who had dealt Nestorius the first blow. A local council met at Constantinople in 448 and excommunicated Eutyches, who called upon Dioscurus, the Patriarch of Alexandria—who found for him (as might have been expected)—and upon the Pope. The Pope was St Leo, the greatest pontiff of the age, who had been instrumental in halting Attila. Flavian, the Patriarch of Constantinople, who had remained loyal to holy doctrine, enlightened him, and the Pope formulated a rule of faith which became famous as the *Tome to Flavian*. It made a considerable impression, but was not sufficient to bring all the wandering sheep back to the wisdom of the fold. A new council met at Ephesus in 449, but the degree of violence was astonishing—the Fathers threatened each other, deposed each other and came to blows. The Monophysites called upon the scum of the port for help and to such good effect that Flavian died of injuries. History describes the painful episode as the 'Robber Council of Ephesus'. What might not have happened had not Pulcheria taken power two years later with her husband Marcian and ordered the convening of yet another council? At Chalcedon in 451 six hundred Fathers condemned Monophysitism and proclaimed that they recognized only one Jesus Christ, the only begotten Son of God, in whom they acknowledged 'two natures without confusion, without change, without division, without separation'.

Everything seemed to be cleared up, and this was so from a doctrinal point of view. And yet the year 451 marked the beginning of that process of separation and division that has continued until the present day. The theologians of the two extreme wings attacked the Definition of Chalcedon, some finding it too biased in favour of Nestorius, others that it was too little in accord with the teachings of St Cyril. One wonders if these doctrinal dissensions would have been enough to set off the process of schism had not other reasons manifested themselves. It is doubtful. It is not too much to assert that the *fellaheen* along the Nile or the Syrian Bedouins could have had only the vaguest notion of the interplay of these ideas. Why should these two deviationist doctrines in particular have led to the founding of substantial, still-enduring Churches, whereas others, such as Pelagianism, sank without trace in the sands of history? Even Arianism itself, after appearing to be adopted by the Germanic conquerors, was driven out by the Church in the West with very little trouble.

Theologians discovered a strong element of support in the masses. In the fifth century the Byzantine Empire was eaten up with internal dissensions; two centuries later, at the time of the Arab invasions, these weaknesses were responsible for its rapid dislocation. In the provinces the Greeks were hated—from their haughty functionaries to their voracious tax-gatherers; and even the prelates imposed on them by Constantinople were no more favourably looked upon. The rivalry between Alexandria and Antioch (allies at least in this aspect) on the one hand and Byzantium on the other made the situation explosive, both the ancient Metropolitanates becoming ever-increasingly irritated under Constantinople's primacy, a primacy which filled it with pride since the emperor had made the city his capital. Both heresies provided the occasion, already long awaited, to shake off the Byzantine yoke. One of the first signs of this liberation was the abandonment in many Eastern countries of Greek as the liturgical language.

Into being therefore came the Monophysite Churches in Syria, as well as among the Copts of Egypt; at the same time there sprang up the Nestorian Churches of Mesopotamia. Even Sasanid Persia was perpetually in conflict with Byzantium; it urged its Christian population to separate from the See of Constantinople by adopting Nestorianism. This was a characteristic attitude of Near Eastern politics where the geographical distribution of the various religions century after century grew still more complicated, each branch of Christianity becoming more and more an ethnic and national community with its own hierarchy, rites, language and courts, and where the religious head was as often as not the political leader of his people as well. All the efforts undertaken by the Basileis to lead their peoples to adopt one common faith failed; they could only retain minorities, contemptuously referred to as Melchites, or Royalists, by the heretics. Islam, which in the seventh century had established political unity throughout its empire (a unity which transcended religious divisions between Christians), finally established them on a secure basis. Founded in the fifth century, the Christian 'communities' have managed to survive after fifteen centuries of persecution and humiliation. They are scattered over a wide area—from Armenia to Ethiopia, from Lebanon to India. Cut off as they are, they have taken on various, sometimes odd, characteristics. Some are very small, poor and weak; others appear wealthy, powerful, in full expansion. All are worthy of respect for the deep conviction that they have of being guardians of the message of Christ and of faith.

2. THE ASSYRIAN NESTORIANS: ONCE SO GREAT, NOW NEGLIGIBLE

Of the two great Christological divisions, that of Nestorius has lost ground. Adherents of Nestorianism now number no more than some eighty thousand, split up into different groups in Mesopotamia, in the Kurdish mountain regions and in Lebanon. There is a small group in the U.S.A. and a still smaller one in India. They are descendants of ancient peoples of Chaldea, whose history goes back four millennia; they might be better described as the descendants of a small minority of believers who, during the Moslem invasion, remained faithful to the Cross of Christ. Their chief characteristic is the Chaldean rite, whose customs are slightly different from those of Byzantium and whose liturgical language is Chaldean (now an unknown tongue for the common people and one which the clergy themselves only just understand). They reject the appellation 'Nestorians'; they have always preferred to be known as 'Assyrians', leaving the label 'Chaldeans' to their separated brethren who in the seventeenth century joined Rome. They are found in Iraq, Iran, Syria, Turkey, Lebanon and Russia and also in America; they have always had difficulty in preserving unity.

They only became Nestorians for the political, administrative reasons we have mentioned. Their Church is a very old one, sprung from the Apostle St Thomas and his disciples, and came into existence early in the fourth century under the Bishop of Seleucia-Ctesiphon whose primacy was recognized under the title of Catholicos—delegate of the Patriarch of Antioch. The majority of Christian Chaldeans lived under the rule of the Persian emperor, the master of Mesopotamia. Under Sapor II there was a wave of persecution led by fanatical followers of the ancient dualist Iranian religion, and the Chaldeans were almost annihilated. But a more tolerant and wiser Shah, at the beginning of the fifth century, came to an understanding with the Christian Church, and in 424 this declared itself independent of Antioch as the Church of Persia.

The Nestorian crisis was now in full swing. Many young Chaldeans came to the famous Byzantine school at Edessa, whose masters were all supporters of the theses of Antioch concerning the two natures of Christ.

When in 489 Emperor Zeno, staunchly Orthodox, had the school closed, the majority of the professors and students emigrated to the Persian Empire. The Shah was delighted to turn the tables on his enemy at Constantinople and welcomed them with open arms. Nestorianism thus became the official religion of the Persian Christians; the law even forbade the teaching of any other creed.

This immigration was the signal for the beginning of an extraordinary chapter in the seven or eight centuries that followed and which concerned half Asia. The Edessans were intellectuals of a high order, well versed in Greek science and thought. The Persian Empire was, as it happened, lacking in such people, and it made use of the newcomers as civil servants, doctors, bankers, even as advisers to the

Shah; the Christian theologians, Nestorians all, were treated with respect. The most extraordinary fact is that they maintained their position even through the troubled times of the Moslem invasion, when this had driven out the Persian overlords. The caliphs of Bagdad made them their friends and advisers, and the Christians played a considerable part in the brilliant literary, scientific and artistic movement which spread from Mesopotamia to Spain.

The Church was not slow to profit from the respect which many of its adherents enjoyed with the caliphs. It prospered, grew and gathered in the majority of Christians under the authority of the Catholicos, who was installed at Bagdad when the city was completed by the caliph Al-Mansur. Its vitality was now of such a high degree that it undertook a vast programme of missionary work. The Kurds of the Upper Tigris were the first to be evangelized. Then the missionaries set off for the heart of Asia, either as merchants with their own caravans or by joining others. They reached Tartary, Mongolia, China, India and even the Sunda Isles, tackling their task with enthusiasm and persuasiveness. Among both Turks and Mongols they made many conversions—to such an extent that veritable Churches arose. They worked to such good effect that—though it is scarcely credible—in the thirteenth century they had established 230 dioceses in 27 provinces. St Louis negotiated an alliance with the Nestorian Mongols at the expense of the Turks, and the famous Franciscan, William de Rubrouk, who was received by the Great Khan at his capital, met Nestorian monks there who acted as chaplains to a part of the court. Even in China there were Nestorian missionaries, for traces have been found of inscriptions left by them; some authorities affirm that they penetrated into Tibet.

But Tamerlane's campaigns of conquest merely finished off what had already begun to rot. Late in the fourteenth century the Nestorians were dragged down at the same time as the Mongol Empire collapsed; the conqueror of the steppes was not one to bother with religious subtleties. The remaining Nestorians in Mesopotamia felt themselves dangerously isolated; on several occasions they made overtures to Rome—in 1552 when the first United Chaldean Church was founded, and again in 1672 when Chaldean Catholicism was founded, headed from 1681 by the Patriarch of Babylon. The precarious situation of the Nestorians and Catholics worsened if anything; there were persecutions and constant wars between Persians and Turks. The most active elements among the Assyrians were forced to settle in the impregnable Hakkiari mountain range near Lake Van. Here they scratched a living with great difficulty, adapting themselves to the ancient tribal customs, in which the social and the religious were one and the same, under the leadership of their *Malik* and their hereditary

Patriarch. This did not put a stop to dissensions within their Church; there were, at one time, three Nestorian Patriarchs. The Patriarchal See, after transferring from Seleucia to Bagdad and thence to Mosul, was finally settled at Kotchanes, a virtually inaccessible spot in Kurdistan, where it is to this day.

The nineteenth century saw the Nestorian Church in complete decay. Many of its adherents, fearful of persecution or at least of interference by officialdom, became converted to Islam. There remained perhaps 100,000. Monasticism, once so flourishing, was in ruins—of two hundred monasteries there remained only thirty, and these had progressively declined in terms of inhabitants. Nothing, it seemed, was going to halt this decline. Throughout the nineteenth century and during a large part of the twentieth they were continually persecuted, some of the campaigns being ferocious. In 1843 the Kurds suddenly turned on the Christians in their midst and massacred thousands of them; a new outbreak took place in 1846 when they murdered what remained of the clergy. In 1860 there was yet another campaign, while the Turkish yoke pressed ever more heavily on them.

The First World War was the occasion for the worst calamity in their history, and they had known many already. Tired of the Turkish yoke, they accepted Russian and allied offers in 1915 to quit their mountain fastnesses and join with the Allies. Britain had promised 'her smallest ally', as they were called, independence on victory.

Their Patriarch mobilized them for the cause of liberty. After fighting as levies alongside the regular British troops the Assyrians were dismayed to see that their country, the mountains of Hakkiari, was ceded to the Turks by the League of Nations. They themselves were settled as inconveniently as possible on the territory of the new State of Iraq, without any serious thought being given to their protection. Year by year tension mounted until the inevitable explosion in 1933; the Patriarch having been confined to his residence, a thousand Assyrian warriors took up arms against the regular Iraqi army on the Syrian frontier. Reprisals were severe, reaching such proportions that they could well be called genocide: villages were razed and burned down and their inhabitants massacred. A few thousand took refuge in Syria, then under French protection; but after independence was declared in 1937 the Assyrians felt uneasy and many of them trekked on to the Lebanon. An unedifying and distressing story, whose sequel is to be seen in the figures: there are now in the Near East no more than seventy thousand Assyrian Nestorians, some ten thousand settling in the U.S.A.

In theory the Nestorian Church retains the same structure now as in the past. It is headed by a Catholicos, who controls five dioceses each headed by a bishop. In reality the diocesan organization is so vague that it cannot be defined properly; as for the Catholicos, though he may be surrounded by pomp and circumstance, he has little enough responsibility. His appointment is arrived at through a curious procedure: it is hereditary and has remained the province of the same family since the fifteenth century, passing by complicated channels from uncle to nephew. No one may be appointed Catholicos if he has ever eaten meat. Candidates for the office are therefore never given any. It happens occasionally that children of twelve are appointed, as was the case in 1920. All candidates are called Simon—Shimoun in Chaldean—in memory of the founder of this priestly dynasty, this forename being preceded by that of the holder and followed by a number. The most recent Catholicos have had chequered histories: Mar Benjamin Shimoun XIX, elected in 1903 at the age of sixteen, was more interested in horses than in theology, and led his people to war against the Turks in 1915; at the time of the Russian debacle he was obliged to flee and was later murdered by a Kurd in Persia. Mar Polous (Paul) Shimoun XX had considered bringing his people back to Rome, but died in 1920 in circumstances that have never been satisfactorily explained. After an interregnum by his sister, Sourma Khanem, her son, then aged twelve, was appointed under the title of Mar Eshai (Jesse) Shimoun XXI, but he was soon in difficulties with the government at Bagdad. After a period of captivity he preferred to emigrate to Chicago, where he decided to remain, even though he had agreed to submit to the government of Iraq. He continues to style himself 'Patriarch Catholicos of the Assyrians of the East', but in the country itself another Catholicos runs the Church, though his authority is in dispute.

Despite so many trials the remnants of the Assyrian Nestorians keep their faith in a manner that arouses respect. Services regularly draw numerous faithful, who participate as best they can in the venerable Chaldean liturgy, which springs directly from that of Antioch, comprising special litanies and gestures such as the 'showing of hands to God' before the Anaphora. It is hard to distinguish speech from song, so much is the former rhythmical and similar to recitative. But despite the sumptuous liturgy everything is poor in their churches. So are the clergy; their numbers are unknown and they receive no training.

The dogmatic differences between them and Rome or Byzantium are not always clear. Assyrian priests have reproached Protestant missionaries for not venerating the Virgin Mary sufficiently, which, for Nestorians, is a strange attitude. Among the seven sacraments two have been modified—penance and extreme unction. Monasticism has all but disappeared. There are reputed to be several small communities left in Iraq, mixed with Monophysite groups, but the most famous monastery, that of Rabban Hormuz, the 'Red' Monastery, from the colour of its walls, is now occupied by Catholic Chaldean monks.

The situation could hardly be worse; but several years ago a movement arose among emigrant Assyrians, whose two main centres are at Chicago and Hassatchiyah in Syria, to give new life to the ancient Assyrian Christian nation. Several members of the ancient dynastic families are concerned in this venture. Material and spiritual help is to be made available to those left behind in Iraq and neighbouring countries; the bigger powers are being asked to ensure independence for the Assyrians and for their resettlement.

The movement does not recognize the present Patriarch, Mar Eshai Shimoun, whom it reproaches for having become a naturalized American with all the advantages that that implies. It has formed an independent Church at Chicago, the American Assyrian Apostolic Church, competently led by one of the members of the Patriarchal family, the Reverend Mar Sadok Shimoun. Locally they appear to be considerably attracted to the Anglican Church and even more to the Catholic Church, both of whose missions, with their schools and hospitals, are far more active and efficient than their own. It is perhaps among these survivors that one should look for the greatest possibilities of unity.

3. THE DESCENDANTS OF JACOB BARADEUS

Monophysitism has maintained its place far better than Nestorianism. It might be better to refer to it in the plural, for, as we saw, the movement quickly split into numerous factions, which century by century led to still further divisions. The most ancient of these Churches, and that which so nearly represents the original Monophysites, is to be found in Syria, with extensions in the Taurus region, Asia Minor and Mesopotamia, where its communities are so intermixed with the Nestorians—as well as the Orthodox Melchites, the Maronites and Catholics of various rites—that a visitor is never sure with what variety of religion he is confronted. It is now called the Jacobite Church.

The name itself deserves some explanation. With its roots in early Christian history it is one of its most curious features. When the Council of Chalcedon in 451 duly condemned the errors of Eutyches the majority of priests and monks in Syria refused to accept the sentence, which they interpreted, wrongly as we think today, as a condemnation of St Cyril. From 451 to 518 there was a succession of Orthodox and Monophysite Patriarchs at Antioch, depending on whether the emperors were indifferent or hostile 'Chalcedonians'. In the sixth century two great Basileis, Justin and his more famous nephew Justinian, adopted radical measures against the dissidents, and all bishops suspected of Monophysite tendencies were shut away in monasteries. But while Justinian was powerful his wife, the Empress Theodora, was scarcely less so. She harboured certain sympathies for the Monophysites and their beliefs. When a certain Bedouin sheik, Harith ibn Djaballah, asked for her help in securing bishops of the sect for his subjects, she put forward one Jacob Zamalos, a monk from Constantinople, a believer in the condemned doctrine.

He was an exceptional personality, a spirit of fire with a temperament to match any trial. Ordained Bishop of Edessa in 543—the date at which the Jacobites set the founding of their Church—on orders from the empress and in circumstances far from clear, he did not remain in his see, protected by Sheik Djaballah, but embarked on an immense propaganda tour throughout all Byzantine Syria. Since he was sought by the imperial police he was obliged to adopt a disguise, that of a beggar, hence his name Jacob Baradeus. He preached in monasteries, enrolled new adherents, ordained bishops, even reaching as far afield as Egypt; he carried out his campaign in the midst of difficulties made worse by the dissensions within his own Church—one of which was the doctrine of 'tritheism', the details of which need not concern us. Despite all these trials, however, the indefatigable Jacob Baradeus continued his work, building up his Church not only in Syria, where a Jacobite hierarchy was set up, but also in Egypt, where he set up a Patriarch responsible for seventy bishops. He died at a great age, still hard at work, while on a missionary journey.

From the end of the sixth century, therefore, the Monophysites had a Church parallel in all respects to the official Church in Syria and neighbouring countries. There was a Jacobite Patriarch, with Jacobite bishops, monasteries and parishes. Since the Patriarch could not reside at imperial Antioch, his see was sometimes at Diarbekir, sometimes at Mardin, outside the frontiers of the empire. The Islamic invasion was to the Monophysites' liking, for they hated the Orthodox Greeks; but the reconquest of Syria in 968 by the Emperor Phocas was a different matter, although even then the Byzantine Church was not successful in bringing them back into the fold. The Jacobites had excellent relations with the crusaders: anything which was bad for the Greeks would always have their support. The Church endured and even grew, though not without some internal stresses, particularly those which aroused rivalry between the 'Patriarch of Antioch and all the East' and his representative in Persia and Arabia, the *Maphrian*.

From the seventeenth century onwards the Church was faced with a new peril. In 1662 a group of its adherents broke away and set up a Catholic Church under Rome. Wherever they could the Monophysites, helped by the Turkish authorities, attempted to crush it, but without success. Decimated and attacked many times the Syrian Catholics demonstrated an astonishing vitality. Their presence even today poses a grave problem for the Monophysite Jacobite Church.

During the nineteenth century the history of Syrian Monophysitism had two main aspects: persecution and resistance to Catholic inroads. Like all other Christian communities the Jacobites suffered the consequences of Western Christian policy towards the Turks; they underwent the same persecutions as the Orthodox Maronites, Catholics and Nestorians. The persecutions which took place during the First World War were especially severe: half of them perished between 1915 and 1923. The expansion of Catholicism—which the Turkish Government recognized officially in 1830, separating the Syrian Catholic Church from the Jacobite—was no less harmful. Between 1831 and 1850 five Jacobite bishops turned to Rome, and between 1913 and 1923 twelve. Well-known personalities such as the Catholic Patriarch Mahmani (1898–1929), and his successor the present Cardinal Tappouni, exercised an influence which the best elements in the Jacobite Church felt keenly. The result of these events has meant a substantial drop in the number of adherents, for whereas in the great days of the eleventh and twelfth centuries there were 1 million adherents in 163 bishoprics and 20 metropolitanates, now there are no more than some 120,000 adherents, spread over Syria and Iraq, with seven Metropolitans and three bishops, some of whom have no jurisdiction. The Patriarch, who resides at Mosul, sees his little flock diminish from year to year.

The Jacobite Church has preserved the primitive rite of the Church of Antioch, just as the Assyrian Nestorians have. It is the most ancient in all Christendom, far older than that of Byzantium. The original Greek has replaced Syriac (the Western Aramaic dialect) as liturgical language, but some parts of the order of service, the Epistle and the Gospel in particular, are read in vernacular Arabic, or sometimes in Turkish or Kurdish. One interesting fact: in the canon of the original Mass, the 'St James Mass', a long list of names has been added, some seventy in all, inserted by theologians who were lacking in originality. The shortest Mass in use is that of St Eustathius. A solemn Syriac Mass has a very complicated musical accompaniment, the singers being provided with no score to assist their memories. As with the Byzantines the range extends over eight keys. It is grave, solemn, melancholic and monotonous, though not without beauty and a certain spellbinding quality.

The Jacobites' religious life is, as with the Nestorians, and indeed with all the Christians of the Near East, vigorous and sincere; centuries of persecution nobly borne have strengthened their faith. Just as with their separated brethren, the descendants of Jacob Baradeus have known how to die for their religion. Doctrinally is it a far cry from Catholics and Protestants? Its basis is less that of Eutyches than of St Cyril; theologians aver that Cyrillian formulas were entirely capable of orthodox interpretations and that the break was due to vocabulary misinterpretations, for the political and nationalist reasons which we saw earlier. Little enough separates the Jacobites from Greek Orthodoxy. As regards Catholicism, the matter is not so simple, for under scarcely understood Byzantine influence it rejects the Pope's authority, allowing only one Head, Jesus Christ. Services are conducted by a very poor class of clergy (Mass is celebrated only rarely and not necessarily on Sundays); they are scarcely trained at all and only just capable of interpreting ritual. Sub-deacons are appointed in some cases as early as ten years of age, though deacons cannot be appointed before the age of twenty-five or priests before the age of thirty.

Unlike the Nestorians the Jacobites have managed to safeguard monastic life to some degree. Of course we are no longer in the age when Syria, from the Taurus region to Mesopotamia, was covered with Jacobite monasteries, nor are there any more Stylites, perched on their columns in life-long isolation, to edify crowds. But there are still a dozen monasteries, and in one of them, Dur-Zafarin near Mardin, the Patriarchal See has been established for a considerable time. The one best known in the West is that of St John Mark at Jerusalem, whose monks guard the obscure little chapel situated behind the tomb of Christ in the Holy Sepulchre. The most impressive one is near Mosul on St Matthew's Mount, known today as Cheik Mattio, a veritable fortress built on the edge of a plateau, its approaches covered on the other side by walls worthy of Carcassone. It is a sanctuary of Jacobite martyrs, faithful keeper of the memory of Bar Hebracus, the giant of Monophysite faith in the thirteenth century. Today there are only four monks there under an abbot-bishop, although during the summer months many pilgrims come there with their families and occupy the cells once given over to monks.

During the last few years a renewal has been observed in this Church—the survivor of an age now gone for ever. In 1914 a group of laity from England set up a National Assembly modelled on Presbyterian lines, which was responsible for running the Church. The present Patriarch has had a seminary built where future priests will study for at least three years. He has also founded religious schools. A new degree of interest in biblical matters has been observed among the monks, especially those from the Mosul area and in Jerusalem. The movement of renewal has been accompanied by a distinct hardening of attitude towards other Christian obediences, particularly Catholicism, whose progress still constitutes the major item of interest to the descendants of Jacob Baradeus.

4. THE ARMENIANS: BLOODY BUT UNBOWED

Even for those who know little of history, Armenia is synonymous with massacre. The very word conjures up the most terrible scenes—villages burned down, their inhabitants murdered or deported—all unfortunately true. This unhappy people, a branch of the Indo-Aryans settled in Armenia during the seventh century B.C., with another colony in the Taurus region, has been dominated in turn by powerful neighbours—Persians, Romans, Byzantines, Arabs, Turks and Russians—unceasingly quarrelled and fought over and persecuted by all of them. A sinister fate seems to have been marked out for this noble and intelligent race, a fate that threatens to wipe them out altogether. But despite every trial Armenia continues to exist, and where its sons have managed to develop their existence in freedom they have shown singular qualities. It is an example of a people capable not only of withstanding dangerous forces bent on their destruction, but also with the ability to build a nation in the midst of a dreadful series of catastrophes.

The statistics available—and these are not complete—are terrible enough. During the nineteenth century there were ten waves of persecution in Armenia. During the period 1894–5 persecution took so grave a turn that the Western powers protested to the Turkish Government, though the latter took little notice. In 1909 butchery again broke out, especially around Adana. From 1915 to 1917 and from 1922 to 1923 there were more persecutions, this time on a more systematic basis. It was estimated that there were nearly 1 million victims, either killed or forced to flee. In 1913 there were 2 million Armenians in Turkey, but there remained only 100,000 in 1924.

This campaign of genocide, carried out mostly by the Turks, is hard to understand or explain. As we saw earlier, the Ottoman sultans were rarely systematic persecutors, and even collaborated with Christian communities, except in times when European politics provoked reprisals. It may be that Armenia was unfortunate in being situated at a point where the ambitions of Russia, Persia and Britain clashed, and this could hardly fail to irritate the Turks. Contingent reasons also had an effect: the Armenians were always hard workers, excelling in crafts, commerce and banking, and their successes provoked ferocious bitterness. But nevertheless the fact remains that it was as Christians first that they were persecuted.

They have been Christian for a very long time, since the origins of the Church itself, if we are to believe the legends concerning the evangelization of Armenia by St Bartholomew and his coadjutor St Thaddeus. At all events, Christianity penetrated into this land in the last years of the third century when Gregory the Illuminator, an Armenian brought up in Greek territory, succeeded in converting King Tiridates II. The young Church had its martyrs; but at the beginning of the fifth century it was on a secure basis thriving under the leadership of Isaak the Great, separated from Byzantium and organizing itself on an autonomous basis. It had its own liturgy, which was in essence Cappadocian, and which had exerted influence on that of Byzantium. A monk named Mesrop had introduced a national alphabet, which enabled the common people to read the relevant texts and so dispense with the necessity of relying on either Greek or Syriac.

Mistrust of Byzantium and of its clergy and civil servants led the Armenian Church to embrace Monophysitism in 551 at the Council of Dwin, solemnly condemning the decisions reached at the Council of Chalcedon. Nothing that the Byzantine Church or its emperors could do, either by persuasion or by force—often ill conceived—had any effect; the sheep remained obstinately outside the fold. In 691 the famous Trullan Council served to make the breach wider still, though it was not total until the early eighteenth century.

Thus the Armenian Church was brought into being; it is also called the Church of the Armenians, but its adherents prefer to call it the Gregorian Church, after Gregory the Illuminator; though again this is at variance with historical truth, for it was in the name of the Church of Caesarea in Cappadocia that the Apostle converted his country and not through any desire of secession.

In fact the expression 'Armenian Church' is incorrect for yet another reason. It should be in the plural. According to that same conception, which we have already observed in Orthodoxy,[1] there is no Armenian Church institutionally constituted as such, but many Armenian Churches, each with its head, its hierarchy, even its own customs. The *Catholicos* (the word Patriarch is still used) of Etchmiadzin has only an honorary primacy, his authority being limited to his Patriarchate; the only unity proclaimed is spiritual unity and the only Head is Jesus Christ. This fragmentation can be explained historically and geographically. There are two Armenias, that of the Caucasus, or Greater Armenia, and that of Cilicia, in the Taurus region, Lesser Armenia. There were other reasons for the division, which emerged in the course of the centuries. The Catholicos was installed firstly at Achtichat, but was obliged to transfer his see several times during the Middle Ages; he finally settled at Sis in Cilicia. But a competing bishop had founded a Catholicate at Aghtamar on the shores of Lake Van, and until 1441 he was looked upon as a usurper. Another division came about in the fourteenth century when the Armenian monks of Jerusalem appointed their own Patriarch; then yet another in the year

[1] See Chapter IV, section 4.

1441 when the bishops of Caucasian Armenia appointed a rival to the Patriarch at Sis, the Catholicos of Etchmiadzin; a further division occurred when the Sultan Mahmud IV set up an Armenian Patriarch at Constantinople in 1461, the sees of Constantinople and Jerusalem not being equal to that of Etchmiadzin. The Armenian Church of Aghtamar disappeared during the massacres of the First World War, and those at Constantinople and Jerusalem have been much reduced in size. There remain therefore only the Catholicates of Etchmiadzin and that of Sis, the latter having no more than a nominal see in Turkey. It is the first of these two which controls the Armenians of the U.S.S.R., India, Persia, Europe and America; the second controls the rest.

The total estimate is of some 3½ million Armenians faithful to the pre-Chalcedonian faith, that is to say separated from both Rome and Byzantium. The greatest number look to the Catholicos at Etchmiadzin, and 2 million among these form a compact group in Russian Armenia and in Azerbaijan, the rest being dispersed mainly throughout Russia, Turkey and Persia. Their relations with the Russians have been complicated. Angered with the Persian Shahs who, during the seventeenth and eighteenth centuries, maltreated them, the Armenians helped the czars to conquer their country in 1828. They were ill rewarded for their trouble. In 1836 Nicholas I, under the pretext of reorganizing the Catholicate, set up a Synodal Council on Moscow lines, complete with Imperial Commissar. The Armenians no longer enjoyed the right to elect their own Catholicos; they were obliged to present a list of candidates, from among whom the Czar made his choice. Protests were so violent that the Russian Government dared not apply the new rule at once. It was modified and brought into effect in 1882 and remained in force until 1917. But the ambition of the czarist regime was to ensure that Armenia became both Russian and Orthodox. In 1903 Nicholas II decided to divest the Catholicos of all his property—some 300 million gold francs—but here again attempts to carry out the seizure were so strongly resisted and provoked such bloodshed that it was abandoned. Administrative measures were used to bring the Armenians to heel; for instance, any priest who baptized a Moslem into the 'Armenian confession' was imprisoned.

This therefore explains why there were reactions in Armenia when the Russian Revolution broke out. By President Wilson's express wish the Treaty of Sèvres established the existence of the Armenian State in April 1920, but at the end of November the Soviet regime took over, and in the following year had to put down an attempted rebellion. For reasons which have never been fully explained the Soviets have treated the Armenians with exceptional leniency. Not only have they been allowed to retain their alphabet, not only also has Armenia been one of the best-aided economic areas of the U.S.S.R., but religious persecution has been less severe. The Catholicos has been able to continue leading his flock from his residence at Etchmiadzin, although with great difficulty; Armenian prelates living abroad have been allowed to enter to attend synods and Patriarchal elections. In return Armenia has helped the Soviet regime in many ways: some of the leaders of Russian Communism are Armenians, such as Mikoyan the politician, and his brother the designer of the famous MiG fighters. The Armenian Church has collaborated with the regime, sending loyal addresses to its masters in Moscow (one to Stalin in particular) signed by the Catholicos of Russian Armenia. The religious authorities of the diaspora have even helped in the Soviet campaign to persuade Armenians outside Russia to return home, with results that were reasonably good. It is difficult to say what this policy will lead to in the future: since 1958 and the stepping up of the anti-religious campaign the policy has shown a tendency to alter.

The vitality of Christian Armenians has not shown itself in their own country alone through heroic resistance to oppression. Exiled from their land by successive waves of persecution, or simply by love of adventure or business, they have created a diaspora of their own, stretching from India to the U.S.A.

They all display the same qualities of reliability, willingness to work and a real aptitude for business; among them are such men as Nubar Gulbenkian and Matosian, the Eastern tobacco magnate. But if these emigrant Armenians are bent on making money—which they donate generously to charitable organizations—they are also very anxious to remain loyal to their nation and in consequence to the faith which has fortified them. Some of the Armenian colonies are large. That of Bulgaria, which numbered some 25,000 adherents in 1924, demanded and obtained religious autonomy in 1928. There are 100,000 Armenians in Persia, 10,000 in Iraq, some 250,000 in Syria and the Lebanon, 10,000 in Egypt and several thousand in India and Indonesia. The refugees from the Catholicate of Cilicia fled to Syria after the bloodbath of 1923. There were 15,000 Armenians in Rumania, but since 1947 the government has endeavoured to encourage them to leave and many of them returned to Russian Armenia. There are many in colonies in Western Europe: 150,000 in France, about 1,000 in Belgium, 2,000 or so in Britain and a number in Switzerland. Those in Manchester, Marseilles and Paris are the most active. But the main centre of the Armenian diaspora is in the U.S.A., where there are more than 200,000 of them, mostly in New York, Boston, Chicago, Providence and in California. Two bishops are responsible for them, one at New York and the other at Fresno in California, with some ninety churches in their care. They have their own historiographer, the famous novelist Saroyan, who depicts their lives with humour and

tenderness. There are some 60,000 in Latin America, the greater part
being in Argentina and Brazil.

What place does Monophysitism occupy today amongst all these
different Christian communities? More so than in the case of the
Jacobites one is justified in asking if it is not more apparent than real.
In any case this is what Pope Pius XII stated in his Encyclical *Orientalis
Ecclesiae*. The doctrine of the One Nature has never, since the fifth
century, been examined profoundly from a theological standpoint.
There is often mention of 'one united nature', which seems to imply
two natures, and can be interpreted in an altogether orthodox manner.
The Athanasian Creed, which is that of the Armenian Church, is no
different in its essentials from the Nicene Creed. What differences
there are spring, it appears, from Byzantine influences—e.g. as
regards the procession from the Father of the Son; and here certain
Armenian ecclesiastical doctors and writers reject the disputed *Filioque*.
Armenians do not believe in purgatory, but in limbo, which leads
them to pray for the dead. Divorce is permitted, but only in the case of
adultery on the part of the woman. As we can see, the barriers which
separate them from the Orthodox Churches, even from the Catholics,
are not insuperable.

The most important feature of Armenian Christianity is the strength
of faith among the masses. As with all persecuted peoples it is an
integral part of national feeling; it was religion which saved the
people during their darkest hours—how could one not remain faithful
to it! What is the precise degree of faith? As regards those Armenians
living in Soviet territory, the reply to this is very difficult to find. It
seems that practice keeps the faith alive and that infant baptism is
universal. But, on the other hand, the clergy are now greatly reduced
in numbers; elsewhere, outside the Russian frontiers proper, faith has
never been very strong because the secular clergy were not of a very
high standard; they had no seminaries, and their knowledge was
limited to the recitation of one or two prayers and reading from the
order of service. Liturgy, as in the Orthodox world, has an important
part to play, being the best method of interesting the faithful in
religious life, since sermons and catechism are virtually non-existent.
The regular clergy, much superior to the secular, has always until now
been the mainstay of the Armenian Church, but recently it has become
but a shadow of its former self. The number of monasteries still open
for the training of monks can be counted on the fingers of one hand,
and even so there are barely a few hundred inmates. The doctors of the
Church, the *Vardapets*, are to be found among them. Only they—a
special corps in the Armenian hierarchy—have the exclusive right to
preach, crozier in hand, before the altar. They represent today the
uniqueness of Armenian monasticism, and are the only candidates for

the bishoprics of the diaspora, as well as the few bishoprics in Soviet Armenia.

If a renewal is imminent in the venerable separated Armenian Church, it will manifest itself only among the Armenians of the Near East, Europe and America; it is here that has been observed, for the last ten years or so, a desire to study the past history of the nation, to go more deeply into the ancient faith and to bring out its spiritual significance. There can be little doubt that this augurs well for further steps forward, which may acquire real importance.[1]

5. A CURIOUS RELIGIOUS PUZZLE: MALABAR

It is already difficult enough to obtain a clear picture of the Christianity of the Near East where, under the apparent display of unity provided by the cloak of Islam, there co-exists a whole range of rival obediences, often disputing the same titles and the same stretches of territory, and whose liturgical customs, to the inexpert eye, are all similar. But this complexity is nothing compared to that reigning in the south-western area of Christian India, Malabar. Here live several million Christians, split into no less than five communities, leaving aside the Catholics who constitute, according to their rite, the Church of Malabar and that of the Malenkars. There are Nestorians and Jacobites, but of very curious aspects, for the latter are former Nestorians linked to the Syrian Church, and the Nestorians former Monophysites linked to the separated Chaldean Church! This confusion underlines the fact that doctrinal questions have had less importance than the rivalries of groups and personalities. Added to this, Catholic, Anglican and Protestant influences close at hand have all exercised a certain degree of influence on some elements in these Churches; the word puzzle is no misnomer. The complications are all the more astonishing when it is considered that the population is everywhere of the same race and that the common language is Malayalam, an old Dravidian dialect, besides the fact that all these Christians, when the necessity arises, are capable of united action. This is borne out by the ten-year-old struggle which they have been waging against Communism in the State of Kerala.

The majority of them style themselves 'Christians of St Thomas', which means that they claim descent from very ancient communities founded by the famous Apostle immediately after the death of Christ, prior to his martyrdom at Mylapore, near Madras, where his tomb can be seen. More to the point, in the fourth century there were

---

[1] The author acknowledges the kind help of Mgr Amadouni, Armenian apostolic exarch in France, who checked section 4.

large groups of Christians in this area. They came under the Patri-archate of Babylon, and when this turned to Nestorianism they adopted the new doctrine, without quite knowing the reasons. At the time when Nestorianism was in full expansion, elements under a certain Thomas Cana joined this Church, especially during the ninth century. The Church declined somewhat after this, as did Nestorianism, and its subsequent history up till the arrival of the Portuguese is unknown.

The latter undertook the work of bringing the separated com-munities back to the Catholic Church, and in 1599, under the Arch-bishop of Goa, Monsignor Menézès, they were successful. The provincial Council of Udiamparus (or Diamper), which included Nestorians and Catholics, duly condemned the heretical theses. But the pendulum swung too far: sacred books were burned, quite legitimate customs were banned and their place taken by Roman usages. This resulted in further upheaval. In 1653, under the leadership of the Archdeacon Thomas Parambil, 200,000 adherents left the Catholic Church; and though the Carmelite missionaries of Alexander VII succeeded in bringing back two-thirds of them, the rest remained obstinately schismatic. They then requested the Chaldean Church to admit them, stating that they were Nestorians as their ancestors were; this recantation meant that they were ineligible and they turned to the Jacobite Church, which welcomed them. The Jacobite Church of Malabar was thus formed and, while it remained associated with the hierarchy of Jacob Baradeus, it continued to teach the doctrines of Nestorius.

The modern history of these Christians is no less complicated. In the eighteenth century their Church was torn by dissension for a very curious reason: a certain Patriarch-elect declined to pay the travel expenses of three bishops who had been sent to appoint him; they excommunicated him and appointed one of their number as Patriarch; subsequently he left to govern the southern half of the country, while the northern half remained faithful to the Patriarch with such a highly developed sense of economy. In the nineteenth century the real problem was one of defence against the inroads of Protestant and Anglican ideas, but this danger in no way stopped the Jacobites—who affirmed that they were 'Orthodox' in contradistinction to those who were tending towards 'Reformed' opinions—from disputing anew on matters of discipline. A new dispute broke out in 1909 when the Patriarch of Antioch, the nominal head of the Jacobite Church, quarrelled with the Metropolitan with regard to ecclesiastical property. The dispute became an open conflict between the 'nationalists', who wished to free their Church from the control of the Patriarch of Antioch, and the 'Patriarchists'. The first group succeeded in appoint-ing their own Catholicos, one Mar Basilios, with the help of a Syrian archbishop who had been deposed by the Patriarch. Thus there were two 'Orthodox Jacobite' Churches, that of the 'nationalists' having its centre at Kottayam; over the next few years the number of actions in the civil courts increased as the two Churches disputed their right to churches—even to cemeteries! In 1940 the two camps were more or less equal, each having some 250,000 adherents. After the Second World War groups of young people took the initiative in trying to bring about reconciliation. They undertook spectacular public fasts in the manner of Gandhi. The campaign had the desired results, and in 1958 Mar Basilios III had the honour of presiding over the ceremony of reconciliation and reunion and also of seeing himself appointed as sole Patriarch of the Orthodox Jacobites of India. Today they number some 650,000. The campaign launched by the younger elements has also brought about a trend towards renewal. It is an open question whether this will leave the Jacobite Church independent, or whether it will bring it closer to the major Churches. Both Catholicism and Protestantism weigh equally with it, and, doctrinally speaking, it is in a dangerous position. In 1913 a Jacobite priest, Father Ghiverghis (George), aware of what was lacking in his Church, founded two 'fraternities', one of men, the other of women, under the name of 'Imitation of Christ' Institutes. He became a bishop in 1925 and a Metropolitan in 1938, and he felt more and more drawn towards Catholicism. He and his disciple Mar Teofilos decided to proclaim their union with it. In order to avoid any possible confusion between them and the Catholics of Malabar of the Chaldean rite, the new Catholic Church of the Syrian rite was called the Church of Malenkar. It exercises a powerful influence on all its neighbours.

But both Protestants and Anglicans have made their mark on the Jacobites of India. Between 1843 and 1875 a priest who had made a study of Anglicanism, Mar Mathew Athanasius, founded, with English help, a new Church called the Syrian Reformed Church, which the Orthodox Jacobites could not crush. The worship of the Virgin and of the saints, belief in purgatory and the dogma of the Real Presence were all removed from the liturgy. On the eve of Indian independence it was felt that the major portion of the Jacobite Church was destined to embrace a hybrid form of religion where liberal Protestantism and even rationalism were taught by priests trained in universities. Today the 'Reformed Jacobites' number some 300,000, and expansion has ceased.

Turning now to the third group of separated brethren in Malabar, their origin is of fairly recent date and is as much a paradox as that of the Jacobites. In 1858 a Catholic priest of the Chaldean rite—in other words a Malabar Catholic—named Antony Thondannata rebelled against his bishop and eventually conceived the idea of founding his own Church. The Patriarch of Babylon, the head of the Catholic Chaldeans, was none other than that Monsignor Audu who made such a stir at the First Vatican Council. He declined to assist in this venture, and the rebellious priest then turned to the Nestorian Patriarch, who was overjoyed to welcome an addition to his small flock, and duly consecrated him bishop. The priest was not a man of stable views; for the second time he abjured and returned to his original Church. In the meantime, however, Monsignor Audu had been in conflict with Rome. In 1874 he dispatched to the remaining Nestorians a certain Mellus, who was charged with the task of putting new life into the sect. From his name the word Mellusian is used to designate the Nestorian Church of India. Mellus governed his small flock from Trichur until 1882, when his friend Monsignor Audu, brought back into the Roman fold by the skill of Pope Leo XIII, requested him to submit also. Was the Nestorian Church to be swallowed up by the Catholic Church? So far as Thondannata was concerned the answer was no. For the third time he rebelled and set up an independent schismatic bishopric of a more or less heretical type, his Nestorianism being of the vaguest kind. Since his death in 1900 his flock has declined in numbers. There was another crisis in 1928 when Thondannata's successor, Mar Ebimilech, undertook to reform his Church and proposed that the Patriarch's election should be in the hands of a synod composed of all the bishops of the Nestorian faith; but, as will be remembered,[1] tradition requires that the Catholicos must be a member of the 'Shimoun' family. The proposition was so badly received that the proposer was ordered out of Iraq and solemnly condemned. The Nestorian Catholicos, Mar Eshai Shimoun XXI, then in exile in the U.S.A., appointed a Nestorian Metropolitan for India. But nothing has succeeded in halting the decline of this curious little Church; where there were 14,000 adherents in 1914 there are only 10,000 today; some authorities even put the figure as low as 3,000.

6. THE COPTS OF EGYPT

The greatest grouping of Christians loyal to the ancient opinions of the fifth century is to be found in Africa. Their very presence highlights a historical fact that the Christians of the West have lost sight of, namely that Christianity first appeared at the crossroads of three continents, and that its first attempts at expansion were in the direction of Africa and Asia as much as towards Europe; equally, that there was a time when Christian spirituality had an African basis at Alexandria

[1] See Chapter V, section 2.

and an Asiatic basis at Antioch, while it was still almost unknown in the West.

It was the descendants of those baptized Christians who made Alexandria into a flourishing intellectual Christian centre—who constitute today the most powerful separated Church in Africa, the Church of Egypt; and this takes into account the secession of the Ethiopian Church, which has now achieved autonomy. They are called, and call themselves, Copts. Nowadays it is not longer believed that the name springs from Coptos, a city twenty-five miles from Thebes and which, as Diapolis Magna, was reported to have been the birthplace of Alexandrian faith. It is more likely that the word is a deformed version of the Greek *Aiguptos* (Egyptian) and the Arab *Qoubt*. They are a very ancient people who settled along the Nile in the time of the Pharaohs. Their language, although little used, is still to be heard in the liturgy; it is a variant of the dialect of the *fellaheen*, transformed by forty centuries of use. The Arabs succeeded in converting nine-tenths of them to Islam when they overran the country in 641, but the remaining one-tenth, at the cost of immense sacrifice, succeeded in remaining faithful to the Christian religion.

Christianity succeeded admirably in Egypt from the earliest times. Linked directly to enlightened Judaism—that of Philo and his disciples —contending with the most intelligent forms of paganism, it occupied a foremost position in all the Christian communities as the fountainhead of thought. Its head, the Bishop of Alexandria, came next in order of precedence after the Pope. During the fifth century he controlled some 16 million adherents, who vested him with spiritual omnipotence. There was an army of half a million monks, as pious as they were ignorant, in complete submission. During the great theological disputes of the fourth and fifth centuries the Egyptian Church played a leading part. Arius was an Egyptian; the Christological quarrel of the time was between Alexandria and Antioch.[1] While Eutyches was teaching his erroneous theses at Constantinople on the union of the two natures in Christ, Dioscurus, the Patriarch of Alexandria, while rebutting the heresiarch's theories, manifested a certain tendency towards Monophysitism by over-emphasis on the rather vague formulas of his predecessor St Cyril. The Council of Chalcedon condemned Monophysitism and deposed Dioscurus, but the Egyptians refused to accept these decisions, delighted with an opportunity to score off the Byzantines. Imperial attempts to bring the erring Church back to the Orthodox fold failed lamentably; soon there were only 200,000 civil servants and merchants who remained faithful to Orthodoxy; they were called, here as in Syria, Melchites— the king's people. During the sixth century Jacob Baradeus, the

[1] See Chapter V, section 1.

champion of the Monophysite cause, gave this Church a more secure basis on Jacobite lines.

The Arabs found Egypt ready to welcome them; the Copts were favourably disposed towards the conquerors and they did little to fight them off, welcoming them, in the words of the Islamic Encyclopedia, 'as liberators'. But they were soon to regret their attitude. In the beginning everything went well. The Moslem authorities treated the Monophysite Copts with respect, reserving their wrath for the Melchites. However, the attractions of a less rigid form of religion, together with the desire to be on the side of the conquerors, led many Christians to embrace Islam. From the seventh century onwards the difficulties began. Churches and monasteries were pillaged, and heavy exactions demanded from Christians. A few attempts at insurrection were crushed. For the next twelve centuries the Coptic Church was in chains, persecuted and humiliated. Certain periods of history—during the reign of the Mamelukes, for example—were far worse than others. From time to time some Coptic leader would make overtures to Rome hoping to obtain help from the West, but all these attempts came to nothing. The Christian flock dwindled alarmingly, even when Turkish domination became less severe. In 1789 there were no more than 150,000 Copts out of a total population of 3 million Egyptians; and they were despised, the French author Volney even castigating them as 'ignorant and barbarous'. Their Church was in complete decay, the higher echelons of the clergy were venal and entirely dominated by the Turks, priests could scarcely read and monasteries were deserted.

The story of the Copts during the nineteenth and twentieth centuries is very different. Today there are more than 4 million of them out of a 23-million population in Egypt. Their Church has been rebuilt and they are showing signs of creative vitality. Their epic of survival is similar to that of the Poles when their country was dismembered. The reason is strange and merits explanation. Those of them who had best resisted the Turks were the intellectuals; the humble *fellaheen* turned to Islam in large numbers. A Christian *élite* was thus formed to which the country's leaders turned to fill the higher posts. From the public scribe to the deputy minister of the Moslem Vizier, not to mention civil servants, bankers, lawyers, doctors and merchants, a very large number were Copts, and it was they who ran Egypt. They had a penchant for intrigue, and were not above amassing large fortunes, which led to an increase in their influence. These were the Christians, alert though questionable, who cleverly took advantage of the times to bring about a renaissance of their people.

The favourable circumstances were not to be found in the era of French occupation from 1798 to 1801, for Bonaparte, as we now know, wanted to be 'Moslem among the Moslems'. One of his first statements on arriving in Egypt was that he would work to 'bring down the Cross'. At first he treated the Copts as 'rogues, despised by the country', but he was obliged to utilize them as tax-gatherers for some time. The Copts were disappointed and withdrew to bide their time. It was not until the second revolt at Cairo and the repressions that followed that Kléber turned to them anew; they came back and occupied many important posts. Christians even received permission to ride on horse-back in cities, a privilege denied to the Moslems! But their triumph was short lived. The commander-in-chief was assassinated and his successor, General Menou, turned to Islam and showed hostility towards the Christians. They were faced with immense taxes, and the police harassed them with impunity. In 1801 a Coptic officer, a fanatical admirer of Desaix, suggested raising a Coptic Legion, which would help the French to liberate Egypt. He enrolled eight hundred men and was promoted to the rank of general. But when he resolved to lead his warriors to fight in Europe they deserted *en masse*—poor General Ya'cob died on the ship bringing him to France. But, a good Christian, he had obtained France's signature to a convention guaran-teeing certain rights to the Copts. It was not unimportant for the future that the first Egyptian to demand independence for Egypt was a Copt.

Shortly afterwards the situation of the Copts improved. An Al-banian officer, Pasha of Cairo, governor of Egypt in the name of the Sultan at Istanbul, threw out the Mamelukes and demonstrated extraordinary qualities of leadership and political skill—to such a degree that on two occasions he was concerned in worldwide events. This was Mohamed Ali (1769–1849). He saw clearly that only the introduction of Western civilization would help to regenerate and develop Egypt. Christian assistance in this task was indispensable, and long before Sultan Mohamed II drew up the Gulhani Charter in 1839, which regularized the position of Christians, the governor of Egypt had taken wide and generous steps to that end. The Copts, who had been sorely persecuted after the French withdrawal, now rallied to Mohamed Ali enthusiastically; apart from the ill-fated General Ya'cob none of them had lent aid to the invader. Numerous Copts now occu-pied high posts in his government, some of them acquiring the title of Bey; even the head of the army was a Copt, though unfortunately he abjured Christianity later. Measures of clemency were increased; Christians were allowed to dress as they pleased, to go to Jerusalem on pilgrimage and to restore their dilapidated churches. The Christian *élite* was functioning once more. Under Mohamed Ali's successors, Said and Ismail, the same favourable 'European' policy was pursued. In 1856 the poll tax—that infamous tax to which the Christian com-munity had been subjected—was abolished, and military equality allowed, a point which the Copts appreciated little at the time. The constitutional status of 1866 drew no distinctions between Moslems and Copts. The latter were elected to the Assembly, others became judges, and the government even financed Coptic religious schools. The closest associate of Ismail was a Christian, the Armenian Nubar.

From this time equality of all classes of Egyptians was legally recognized, and the Copts could develop their society in freedom. There were some repercussions brought on by fanatical Moslems— even in 1954 there were outbreaks of violence! Copts took an ever-increasing share of government; in 1910 a British report showed that 32 per cent of its employees were Copts, whose salaries amounted to 40 per cent of public expenditure. Banking and the upper echelons of business were in their hands. A Copt, Ghali Pasha, was head of the government in 1908, but was assassinated in 1910 in mysterious circumstances. The demands set down by the Copts in their Congress at Assiut in 1910 were opposed by the Moslems assembled at Heliopolis, but the progress of the Christian community went ahead seemingly irresistibly.

On the religious level, there came about an event which caused the Coptic Church to acquire certain characteristics. Certain of the *élite* among them considered that the official Church was not keeping up with modern developments, and that to maintain the Christian minority in their special position a strong and determined hierarchy was necessary. (This was not the case.) The laity therefore took a firm step calling on the Moslem authorities for help. In 1873, taking advantage of a grave financial crisis in the Patriarchate's affairs, they set up a lay council to administer the Church's property. The clergy fought against this for twenty years, but the lay council remained in being. The influence of the laity is so great that the Grand Assembly, which elects the Patriarch, is largely lay in composition. For a long time there were no more than 24 bishops out of a total of 72 members. The 1957 reform enlarged the electoral body to include 29 bishops, 31 diocesan priests, several monastic superiors, 108 lay members representing dioceses and other members representing various other associations.

From 1873, therefore, the destinies of the Coptic Church have been as much in the hands of the laity as of the clerics. The Copts, always the first to demand Egypt's independence, allied themselves with the Moslems in pressing for this. Every nationalist movement gained their support. In 1919 the flags of the Crescent and the Cross combined; when the Wafd Party began its struggle the Coptic daily newspaper, *Misr*, lent support. In 1935, at the time of the Italian invasion of Ethiopia, whose Church was linked to theirs by religious ties, the Copts were in the front rank of the struggle against the Fascists. When

Egypt was granted independence by the British there was not one ministry without a Coptic leader in it. Today Nasser treats the Patriarch with great deference on all occasions. Though there are, from time to time, outbreaks of violence, these are the work of extremists with no official backing.

With its 4 million or more adherents and its thousand priests the Coptic community is undoubtedly a power to be reckoned with in Egypt. It is expanding in numbers and influence. The Copts attend State schools, secondary and technical schools and the universities in large numbers. There are three Coptic students for every five Moslems; it is not difficult to see the day when every higher post will be filled by Copts. This applies also to the landlord class, for the Copts buy land and businesses. These signs of progress are not without certain disquieting elements. To attain equality between Christian and Moslem some Copts are tending towards a degree of secularization. One of the leading Coptic personalities, Salam Mussa, congratulating Colonel Nasser on having suppressed the Moslem Brotherhood, said: 'What we require is a secular State.' It is possible that if they lost contact with their living religious community they would sink into the masses and would lose their existence as a separate people.

At the cost of age-long effort the Christian Copts have not only managed to survive but have inspired a respect for their faith. Their religion, a shield for centuries against persecution, has acquired certain peculiar characteristics—though not so much of a theological order, for Monophysitism is more apparent than real. The formulas employed, being largely those of St Cyril, can all be interpreted in an Orthodox and Catholic sense. If the split continues it will be principally because of habit—ancient hostility towards Byzantium on the one hand, and towards Rome on the other, the latter being looked upon as the expression of the Western world. A full and frank discussion between theologians would demonstrate that the obstacles to unity are far from insuperable.

Apart from its more or less anti-Chalcedonian creed, Egyptian Christianity has some singular aspects. Certain historians and sociologists find in its customs traces of pantheism, from the time of the Pharaohs in the earliest Christian era. For example, they prefer to use the Pharaohs' ancient symbol of eternity, the ansated cross, rather than the Greek cross; saints are represented with attributes of heathen divinities—St George as the god Horus, for example, with a hawk's head; liturgical ceremonies are still accompanied by the poignant rattle of the sistrum, a throwback over three thousand years to the death of Osiris. There are other features of Coptic practice which show Jewish influence: circumcision is still practised among the masses, for, it is alleged, hygienic reasons; biblical instructions concerning the meat of impure animals are still in force. Do these scrupulous observances of ritual purity spring from Mahomet or Moses? It is hard to say. The Copts have adopted one custom from the Moslems—the habit of removing their shoes before entering any holy place. They also have a special calendar, a year of twelve months of thirty days each, the remaining five or six days being treated separately; it begins in the month of Thot, on the 10th day of September, as it did in the Pharaohs' time; their era is counted from the time of the great persecution of the Emperor Diocletian, the 'Martyrs' of 284. With all these customs the Coptic Church affirms that it is Orthodox, its official title being the Orthodox Coptic Church, though this has nothing to do with the Orthodoxy of Constantinople or Moscow.

Among the people faith is very much alive, much more so than among the middle and upper classes, where religious indifference so often goes hand in hand with that type of demoralization so well described by the English novelist Lawrence Durrell. Among the lower classes practice is general, but so is an ignorance of the truths of their faith, and this generates numerous superstitions. But on the whole the Coptic community shows an intense desire for education, and no sooner has a school opened than it is overfilled. Immediate religious authority is exercised by the *ghomos*, a title which corresponds roughly to that of dean in the Catholic Church. He is recognized by his black cowl, and the cross of iron worn on his chest. He runs several parishes, orders the services and assigns to each his part in the liturgy.

The liturgy is that of Alexandria, and plays a large part in religious life; with its numerous readings it is also a highly important medium of education. The churches are quite different from those of Rome or Byzantium. They are huge rectangles divided into four sections. One of these, the sanctuary, is linked to the others by only one door in the *iconostasis*; its walls are pierced with circular holes, these being spaced round the circumference of a larger one, filled with motifs in alabaster or with stained glass resembling abstract art. Celebrants wear a curious conical mitre and a white alb. The long slow services are accompanied by monotonous but rhythmical music, often interrupted by exhortations to the congregation by the deacons and by numerous prostrations in the Byzantine manner, punctuated by the strident notes of the sistrum and the chants of the faithful directed by the *asif*. The community aspect of the service is very marked, all the congregation raising their arms in unison, praying with one voice. The Coptic language, which not all the faithful understand, is used for the liturgy, with several of the prayers in Greek; vernacular languages are increasingly employed, as in the West, for the Epistle and Gospel (Arabic in this case) as well as several prayers.

The Coptic Church has suffered considerably from mediocre clergy, for, though it is sufficient in terms of quantity, it is only since the end of the nineteenth century that seminaries, under pressure from the laity, have been opened; today there are four of them, though it is not certain that all priests pass through them. These were chosen originally from among small artisans who, married and usually poor, were for too long incapable of educating their flocks spiritually. Deacons are very numerous despite the canon which insists that there should be no more than six per church; nothing distinguishes them from the ordinary believer in everyday life.

In past ages the power and influence of the Coptic Church were vested in its monks. Prior to the Arab invasion there were half a million of them—an enormous number. During the fourteenth century, after eight centuries of Moslem domination, there were still eighty monasteries, but such is not the case today. The monasteries have been pillaged, attacked and closed so often throughout the centuries that decline was inevitable. Today there are only eight monasteries, those of St Antony and St Paul in the Red Sea area, four more in the Wadi Natrun desert area and two in the Nile valley. There are no more than 390 monks in all, including several hermits who live close to the monastery, attending services there on Sundays. There are four convents, housing about a hundred women.

None of these conditions promises an outstanding future for the Coptic Church. Some observers have even gone so far as to ask if it is not simply an imposing façade, behind which complete collapse is threatening, but this seems to be too exaggerated a view. For the last fifteen years the signs point to a more optimistic view of the situation.

Under pressure from an enlightened laity, many of whom have studied in Europe and have there seen for themselves the religious renewal in progress, and with increasing approval of the hierarchy, steps have been taken which will lead to a renewal here also. The seminaries were reorganized in 1953, and a certain minimum standard of education was laid down before candidates could enter them. A faculty of theology was opened, whose teachers had undertaken work on dogma and the history of their Church. Several of them took up teaching posts in seminaries. A movement has been started, similar to Catholic Action, to promote a Christian renaissance among the masses. Under its aegis students organized Sunday schools in 1954, which they held in city and rural parishes with the object of teaching catechism to the young. A very lively review backs up their campaign. The outlines of monastic renewal can also be seen. Whereas yesterday the monks were merely good people, pious and withdrawn, able to celebrate the liturgy with proper decorum and capable of little else, there are now young and able men entering the ministry, trained along the same lines as their counterparts the Benedictines and Cistercians in the West. Providing this type of recruitment is maintained, taking the place of the former more or less peasant type of postulant, there is reason to suppose that Coptic monastic life could be profoundly altered. A special seminary has been opened for training monks. There has been in recent years an increased degree of interest in the great spiritual leaders of Egypt, the Fathers of the Desert in particular.

The Coptic Church has now rediscovered its ancient vocation in missionary fields; it is directed principally to Africans of the same faith in the Sudan, South Africa and principally Ethiopia. Students from these countries take courses at the faculty of theology and even at the seminaries. In Jerusalem Coptic presence at the Holy Places has been placed on a more up-to-date footing. For the ancient Church of St Cyril the future seems promising.[1]

7. ETHIOPIA, BASTION OF CHRISTIANITY

Very little is known of the Ethiopian Church, probably because it has existed in a vacuum, cut off by both the terrain and a ring of hostile neighbours. Other Christians seem to know only its curious customs—as though this were sufficient to explain the heroism which it has manifested throughout the centuries. Its history is one long story of resistance to different conquerors. Often the country was overrun, but freedom always returned, a freedom of which the guiding principle was faith. Prester John was not entirely mythical; the Middle Ages looked upon Ethiopia as a bastion of faith in the midst of pagan powers. It was rather like a lighthouse standing firm against the assaults of the waves.

That the Ethiopian Church is of very ancient origin there can be no doubt. The historian Rufinus stated that Christianity arrived in the year 340 with Frumentius and Aedesius, kidnapped by pirates, who served their new master the King of Ethiopia as zealous apostles. Frumentius sought the help of Patriarch Athanasius at Alexandria in providing a bishop for Ethiopia—and was himself appointed. A second stage in the evangelization of the country took place at the end of the fifth century with the arrival of nine Syrian monks, the 'nine saints', who converted the king and his court.

Whether it was due to Egyptian influence or to that of these monks —who were accused, though there seems to be no foundation for the charge, of being exiles, expelled from their country as heretics—the fact remains that Ethiopia became Monophysite and still is today. It is difficult to explain its significance, but it seems that Ethiopia was too

---

[1] The author gratefully recognizes the assistance given by Père S. Chauleur, director of *Cahiers Coptes*, who read section 6.

far away to be intimately concerned in the Christological debates and that, early in the seventh century, it followed the teachings of an Egyptian bishop named Kerillos (Cyril). It supported the 'one nature' thesis, though in the Coptic fashion—hostile to Eutyches and also to the Council of Chalcedon which condemned him, but agreeing with Dioscurus and even more with St Cyril. Ethiopia thus moved from traditional aspects of faith to Monophysitism without realizing it, becoming conscious of this separation only during the fifteenth century. Opinions on Ethiopian theology vary greatly. The Jesuits of the sixteenth and seventeenth centuries found nothing to quarrel with. The Capuchin Massaia (1809–89), who spent thirty-five years in Ethiopia and ended his life as a Cardinal of the Roman Church, considered that there was only an error of vocabulary, the concepts of nature and person being little understood by the Ethiopians. Today Monophysitism is a fact in certain monasteries, but in practice popular faith accepts the human nature of Christ just as do Catholics and Orthodox; this explains why the Catholic Church of Ethiopia has adopted the majority of liturgical prayers employed by the national Church without any important modifications.

But this does not mean that the Ethiopian Church is ready to merge with one or other of the great Christian Churches. There was talk of a merger with the Catholics during the seventeenth century when the Spanish Jesuit priest Paez converted the emperor, Sussenios Seltan Sadag, who in turn wanted to convert his people by force, which set off religious wars. Paez's successor, Father Mendez, was brutal and maladroit and succeeded only in bringing about the collapse of any hopes there may have been. From all these efforts there remain but two features—the ruins of a Catholic cathedral on the shores of Lake Tana, and a deep mistrust of Catholicism which has only recently begun to abate. The Orthodox Church, which made great efforts during the last quarter of the nineteenth century, with the aid of Greek and Russian monks, has had no more success than the Catholic. On several occasions unity was about to be proclaimed, but the emperor, Menelik, looked upon as the incarnation of the Ethiopian nation ever since his defeat of the Italians at Adowa in 1896, saw that any association with Constantinople or Moscow would mean that the Ethiopian Church would lose its identity. He declined to sign any formal engagement.

Ethiopian resistance to Islamic pressure was no less rigorous. The expansion of Egyptian power led the nation's elements to close their ranks round the throne. The emperors were defenders of the faith as much as they were defenders of the nation. The attacks from the north were countered by the emperor, Theodore II, not only by force of arms but by religious counter-measures; the Moslems were forced to adopt Christianity, freedom of worship not being granted to them until 1899. The situation reached crisis proportions in 1916, when the then Negus became converted to Islam, claiming descent from the Prophet. He repudiated his Christian wife, set up a harem, built mosques and placed his empire under Turkish religious control. But the Christians reacted, and while the Church excommunicated the apostate sovereign the Choa tribes marched on the capital. Menelik's daughter was proclaimed empress with Ras Tafari as heir and regent. The latter came to the throne in 1930 as Haile Selassie. Christian Ethiopia had triumphed once more.

The battle was won in another important respect also, for since time immemorial the head of the Ethiopian Church (the Abuna) had always been appointed by the Coptic Patriarch of Alexandria from among the Egyptian monks of the monasteries along the Red Sea. Ethiopia was in the curious position of having a foreign bishop appointed who knew neither the liturgical nor the vernacular languages of the country. After the First World War, when Ethiopia came more into contact with the outside world—it had a representative at the League of Nations—a strong current of opinion demanded an end to this situation. In 1929 the Patriarch was forced to ordain four autochthonous bishops and appoint their head from among Ethiopian monks, the Ichege, the head of the great monastery of Debra-Libanos. The Italian invasion accelerated developments. After attempts to persuade the Abuna, then in exile in Cairo, to rally to their cause the occupants set up a separatist movement with the help of the Ichege, who had himself proclaimed Abuna and ordained 'collaborating' bishops. A synod at Cairo excommunicated them. But there was no question, after the Italian defeat in 1941, of putting the national Church under Egyptian tutelage. Haile Selassie himself led negotiations, which lasted for ten years. A preliminary draft of the agreement was signed in 1948, stating that on the death of the Abuna his successor would be Ethiopian. In the meantime he would have an Ethiopian coadjutor. Complete religious autonomy was proclaimed in 1951, the Coptic Patriarch of Cairo enjoying only spiritual and moral primacy.

The Ethiopian Church, then, is an integral part of the nation, in a manner similar to that of ancient Byzantium. The Negus, like the Byzantine emperors, is a sacred personage, head of the Church, to whom religious honours are granted and who must at all times defend the Church; the Abuna, on the other hand, has indisputable powers which the secular authorities respect. He crowns the emperor, appoints the bishops and disposes of the right of absolution and excommunication; no council has sought for a long time to limit these powers, though since 1948 he is assisted by a synod, which is, however, by no means modelled on the lines of the lay council in the Coptic Church of Egypt. His only serious rival (since he has no mandate to teach religion) is the Ichege, who incarnates spiritual tradition and whose prestige is great. Though there are sometimes internal dissensions the clergy as a whole are agreed that they must continue to exercise a wellnigh medieval tutelage over the people.

The people of Ethiopia retain, in general, an indisputable loyalty to their faith. While it may be difficult to obtain reliable figures in the absence of proper censuses to evaluate the total number of Christians in Ethiopia—figures vary between 4 and 7 million—every traveller there is agreed that there are innumerable proofs that modern secularization has not dented faith. The Blessed Virgin Mary is worshipped there in the same degree as in a Catholic country. Tattoo marks in the form of a cross are often seen on the foreheads of believers, and religious festivals are so numerous—another medieval trait—that there is one every week. On Saturdays and Sundays great throngs of people crowd into the churches, all uniformly dressed in a type of white alb, the *shemma*. No Ethiopian would neglect to make some sign of reverence when entering church or chapel. Education may have been scant or even non-existent, but the people nevertheless are well aware of their Christian past, and sacred edifices are venerated.

Ethiopian Christianity has some characteristics which at first sight may appear disconcerting. It is extremely austere, very formalist, the Lenten period being the longest in the world and lasting fifty-five days, with fasting on Wednesday and Friday at least until midday, sometimes until 3 p.m. Prayers and prostrations without number are also required, and in this it resembles the Greek Church. But there seems to be little discipline in moral life; confession is no longer the custom save *in articulo mortis*, when it is superimposed on a form of extreme unction which is also a confirmation.

One of the most remarkable features of Ethiopian Christianity is its insistence on biblical texts, for there is an extraordinary attachment to the Old Testament and especially to the Psalms. It is not for nothing that the Ethiopian dynasty claims descent from King Solomon and the Queen of Sheba, with their son—the first King of Ethiopia—born after the famous visit, nor that the arms of the Negus include the Lion of Judah. Mosaic customs, similar to those we saw among the Copts of Egypt, are even better observed among the Ethiopians, especially circumcision, which is carried out before baptism. The first-fruits of the earth are always offered to the 'Lord of the Universe'; the Sabbath has been observed for almost as long as Sunday itself; no unbled meat is eaten; weddings are performed according to the biblical ceremony in the manner of the marriage of Cana. Brothers should marry the widows of deceased elder brothers, if the woman so requests, according to the Levirate. Let us add merely that the biblical precepts concerning welcome to strangers and charity towards the poor are fully observed.

Architecture, art and liturgy all combine to give Ethiopian Christianity its especial stamp. Here again, as among the Egyptian Copts, some of the customs seem to come down from far-off pagan ages from the Egypt of the Pharaohs or from autochthonous sources. The habit of celebrating St Michael's or St George's Day or the Feast of the Assumption or the Nativity once a month is evidently taken from a very ancient lunar calendar in which every phase was celebrated religiously. The liturgical language used is from the Tigré region and is prehistoric; as for the sistrum, the gestures used in its execution are the same as those seen in frescoes at Thebes or the Valley of Kings.

There is extensive clergy, though thousands of priests are priests in name only or officiate at certain festivals. For a long time it was not necessary to have had any training to be a priest. It was only necessary to go to the Abuna, along with a group of others at the same time, to pay the prescribed taxes—in olden times this was in blocks of salt—to be ordained and to depart, still in a group, to seek some village which was in need of the services of a priest. But, apart from the 'ecclesiastical clerics', for a long time there have been 'secular clerics', who are much better trained and who have often received secondary education. There are even some teachers among them—it is they who, as deacons, instruct the people during the services and form the corps of singers and poets so indispensable to liturgy of any importance. For the 'ecclesiastical clerics' they have proverbial contempt.

In Ethiopia, as among the Orthodox, the most vigorous elements are to be found among the monks. Monasticism in Ethiopia is as old as Christianity itself; it was implanted here from Egypt, that classic source of hermit saints. The great monasteries have played a very important part in the national history—bastions of faith which today are still centres of intellectual and spiritual life. The most famous, that of Debra-Libanos founded in the thirteenth century by the reformer Haimanot, is at the head of the order founded by the saint—it is its abbot who is Ichege, the recognized head of national monasticism. Others follow the so-called Eustathian tradition and have no hierarchy. Today there are a dozen monasteries and six convents, well attended, whose inmates are in practically complete withdrawal from life. All of them have preserved, despite Moslem invasions, vast treasures; an inventory has scarcely been attempted yet. The ancient manuscripts are for the most part decorated with miniatures in hieratic or barbarian style. Within the monasteries a renewal has been observed over the last few years in theological and biblical studies. This has been undertaken in concert with the Copts of Egypt and the Orthodox Patriarchates of Constantinople and Alexandria, and even with some of the Protestant

Churches. The secondment of young people to universities and seminaries in Egypt, Greece and Istanbul represents a stake in the future for the Ethiopian Church. The development of an Ethiopian Catholic community, helped by the return of Eritrea to Ethiopia after the Second World War, has meant the opening of a seminary, of a Cistercian monastery, of religious schools (most of which are run by Ursuline nuns), and in Rome itself the setting up of an Ethiopian College (1919); this is not without significance.

Taking into account these circumstances and the influence exercised by Rome and Orthodoxy, as well as by the Coptic Church of Egypt, the Ethiopian Church may find renewal. In maintaining its traditions on a secure basis, it will need to make some considerable effort to raise the moral and intellectual level of its priests and of its faithful, and to combat the growth of magic and astrology. The role of the 'crossroads of Africa', which the emperor has marked out for his country, brings the outside world much closer. The wind of change which blew through the Vatican at Pope John's behest has not left the 'elder sister' of the African Churches indifferent—the Abuna himself sought to be represented at the recent Council.[1]

8. Between the Past and the Future

Some 14 or 15 million Christians are members of the ancient Churches, separated both from Rome and Byzantium, and strangers equally to the Protestant phenomenon. They are to be found in all parts of Asia and Africa, with groups in Europe and America. For the most part they are an unknown quantity to the rest of the baptized, not only do they survive, a fact which merits respect when one considers the conditions under which they have had to live for fifteen centuries, but they also show signs of increased vitality in various parts of the world. It would be impossible not to pay tribute to them and their venerable Churches, or to refuse them friendship.

So far as historians of Christianity are concerned, they are all of absorbing interest, as though they were in truth vestiges of a medieval past still more or less intact today. Whether they present themselves, as in Ethiopia today, as breakwaters against the violence of the waves, or as islands—all that remain of vanished continents, surrounded by the sea of Islam—they are all survivals, in the strictest sense of the term. They live today as they lived in ages past when the Christian West was only just emerging from the shadows of barbarian rule and when 'Christianity' was only just beginning to be aware of itself.

[1] Section 7 was read by M. l'Abbé Bernard Velat, Professor of Ethiopian at the *Institut Catholique de Paris*, to whom the author is indebted.

There are valuable lessons to be learned from these fifteen centuries. Everywhere these communities have demonstrated an astonishing degree of vitality, resistance to the worst kinds of persecution, often forced into distressing exile, and yet everywhere they have seized the smallest chance to readjust and reaffirm themselves.

TABLE OF EASTERN CHURCHES
(not including Orthodox Churches)

NESTORIANS

Mesopotamia and environs	80,000
Malabar	2,000

MONOPHYSITES (JACOBITES)

Patriarchate of Antioch	120,000
Orthodox Malabar Jacobites	650,000
Reformed Malabar Syrians	300,000
Armenians	3,100,000
Egyptian Copts	4,500,000 (?)
Ethiopians	5,000,000 (?)

Total between 14 and 15 million

The resistance of Polish Christians, or those of Greece, Serbia and Bulgaria, to Turkish oppression is much admired in Western historical works; for these the period of trial has been much shorter than for the Christians of Mesopotamia, Armenia or Egypt. It required great strength throughout fifteen centuries to stand up to torture, death and insults of all kinds and to remain faithful to ideals; resistance was possible only because the adherents of each Church had a sense of community. Even before they considered themselves as citizens, or nationals of a State, they looked upon themselves as members of a religious community, which conditioned their own personal existence. Today, in a country such as the Lebanon, an original development has been the juxtaposition of various religious communities, including Moslems. Nor can it be forgotten, when one studies the history of the East from the invasion of the Arabs to the present day, that the Christian communities have all played a role in it, sometimes obscure, but always effective.

As vestiges of the past, and as we find them today, all the Christian communities of the East can furnish the Christians of the West, whether Catholic or Protestant, with concrete facts and ideas of great value. Their communities have often been criticized for mixing religious and social aspects too intimately, but this has been due partly to the influence of Islam and partly to the conditions in which the communities found themselves, their existence as peoples being dependent on the existence of their Church. Everywhere there is a sense of unity among Christians, of fraternity and of community which approximates to the best in the movement of renewal among both Catholics and Protestants. In strictly religious matters liturgical renewal, so much in evidence in current thinking in Catholicism, has a great deal to learn from these Nestorian or Monophysite Churches, for they have preserved incomparable liturgical treasures, sprung from cultures so different from those of the Greek and Latin West.

To look upon these ancient Churches as museums or venerable fossils and upon their faithful as relics of the Middle Ages would be quite wrong. One cannot see an Armenian or a Copt accepting this mute role. The Reverend Father Edelby, in the Jerusalem *Near East Christian Review*, wrote: 'Eastern Christianities are not mummies presented for the inspection of archaeologists or indolent aesthetes; they are not relics which one tolerates condescendingly for atavistic reasons; they are not closed-in, stagnating communities incapable of growth, committed to inertia while everything else around them is in a state of flux.'

These words connote more than a pious wish: they imply promise for the future. If the elder Christianities of the East will listen to appeals of this kind, then they can expect to benefit from the advice given and face the future. Their main problem is to hold fast to their traditions, failing which they will soon find themselves swallowed up in the Moslem sea around them. In addition to keeping up to date, they will also have to escape from rigid confessionalism and to participate in the new trends which are evident everywhere in the East. Each of these two factors is dependent on the other being observed.

There is no reason why the Christians of the East—and here we include the Orthodox Greeks and the Catholic minorities—should not consolidate their position. From the beginning they have been independent of the West, some by opposing unity with Rome, others by separating themselves from Byzantium. In no case can they be suspected of collusion with 'colonialist' Europe. They are authentically Asiatic or African and well able to speak in the name of those peoples who are only now beginning to awake to their place in the world. Their role as forerunners of the uncommitted third of the world can be considerable. This is the desire of the best Christian elements in Malabar who are, in the state of Kerala, in the forefront of the fight against famine. Haile Selassie has clearly understood this aspect of the matter, for his aim is to make Christian Ethiopia the crossroads of Africa, the crossroads even of all non-aligned nations Moslem as well as Christian.

Islam provides the channel whereby the Eastern Christians may achieve this goal. Their relations with Islam go back twelve centuries, and though they have suffered at its hands, and still do, there is no reason to suppose they they could not play an essential part in the relations between Islam and the rest of the world; firstly, as witnesses to a Christianity despite the growing strength of Islam. Religious attitudes, here more than ever, govern the whole scene. Might not true Christians become living links between two worlds, act as a channel of friendship and fraternity? At the Islam-Christian conferences of 1954 in Lebanon and 1955 in Egypt, similar perspectives were envisaged. (At the latter conference the Copts played an important part.) We are still in the early stages of vague resolutions and hopes, but nevertheless these events are all pointing in the right direction.

The future of the Eastern Churches is directly related to the amount of effort they are prepared to expend in the process of renewal, in raising the moral, spiritual and intellectual level of their clergy and their faithful. They will surely heed the spirit of Pentecost, which for more than a century has moved every obedience of the whole of the Church of Christ. It is not too much to hope that this spirit will one day lead the entire flock faithful to the Cross towards the fold of unity.

CHAPTER VI

THE SEAMLESS COAT

1. 'May They be One'

In the spring of 1848 Western chancelleries, although preoccupied with graver matters, received news from their embassies in the Near East of a serious incident: the silver star had been stolen from the Church of the Nativity at Bethlehem. The star carried a Latin inscription, which had for a long time been a source of irritation to the Greek Orthodox clergy. The disappearance of the star caused concern in Western capitals. An envoy, Eugène Boré, was sent specially from Paris; his investigations on the spot left no doubt as to the identity of the culprits. A protest was then addressed to the Turkish Government by the French ambassador. Russia, the protector of Eastern Christians, also intervened, dispatching a veritable army of Embassy officials to Constantinople, so numerous that this appeared to constitute the advance guard of a military force. There were discussions, threats and intrigue to such an extent that the great powers soon found their most vital interests at stake—all this stemming from a dispute between rival monks. The upshot was nothing less than the Crimean War.

This incident of the star was only one of many. Ever since the West and the East had knelt together in the Holy Land to pray to the same Saviour, the disputes between them for the privilege of guarding the Holy Places and celebrating services there had never ceased. Under the Turks' cynical and contemptuous eyes the Christians of the Holy Land had indulged in pointless quarrels about precedence, rites, calendars and time-tables, all of which would have been comical had not the disputes been of a sordid and sometimes dangerous nature. For example, in 1834 the Orthodox Easter ceremony resulted in an inter-confessional riot of such proportions that four hundred corpses were reportedly collected from the streets afterwards. Nowadays the antagonism is not so violent, and a *modus vivendi* has been established among the different communities. But nevertheless the situation is a distressing one, particularly for the visiting believer. The Holy Sepulchre is looked after by five different and rival confessions: Latins, Orthodox Greeks, Armenians, Syrian Jacobites and Copts, each bitterly disputing every inch of ground, every nook and corner, the ownership of the rods on which the lamps hang, even the benches on which the pilgrims' offerings are collected. In the labyrinthine, chaotic architecture of the place, amidst the atrocious ornaments, the framed chromolithographs, the gimcrack artificial flowers, the rivalry between the clergies is the last straw in a distressing spectacle where faith finds little glory. It needs great strength of mind and deep humility to accept that in this place and in these conditions the God of love and human brotherhood reigns.

Jesus stressed many times the need for brotherly love and for unity: 'By this shall all men know that ye are my disciples, if ye have love one to another' (John xiii. 35). And: 'Neither pray I for these alone, but for them also which shall believe on me through their word . . . that they may be one, even as we are one' (John xvii. 20–2).

Jesus had stressed this need for unity many times during his public teaching. The most striking comparisons were employed in his parables—his disciples must be linked like the vine, like the flock of which he was the shepherd; more, they must constitute one living body, the Body of Christ, who was the soul. Moreover all the signs were of unity in that little community—equal participation in the bread and wine of the sacrament, equality in election, equality in God's call to each and everyone, equal allegiance to the Messiah, the Lord and the Saviour. Later, when Christ had vanished from the earth, in the young Church illuminated by the Holy Spirit, the sense of unity was even stronger, founded as it was on the common belief in the return in glory, the common certitude that they were all guardians of the same Message and the same Promise, with the same destiny, common resolution in the face of the challenges of destiny.

We know only too well what Christians have made of this unity, imposed by the Master as a basic characteristic of the Church. A glance at the spectacle of the Holy Sepulchre suffices to give an idea, but a clearer picture can be had by surveying the Christian world as a whole. Of every three men in the world today, after centuries of evangelization, a fraction less than one is a Christian, a curious and distressing fact. And even more distressing and shameful is the fact that the so-called Christian world is split into Churches, obediences, denominations and sects, all of whom either ignore one another or hate one another, vie with each other or fight one another. The whole basis of Christianity is thrown into question thereby: it could be argued that the Word of the Lord has not conquered the world—that the Gates of Hell have prevailed against it.

'Is Christ divided?' said St Paul (I Cor. i. 13) to his disciples in Corinth; even then one was for him, one was for Peter and another claimed the sole right to speak in the name of Jesus. Since that time Christians have followed other masters with a result worse still: Christ is put aside.

A conclusion such as this is inevitable when one considers the strange puzzle which is the Church of Christ, or attempts to follow through history the kaleidoscope of schisms and divisions. Even a Catholic, however deeply convinced he may be of his belonging to the community which has kept the authentic message of the Lord, however proud he may be of belonging to the greatest group of baptized, cannot accept a situation such as this. May he not feel in some measure responsible for all those sheep that have quitted the fold? Merely to ask such a question is to conjure up the 'great distress' that is disunity, so well described by the Abbé Couturier in unforgettable words. What Christian worthy of the name has not felt this distress? It was Calvin in the sixteenth century who said: 'Among the worst evils of our age is the separation of Churches, to such an extent that there is scarcely any pretension to community, even less to that communion of the members of Christ, which each professes with his lips, but which few carry into reality.'

2. The Nostalgia for Unity

The allusion to the 'second father of the Reformation' is significant: it illustrates to what degree, among true Christians, the nostalgia for unity existed and also to what degree each felt responsible for the split. The history of the heresies and schisms which have been responsible for shattering unity can be matched by yet another containing all the regret expressed for this, and of the efforts made to remedy it.

Leading figures have stressed, throughout the Church's history, that disputes were damaging and must end. This explains why in the year 210, in his treatise against Marcion, Tertullian made use of the famous analogy of the 'seamless coat', employed as a symbol to denote the One Church, which must not be 'rent': '. . . took his garments, and made four parts . . . and also his coat: now the coat was without seam, woven from the top throughout' (John xix. 23–4). St Cyprian, St Augustine and St Jerome, and patristic tradition after them, saw in this intangible garment the image of that other supernatural garment, the Church, which the disloyalties of its sons have rent to shreds.

As the theological discussions grew deeper and more complicated, so the conciliators grew in number, each seeking to explain the misunderstandings, to pour oil on the waters and to seek compromises. Until the year 1054, when the split between Rome and Byzantium became open and final, the seven ecumenical councils, at which all Christians were represented, could claim credit for their untiring work in the cause of unity. Points at issue were debated: one of the solutions proposed was then adopted and became official; those disagreeing with it then had either to accept it or to leave the Church. Some adopted the latter course, Nestorians and Monophysites among them, but these were minorities who did not seriously compromise the authority of the true Church; they were many times offered opportunities to return to the fold.

The break in 1054 did not leave the Church resigned to the tragic situation thus created. The majority of Christians of the epoch had no idea that the wrongs were as much on one side as on the other, a fact that historians see only too well.[1] Several believers at that time regarded the break as a cruel wound; the letter sent by the venerable Peter of Antioch to his colleague in Constantinople, Michael Cerularius, is one which cannot be read without emotion. In it he besought him not to push the argument to a final break, warning him in prophetic terms of the catastrophic results which would ensue. . . . Once the break was open and evident there were men who had the courage to deplore it aloud, even to praise their separated brethren, such as George the Hagiorite, who in 1064 boldly affirmed that he found no deviations in the Latin faith. Or John II, Patriarch of Kiev, who stated that whatever criticisms one could level at the Latins it was not on dogmatic matters. Or Theophylact, Patriarch of Ochrida in Bulgaria, who devoted a long treatise to the errors of the Latins, concluding that nothing in these errors justified a schism and that, at bottom, it was principally a question of persons and races. . . .

In reality for many years, especially in the West, no one thought that a break had taken place, The knights of the First Crusade were in no doubt that the sacraments received from Eastern priests were valid. In any case relations between the Catholic West and the Byzantine emperors remained constant. Political considerations as much as religious ones urged *rapprochement*. There was a special envoy from the Basileus to the coronation of Gregory VII; other emperors poured out their gold bezants to assist Western monasteries, such as that of Monte Cassino. Thirty-five years after the break, in 1089, a synod met at Rome to examine relations between it and Byzantium and to seek ways of eliminating the causes of the division. During the following decades many popes voiced the hope that all Christians would come together again (Alexander II, Paschal II and, later, Innocent III). Even the unfortunate Fourth Crusade (1202–4), which took Constantinople and launched the Frankish Eastern Empire and which widened the gap between Greeks and Latins, did not stop these appeals. There was even an attempt at reconciliation soon afterwards.

This was the work of St Gregory X, a Visconti, a contemporary of St Louis, who was frightened that the Turks were going to burst across the Byzantine ramparts and flood into Europe. Since the emperor, Michael Palaeologus, was of the same opinion, a council was convened

---

[1] See Chapter IV, section 2.

at Lyons in 1274 where, for the first time since the break in 1054, the representatives of the Orthodox world (two archbishops and several dozen prelates) met their Catholic counterparts and even celebrated Mass together. The climate was highly propitious—even on the disputed question of *Filioque* a solution was found. But it was all too short lived. The successor of Gregory X, Nicholas III, was as imperious and curt as his predecessor was accommodating, and the Greek clergy far from welcomed the Fathers when they came to discuss reconciliation. The emperor, Michael, a logical Unionist, died a Catholic, but his son Andronicus II did not follow his father's example and remained outside Rome, an attitude which was responsible for a further hardening of the Roman position.

It was all a very unfortunate series of events. However, even during the fourteenth century, with Turkish power growing in the East and taking into account the distressing incident of the Pope's exile to Avignon, and the Great Schism, when rival pontiffs fought each other, there were still many who held on to their hopes for unity. John Palaeologus, Emperor of Byzantium, even went so far as to become a Catholic, but he did nothing to rally his people, still less his clergy, to the cause of Rome. At the beginning of the fifteenth century there were men in both camps who were clear-sighted enough to see that Western safety lay in unity, and of sufficiently spiritual endowment to see that the true traditions of the Church provided the means towards achieving this. Some examples: Pope Martin V, the victor at the Council of Constance in the terrible crisis of the Schism, and his successor, Eugenius IV; on the Eastern side, Bessarion, one of many theologians holding similar views. Firstly at Basel, then at Ferrara in 1438, later at Constance in 1439, a council met to consider the matter; the Byzantine emperor attended, accompanied by his Patriarch and a large number of archbishops. After much discussion agreement was reached on the *Filioque*, there were embraces and, amid general enthusiasm, it was proclaimed that the wall between East and West had been demolished. But on their return the Greek prelates soon discovered that the wall between the Churches of East and West was a solid as ever, for they found that others had not come to the same conclusion; the monks remained obstinately hostile to the Latins; many Metropolitans reached open defiance of the decrees agreed upon at Florence. The efforts of the Basileus to maintain unity came to nothing, and in 1452, while a pro-unity cardinal was celebrating Mass at St Sophia, trouble broke out. The general opinion prevalent among the Greeks was expressed thus by Admiral Notaras: 'It would be better to see the Turkish turban dominate Constantinople than the Latin cardinals' hats'—a wish that was granted a year later.

And yet, despite the gulf created by incomprehension and bungling, the separation between the two great portions of the Church was never complete, never wholly accepted. In 1583, when his reform of the calendar was being discussed, Gregory XIII entered into friendly correspondence with the Patriarch, Jeremiah II, and when he opened the St Athanasius Greek seminary at Rome, to which all Easterners were admitted, he received warm thanks from Byzantium. In 1630 the Patriarch, Cyril of Berea, made attempts to renew the links with Rome, but three years later he was deposed by an Eastern Council and subsequently murdered. Some of the men of goodwill who sought to unite the Church, in the face of an almost totally hostile climate of opinion, did succeed partially in founding 'Uniate' Churches which were associated with the Church of Rome. Others who strove all their lives, but with no success, were the Croatian priest Krijanich, who sought to prepare the way for unity between Rome and Moscow, killed in 1688 when chaplain to the Christian armies defending Vienna against the Turks; Czar Alexis, whose education was undertaken by an apostate Catholic and a Russified Pole, haunted by the problem of Church unity, dispatched the Catholic Scot Menzies to Paris in 1672 to study the problem (the latter had excellent views on the subject, but no court in Europe—and certainly not that of Louis XIV—took them seriously); Peter the Great was interested in the question and discussed it with Dr Boursier and other masters of the Sorbonne during his visit to Paris in 1718.

At this time, moreover, it was not only vis-à-vis the East that the Catholics were pondering the problem of unity. The Protestant Reformation had served to disrupt habits and multiply the causes for outbreaks of hostility between Christians, made even worse by the fact that temporal considerations had entered into the matter. And yet, here again, it would not be correct to say that the rents in the coat were lightly accepted. Let us leave aside the efforts undertaken within Protestantism itself by such men as Bucer, Melanchton, Oeclampadius and others to maintain unity, distressed as they were to see it torn between followers of Luther, Zwingli, Calvin or the Anabaptist faith (and also the numerous conferences which took place, laying the groundwork for the now characteristic Protestant preoccupation with internal consolidation). Even in relations between Protestant and Catholic, not all were ready to admit that there were no chances of reconciliation. Erasmus, for example, criticized so unjustly by so many Catholics, did his best to re-establish the links between the Roman Church, the Czech Utraquists and the Moravians. Among the Protestants, with George Mitzel, author of *Via Regia*, and among the Catholics, with Julius von Pflug, Bishop of Nuremberg, the spirit of reconciliation was to be seen at work. There were also official attempts, not merely for political reasons—such as the Poissy colloquy in 1561 at the request of Catherine de Medici, or the meetings at Hagenau, Worms and Ratisbon at the instigation of Charles V. Representatives of the Reformed faiths were invited to the Council of Trent; many Fathers nourished the hope that the Lutherans at least might be persuaded to return to the fold.

In the darkest moments, when the religious split was marked by bloody affrays, there were always in both camps men of goodwill, energetic and daring enough to oppose the fury of princes. There was Adam of Schwartzenberg, a friend of the Protestant Elector of Brandenburg; there were bishops such as the Pole Lubiensky; there was the Milanese Capuchin Valeriano Magni, whose role in Bohemia after the Protestant defeat was an admirable one; there was the Benedictine Leander of St Martin, a skilful apostle of Anglican return to Rome. These men were all forerunners of the ecumenical movement. Nor should we forget the famous Father Joseph, *éminence grise* behind Richelieu, who set down some memorable words on the subject of unity. As for the other camp, respect is due to men like Hugo de Groot, who once confessed to a friend that he 'burned with desire to reconcile the Christian world'; to Georges Calixte, who somewhat naïvely but nevertheless sincerely proposed a set of 'simplified dogmas' which both Catholics and Protestants could accept. In the middle of the seventeenth century the confessor to the court at Vienna, Cristobal de Rojas y Spinola, Bishop of Dalmatia, an indefatigable apostle of unity, spent long years travelling between European capitals and the German courts in preparation for reconciliation, even at one stage being convinced that he had wellnigh achieved it. . . .

All these efforts were in vain, although from the middle of the sixteenth century to the end of the eighteenth century one important step forward was taken.[1] The controversy between Catholics and Protestants altered in character. In the early days it was purely polemical; e.g. 404 errors were ascribed to Luther by Eck at the Diet of Augsburg, and an unnamed Franciscan criticized Calvin's 1,400 theological monstrosities! This polemical style of controversy, perpetrated by both sides, tended to amuse the gallery.

Later it took on an irenical turn, and, while still remaining firmly attached to principles, the controversy was led by men who deliberately chose a more placid vocabulary for their accusations. St Peter Canisius is an example; he was perhaps the first to employ the term 'separated brethren' instead of 'erring brethren'. St Vincent de Paul, firm but charitably disposed towards the Protestants, is another example—as is St John Eudes, who prayed to the Blessed Virgin for the separated brethren. The discussions went on, but without the heat of

[1] See section 4 of this chapter.

earlier ages. Humbert de Romans demonstrated a comprehensive understanding of the position of Orthodoxy. François Véron, curé of Charenton, proposed that the anti-Protestant dispute be cleansed of minor questions concerned with scholastic differences, of wounding attacks and of mockeries in order to tackle only the vital questions of dogma. Bossuet took up this idea in his own inimitable style and set it down in his work, *Exposition of the Doctrine of the Catholic Church*; he also embarked on a most interesting correspondence with Leibnitz on the subject, in which both writers defended their standpoints with all their resources of knowledge and dialectic, avoiding any personal or offensive attacks. There were many other such dialogues, indicating that in the absence of a real climate of unity there was at least one of mutual respect.

During the eighteenth century it was clear that there were many individuals who clung to the dream, although every attempt at union on a wider front came to nothing. Those individuals were to be found in both camps, exemplified by Locke in his essay *On the Reasonableness of Christianity*, which advocated a more enlightened religion, and the Pietists, who, by stressing personal piety, hoped to take the sting out of their antagonists' blows. Among these mention must be made of the founder of the Herrnhut community, Count von Zindendorf, a generous and somewhat naïve personality; before him the Anglican pietist, John Dury, had advocated a similar approach; Wesley, although he founded the Methodist Church, was also a convinced unionist. Others were less swayed by feeling, more rational in their approach—such as the Protestant magistrate Rouvière, and the Anglican priest Dutens; both worked out detailed plans for reunion, maintaining that the charges against Rome were not worth the schism and all its attendant afflictions. At the end of the eighteenth century there appeared through Planck and Marheineke the first concretization of the bases of modern ecumenicalism, which Moehler later expanded.

The above list is restricted and gives only a minimal idea of the many efforts undertaken—often in the most dispiriting circumstances —to keep alive the hopes of unity.

3. THE NINETEENTH CENTURY MOVES TOWARDS ECUMENICALISM

The nineteenth century was an important step forward to what is now called ecumenicalism. There were many reasons for this, some profound, some merely contingent and some controversial. A certain degree of *rapprochement*, brought about by closer personal contact, could be seen in many circles. For example, there can be no doubt that during the Revolution the presence of many exiled priests in Britain and Germany contributed to a better understanding of the Catholic clergy; among the influx of Catholic priests there were some who gained a better understanding of the Protestant positions, even to the extent of adopting them, as was the case with the future apostle of Methodism in France, du Pontavice. In 1810 a Catholic historian, Antoine Caillot, published an anthology of the finest Protestant sermons with the object of paying a tribute 'to all Protestants for their generous and heroic assistance towards those French ecclesiastics forced by persecution to seek asylum in foreign countries'.

In both its good and bad aspects, this era is one which tends towards a *rapprochement* between Christians. The universe is expanding and there is a trend towards what one might call 'cosmopolitanism'. Schleiermacher, one of the masters of Protestant thought, declared that he could perceive 'the idea of a Church in a peaceful and cosmopolitan union of all existing communions, each as near perfection as possible within its type'. This idea smacks of liberal Protestantism and also of a certain degree of rationalist liberalism in which dogma becomes diluted. But, at the same time, we live in an age where the tendency is all towards centralization, uniformity and interdependence, and it would be odd if the Christian communities alone did not follow this tendency—particularly after the experience of the nineteenth century when Christianity was following a different line. The missionary movement, in full flood among both Protestants as well as Catholics, has led Christians of all faiths to realize to the full the shame of their disunity. There is a story, current in missionary circles, of a Brahmin who confided to a Christian friend that he had abandoned his ancient Hindu religion and wished to enter his Christian friend's Church. The latter smiled sadly: 'Which one?' he asked. 'There are seventy in my country.' It is not only heathen peoples who pose the Christians this cruel question—it is a problem within Christianity. The ever-increasing threat of atheistic humanism in all its forms— Nietzscheism and Marxism—may perhaps force Christians to close their ranks. Obviously this on its own would be a paltry reason for union. The increasing importance that was given to theological and biblical studies throughout the nineteenth century has made itself felt, tending to bring different obediences together and resulting in impressive renewals.

The drive towards unity is not one which can be defined precisely. It is a movement in the loosest sense of the term, and because it springs from deep down in the soul it cannot be pinpointed and described accurately. In outline it can be described as a general decline in polemics, a mutual desire to understand the separated brethren, and the wish to respect their beliefs, thus preserving charity, Christ's true link between Christians. But it would be wrong to suppose that these feelings were universal. For many believers in both camps, the other is the enemy. A writer of the standing of the Spaniard Jacques Balmes expounded the following naïve thesis in his vast work, published between 1841 and 1844, *Protestantism and Catholicism Compared*: 'Protestantism is a basically corrupting influence; it destroys all virtues!' A Catholic apologist, the Abbé Audin, offered an 'explanation' for the Reformation by saying that Calvin and Luther were guilty of the grossest vices. But, on the other hand, anti-Roman prejudices are fully exploited by Protestant apologists, and are just as absurd and deplorable. The untruths which are even today still printed in Protestant writings against the Vatican or the Society of Jesus are beyond the limit of stupidity. Worse, the Missouri American Lutheran Synod printed in a report, which is used as doctrinal material, the statement that as regards Antichrist, one must accept that the prophecies (found in II Thess. ii. 3, 12, and I John ii. 18) have been fulfilled in the most horrible way in the person of the Pope and his sphere of influence.

It is therefore very important to remember that, against such examples of Christians misled by routine and passion, there were, throughout the century, men who strove to weave the coat of Christ anew. There have been so many of them, and their efforts have taken on so many different aspects, that it would be impossible to enumerate them all here. Some have carved out places of renown for themselves as forerunners in the history of ecumenicalism; others are more or less unknown and merit no more. On one occasion Pope Pius IX received in audience an English Catholic priest who, since 1832, had undertaken a campaign of prayer for the conversion of the Anglicans; the Pope was somewhat surprised when, in defiance of protocol, the priest addressed him first, and entreated him to remove the term 'heretic' from officials texts when referring to Anglicans and other separated brethren. This was done, all Roman documents thenceforth using the term 'acatholici' (non-Catholics). Who has ever heard of this admirable believer, Father Ignatius Spencer? Or of a Russian, Father Tolstoy, who fifty years later journeyed to Rome to tell Pope Leo XIII that, although he was a true Orthodox believer, he believed also in all that the Catholic Church—'One and Indivisible'—taught and, as an integral part of the Church, he demanded the same rights as any Catholic priest, especially as regards celebrating Mass; these rights were granted to him.

Even in the most obstinate citadels of Protestantism there have been minds who considered unity with as much lucidity as they considered the strengthening of their own faith. The most outstanding phrase is one from Vinet, the great spiritual thinker of Lausanne: 'One separates only to reunite; Protestantism will return to Catholicism, as Socialism leads to unity.' There is also this extraordinary sentence from the writings of Kierkegaard: 'Catholicism and Protestantism are as parts of the same building which cannot stand upright unless each part bears on the other.' Nicholas Grundtvig, the Danish Protestant Church's great revivalist, used some admirable phrases on the subject: 'The Church which was, is and will be, the doctrine of which manifests itself clearly throughout history in the name of the unique, the true, the historic Church of Christ'. Did he not call on the Holy Spirit, in a burning passage, to 'move all those who have the same hopes, the same Lord, the same faith, the same God who is the Father of all'?

Are these all isolated cases? In a sense they are—as the Metropolitan Philaret of Moscow was an isolated case when he refused to condemn the Churches separated from Orthodoxy: as surprising as William Palmer, a partisan of the 'three branch' theory, who set out to harmonize in one faith the Catholics, Anglicans and Orthodox; as Monsignor Strossmayer, the *enfant terrible* of the First Vatican Council, who dreamed all his life of bringing the Orthodox Balkans into the Roman fold; as Abbé Guettée, founder of *L'Union Chrétienne*; or as Monsignor Szeptyckii, who for more than forty years strove to link the Catholic West and the Orthodox East.

But let us turn to other matters. If we attempt to classify all these efforts towards unity we see that there are distinct kinds of apostles of reconciliation. Some have taken the view that the only agency of unity could be God, and that it was to Him that one must turn—to the Holy Ghost and to Christ who taught the necessity of unity. Throughout the nineteenth century this purely spiritual current manifested itself on several occasions—with Father Spencer as we saw earlier; with St Vincent Pallotti (founder of the Missionary Union of the Clergy) who, in 1835, marked the feast of Epiphany as a time of prayer for Christian unity; with the German Catholic publicist Riess, who founded a pious association the members of which prayed for the return of the Reformed adherents to the Catholic Church. Bigger campaigns were undertaken in England with the Association for the Promotion of the Union of Christendom, in which the Catholic convert, Ambrose Phillips de Lisle, and the Anglican, Dr Lee, were concerned; all those who desired to pray for Christian unity were welcomed. But the time was not ripe for such a move, and in 1864 the Holy Office, disturbed by reports of these activities between Catholics and non-Catholics, forbade its faithful to attend the association's meetings. Yet it is difficult not to see in all these activities the forerunner of today's Week of Prayer for Unity, besides other similar activities.

Other believers considered that it was more essential to get to know one another, and, that by working together, serious theological questions would be solved more quickly. The volume of private contacts grew; there were unofficial ones at Madame Swetchine's *salon* and contacts of a more official type through the offices of the English Church Union or groups of liberal Protestants. These meetings were the forerunners of other inter-confessional ones, such as those in 1960 at Taizé when there was a conference of bishops and pastors. The most spectacular meeting during the nineteenth century was the Parliament of Religions at Chicago in 1893. This congress embraced not only Christians of every denomination, but all those who believed in a supernatural and divine reality. The two Catholic archbishops of the U.S.A., Ireland and Gibbons, agreed to attend some of the sessions of the parliament. The rector of the Catholic University of Wisconsin acted as speaker to this parliament, and for seventeen days there were speeches from pastors of different obediences, as well as from archimandrites and even several Brahmins. All the speakers confined themselves to stressing the value of faith to humanity and left aside all dogmatic questions. But unfortunately this did not stop the authorities at Rome from being extremely suspicious of the whole proceeding, Catholicism at that time being riddled with 'Americanism', the precursor of modernism.

4. FROM MOEHLER TO LEO XIII: THINKERS FOR UNITY

Apart from the efforts made either to establish links between different shades of belief, or to bring the different believers together in prayer for unity, there have been other attempts made by several thinkers to plan and establish a basic theology of unity. The fact that the leading thinkers in this have represented all the different confessions has been of the greatest importance. It is to them that we owe the changed climate, from one of controversy to one of discussion. The spirit of ecumenicalism today owes a great deal to their work.

The first and the most important among them was Johann Adam Moehler (1796–1838), whose works have recently been reissued. This young German priest, a gifted orator, was one of the prime movers in the spirit of renewal in his country, and his three great works are full of inspiration. The first, *The Unity of the Church*, written when he was twenty-nine years old, demonstrates a thorough knowledge of the Fathers of the first three centuries; the second, *Athanasius*, examines the life of the saint of Alexandria during the existential crisis brought about by the heresy of Arianism; the third, *Symbolism*, his principal work, in which he analyses Protestantism, going beyond thesis and antithesis to point out the essential idea of each religion, demonstrating that Catholic Christianity contains the synthesis. The work is dominated by the central theme of unity, and sets out to formulate an answer to the problems posed by Christian disunity.

As a student Moehler followed the teachings of the most highly respected masters of Protestantism in Berlin, and these instilled in him a profound respect for Protestant believers as well as a deep distress at the gulf which separated him from them.

As an historical theologian he was convinced that, though illumination came from the Holy Spirit, he was nevertheless entitled to ask himself what significance could be attached to the split. His work replies to just this question. The unity of the Church appeared to him to be nothing less than 'the Unity of the Spirit in the heart of all Christians'.

As a Catholic he had no doubt that the Church was an institution, but he also considered that it was 'above all, the effect of Christian faith, the result of the living love among the faithful brought together by the Holy Spirit'. His idea of the Church was not of a thing closed in on itself, a stagnant pool of doctrine, an institutional conglomeration to which nothing new might be added. He saw it as living, dynamic, open to all, infinitely fraternal—the Incarnation of Universal Love. Should it therefore allow itself to be open to error? By no means; in Moehler's view, Protestantism constituted an error, for it claimed to possess for itself alone certain truths which were the property of the whole Church. It was, however, vital to recognize that even an error could contain some truth, and that this truth should be extracted. A true Catholic therefore should be able to understand a Protestant in his submission to an all-powerful God, in his respect for Holy Scripture, in his recourse to the guiding light of the world—the Holy Spirit. A whole brotherly attitude has grown out of these certitudes—what greater achievement has there been over the past hundred years than the confirmation of them?

Half a century after Moehler another great Christian personality, who had read Moehler's works, took up his ecclesiology of the Holy Spirit and the love which it manifests, and transposed to another framework the question of the relations between Catholics and non-Catholics. He was a Russian, one of the masters of Russian spirituality and literature—Vladimir Soloviev (1858–1900),[1] whose great work, *The Spiritual Foundations of Life*, appeared in 1889. Since he was from birth an Orthodox Christian and a Russian with Slavophile tendencies, he conceived the Church quite naturally as universal—as 'the whole of humanity itself united in love; each believer within the Church must be united to all others through love'. Early on he came to the question of disunity and the problem of a return to unity. Christians had divided Christ because they did not practise universal love, and it

---

[1] See Chapter IV, section 12.

would require an effort of fraternal affection to establish its reign once more.

Soloviev then turned to that part of the Universal Church which stands out as a question mark, a judgment or a reproach for all Orthodox Christians—Rome. But he did not altogether reject Catholicism, as Moehler had not rejected Protestantism. On the contrary, he saw the Roman Church as a complement to the Eastern Church—the first had had the courage to put its hands to earthly tasks to effect men's salvation; the second had saved the spirit by withdrawing into meditation. The unity of the Church would come about through a synthesis between the Church which prayed and the Church which acted. In such a perspective all antagonisms were pointless, and the sole duty of all Christians was to love one another and so to understand one another. The Holy Ghost would do the rest. Soloviev went still further along the road to unity. He declared that, as a living body, Church unity must be manifested, and that it must have a head which directs the body. 'The Church must correspond to Christ, *the* being and centre of all beings; it must represent the common desire towards perfect unity.' His conclusion led him to state that 'universal truth perfectly achieved in one being [Christ] draws to it the faith of all, this being infallibly determined by one man alone—the Pope'. He was condemned and excommunicated by the Orthodox Church, and in 1896 became a Uniate Catholic, refusing to abjure the faith in which he was baptized, declaring that he remained faithful to the Pope besides remaining 'a member of the true and authentic Orthodox Church'; he was a fine example of the soul-searching demanded of the early prophets of ecumenicalism.

There were two other theologians of the nineteenth century who entertained advanced views on the subject, making use of formulas which a Catholic could not accept. Frederick Dennison Maurice (1805–72), who played an important part in Anglicanism with his great work, *The Kingdom of God*, occupied an important place in the nineteenth-century current of thought which was leading to unity. Convinced that Anglicanism was the most perfect form of Christianity, he stated nevertheless that he could see the importance of the principle of Protestantism—that its true goal was the Catholic Church. In his view the different Churches were living members of the divine Kingdom. The duty of a true Christian faced with his separated brethren was to unite his faith with those who were separated in order that they might become integral members in the body of Christ. This may seem paradoxical language to any Catholic used to looking on all Anglicans at least as 'separated brothers'.

The theologian Ignace von Döllinger (1799–1890) was less paradoxical. He was the leader of the anti-infallibility faction at the First

Vatican Council,[1] the promoter of the schismatic Old Catholic Church. He had, however, profound views on unity, not all of which were worthless. In an attempt to make evil do good, he dreamed of making his little Church into a meeting ground for all true Christians. His work, *The Unity of the Churches* (1880), condemned schism as a 'massive error', entreated the different Churches to pool their knowledge and their privileges and thus achieve, in the noblest sense, community of property. He called upon them to refashion the Church along the lines of the primitive Church, which would receive within it all those now separated from it, and concluded that 'hope cannot be absent when faith and love are present'. Then Döllinger left the field of theory to embark on a plan of action, and in 1874 and 1875 he arranged meetings between Anglicans, Lutherans and Orthodox as well as Old Catholics. This schismatic, who so easily mixed errors and truths, caused some surprise, but nevertheless one could not ignore a Christian who stressed to his brothers: 'Come closer one to another, help one another, the better to understand and love each other.'

A question remains: What was Rome's attitude in the face of this many-sided agitation in favour of Christian unity? It was obvious that all popes desired unity, but, conscious as they were of possessing the sole truth, they could conceive it only as a 'return', to use the traditional expression. It is also true that, in a certain sense, reconciliation among the baptized would be a 'return'; but were allusions to the return of the prodigal son, of the lost sheep, the best ones to use in the circumstances? Even when swayed by the most sincere desire for unity, the Catholic Church cannot renounce its *raison d'être*, the certitude that it alone is the guardian of the authentic message of Christ. In 1682 the Assembly of French clergy addressed a warning to the Reformed Churches, couched in language that was generally believed to be that of Bossuet. It read: 'The Church seeks you as she seeks her lost children; she calls to you as the ewe calls to her lambs; she strives to gather you under her wings as the hen her chickens; she entreats you to undertake the way to the heavens as the eagle entreats her young.' The generosity of the language employed cannot be doubted, but what Protestant would agree that he is a lost child or that he needs to be shown the way to heaven?

It is therefore within this rigid framework that one must see the attitude of the popes to unity. The two greatest among them during the century were aware of the gravity of the problem and were sincerely desirous of finding a solution to it. Each of them set about his task in a way befitting his temperament.

Until he convened the Vatican Council Pius IX manifested no great interest in this question. There were two Roman documents which

---

[1] See Appendix 1.

mentioned it, but only to stress that it must be approached with circumspection. The letter from the Holy Office in the autumn of 1864 forbade English Catholics from participating in the work of the Association for the Promotion of Unity among Christians; a year later there was another communication from the Holy Office on the same subject; these were merely restrictions imposed on a purely local level. The Pope nevertheless remained preoccupied with the question. This can be seen when, having convened the Council with the Bull *Aeterni Patris* on 29th June 1868, he followed it up with two others: one a letter addressed to 'all bishops of Eastern Churches which are not in communion with the Holy See' and, a week later, by another addressed to Protestants and Anglicans inviting them to attend the Council. Both attempts met with failure. The Orthodox bishops, who were in any case irritated by the Bull *Reversus*, of 1867, which signalled the interest of Rome in the Eastern Churches attached to it, maintained for the most part a contemptuous silence. The Ecumenical Patriarch of Constantinople, referring to an allusion to the councils of Florence and Lyons, answered that the decisions taken at those councils had been nullified by the fact that the Pope did not take part as a Patriarch equal to all the others. As for the Reformation Churches, their attitude was more complex. The Lutheran pastor Baumstarck stated that he was in favour, but his lone voice was lost in the controversy. In France Guizot's conciliatory tendencies were largely nullified by Pressensé's more intransigent attitude. In England the proposition got off to a good start: Anglican bishops such as Cobt and Urquhart, and the Scot Forbes, were well disposed towards participation in the work of the Council, but they came up against Pusey, who feared that the Anglican High Church would follow Newman's lead to rejoin Rome. In the end not one 'separated brother' went to the Council. It was obvious that the dogma of Papal Infallibility was not helping to bring about a climate favourable to a 'return'.

This did not stop Leo XIII from undertaking and pursuing throughout his term of office a policy of *rapprochement*. It was part of his policy to widen the perspectives of the Church and bring about a closer degree of contact with the modern world. The tragedy of disunity moved him as much as did another scandal—social injustice—which he denounced strongly in *Rerum Novarum*. In the twenty-five years of his pontificate there were no less than thirty-two documents issued which dealt, in some degree or other, with the question of reconciliation. He was especially interested in reconciliation with the Christians of the East, entreating them to 'remove the idea that the Latins wanted to abolish or attenuate their rights, their privileges and rites'. He proclaimed in the Encyclical *Praeclara Gratulationis* that 'apart from one or two points, agreement between Catholics and

Orthodox was virtually complete'. But his efforts towards the goal of reconciliation were ill received: in October 1895 a document, styled 'Patriarchal Encyclical', was published, signed by twelve Greek Orthodox bishops, which began with the words: 'The Devil having inspired the bishops of Rome with an intolerable pride, from whence come innumerable impious innovations. . . .' Leo XIII nevertheless pursued his irenical goal: 'We may not live to see the unity of the Churches accomplished, but we should not qualify this as vainly utopian'. The novena of prayer in 1895, which he launched, was the expression of this invincible hope, expressed in spiritual terms while awaiting concrete realization.

Undoubtedly Leo XIII directed his efforts principally towards the Eastern Churches, but when he heard of the contacts made between Catholic priests and Anglican leaders he was happy to encourage them, urging Father Portal to spare no efforts. Nothing came of it, perhaps because the time was too early or perhaps because of the lack of solid canonical or historical bases. When he was obliged to terminate these discussions everyone agreed that he did so with a heavy heart, but that he in no way despaired of the sublime cause.

5. The Attempt at Corporate Reunion between the Anglicans and Rome

The winter climate of Madeira is beneficial, and for this reason Lord and Lady Halifax, accompanied by their children, went there in December 1889. Of Lord Halifax's four sons two had died of consumption; of the remaining two, Charlie was suffering from chronic pleurisy.

Lord Halifax (1839–1934), though a Protestant, spent much time visiting the Catholic churches of the island, even taking part in the services. In the chapel of the Doña-Maria hospice he met Father Fernand Portal (1855–1926), then acting as an auxiliary chaplain, and a firm and lasting friendship sprang up between them.

The problems which were preoccupying Lord Halifax were not concerned with faith—he was an Anglican by birth and belief; he prayed daily, was often present at services and even undertook an annual retreat. The two blows which he had suffered had done nothing to diminish his belief in Providence. His preoccupation was of another kind—since his youth he had been haunted by the shame of Christian disunity. One of his uncles had presented him to Newman, with whom he had conversed many times on the problem of possible reunion between the Anglicans and the Church of Rome. Without offering any criticism of the conversion of the leader of the Oxford Movement the young Lord Halifax had preferred the attitude adopted by Dr Pusey [1] who, while criticizing certain lacunae in the Anglican Church, remained faithful to it, affirming that it remained an integral part of the universal Church and that it was within this framework that work towards reunion should take place. At twenty-eight Lord Halifax was elected leader of the English Church Union, whose thirty-five thousand members, including thirty bishops, were 'ritualists' who believed in 'Catholicizing' the Anglican Church.[2] He himself had never concealed his 'Anglo-Catholic' views, believing that these were a stage on the road towards a much greater degree of reunion. While he had not directly participated in the founding of the Order for Corporate Reunion in 1877 (which had taken over the pious intentions of the Association for the Promotion of the Union of Christendom, condemned by Pius IX in 1864, and had added a radical programme of reform for the Church of England), many of its most outspoken views were his. In 1889, when he arrived at Funchal, his views on the means to be used towards a *rapprochement* between the Anglican Church and Catholic Church, and the possible chances, were already clear cut, even though he had never had the opportunity to put them to the test. At the last meeting with Newman the latter had said: 'It is among the French that the best chances of helping the campaign for reunion are to be found, not in England.' Discussions with Father Portal confirmed this view.

Their meetings resulted in one of the most important chapters in the history of Christian unity. Henceforth Lord Halifax was an untiring worker in this cause—speaking, writing, travelling widely, sowing the seeds of future action even when he realized that he himself would not live to see the results. Some, such as his friend Archbishop Benson, compared him to a solitary chess player, who, lacking an opponent, manœuvred the pieces himself on the board. It should not be forgotten, however, that if the cause of reunion between Anglicans and Catholics was much talked about on two occasions and if—under very different forms—it still interests many people today, it was due wholly to Lord Halifax and to his friendship with Father Portal.

The latter knew nothing of the Anglican Church; he had never read the Prayer Book, until a copy was given to him by Lord Halifax. He could not have said which of the Thirty-nine Articles might be heretical. If the idea of *rapprochement* with the 'separated brethren' had crossed his mind at all, it would most likely have been with the Orthodox Churches. He had no reason to doubt Halifax's statement that the overwhelming majority of Anglican bishops preferred the possibilities of appeal to Pope Leo XIII rather than to the Queen's Privy Council, and that the majority of Anglicans rejected not the *real*

[1] See Chapter III, section 6.   [2] See Chapter III, section 6.

presence of Christ in the Eucharist but the corporeal. The standpoint of Lord Halifax with regard to the problem of conversion seemed to the Catholic priest to be an admissible one: instead of trying to convert Anglicans one by one, a method which might last centuries, it would obviously be better to try to find some way in which the entire English hierarchy could be converted to Rome, a reconciliation which Lord Halifax viewed as the logical outcome of Anglo-Catholicism. It would constitute corporate reunion, for which there were previous examples in history: the conversion of a Constantine, of a Clovis, was followed by the mass conversion of their peoples, the Romans and the Barbarians. In the other sense, the conversion of the higher echelons of the clergy in Germany and Scandinavia to Lutheranism brought about the 'Protestantization' of the masses. The objections to this mode of reasoning were that in the cases cited people were still living in an age when the conversion of all-powerful kings and princes was automatically followed by conversions *en masse*.

In any case the Anglican clergy—and especially the theologians—had to be urged to study the causes and the nuances of the break with Rome. To this end a press campaign would be needed, with careful choice of the subject to be debated. Both men knew that the real obstacle to reunion was, and was likely to remain, the primacy of the Pope, and that the proclamation of the dogma of Infallibility put this out of court. It was therefore necessary to tackle the matter by another, roundabout, route. In Father Portal's view the question of Anglican ordinations offered the best terrain for discussion. It could be very simply stated: 'Are English bishops true bishops? Do they enjoy Apostolic Succession and do the priests they consecrate receive valid orders?' It must be said that this, although it proved to be a mistake, seemed in 1894 the best proposition, for only eighteen months later the Benedictine, Dom Gasquet, found and published the text of the Bull of Pope Paul IV, *Praeclara Carissimi*, of 20th June 1555, and the Brief of 30th October, *Regimini Universalis*, which dealt with the matter dogmatically. Father Portal, mindful of the doubts surrounding the subject, published in 1894, under the pseudonym of Dalbus, a brochure entitled *Anglican Ordinations*, which went into two editions in two months. From a careful analysis of the documents, and the historical facts available, he concluded that the Anglican rite of ordination was certainly valid, that Bishop Parker, from whom all Anglican ordinations sprang, was certainly empowered to ordain (though a certain doubt existed as regards the intentions of the ordainer), and, finally, that if Anglican ordinations were to be declared invalid, then this was solely because a detail had been left out of the liturgical ceremony in Anglican ordinations: the 'porrection of instruments' (presentation to the ordinand of liturgical objects—the paten and chalice—for him to touch). The subtlety of this was evident; this liturgical detail was not introduced until the Middle Ages and therefore Anglican bishops had not suppressed anything essential, having only disobeyed a decree of Eugenius IV, which a pope might correct.

The brochure was an immense success. Visitors flocked to Cahors, where Father Portal had taken over directorship of a seminary. The second edition carried several letters from eminent personalities, among them Cardinal Bourret and an Anglican bishop, severely critical on certain points of the 'Dalbusian' theses, but nevertheless attentive and sympathetic. Abbé Duchesne, the most famous historian of the early Church, a future Academician, sent the author a letter couched in friendly terms, and in which he even stated that all Anglican ordinations were valid. This letter was first published in the *Bulletin Critique*, and reproduced in the three leading French newspapers of that time, *Le Temps*, *L'Union* and *L'Univers*. Feeling that the wind was fair, Father Portal prepared to launch a review, hesitating between two titles: *L'Union des Églises* or *La Revue Anglo-romaine*, both of which augured well.

The summer of 1894 was rich with promise. Invited to England by his friend, Father Portal visited numerous Anglican parishes and religious communities—they were in full expansion at this time [1]—as well as Anglican personalities in the hierarchy. The result of these meetings convinced him that reunion was not only possible, but even nearer than he had believed. An Anglican theologian of note, the Reverend Mandell Creighton, affirmed that no sensible person could dispute the Pope's primacy. The Archbishop of York told him that St Charles Borromeo and Monsignor Dupanloup were his own guiding spirits. The Archbishop of Canterbury himself, while counselling prudence in order not to split the Anglican Church, was confident that the undertaking would succeed.

Rome meanwhile had been kept informed of the discussions between Father Portal and Lord Halifax. Summoned to the Vatican, the former gave a detailed account of his negotiations and his hopes to Cardinal Rampolla. The next day Father Portal was received in audience by the Pope, who questioned him closely, and appeared to entertain the highest hopes. 'With what joy I should sing *Nunc Dimittis* if I could do the slightest thing to usher in reunion,' said Leo XIII. Optimism was in the air. In the unionist camp there could already be discerned the time when the noble Anglican Church as a whole would cross the threshold to enter the Universal Church.

But perhaps things were going a little too quickly. 'The slightest thing' of which the Pope had spoken—what was it? Lord Halifax suggested that this could take the form of a letter officially announcing

[1] See Chapter III, section 6.

that Rome had shown interest in the question raised by the enterprising propagandists of reunion. Originally it was decided that this letter would be addressed directly to high dignitaries of the Anglican Church—as had been the case with the Eastern Church, though with notable lack of success—but the Vatican observed that if the Pope's letter was greeted with derision the failure would be final. It was therefore decided that Cardinal Rampolla would write to Father Portal and that the contents would be communicated by Lord Halifax to the Anglican primates. If their reaction was favourable, if they replied positively to the Pope, he would answer them personally. Obviously this was a step backward, and the Anglican bishops took it as such, apart from the fact that certain of the terms used by Cardinal Rampolla concerning Rome—'Mother and mistress of all Churches'—were lacking in finesse. The reply which Lord Halifax received from the Archbishop of Canterbury was disappointing. Was the traditional Anglican position stiffening?

Father Portal was not discouraged, nor was the Pope. The Church of England had announced that it would be celebrating the thirteenth centenary of the conversion of England by the missionaries of St Augustine of Canterbury. Might not the Pope, considering his seniority, issue an Encyclical prior to the opening of the celebrations, recalling that the mission in England was the work of a Roman pope, Gregory the Great? This was agreed, and on 14th April 1895 the admirable *Ad Anglios* was issued, one of the most noble works of that noble pope, Leo XIII. Addressing all those in England who sought the Kingdom of God in the unity of faith, he invited them to work for the cause of unity, whatever their community or their institution. He announced that a commission would be set up to study the question of Anglican ordinations. The tone of the letter was generous from beginning to end and touched many English hearts. If some prelates manifested their annoyance at the Pope for addressing their flock over their heads, reactions were in general favourable. Opening the Congress of the Church of England in October of that year in Norwich (to which the Orthodox Churches were invited), the Archbishop of Canterbury said: 'Unity is in the air—a voice from Rome speaks of it also in a spirit of paternal love.' Gladstone, who had published a virulent pamphlet against Rome on the eve of the Vatican Council, now greeted with deference the 'first bishop of Christendom'.

But the difficulties were nevertheless real and had not all vanished. The most serious ones came from a sector where one could have expected it least—the English Catholics. They were of course only a minority, but they were active, and since the conversion of Newman and his friends in the Oxford Movement they had become ambitious, bent on the conversion of all England. For them corporate reunion was an impossibility, since the Anglican Church was too closely linked to the State to break free. All that counted in their view was individual conversions. Opposition was incarnate in Cardinal Vaughan, Manning's successor in the See of Westminster. He was brusque, straight-talking, a man who bothered little with shades of meaning, and he regarded the attempt at corporate reunion as an invention of Satan. All the theologians who had encouraged it or even tolerated it— the Duchesnes, Portals and Gasparris—were 'mere unknown scribes without any mandate'. A report issued at his instigation accused the unionists of wishing to force in the theory of the 'three branches', according to which Anglicanism, Orthodoxy and Catholicism would be on an equal footing. What was the cause of this furious attack? Malicious tongues attributed it to jealousy, for the cardinal would be aware that in a united English Church his place in the hierarchy would be of lesser importance. This is an unworthy argument, scarcely to be believed, especially when one considers the character of the cardinal himself. What is more to the point is the fact that the cardinal, like many other converts to Catholicism, entertained a hearty contempt for the Church of England; disunited, subject to secular control and spiritually lacking in vigour.

While the cardinal left for Rome, there to plead his cause, Lord Halifax continued with his campaign, making a stirring speech at Bristol which earned the approval of what he believed was the whole of the English people, and even obtaining words of encouragement from a number of Anglican bishops. But again none of this touched on the crux of the matter, dealt with in Father Portal's brochure—the validity of Anglican ordinations.

Then a curious incident took place which threw the whole question into sharp relief. A schismatic Spanish priest, Cabrera, who was working for the establishment of a small Protestant Church in his country,[1] had himself ordained in Ireland by the Archbishop of Dublin. In the name of the English Church Union, of which he was still the leader, Lord Halifax protested. A violent dispute broke out. Was the ordination valid or not? Cardinal Vaughan was only too pleased to join in, stressing that the Anglican archbishop had agreed to ordain a Protestant, and proclaimed that, whether English or Irish, Anglican ordinations were equally invalid. He wrote a letter to the Cardinal of Toledo, and *The Times* newspaper (through some unknown source) got hold of a copy and printed it. The letter stated that Lord Halifax was the leader of an insignificant sect and had no following among the official Church; and, furthermore, he had no right to the label 'Catholic'.

In Rome the climate was changing. Though coolly received by

[1] See Chapter II, section 7.

Leo XIII, Cardinal Vaughan conducted his offensive skilfully. Only a last-minute intervention by Cardinal Rampolla stopped a monition being issued by the Holy Office against Father Portal and Abbé Duchesne. Even the Pope himself had grown less enthusiastic, and to his *entourage* he was heard to say: 'The good Lord Halifax is making a mistake, the Church is One. . . .' But this did not prevent him from sending him a large photograph of himself. Everything now depended on the result of the Pope's commission on ordinations. This had been made up with evident care for impartiality. Among its eight members, and leaving aside Cardinal Mazzella the chairman, and Monsignor Merry del Val the secretary, two of the members, Abbé Duchesne and Father de Augustinis, a Jesuit, were on record as voting for validity; a third member, the Englishman Abbot Scannell, was understood to be favourable; three other members, all English, were hostile to it— the Benedictine Dom Gasquet, the Franciscan David and Canon Moyaes. The remaining two members, Monsignor Gasparri and Father Jose Calesanz, a Spanish Capuchin, had no preconceived ideas. Little by little the commission was forced to see that there was no majority for approving the validity of Anglican Orders. Furthermore Dom Gasquet had resuscitated sixteenth-century pontifical texts which settled the question in the negative.

At this point the great statesman Gladstone intervened. He looked upon himself as the standard-bearer of the 'ritualist' or Anglo-Catholic faction. A statement signed by him explained that the basis of true union between all Christians should be sought in their common affirmation of the great basic truths of Christianity, so that they could all join together against the assaults of atheism. It was obvious that Rome could never accept this type of 'basic Christianism'. Leo XIII brought the argument into line; the Encyclical *Satis Cognitum* of 29th June 1896, which dealt with the true unity of the Church, recalled that it was firstly a unity of faith; to preserve this unity of faith and guard against its undergoing different interpretations Christ had established a *magisterium* which was perpetual and infallible. . . . Was the question of ordinations to be relegated to the background and the question of the primacy of the Pope to be brought to the forefront, thus breaking off the negotiations? In any case the traditional conception of Anglicanism regarding the 'three branches' was severely shaken. An article in *The Times*, which bore traces of the pen of Cardinal Vaughan, concluded that there was no excuse for the illusions nurtured by Lord Halifax and his friends; for Rome there could be no reunion unless it was accepted that the Roman Pontiff enjoyed primacy not only of honour but also of jurisdiction.

The Commission's decision had been taken; in circumstances which are still unknown, with a majority that the Vatican archives will only reveal only in later years, it had reached its decision, declaring on 13th September 1896 that Anglican ordinations were invalid. Was it simply that the Commission had not found sufficient proof of the validity of Anglican ordinations to be able to accept them, or would it be made the subject of solemn declaration? Cardinal Vaughan and his friends opted for the second solution, employing the somewhat curious argument that in seeing their Church reduced in status in this way there would be many Anglicans seeking conversion.

On 13th September 1896, in his Encyclical *Apostolici Curae*, Leo XIII declared that in conformity with all the decrees of his predecessors, and in agreement with them, ordinations under the Anglican rite were invalid.

Lord Halifax, Father Portal and all the partisans of union were grieved by the blow. Father Portal announced that the *Anglo-Roman Review* would appear no longer. Cardinal Vaughan was pleased that the manœuvre, which he regarded as a trick of the devil, had been stopped in time. In the Anglican camp the Low Church was delighted; the Reverend Fillingham, one of its leading members, wrote that for real Protestants the question was unimportant; they were quite sure that their orders were not Catholic ones. The High Church was somewhat ruffled. As it happened, the flood of conversions predicted by Cardinal Vaughan did not take place.

The attempt launched by Lord Halifax and Father Portal had thus failed. They both accepted it without bitterness and turned once more to prayer, meditation and work, remaining friends, always ready to re-enter the scene if circumstances proved favourable once more. Their efforts were not wholly wasted. After these events Anglicans were at least now asking themselves questions that hitherto they had totally ignored. The fairness of Leo XIII had impressed the Anglican dignitaries so much that at the 1897 Lambeth Conference a total of some two hundred prelates voted a resolution on the Unity of the Church, which undertook that the entire Anglican Church would work without cease for the visible unity of all Christians, a copy of which was sent to Leo XIII together with a Latin address in which he was addressed as 'brother' and 'father'. Among continental Catholics the 'corporate reunion' affair had aroused interest anew in Christian unity. One should not overestimate the importance of the abortive attempt which was made, nor underestimate it—as one Anglican historian has done—by passing it over in silence. Among the many rivulets which have now begun to run together into the great river of ecumenicalism, we must not forget a source which sprang up in Madeira in 1889.

6. THE WORLD OF THE REFORMATION MOVES TOWARDS UNITY

The Protestant Churches as a whole deserve our admiration for having taken the first practical steps inspired by the longing for unity. It can truthfully be said that until January 1959, when the situation was reversed, the ecumenical movement was undeniably Protestant and Anglican.

It is therefore within the framework of Protestantism that one must recognize the stream which from the early years of the twentieth century began to sweep the Churches towards mutual understanding. Until the end of the eighteenth century there appeared to be a tendency to indefinite fragmentation, typical of the Protestant genius; but thereafter the movement took an opposite direction, and many of the Churches seemed resolved upon a concentration of their forces. That concentration was made manifest in two ways, depending mainly upon two different Protestant interpretations of the word 'Churches'. The religious world deriving from the Reformation appears as split up into 'Churches' distinguished from one another by different professions of faith, in the sense that one can speak of a 'Lutheran Church' or a 'Methodist Church'. But it is also true to say that within a community accepting a rule of faith there may be differences between groups, which are likewise described as Churches, and which are separated from each other by the historical and geographical circumstances in which they were established, and even by certain dogmatic or spiritual attitudes. Thus we now refer to the 'Lutheran Churches of Germany', just as within the field of Calvinism official Churches have found themselves confronted by 'free Churches'.

The tendency towards concentration is apparent in both cases. Within the chief doctrinal groups it was in the middle of the nineteenth century that alliances were formed. As early as 1847 the Universal Evangelical Alliance invited all the Protestant Churches to unite in a common 'effort of testimony and intercession', but that appeal found few echoes outside the larger bodies. In 1877 the Reformed Churches summoned a congress at Edinburgh, which gave rise to the 'Universal Alliance of Reformed Churches established according to the Presbyterian system'. Every ten years thereafter the movement was seen to have gained ground: all the great Christian communities of the same tradition realized that the points of doctrine and administration which separated them were much less important than those which united them. Baptists, Congregationalists, Lutherans, Methodists and others formed 'organic unions' among themselves. In 1911 there were no fewer than fourteen either localized or tending to include the worldwide total of believers belonging to the same faith. The movement was destined to continue, vigorous and with such important results as the birth of the 'Anglican Communion'.

This process of concentration was effective also between religious groups which had not the same professions of faith but which, in order to defend their interests and to combine their charitable undertakings— and also sometimes with the more spiritual purpose of mutual under-understanding, united in federations or inter-confessional unions. The first in date was the Federation of French Protestant Churches (1905–7), followed (1908) in the U.S.A. by the Federal Council of the Churches of Christ. The example had many followers: today there are no fewer than twenty-two federations or federal unions, and the tide seems to be in full flood.

In neither case, intra-ecclesial or interecclesial, can one truthfully claim an example of ecumenism, since there is no question of universal Christianity: we are still within the framework of a world deriving from the Reformation. But a first favourable note was struck in 1919 when the Council of Churches, in the U.S.A., admitted Orthodox representatives. Meanwhile, however, a significant step had been taken by the appearance of two movements, both of which were Protestant and Anglican in origin, but were destined soon to enlarge their framework and so to become truly ecumenical; two movements whose fusion was to beget the World Council of Churches, which is today one of the opportunities for achieving Christian unity.

The origin of those two movements, that is to say of the World Council, is manifold. It has been observed that during the nineteenth century certain currents of thought had permeated all groups deriving from the Reformation, irrespective of sectarian limits. On the practical level also, collaboration was achieved for purposes of charitable work or social action in which no account was taken of dogmatic or administrative differences. The ecumenical character was clear in the *Union chrétienne de jeunes gens*, founded in 1844 and granted a charter at Paris in 1855, and even more so after 1878, when, having become worldwide as the Young Men's Christian Association (Y.M.C.A.), followed in 1898 by its feminine counterpart (Y.W.C.A.), the union included thousands of young Protestants. Likewise the Universal Federation of Christian Student Associations, founded at Vadsten, in Sweden, 1895, took no account of confessional differences among its members. Thus the Protestant youth movement made for co-operation between the Churches. John Mott, a great American leader of students, was also one of the pioneers of ecumenism.

Another decisive influence was that of the missions, which, as we have seen, flourished during the nineteenth century; youth movements took a great interest in them. Missionaries at work in non-Christian lands suffered most from the unhappy error of division. Where they were not confronted with Catholic missionaries, whom the majority of them considered as rivals, they were in competition with one another, zealots belonging to many Churches in the same area. In some parts of the world missionaries of various denominations agreed not to compete in presence of future catechumens, and in 1866 the Continental Conference of Missions was established to generalize such agreements. It grew to worldwide stature and became the World Missionary Conference, including more than one hundred and sixty evangelical societies. In 1910 twelve hundred delegates met at Edinburgh, where they heard, among other reports, one from a Chinese who put the matter fairly and squarely thus: 'You have revealed Jesus Christ to us, for which we thank you. But you have also brought us your distinctions, your divisions: some preach Methodism, others Lutheranism, while others again are Congregationalists or Episcopalians. We ask you to preach the Gospel.' The shock caused by those words was such that the whole assembly resolved to take steps to end the scandal. That gathering of missionaries appeared, in the words of William Temple, Archbishop of Canterbury, as 'the greatest event in the life of the Church for a whole generation'. It was the source of capital achievements in the Protestant world as a whole, particularly as regards the missionary field. The Edinburgh meeting gave rise to the International Missionary Council, which was formed in 1921 and included 173 evangelical societies. Thoroughly well organized, the Council has since forged a firm link between the various Churches, and it remained active after the foundation of the 'World Council' with which it was fused at New Delhi in 1961. Its regular meetings, at Jerusalem in 1928, at Madras in 1938, at Whitby in 1947, at Willingen in 1952 and, finally, at Accra in 1958, all marked progress in the linking together of the several groups.

The Edinburgh meeting, however, had many other results. Charles Brent (1862–1919), an Episcopalian bishop of the Philippine Islands, was particularly moved by what he heard about the scandal of disunion. 'During these days', he declared at the final session, 'God has given us a new vision in order to lay upon us a new responsibility. You and I will all leave this assembly with new duties to fulfil.' Returning to the U.S.A. he kept his word, striving through personal contacts, as well as through books and lectures, to awaken the Protestant world to its responsibility in face of the scandal of disunion. His own Church decided to set up a permanent committee entrusted with the preparation of a universal conference for the study of questions concerning 'the Faith and Constitution of the Church'. The two words Faith and Order found an echo, and were used thenceforward to denote the movement inaugurated by Bishop Brent. Its aim was to lead all

Protestants to study those factors which separated them one from another, in the hope that a better understanding of the different points of view concerning faith would prepare the way for unity. The movement was highly successful in the U.S.A., where Brent received valuable help from a layman, Robert H. Gardiner; but less so in Lutheran countries, particularly Germany, which distrusted Anglican laxity. Certain declarations by a number of partisans more or less tainted with liberal Protestantism gave grounds for the idea of a sort of 'pan-Christianity', which was no less disquieting to Catholics. But Bishop Brent was not discouraged: not even the First World War prevented him from continuing his efforts, and he established contact with Pope Benedict XV.

Meanwhile another movement had been born in various Protestant circles, less concerned with dogmatic precision than with practical results. One man embodied the determination to 'do something', to unite all the Churches of Christ for the defence of Christian values: Nathan Söderblom (1866–1931), Archbishop of Upsala and Primate of the Lutheran Church of Sweden, a man of action as well as a man of prayer. The sensational campaign for peace launched by him in November 1914 won him worldwide celebrity and prepared the ground for later efforts. The climate of the immediate post-war years was clearly favourable to Söderblom's great plans. *Life and Work* came into being and at once placed itself beyond the strictly Protestant framework by introducing itself to Pope Benedict XV and by making contact with the Ecumenical Patriarch of Constantinople, who in 1920 replied on behalf of Orthodoxy with a kind of encyclical 'on a possible *rapprochement* between all those who believe in the True God and the Trinity'.

In 1920, therefore, there existed two movements tending towards union of the Protestant Churches and both admitting, though still somewhat vaguely, that the effort for unity went further than the Protestant boundaries. One, *Faith and Order*, concerned itself mainly with finding doctrinal bases for unity. The other, *Life and Work* (practical Christianity, as it was called in France), thought it simpler to unite believers by making them act together. There was no insurmountable barrier between the two, and many men took an interest in both. But they remained independent until 1948, each following its own paths according to its specific purposes. It was none the less certain that an important stage had been reached on the road to unity between Christians born of the Reformation, and even between them and their Catholic and Orthodox brethren.

Thus was established, in its two aspects, the 'Ecumenical Movement', whose influence was to be considerable. It had the good fortune to be led by a number of men, deeply spiritual and thoroughly practical, who devoted their lives to the cause of unity. Brent, Söderblom and John Mott (1865–1955), founder of the Y.M.C.A., were followed by Archbishop William Temple, Bishop Anders Nygren of Lund and Bishop Bell of Chichester. It must be emphasized that all these leaders of the ecumenical movement belonged either to the Scandinavian Lutheran or to the Anglican Church, both bodies, the first more than the second, having retained dogmatic and liturgical elements closer to Catholicism than those found in Calvinism. Nevertheless within the French Protestant fold there were Élie Gounelle and Tommy Fallot, who both came to ecumenism by way of social Christianity; Wilfrid Menod, for whom unity was above all a spiritual duty; and, finally, Marc Boegner, a young pastor, Alsatian by birth, who in 1914 won his theological doctorate with a thesis on the *Unity of the Church* and who has devoted himself ever since to that cause.

Impelled by such men, the two movements flourished and expanded during the inter-war years, each endeavouring to carry out its original purpose. As soon as conditions allowed each held a great assembly: *Life and Work* at Stockholm in 1925, *Faith and Order* at Lausanne in 1927. Both were highly successful. At Stockholm the two hundred delegates, representing thirty-one great Churches, were mainly concerned with means of extracting from the Gospel rules applicable in politics and sociology and giving them effect; the conclusions, it must be admitted, were rather like those drawn by those who attended Catholic Social Weeks. At Lausanne the atmosphere was equally uplifting. Under the presidency of Brent, assisted by a Congregationalist, a Swedish Lutheran (Söderblom in person), a French Calvinist and an Orthodox, five hundred representatives of ninety great non-Roman Churches studied an enormous programme dealing with the sacraments, the ministry and ecclesiology, examined from the standpoint of unity. The final motion contained these words, which have so often been repeated: 'We can never be the same again.'

Two major ideas were now abroad: on the one hand, that all Christian Churches must together find the answer to the problems raised by atheistic materialism; on the other, that confessional differences cannot stand in the way of so indispensable a task. The two ideas were of course complementary. They did not, however, immediately combine. Each of the movements set up a 'committee of continuation', whose duty was both to prepare for new meetings and to organize propaganda in favour of 'ecumenical' ideas. And, without waiting for new assemblies to make decisions for the future, immediate results were achieved, in the same spirit of unity, such as the International Institute of Social Christianity founded by Söderblom.

Ten years later, in 1937, each of the two movements again held a meeting, *Life and Work* at Oxford, *Faith and Order* immediately

afterwards at Edinburgh. Resistance to totalitarianism was the substance of all the numerous addresses at Oxford, while Edinburgh
concerned itself with the doctrinal justification of that resistance. The
influence of Karl Barth began to be felt throughout the ranks of
Protestantism: the social Gospel became once more 'the Gospel of
historical redemption in the Son of God made Man'. The conjunction
of the two movements appeared more and more necessary. Before the
end of 1937 there was founded near London, under the direct influence
of William Temple, a Committee of Action, including, besides the
delegates of the two movements, those of the International Alliance
for Friendship, those of the Y.M.C.A. and Y.W.C.A., of Christian
students and of the missions. This event indicated a definite move
towards fusion.

7. CATHOLICS AND THE MOVEMENT TOWARDS UNITY:
I. THE POPES AND DOCTRINE

What was the attitude of the Catholic Church in presence of this
tendency, which was clearly leading Protestantism towards the
supreme goal of the reunion of all Christians? She has often been
severely criticized; most Protestant authors have accused the popes of
downright hostility to the ecumenical movement. The facts are not so
simple.

The official attitude of the Roman Catholic Church in face of the
problem of unity was inevitably determined by her certitude of being
the sole guarantee and guardian of that unity willed by Christ. The
'separated brethren' were, strictly speaking, men who had voluntarily
separated and who could not restore unity except by removing the
causes of separation. That is the canonical point of view, which
considers the separated Churches as abstract types of schism or heresy
without implying a judgment condemning the conscience of their
members. The expression most commonly used to denote the step
which would bring back the separated brethren to unity continued to
be 'return'.

Such an attitude of principle does not of course exclude a fervent
desire to re-establish unity, which all the popes have expressed
emphatically; but it does place an obstacle between the Catholic and
the non-Catholic Churches. It is hard to see how it could have been
otherwise; the popes considered that in voicing this point of doctrine
they were simply giving proof of honesty, by not leaving the dialogue
to hinge upon an equivocation. Such is the underlying cause of the
'rigidity' and 'lack of understanding' attributed to the sovereign
pontiffs who, during the first half of the twentieth century, had to

determine the Roman attitude. Subsidiary reasons helped to render their position somewhat unyielding, which certainly does not mean that they were fundamentally opposed to the current which was sweeping so many Christian souls towards unity.

Leo XIII had laid the foundations of Catholic thought in the matter of ecumenism and had clearly indicated what should be the hope of all. 'To consider union of the Churches as utopian', he said, 'would be a sentiment unworthy of a Christian.' Originator of the Novena of Prayer for union, active artisan of *rapprochement* with the Christian East, he had also, as we have seen, encouraged attempts by Lord Halifax and Père Portal for reunion of the Anglican Church; and he had renounced that grand design only because the canonical obstacle of Anglican Orders appeared to him insurmountable.

Although Pius X was personally attentive to the problems of Christian unity, his pontificate was not favourable to ecumenical efforts. It was a time of crisis in which he was confronted with the problems of modernism and Christian democracy, resulting in a hardening of papal attitudes; though there was not, strictly speaking, any confusion between the ecumenical movement and suspect ideologies, but circumstances created a rather delicate situation. Consequently Pius X took no direct part in the matter of unity. In 1910, when the World Missionary Conference met at Edinburgh, the Vatican did not of course react. But a Catholic voice was heard there and incurred no papal thunderbolt. It was that of Mgr Bonomelli, the famous Bishop of Cremona, who was always a man of strongly 'progressive' views. He sent the assembly a message which was read by an American delegate: in it he spoke of the necessity for union, insisted on the unity of faith for which men should strive, suggested as bases of accord belief in the same Creator, the same Redeemer, the same Incarnate God; and he saluted the 'noble aspiration on the part of various Churches and denominations for the making of Holy Church one in all the children of the Redemption'. Not a word in that message could offend Protestant consciences. It constitutes one of the first and finest tributes paid by a Catholic dignitary to the ecumenical movement.

Was it possible to go further? Shortly before the outbreak of the First World War one of the founders of *Faith and Order*, the American Robert Gardiner, established contact with Cardinal Gasparri, who was favourable towards ecumenical relations. Letters were exchanged in November 1914: the promoters of the movement wished to obtain a papal audience, which was granted by Benedict XV on 16th May 1919 to a delegation of the Protestant Episcopalian Church of the U.S.A. The Pope declared that the efforts of the movement had all his sympathy. But he recalled the Catholic doctrine by assuring his hearers that he prayed that those taking part in the forthcoming ecumenical congress would 're-unite themselves to the visible Head of the Church, by whom they would be received with open arms'. What else could he have said? The Secretariat of State notified the Lutheran primates of the Scandinavian countries that the Catholic Church would not take part in the congress that was to meet at Stockholm; an official invitation extended two years later received the same answer.

The pontificate of Pius XI was a period of concern with the social preoccupations of mankind, with the need (rendered more imperious by the rise of totalitarianism) to defend the human person and his freedom. It would therefore have been inconceivable that the problem of Christian unity should be ignored. And in fact Pius XI gave many indications of his constant interest in the cause: towards the Christians of the East he proved himself as accommodating as possible, helped the foundation of groups which would work to make them better known and encouraged conversations between Catholics and their separated brethren. On several occasions he insisted on the idea that one must 'abandon the false notions adopted in the course of centuries as to the non-Catholic Churches, and make a deeper study of the Fathers with a view to discovering a common Faith'. During an allocution to young people in 1927 he uttered these beautiful words charged with poetry: 'Do we realize all that is good, all that is precious, in those fragments of ancient Catholic truth? The separated parts of a gold-bearing rock are themselves auriferous also.' He was actually referring to the oriental Churches, but surely his words are valid in respect of *all* separated brethren.

Thus an important step was taken by Pius XI in the acceptance of that doctrine of 'Vestigial Churches', in which some theologians see an opportunity of reunion. In practice it was impossible for him not to follow his predecessors. No Catholic was authorized to take official part in the meetings of the two ecumenical movements in 1925 and 1927, but a few, among them Max Metzger, were not forbidden to attend in a private capacity. Pius XI went further: on 6th January 1928 he published an encyclical, *Mortalium animos*, in which he ventured upon a calm but severe criticism of the Protestant movement. With what exactly did he find fault? *Life and Work* had talked too much about 'common bases for the spiritual life', as if there were question of establishing a kind of pan-Christianity with very little dogmatic content, implying that 'all religions are more or less good and praiseworthy'. *Faith and Order* had sought too much to compare the external aspects of professions of faith without attempting that work of doctrinal deepening which Pius XI regarded as indispensable. The criticism was pertinent, so pertinent indeed that in the assemblies of 1937 the representatives of both movements abandoned activism in favour of more solid tasks. Though outmoded today by the evolution of the ecumenical movement itself, yet retaining the whole of its doctrinal significance, since it formulates the traditional thought of the Church, *Mortalium animos* was not directed against Protestant ecumenism but against certain tendencies from which it was not exempt.

8. CATHOLICS AND THE MOVEMENT TOWARDS UNITY: II. DIALOGUE BECOMES POSSIBLE: MALINES

It would moreover be quite unfair to conclude from those papal admonitions that the Catholic Church assumed a purely negative attitude in presence of a movement which seemed to be carrying the dissident groups in the direction of unity. On the contrary. The period that saw the laying of the foundations of Protestant ecumenism coincided with years fruitful for Catholicism itself, years that witnessed achievements which would prepare the way for that truly ecumenical spirit characteristic of the present day.

While Catholics refused to take part in the great assemblies to which the Protestants invited them, they certainly did not hold aloof from any form of dialogue with their separated brethren. In two cases especially the dialogue was undertaken and carried to considerable lengths. First, with the Orthodox. In 1907, under Pius X, distinguished Catholic and Orthodox scholars met for days of historical and theological study at Velehard in Bohemia. Those gatherings, though the attendance was never very large, were held again, more or less regulaly, in 1909, 1911, 1924, 1927, 1932 and 1936. It was on the occasion of their resumption after the First World War, in 1924, that Pius XI wrote to the Bishop of Olmuz, an important figure in the young Czechoslovak State, one of his most important messages on the need for Catholics 'to acquire knowledge of the historical facts and vicissitudes of the Oriental peoples, of their habits and customs as well as of the venerable rites and institutions of their Churches'.

It was, however, with the Anglicans that contact was established in the most spectacular manner. About twenty-five years earlier Leo XIII had refused to recognize the validity of Anglican Orders and thereby put an end to the efforts at reunion begun by Lord Halifax and Père Portal. Since that date there had been men in both camps who believed that the hour would strike when a new experiment could be made. That hour seemed to be proclaimed in 1920 by an initiative of the Lambeth Conference.[1] On several occasions the prelates meeting at the Archbishop of Canterbury's residence had expressed fervent longing

---

[1] See Chapter I, section 9.

for Christian reunion. In 1888 they had defined the common bases of faith and of the structure of the Church, without which no effort at reunion would be valid: the Bible, the Nicene Creed and the two sacraments of Baptism and Holy Communion, the episcopate receiving the interior call of the Holy Spirit. More than once since then the Anglican hierarchy had suggested to various Churches—Swedish Lutherans, Old Catholics,[1] Nonconformists and even Orientals—that they should consider understandings on the basis of the Lambeth Quadrilateral. In 1920 the 252 bishops assembled at Lambeth gave to the expression of that desire an unusually warm turn: 'A new age is opening', they said, 'which demands a new way of conduct; one must forget the past and pursue the idea of a Church eventually one.' Not only was the Lambeth Quadrilateral reaffirmed as the necessary and sufficient basis of union, but decisions were taken that might help towards agreement. Thus it was declared that 'ministers of sacred things should not only be called interiorly by the Holy Ghost, but should also be fortified with a commission from the Church, which can be delivered by none but the bishops'. Furthermore it was declared that in cases where the validity of Anglican Orders was not acceptable to other Churches a supplementary form of ordination might be imposed on Anglican ministers if necessary for the restoration of Christian unity. These two decisions were manifestly Catholic in spirit, although apparently the Lambeth bishops were thinking not of Leo's condemnation of Anglican Orders, but of certain requirements of the English Free Churches. Those Catholics who still dreamed of union saw therein an opportunity, especially as the Archbishop of Canterbury, Randall Davidson, sent the text of the Lambeth appeal to several Catholic bishops and even to the Pope.

The two great Christians who a quarter of a century earlier had led the attempt at reunion were still alive. Lord Halifax was now an octogenarian; Père Portal was gradually succumbing to the disease which had afflicted him from youth upwards; but both were equally enthusiastic, equally determined. They were joined by a third man, so distinguished that he seemed in his own person alone to assume the responsibility and the glory of the new enterprise: Cardinal Mercier (1851–1926), a noble image of the priesthood, learned and full of common sense, deeply spiritual as well as highly intellectual, to whom Catholicism owed in large measure the revival of Thomism, the rebirth of learning and the spread of social teaching. Désiré Joseph Mercier, Archbishop of Malines since 1906 and a cardinal since 1907, had acquired during the First World War an unrivalled moral authority. He had embodied the determination of his heroic little people to remain free, and had even impressed the Germans. He was well

[1] See Appendix.

known throughout the civilized world, and on the death of Benedict XV some had imagined him as a likely successor.

Lord Halifax and Père Portal thought that if a man of such stature as that of Cardinal Mercier would patronize a new attempt at *rapprochement* between Anglicans and Catholics, the chance of success would be greatly increased. In order to explore the ground, Père Portal sent the cardinal a complimentary copy of the pamphlet he had recently dedicated to the Sisters of Charity, together with a letter in which he made clear his own position by recalling the events of the 1890's, and which he ended with an assurance that the Lambeth declarations constituted a new factor. He received in reply a most cordial note, in which the cardinal promised to do his best to help the cause of unity, a promise which he had already made in acknowledging receipt of Archbishop Davidson's copy of the Lambeth document. In the autumn of 1921 Lord Halifax and Père Portal, happening to be on the Continent, called, apparently without notice, at the archiepiscopal palace in Malines. The cardinal invited them to dinner; they remained with him for several hours and ended by asking him whether he would agree to lend his name to serious talks between Catholics and Anglicans. Such was the origin of the Malines Conversations, which continued for five years in the cardinal's own palace.

These conversations marked a stage further than those which had taken place thirty years before. It was not in a merely private capacity that the participants debated with a view to obtaining a decision from Rome; but nor was their capacity official, since none of them had received a mandate from the Holy See. Yet the quasi-official nature of the conversations themselves was never in doubt, since one of the highest dignitaries of the Catholic hierarchy was closely associated with them, and the names of those taking part had certainly been submitted to Rome. Furthermore Cardinal Gasparri, the Secretary of State, wrote to Cardinal Mercier: 'The Holy Father authorizes Your Eminence to tell the Anglicans that he encourages your conversations and prays God with all his heart to bless them.' The immediate goal envisaged was not to negotiate reunion between Canterbury and the Vatican. Everyone realized that such an ambitious project was for the time being unrealizable. The purpose was to undertake preliminary work for a better mutual understanding and to determine the points at which Anglicans and Catholics could meet on equal ground. 'Our task', said Cardinal Mercier more than once, 'is to remove the obstacles to union; union itself will be the work of Grace at such time as Divine Providence sees fit.'

The first two meetings were attended by only three Anglicans and three Catholics. Halifax was accompanied by Dr Armitage Robinson, Dean of Wells, and Dr Walter Frere, superior of the Community of the Resurrection and later Bishop of Truro. At the cardinal's side were Père Portal and Mgr van Roey, vicar-general of Malines. The initial meeting (December 1921) was little more than introductory. Fifteen months later, in March 1923, Lord Halifax arrived in Malines with a memorandum setting forth what would happen if reunion were accomplished. It was clearly altogether hypothetical, and it is hard to see how discussion of such topics could remove the obstacles. While recognizing the theoretical right of the Pope to universal jurisdiction, the Anglican Communion, with its 368 dioceses, refused to admit any foreign interference. There matters rested, the Catholics standing firm upon doctrine by declaring that as regards questions of mere discipline, e.g. communion under both species and the marriage of priests, solution was always possible.

It was necessary to go beyond such generalities; and so for the third meeting (November 1923) both sides were reinforced. The Anglicans were joined by a distinguished historian, Dr Beresford Kidd, and, more important, by the Rev. Charles Gore (1853–1932), an eminent theologian whose thought was a synthesis of Pusey and Dennison Maurice and in whom the Archbishop of Canterbury had complete confidence. The Catholic side was strengthened by Mgr Pierre Battifol, celebrated historian of the Church, and by Canon Hemmer, a specialist in patristics. The examination of problems was now carried a stage further. In November 1923 there was question of St Peter's place in the primitive Church, of the use of documents relating to St Peter until 461, of the repudiation of Peter's authority by the Reformation. The Anglicans admitted that the See of Rome was founded by the Apostles Peter and Paul, and that the only Apostolic See known to history is that now occupied by the Pope. The results were not startling, but such reserve was better than the bickerings of a century ago.

At this juncture, however, the Malines Conversations, hitherto veiled in partial secrecy, became known to the general public. At Christmas 1923 the Archbishop of Canterbury addressed a message to the English episcopate, showing above all that these discussions were in fact an answer to the Lambeth appeal. In order not to be left behind, Cardinal Mercier published a letter to his diocesans explaining the conversations, asserted that the participants were 'in step with the supreme authority and encouraged by it', and argued against those who relied exclusively upon individual conversions. The cardinal was obliged to admit that the 'time for results was still a secret of God'; in the light of such high talk no one could prevent opinion in either camp from believing that reunion was at hand.

The fourth conversation, however, in May 1925, followed the same cautious method as the other three. It studied memoranda on the episcopacy and the Papacy from the theological standpoint, on their historical relationship and, above all, one by Charles Gore on 'Unity in Diversity', to which Mgr Battifol replied. All this work was extremely thorough and threw a flood of light on the various problems. It was less sensational, however, than a short paper read by Cardinal Mercier, but written by Dom Lambert Beauduin,[1] a Benedictine devoted to the cause of ecumenism. This historical study of relations between Canterbury and Rome before the Reformation maintained that the English had been tacitly allowed freedom. The formula 'Anglican Church united but not absorbed' became known to the public and proved most acceptable.

Unfortunately two principal leaders of this project disappeared from the scene in 1926: Cardinal Mercier died in January, Père Portal in June. Lord Halifax alone was left, aged almost ninety; to him Mercier had bequeathed his episcopal ring, which he wore on his breast until his own death, when he left it in turn to York Minster. The great cardinal's successor lacked his authority, his prestige and perhaps also his zeal for the cause of unity. The climate was much less favourable. The British Parliament was about to begin its great debate on the Prayer Book,[2] and while it was certain that in the House of Lords the Anglo-Catholics would obtain a majority for the new text, it was known in advance that such would not be the case in the House of Commons. At this juncture also the two Protestant 'ecumenical' movements, *Faith and Order* and *Life and Work*, were attracting a good deal of attention and confronting Rome with the difficult problem of eventual Catholic participation. All these facts were bound to result in an end to the conversations. The fifth meeting (October 1926) confined itself to drawing up for the benefit of posterity a balance sheet of what had so far been done. In the following year Lord Halifax, passing through Rome, was received in audience by Pius XI, but more briefly than usual; and on his arrival at Malines he was grieved to learn that because of the state of mind prevailing in England there would be no further conversations. Moreover on 15th February 1928 the *Osservatore Romano* considered it necessary to affirm that the Pope, 'though he had followed the course of events, had never taken official note of them, regarding them merely as something that had taken place between private individuals without mandate of any kind'. The Encyclical *Mortalium animos*, written mainly for the Protestants, put a full stop to what had been too hasty an attempt at *rapprochement* with the Anglicans.

What survived of this experiment? Many have quoted some words spoken by Archbishop Davidson in 1929, when the Churches of Scotland were reunited: 'We have long sought unity by turning to Roman Catholicism; that is now over. It is to our Protestant friends that we wish to turn in future.' Such pessimism seems exaggerated. It was rather chimerical to think that a few meetings would suffice to bridge a gulf of four centuries, but those conversations had been useful. At all events they had proved that dialogue between Catholics and Anglicans was possible, that there were men of goodwill in both camps, and that they could discuss the most burning topics in a spirit of friendship and loyalty. Those conversations, too, paved the way for a whole series of more or less secret gatherings, which were later held in many places and in their turn advanced the cause of unity. From time to time a more striking demonstration would show that the dream had not been abandoned. For example, in 1932, the centenary of John Keble's famous sermon which started the Oxford Movement, fifty Anglican clergymen declared reunion with Rome to be 'the logical and supreme goal, the natural outcome of the Movement'. The Malines Conversations had produced no tangible results, but they helped to create the atmosphere in which later discussions would take place. One cannot but be moved by this sentence written by Cardinal Mercier in his *Testament*: 'To unite, we must love one another; to love one another, it is necessary to know one another; to know one another we must meet one another.'

9. CATHOLICS AND THE MOVEMENT TOWARDS UNITY: III. A CREATIVE FERMENT

The failure of the Malines Conversations, or rather their lack of concrete results, must not deceive us. To study the ultimate reunion of Anglicanism was sufficiently interesting in itself; but, apart from that initiative, there emerged within the Catholic fold a relatively important number of other attempts, aiming in various directions but all with a view to restoring unity. The period that opened with the beginning of the twentieth century and closed with the Second World War was altogether remarkable, an epoch of ferment and uncertainty during which the Catholic pioneers of ecumenism were continually asking themselves to what extent they were covered by the hierarchy, whether they did not risk a rap over the knuckles if they went too far—which is just what some of them received—and whether the boldness of their thought was sufficiently embodied in such cautious formulas as would not involve them in trouble with the Holy Office, but would at the same time offer a starting-point for future pioneers.

To love one another, understand one another; to understand one another, go and meet one another: most of the initiatives in the period 1910–38 were fundamentally due to Cardinal Mercier's advice. Hitherto Christians in all camps had misunderstood one another. For centuries the same follies, the same calumnies, had been repeated up and down the world. Catholics were unacquainted with Protestant theology and Orthodox spirituality, while the separated brethren told the same lies about Rome, the Pope, the Vatican and its ways. To penetrate the thought of Orthodoxy and that of the Reformation, to understand the confrontation from within, would be a long stride on the road to fraternal reconciliation. Such was the purpose of some small centres of liturgical and theological training, as well as of several religious writers, reviews and collections of works.

In the foreground stands a figure to whom scant justice has been done: Dom Lambert Beauduin, the Benedictine monk whom we have already noticed in connection with the Malines Conversations. He was among the promoters of the liturgical revival, and may be associated with the Social Catholic Movement by virtue of his experiment as a young priest in the suburbs of Brussels. His name moreover is inseparable from one of the high places of Catholic ecumenism—the priory of Chèvetogne. One of the first documents of Pius XI's pontificate was the apostolic letter *Equidem Verba* (1924) dealing with the reunion of Christians. It was especially concerned with the small parties of Russian refugees arriving in the West; the former nuncio in Warsaw was anxious about them, and his letter ended by expressing a hope that some monastic institution would dedicate itself wholly to the task of their conversion. Dom Lambert Beauduin, a monk of Mont César, was at that time teaching at San Anselmo in Rome. Did Pius XI think of him for the foundation he desired, or was it the Benedictine himself who suggested to the Pope that he should undertake the work? A document preserved at Mont César appears to support the second alternative. At all events, in 1925–6 Dom Lambert established the Monastère d'Union at Amay-sur-Meuse, near Liège. The famous Uniate metropolitan of Lvov, Mgr Szeptyckii, took a keen interest in the project. Candidates were soon flocking to the new priory, coming from various countries, including England.

The goal envisaged by Dom Lambert Beauduin was not the immediate 'conversion' of the Russians, but the finding of common ground between Orthodox and Catholics where they might learn to understand one another. The Benedictine Order was particularly well qualified to succeed in this task, its great liturgical traditions according with the profound aspirations of the Russian faith. Six years after its foundation Amay was already a centre that might be called ecumenical when a crisis occurred. Dom Lambert, whom some had never forgiven for his initiative in the matter of Malines, had to retire from his work, to which he was not destined to return until 1951. But that work continued to develop none the less. In 1939 it removed to Chèvetogne because its growth necessitated larger premises. Its review, *Irenikon*,

had acquired considerable authority in everything concerning Orthodoxy. Some eminent men followed one another at its head, e.g. Dom
Thomas Bequet and Dom Olivier Rousseau. The whole Benedictine
Order watched the efforts of the Belgian monastery. Later certain
houses were entrusted more specially with the duty of supporting its
efforts. A milestone had been erected on the road to unity.

Others were planted soon afterwards. A year after the foundation of
Amay some French Dominicans, under the direction of Père Christophe J. Dumont, decided to found a centre for the study of Orthodoxy. More precisely, they intended to consider 'the problems posed
by Russia in the religious field'. This centre was known as *Istina*; it
was established first at Lille then in Paris itself, where its splendid
Slavonic liturgy drew enormous congregations, and where, more
important, meetings between Catholic and Orthodox theologians were
arranged. On the eve of the Second World War *Istina* was turning
rather to a general study of ecumenical problems, to which four
reviews and a whole group of publications were devoted.

It was not, however, the Orientals alone that attracted the attention
of Catholics eager for unity. In Germany the Moehler Institute was
founded at Paderborn in 1917; it was approved by the hierarchy and
arranged annual meetings of theologians representing various
denominations for the common study of papers on Christian dogma
and Catholic thought. In England efforts at agreement with the
Anglicans were mainly the work of the Benedictine community at
Prinknash: its bulletin *Pax* was markedly ecumenical in tone. In the
U.S.A., from 1926 onwards, the abbey of St Procopius at Lisle
(Illinois) interested itself chiefly in contacts with the Orthodox, in
alliance with the Institute of SS. Cyril and Methodius in the Byzantine
Catholic diocese of Pittsburgh. In France an important place in the
effort towards unity was occupied by the Augustinians of the Assump-
tion, whose famous Institute of Byzantine Studies, founded in 1897 by
Mgr Louis Petit, had opened up the field of Orthodox spirituality.
Their review, *Unité de l'Église*, laboured until 1938 to familiarize its
readers with the Oriental Churches.

Of all attempts to prepare the reconciliation of Christians, the most
moving, because it was sealed with blood, was that of a German priest,
Max Josef Metzger (1887–1944), who was led to the cause of
ecumenism by his love of peace. In 1916, at the height of the First
World War, he had founded a sort of congregation or institute called
the League of the White Cross, later known as the Society of Christ
the King. In 1918 he assigned as the purpose of its members universal
reconciliation between Christians. His voice found an echo here and
there, notably in university circles at Munich and Tübingen. But this
roused the ire of the Nazi regime, which twice imprisoned him. Nothing,

however, could stop this priest, whose gentle exterior concealed iron determination. From 1927, when he attended the ecumenical assembly at Lausanne, in a private capacity, he gave himself heart and soul to the cause of reconciliation. In Germany, Sweden, Holland and Switzerland he made numerous contacts with Lutherans, Calvinists, Anglicans and even Old Catholics. In 1938 he founded the *Una Sancta* Fraternity to canalize all the goodwill scattered in the two camps; each member retained his complete confessional freedom, but undertook to pray and work 'that they may be one'. During the war, in 1940, Father Metzger dared to hold a congress at which he set forth his ideas. The Nazi response was not long in coming. Arrested for pacifism and convicted of treason, the heroic priest was executed on 17th August 1944. From his prison he wrote to Pope Pius XII an astonishing letter, using the very phrases that are today forever on the lips of 'ecumenists'.

Thus the clock of Providence was striking loud and long at a time when it hardly seemed that the Christian world in general, and Catholicism in particular, were preoccupied with what we understand by ecumenism. Of those pioneers who ventured to take risks and speak in unwonted terms, several are recognized today as having accomplished a decisive task and set the Church upon that road where we now see her.

The most important of all, in the sense that he appears as a leader of the column, is Père Yves Congar, a Dominican. There was nothing in his exterior to suggest his amazing courage and resolve. As a young professor at the Saulchoir he interested himself in the cause of unity by studying the Fathers and particularly ecclesiology. In 1937 he published a book, *Chrétiens désunis*, which, read today with hindsight, must be recognized as one of the most important of that period. For the first time a Catholic theologian sought to understand why and how Christians were separated. Deliberately avoiding all polemic, Père Congar analysed the differences among Christians in their origins, in history and in their present state. At the same time he drew up an entirely new programme of possible union, examining the bases of the Church's catholicity and unity. 'That unity', he said, 'exists here and now in the Church. But her catholicity is not fully actuated and there is a sense in which it is true to say not only that the catholicity of the Church is only imperfectly explicit, but also that the fact of division plays a part in that imperfection. . . . *What our separated brethren hold unduly outside the Church is lacking to the actual catholicity of that Church.*' [1] This last sentence in particular was of capital importance. It amounted to telling the separated brethren that the Church did not ask them to renounce what was positive in their Christian faith, but only 'the negations and limitations which make those values

[1] Daniel-Rops's italics.

schismatic and separated realities'. There was no question, then, of a 'return' pure and simple; the perspectives were greatly enlarged. Reunion presented itself as 'an accomplishment in the plenitude of communion and of the heritage of Christ'.

Such theories, it need hardly be said, were regarded as extremely rash, even though Rome did not react until long after their publication, not indeed until after the Second World War. They were none the less the origin of a whole stream of thought. While a collection published under the title *Unam Sanctam* brought together some great books on analogous themes, a growing number of theologians manifested their interest in this kind of problem. Almost everywhere it was evident that Catholic writers were interested in the great leaders of the Reformation, notably Luther, and abandoned the systematically critical and even insulting vocabulary which until then had been fashionable.

Admittedly all this represented as yet nothing more than straws in the wind. Hostility and resistance were not lacking. The pioneers of unity were all more or less subjected to mud-slinging; Cardinal Mercier himself suffered more than his fair share. More serious was the fact that the movement for unity was still confined to a relatively narrow field; it was a matter for priests, theologians, members of the universities—all specialists. How many years would have to pass before the Christian soul was truly stirred?

10. PRAYER FOR UNITY

In order that the day might dawn when an advance would become possible, the light of the Holy Spirit was indispensable. A few believers set about asking for it. Such was the history of Prayer for Unity. Surprisingly enough, its beginnings are to be found in the Protestant Episcopalian Church of America and her elder sister the Anglican Church, though its earliest achievements were Catholic. It constitutes the most striking manifestation of that 'spiritual ecumenism' whose effectiveness in our own day cannot be overestimated.

'Our first move will not be to lecture and debate, but to kneel down together at the Cross of our common Saviour. . . . In that attitude of repentance Christians purify themselves and discover the climate—the only climate—favourable to Christian unity. That climate can be none other than that of Christ's own prayer—or that of His agony, which is its extension.' Those words, written by one of the great pioneers of ecumenism,[1] express a conviction shared today by all conscientious Christians. But time, effort, suffering and the long patience of a few apostles were necessary in order to spread that conviction. No less than

[1] Père Maurice Villain, *Introduction à l'œcumenisme*, 1958, 2nd edition 1964.

one-third of a century elapsed before 'prayer for unity' became general.

It will be recalled that Leo XIII's Encyclical *Provida Matris* (5th May 1895), inaugurated a novena to take place between the Ascension and Pentecost, during which Catholics were asked to pray for the return to the Church of their separated brethren. That step, to say the least, had not proved a great success; and the Pope himself, during his last years, made little effort to awaken souls to this devotion.

In 1906, in a very different setting, the idea was taken up and amplified. The initiative came from a minister of the Episcopalian Church of America. Lewis Thomas Wattson (1863–1940) had started his career as rector of Graymoor, a parish in the state of New York, where he had won quite a reputation as a preacher, but, obsessed with the desire to live a more exacting religious life, as well as by the longing for unity he experienced whenever he talked with a Protestant pastor, he had decided to found a Franciscan community with that end in view. A female branch had followed, then a third order, without any objection from the authorities of the Episcopalian Church, of which 'Father Paul' Wattson considered himself a faithful son. Becoming more and more convinced of the Pope's primacy over the whole Church, he declared himself a member of the 'Catholic' Church, according to the 'three branches' theory.

It was then as superior of that Anglican Franciscan community that Tommy Wattson launched the idea that all believers should pray for unity. At the same time, in England, Spencer Jones, a highly educated Anglican parson, had published a sensational book on *The Church of England and the Holy See*, to which Lord Halifax contributed a preface and to which Wattson extended a warm welcome in the American press. The two men linked themselves in friendship, and together started to propagate the idea of Prayer for Unity. The Society of St Thomas of Canterbury, founded under the presidency of Spencer Jones, devoted itself to that task. The Englishman proposed a single day of prayer, 29th June, feast of St Peter and St Paul. The American, more ambitious, secured a whole octave running from 18th to 25th January, i.e. from the feast of St Peter's Chair to that of the Conversion of St Paul. A review was inaugurated to spread the idea, and it was echoed by the voices of some authoritative Catholics. In 1909 the octave was celebrated with fervour in many Catholic and Anglican parishes, and was soon afterwards officially approved by Pius X.

The spiritual evolution of Father Wattson did not damage his undertaking. His convictions, especially on the papal primacy, led him to join the Roman Catholic Church, together with all the religious of both sexes who had followed him to Graymoor. Spencer Jones remained within the Church of England, though continuing to pray that it might return to Rome. From 1910 onwards the octave was celebrated by an increasing number of believers. Pius X approved it; Benedict XV indulgenced it; Pius XI promised to say Mass on the first day of this crusade for the Seamless Robe.

The mere account of its origins shows that this prayer aimed at first simply and solely to conversion, to a 'return' to the fold of all stray sheep. Day after day believers prayed for the *return* of all dissident Christians, and also for the conversion of Muslims, pagans and Jews, not forgetting bad Catholics. Protestant believers and even Anglicans less committed to the road towards Rome could not of course share the intentions of a prayer thus formulated.

It was then that there came upon the scene the Abbé Paul Couturier (1881–1953), a man of God who was destined to give Wattson's initiative its truly ecumenical direction. He was a priest of the diocese of Lyon, teaching mathematics, physics and chemistry at the Collège des Chartreux. He had scarcely begun to consider the problem of unity when in 1920 his friend Père Albert Valensin, a Jesuit, led him to take an interest in the ten thousand Russian refugees whom the Bolshevik Revolution had driven to Lyon. Through this contact, and especially through daily meetings with the Orthodox clergy, he discovered their spiritual life, their faith, their charity. Precious friendships were then forged, which orientated Couturier towards his providential destiny.

Henceforward he experienced that longing for unity from which others suffered no less than he, and he set about propagating Leo's novena and Wattson's octave in the parishes. This still seemed to him insufficient. Having learned of the work in progress at the Benedictine priory at Amay-sur-Meuse, under the direction of Dom Lambert Beauduin, he went to stay there, studied the founder's writings on 'the true work for Christian unity', pondered Cardinal Mercier's notes and the appeals of Pius XI. Returning to Lyon he made up his mind to do something that would enlarge the framework of Wattson's octave and enable non-Catholics to join their prayers to those of the Catholics. In 1933 a modest triduum; in 1934 an octave for Catholics only; in 1935 another octave, but this time one with which all Christians could associate themselves in complete spiritual independence and in which the Orthodox of Lyon actually took part: such were the stages that led to the Week of Universal Prayer for Unity.[1]

The Abbé Couturier's idea appears very obvious and simple to present-day Christians. Thirty years ago it was somewhat audacious, emanating from a Catholic priest. The octave of prayer had to be universal 'in order to offer the world the spectacle of unanimous prayer on the part of all Christians'. 'Neither Catholic prayer, nor Orthodox

[1] The word octave was abandoned as too 'Catholic'.

prayer, nor Anglican prayer, nor Protestant prayer suffice,' he said; 'all together are needed.' In order that this might be so, it was indispensable that the appeal for common prayer should be formulated in such a way as to offend no one. Consequently emphasis must not be laid on 'return', 'conversion', but on the 'sanctification' of all, on the common responsibility of Christians before the scandal of disunion, and on their common faith in the Master's eternal promise. The octave was to rest on three pillars: a *Confiteor* of all in presence of Christ who calls His sons to unity; universality of participation in the prayer; spiritual independence of each group of participants. Thus God would be asked for unity, the final nature of which would remain a secret of Providence, sought not in discussion but in the offering of souls and self-dedication. God alone knew when and under what form that unity would come about.

One cannot withhold admiration at the audacity of that humble priest who, without official mandate, led the whole Christian world on to the road along which we see it moving today. The extraordinary fact is that his enterprise succeeded. It must, however, be said also that, in order to bring about its success, the Abbé Couturier devoted the whole remainder of his life and the last drop of his strength. As self-appointed crusader in the cause he made it his duty to visit all those who might understand and share his labours. The highest authorities of Orthodoxy were approached. In England he visited archbishops, bishops, theologians and Anglican communities. The Rev. Spencer Jones and Dr William Temple received him fraternally. Among Protestants, where there had been at first more reserve, his transparent sincerity brought about the same results: in 1937 some Swedish Lutheran ministers were won over; Swiss pastors agreed to meet the abbé, first at Erlenbach, then in a study session at the Trappist abbey of Notre-Dame-des-Dombes. In France the Protestant Federation allowed the prayer in 1936. On the eve of the Second World War the Week of Prayer was so well on its way that nothing could stop it. The Abbé Couturier now presided over a veritable ecumenical centre at Lyon; after his death in 1954 Cardinal Gerlier gave it the name *Unité Chrétienne*. Among those who had joined Couturier, and would later deepen and radiate his thought, were Père Maurice Villain, a Marist, and Michalon, a Sulpician; and in the autumn of 1940 he welcomed Roger Schutz, a young Genevese pastor whose initiative at Taizé was to continue and enlarge his own.

Thus was established what the Abbé Couturier used to call 'the invisible monastery', formed of all those souls—only God knew how many—who in all parts of the Christian family held high hopes of ultimate unity. Standing at the very heart of the Church, sharing in the profound mystery of her union with Christ, it was he who gave the ecumenical movement its 'mystical' character in the twofold sense that the Church and Péguy attach to that word.

11. THE WORLD COUNCIL OF CHURCHES

Meanwhile the impetus given by Protestants since the formation of *Faith and Order* and *Life and Work* had not slackened. The considerable success of the two great conferences at Oxford and Edinburgh in 1937 had placed them in the front rank of Protestantism. Their attitude in face of totalitarianism had made a deep impression. But above all the two movements had appeared to complement one another: *Life and Work* seemed destined to put in practice the theories elaborated by *Faith and Order*. It was natural to expect that they would eventually unite.

The first step was taken during the conferences in 1937. At Westfield college, near London, representatives of the seven main Protestant movements, those of worldwide standing, studied the chances, the difficulties and the means of an ultimate fusion of *Faith and Order* and *Life and Work*. Thanks to the influence of Archbishop Temple, a great deal of mutual mistrust was laid aside, and it was envisaged that a single organization might be created, in which the two movements would combine their efforts without renouncing their specific characters. A Committee of Fourteen, including seven delegates from each movement, was set up—though not without some difficulty, because the representatives of *Faith and Order* demanded explicit statements of the Christology of certain Churches belonging to *Life and Work*.

In the spring of 1938, at Utrecht, a meeting was held of the same committee, which had been enlarged. Two important decisions were taken: one doctrinal, a unanimous declaration that the Nicene Creed was and would remain the dogmatic basis of all those taking part; the other administrative but paramount, that the members of the committee would be the delegates 'of the Churches', that is to say there was no longer question merely of individuals concerning themselves with the prospect of unity but not necessarily with a mandate. This meant that if fusion came about it would be in order to found not an 'ecumenical movement' acting apart from the Churches, but a World Council of Churches, which every Protestant Church would join. In 1939 the Provisional Committee of Utrecht held a second plenary session at Saint-Germain-en-Laye. It discussed international problems that would be raised by union; it drew up a letter to the Pope suggesting an unofficial exchange of information; it resolved that the first General Assembly should be held in August 1941; and, finally, it appointed a secretary-general, Pastor W. A. Visser't Hooft, who would reside at Geneva, with two assistant secretaries in London and New York.

The Second World War prevented the General Assembly, but did not lessen the ardour of those concerned. In 1945 the Norwegian Bishop Berggrav was fully justified in declaring: 'During these dark years we have drawn closer to one another than at times when communications were easy. We have prayed more together; we have paid more attention to the word of God; our hearts have been more united than ever.' The fact is that after the conclusion of hostilities the ecumenical task was resumed with fervour. The committee set up a 'department of reconstruction and mutual aid', which did some excellent work. Together with the International Missionary Council it instituted commissions to follow the labours of U.N.O. and kindred organizations. Before the war a Department of Studies had elaborated a rich body of doctrinal material. At Bossey, near Geneva, a centre was opened where students could familiarize themselves with the problems of unity. Representatives of certain Churches met at Geneva, Cambridge and Buck Hill Falls (U.S.A.). The ground was so well prepared that Pastor Marc Boegner, opening the World Assembly at Amsterdam on 23rd August 1948, was able to announce the official birth of the World Council of Churches.

That meeting at Amsterdam was the most important ever held by the World Council. Not only was it attended by delegates from 147 Churches in 44 countries almost 900 participants, including Orthodox and a few Old Catholics—but it also laid foundations for the future. Carefully prepared, it proposed to consider the 'disorder of Man and the purpose of God'. Several very important motions were accepted: one which ruled that all member Churches should recognize 'Our Lord Jesus Christ as God and Saviour'; another which rejected certain 'liberals' who disputed the divinity of Christ; another which declared that every Church remained completely free, but that the Council, as such, must place itself on the level of a unified Church and judge everything from that point of view; and, lastly, one that refused to condemn the world, choosing rather to recall Christianity to its own responsibilities.

Four years later, in 1952, another meeting was held at Lund in Sweden. Though taking place within the framework of the World Council, it was not a plenary gathering. Responsibility for this lay with *Faith and Order*, whose members considered that an effort at doctrinal precision was indispensable. Under the twofold influence of Tomkins, an Anglican, and Edmund Schlink of Heidelberg, a Lutheran, the meeting studied three great subjects: the nature of the Church, forms of worship and the problems raised by intercommunion. Liturgical questions were now included in the schema of ecumenism.

This was an advantage in helping the liturgical revival towards unity, of restoring a communal sense of action and of rediscovering the value of Tradition expressed in worship. Even from the Catholic standpoint it marked progress.

Two years later again, during the summer of 1954, an assembly of the World Council was held at Evanston in the United States. It took place in an atmosphere less irenic than its predecessors, amid incredible publicity through the press, radio and television, against the background of the 'North-western University' which was well known as a militant centre of activist Protestantism. It was marked not only by a vehement attack upon Rome by an Argentine Methodist bishop. Santos Barbieri, but also by some disagreement among the members themselves concerning the divine election of Isreal and criticism from the Orthodox on the doctrine of free examination. Nevertheless that meeting, whose general theme was 'Christ, the hope of the world', represented a new stage in the march of the ecumenical movement towards real reform according to the spirit of the Gospel. The moving appeal delivered by the Council to all Churches had a certain resonance: 'Does your Church study seriously its relations with other Churches in the light of Our Lord's prayer that the truth may sanctify us all and that we may be One? Does your parish, in union with its neighbours, do everything possible to enable all to hear the voice of the One Pastor calling all men to a single fold?' The accent was undeniably ecumenical and fine.

Here we reach the end of the period covered by the present volume. The World Council of Churches was thenceforward considered as a great institution of Protestantism, of Anglicanism and even of Orthodoxy. So far it had done little more than lay down principles, establish certain bases for common action. But it existed, and there was no longer any likelihood that a counter-current would sweep the non-Catholic world back to indefinite division. There was still the question of the existence, outside the World Council, of the International Missionary Council, where the reformed Churches encountered one another against a different background and according to different methods. Many members desired that agreement between the two organizations should not be limited to theoretical collaboration within a committee of co-ordination, but should lead to genuine fusion; to which others objected, not without reason, that since the World Council wished to be open to the non-Protestant (Orthodox and Old Catholic) Churches, it was impossible to combine with an organization whose declared purpose was to spread Protestantism throughout the world. Despite these reservations it seemed in 1958 that fusion was inevitable; the tendency became stronger from one gathering of missionaries to the next. In January 1958 the Missionary Council, assembled at Accra in Ghana, accepted the principle of fusion by fifty-eight votes to seven, leaving the meeting that was to be held at Delhi in 1961 to give effect to the decision.[1] Some asked whether this momentous step would favour the ecumenical cause: would not the Orthodox and the Old Catholics regard the Council henceforward as an organization for Protestant proselytism? And would not the Anglicans themselves, at any rate the Anglo-Catholics, feel some embarrassment at finding themselves thus qualified as Protestants?[2]

What then is the World Council of Churches, such as it has existed since 1948? It is a council of *Churches*, which means that it is as representative of a religious group that each member takes part. The official definition in its final form (1961) runs as follows: 'The World Council of Churches is a fraternal association of Churches which confirm that the Lord Jesus Christ is God and Saviour, according to the Scriptures, and which endeavour to respond in unison to their common vocation, for the glory of God, Father, Son and Holy Spirit.' The definition of the word 'Church', moreover, is very wide; in 1950, at Toronto, the Central Committee decided that the member Churches 'are not bound to recognize other member Churches as Churches in the full acceptation of the word, but only to admit that they reveal elements of the true Church'. This has enabled Pentecostal Movements to obtain admission. The World Council of Churches constitutes the central organism of all Churches which have joined the ecumenical movement, but it is by no means a sort of super-Church, nor even a superior administrative body which can impose its decisions on the Churches.

How many are those member Churches? In 1958 they numbered 172; in 1964 the figure had exceeded 200. Actually, however, the term 'Churches' here is deceptive. It is not a matter of 172 different confessions! Most often we are dealing with national variations of the same confession: e.g. the Churches of Sweden, Norway and Denmark have joined the Council individually, although they are identically Lutheran. The detailed list too shows some rather singular complications. Thus the reformed Church of Alsace is considered as a member Church because it was originally concordatory and thereby differs from the reformed Church of France, itself a member of the Council. Conversely, the Lutheran Church of Missouri, although a member of the World Lutheran Federation, a pillar of the Council, has always refused to take part in the ecumenical movement. The member Churches belong to very many peoples of the world and cover a huge field of non-Catholic faiths. Lutherans, Calvinists, Anglicans and Methodists occupy the foremost place, along with a section of the

[1] This was done.
[2] In fact this fusion has done good at the ecumenical level. Since then there has been a change in many missionary fields.

FORMATION OF THE WORLD COUNCIL

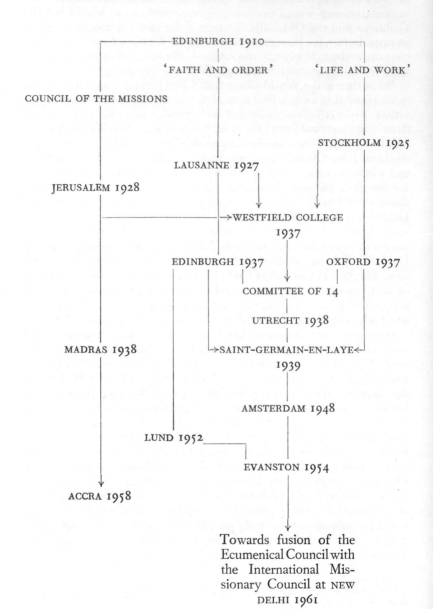

EDINBURGH 1910

'FAITH AND ORDER'   'LIFE AND WORK'

COUNCIL OF THE MISSIONS

STOCKHOLM 1925

LAUSANNE 1927

JERUSALEM 1928

→WESTFIELD COLLEGE
1937

EDINBURGH 1937   OXFORD 1937

COMMITTEE OF 14

UTRECHT 1938

MADRAS 1938   →SAINT-GERMAIN-EN-LAYE←
1939

AMSTERDAM 1948

LUND 1952

EVANSTON 1954

ACCRA 1958

Towards fusion of the
Ecumenical Council with
the International Mis-
sionary Council at NEW
DELHI 1961

Baptists; the Orthodox, far behind, form a second group, representing both the Greeks and the Russians; there are also the Old Catholics, precious in the eyes of the Council, for they would enable it still to call itself ecumenical if the Orthodox withdrew. The presidency was held briefly by a 'Syrian' Christian from India, i.e. a Monophysite, but that was chiefly for the sake of principle. In recent years even the Salvation Army has been admitted—surprisingly, since it is hardly a Church—as have some Pentecostal Movements. But the Mormons and Jehovah's Witnesses have been barred, because their faith rests upon a revelation that is not exclusively biblical.

The organization of the World Council is reminiscent of that of the United Nations, which took shape at about the same time and in a similar climate. At the summit, all-powerful, is the World Assembly, which may include between seven hundred and a thousand delegates, and which is supposed to meet every six years. For that period it appoints six presidents, with whom are joined one or more honorary presidents, chosen from among those who have distinguished themselves in the movement, and a central committee of a hundred members who assist the presidents in their work. The really active element, however, is the executive committee, which works in association with the general secretariat.

As for the activities of the various organisms which are animated and controlled by the central authority, they are divided into two main sections, corresponding to the two movements from which the whole vast enterprise developed (*Faith and Order, Life and Work*). Intellectual, theological and religious work belongs to the Study section; the remainder with the Action section. All work done by both sections passes to the general secretariat, whose duty it is to give effect to the ideas put forward and the observations made. For this it disposes of a vast administration consisting of four departments: Finance, International Affairs, Mutual Aid and Information. The whole is impressive; its organization is certainly more rational and logical and national than that of the Catholic Church as seen at the Vatican; but the gigantic ministry functions very slowly because of the obligation to bring the member Churches strictly into line, and also because of the extremely varied origins of those who, in practice, have charge of affairs.

All these facts show how delicate is the position of the World Council. Not being a super-Church, it cannot command its members. It cannot even legislate, and it acts only in so far as it has a mandate to do so. In the Catholic Church a decision taken by a General Council and promulgated by the Pope is the last word in any dispute. An opinion formulated by the World Council of Churches is never anything but the first word, opening the door to endless debate; and the Council is faced with this further difficulty, that it must maintain equilibrium between insistence on loyalty to true Christian principles and the desire to extend an all-embracing welcome. In a phrase, it can be like all assemblies of parliamentary type, subject to attacks of fever and uncontrolled reflexes.

The movement which sways the World Council seems to obey the demands of feeling rather than of a clearly defined purpose. Moreover if that purpose, namely unity, were achieved, is it not true that the movement, the World Council and the member Churches themselves would be bound to disappear? A spirit of self-sacrifice is necessary if such a prospect is to be accepted. And indeed some speakers in one or other of the Assemblies have dared to say that that was the only desirable outcome. Among them was a pastor of the Disciples of Christ, who declared at Lausanne in 1927: 'Let my Church diminish so long as I see the image of Christ increase.' Another was O. S. Tomkins, secretary of the Lund conference and later Anglican Bishop of Bristol: 'The mere fact of our meeting here attests our readiness to see the disappearance of our respective confessions. . . . The Council has been born for no other reason than to strike the death-blow.'

Did those who took part in the Assemblies share these sacrificial notions? Nothing is less sure; nor is it certain that the rapid stream which bore the associates of the ecumenical movement was accepted by the sum total of non-Catholic Churches. The Orthodox are a case in point. They have delegates at all the Assemblies, and presidents of the World Council have been chosen from among them. But does that mean to say that they are fully at ease in those strongly Protestant gatherings, where they seldom find their own liturgical usages or their characteristic spirituality? It should be noted that they have never been numerous: Evanston was attended only by the Orthodox resident in America. More serious still: are they agreed upon those principles in whose name the Protestants desire unity? At nearly every meeting they have tabled reservations in one form or another. At Evanston, for example, all the Orthodox signed the following declaration: 'The Orthodox Church cannot accept the idea that the Holy Spirit speaks to us only in the Bible. The Holy Spirit dwells and testifies in the whole of life and experience. The Bible has been given to us in the context of Tradition, in which we also possess the interpretation and authentic exposition of the word of God.' While a Catholic warmly approves such phrases, it is hard to see how a Protestant, no matter to what obedience he belongs, could underwrite them.

It is certain, however, that even in the Protestant world itself the ecumenical movement has not won unanimous assent. True, it represents a great majority of the Churches, but not of *all*. There are many signs of a certain reserve towards certain aspects of the ecumenical movement. . . . It is rather significant that Protestants of southern countries, especially South America, do not feel at home in these gatherings dominated by Anglo-Saxons. But other critics look more to essentials. The Protestant orthodox, called in the U.S.A. 'fundamentalists', are mistrustful of a movement which welcomes upon equal terms with true believers people whom they themselves regard as heretics. When the first meeting of the World Council was held at Amsterdam, opponents of this type also held there a small congress which openly criticized that initiative. An official organization known as the International Council of Christian Churches loses no opportunity of hitting at the World Council. It reproaches the latter with fostering doctrinal confusion, of violating the independence of local Churches, of preparing a form of unity modelled upon that of Rome and of seeking to re-establish clericalism; but none of this prevents it from favouring Modernism and Communism. It is very difficult to assess the exact importance of this counter-movement, which seems to be fairly widespread in the U.S.A. and is active in Scandinavia also. But it is certain that some of those grievances have been echoed by other fractions of Protestantism which have remained outside the ecumenical movement, e.g. the powerful Southern Baptist Convention in the U.S.A.

While it seems, however, that the World Council need not be much embarrassed by such resistance, there exists also in the Protestant world another tendency which manifested itself a short while ago and might come to dominate the World Council. It is represented by men who think more about immediate practical unity than about safeguarding doctrinal values, and who care nothing for the difficult equilibria which the ecumenical movement has sought to maintain. This tendency has won a victory in southern India, which forms an object lesson. Where will it stop?

12. THE SOUTH INDIA CHURCH

Catholics, who judge Protestantism from the outside, tend to think of all Protestants as tarred with the same brush—all equally heretics. And no doubt Catholic readers of the present book may have been surprised to discover that there exists a greater doctrinal difference between a Unitarian and an Anglican than between the latter and themselves. In fact the main non-Catholic groups are keenly aware of their specific differences; the Anglican Church in particular is fully conscious of what makes it different from the rest. The fraternal collaboration for which the World Council of Churches strives has limits which its leaders know full well.

Until about twenty years ago the idea that some of those limits could be overstepped seemed quite out of the question, as had been shown, for instance, by the Kikuyu affair. In 1918 the missionaries in central Africa held a meeting with a view to studying means of collaboration among themselves. They did not much alter the existing situation and, while there was talk of one day uniting all the Churches of Black Africa, the project remained a mere hope. At the end of the meeting, however, the two Anglican bishops of Mombasa and Uganda held a communion service to which were invited members of the non-Anglican groups, who attended and received communion. This let loose a storm of protest. A cloud of incendiary pamphlets flew in the British sky; the Bishop of Zambezi accused his two colleagues of heresy. The matter was submitted to Lambeth, and one wonders where the affair would have ended, but for the Second World War, which gave the Anglican Church other things to think about.

In 1947 the Protestant world received some astonishing news. In India four Churches—six by another reckoning—some episcopal and the others synodal, had decided to amalgamate. They were the Anglican Church of India, Burma and Ceylon, the Methodist Church of Southern India and the United Church of Southern India, itself the result of an earlier union (1908) between Presbyterians and Congregationalists with the addition of some Swiss (Calvinist) and German (Lutheran) missions. The new formation called itself the South India Church.

This amazing decision was the result of long and detailed negotiations. The question of agreement between Anglicans and the United Church had been raised in 1919. After that date there was continuous discussion, the Congregationalists fearing that the Anglican element would absorb all the rest, the Anglicans declaring that the integration of so many Protestants was likely to Protestantize the Church of England. After many exchanges it was agreed to set up an entirely new Church that would be in no way a branch of Anglicanism, but would present itself as a regional Church on the pattern, for example, of that of Sweden or Finland; once it was fully established, its relations with the Anglican communion would be determined. The Second World War led many to think that union of the Churches should be effected without delay. The final agreement, therefore, was signed in 1947 in a very tense atmosphere; the majority of Anglicans saw the four dioceses of southern India leave their Church for what appeared to them as an uncertain venture and to the Anglo-Catholics as virtual apostasy, while the more Protestant of the newly 'united', especially the Congregationalists, remained mistrustful of certain aspects of the Anglican worship.

Results, however, on the whole were satisfactory. The ex-Anglican episcopate tried hard to convince its followers and its former colleagues that the operation served higher interests, and in 1955 the Church of England admitted that ordinations conferred in the new Church were valid. The Presbyterians, who had shown some hesitation in joining the union, now showed themselves extremely active and confident; one of their leaders, Leslie Newbiggins, who had become a bishop in the united Church, proved himself its ablest theologian and wrote a book to justify his attitude towards the paramount problem of the Church. Only the Lutherans and a few American 'fundamentalist' missions finally rejected the union. Nor, contrary to what some had expected, was there a 'mass defection from Anglicanism to Catholicism'—not even from among members of the 'Annunciation', a group which represented the extreme Anglo-Catholic tendency.

It may therefore be said that the amalgamation has succeeded, which means to say that the 'bases of union' were well chosen. One Catholic observer, speaking to me about this curious achievement, said he thought that its success was due to the fact that it was centred upon the episcopate and its powers, thereby enabling the Anglican and Methodist bishops to retain their rights and satisfying the secret nostalgia for authority and prestige which existed among ministers of the Churches which had no episcopate. The remark, though perhaps tinged with sarcasm, is not altogether false. The South India Church is *episcopal*; it expressly includes in its hierarchy the episcopate envisaged as an historical reality, but does not define its nature, so that everyone can think of it as he chooses. It wears the guise of Apostolic Succession, since the Anglican bishops who belong to it were not re-consecrated, while the Protestant ministers chosen for the episcopate were consecrated by bishops. As for the pastors and ministers of parishes, though they were ordained by a bishop they remained in office, with this reservation, that a minister cannot be imposed on a community if he would offend against its customs.

As an organization and administrative body the South India Church is thus well conceived and well constructed. But upon what doctrinal bases does it rest? Extremely wide: acceptance of the Holy Scriptures as the foundation of all faith; full assent to the Apostles' and Nicene Creeds; belief in two sacraments, Baptism and the Holy Supper, of which it is said only that they are 'means of grace whereby God operates in us'—though the existence of others is not expressly denied; a liturgy fairly akin to the Catholic. One article of the constitution states that doctrines and customs of which there is no mention are not suppressed and that each Church is free to retain them.

Hence we see the true meaning of the operation: 'Let us unite in practice; let us raise as few doctrinal questions as possible; a creed will emerge from within those Christian masses.' And, it may be added, an interesting programme of theological agreement has been accomplished. For example, the very notion of the Church varies enormously: among Calvinists the Church is a voluntary union of believers; among Anglicans (and Catholics) the mystical and social body of Christ; among pietist Lutherans and many new Churches a community where the Holy Spirit speaks. Bishop Newbiggin has shown with extraordinary dialectical ability that those three notions complement and overlap one another, and, in the final analysis, apply to the same undivided Church.

After fifteen years of existence, therefore, one must acknowledge the South India Church as a success. It has lasted, it has survived two or three crises. But in what direction is it moving? In trying to combine all the elements of which it consists is it not likely to accept a simplified creed, a kind of elementary Christianity such as that whose danger was apparent in the beginning of *Life and Work*, which was too ready to combine with certain elements of the American 'social Gospel'? [1] Others asked themselves whether it would not be led by force of circumstances to become more and more Anglican, and even Catholic. This is why many Catholic theologians follow with great interest the experiment of the South India Church.

The future of this 'Pilgrim Church', as it is often called, is all the more important in that it is undoubtedly a pilot Church, whose experiment is watched by the whole non-Catholic world and which has already been imitated. As early as 1947, in Ceylon, the representations of five great Churches (including the Baptists) thought of copying their Indian neighbour and set up the united 'Church of Lanka'. Long discussions were held between the Churches of northern India and of Pakistan: in 1958 they were on the point of success. In Siam an agreement was reached between the Presbyterians and the Baptists, in the Philippines between five Churches. In China and Japan agreements fell short of amalgamation, and there were negotiations in Persia, Madagascar and Australia. A movement had been started which tended to associate different Churches in an administrative framework without asking them for an immediate renunciation of their specific characters, and leaving Providence to bring about a complete reunion of minds and souls.

The most interesting fact is that this movement, starting from young missionary Churches in which agreement seemed to be required by confrontation with the pagan world, is in process of winning over countries in the old tradition. Thus in 1957, in the U.S.A., an organic union was accomplished between Congregationalist communities and the 'Disciples of Christ', so as to form the United Church of Christ. Still more remarkable, in Scotland, where, as we have seen, the official

---

[1] See Chapter II, section 10.

Presbyterian Church stands over against the Anglican Church (considered as dissident), there has been a patient effort towards unity; doctrinal agreements have already been reached, though union was rejected in 1959. But this has not prevented some from concluding that it is necessary to enlarge the project and extent it to the kindred Churches in England.

Thus there is developing in the Protestant world an apparently strong movement towards practical unity. Originating outside the World Council, it has been approved thereby, despite resistance, and may be regarded even today as a kind of experimental field in which the union desired and studied by the Council is accomplished. In 1958 the results achieved were still too recent for the success or failure of such Churches as that of South India to be evaluated. But it is not impossible that a new theology may emerge capable of playing an important part in the 'ecumenical' movement.

13. Towards 'Ecumenism'

Now what has been the attitude of the Catholic Church faced with the considerable growth of the Protestant ecumenical movement? Doctrinally of course her attitude has not changed; but has there not been some alteration in practice? Soon after his election to the Papacy, in *Dum Gravissimum* (3rd March 1939), Pius XII spoke with fatherly kindness of 'all those who are outside the fold of the Catholic Church', and his Christmas address in the same year was a vibrant appeal to 'all those who, without belonging to the visible body of the Catholic Church, are close to Us by their faith in God and in Jesus Christ'. In answer to the question whether those words really altered the situation, we must distinguish two different spheres. There was no veto upon exchange of information or upon private and confidential contacts; but in the matter of a more spectacular demonstration of feeling the question was different.

On the eve of the World Council at Amsterdam the Holy Office repeated its warning: no Catholic would be authorized to attend the meetings; but at the same time the Dutch episcopate appointed a day of prayer that the Holy Spirit might enlighten those taking part. Then, on two subsequent occasions, the Holy Office returned to the question, laying down in particular (December 1949) a regular charter of Catholic ecumenism. It recognized the historical and sociological importance of the Protestant movement and invited the bishops to take note of it. It went so far as to say that those efforts towards unity constituted 'a source of holy joy'. The evident interest of the Catholic press in the work at Amsterdam is sufficient proof that such words re-echoed a deep-seated longing.

Two years later, when *Faith and Order* announced its forthcoming assembly at Lund, there was again question of Catholic participation. Yngve Brilioth, Lutheran Bishop of Uppsala, had a meeting with the Vicar-Apostolic of Sweden, and was so persuasive that Rome did not refuse. It was agreed only that the Catholic representation would not be 'delegates' to the assembly, but only 'observers'. Four priests were nominated: three resident in Sweden and Père C. J. Dumont, founder of *Istina*, whose competence in the matter of ecumenism was outstanding.

This decision might have seemed to form a precedent. At Evanston, however, it was not so. But the *Istina* group had taken a constructive initiative; it had published, translated into English and addressed to all participants a document making clear the Catholic position with regard to the problems about to be studied. In America, on the other hand, relations between Catholics and Protestants were not friendly at that time. Evanston itself was considered as a Calvinist stronghold. Thus Cardinal Stritch of Chicago ruled that no permission to take part in the Assembly could be given without consent of Rome; and the deplorable behaviour of the Methodist Bishop Barbieri seemed to justify his decision.

Consequently it may be said that in 1958 the situation had not altered. Officially Catholics took no part in the proceedings of the World Council. But they were not forbidden to establish friendly relations with their separated brethren in order to reach a better mutual understanding. It must, however, be added that this wise restriction was imposed within the framework of a wide tolerance often defined by Pius XII. For example, on 6th October 1946, addressing members of the Rota, he said: 'There is a political, civil and social tolerance towards the adherents of other faiths which is morally binding upon Catholics.' And on 6th December 1953, speaking to the Union of Jurists: 'The day of suppressing moral and religious errors cannot be an ultimate norm of action; it must be subject to those higher and more general norms which in certain circumstances allow and sometimes demonstrate as more perfect the tolerance of error with a view to promoting a greater good.' Such words make clear how far removed were relations between the 'separated brethren' from the former climate of hostility. Systematic criticism could make way for mutual respect. Did not Pius XII speak later of the 'religious value' of certain non-Catholic testimony? Would the famous expression 'No salvation outside the Church' cease to be a weapon of warfare? In 1949, in the U.S.A., when Father Feeney declared from the pulpit that Protestants were inevitably damned, Mgr Richard Cushing, Archbishop of Boston and later cardinal, vehemently denied the statement and asked the Holy Office for a letter setting out the Catholic doctrine on this subject.

In fact from 1945 onward relations between Catholics and their separated brethren greatly improved. In London, at the beginning of the war, the archbishops of Canterbury and Westminster arranged meetings with a view to friendly relations between Anglicans and Catholics. After the war there was a real combination of forces, striving for the unity of Christians of all denominations. The immediate and constant threat of totalitarian dictatorship, inspired by atheism, has counted for much in the growing determination of all Christians to unite in defence of those sacred values which they hold in common. The changes brought about by decolonization confronted all Churches with the same problems. We see within the Christian conscience a flow of thought towards unity; since the publication in 1943 of the Encyclical *Divino afflante Spiritu* the biblical revival has gained strength year by year among Catholics, who find themselves thus drawn closer to the Protestants; it was followed soon afterwards by a new interest in patristics, which, by concentrating attention upon the Greek Fathers, has produced a better understanding of the Orthodox. Conversely, a newly awakened interest in the liturgy in certain Protestant circles has led them to make contact with the Catholic liturgical revival, while those who endeavour to reanimate the Orthodox Church in Greece, the Near East and even Russia, borrow a great deal from Catholic Action, from community parishes and from the young secular institutes.

It is therefore in a much more favourable climate that there worked and developed those organisms which we have seen arise during the inter-war years in the cause of unity; others may be added to the list. Spiritual ecumenism gained ground with the spread of the 'Week of Universal Prayer for Unity', warmly recommended to Catholic devotion by the Pope and adopted by more than half the Protestant Churches. Father Wattson's Society of Atonement became the most important of Catholic organizations working for unity in English-speaking lands. At Lyon the *Unité Chrétienne* centre was established in 1954 to continue the work of the saintly Abbé Couturier, whose death in 1953 was the result of his detention in Nazi gaols and to his own exhausting labours. His disciple, Père Michalon, a priest of Saint-Sulpice, took charge of the centre and gave it a vigorous life; his friend and biographer, Père Maurice Villain, spread his message through books, newspapers and lectures. *Istina*, founded by Père (afterwards Mgr) Dumont to study 'the problems raised for the Catholic Church by Russia in the religious field, extended its horizon to unity in general, concerning itself with the Protestants no less than with the Orthodox: its house at Boulogne-sur-Seine became more and more a place of meeting and discussion, while Chèvetogne, the Benedictine centre, though keeping knowledge and penetration of the Orthodox world as its principal duty, organized the Catholic Ecumenical Conferences and published the review *Irenikon*, which, under the learned editorship of Dom Clément Lialine, studied in great detail the problem of unity. In Germany the Moehler Institute at Paderborn, under the direct influence of Archbishop (later Cardinal) Jäger, went from strength to strength, its activity, however, being limited exclusively to Protestant affairs. *Una Sancta*, Father Metzger's foundation, had been taken over by the Benedictines of Niederaltach.

In 1947 a centre of ecumenical work was established in Rome itself, strongly encouraged, it is said, by the Pope, and certainly linked with the famous Gregorian University run by the Jesuits. Its founder, Père Charles Boyer, was at that time one of the most distinguished members of the Society. *Unitas* was the title and also that of a review, both patronized by eminent Catholics; Père Boyer chose his collaborators not only from among the sons of St Ignatius but also from among the Augustinians of the Assumption and the Fathers of Atonement. The purpose of this undertaking was threefold: to remind Catholics of the advantages of unity and to invite them to work for it less by discussion than by holiness of life; to show the Orientals all that is similar between Catholics and themselves—the grandeur of their common heritage; and to reveal to Anglicans and Protestants the real nature of the Catholic Church, i.e. that it regards ecumenism in the most strictly Catholic fashion.

Apart from the centres working for concrete unity, aiming at a better mutual understanding, the period following the Second World War witnessed the establishment within the Catholic Church of many hearths upon which the flame of ecumenism burned brightly. Besides the Benedictine abbeys already mentioned there were the Maison Saint-Jean at Louvain University, the Olivetan centres of Gelrode and Schotenhof, and the Russian centre at Fordham University in the U.S.A. Even Spain, so mistrustful of Protestantism, began to awaken to ecumenical problems. All were indubitable signs of a manifest evolution. But there were many others. In France, when on 1st April 1953 the Dominicans of Paris founded a new periodical, *L'Actualité religieuse dans le monde*, it was to Mgr Dumont that they turned for the leading article, 'L'appel de l'Unité'. In 1958 a preacher at Notre-Dame, Mgr Blanchet, rector of the Institut Catholique, dealing with 'The Church of God', devoted an entire sermon to 'The Church and the Churches', and spoke frankly about the problem of unity. 'Who shall say', he asked 'that Catholics were not in part responsible for the birth of Protestantism?' And again: 'Let us make no mistake as to lofty Christian values they have preserved.'

Another clear symptom was the increasing number of Catholic theologians who interested themselves in the problem of unity. One pioneer, Père Congar—whose book *Vraie et fausse Réforme dans l'Église* created a mild sensation—became less and less an isolated figure. An 'ecumenical theology' emerged which was defined by Canon G. Thils, one of its promoters, as 'the theological science in so far as it is constructed and presented so as to take account of the aims and intentions of the ecumenical movement'. Of this science Père Congar rightly said that it must undertake the twofold effort of 'purity' and 'plenitude'. The names of those theologians of ecumenism are so numerous that we cannot hope to cite them all here: Karl Adam, Josef Lortz, Max Pribilla, W. H. van der Pol, Père (later Cardinal) Bea; Father Bernard Leeming, S.J., who introduced theology into English ecumenism; in the U.S.A., Dom Columba Carey-Elwes, John Todd and the French Assumptionist Georges Tavard, whose work contributed enormously towards making the separated brethren better known. In 1951 Mgr Willebrands, a Dutch prelate, founded the International Catholic Conference for Ecumenical Questions, composed of some fifty men of worldwide reputation; it was to meet annually, and the first Assembly was held at Fribourg (Switzerland) in August 1952. Its purpose was to bring Catholic ecumenism into relations with that of the World Council of Churches, to study problems common to all Christians and to establish contact with the general secretariat at Geneva. Year by year this conference so enhanced its position that when Pope John XXIII set up the Secretariat for Unity, preparatory to the Vatican Council, it was Mgr Willebrands whom he appointed first secretary-general.

During those fruitful years between the end of the Second World War and the accession of Pope John, we find the Catholic Church borne along by an irresistible drive towards unity. We must, however, face the fact that, while the 'ecumenical' preoccupation was discernible among a large part of the intellectual *élite*, it did not seem to affect the masses. Lack of understanding persisted; the partisans of unity were often attacked in certain papers. Even so brilliant a man as Claudel seized every opportunity to vilify Protestantism, and spoke of toleration in terms which, though witty, were odious. Rome, moreover, though she had approved, in general and subject to certain conditions, the project of going to meet the separated brethren, remained none the less fearful that the movement was too fast. Hence a number of clashes, some violent: Père Congar was exiled for some time in a British house of his Order and subjected to censure. *Unitas* also was victimized; it had been allowed, upon conditions, to admit non-Catholic members, but that permission was withdrawn.

Nevertheless the atmosphere in 1958 to the search for unity was more evident than it had been twenty or thirty years earlier. On the Protestant side a very similar development was apparent, both inside and outside the World Council of Churches. The theological revival, so manifest within the Protestant fold, helped to advance the idea of agreement not only among the Protestant Churches themselves, but also between them and others, including Catholics. Karl Barth particularly, whose theories won so much attention in Catholic circles, worked in this direction; but Bultmann's neo-liberalism was equally widespread. The studies of Oscar Cullmann on the origins of the Apostolic Succession and the residence of St Peter in Rome revealed an altogether new Protestant attitude towards the question which was still, apparently, the most insurmountable obstacle between Protestants and Catholics. One of the most curious attempts to effect a confrontation of Protestant and Catholic theology was a German movement, *Die Sammlung*. Founded in 1954, in 'High-Church' Lutheran circles, it was intended to fulfil the hope that 'the Reformed Churches, for their own perfection and for the future benefit of the whole Church of God, may be able to find their indispensable place in the one, holy, catholic and apostolic Church'. Its promoters, however, exercised great freedom of criticism in respect both of the Catholic and of their own Church, demanding of both a 'return to the sources'. A similar movement was the Dutch 'Hilversum Group'.

It is of course true that the religious communities which we saw [1] re-established within the Anglican and in the Protestant fold, and which seemed living bridges between their own Churches and Catholic tradition, did not fail to serve the cause of unity. That is eminently so in the case of Taizé in Burgundy. But the desire to serve the cause of unity was no less keen among the nuns of Grandchamp, the retreatants of Pomeyrol, the 'Marian Sisters' of Darmstadt and the Anglican Benedictines of Nashdom.

In this delicate business of mutual seeking and approach it is always possible that a step taken by one or other side, in the fullness of what it conceives as its most sacred rights, may give such offence in the other camp as to imperil the entire ecumenical movement. Thus the promulgation of the dogma of the Assumption (1st November 1950) was, as Père Congar said, 'a cruel blow to ecumenical activity; in many places groups which had been full of life ceased to exist'. And yet every Catholic knew that in promulgating that dogma Pius XII had acted in the plenitude of his infallible authority and in accordance with tradition.

Shocks of that kind are always possible so long as Christian unity has not yet been accomplished. That unity can come about in a profound renewal of all Christianity, a fact which was understood and proclaimed in 1958 by Angelo Roncalli, Pope John XXIII.

[1] See Chapter III, section 14.

14. THE HOUR OF JOHN XXIII

On 25th January 1959 Pope John XXIII went to the basilica of St Paul Outside the Walls. The Unity Week was ending; the Vicar of Christ had always taken a fervent part in its prayers, and it seemed natural that this journey outside the Vatican, the tenth since his election, should mark his interest in this mystical undertaking. The seventeen cardinals, all of the Curia, who had been invited to attend had thought the occasion to be no more than one of those departures from protocol of which the Pope seemed to be making a habit. Their eminences therefore did not expect an important announcement when they were informed that the Pope wished to see them in the adjoining monastery after the service; only one of them, Cardinal Tardini, knew what was afoot.

What they heard surprised them, to say the very least. That same evening a communiqué from the Vatican press agency announced that the Pope had made known to his hearers some thoughts suggested to him by the first three months of his pontificate. As Bishop of Rome he was worried about the serious problems arising from the rapid growth of the city. As Supreme Shepherd he was deeply troubled by the dangers that threatened the spiritual life of the faithful. In order to meet those perils he announced three decisions. A diocesan synod would meet without delay in order to study the life of souls in the City of Rome. The Code of Canon Law, in force since 1917, would be revised and brought up to date. And a General Council would be summoned to study the whole body of problems confronting the Church. It was of course the third decision which amazed the *porporati*. A council! Since the Piedmontese cannon, thundering at the Porta Pia, had suspended the Vatican Council eighty-eight years earlier, there had been occasional talk of its resumption, but no such step had been taken, and John's latest decision was thought by many to be highly imprudent—though they kept that thought to themselves.

But the official communiqué, as printed in *Osservatore Romano* on 26th January, contained some words which were at once picked out and roused lively comment: 'The Holy Father not only regards the General Council as a measure for the spiritual good of the Christian people; he intends it no less as an invitation to the separated Churches to join in the search for unity, for which so many souls today are longing in all parts of the world.' That sentence was of paramount significance: the Vicar of Christ not only recognized the yearning for unity which was stirring so many souls, but also made it his own. His words invited all Christians to a common search for unity and committed the entire Catholic Church to that pursuit. The ecumenical movement, hitherto the preoccupation of a limited number of believers, more or less firmly encouraged by the authorities, was to be henceforward the Sovereign Pontiff's own concern.

How had Pope John come to take so deep an interest in the problem of unity? As a young priest he had been trained by one of the most 'advanced' Italian bishops, Mgr Radini-Tedeschi of Bergamo, who shared the views of Mgr Bonomelli. Later, as a papal diplomat representing the Holy See in Bulgaria, Turkey and Greece, Angelo Roncalli had forged many links with the Orthodox in those countries, and enjoyed the true friendship of the Ecumenical Patriarch Athenagoras. On Christmas Day 1934, preaching a farewell sermon in the Catholic cathedral at Sofia, he had spoken particularly to the 'separated brethren', assuring them of 'that brotherhood, that sincerity of feeling taught by Jesus Christ in the Gospel' and declaring his conviction that eventually there will be only one flock and only one shepherd, 'for such is the will of God'. During his nunciature in Paris his *entourage* often heard him speak of the spiritual treasures of the Orthodox Church, about the fifteenth-century Council of Florence, and also about the Protestant Churches of France, for which he expressed great respect. The same desire for unity continued to occupy his mind after his appointment to the Patriarchal See of Venice. In 1957, taking part in a unionist congress at Palermo, he spoke with much fervour and quoted especially some words of Dom Lambert Beauduin, founder of Amay-Chèvetogne, whom he called 'my very dear Belgian friend'. 'We must create in the West, with a view to reunion of the separated Churches, a movement akin to that of the Propagation of the Faith.' And that is exactly what Roncalli himself was to do on 25th January 1959.

It is important to notice that Pope John did not separate the duty of working for unity from that of renovating the Church, of 'bringing her up to date'. The word *aggiornamento*, which now became so fashionable, was exactly in accord with the purpose of many Catholic theologians. The Encyclical *Cathedram Petri* (29th June) formally associated the idea of unity with the 'development of Catholic faith, with the moral revival of Christian life, and with the adaptation of ecclesiastical discipline to the needs and desires of our time'.

Pope John's appeal re-echoed round the world. Père Villain has related how, while visiting the Protestant ecumenical centre at Bossay, he heard Pastor Visser't Hooft read the communiqué in *Osservatore Romano*, and how all present were most deeply moved. The Protestant press devoted considerable attention to the announcement; many pastors wrote to their Catholic friends expressing their great joy; and at Constantinople the Patriarch Athenagoras made an announcement full of enthusiasm.

Though some commentators appeared to expect too much too soon, the decisive impulse had been given, and during the months that followed Pope John managed to sustain it. One declaration made it clear that the work for unity must be envisaged in three stages: 'first an approach, then the making contact, and finally brotherly reunion'. In private conversation, or when addressing small groups of visitors, he expressed himself even more clearly. Thus on 19th January 1959, speaking to the parish priests of Rome, he said: 'We shall not seek to discover who was right and who was wrong. Responsibility is shared. We shall only say, "Let us unite, let us have done with disputes."' Action followed closely upon words: the foundation of a Secretariat for Unity, and the announcement that non-Catholic observers would be admitted to sessions of the Council. Beyond doubt a new climate had come into being throughout the world and among all men who owe allegiance to Jesus Christ.

Upon that image haloed in light we may conclude our story of the efforts made by Christians in the hope that Christ's robe may once again be seamless. With Vatican II a new page of history will inevitably be written.

APPENDIX

1. The Old Catholics

The Old Catholics occupy a special place among the Christian communities separated from Rome. As their name implies, they claim their right to the use of the name Catholics; more, they affirm loyalty to authentic tradition, leaving aside everything which seems to them to be pointless innovation, especially the dogma of Papal Infallibility.

Historically, in the strict sense of the term, the Old Catholics are those who in 1871 refused to accept the Vatican Council's decision. Their leader was the theologian, von Döllinger (1799–1890), one of the masters at Tübingen and a friend of Moehler. Violently opposed to the proclamation of the dogma, he contended that it 'had founded a new Church'. Although he was excommunicated, he showed no desire to break completely with the Catholic Church, and advised his disciples to remain in the Church the better to disseminate his theses. In point of fact he was soon overtaken by those who followed him. They set up a schismatic Church, the Old Catholic Church, which, like the Orthodox Church, recognized only the decisions of the Seven Ecumenical Councils, rejected auricular confession, celibacy of the priests and, furthermore (and this was distinctly a Protestant attitude), dropped the worship of saints and the practice of indulgences. The ministers of this Church were elected and the services were conducted in the vernacular languages. These schisms were to be found mostly in Germany and in Central Europe. But in Switzerland, where the famous Father Hyacinthe Loison took refuge (he was another opponent of Papal Infallibility), there was another schism—that of the 'Catholic Christians'.

These new groups soon came up against the age-old problem which was inherent to all schisms—the ordination of their priests by a legitimate bishop, one to whom Apostolic Succession incontestably applied. They turned to Utrecht for help. Here were many other schismatics, none of whom recognized Papal authority—and this ever since the Bull *Unigenitus*! The diocese of Utrecht during the Reformation was a Catholic island in a Calvinist sea; it was looked upon as mission territory and in this light was directed by an apostolic vicar. Since 1580 it had been directly attached to Rome, a fact which caused difficulties with the local clergy. Jansenism was very successful in Utrecht, and this brought about a violent conflict with Rome in the years 1703–5. An inhibited missionary-bishop, Varlet, Bishop of

448

Babylon, then came to Utrecht and consecrated Cornelius Steenhoven, leader of the Jansenists (who had rebelled against *Unigenitus*) as archbishop. The new Church was now (1723-4) on a firmer footing. It had its own theologian, Van Espen, former master of Louvain. Jansenists fleeing from France were warmly welcomed. In 1750 there were three dioceses.

In calling upon the Church of Utrecht (which some refer to as 'Old Catholic') the disciples of Döllinger and others who were equally against Papal Infallibility considered that their clergy would be thereby officially recognized. Bishop Varlet was certainly recognized, even if inhibited. The first 'Old Catholic' bishop consecrated was Reinkens; the 'Catholic Christians' consecrated Herzog. But these various groups were well aware of their weak position and in 1889, under Bishop John Eynkamp, of Utrecht, they convened a Lesser Council. This arranged for the merging of the three groups. They decided that the basis of their faith would be 'that which had everywhere and at all times been believed in the Church' from the famous maxim of Vincent de Lérins. A solemn declaration recorded the membership of small groups with similar ideas from Poland, Bohemia, Croatia, etc. To the resulting united group the name 'Old Catholics' was applied.

It is curious to note here that these schismatic groups, who had broken with the Catholic Church, were of the opinion that the Old Catholic Church could serve as a model for the other great Churches towards better understanding and even *rapprochement*. As we saw, Döllinger [1] was a fervent believer in Christian unity, and in this matter he was a not insignificant theologian. The *Revue Internationale de Théologie*, founded in Zürich in 1893 by the Old Catholics, often printed very interesting studies on the problems of unity. Moreover the Old Catholics organized Assemblies from the year 1875 onwards, and these would be characterized today by the adjective ecumenical, for they were attended by the representatives of several Protestant Churches and Orthodoxy.

There was even an attempt at merging between the Old Catholics and the Orthodox Church in 1902. But the die-hards among the Orthodox considered that the Old Catholics were more or less contaminated by the Roman virus. For their part, the Old Catholics were proud of their links with the chain of bishops and of faithful, untouched—like true Catholics—by any heresy, and the merger was dropped, though this did not stop the friendly relations between the two camps.

On several occasions the Old Catholics have made their name in public affairs. They provided Bismarck with one of the pretexts for unleashing the *Kulturkampf*: the Catholic bishops had forbidden their

[1] See Chapter VI, section 4.

theologians to teach in the universities, but Bismarck upheld them, pleased with the 'national' character displayed by this little Church. And in the thick of the dispute between Berlin and the Vatican he attempted to call upon the Old Catholic clergy as a replacement for the Catholic clergy. The same thing occurred in Switzerland, when *Kulturkampf* broke out on a smaller scale. But in neither Germany nor Switzerland did the matter go very far.

They came to the fore again when there was talk of union between Anglicanism and Rome under the guidance of Lord Halifax and Father Portal. When Leo XIII was obliged to declare Anglican ordinations invalid, there were some who asked themselves what would happen if Anglican bishops were re-consecrated by Old Catholic bishops— could Rome still maintain that they did not qualify for Apostolic Succession? In point of fact this idea remained hypothetical, since no Anglican bishop doubted the validity of his ordination. It has been said that the Anglican, Doctor Lee, founder of the Order of Corporate Reunion (1877), had himself consecrated as a Catholic bishop in secret, but it would appear that this was carried out by an Italian bishop and not by an Old Catholic.

It is mostly in the ecumenical movement, conceived since 1910, and operative within Protestantism and Anglicanism, that the Old Catholics have made their presence felt. They joined the World Council of Churches at its inception, and have always had several of their members at work in the general secretariat. It is here, despite their small numbers, that they exercise real influence, for they guarantee the ecumenical nature of the Council; if they were to leave it there would be but two participants, Protestantism and Orthodoxy; and, on very serious questions, we know that the Orthodox Churches are not always in agreement with the Protestants; the Old Catholics therefore act as the arm of the balance.

Today the Old Catholic Church numbers some 600,000 adherents, of whom there are 360,000 in the U.S.A. (four bishoprics), 30,000 in Germany and Austria, 30,000 in Switzerland and 100,000 in Poland. There are very few of them in France (where some people confuse them with the members of the *Petite Église*, which declined to subscribe to the Concordat regime). They maintain an excellent Faculty of Theology at Bern. The *Revue Internationale de Théologie* has survived the death of its founder, the indefatigable Old Catholic abbot, Michaud. It prints its articles mostly in German or in English. The Old Catholics were among the first to welcome the initiative of John XXIII in giving the Vatican Council, among other goals, that of ecumenicalism. Recently there have been colloquies held between Old Catholics and Catholics. The Old Catholics have sent observers to the Council from its inception.

2. SHORT LIST OF CHURCHES, HERESIES, DENOMINATIONS AND SECTS OUTSIDE THE CATHOLIC CHURCH

ANABAPTISTS. Separate Protestant groups which came into being in Germany, Switzerland and Holland during the Reformation. Their common features are adult baptism and the re-baptism of converts. Their doctrine was very imprecise. Decimated during the Peasants' War and the 'City of God' experiment of Leyden, Anabaptists arose anew with the Mennonites (q.v.).

ANGLICANS. Adherents of the Church which emerged in England under Henry VIII, gradually infiltrated by Protestantism. The Thirty-nine Articles of 1563 are the basis of the Anglican faith, but there are three tendencies in Anglicanism—High, Low and Broad Church. The Church of England lies at the centre of the Anglican Communion, which also includes the Episcopalians of the U.S.A. Total: about 30 million.

ARMENIANS. Eastern Christians settled in the Caucasus and Taurus regions; since 551, Monophysite outwardly if not doctrinally. The Armenian Church was savagely persecuted by the Turks. Some $3\frac{1}{2}$ million adherents today. (There are also Catholic Armenians.)

ARMINIANS. Calvinists, so called after Arminius, a professor at Leyden who, early in the seventeenth century, propounded liberal theses on predestination against Gomar, who held stricter views. Condemned at the Dordrecht Synod in 1619. Some small groups remain today totalling about 25,000 adherents.

BAPTISTS. Protestant groups which arose in the eighteenth century outside the Established Churches and main faiths, in England and later in the U.S.A., under Arminian and Anabaptist influences. Their main characteristic is adult baptism. Their creed is very simple, based solely on the Bible and especially on the Gospels. Their very simplicity in doctrinal matters explains their success in the U.S.A., where they are the leading Protestant denomination; this, however, is split into numerous branches, not all of which are members of the Baptist World Alliance. Total: 30–40 million.

CALVINISTS. Protestants in the tradition of Calvin. There are no 'Calvinist' Churches as such, though the doctrine of Calvinism has provided a basis for many Churches, who style themselves 'Reformed' or 'Presbyterian' (some 30–40 million adherents). Calvinism has great influence on all forms of Protestantism. *See also* REFORMED CHURCHES, PRESBYTERIANS, PURITANS.

CONGREGATIONALISTS. Protestants of differing origins (mostly Presbyterians and Anglicans) who, in their conception of the Church, differ from the Presbyterians and the Episcopalians. They hold that all authority is vested in the local church and no hierarchy, even elective, stands above it. They landed in the U.S.A. with the Pilgrim Fathers. Congregationalism today has an influence out of proportion to its small numbers—only 1½ million in the U.S.A.

COPTS. Christians of Egypt, descendants of the pharaonic *fellaheen* and Christians of the first centuries, whose centre was Alexandria. Under the influence of Jacob Baradeus they became Monophysites, resisting the pressure of Islam. Today they number some 4 million. (There are also Catholic Copts.) *See* MONOPHYSITES.

DARBYITES. Protestant sect founded at the beginning of the nineteenth century by the Anglican minister, John Nelson Darby. They merged with the Plymouth Brethren (q.v.). Darby taught a new form of Protestantism, simplified, based on piety and brotherly love. He acknowledged no ecclesiastical organization, reducing ritual to the feast of bread and wine and to public prayer. There are nowadays some 300,000 Darbyites around the world. But the influence of Darbyite missions has been felt even in those Protestant circles which had remained loyal to the older Churches—the Calvinists of the Cévennes, for example.

DISCIPLES OF CHRIST. A variety of Baptists (Reform Baptists) in the U.S.A., founded at the beginning of the nineteenth century, in the wish to live a life based on early Christianity. They flourished at the time of the westward expansion of the U.S.A. in the role of apostles. The climate being influenced by liberal ideas, they have gained ground principally in intellectual circles; they have a strong cohesion, both in the moral and social sense, and are very ecumenical in outlook, being strongly opposed to disunity among Christians. They number about 1½ million.

DOUKHOBORS or 'Spiritual Christians'. Russian sect, founded during the eighteenth century, whose religion has no outward signs, with no churches, no icons, no public worship. Persecuted by Moscow, they were later settled by Alexander I along the Black Sea coast in 1820–6. In many ways they resemble the Quakers. Numbers unknown, though certainly not high.

EPISCOPALIANS. Part of the Anglican Communion situated in the U.S.A. and who, for this reason, can no longer be linked to the British Crown, but who retain the Thirty-nine Articles and the customs of Anglicanism. The Protestant Episcopalian Church has about 1½ million adherents and wields considerable influence.

ETHIOPIAN CHURCH. Christians of north-east Africa. One of the oldest Christian Churches in the world. Monophysite beliefs were introduced from Egypt in the sixth century and have continued, at least in theory, until today. There are between 4 and 7 million adherents, and the Ethiopian Church is an integral part of the nation. It has preserved quite distinctive characteristics of liturgy and piety. (There are also Catholic and Protestant Ethiopians.)

EVANGELICALS. This term does not indicate a denomination, for most Protestants qualify themselves as evangelists. It is applied more especially to Calvinists hostile to liberal tendencies (and in this sense it approaches the Fundamentalist ideas). But there are also Baptist, Methodist and Pentecostal Churches which claim this quality. In England the Evangelists were, around 1800, fervent Anglicans, sometimes influenced by Methodism, who sought to regenerate the Church of England. Today the term is applied to members of the Low Church.

FRIENDS OF MAN. A sect which styles itself 'The Army of the Eternal' or 'The Church of the Kingdom of God'; founded in 1916 by dissident Jehovah's Witnesses. Their doctrine is simple, affirming man's immortality provided he avoids sin and 'offence to the body'. Certain naturistic customs are imposed on adherents. It is far from being a true religion, and the Protestants do not admit this sect as one of their Churches.

FUNDAMENTALISTS. In the U.S.A. this term refers to an attitude of mind, not a Church or denomination: unswervingly strict faith, literal interpretation of the Bible, austere moral life, etc. This attitude is found equally in Presbyterians, Baptists or Methodists. The southern states of the U.S.A. are more inclined towards it than are those of the north, which are more liberal in outlook.

HINSCHITES. Small groups of dissident Calvinists from the Montpellier area of France. The Hinschite (Evangelical) Protestant Church was founded by Coraly Hinsch in the middle of the nineteenth century. It has a dualist theology with emphasis on the blessings which flow from the Holy Ghost. The Hinschites also undertake social works.

HUTTERITES. Strict Lutherans, with emphasis on piety and baptism. The Hutterite Brethren were founded by Hutter at the beginning of the seventeenth century, but little was heard of them until 1945, when they left Germany to settle in Paraguay. Here they were to be very successful: there are 450 communities with possibly some 100,000 adherents.

IRVINGITES. Protestant sect founded at the beginning of the nineteenth century by the Scots Presbyterian minister Edward Irving, under the name of the Catholic Apostolic Church. Irving's object was to reconstitute the early Church, including the charismatic phenomena of prophecy and the gift of tongues. Irving overlaid this with the observances based on the seven sacraments, a very complicated ecclesiastical organization and a liturgy which was Byzantine in origin. This ambiguous theology was not conducive to the success of the sect, which numbers only some 50,000 adherents. *See* NEO-APOSTOLIC COMMUNITY.

JACOBITES. Eastern Christians, followers of Jacob Baradeus, an astonishing person who organized Monophysite resistance to Byzantine repression during the sixth century. The Copts of Egypt and the Ethiopians are Jacobites.

JOANNITES. One of the many sects which have emerged recently in Soviet Russia. Followers of the great figure of Blessed John of Kronstadt, a popular and mystic apostle of the early twentieth century. They see in him the reincarnation of Christ.

JEHOVAH'S WITNESSES. This sect sprang from the Seventh Day Adventists, but the majority of Protestants refuse to admit it into their circle of Churches. They are violently anti-trinitarian, recognize only the God of the Bible, reject all other revelations, deny the immortality of the soul and are strongly pacifist. They have an excellent organization and true sense of mission, and this has helped them to make considerable progress, especially between the years 1925-55.

LUTHERANS. Protestants, followers of Martin Luther. The Lutherans constitute the greatest single unit in the Protestant world, totalling some 75 million, mainly in Germany, Scandinavia and the U.S.A., divided into Churches according to their doctrinal bases or national boundaries. In the U.S.A. they are organized in synods, of which the most important is that of Missouri.

MENNONITES. Protestants whose communities were founded in the middle of the sixteenth century by the former Dutch Catholic priest Menno Simons on a basis akin to that of the Spanish *alumbrados* of the Middle Ages, embracing what was left of Anabaptism. The Mennonites are characterized by an exceptionally liberal creed, adult baptism and the re-baptism of converts and great simplicity in everyday life. There are about 500,000 of them, half of these being in the U.S.A. and Canada.

METHODISTS. Founded by the former Anglican, Wesley, in the latter half of the eighteenth century, professing a form of Christianity without doctrine, reduced to broad principles of charity, morals and piety. They are grouped into Churches, some forty in all, most of them members since 1951 of the World Methodist Council. Total: some 30 million, of whom two-thirds are in the U.S.A.

MONOPHYSITES. Follow the teachings of certain theologians such as Dioscorus and Eutychus (fifth century) recognizing only one nature, the divine, in the person of Christ. Condemned in 451 by the Council of Chalcedon, the Monophysites nevertheless resisted Byzantine pressure, mainly through the leadership of Jacob Baradeus (*see* JACOBITES). The three important Churches are Monophysite (at least outwardly)—the Armenian, Coptic and Ethiopian (qq.v.).

MORAL REARMAMENT. This formation is neither a Church nor a sect. Founded under the name of 'Oxford Group' after the First World War by the Lutheran minister, Frank Buchman, M.R.A. has no dogma, but stresses the importance of personal witness, human brotherhood and living a Christian life. Very distinctly Protestant in its principles, it has nevertheless opened its ranks to non-Protestant Christians, and today to non-Christians.

MORAVIANS. These derived from Hussite sects, and are found mostly in Moravia. They are linked with the Lutheran Augsburg Confession, but have autonomous communities in Bohemia, England, Germany, the U.S.A. and South America. Scarcely more than 1½ million adherents, but considerable missionary activity.

MORMONS. Although recognized in the U.S.A. as a Church, the Mormons are generally considered as heretics by the Protestants. To the revelations of the Bible they have added the 'Book of Mormon', the work of Joseph Smith at the beginning of the nineteenth century. For a long time they were celebrated for 'biblical' polygamy; their trek across the U.S.A. to settle in the Salt Lake area is also famous. Nowadays monogamous, the Mormons are not unlike certain types of Protestants, such as the Quakers or certain Methodists; they have, however, dogmas and customs of their own, some taken from Judaism, others being originated by themselves, such as the baptism of the dead by proxy.

NEO-APOSTOLIC COMMUNITIES. These were founded in 1860 by dissident Irvingites (q.v.). They were subsequently strengthened and placed on a firm basis by Niehans and Bischoff. They hold that they are the only true Church. They have retained a number of the features of the Irvingites but have only three sacraments. A considerable degree of importance is accorded to their leader, the 'Apostle', who alone has the power to save souls. Many of them believe that Christ's return to earth is imminent. Total: about 540,000.

NESTORIANS. Eastern Christians who are descendants of the adherents of the heresiarch Nestorius (fifth century), who made a radical distinction between God and man in the person of Christ and refused to attribute to God the characteristics of Jesus the man, and therefore concluded that the Virgin Mary was not 'The Mother of God' (*Theotokos*) but simply the Mother of Jesus. Condemned by the Council of Ephesus in 431, the Nestorians exist today in very small groups in Mesopotamia and India.

OLD BELIEVERS. Russian Christians separated from the official Orthodox Church since the schism of Raskol in the seventeenth century, because they would not accept certain innovations. Much persecuted by the Soviets, they still number some 20 million, split into different elements, of which the main one is the Old Believers Orthodox Church.

OLD CATHOLICS. Schismatics who left the Roman Church because they declined to accept the dogma of Papal Infallibility (1871). Later they became attached to the Jansenist Church at Utrecht; they became more and more Protestant. There are some 600,000, of whom 360,000 are in the U.S.A.

ORTHODOX CHURCHES. The term today is taken to mean those Christians separated from Rome by the Greek Schism of 1054 (it can be construed as 'teachers of the true faith'). Minor points of doctrine, not heretical opinions, separate them from the Catholics. The Orthodox Churches have some 150–180 million adherents assembled in autocephalous Churches, over which the Ecumenical Patriarch of Constantinople (Istanbul) maintains honorary primateship. They are found in the Balkans, in Russia, and have strong groups in Western Europe and the U.S.A. In Protestantism the term 'orthodox' is roughly synonymous with 'fundamentalist' and signifies 'anti-liberal'. In the smaller Churches in India the term is applied to Jacobites who opposed the trend towards Protestantization which affected certain Monophysite groups.

PENTECOSTAL CHURCHES. The Pentecostal communities or 'Assemblies of God' are the most active of all Protestant sects. Founded early in the twentieth century by the Welsh miner Evan Roberts and the Negro Baptist preacher W. J. Seymour, their religion is based on the guidance of the Holy Ghost, this being manifested by miraculous cures and the gift of tongues. Religious observance is of an uncomplicated type, and charitable works abound within the communities. The Pentecostal Churches have some 4–10 million adherents; they are making considerable progress in the Americas, especially in Chile.

'PETITE ÉGLISE'. Very small groups of schismatics who left the Roman Church rather than accept Napoleon's Concordat. There are several thousand of them still, mostly in the Charente region and Lyon in France. All of them affirm complete Catholic orthodoxy (a part of this Church did return to the Catholic Church in 1963 and 1964).

PIETISTS. Protestant elements, especially among German Lutherans, who attach supreme importance to piety and to emotional religious fervour. The movement was of great importance in the eighteenth century under Count von Zinzendorf and his emulators at Herrnhut, but has never developed into an autonomous Church. Nowadays one can link pietists with Moravians (q.v.).

PLYMOUTH BRETHREN. At the end of the eighteenth century the Plymouth Brethren were a collection of small pietist communities, analogous to the Moravians. They were given an initial stimulus by John Walker and were then taken in hand by Darby, with whose movement they are now fused in all but name, though the title of Plymouth Brethren is more often used in the U.S.A. *See* DARBYITES.

PRESBYTERIANS. This appellation can be used to designate all those Protestants who accept the system of the 'presbyterium' in the organization of their Church as it was established by Calvin (a council of pastors and laity), that is to say, those who are neither Episcopalians nor Congregationalists. In point of fact the term designates the Calvinists of Scotland, England and the U.S.A., their counterparts in continental Europe being termed 'Reformed'.

PURITANS. A type of very austere Protestant. Historically speaking, the Puritans are strict Presbyterians who dominated England for a time with the Roundheads of Cromwell, and who took part in the first colonization of America as passengers in the *Mayflower*. There have never been Puritan Churches; Puritanism is, in its widest sense, an attitude of mind which has had considerable influence throughout the Protestant world; it is not far removed from the Jansenism of the Catholic world.

QUAKERS. (Protestant) members of the 'Society of Friends', referred to as 'Quakers'. Founded by George Fox in England in the seventeenth century, spread to the U.S.A., regenerated at the beginning of the nineteenth century by Bénézet, de Grellet, Woolmans and Whitter. They practise a rudimentary form of Christianity, based on silent meditation while awaiting the inner call of the spirit. Their moral standards are very austere. There are some 200,000 in England and the U.S.A. Their social and charitable works earned them the Nobel Prize for Peace in 1947, two of their Relief Committees being so honoured.

REFORMED CHURCHES. This term designates Calvinists in general in France, Switzerland, Holland, Germany and central Europe. It corresponds to the term 'Presbyterian' in Anglo-Saxon countries.

SALVATION ARMY. Protestant military-style organization, well-known through its uniform, but principally for its outstanding social works. Founded by William Booth at the end of the nineteenth century, it has spread all over the world. Some authors consider it a sect, but it has in reality no dogma and only counsels its adherents to observe a spiritual life based on charity.

SEVENTH DAY ADVENTISTS. Protestant sect or Church of American origin, founded by William Miller in 1840; subsequently strengthened and developed by Ellen Gould White. The Adventists await Christ's early return to earth, observe Saturday as the Sabbath, base their faith on the Bible and have conceptions of personal life hereafter. There are 1 million of them throughout the world. They are recognized by the Protestants and take part in the World Council of Churches.

SKOPTSY. (Castrates.) A strange Russian sect who practise emasculation, thus avoiding the sin of the flesh. The *Great Soviet Encyclopedia* states that in 1930 there were still a few adherents.

TRUE ORTHODOX CHRISTIANS. One of many sects which have arisen in Russia during the last fifty years. Hostile to all forms of official Communism, they nevertheless live in tightly knit communities, decline to consider themselves as a Church and await the end of the world, which they consider near at hand (as do the Seventh Day Adventists among the Protestants).

UNITARIANS. Groups which have emerged from various Protestant denominations, which in their hostility to the dogma of the Holy Trinity have prolonged the heresies of the first centuries and the Socinianism of the sixteenth century. Established in the U.S.A., where Harvard University was to become its centre, Unitarianism has evolved as a form of Christianity without either moral or social dogma. There are some 125,000 Unitarians in the U.S.A., some 40,000 in England.

WALDENSES. Descendants of heretics of the Middle Ages, still called the *Pauvres de Lyon*, of which some small groups still exist in the upper Alpine valleys, they are survivors of ancient persecutions. Today they are attached to the Italian Reformed Church and exercise a certain intellectual influence.

CHRONOLOGICAL TABLE

CHRONOLOGICAL TABLE

DATE	POLITICAL, INTELLECTUAL AND SOCIAL EVENTS	EVENTS CONCERNING THE CATHOLIC CHURCH
1789	French Revolution.	
1790		Civil Constitution of the Clergy in France.
1791		Religious persecution begins in France.
1792	10th August—fall of the monarchy in France.	
1793	21st January—execution of Louis XVI. Second partition of Poland.	Religious persecution worsens—many priests emigrate. Feast of the Goddess Reason.
1794	The Terror in France.	Robespierre and the Feast of the Supreme Being.
1795	Third and final partition of Poland.	
1798	Napoleon lands in Egypt. Rome occupied by the French.	
1799	Napoleon seizes power (18th–19th Brumaire).	Religious peace returns to France. Death of Pope Pius VI.
1800		Election of Pope Pius VII.
1801	Alexander I Czar (1801–25). French troops leave Egypt.	The Concordat in France.
1802	The Montbéliard territory (Lutheran) is returned to France.	
1803		
1804	Coronation of Napoleon by Pius VII. French Empire proclaimed. First Serbian insurrection against the Turks.	
1806	Hegel's *Phenomenology of the Mind.*	
1807	Abolition of slavery.	
1808		Napoleon's conflict with Pius VII.
1812	The Russian campaign.	Pius VII at Fontainebleau.
1813		
1814	Napoleon's first exile.	Pius VII returns to Rome.
1815	Battle of Waterloo. Fall of Napoleon. Congress of Vienna. Government of Louis XVIII.	
1816	Serbian autonomy.	
1817		
1818		
1821	Greek War of Independence.	
1822	Massacres of Chios.	
1823		Death of Pius VII. Election of Leo XII.

460

DATE	EVENTS CONCERNING THE EASTERN CHURCH	EVENTS CONCERNING THE REFORMATION CHURCHES	EVENTS CONCERNING THE HISTORY OF UNITY
1789 1790			
1791		Death of Wesley, founder of Methodism. In France the Protestants obtain equality of rights.	
1792		The Baptist Missionary Society.	
1793	The *Philocalia of the Saints* translated into Russian.		
1794	Death of the great *starets*, Velochkovsky.		
1795		The London Missionary Society.	
1798			
1799			
1800 1801			
1802			
1803 1804		Death of Herder in Germany. London Bible Society.	
1806 1807 1808 1812 1813		Expansion of Baptists; setting up of Baptist Union. Birth of Kierkegaard.	
1814 1815			
1816		Revival in Geneva. American Bible Society.	
1817		Frederick William III and the 'United Church' in Prussia.	
1818		French Bible Society.	
1821	The Patriarch of Constantinople hanged by the Turks.		
1822 1823			

DATE	POLITICAL, INTELLECTUAL AND SOCIAL EVENTS	EVENTS CONCERNING THE CATHOLIC CHURCH
1824	Charles X King of France (1824–1830).	
1825	Nicolas I Czar (1825–55).	
1827	Turkish defeat at Navarino.	
1828	Russians in Armenia.	
1829		Death of Leo XII. Election of Pius VIII.
1830	Kingdom of Greece constituted. Independence of Belgium. Occupation of Algeria by the French. Fall of Charles X. Accession of Louis-Philippe.	Death of Pius VIII.
1831		Election of Gregory XVI.
1832	Mohamed Ali, Pasha of Cairo, revolts against the Sultan.	
1833		
1834		
1835	Strauss publishes his *Vie de Jésus*.	
1836		
1837	Accession of Queen Victoria.	
1838		
1839	New Turkish-Egyptian conflict.	
1840	Treaty of London (Eastern Question).	
1841		
1842		
1844		Anti-Catholic movement in the U.S.A.
1845		
1846		Death of Gregory XVI. Accession of Pius IX.
1847		
1848	Revolution in Paris. Fall of Louis-Philippe. Karl Marx publishes his Communist *Manifesto*.	
1849		

DATE	EVENTS CONCERNING THE EASTERN CHURCH	EVENTS CONCERNING THE REFORMATION CHURCHES	EVENTS CONCERNING THE HISTORY OF UNITY
1824		Paris Missionary Society.	Moehler's Unity of the Church.
1825		Death of Oberlin, pastor of Ban de la Roche.	
1827			
1828		Irving and the apostolic communities.	
1928		Death of Felix Neff, pastor of Queyras. Abolition of the Test Act (1829–33).	
1830	The Greek Church declares itself autocephalous.		
1831			Moehler's *Symbolism*.
1832		Adolphe Monod's Revival in Lyons. In Scotland, the Haldanes. In Germany, Wichern sets up his *Rauhe Haus*.	
1833	Death of Seraphin of Sarov.	Beginnings of the Oxford Movement in Anglicanism. Congregational Union.	
1834		Death of Schleiermacher.	
1835			
1836	The Russians attempt to control the Armenian Church.	Fliedner founds the German deaconesses.	
1838		Founding of the Disciples of Christ in the U.S.A.	Death of Moehler.
1839	The Sultan grants civil equality to the Christians of the Turkish Empire.		
1840		General Welfare Association in Germany. Elizabeth Fry and prison reforms in England. Frederick William IV of Prussia (1840–59), religious reformer.	
1841		First Anglican nuns.	
1842	Kurds massacre Armenians.		
1844			
1845		G. Williams founds Y.M.C.A. Norway grants freedom of worship to all religions.	
1846			The Evangelical Alliance.
1847		Death of Alexandre Vinet.	
1848	Letter from the Metropolitans in reply to that of Pius IX.	Founding of Presbyterian Alliance, in Scotland. Wichern sets up Inner Mission in Germany. John Bost Homes. Separation of Church and State in Holland.	Pius IX's letter, *In supremo patri*, to the Christians of the East.
1849		Denmark grants freedom of worship to all religions.	

DATE	POLITICAL, INTELLECTUAL AND SOCIAL EVENTS	EVENTS CONCERNING THE CATHOLIC CHURCH
1850		
1851	2nd December—Louis Napoleon seizes power.	
1852	Second French Empire.	
1854	Crimean War.	Dogma of Immaculate Conception.
1855	Alexander II Czar (1855-81).	
1856	Treaty of Paris (Eastern Question).	
1858	Rumanian autonomy.	Apparitions at Lourdes.
1859	Darwin publishes his *Origin of Species*.	
1860		
1861	Founding of the kingdom of Italy. Abolition of serfdom in Russia.	
1863	Renan publishes his *Vie de Jésus*.	
1864		Encyclical, *Quanta Cura*, and the Syllabus.
1865		
1866	The First International. Austria defeated at Sadowa. Constitutional status proclaimed in Egypt.	
1867	Serbian independence. First volume of Marx's *Das Kapital*.	
1868	Beginning of the Mei-ji era in Japan.	Bull, *Aeterni Patris*, convoking the Ecumenical Council.
1869		Opening of the Vatican Council.
1870	Capture of Rome by the Piedmontese, interrupting the Vatican Council. Franco-German War. Fall of the French Empire and proclamation of the Third Republic.	Definition of the dogma of Papal Infallibility.
1871	German Empire proclaimed.	Old Catholics schism. *Kulturkampf* begins in Germany.
1872		Monsignor Mermillod and the Swiss *Kulturkampf*.
1873	Turkish atrocities in Bulgaria.	
1875		
1877		

DATE	EVENTS CONCERNING THE EASTERN CHURCH	EVENTS CONCERNING THE REFORMATION CHURCHES	EVENTS CONCERNING THE HISTORY OF UNITY
1850		Darby and the Plymouth Brethren. Pusey and the beginnings of Anglican ritualism.	
1851			
1852			
1854			
1855			
1856	Christians in Turkey obtain, at least in principle, equal political rights.	Death of Kierkegaard.	
1858			
1859		Increasing importance of liberal Protestantism.	Abbé Guettée founds Christian Union.
1860	Druses massacre Christians in Lebanon.	Ellen Gould White and the Seventh Day Adventists. Vermeil and the French deaconesses.	
1861			
1863		The Colenso affair in South Africa.	Publication of the *Union Review*.
1864		First African Anglican bishop.	The Holy Office condemns the English Association for Unity.
1865	*The Story of a Russian Pilgrim* appears.	William Booth and the Salvation Army. The Social Gospel in the U.S.A.	Anglican and Eastern Churches' Association.
1866		Pressensé denounces the excesses of 'free criticism'. The Ku-Klux-Klan in the U.S.A.	Founding of the Continental Missions Conference.
1867		Constitution of the Anglican Communion (Lambeth Conference).	
1868		Monumental statue to Luther set up in Germany.	
1869	Orthodox hierarchy decline invitation to Vatican Council.		Bull, *Aeterni Patris*.
1870	Foundation of the Orthodox Missionary Society. The Bulgarian Church becomes autocephalous.		
1871			
1872			Monsignor Strossmayer's campaign.
1873	The laity set up a Supervisory Council in the Coptic Church.	Sweden grants freedom of worship to all religions.	
1875		World Alliance of Reformed Churches.	
1877		Founding of the Salvation Army.	

DATE	POLITICAL, INTELLECTUAL AND SOCIAL EVENTS	EVENTS CONCERNING THE CATHOLIC CHURCH
1878	Treaty of San Stefano (Eastern Question); Congress of Berlin.	Death of Pius IX. Accession of Leo XIII.
1879		*Kulturkampf* ends in Germany.
1881	Alexander III Czar.	
1882		The Uganda martyrs (Anglicans among them).
1884	Death of Karl Marx.	
1885		
1888	Accession of William II in Germany.	
1889		
1890	Renan publishes his work *L'Avenir de la Science*.	
1891		The great social Encyclical, *Rerum Novarum*.
1893		
1894	Nicolas II Czar.	Appeal to Leo XIII to Christians of the East.
1895		
1896	Italian defeat at Adowa in Abyssinia.	
1897		Hecker's *Americanisme*.
1898	The Dreyfus Affair in France.	
1899	The Boer War.	
1900		
1901	Death of Queen Victoria—accession of Edward VII.	
1902		Commencement of modernism.
1903	Founding of Bolshevik movement.	Death of Leo XIII. Accession of Pius X.
1905	Russian defeat at the hands of the Japanese — revolutionary agitation in Russia.	
1907		Condemnation of modernism.
1908		

DATE	EVENTS CONCERNING THE EASTERN CHURCH	EVENTS CONCERNING THE REFORMATION CHURCHES	EVENTS CONCERNING THE HISTORY OF UNITY
1878			
1879			
1881	Death of Dostoyevsky.		
1882			
1884			
1885	The Rumanian Church becomes autocephalous.	Ten-year period of expansion of Stöcker's Christian Socialism. Charles Gide's School at Nîmes.	
1888			
1889			The Utrecht Union embrace-Jansenists and Old Cathos lics. Lord Halifax and Father Portal meet.
1890			
1891		And following years—renaissance of Anglican monasticism.	
1893			'Parliament of Religions' at Chicago.
1894	Encyclical, *Praeclara*, is rejected by the Orthodox Church. Death of Theophanes the Recluse. Widespread massacres in Armenia.		
1895	Massacres extend to the Taurus region.		
1896			*Apostolici Curae* declares Anglican ordinations invalid. Leo XIII establishes a novena for unity.
1897		Auguste Sabatier's *Philosophie de la Religion*.	
1898			
1899			
1900	Death of Soloviev (1858–1900).	Founding of the Lutheran Alliance.	
1901		Liberal publications of Albert Schweitzer on Christ.	
1902			
1903	Russia pillages the Armenian Church.	Central Commission of Evangelical Churches in Germany.	
1905	Beginning of a reform movement in Russia.	Baptist World Alliance. Founding and rapid spread of Pentecostal movements. French Protestants accept the *Associations cultuelles*.	
1907		French Protestant Federation Rauschenbusch and social Christianity in the U.S.A.	
1908	Death of John of Kronstadt. *I Zoï* movement launched in Athens.	Baden-Powell founds the Scout movement.	Father Watson creates octave of prayers for unity.

DATE	POLITICAL, INTELLECTUAL AND SOCIAL EVENTS	EVENTS CONCERNING THE CATHOLIC CHURCH
1909		Foundation of the Biblical Institute.
1910	Death of Edward VII. Accession of George V.	
1912 1913	Balkan wars (1912–13).	
1914	First World War (28th July).	Death of Pius X. Election of Benedict XV.
1915		
1917	Russian Revolution: 2nd March—Liberal and Socialist; 25th October—Communist.	Founding of the Congregation of Eastern Churches.
1918	11th November: First World War: Armistice.	
1919	Greeks attack Turkey in Anatolia.	
1920	Famine in Russia. The Treaty of Sèvres. Armenia gains independence to become a Soviet republic.	
1921	Anti-Soviet revolt in Armenia crushed.	
1922	Lenin brings in the N.E.P. Turks defeat Greeks. Mussolini comes to power in Italy.	Death of Benedict XV. Election of Pius XI.
1923	Mustapha Kemal becomes dictator of Turkey.	
1924 1925	Death of Lenin (1870–1924).	
1926 1927	Stalin now all-powerful.	
1928		Appeals by Pope Pius XI to Christians of the East.
1929		Lateran agreements put an end to the Roman Question.
1930	Haile Selassie becomes Emperor of Ethiopia.	

DATE	EVENTS CONCERNING THE EASTERN CHURCH	EVENTS CONCERNING THE REFORMATION CHURCHES	EVENTS CONCERNING THE HISTORY OF UNITY
1909	New wave of massacres in Armenia.		
1910	Death of Tolstoy (1828–1910).	Success of the Berlin Congress (liberal Protestantism). Resurrection of the Desert. Museum of the Desert.	Edinburgh Conference (origin of the ecumenical movement).
1912			
1913	Widespread demand for restoration of the Patriarchate in Russia.		
1914			Founding of the Universal Alliance for Friendship by the Churches (2nd August).
1915	Further wave of massacres in Armenia and in all Christian regions of Near East.		
1917	Restoration of the Patriarchate of Moscow (28th October). Commencement of persecution in Russia.		
1918	Separation of Church and State and violent persecution in Russia.		
1919		First of Karl Barth's works appears (born 1884). Frank Buchman sets up the Oxford Groups, later M.R.A.	
1920		Remarkable Dutch law on schools. Lambeth (Anglican) Conference.	
1921		International Missions Council.	The Malines meetings (until 1925).
1922	The Serbian Church becomes a Patriarchate. Massacre of Christians in Turkey recommences.	German Churches' Federation.	
1923	The Patriarch, Tikhon, accepts the Soviet regime. Persecutions die out almost completely.		
1924			
1925	Expansion of the 'Godless' movement in Russia.		Founding of the Monastère de l'Union at Amay. Stockholm Congress (Life and Work).
1926			Founding of the Istina Centre.
1927	Monsignor Sergius allies himself with the Communist regime.	The Prayer Book affair in England.	Lausanne Congress (Faith and Order). Founding of the Centre for Unity of the Churches at the Catholic Institute in Paris.
1928	New wave of persecutions in Russia.		Encyclical, Mortalios animos.
1929			
1930			

DATE	POLITICAL, INTELLECTUAL AND SOCIAL EVENTS	EVENTS CONCERNING THE CATHOLIC CHURCH
1931		*Quadragesimo anno.*
1932		
1933	Hitler becomes German Chancellor.	
1934	The great purges in Russia.	
1935	Mussolini invades Abyssinia.	
1936	Civil war breaks out in Spain. Death of George V. Accession of George VI.	
1937		Pius XI's encyclicals against Communism and National Socialism.
1938	New wave of purges in Russia. The Austrian *Anschluss.*	
1939	1st September—Hitler invades Poland. Second World War breaks out.	Death of Pius XI. Election of Pius XII.
1940		
1941	Hitler attacks Russia.	
1943		Encyclical, *Divino afflante Spiritu,* on the Bible.
1944		
1945	Yalta Conference—partition of Europe favours the Russians.	
1946	Collapse of Germany. Indo-Chinese War breaks out.	
1947	The British leave India.	
1948		
1949	People's Republic of China.	
1950	The Iron Curtain. The Korean War.	
1951		

DATE	EVENTS CONCERNING THE EASTERN CHURCH	EVENTS CONCERNING THE REFORMATION CHURCHES	EVENTS CONCERNING THE HISTORY OF UNITY
1931			
1932		Commencement of Barth's *Dogmatics.*	
1933	Persecution of Assyrians in Iraq.	Hitler attempts to set up the German Evangelical Church.	Abbé Couturier gives true meaning to the Week of Prayer for Unity.
1934		The German 'Confessional' Church.	
1935			
1936			
1937			Reverend Father Congar publishes *Christians Disunited.* Oxford and Edinburgh meetings (*Faith and Order* and *Life and Work*).
1938	Further wave of persecutions in Russia.		Max Metzger's *Una Sanctis.*
1939		Billy Graham's campaigns begin.	
1940		Founding of the Central Maronite Committee. Roger Schutz comes to Taizé.	
1941		Bultmann (born 1884) publishes his *New Testament and Mythology.*	
1943	Normalization of relations between Church and State in Russia. Suppression of the 'Godless' movement.		
1944	Death of the Moscow Patriarch Sergius. Election of Alexis.	Baptist Union in Russia.	Pius XII's Encyclical, *Orientalis Ecclesia,* praises St Cyril of Alexandria.
1945	Renewal of the Church in Russia.	Roger Schutz definitely launches the Taizé Community. The Hutterite Brethren in Paraguay.	
1946		World Bible Alliance.	
1947	The 'Godless' movement reconstituted in Russia.	Lutheran World Alliance.	Founding of the Church of South India. Reverend Father Boyer founds *Unitas* Centre at Rome.
1948			Founding at Amsterdam of the World Council of Churches.
1949			The Holy Office lays down conditions for Catholic participation in ecumenical activities.
1950			
1951	The Ethiopian Church becomes independent, leaving the Coptic Church of Egypt.	World Methodist Council founded. Tillich (born 1886) publishes his *Systematic Theology.*	Monsignor Willebrands founds the Conference on Ecumenical Questions.

DATE	POLITICAL, INTELLECTUAL AND SOCIAL EVENTS	EVENTS CONCERNING THE CATHOLIC CHURCH
1952	Death of George VI. Accession of Elizabeth II.	
1953	Death of Stalin (1879–1953).	
1954	Crisis in Russia—Kruschev takes control.	
1955		
1956	Hungarian revolt suppressed by Russians. Suez crisis.	
1958		Death of Pius XII, accession of John XXIII.
1959		John XXIII announces Ecumenical Council (25th January).

DATE	EVENTS CONCERNING THE EASTERN CHURCH	EVENTS CONCERNING THE REFORMATION CHURCHES	EVENTS CONCERNING THE HISTORY OF UNITY
1952			Lund meeting (*Faith and Order*).
1953			
1954	Coptic Patriarch sequestered by his people.		Evanston meeting of World Council of Churches. Founding of *Die Sammlung*.
1955	Antichristian riots in Constantinople.		
1956			
1958			
1959	New wave of persecution in Russia. Expansion of atheistic movement.		John XXIII announces that one of the aims of the Vatican Council will be Christian unity.

SELECT BIBLIOGRAPHY

THE following are the principal works named by the author in his bibliographical notes.

GENERAL

J. Dedieu, *Instabilité du Protestantisme*, 1928; Père Y. Congar, *Chrétiens désunis*, 1937; G. Tavard, *À la rencontre du Protestantisme*, 1954, and *Le Protestantisme*, 1958; A. D. Toledano, *L'Anglicanisme*, 1957; G. Viatte, *Œcuménisme*, 1964; J. Guitton, *Le Christ écartelé*, 1964; Père M. Villain, *Introduction à l'œcuménisme*, 2nd ed., 1964; E. G. Léonard and J. Boisset, *Histoire générale du Protestantisme* (with 67-page bibliography), 3 vols., 1964.

SPECIAL

CHAPTER I. DAUGHTERS OF THE REVOLUTION

LUTHERANS: R. Jung, *Histoire résumée de l'Église luthérienne en France*, 1928. CALVINISTS: J. Clavier, *Études sur le Calvinisme*, 1936; J. Rilliet, *Calvin*, 1964. CONGREGATIONALISTS: F. G. Flagey, *Story of the Congregational Christian Churches*, 1941. ANGLICANS: C. Garbett, *The Claims of the Church of England*, 1947, and *The Church and State in England*, 1950; J. R. H. Moorman, *A History of the Church in England*, 1953; S. Neill, *Anglicanism*, 1958. BAPTISTS: H. W. Robinson, *The Life and Faith of the Baptists*, 1947; G. Rousseau, *Histoire des Églises baptistes dans le monde*, 1951; G. M. Smith, *Story of the Mennonites*, 1957. METHODISTS: J. F. Hurst, *History of Methodism*, 7 vols., 1891; M. Piette, *La Réaction Wesleyenne dans l'évolution protestante*, 1925; Agnès de la Gorce, *Wesley, maître d'un peuple*, 1940. QUAKERS: H. van Etten, *George Fox et les Quakers*, 1956. NEW CHURCHES AND SECTS: G. Welter, *Histoire des Sectes chrétiennes*, 1950; E. Gerber, *Le Mouvement adventiste*, 1950; G. Dagon, *L'Église et les Sectes*, 1951, and *Petites Églises and Grandes Sectes*, 1960; M. Colinon, *Faux prophètes et sectes d'aujourd'hui*, 1953, and *Le Phénomène des Sectes*, 1959; H. Ch. Chéry, *L'Offensive des Sectes*, 1954; B. Lavaud, *Rites modernes et foi catholique*, 1954; J. Séguy, *Les Sectes protestantes dans la France contemporaine*, 1956.

CHAPTER II. THE PROTESTANT WORLD

SCANDINAVIA: J. G. Hoffmann, *Les Fondements historiques des Églises du Nord* (no date); J. Maurice, *Voyages chez les Protestants*, 1964. GERMANY: G. Goyau, *L'Allemagne religieuse, le Protestantisme*, 1898. ENGLAND: G. Coolen, *Histoire de l'Église d'Angleterre*, 1953; A. D. Toledano, *Histoire de l'Angleterre Chrétienne*, 1955; Berthe Garalda, *Églises en Grande-Bretagne*,

476   SELECT BIBLIOGRAPHY

1959. FRANCE: E. G. Léonard, *Le Protestant français*, 1953; R. Stephen, *Histoire du Protestantisme français*, 1961. UNITED STATES OF AMERICA: W. Herberg, *Protestants, Catholics, Israelites*, 1960; C. Jullien, *Le Nouveau Nouveau Monde*, 1960. LATIN AMERICA: E. G. Léonard, *Formation d'une société protestante au Brésil*, 1953; A. Gorete, 'Les Pentecôtistes au Chili' in *Recherches et Débats*, May 1956; W. Stanley Rycroft, *Religion and Faith in Latin America*, 1958. THE PROTESTANT MISSIONS: K. S. Latourette, *History of the Expansion of Christianity*, 1935; G. Mondain, *Un Siècle de Missions protestantes à Madagascar*, 1948.

CHAPTER III. THE SOUL AND SPIRIT OF PROTESTANTISM

REVIVALS: L. Maury, *Le Réveil religieux à Genève et en France*, 1898; E. Bois, *Le Réveil au Pays de Galles*, 1906; Y. Brilioth, *The Anglican Revival*, 1925; J. Blocher, *Le Réveil du XVIIIᵉ siècle en Amérique du Nord*, 1952. KIERKE-GAARD: K. Koch, *S. Kierkegaard*, 1932; P. Mesnard, *Le Vrai Visage de Kierkegaard*, 1948; J. Wahl, *Les Études Kierkegaardiennes*, 1949; Marguerite Grimault, *Kierkegaard par lui-même*, 1962. SCHLEIERMACHER: Studies by Tissot (1853) and Goy (1868). THE SALVATION ARMY: A Peyron, *Réflexions*, 1924; Mildred Duff, *Catherine Booth*, 1941; G. Brabant, *William Booth*, 1948. BIBLICAL AND THEOLOGICAL RENEWAL: G. Casalis, *Portrait de Karl Barth*, 1940; Suzanne Dietrich, *Le Renouveau biblique*, 1945; J. Rilliet, *Karl Barth, théologien existentialiste*, 1952; O. Cullmann, *La Tradition*, 1953; G. Miegge, *L'Évangile et le mythe dans la poésie de Bultmann*, 1958; Père Marle, *Le Problème théologique de l'herméneutique*, 1963. MORAL REARMA-MENT: D. Lazard, *Le Réarmement moral*, 1949; F. Buchman, *Remaking the World*, 1953. PROTESTANT MONACHISM: C. E. Babut, *Adolphe Monod*, 1902; C. Leenhardt, *Oberlin*, 1910; R. Weiss, *Daniel Legrand*, 1926; W. Monod, *La Nuée des témoins*, 1928; A. Lavondes, *Charles Gide*, 1958; R. Lescure, *John Bost*, 1959; F. Biot, *Communautés protestantes*, 1961.

CHAPTER IV. THE BYZANTINE HERITAGE—THE ORTHODOX CHURCH

GENERAL: Père R. Janin, *Les Églises séparées d'Orient*, 1927, and *Églises orientales et rites orientaux*, 1955; A. Fortescue, *The Orthodox Eastern Church*, 1932; C. Galli and C. Korolevskij, *I Riti e le Chiese orientali*, 1942; G. Welter, *Histoire des sectes chrétiennes*, 1950; G. Boulgakov, *L'Orthodoxie*, 2nd ed., 1959; P. Evdokimov, *L'Orthodoxie*, 1959; J. Meyendorff, *L'Église orthodoxe, hier et aujourd'hui*, 1960; O. Clément, *L'Église orthodoxe*, 1961; Père Le Guillou, *L'Esprit de l'Orthodoxie grecque et russe*, 1961; G. Zananiri, *Pages et Patriarches*, 1962. SPIRITUALITY: V. Lossky, *Essai sur la théologie de l'Église d'Orient*, 1944; 'A Monk of the Eastern Church' in *La Prière du Cœur*, 2nd ed., 1959; J. Meyendorff, *Saint Grégoire Palamas*, 1959; L. Ouspensky, *Essai sur la théologie de l'icone dans l'Église orthodoxe*, 1960; O. Clément, *Byzance et la Christianisme*, 1964. THE GREEK AND MELCHITE CHURCHES: P. Rondot, *Les Chrétiens d'Orient*, 1955; J. Décarreaux, *Une République de moines*, 1956; J. Leroy, *Moines et monastères du Proche-Orient*, 1957.

CHAPTER V. SEPARATED BRETHREN OF ASIA AND AFRICA IN EARLIER AGES

Dictionnaire de Théologie catholique; *Dictionnaire d'Histoire et de Géographie ecclésiastique*. H. Musset, *Histoire du Christianisme, spécialement en Orient*, 1943. ARMENIANS: Mgr M. Ormanian, *L'Église arménienne*, 1910; K. J. Basmadjian, *Histoire moderne des arméniens*, 1922; B. Kassardjian, *L'Église apostolique arménienne et sa doctrine*, 1943. THE MALABAR COMMUNITIES: A. Fortescue, *The Lesser and Eastern Churches*, 1913; J. C. Panjikaram, 'Christianity in Malabar' in *Orientalia Christiana*, 1926. THE COPTS: J. B. Coubleaux, *Histoire politique et religieuse d'Abyssinie*, 1929; J. Doresse, *L'Éthiopie antique et moderne*, 1956; M. Cléret, *Éthiopie fidèle à la Croix*, 1957; Père S. Chauleur, *Histoires des Coptes*, 1960.

CHAPTER VI. THE SEAMLESS COAT

FROM THE PROTESTANT AND ANGLICAN STANDPOINT: R. Werner, *L'Unité protestante, les faits et les idées*, 1925; A. Paul, *L'Unité chrétienne*, 1930; W. A. Visser't Hooft, *Le Protestantisme et le Mouvement œcuménique*, 1935, and *Le Conseil œcuménique de Églises*, 2nd ed., 1962; M. Boegner, *Le Problème de l'Unité chrétienne*, 1946; Spencer Jones, *The Church of England and the Holy See*, 1951; Ruth House and S. Neill, *A History of the Ecumenical Movement*, 1954; Berthe Gavalda, *Le Mouvement œcuménique*, 1959. FROM THE ORTHODOX STANDPOINT: P. Kovalevski, *L'Unité de l'Église*, 1946; L. A. Zander, *Vision and Action: The Problems of Ecumenism*, 1948; J. Kotsonir, *Intercommunion*, 1957. FROM THE CATHOLIC STANDPOINT: Abbé Couturier, *Rapprochements entre les chrétiens au XXe siècle*, 1944; J. de Bivort de la Saudée, *Anglicans et catholiques, le problème de l'Union anglo-romaine*, 1948; K. Adam, *Vers l'Unité chrétienne*, 1949; Père Y. Congar, *Vraie et fausse réforme dans l'Église*, 1950, and *Chrétiens en dialogue*, 1963; Abbé A. Gratieux, *L'Amitié au service de l'Union*, 1951; C. J. Dumont, *Les Voies de l'Unité chrétienne*, 1954; G. Thils, *Histoire doctrinale du Mouvement œcuménique*, 1955; Father B. Leeming, *The Churches and the Church*, 1960; J. Guitton, *Dialogue avec les précurseurs*, 1964; P. Michalon, *L'Unité des chrétiens*, 1965.

INDEX

INDEX